KEY TO SECTIONS, REGIONS AND DEPARTMENTS

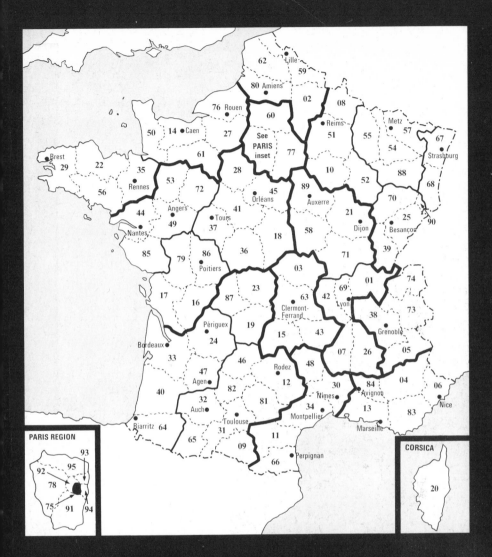

Map labels:

62 · Lille
59
80 Amiens
76 Rouen
60
02
08
50 14 ●Caen 27
See PARIS inset
●Reims
51
55
Metz
●
57
67
Strasbourg
Brest●
29 22 35
Rennes
53 72 28 77
●
45
89
52
88
70
68
Angers●
44
49 37 41
Orléans
●Tours
●
18
58
Auxerre
21
Dijon
●
25
Besançon
90
Nantes●
85 79 86
Poitiers●
36
03
71
39
01
74
17
16 87
23
63
Clermont-Ferrand
42
69
Lyon●
38
73
Périguex●
19
15
43
Grenoble●
05
Bordeaux●
24
46
Rodez●
48
07
26
33
47
Agen●
82
12
30
Nîmes●
84
Avignon●
04
06
Nice●
40
32
Auch●
81
34
13
83
Biarritz●
64
Toulouse●
31
Montpellier●
Marseille●
65
09
11
66 ●Perpignan

PARIS REGION
93
92 95
78
75 91 94

CORSICA
20

The Shell Guide to France

The Shell Guide to

France

Edited by Edward Young

Introduction by John Ardagh

Introductory essays by
Jane Grigson
Hammond Innes
Joy Law
George Rainbird
Christopher Tadgell

Regional introductory essays
and gazetteer entries by
Pauline Devaney and Edwin Apps
Gerald Barry
David and Anne Lockie
Michael Peppiatt
George Savage
Edward Young
H.W. Yoxall

Michael Joseph

First published in Great Britain by Michael Joseph Ltd
44 Bedford Square, London WC1, 1979
This softcover edition first published by
Michael Joseph Ltd 1983

ISBN 0 7181 2255 0

This book was designed and produced by George Rainbird Ltd
40 Park Street, London W1Y 4DE

House Editor: Georgina Dowse
Picture Research: Georgina Dowse
    assisted by Marion Smith and Hugo Kondratiuk
Design Yvonne Dedman and Judith Allan
Production: Clare Merryfield
Cartography: Tom Stalker Miller
Index: Mary Young

Printed and bound by Jarrold and Sons Ltd, Norwich, Norfolk

Maps 1–7 at the back of the book were produced by Recta-Foldex
and are based on those of L'Institut Géographique National, Paris
Copyright Shell Française

The picture on the cover: A view of the Dordogne at
La Treyne southeast of Souillac (*Photo: Ronald Sheridan*)

Contents

Colour Plates

The page numbers given are those on facing pages

Editor's Foreword

The four previous volumes in this series of *Shell Guides* have dealt separately with the individual countries comprising the British Isles – Scotland, Ireland, Wales and England. France is four times the size of England, and almost twice the size of the whole of the area to which those four volumes were devoted. The challenge facing the compilers of this *Guide to France*, therefore, was how to compress within the allotted span of words the variety of landscape and peoples, the stormy history, the rich architectural heritage, indeed the whole character and flavour of this great and resilient nation. Success in such an endeavour could only be partial, but our modest hope is that we have provided enough information to whet the appetite, to enable readers to plan their holidays, and to give pointers to the places they would perhaps be sorry to miss.

This is a tourist guide to places. It does not cover hotels or restaurants. There are enough guides already available which specialize in such information – which in France requires a whole volume to itself. Nor does this guide give times and prices of admission to museums and other places open to the public, since these are liable to change, but there is a general note on the subject under 'Tourist Information' at the end of the book.

The plan of the book is the same as that of *The Shell Guide to England*. The introductory section, consisting of essays on aspects of France in general, is followed by a breakdown of the country into a number of areas, starting with the section devoted to Paris. Each of these sections has its own introduction, followed by a descriptive gazetteer covering the important and interesting places within that area. Proportionately more space has been given to the areas most likely to attract the tourist – namely Paris and its environs, Normandy and Brittany, the Loire valley, the Southwest, and Provence.

In the gazetteers the name of each place is followed first by the name of its *département*, then by a map-reference indicating the relevant page and square in the coloured map section which follows this Foreword. It has not been possible to include every single place-name on the maps, but where a place is not shown on the map the map-reference gives a distance and compass direction from a place that *is* on the map. The distances given here are 'as the crow flies' and not road distances – sometimes two very different things, as those who drive in mountainous regions will soon discover. In the Paris section the entries are keyed to the numbers on the Paris map which appears on page 8 of the map section.

Where they would seem useful to the reader, cross-references are made to other gazetteer entries in the book. If such references are to entries in the same section, they are given simply as '(*see —*)'; if to entries in another section they are given as '(*see — in the — section*)'.

In a long entry describing a large city (e.g. Bordeaux), to assist the reader the main tourist sites are printed in capital letters. This has not been considered necessary in the shorter entries.

In some cases, a place of comparatively minor importance is included in bold type as a short sub-entry under the gazetteer heading of a more important place in the vicinity. The Index at the end of the book lists all the places which have entries or sub-entries in the gazetteers.

No book of this kind could be compiled *de novo* from original research without being out of date by the time of its completion. The gazetteer contributors in particular are inevitably indebted to the help derived from a large number of historical, topographical and architectural works and other books of reference. A selective list of reference sources is given in the Bibliography at the end of the book. Thanks are also due for assistance received from the French Government Tourist Office and from the Syndicats d'Initiative, the tourist offices to be found in most towns throughout France.

For myself, I gratefully acknowledge the immense amount of interest and help I have received from friends in France: in particular M. Pierre Blondet, Mme Renée Dandurand, and Mme Marie-Louise Thomassin, who have lent me books, pamphlets and old news-cuttings, and generally helped me with advice and information; Mme Olga Costet, who provided me with notes from personal experience of Corsica; Mlle Amélie Gaillard, who read and checked the Southwest gazetteer, put me right on a number of points, and gave me a splendidly apt metaphor for the colour of a particular mountain river; and not least Bill and Ann Merryfield, who also checked the Southwest gazetteer and lent me books, and in addition made several arduous journeys on my behalf and came back with reams of notes and observations.

I would also like to thank my contributors, both for their contributions and for so generously accepting the amendments I had to make in order to achieve a measure of unity and balance throughout the book. I thank especially Dr Christopher Tadgell, not only for his illuminating survey of French architecture but also for checking and correcting the architectural terms in the Glossary. Out of the many at Rainbird's who helped to edit, design and produce the book, I would especially like to thank, first, my former colleague John Hadfield for his experienced advice and timely encouragement, and above all Georgina Dowse who, as House Editor, cajoled, bullied, soothed, supported, and tactfully steered me towards completion of my assignment.

Finally I thank my long-suffering wife who, besides undertaking the arduous task of compiling the Index, has accompanied me on all my fact-finding journeys and generally been a tower of strength with her constructive criticism and patient encouragement.

E.Y.

Introduction: France Today

John Ardagh

I have, like many other francophiles, a long-standing love-hate affair with the French. They can be maddening at times, especially Parisians – offhand, conceited, inconsiderate – yet I also find them stimulating. They are confident that theirs is the world's most civilized land – and possibly they are right. It exudes a sense of continuous civilization, from the Roman ruins and Gothic cathedrals to the latest *haute couture* boutiques and futuristic culture-palaces. The French are a nation of eloquent talkers who do not suffer fools gladly; of stylish hedonists who also work furiously; a nation today uneasily balanced between new-found modernism and a hankering for tradition.

The essence of France is diversity adding up to harmony. Its very shape is harmonious, a neat hexagon. And compared to its neighbours it is still quite an empty country – four times the size of England but with a similar population. Yet it is not arid, like much of Spain: most of it is lushly fertile and neatly cultivated. France has that rare commodity in this crowded continent – elbow-room for development and replanning.

More than any other country, it belongs both to north and south Europe. The Lille area, with its cobbled streets, and coal-tips dotted across a sombre plain, seems as northern as Leeds or the Ruhr, and so do its solid, phlegmatic people. Yet nowhere could be more Mediterranean than Provence with its cypresses and olive-groves, where old men with the twangy accents of the *Midi* drink *pastis* in the dusty squares of ancient hill-villages. Paris itself is a Latin city strayed into a semi-northern clime. The ethnic variety of France is as great as the scenic. Bretons are very different from Corsicans, or Basques from Alsatians, and at these peripheries there are people dedicated to keeping the old languages alive or even nourishing dreams of separatism. But the diversity of the many provinces has been welded across the centuries into a common Frenchness, in this most centralized of modern States.

After World War II the French brilliantly modernized their hitherto backward country, at least on a material level. Prosperity brought with it a zealous new faith in the cure-all of growth and technical progress. But in the past few years this climate has changed. Not only has the novelty of modernism worn off, but recession has begun to bite, undermining the faith that prosperity would continue without interruption. In May 1981, after twenty-three years of Right-of-centre rule, a Socialist Government came into power, pledged to reduce the inequalities of this unequal society and to lighten and humanize France's centralized bureaucratic structures. But recession has obliged the Socialists to give a lower priority to these reforms than to the grinding daily struggle against inflation, trade deficits and rising unemployment. It is all drearily familiar. At the same time, the mood of the French has changed in the past ten years or so: insecure in the new world of self-doubt in the 1970s and 1980s, they have been noticeably turning back to their roots and traditions, after their love-affair with modernism.

However, this trend has not yet negated the spectacular post-war French renewal which is a mighty saga. Paradoxically, it was the humiliation of the defeat in World War II and the occupation that shocked the French out of their pre-war decadence and paved the way for their new energy and self-confidence. In the 1950s and 1960s they seemed to be moving traumatically in one swoop from the eighteenth to the late-twentieth century: hence the conflicts and contrasts between old and new were sharper than in most western countries. Clochemerle no longer got worked up about a *pissotière*, but instead over a hypermarket or a new motorway slip-road. The French carried through a belated industrial revolution, and today theirs is no longer an economy based mainly on agriculture. Technical improvements on the farms have led to a huge rural exodus: only 8 per cent of the French today work on the land, against 35 per cent in 1945. The peasantry used to be an archaic world apart: today farmers are more like businessmen, as in Britain, and are finally integrated into society. The old reactionary peasant, sozzled, half-illiterate, living scarcely better than his animals, does still exist in some areas: but he is a dying species. The rural emigrants made for the towns, and this plus the high post-war birth-rate led to the kind of rapid urbanization that Britain knew in the nineteenth century. Many cities have doubled or trebled in size since the end of World War II: Grenoble has risen from 80,000 to 400,000 inhabitants. This revival of the provinces has been one of the most striking of post-war changes. Towns that formerly looked so charming, but in fact were lethargic and narrow-spirited, became bustling industrial and cultural centres forging new links with the outside world.

Pushed on by eager State planners, industry surged ahead, far overtaking Britain's both in output and technology. It was helped by wartime devastation, which forced much of industry to start again on a modern basis. And today France leads Europe in aeronautics, electronics, and space technology. The housing short-age once such a disgrace, has been largely solved, and every city is ringed with white megaliths: new high-rise blocks, some of them ugly and ill-planned during the crash programme of the 1960s. Outside every town, too, there are huge new hypermarkets, for the French – who do nothing except by extremes – have moved in one leap from the local corner-shop to the largest modern stores in Europe. Finally, even the telephone service, for so long a joke in France, has at last been pulled into the modern world. The number of lines has increased since 1970 from four to over twenty million.

Private affluence rose steadily in the boom years before recession, and it seems to have pushed the French closer to Anglo-Saxon spending patterns. In absolute terms they spend as much as ever on food and drink, but proportionately this item has dropped since 1939 from 50 per cent to 23 per cent of the average family budget, while consumption on health and hygiene has risen from 6 per cent to 12.3 per cent – so the French have been getting cleaner (have you noticed how the Métro smells less?). They used not to care so much about their homes, but today they spend as large a share of the budget on them as the Americans or British. They have one of Europe's highest levels of car ownership, and have developed a taste for all sorts of modern gadgetry. In fact, in the post-war decades the French businessman developed a naïve faith in material progress. In State planning offices, tidily dressed technocrats would eagerly brandish their blueprints for implanting new airports, ports and factory complexes in 'Europe's Texas', excited by the challenge of a virtually virgin land. Young industrial executives acquired an American ethos together with their Harvard business diplomas, and would enthuse about *le management* or *le merchandizing*.

And yet, although the French have adapted readily to the material benefits of economic advance, when it comes to their personal routines and traditional ways of thinking, or their social attitudes, they remain more conservative. An example: in 1959 the 'new franc' was introduced (100 old francs), yet over twenty years later a large proportion of people, even educated people and young ones born since the change, are still unwilling to calculate in anything but old francs. Custom dies hard and French society is still in a confusing state of transition. On the suburban estates, for example, 'new-town blues' are chronic, for although the ex-slum-dwellers and ex-peasants have moved into homes far more comfortable than their old ones, their French habits of family privacy and lack of neighbourliness inhibit them from creating a new friendly community.

Happily, today there are signs of a changing attitude; but in general the French have adapted badly to the strains and stresses of big-city living, especially in congested, nerve-racking Paris. They get away from it whenever they can: hence the

French industry: Solar furnace at Font-Romeu

craze among the middle classes for country cottages where they retreat every weekend, leaving the city empty and clogging up its exits with monstrous Sunday-night traffic-jams. And even stronger than the weekend mania is the post-war holiday mania. The French work hard and late each day, they have little evening leisure, so they live for their holidays – the longest in Europe, now five weeks legal minimum. Among the bourgeoisie, the phenomenal success of the *Club Méditerranée*, where 'nice' members play the noble savage, with straw huts and beads for money, seems to mark a yearning to get back to some rural idyll and to escape from the rigidness of city society into a world of un-French camaraderie where everyone is on *tu* terms.

The French want new cars and holidays, yet they cling to the convention of going away only in July and August, thus jamming the roads and resorts. This is one more example of French reluctance to bend old habits to suit new conditions – and so, arguably, is the ritual of the big family lunch. In Paris, it is true, many people now commute to such far-flung suburbs that they cannot get home at midday, and firms have been moving over to the shorter Anglo-Saxon-style break. But in the provinces, many towns still close down from midday to 2 p.m. while the family ritual is observed – a pleasant custom in itself, but not always sensible in cities with heavy traffic. Lunch is still the main meal, yet *cuisine* in France is changing, like so much else. The French still eat better, and with more care for quality, than other Western nations. But their glorious tradition is under assault, as fast-food eateries and cafeterias line the boulevards, and as younger housewives will sooner toss a steak under the grill than spend hours on a *plat mijoté* as their grandmothers did. However, the gourmets are counter-attacking. The really good restaurants are as good as ever, and as full; and although the vogue for *nouvel le cuisine* may no longer be so new, its success has shown how much the French still care passionately about cooking as an art. It seems that eating in France is fated to polarize: on the one hand, serious gastronomy for the few, or for special occasions; on the other, the inevitable spread of convenience foods for every day. Sad, in a way.

So we come to a key question: in modernizing, have the French been able to preserve their Frenchness, their flair and sense of style? Or have they become Americanized? At first sight, some portents are not encouraging. The tongue that Proust and Balzac spake has been invaded by the newspeak of *franglais*, whereby a man does *le jogging* before applying *l'after-shave*, to go and be *interviewé* about *le marketing* and have *un drink* with friends. But this *franglais* craze is now well past its prime. And in many areas of life, whereas in the 1960s the French seemed to be blindly copying the Americans, today they have digested this and have proved they are able to innovate in their own style, with a French inventiveness and elegance. Like it or not, look at the Pompidou Centre in Paris. Or take *le drugstore*, where the French have borrowed an American term and formula, and turned it into something of their own. Other French innovations range from the *Club Méditerranée* holiday formula to the new musical public WCS (*sanisettes*) in Paris. So judgment must be suspended. More worrying is the fact that in recent years the nation has seemed so absorbed in its economic changes and crises that it has not focused its energies on the creative arts as in harder times. Paris intellectual life today is dazzle and frenzy more than substance; literature has lost its universality; where are the new playwrights and painters? Only music shows signs of a renaissance. This seems to be an age that favours the dissemination of culture to new mass audiences – and here the French are certainly active – rather than individual creative power.

And have modern developments been making an impact on the subtle world of French social and personal relations? By many Anglo-Saxon criteria this is still a rigid society – but less so than it used to be. It all depends on your point of reference. I would say it is less class-obsessed than British society, but more class-divided. Social change was slower than in post-war Britain. The process may now speed up under Socialism. But France is still a land where the working class feels apart and rarely penetrates into positions of prominence. Maybe society would shift faster, were it not for the powerful family ties that still command many first loyalties. Here again, all is relative. To an English or American eye, a Frenchman may still seem to spend an inordinate amount of leisure time with his cousins and aunts and his brother-in-law's second cousins. Yet this clan-life is gently on the wane. Within the family, too, teenagers have won a new freedom from parental authority since the student uprising in May 1968. Sexual permissiveness has grown, as old-style Catholic piety declines: many couples now co-habit openly before marriage, and this is widely accepted. Women have won a fuller emancipation, legally and socially; and abortion and contraception are at last fully legalized.

Social formalities, too, are easing. True, an Anglo-Saxon may still raise his eyebrows at a respect for hierarchies that can seem almost Teutonic. Any ex-chairman expects to be addressed until his death as 'Monsieur le Président', and letters still ask you to agree to the assurance of most distinguished sentiments. But this formality should not be mistaken for coldness: courtesy may be stylized, but it can be a channel for expressing warmth. Anyway, a younger generation is now breaking with the old styles. It is steadily adopting the Anglo-Saxon habit of Christian names. And it is entertaining at home more casually, in defiance of the bourgeois tradition that a dinner-party must be given with lavish ceremonial or not at all.

It has never been true that the French do not invite you to their homes. Most Anglo-Saxon stories about French inhospitality are based on stays in Paris: visit other towns and you will find a people as welcoming as any in Europe. Even Parisians are hospitable when away from the Parisian rat-race. I knew an English married couple in official jobs in Paris who became friendly with two French civil servants. There were cordial business lunches, and sometimes the couple asked the French to parties and were then assured, '*Vous devez dîner chez nous, on vous fera signe*' – and, of course, nothing happened. Until, one day, the English couple and both the Frenchmen and their wives found that, by chance, they were all going to spend August in villas in the same part of Auvergne. Addresses were exchanged, plus the usual promises of hospitality, which my friends took with a pinch of salt. But lo! – in Auvergne, the telephone rang, dates were fixed, their French hosts piled lavish meal upon lavish meal with the utmost grace and warmth. The English had broken through the barrier. But, back in Paris, it simply descended again.

Confronted with the frequent brusqueness or unhelpfulness of Parisians, many foreign tourists take it personally. 'They're so anti-American,' thinks an American; 'They still hate us,' thinks a German. But probably it is not this at all, not even a general xenophobia. The Parisians are just as prickly with each other; they live in a

Modern high-rise flats, Paris

city where the pace of life is too fast for the nerves and *sauve qui peut* is the rule, and they take it out on others. I do not think that the French as a whole, though convinced that their own way of life is best, are any more anti-foreigner than other peoples. Their old insularity, springing from the Gaullist vision of *la gloire*, is on the wane; they are travelling more, the young are more internationally minded. What does persist is a French assertive competitiveness. Sometimes arrogantly scornful, sometimes defensive, they are always trying to score points off other nations or exploit them for their own purposes. This can be tiresome but it seems to me positive and realistic. They are eager to make contact, even to learn. Witness how, in the years since de Gaulle's death, they have been giving up their proud refusal to speak anything but their own illustrious tongue. With understandable resentment, they have seen it far overtaken by English as the world's global vehicle, and they have now regretfully decided, 'If you can't lick 'em, join 'em.' In the interests of promoting their trade and world position, they have no choice but to use the world's new *lingua franca* like everyone else. And so the learning of English, in schools, colleges and on adult courses, has been making giant strides. So, at least in the modern professions, the average young educated Frenchman today speaks good English, as was not the case in the 1960s.

The supremacy of their language, like that of their culture and their classic education system, is one of the *idées reçues* that the French have been forced painfully to reappraise under changing conditions. The old structures that held France together so well in the past, centralized, hierarchic, legalistic, have proved increasingly unsuited to a more modern, open society, and growing frustration over them culminated in the 1968 explosion. Politically, this proved a non-revolution: but in education it did crack an archaic framework. Universities are now at last semi-autonomous; school life is less hidebound. But sterility has given way to a certain cheerful chaos; and as the French dismantle parts of their old purist academic system, they do not seem quite sure what kind of more humane, egalitarian education to put in its place. Again, it is their national dilemma: how to promote liberal reform without sacrificing the best of tradition.

During 1958–81 the Right-of-centre governments of Presidents de Gaulle, Pompidou and Giscard d'Estaing did carry through a large number of valuable reforms. But by the late 1970s the French were growing bored with having similar *régimes* in power for so long; France badly needed the alternation of power that is normal and healthy in a democracy. So in 1981 the French voted for change, by electing President Mitterrand and a Socialist government, with their troublesome Communist partners relegated to a junior side-role. The Socialists quickly made it clear that their aim was moderate democratic reform, not Marxist radicalism. They did promote a few doctrinaire measures – notably the nationalization of some large industrial firms and private banks – but apart from this they concentrated on practical steps to deal with the recession.

At the same time they embarked on two important series of reforms that had a wide degree of public support: to reduce social inequalities, and to curb the centralized power of the State. These were two of the great unsolved problems that the prosperous modernized France still bore round its neck like albatrosses. France has long been a less egalitarian society than most advanced nations: wage differentials have been wider than elsewhere in the EEC. Furthermore, the real power in France – in politics, business, and the civil service – has tended to be concentrated in the hands of bourgeois cliques, notably those emanating from the elitist colleges known as the *Grandes Ecoles*. The Socialists in 1981–82 slapped new taxes on the rich and increased minimum wages, thus reducing the differentials a little. They hardly altered the *Grande Ecole* system: but they did begin to introduce measures for a degree of co-management in industry that could lead to a wider sharing of power. They also set in train a process of devolution that would give more autonomy to the regions, to town councils and other local bodies, and reduce the heavy central power of the State. Most people welcomed this, though some Jacobin diehards feared that it might lead the nation to fly apart, among a people so contentious and politicized as the French. The Socialists were clearly embarked on a bold gamble, in their bid to bring France's out-of-date structures in line with her modernized economy.

Long before the Left came to power, in fact ever since the water-shed of May 1968 and the onset of the world energy crisis, the mood in France had been subtly changing. Modernism was losing its glamorous appeal. The French were also shunning formal public institutions and returning to private satisfactions, to a renewal of links with the traditional past, and to a search for new kinds of community on a local level. Oddly, this trend seemed to be at once a defence against economic crisis *and* a reaction against the too-rapid material change that preceded it. Today, the French are more concerned with the 'quality of life' than with the gigantism in fashion in the 1960s: *le petit* is now *beau*. They are seeking renewal of contact with their rural roots (one reason for the popular weekend-cottage) and are showing a new absorption in folk-cultures, in history, music, and in traditional *cuisine*. Nostalgia is in vogue. For this trend to progress too far could be harmful, even decadent; it could lead the French as individuals to retreat into self-centred privacy, leaving a social void. Happily, in the new towns and suburbs, there are also signs of the pioneering of new kinds of local-community activity – a bid, finally, to re-create in a new urban setting some of the old lost warmth of the villages. The French are learning the Anglo-Saxon virtues of self-help – what they call *la vie associative*.

This is a new uncertain era for the French as for others. After the years of strenuous modernization, they are now tiring of the rat-race and losing some of the potent work ethic that propelled them to rebuild their nation. Young people are not prepared to work as hard as their fathers did. The French now seem to be tempted towards a society maybe closer to the British model, a gentler society, less hectically ambitious, with more accent on leisure, environment, and local self-help. If they work less, there will be a price to pay in terms of lower living standards; this will cause moans, for the French will want to have their cake and eat it. But they still retain their vital qualities of resilience, flair and enthusiasm. They seem to me as well equipped as any Western nation to survive into the difficult post-industrial era that lies ahead.

Food in France

Jane Grigson

Food is a main pleasure of holidays in France. The fact that French hotels are too expensive for most families has turned out to be a blessing. We have to camp and rent houses, and cater for ourselves these days. We soon discover that shopping can be a delightful exploration, the occasional meal out a revelation of skill. We are not prepared for the variety of food in France. Obviously the wet north will eat differently from the Mediterranean south, but within that expected difference there are subtle changes of emphasis between neighbouring regions that even the informative articles in the green Michelin guides cannot convey.

The first thing to do on arriving is to inquire about local markets. Market day means open banks (the idiosyncratic banking hours can be unnerving in France). It also means excitement and good food, as prices really are lower than in the shops, so that everyone comes in for the day. As well as luxuries from further afield, you will find regional specialities – there are young people selling goat cheeses or oysters, old women with chickens, herbs, vegetables, farmers with bags of late apples, trusses of garlic, shallots, bunches of basil. In the autumn in Périgord, *foie gras* and truffles will be displayed. There will be cheese merchants with huge Gruyères and Cantals; pickle merchants with buckets of different olives, prunes from Agen, angelica in foot-long stalks, nuts, dried fruit; *charcutiers* specializing in Spanish, Portuguese or Arab sausages for immigrant workers. Fresh fruit and vegetables are a major attraction. Peaches, apricots, greengages, brugnons (peach/plums), mirabelles can be bought cheaply in trays (*plateaux*) of 4 or 5 kilos. Huge Marmande tomatoes, plum-shaped Rome tomatoes, grown out of doors, come with a shock of delight after the poor tomatoes sold in Britain.

You soon see that food is going to be an important part of the holiday, that shopping is something to enjoy, whether from the market, or from the specialized shops that are still such a feature of French towns. Incidentally, although most places have taken to Monday closing (unless it happens to be market day), there is usually one bakery, one *charcuterie*, one grocery shop open in the morning.

Charcuterie

This means 'cooked meat shop', which it was originally, the meat being pork. Nowadays uncooked pork is sold as well as tripe, couscous, and sauerkraut for reheating at home, occasionally even fish dishes, such as salmon mayonnaise or, in Lent, *brandade de morue* (creamed salt cod). There are salads (*céleri-rave*, mushrooms *à la grecque*), and dishes verging on *pâtisserie*, such as sausage in *brioche*, pizzas, *pissaladières*, gnocchi (small cheese tartlets or rolls, with whiskers of grated Gruyère), sausage rolls (*friandises*), *quiches* and meat pies sold by the wedge (*un part*), or whole. A weekend item may well be hot roasted chicken, handed to you in a special bag that keeps in heat and juices; moreover the whole thing can go straight into the oven for reheating. Such things and many more, according to district, can usually be ordered – if you ever watch a First Communion feast being loaded up for delivery at the side door of the shop, you will be amazed at the skill and range of dishes. If you are in France at Christmas time, the *charcutier*'s window will be full of game pies and pâtés.

The main repertoire of every *charcuterie*, whatever the *jeux d'esprit* consist of, depends on pork. It's varied enough to be puzzling. My advice is not to be flurried into the obvious, but to start with unfamiliar sausages, delicate white pudding (*boudin blanc*), black pudding (*boudin noir*), lighter than ours and good with fried apple and mashed potato; well-peppered, knobbly, chitterling *andouillette*, which must be eaten with mustard; small packages of sausagemeat, flavoured with parsley or chestnuts, or truffles, and wrapped in a white veil of caul fat (*crépinettes*). A sausage new to the repertoire is the reddish-brown Algerian *merguez*, a spiced mutton sausage, ideal for hot dogs when stuffed, with fried onion, into a length of *ficelle* or a *pain au lait*. Try out the pâtés, brawns and galantines, too, keeping an eye open for *rillettes*, a piled mass of spiced pork to be spread on bread as a first course or snack – sometimes they are smoothed into moulds and sliced, but the thready browner kind that is dolloped on to a paper, or into a carton, is much better.

When it comes to ham, pass over *jambon de Paris*, or *de York* (often as boring as our own supermarket ham), in favour of thin slices of Bayonne or cheaper country hams; eat them with butter, or with figs, or wrapped round peeled slices of melon. Most *charcutiers* stock branded salami-type sausage (*saucisson sec*), but they will make one or two of their own as well; some of the dried mountain sausages are

A local market, Villefranche-de-Rouergue

Denis Hughes-Gilbey

particularly good, so are the more famous *rosette de Lyon*, the mellow *saucisson d'Arles*, or the little fat *Enfant Jésus de Lyon*, swaddled in a mesh of string. I would also put in a plea that you try the pig's ears: they are ready cooked, all you need do is heat them up in their own jelly, or sprinkle them with crumbs and butter and put them under the grill – you can eat the whole lot with a vinaigrette sauce thickened with chopped herbs and onion, or just the soft jellied meat surrounding the inner cartilage.

Every *charcuterie* seems to have a vast bric-à-brac – tubes of mustard and mayonnaise, pickled olives, gherkins, capers, bags of potato crisps, packages of Breton pancakes (Breton *charcutiers* may sell grey-looking buckwheat pancakes to wrap round their sausages and pâtés, instead of bread), marmalade, tomato ketchup (reckoned to be chic at French barbecues), dried mushrooms, packaged and canned soups.

In other words, the *charcuterie* is the traveller's mecca, the work-saver of people who camp or rent houses, the picnicker's delight, once its mysteries begin to unfold themselves. On any shopping expedition, you will be wise to go there first, and make the rest of your purchases accordingly.

Boucherie
As well as the *charcuterie*, there are three other kinds of meat shop – the *boucherie chevaline*, selling horsemeat (try it once at least, cooking it like beef, but do not expect to find it cheap) and occasional oddities like kid, in the spring when herds are being culled; the *triperie* specializing in tripe, cow heel and calf's head, which is a great treat as it is difficult to buy in England; and the general *boucherie* which sells the range of meat we are accustomed to at the butcher's, with a greater emphasis on veal (lamb is the most expensive, followed by veal and beef, then pork); it also has farm chickens, duck, and guineafowl which can be cooked most successfully in a pot on top of a single burner with onions and green peppercorns, and a little stock and alcohol. Battery poultry does not seem to have caught on in France, as it is tasteless.

When you go to the butcher's take a book or newspaper unless you go early in the day. Every customer is dealt with individually, the meat cut and trimmed to her very firmly expressed desires. This means a long wait sometimes. You may think the meat expensive, but it is usually of the highest quality, free of all waste, and elegantly cut, so you need a smaller weight than you would think of buying at home. To me the butcher in France means the luxury above all of veal escalopes, meltingly tender calf's liver, and large calf's sweetbreads, and the superb corn-fed poultry.

Many butchers also sell pâtés, *rillettes* and sausages, etc., overlapping with the *charcutier*. Sometimes they call themselves *boucher-charcutier*. There is the same kind of difference between them as there is between the baker and *pâtissier*; the products of *charcutier* and *pâtissier* depend on hand-skill and taste, so that their products tend to be finer, less rustic – and slightly more expensive.

Poissonnerie
I have the feeling that travellers neglect fish in France. What could be nicer, more of a treat, than a picnic starting with oysters – at a sensibly low price – shrimps or prawns (*bouquets roses*) and a glass of white wine? And going on to eel or sardines, grilled over vine prunings (sold in plastic bags, in some supermarkets, as *sarments de*

vigne) or a wood fire? I like mild *harengs saurs*, the lightly cured Boulogne bloater, conveniently sold in fillets in packages: they can be decanted, dressed with olive oil or cream and chives, and eaten with plenty of bread, or potato salad.

The variety of fish inland is surprising, but on the coasts you will find an even more ambitious choice. Take the chance to try tunny (*thon*), swordfish (*espadon*) or tope (*veau de mer*), squid (*encornets*) and octopus (*poulpe*). Another delight is the tiny mussels labelled *bouchots*, from the mussel beds where they grow on posts stuck in the shallow water: they are sweeter and more piquant than the large kind. In a restaurant be sure not to miss *praires, palourdes* or *moules farcies*, should they appear on the menu. They come to table sizzling with hot garlic butter and crunchy from the breadcrumbs on top.

A dish that may surprise you in the south, fresh anchovies apart, is the salt cod *ailloli garni* (boiled cod, raw and cooked vegetables, eggs, with garlic mayonnaise). Cod is an Atlantic fish, but since the Middle Ages it has been sent down in exchange for Mediterranean goods, to the extent that southern cooks have evolved far better ways of eating it than the people who produce it. Another great southern dish, *bourride*, may be made from *lotte de mer* (*baudroie*), a fish of firm, sweet texture that we can occasionally buy in Britain as monkfish (most of ours goes to France where it sells at Dover sole prices). When you are in the Alps or Pyrenees, you may come across char-type fish from the lakes, *lavarets, ombles chevaliers*, and – best of all – the trout of mountain streams, *truite du gave*. It is exquisite. One forgets, after fish-farm trout, how good the real thing can be. Perhaps this is the place to say that the best snails we ever ate were served at Mas d'Azil in the Pyrenees, not in Burgundy as you would expect. But then people have been eating snails at Mas d'Azil since the Middle Stone Age.

Pâtisserie

A main shopping ritual is choosing cakes for Sunday lunch. Market day apart, Sunday morning is the great shopping time. Shops put on their best displays. People queue in their best clothes after mass, to buy treats for the family party.

I shall declare unrepentantly that nowhere in Britain can you find cakes comparable in elegance and skill with those you buy in Parisian and good provincial pastrycooks. They altogether lack coarseness and stodge. In consequence they are expensive, to be savoured slowly. Has anyone ever listed the cakes of France? There are large cakes and small, tiny biscuits, *petits fours*, special sweets and chocolates, candied fruit in baskets, sugared almonds in jars, *brioches* and *croissants* richer and lighter than the baker's. How can you choose between the *présidents*, the *religieuses*, babas, *savarins, barquettes aux marrons . . . au chocolat . . . au café*, the *meringues, tartelettes aux fraises . . . aux amandes, financiers, madeleines, oreillettes, bras de Vénus, merveilles, fouaces*, the large *Paris-Brest, St-Honoré, Pithiviers feuilletés* and *fondants, gâteaux moka*, etcetera, etcetera? Every pastrycook of any pride has a speciality, tiny biscuits scented with orange-flower water or crunchy fingers of almond *croquets* or marzipan 'cheeses'. At Easter his windows burst out with chocolate fish, rabbits, hens, eggs, nests, decorated with coloured icing and bows. On May Day pale-green and white cakes are stuck with tiny artificial sprigs matching the lilies of the valley the children sell in the streets.

Some pastrycooks go in for iced confections that rival pictures in Victorian cookery books. Others incline to the savoury, with Easter pies from Berry (sausage meat and halved hard-boiled eggs) or *petits pâtés* of mutton, brown sugar and lemon or raisins, such as they make in Languedoc at Béziers and Pézenas, to a recipe left behind by Clive of India's chef, when his master stayed in those parts.

All these things are for taking away in ribboned parcels and boxes, but you can sit and eat them, too, with tea or coffee and fruit juice for the children. In some towns, the *pâtisserie's* decor will be as twirled with rococo fancies as the cakes. On a Thursday, they are full of large ladies sharing forbidden delights of richness with children and grandchildren, off school for the weekly holiday.

Boulangerie

By law every village in France must have either a baker, or a *dépôt de pain* where bread is delivered daily. Because of the flour, a soft flour, bread needs to be bought at least once daily – most bakers bake twice, in the early morning and at midday – unless you go for wholemeal (*complet*), rye (*seigle*), or the vast *pain de campagne* and *gros pain* which keep for two or three days. People claim that French bread is uneatable next day. This is not entirely true. It can be brushed with water and heated in the oven, it can be toasted or fried. Never throw bread away in France, if you value your neighbours' good opinion. Keep it and give it to people with dogs, who will use it up in the dog's soup.

France is famous for its different breads and their light textures. My favourite is the *ficelle*, the smallest and thinnest and crustiest, ideal for sandwiches and for breakfast. Next in size comes the *baguette*, then the pound *pain de livre* (the French have not yet given up their pre-metrication weights as you will find out when you go shopping), then the large loaves mentioned above. You will find varying specialities, the oval *Viennois* or *bâtard*, the round *couronne*, and the *pain de mie*, which looks like an English tin loaf, except that it is baked a metre long, in sections that can be pulled off for sale. A practical bread for picnics is the *épi, baguette* length, but consisting of little pointed knobs of dough stuck together like an ear of corn. There will be bread rolls very likely, and the milk rolls known as *pains au lait*, certainly *pains au chocolat*, made from an enriched dough with a stick of chocolate in the centre, for children's tea.

The baker also sells *croissants, brioches*, éclairs, apple turnovers and a horrible floury yellow custard tart called a *flan*, much favoured by children. I cannot understand why the French tolerate such a monstrosity when they could make much nicer versions for themselves at home, as we do in England. The truth is that the French housewife is not much of a cake or bun-maker, such things being regarded as occasional treats, for Sundays and family feasts.

Épicerie, supermarché, le self-service

These cover the same range, sometimes under the same umbrellas of SPAR and CO-OP, as they do in Britain, with the bonus of intelligent advice. The French manage to have the best of both worlds. In a Normandy store, I saw shelves of litre cans beside the bottled milk. The manager was filling the cans from a churn – 'Many of my customers prefer farm milk.' There's no doorstep delivery of milk in France, but that kind of attitude is a compensation. We have learned to value help in choosing fruit, vegetables, cheeses. Kindly hints have directed us towards certain packaged

A cheese merchant on market day, Nice

brioches and cakes, away from others, towards certain canned foods – tiny undyed *petits pois*, green or haricot or flageolet beans, salsify, sardines, mackerel in white wine, tunny *au naturel* rather than in oil; fish soups, cassoulet and tripe in tins are a splendid basis for improvements. Apart from commercial icecream, far better than ours, freezer goods are best avoided; familiar international brands cost twice as much as in Britain.

From the dairy cabinet, try different *fromages frais*, the delight of summer meals in France, and the cream, which is 'ripened', a little sharp, making it ideal for fruit and sauces, but useless in coffee. At the butchery counter, meat can be as excellent as an independent butcher's, but the factory *charcuterie* will be blander. Look out for smoked whole chicken (the boned and rolled kinds have a denatured texture and taste); in hot weather it makes a delicious cold meat with salads, or you can joint and reheat it with vegetables.

Such shops, particularly in their grand Parisian form at Fauchon, Hédiard and Corcellet, provide treasures to take home after the holiday. Even from our small town, we can load the returning car with jars of salted anchovies, grey Breton sea salt, walnut oil, vanilla pods, *quatre épices* for flavouring pork, juniper berries, harissa, couscous semolina, slate-green lentils, split green peas, smoked cod's liver (*foie de morue fumé* – excellent), fine biscuits, orange-flower water, bilberry jam.

A last word, do not despise the hypermarket. You can buy everything there, and go to the bank, while the children have an ice or pancakes. Range and quality of food, including cooked items, are outstanding. They are a godsend if you cater for a family, and the weather's too good – or too bad – for you to indulge in a daily amble round the specialized shops of the nearest village or town.

Wines of France

George Rainbird

Vines are grown in most of the departments of France and by some hundreds of thousands of growers, and it is not in the province of this short essay to enter into any detailed or technical account. One will assume that the reader has drunk wine, likes drinking wine, and would like to know what to expect and where to find it. Most of the wines made are *ordinaires*, some are good wines, many are fine wines and few, very few, are great, and not even then in a bad year. The traveller will get the cheapest local wine there is if he is supplied with a meal inclusive of wine, and this does not necessarily mean a bad wine – very far from it. Most of the *ordinaires* that come to the café table or restaurant table at a *prix fixe* meal will be from Roussillon at the eastern end of the Pyrenees. They are rich and fruity and perfectly good honest wines and can be bought at most *alimentations* or supermarkets for a few francs for a litre bottle if you take your own bottle. Go to the other extreme and you will find bottles of the great burgundies and Bordeaux wines for – I am not joking – as much as £30–40. Choose according to your purse, and you will not choose the very expensive wines for indiscriminate drinking.

I think my advice would be, if you wish to undertake a tasting of the wines of France, to go on a *tour vinicole* which starting at Calais or Boulogne will take you round the vineyards of France comfortably in two or three weeks, and will give you an opportunity of really sampling wines great and small in the places where they are made, which are themselves mostly places of great beauty. I have recently completed such a trip myself (the last of many such), and my route took me from Calais to Champagne, from Champagne to Alsace, thence to Burgundy, from Burgundy to the Dordogne, and thence to Bordeaux, returning by way of Cognac and the Loire. It was a most delightful experience, taken at the time of the vintage when the vines had turned in colour and when the famous Côtes d'Or of Burgundy had turned into real, brilliant, gold.

Now I shall say a word about tasting. There is no difficulty about sampling wine at any place in France where they make it. The traveller will get used to the word *dégustation*, which usually means that a local vineyard has a room or rooms arranged with samples of its wine for the traveller to taste and, hopefully, to buy bottles to take away. Mostly they do. Sometimes the tasting is free, sometimes not. On the other hand, in the great vineyards of Burgundy, Bordeaux, Champagne, and so on, the traveller will need an introduction if he is to be taken into the world-famous cellars; this is easily obtained from your local wine merchant, who will be delighted to arrange matters for you. After such an introduction you will almost certainly be able to taste, and you will not be expected to buy unless you wish to place a fairly large order, which would be supplied through your local wine merchant.

So to our travels. The road will take you from Calais or Boulogne through

Champagne cellars

Amiens, Compiègne, Soissons, and there you will decide whether to go to Reims or Épernay. It does not really matter which if you are going for the wine. Reims has, of course, its marvellous cathedral where the kings of France were crowned. Épernay has its *Avenue de Champagne* where most of the great houses have their cellars, and there you will be received at any one of them. No appointment is necessary and arrangements are made for periodic tours of the cellars, some of which run for literally miles in the solid chalk. Here the mysteries of champagne will be explained and, hopefully, you may be able to taste. At the end of it you will be surprised at the extremely moderate price of champagne, because the making is, to say the least, a very expensive process. Champagne is made from both black and white grapes, usually a mixture, although nowadays *blanc de blanc*, or champagne made only from white grapes, is deservedly popular. Champagne itself denotes a process as well as a district and it is more than just sparkling wine. Sparkling wine may be made by other processes such as injection of carbonic acid gas (the worst) and also in what is called a *cuvée close* which is fermented in vat and not in the bottle. There is no substitute for champagne: true champagne is a very long process and the wine is not put on the market for some years.

Between Reims and Épernay is the 'Mountain of Reims' which is largely forest and where the wild boar is still hunted. On either side of the forest are the great champagne vineyards where the tiny pinot grapes are grown on shallow chalky soil which has no peer anywhere else in the world.

After leaving Champagne the road will take you through Nancy (where the Place Stanislaus is not to be missed) down through delightful scenery to Colmar in Alsace. To the north are the famous wine villages of Riquewihr, Ribeauvillé, and so on, where the delicious Alsatian wines are grown. The scenery is almost as good as the wine, and in Riquewihr, which is a walled village with vines growing right up to the walls, every house seems to have its main concern in wine and the making of wine. There you will have no problems about *dégustation*. Restaurants and cafés will suit every purse and the wine is the wine of the village and made in it. I am not going to tell you what the wine tastes like – that I must leave to people who can explain taste better than I can – but my advice is to go for yourself and be happy, because then there is no question that you will enjoy every mouthful.

From Colmar your road will take you through to Dijon, again through lovely country, and from Dijon to Beaune is where the great burgundies are grown and made. Chablis means a detour on this road but again is well worth the visit, for chablis is very delicious wine and there is not much of it. But the road from Dijon to Beaune is bordered by very famous vineyards; red wines to the north such as the great Chambertin, Chambolle Musigny, the Clos de Vougeot which may be visited and should not be missed, Vosne-Romanée, and the famous vineyards of Echézeaux, La Tâche, Corton, Romanée-Conti, Richebourg, and so on to Beaune, which I think has been well described in the section in this book on Burgundy so I will not repeat it here.

South of Beaune you have the great white burgundies as well as some red. Here are Montrachet, Meursault, Blagny and many other world-famous vineyards. There are plenty of places to buy them in Beaune if you can afford them, but you must remember that the output of these vineyards is miniscule compared with the rest of the wines of France and you must expect to pay a lot of money for your good bottles, comparatively at any rate. Burgundy is by regulation subject to *chaptalisation*, which is to say that because the vineyards are northerly and the grapes do not always obtain their full sweetness, the vinegrower is allowed by law to add sugar, and this method has developed, although it is strictly regulated. Only

The Château and vineyards of Clos de Vougeot

Peter Baker

experience and taste can show whether the wine has been oversweetened but the great burgundies are not oversweet.

Continuing further south you will come to the famous country of the Beaujolais, where (I may remind you) it has been said that Paris alone consumes twice the annual product of all the vineyards of Beaujolais. It is a much-faked wine, but the true Beaujolais (and here you must rely on the integrity of your wine merchant) is a delicious wine which used to be cheap but is no longer. The wines are much better than their popularity would seem to indicate, and some of the estate-bottled wine can last to a great age and attain great perfection. A good *Moulin-à-Vent* can achieve greatness. In between Beaune and Beaujolais is the Mâcon, which produces a large quantity of excellent white and red wine, including the *Pouilly-Fuissé* wines and the *Mâcon Blanc* and *Mâcon Rouge* which are somewhere between the Beaujolais and burgundies, and all are very good and reasonably inexpensive wines. Again you will have no trouble about *dégustation* in these districts.

If you proceed further south still you will come to Provence on the other side of Lyon, again travelling through some lovely country, and arrive at the home of *Châteauneuf-du-Pape* which makes an excellent Provençal wine; and on the other side of the Rhône at Tavel are made some fine *rosé* wines from both white and red grapes, sometimes from three black and two white grapes, to a formula that has been handed down from father to son for generations – a lovely colour and a rather special flavour, and like all Provençal wines they should be drunk cold rather than at chamber temperature. There are no really important wines between Provence and the Pyrenees and it is in this district that most of the *ordinaires* are made and exported in tankers all over France and indeed Europe. The soil is rich, the grapes are large and bountiful and there is no *finesse* about them, but they are none the less a very good drink for ordinary rather than special drinking.

Here your road can take you two ways towards Bordeaux: either along the foothills of the Pyrenees through Carcassonne, or northwest through the lovely valley of the Dordogne. The wines are better on the more northern route, and rather sweet wines are made at Bergerac and Monbazillac. The gentle scenery of the Dordogne is not to be missed and good sound wines can be drunk everywhere. The road is a pure joy, with ancient castles amid the gentle hills and lovely landscape, and for those who like caves and for the archaeologists there are the wonders of Les Eyzies.

So, enjoying every moment of the drive, we arrive at St-Émilion, which is the outpost of the Bordeaux *appellation contrôlée*. St-Émilion itself is a lovely town, with many architectural wonders, especially the great church carved out of solid rock in the tenth and eleventh centuries, but the vineyards of St-Émilion are its chief attraction, with great names one upon the other. Château Ausone is built on the site of the villa of the Roman poet Ausonius who wrote poems in honour of wine, and his vineyards are still under cultivation today. Here also is the Château Cheval Blanc which achieved a miracle wine in 1947 and which now when it is found can only be bought by millionaires. St-Émilion wines are not cheap and many of them are truly great. The same may be said of the adjoining communes of Pomerol, where the wine is slightly fruitier and probably the nearest a claret can ever get to a burgundy, and there you have the famous Château Pétrus, a small vineyard which had phylloxera-free vines up to 1956, when they were destroyed by late frosts. They still make a small quantity of excellent wine. There are so many good vineyards in or about St-Émilion that it would seem invidious to choose one above the other; there certainly is no lack of opportunity of *dégustation* in this very lovely town.

From St-Émilion you may travel by way of Libourne straight into Bordeaux. Libourne is the port for St-Émilion and where most of the wine *négociants* and merchants have their cellars, but to visit them you will need an introduction. Next you may travel across country, and this I recommend should be through the country of *Entre-Deux-Mers*, where are made vast quantities of sweetish good white wine which is deservedly popular and inexpensive, and eventually arriving at Langon at the other end of the Graves-Sauternes district. At Langon the Sauternes and Barsac vineyards start, and soon the traveller will find himself amid famous names, none more so than Château d'Yquem where is made probably the most famous white wine in the world. The grapes are kept on the vine until they are rotten with age, when they have become almost entirely sugar alcohol. They are covered with a mould, the famous *pourriture noble*, and they are literally picked one by one (I have seen this more than once) day by day as they grow to sufficient ripeness. The pickers start at one end of the vineyard and go through it picking these single grapes, and come back the next day when more have become sufficiently ripe, and from these mouldy-looking grapes is pressed the sweetest and most beautiful wine that the gods have allowed to come into our mouths. The French like to drink *Château d'Yquem* with *foie gras*; I think they are probably the only nation that can afford it, because *d'Yquem* by reason of its rarity and difficulty is one of the most expensive white wines in the world, and we all know about the cost of *foie gras*.

Thence we travel towards Bordeaux through the other famous sweet-white-wine vineyards: Climens, Coutet, and other well-known names until we come to Graves, where much white wine is made but even more red. The red wines are not so full as the *Médocs*, they are fine wines and are mostly delicious. There again you will find great names such as Smith-Haut-Lafitte, Pape Clément, culminating as one gets into Bordeaux with the two great vineyards of Graves, Haut-Brion and La Mission-Haut-Brion, nearly opposite one another and both of the very highest order; in fact Château Haut Brion is one of the five first growths of Bordeaux, the other four all being in the Médoc to the north. If you happen to be in Bordeaux itself during the weekend, when you will not be popular if you visit vineyards (although there are plenty of places for *dégustation*), go to Arcachon which is the sea resort for Bordeaux and where one can still buy oysters at a few francs a dozen – not very big ones certainly, but washed down with some of the local white wine you will find them excellent. In Bordeaux itself the wine trade is centred along the banks of the river on the *Quai des Chartrons*, and here are some of the greatest wine shippers in the world – Calvet, Cruse, Sichel, and so on. You will need an introduction from your wine merchant to visit them but it is well worth the trouble – you will be courteously received, shown some of the most fantastic collections of wines anywhere, and you could even be given some to drink.

After Bordeaux, the Médoc is the mecca of all wine lovers. It is about 20 kilometres to the north and here you will find some of the greatest wines in the world. The vines grow on stony, gravelly soil with a very small yield; the soil is so perfect that if the resulting wine is properly made (and all wines are not properly made in the Médoc) they produce wines of incomparable quality. It is the salts and

Cahors vineyards in the Lot Valley

minerals of the soil which are responsible for this fantastic quality, and they are not found all over the Médoc. There can be a difference in the soil between one field and the next, and in travelling through the country one can pass for miles where no vines are grown and then possibly a further stretch of several miles with nothing but vines. And let there be no mistake, the wine does vary from one vineyard to another. All the names that you remember from your wine labels will come one after the other – Macau, Margaux, St-Julien, Pauillac, St-Estèphe, with their smaller communes on either side. Here in the Médoc are four of the greatest vineyards in the world and so classified as *Premiers Crus*: Lafite, Latour, Margaux, and Mouton-Rothschild. Here is wine made regardless of its cost; it can only be bought *mis en bouteille au château* and at prices which can rise to £80 or £90 a bottle for a 1945 vintage. Here are also the other fifty châteaux which were granted the five *Grand Cru* classifications in 1855, and here also are some two thousand or more minor châteaux (châteaux in this sense means little more than a farmhouse in some cases) where are made the excellent Bourgeois wines which one buys under their own label, or as *Médoc*, or in some cases merely as *Bordeaux*. There is plenty of *dégustation*, but introductions, I am afraid, are needed for all the principal châteaux.

The trip from Bordeaux through the Médoc is fascinating, with all the great names of wines spread on small signposts in the vineyards one after the other like a mighty procession of giants. Some of the châteaux are beautiful, others are not, but Château Beychevelle is a joy and Lafite is very pretty, and d'Issan a marvellous example of a medieval château. Pauillac, the centre of the Médoc, is a seedy little town on the Gironde and with no good restaurants but one or two minor ones not worthy of the great wines it serves. If you do not want to go back through Bordeaux you can cross the Gironde by ferry at Lamarque near Margaux to Blaye on the other side, and in this country on the low hills above the river are grown some very excellent wines which have improved greatly in recent years due to more modern methods of filtration and technique. The Blayais wines are usually sold under *appellation contrôlée* Bordeaux or *Premières Côtes de Blaye* and they are good soft wines but without the unique character of the Médoc.

It is now time to start the long trek back home. Passing through vines all the way on the road to La Rochelle you come to Cognac, where there will be no difficulty in *dégustation* at all. Here are the great brandies of France, equalled only by those of Armagnac south of Bordeaux. Cognac is made from the distilled wine of the St-Émilion grape, which has nothing whatever to do with St-Émilion; it is merely the name of a rather sourish type of grape which when distilled makes superb brandy; one is told that the river Charente which flows through Cognac has something to do with it too – I am not quite sure why or how. The finest cognac comes from a very small district round Cognac itself called Grande and Petite Champagne because the soil is similar to that of the champagne district in the north, but the Fins Champagne of Cognac has nothing whatever to do with sparkling champagne. There are five or six main classes of soil upon which the grapes grow from which the cognac is distilled and the finest are the Grande Champagne and Petite Champagne, after which come the Fins Bois and the Bons Bois, and lastly the Bois Ordinaires.

If you have time call in at La Rochelle, which is a very lovely town with some good restaurants, otherwise proceed to the Loire and make for Sancerre about the middle of the Loire vineyards. Good wine is made throughout the length of the Loire, and well worth the special journey as Monsieur Michelin would say. It might be a good idea to start at Nantes and drink the *Muscadet* of the district, which is rather dry but delicious on a hot day, and then follow the Loire as far as you want to, visiting on the way the very famous fifteenth-, sixteenth- and seventeenth-century châteaux which were so beloved by the court of France, all of which are of great beauty in marvellous settings. You will sample the wines of the Côteaux de la Loire on the lovely hills south of the Loire itself between Angers and Saumur, the Côteaux du Layon, and all round Saumur is made excellent wine. After Saumur you will get to Pouilly where you may drink the *Pouilly-Fumé* and the wines of Reuilly and Quincy. At Saumur are made many sparkling wines but not all by *méthode champenoise*. All these wines have their own character, not forgetting the very good red wine of Bourgueil. If you are travelling north to Calais from this point there will not be much of vinous interest and you will have to complete your education by what you can find on the menus of hotels and restaurants.

I am quite well aware in this brief dissertation on wines of France that I have missed some important vineyards, including the quite important wines of the Rhône valley which are universally good and of a fairly high alcoholic content. But as I have said before and repeat again, wine is made all over France with the exception of the northwest corner. The reader must follow his nose, for there will be no lack of opportunity, and I wish you all *bon voyage* and *bon appétit* and success with your tasting.

The Caves of Prehistoric Man

Hammond Innes

The cave area of France lies in a great half circle stretching from Biscay to the Mediterranean and up the Rhône Valley as far as the Côte d'Or. But it is in Périgord and Quercy that the most interesting caves are found, and it is here that France holds in trust one of the great treasures of the world.

Far back in geological time the great bare plateaux of the *causse* emerged out of the sea to stretch long limestone fingers down towards what is now the Garonne, channelling rivers and streams that grooved out great overhangs and disappeared underground to tunnel the endless caverns. It was ideal country for Neanderthal man, and his first known habitation in the area was at the Le Moustier site, which gave its name to the whole Mousterian period.

For the better part of 70,000 years our ancestors found shelter in the caves and overhangs of this limestone country, hunting reindeer, bison, horses, even mammoth and woolly rhinoceros. The evidence of man's carnivorous occupation is to be seen wherever archaeologists have cut vertically through the middens at the entrance to old cave dwellings, exposing layer upon layer of habitation marked by the ash of hearths and discarded bones. The weapons with which he killed his prey have also been unearthed, artefacts fashioned out of antlers and bones, chipped from rock or flaked from the cherty flint characteristic of the Dordogne.

Speleologists have explored more than 1200 caves in this area alone. Pierre Vidal, leader of a local group, examined over seven hundred in a period of twenty years searching for evidence of prehistoric occupation. Only about fifty have been classified as *gisements* – i.e. those showing evidence of prehistoric habitation. But – and here is the treasure – no less than half of these include examples of prehistoric engravings and paintings.

The work of those early cave artists dates back 30,000 years, and most of it is in the vicinity of the Vézère river, which meanders between pale grey limestone cliffs to make its junction with the Dordogne just below Les Eyzies. This small town is the centre of the greatest concentration of early habitation. To the north, within walking distance, is the Gorge d'Enfer, Le Grand Roc, Laugerie Basse and Laugerie Haute, where archaeologists have cut down through layers of occupation 10 metres deep; to the south and east are La Mouthe, Bernifal, Combarelles, La Grèze, Cap Blanc. Les Eyzies is indeed the French 'Capitale de la Préhistoire'.

There is an excellent museum built on the site of the Cro-Magnon *abri* or shelter where the skulls, unearthed in 1868, gave the name Cro-Magnon man to a species of *Homo sapiens* living in the Aurignacian period of 20,000–30,000 years BP (Before the Present). It was from Cro-Magnon man that most of the cave artists were descended.

For convenience it is probably best to visit Les Eyzies in the tourist season, but my

Cave drawings at Les Eyzies

wife and I were there to study the caves for the background of my novel *Levkas Man*, and in winter it is more peaceful. La Mouthe was the one we wanted to see first and there was snow on the ground as we drove under a great limestone overhang and up the road to the farm. The cave is just below the farm buildings and it was Marie Lapeyre herself who showed it to us, looking like a Mother Superior in her black Périgord habit, carrying an old acetylene lamp and unlocking the wooden door of the blocked-up entrance with a huge key.

It was the discovery of painted animals in this cave that started the archaeologists searching for prehistoric art. This is where it all began, and it happened by accident. Even when we were there the cave was still being used as a storeroom for farm produce, gourds, potatoes, and a great pile of carrots laid out on the floor. For years it had also been used as the *cave*. Marie Lapeyre was a young girl in 1895 when workers enlarging the *cave* so that it would hold more of her grandfather's wine broke through into the long gallery with its paintings of animals. The great French archaeologist, the Abbé Breuil, happened to be in the neighbourhood and it was his study of the paintings that started the frantic search for further examples of prehistoric cave art.

Marie Lapeyre worked with him at La Mouthe. It was important, she told us, to see the paintings by lamplight since it was then possible to see them the way the artists had envisaged them as they worked by the light of animal fat burning in stone lamps. One of the original lamps was still there on the floor, but the others had been removed to a local museum. Holding her acetylene lamp aloft, she traced for us the faded outlines of bison, reindeer, cattle and horses; there was the vague shape of a mammoth, a large rhinoceros, and at the far end of the cave, 128 metres from the entrance, a primitive hut engraved on the rock surface and painted in black and red.

A much earlier discovery is the vast Grotte de Rouffignac. This is the 'Cave of the 100 Mammoths', complete with its own railway, where vandalization of the *gravures* dates back as far as the early-seventeenth century. The scratchings on the walls would have had no scientific significance until Breuil examined La Mouthe, and those who entered it by the light of candles so long ago would have come for the excitement of exploration.

Rouffignac is one of the many caves that are privately owned and when we were there we had to persuade Monsieur Plassard to leave the re-tiling of his farmhouse roof. The humid air drifted like smoke in the frosty sunlight of the entrance as we descended to the tramlines of the miniature railway. There are 10 kilometres of explored galleries and, unlike the lesser caves fashioned by the rivers, this is a sea cavern. Where the railway ends, which is the furthest point penetrated by ancient man, there are a great number of *gravures* of mammoths slashed with the 'macaroni' lines that scientists believe represented the spears or arrows of the hunters.

The theory that the caves were temples of a very primitive religion and that the hunters came there to have the 'witch doctor' artists engrave or paint their hopes for a successful kill is a possibility that can never be proved. The owner of Rouffignac certainly believed that our early ancestors worshipped an earth goddess and that they penetrated to the greatest depth to be as close to her as possible; there the beast they hoped to kill was engraved on the rock and marked with the hunter's weapons. There are other, deeper scratches on the walls of Rouffignac, but the cause of this is obvious, for the cave is pitted for half its length by great hollows made by generations of hibernating bears.

Combarelles is another sea cavern, but only 237 metres in extent. The grandfather of the man who showed us round discovered its paintings in 1901. It was the fire marks at the entrance, with natural chimneys for the smoke, that encouraged him to penetrate deeper into the twisting passages. There are sections of wall here that have been painted over and over again – bison, horses, deer, woolly rhinoceros, a bear, several mammoths, even a giraffe and a lion. The old man died at the age of 112 and either his theory, or his grandson's, was that those early men had tried to record all the animals they had seen on their long trek over the land-bridge from Africa to the Dordogne.

Here the oxide and iron-oxide pigments of the paintings are very faint, probably because they did not use grease to impregnate the rock first as the artists did in nearby Font-de-Gaume. This cave, with its narrow passages and its superb reproductions of animals – there are 80 bison, 40 horses, 23 mammoths, 17 deer and a number of other figures including a wolf, a bear and a man – is the greatest art treasure you can now see, for the most magnificent of all, Lascaux, has been closed to the public for a long time. The reason for its closure is apparent at Font-de-Gaume. Because the paintings are open to the air, and also subject to the breath of visitors, their colours, already faint, are gradually deteriorating.

This is the problem the authorities had to face at Lascaux, which is further up the Vézère on a hill above Montignac, for Lascaux is without question the finest example of prehistoric art in France, probably in the world. It was not discovered

until 1940 when four boys, attracted by vague stories of treasure associated with the
area, went searching for it. The roof hole into the cave had for years been used as a
rubbish dump and had been stuffed with branches to prevent cattle from falling into
it. Jacques Marsal at fifteen was already a keen cave explorer. It was he who went
down the hole with a torch, found himself in a narrow chute and, wriggling
backwards, dropped into the great three-roomed art gallery of priceless paintings.
And it was Jacques Marsal who showed us round when we went armed with the
necessary official letter that would secure our admission.

The impact of the galleries is immediate and in a sense shocking, for not only were
these men great artists, but their subject was slaughter. In the light of our torch,
ceilings and walls were a terrible charnel-house red. And it was not just the colour
that was startling, it was the wonderful sense of movement, sometimes relaxed, but
more often expressive of fear. Bulls and horses, two startled bison, the shapes
getting larger as you proceed until the whole roof bears the sprawling image of a
great bull. There is a frieze of deer swimming a river, just the heads, but still
conveying the fearful struggle against the current. There is a little horse that is a
masterpiece, and then a whole herd of horses being driven over a cliff, one of them
falling upside down, another with its neck flung back in terror, its forefeet treading
air. The last gallery of all is full of animals either wounded or falling into traps.

This is the art form of Man the Killer. Painted 15,000–20,000 years ago, it remains
in my mind as a nightmare representation of instincts we still possess.

The paints they used had a base of iron or manganese. When applying wet paint
they used a stick brush, either stroking or dabbing it on; in powdered form they blew

Animal drawings in the caves at Lascaux

it on. Usually they engraved the outline first, and the extraordinary thing is that in painting the cave roof they not only worked lying on their backs, but also managed to maintain the proportion and the flow of the animals' movement, though the curve of the rock made it impossible for them to see half the 'canvas' they were working on.

To preserve these paintings Lascaux is now like a combination of pressure chamber and laboratory. The entrance is through a series of airlocks; there is an air circulation plant, instruments to check temperature and humidity and a whole range of gadgets designed specifically for checking and recording the work of preservation. Everything is designed to reproduce the natural condition of air circulation that existed before the cave was first opened to the public in 1948. It was the interruption of the normal circulation, and human breathing, which caused the damaging green algae to form. We were just three people and in less than an hour the sensitive instruments had recorded a significant change in the cave's atmosphere.

Bearing this in mind, the natural disappointment at being excluded should be alleviated by appreciation of the fact that the French authorities are doing everything possible to preserve this great treasure for posterity. There are reproductions available on the site and the Mousterian excavations at Regourdou are only 500 metres away. And anyway there is so much else to see in this area. All through the Vézère valley there are superb walks among the truffle oaks and the limestone cliffs, and always that sense of treading in the footsteps of prehistoric man – always the possibility of finding some unlisted *gravure*, even of stumbling upon another treasure like Lascaux!

Drawings in the caves at Niaux near Foix

Jean Vertut

A Brief History of France

Joy Law

See also Chronology of Principal Events, page 450

History in France, if not French history, could be said to start with the cave paintings of Lascaux, in the fertile valley of the Vézère where over two hundred sites are known to have sheltered Early Man as early as 30,000 BC. The other striking monuments of prehistoric France are the megalithic tombs at Carnac in Brittany, where the mysterious stone alignments are the only remains of a civilization, of about 3000 BC, of which we have no other records.

Gauls, Romans, Visigoths

The first peoples of whom we have more informative evidence are the Gauls, as the Celts are commonly known in France. They established themselves from about the fourth century BC and their many tribes achieved a stable form of government for some three hundred years.

Towards the end of the second century BC, the Romans, needing a wider base for operations against the Carthaginians, colonized Provence, and their grandiose buildings may still be seen at Nîmes, Arles, Orange and the Pont du Gard. Julius Caesar spent from 55 to 52 BC putting the rest of Gaul, with uncharacteristic brutality, under the Roman yoke, and his conquest was complete when he defeated the last Gallic chieftain, Vercingétorix.

The Gallo-Roman era was one of relative prosperity and peace for the five subsequent centuries until it was brought to an end by barbarian invaders from the east. Of these, the Visigoths were the most tenacious; in the fifth century AD they created a kingdom which stretched from the Loire to the Pyrenees, until they in their turn were ousted by the Salian Franks.

The Merovingian and Carolingian Kings

Clovis, the pagan leader of the Franks, was the grandson of Merovius, who gave his name to the first 'French' dynasty, the Merovingians. It was he who, by becoming a Christian through the influence of his wife Clotilde, created that link between crown and church that was to become such a feature of later dynasties. His heirs ruled France for longer than either the Valois or the Bourbons, but the last rulers of his house, known as *les rois fainéants*, were effete and corrupt, and were replaced by their palace mayors, the Carolingians.

The first Carolingian, Charles Martel, defeated the Moors at the decisive battle of Poitiers in 732 and saved continental Europe from Islam. His grandson Charlemagne restored to western Europe something of its Roman order and territorial unity in his creation of the Holy Roman Empire, and laid the foundations from which feudalism was to spring. His grand scheme did not long outlast his death, for his descendants divided his inheritance and then had to contend with

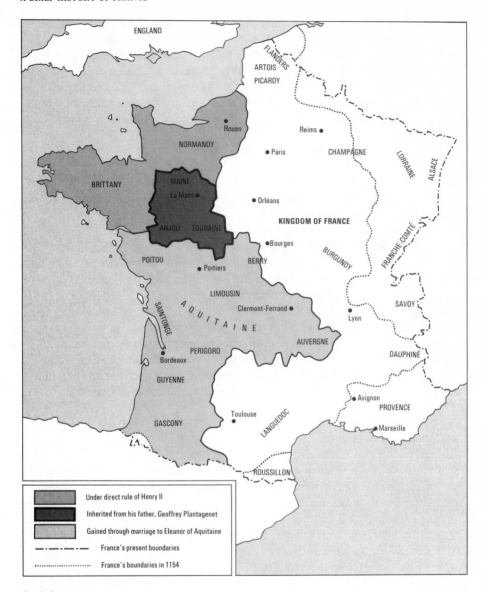

English possessions in France in 1154

invasions not only from the Moors but also from the Norsemen. In the loosening of central power that followed, the barons of France emerged as powerful local magnates, until one of them rose above his peers, and was made king.

Capets and Plantagenets

Hugues Capet, Duke of the Franks, was consecrated King at Noyon in 987, and though he only controlled modest estates in the Ile-de-France, his successors, who reigned from father to son until 1328, established the principle of hereditary monarchic power and created the base from which the nation state of France was to grow. The English soon became the greatest threat to Capetian territorial control. Henry Plantagenet, when he inherited the English throne in 1154, ruled not only the whole of northwestern France but had also acquired Aquitaine on his marriage to the French king's divorced wife, Eleanor. The area of France which acknowledged the overlordship of the English king thereby far exceeded that of the French, and the long love-hate relationship between the two countries began.

The English in France and the Hundred Years War
War between England and France was continuous but spasmodic throughout the thirteenth and fourteenth centuries, but since it was localized it did not prevent the growth of new towns and cities, whose increasing population and wealth was reflected in the great Romanesque churches and Gothic cathedrals then built. A national consciousness was being born, to be tested and strengthened throughout the long struggle of the Hundred Years War. The English defeated the flower of the French chivalry at the battle of Crécy in 1346, and again at Poitiers ten years later when the French king, Jean II, was taken prisoner and sent to England, where he later died. The French crown was further weakened by internal dissent, exemplified by the revolt of Étienne Marcel in Paris and by the defection of semi-independent nobles like the Duke of Burgundy. Another victory by the English, at Agincourt in 1415, enabled Henry V five years later to stipulate that his son by the French king's daughter, Catherine of Valois, should inherit the French throne. The Treaty of Troyes was the nadir of French fortunes, which did not improve until Joan of Arc inspired the French to military victories and enabled the Dauphin to be consecrated as Charles VII at Reims in 1429.

The Renaissance in France
With the English evicted from all of France but Calais, following on their defeat at Castillon in 1453, the French cast their eyes beyond their own boundaries, and Charles VIII and François I led a series of ultimately unsuccessful expeditions to Italy. Although François I was captured at Pavia in 1525 and imprisoned by the Emperor Charles V, on his return he opened the cultural gates to admit Italian artists and craftsmen; the result was that brilliant marriage of styles to be seen in Renaissance châteaux such as those of the Loire and at Fontainebleau. Meanwhile Burgundy had reverted to the crown in 1477, and Brittany was re-united to it by the marriage of its duchess to two successive kings, Charles VIII and Louis XII, who also acquired a further ten provinces.

The Wars of Religion
The kingdom, so recently united territorially, was then torn apart by religious strife. The Protestants (Huguenots) rapidly became, as did their counterparts in England, a party held together as much by political as by religious beliefs. Their threat to the stability of the predominantly Catholic country was made the more dangerous by the fact that so many of them were members of the establishment. The Wars of Religion, which finally erupted in 1562, were marked by the savagery that often characterizes civil war, and culminated in the Massacre of St Bartholomew's Eve. Most of the influential Huguenots were gathered together in Paris for the marriage

Mansell Collection

The Massacre of St Bartholomew's Eve 1572. Contemporary engraving

of Henri of Navarre and Marguerite of Valois in August 1572, and on the night of the 24th over two thousand of them were killed by Catholics in Paris alone.

It took six years and a man as resolute and crafty as Henri IV, the first Bourbon king, to heal France's wounds. His politically adroit conversion to Catholicism from Protestantism, the promulgation of the Edict of Nantes in 1598, which allowed Protestants a limited freedom of worship, and the policies of his chief minister, Sully, who encouraged agriculture as the basis of a sound French economy, went a long way to re-establish harmony and encourage trade and commerce.

The Sun King: Le Grand Siècle

The assassination of Henri IV in 1610 and the succession of a minor saw the first of a series of powerful and worldly cardinals who were to be responsible for the government. Richelieu, whose 'first goal was the majesty of the king, and whose second was the greatness of the realm', went far to establishing the base from which Louis XIV was to build his centralized and autocratic government. The *roi soleil*, adept in his early and middle years in his choice of public servants like Colbert, Turenne and Vauban, reigned for seven decades, until his death in 1715, over a France whose frontiers he enlarged and whose arts he enriched. He conducted the *grand siècle* from his palace at Versailles, created to muzzle the nobility and stun the world. But the Revocation of the Edict of Nantes in 1685 resulted in many of his most hard-working subjects fleeing the country, and his lavish spending ultimately antagonized his people. This, combined with his wars of aggrandizement, enfeebled the country and, by upsetting the European balance of power, provoked his neighbours, the English in particular. The Duke of Marlborough's victories in the early 1700s, combined with disastrous winters and harvests, left the French people starving and the aristocracy disillusioned.

Cliché des Musées Nationaux

The Palace at Versailles in 1722, by P-D. Martin

The Revolution

Reaction against the classical grandeur of the seventeenth century led easily on the one hand to the extravagances of the Regency and Rococo, and on the other to the radicalism of the *Encyclopédistes*. The monarchy, which until then had been a stabilizing factor between opposing political and social forces, came to be seen by the *philosophes* and their followers as the barrier to the reforms which they thought reason and natural justice demanded. The institutions of the monarchy and the attitudes popularized by Voltaire and Rousseau were incompatible. The aristocracy took note of the success of the American revolt against the English; the middle class resented the privileges of the aristocracy; and the peasantry found its antiquated feudal burdens ever more intolerable. The writings of the *philosophes*, the legacy of Louis XV's wars which lost France her Indian and Canadian colonies, bad harvests and inflation, and the well-meaning but inept attempts at reform by Louis XVI, were a potent mixture. With hindsight the Revolution seems to have been inevitable.

The National Assembly, established on 9 July 1789, and the fall of the Bastille on 14 July, celebrated since 1880 as a national holiday, were the opening events of a movement that was to go far beyond the intentions of its instigators. In its early days, led by Mirabeau, who believed with Montesquieu in the separation of powers, it was essentially a republican movement where the nation was to be sovereign but with the monarchy at its head. But the government's feeble reaction to a programme of reasonable reforms was fuel to the fire of the radical party.

The Jacobins, and extremists such as Danton, Marat and Robespierre, emerged as the men in command. The King was guillotined in 1793, and the Terror, which lasted fourteen months and claimed 2800 heads in Paris and 14,000 in the provinces, cowed opposition. But as the violence grew, so it brought reaction; on 27 July 1794 Robespierre was removed and suffered the fate of so many of his victims.

Napoleon
The Convention, one of the many self-constituted governments of the time, was succeeded by the Directory; this in turn was ended five years later by a *coup d'état* in which a rising young soldier who had distinguished himself in the wars of France, Napoleon Bonaparte, became First Consul. It was a short step for General Bonaparte to transform himself into an Emperor. Napoleon crowned himself in the presence of the Pope in 1804. He enforced reforms long since seen to be desirable, though his dictatorial methods aroused opposition. He founded the Bank of France, established a legal code which still holds sway and restored official recognition of the church, which had been persecuted during the Revolution. But a France led by a military genius with imperial ambitions, who put a series of his own nominees on half the thrones of Europe, was too much for France's neighbours, and after the disastrous retreat from Moscow, Napoleon's days were numbered. He was exiled to St-Helena after the battle of Waterloo (1815) and left behind him a legend which still haunts European history.

The Restoration
Although the Restoration put the Bourbons back in power from 1815 to 1830, they ruled over a new France. The *ancien régime* was finally done with, as the country, dispensing with the rationalism of the eighteenth century, embraced first the romanticism and then the capitalism of the nineteenth. In the aftermath of the Revolution the bourgeoisie prospered; its conservatism and devotion to making money enjoyed mass support and are memorably recorded in Balzac's great series of novels, the *Comédie Humaine*.

The July Revolution of 1830 was a middle-class reaction against an ultra-royalist movement, but was checked before it got out of hand. Louis-Philippe, by a nice semantic quibble, was installed as 'King of the French' and ruled for eighteen years over a country which set about coming to terms with the problems of raising the finance needed to develop industry and modernize its transport system.

Improvements in the roads, and the rapidly spreading network of railways which started in 1848, radically changed the face of France. But parliamentary reform was not among the achievements of the Orléans monarchy or its ministers Thiers and Guizot, and the monarchy fell, ostensibly on this issue, to be replaced by the short-lived Second Republic (1848–52).

The Second Empire
The Second Empire was presided over by Louis-Napoleon, a nephew of the first emperor; like his uncle he believed that the fortunes of France depended on the principle of nationality. He set out to redraw the map of Europe; by supporting the Italians in the war of independence from the Austrians, the Poles in their fight against the Russians, and by seizing Nice and Savoy for himself, thereby alienating the English, he effectively broke up the alliances that had held the balance of power since the Congress of Vienna. He compounded this error by encouraging the unification of North Germany under Prussian leadership. His reward was his own defeat at Sedan in 1870. The humiliation of the French in seeing the Prussians march through a Paris so spaciously and ruthlessly rebuilt by its prefect, Baron Haussmann, the cession of Alsace and Lorraine to the Germans, and the latter's increasing militarism, played a large part in reconciling the English and the French, and eventually led to the *entente cordiale*.

The collapse of the Second Empire ushered in a period of intense political conflict in which the power of the conservative monarchist 'Notables' – the old aristocracy, the high bourgeoisie and the landed proprietors – was challenged by the professional classes who were becoming increasingly liberal and even radical. The rising of the Commune in Paris in 1871 was put down by the army, with a horrifying total of 18,000 deaths, and the Communards were exiled. Attempts at yet another restoration foundered, and it was not until 1875 that a parliamentary republic came into being.

The Third Republic and World War I
The first phase of the Third Republic was characterized by a series of ephemeral and unstable governments which had to deal with financial crises, social unrest, political extremism – and the Dreyfus case. Nonetheless it achieved much: in 1884 the workers, who had already won the right to strike, were permitted to belong to trade unions (*syndicats*); Jules Ferry brought in compulsory and free primary education and created schools for training women teachers; acquisitions in Africa were transformed into an empire; and the arts – painting, music and literature – which had moved from romanticism to realism, saw an astonishing flowering in which France led the world once again as she had done in the *grand siècle*.

Thus, despite difficulties, France found herself in confident mood when World War I broke out, and her renewed prestige ensured that she was given the high command. But she was ill-equipped for the long war of attrition and the high death toll that followed. The victory of the Allies was as costly to her as defeat would have been.

The post-war problems of the Third Republic were much the same as they had been before: the instability of succeeding governments increased as they had to contend with financial difficulties, caused by the need for reconstruction, and the growth of disaffection engendered by increasing industrialization. The re-occupation of the Ruhr by France in 1923 to enforce reparations shook European confidence and the franc slumped. Crisis bred extremism, on both the left and the right. The year 1936 saw the election of the Popular Front – a union of the three left wing parties – led by the Socialist, Léon Blum. It was followed by a wave of strikes and the devaluation of the franc, and lasted barely a year. Domestic politics were played out against the background of the rise of fascism in Italy and Germany and the outbreak of civil war in Spain. The Anglo-French policy of non-intervention in central Europe was abruptly ended by the declaration of war in 1939.

World War II: The Occupation

The Germans invaded France in May 1940, and by the terms of the armistice signed on 22 June the defeated country was divided into two. The Third Republic was thus ended by war, as its successor was to be eighteen years later. Marshal Pétain installed his government at Vichy in the 'unoccupied zone', while in England General de Gaulle was trying to convince his fellow-countrymen and Winston Churchill that he was the natural leader of the Free French. When the Allies landed in North Africa in 1942, the Germans occupied the whole of France, and the French fleet at Toulon scuttled itself rather than fall into German hands. Two and a half months after the Americans and the English landed in Normandy in June 1944, General de Gaulle entered Paris at the head of a provisional government, which lasted little more than a year.

The Fourth Republic: Towards European Unity

The Fourth Republic, with a new constitution, was founded in 1946, and saw a series of uneasy coalitions between varying combinations of Catholic Democrats (MRP), Socialists, Radicals and Communists. It was largely due to the vision of a Frenchman, Jean Monnet, that the first steps towards European unity were taken in the 1950s with the foundation of the Coal and Steel Community (1951), the European Defence Union (1952), and the European Economic Community (1957), to all of which France adhered. But her colonial empire was beginning to disintegrate; independence was granted to Cambodia in 1949, and to Morocco and Tunisia in 1958. Algeria was a special problem since it had been treated as an integral part of metropolitan France; terrorism by Arab nationalists led to drastic counter-measures by the army, which in May 1958 assumed power. The government, and the Fourth Republic, fell, and in December General de Gaulle, who had been waiting patiently and astutely in the wings for his moment to come, became President of the Fifth Republic.

The Fifth Republic: De Gaulle and After

The feature of the new republic's constitution, written into it at de Gaulle's insistence, was the greater independence of the executive from parliament and de Gaulle eventually resolved the Algerian crisis by granting its independence. The rate of modernization and the expansion of the economy, so fast in the 1960s, slowed down in the decade which followed de Gaulle's death in 1970 and today, under a Socialist government elected in 1981, France is suffering from the common European problems of inflation and unemployment.

Architecture in France

From Charlemagne to Le Corbusier

Christopher Tadgell

Note: For definitions of architectural terms *see* Glossary, page 446. Footnotes refer to illustrations on other pages of the book.

Comparatively rich in Roman remains,[1] France preserves little Gallo-Roman architecture from the Christian era, though its few known traces – for instance the foundations of St-Denis in Paris (Fig. 1) – indicate that its churches followed the form of the early Christian basilica. The Merovingian age, in which almost all France's cathedrals were founded on an impressive scale, left considerable documentary evidence but few actual remains. Many later texts, again, tell us of the renovation or reconstruction of most of these great churches under Charlemagne. Though his work was subsequently effaced in further rebuilding, it had lasting influence – for it achieved a truly imperial synthesis between Roman or Early Christian forms and those passed down by the early northern barbarians. France has little to show of this – the main elements of both church and palace at Aachen in West Germany incorporate the most prominent examples.

Romanesque

As with later renaissances, in which the forms of a prestigious Antiquity were adapted to modern needs, the element of innovation in Carolingian architecture was significant, formulating the great church with its many towers, its 'west-work', its east end with apse and transept separated by a choir, its composite piers bearing arcades to define the main spaces and, above all, its scale. The perfection of the great church was the aim of builders throughout the Middle Ages, but the consolidation of these elements in the Romanesque period was the achievement largely of the religious Orders, for in the eleventh and twelfth centuries culture was the monopoly of the monastery, a haven of peace in the otherwise strife-torn feudal system. Funds were readily proffered by the great and the small seeking indulgence, and pilgrimage provided the channel for ideas.

Developed in the context of feudalism there is no one Romanesque. The styles of Burgundy, Normandy, Provence, Poitou, for example, are readily enough distinguishable in their use of materials, in their approaches to massing, in their sumptuousness or simplicity. But given the far-flung network of the pilgrimage routes and the still more pervasive network of relationships between the Orders – especially the almost imperial position of the Abbey of Cluny in the Benedictine network – no single approach was confined to a particular region. Thus no one alternative to the most common combination of barrel-vaulted main spaces, flanked by groin-vaulted aisles and galleries,[2] was the preserve of any particular area. Even the spectacular combination of domes popular in Aquitaine (notably Angoulême, Cahors and Périgueux[3]) occurs in many examples beyond the old province between the Loire (Fontevrault) and the Garonne (Agen). Thus, too (except, admittedly, in

---

1. Orange page 419, Pont du Gard page 358, Arles page 397   2. Conques page 281
3. Périgueux page 300

Provence), naves are usually flanked by aisles which vary in form in accordance with no regional pattern: they may be lower than the nave, as in the old basilican form, permitting a clerestory with or without a triforium below it (St-Philbert at Tournus, Vézelay,[1] St-Benoît-sur-Loire); they may approximate its height (St-Martin de Canigou, Notre-Dame-la-Grande at Poitiers, St-Révérien in Burgundy); they may support a gallery (Notre-Dame-du-Port at Clermont-Ferrand, Issoire, St-Martin at Tours, St-Sernin at Toulouse[2]); and they may be surmounted by both gallery and clerestory (St-Étienne at Nevers, St-Rémi at Reims, Mont-St-Michel). After the late Carolingian example of St-Philbert-de-Grandlieu (near Nantes), many east ends throughout France were terminated by several apses *en échelon* (Cluny II and Fig. 2a), but following the arrangement on the lower level of the same church, later developed in St-Martin at Tours, the semi-circular ambulatory with radiating chapels became generally the most popular form (Cluny III and Fig. 2b). St-Martin at Tours was, in fact, the direct model for the truly international pilgrimage church – with its ambulatory and radiating chapels, its nave with barrel vaults

Fig. 1 St-Denis: plans of successive structures including the Carolingian basilica (8th-c.) and the work of Abbot Suger (1137–44)

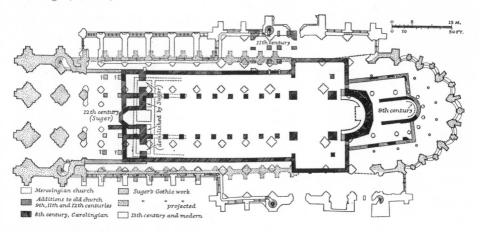

Fig. 2(a) St-Philbert-de-Grandlieu (9th-c.): plan – note apses en échelon

Fig. 2(b) Ste-Foy at Conques: plan – note ambulatory with radiating chapels

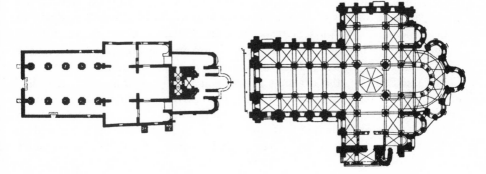

1. Vézelay page 347   2. Toulouse page 313

on transverse ribs, its aisles surmounted by galleries, its restrained exterior directly expressing the interior spaces – which reached its apogee via St-Martial at Limoges and Ste-Foy at Conques,[1] in St-Sernin at Toulouse[2] and St-Iago at Compostella.

St-Martin at Tours also contributed to the development of the eleventh-century Norman churches which, with Cluny, were to provide the basic premises for a new style. Dome-like vaults in the towers at St-Martin were crossed in the middle by an extra rib, and this seems to have been the key to the adaptation of the Lombard square-bay rib vault to a support system based on double nave bays crossed in the middle by an extra arch in St-Étienne and Ste-Trinité at Caen, when stone vaults were substituted for the original wooden roofs in the early eleventh century.

Behind all this unity and diversity of style and form lay one common aim: the great church was to be an enduring structure. This meant, ideally, that it was to be of stone, and sophistication in the handling of stone was acquired through reference to Roman antiquity. Antiquity, too, provided the models for the arcades[3] carried on more or less complex piers, universally adopted inside, and for the vaulting – barrel and groin – at first confined to east ends for the security and dignity of altars and relics. Antiquity also provided a repertory of decorative detail, and its translation was often literal in Provence and Burgundy (Arles, Autun, Cluny) until the austere St Bernard of Clairvaux, founder of the Cistercian Order, preached against sumptuousness in general and pagan forms in particular. Before and after St Bernard, however, one of the most consistent concerns of architects was to effect a complete system of interrelated arches through the systematic application of pillars, columns, colonnettes, capitals and moulded voussoirs, to all apertures – from the triumphal entrance, symbolizing the threshold of heaven,[4] to the great bays of the nave, and ultimately even across those bays to the vaults symbolizing heaven itself.[5]

Gothic

Though this system was the prerequisite of the Gothic style, its achievement in mid-eleventh-century Normandy was by no means Gothic. The transformation took place in the Ile-de-France at the behest of Abbot Suger of St-Denis, friend and principal adviser to Louis VI. Undertaking the first major building campaign there for generations, he had to call on experts in the quest for a style that was to serve at once a more optimistic interpretation of Christianity – based on a conception of light as a divine healing agent – and the imperial pretensions of the dynasty. Significantly, the great sees of the heartland of the French monarchy – principally Sens, Noyon, Laon, Paris, Chartres, most of whose incumbents were at the consecration of Suger's great church of St-Denis in 1144 – gave the new style its initial impetus, though the Cistercians were also in the van of the movement.

The decisive achievement of Suger and his unknown aides was the synthesis of elements variously present in Romanesque – the pointed arch and flying buttress of Cluny and Durham, the rib-vault of Caen and Durham, Lassay, Évreux and Morienval – to form an essentially new structural system, relying not simply on gravity and the dead weight of the enclosing fabric but on the counteraction of finely calculated forces. With emphasis on the verticals, rather than on the horizontals as in Romanesque, the result was aspiring and, with a predominance of void over solid, it was essentially light – until the triumph of stained glass.

1. Conques page 281   2. Toulouse page 313   3. Pont du Gard page 358
4. Laon page 121   5. Conques page 281

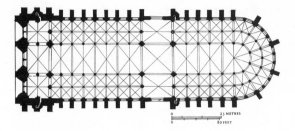

Fig. 3 Notre-Dame, Paris (1163): plan

All this may be seen as a natural outcome of the Romanesque achievement of an interrelated, if additive, system of arched units; and in fact, once formulated, the Gothic synthesis – producing unified designs divided along structural lines (Fig. 3) – was continuously modified to achieve the full integration of all the parts. For this the pointed arch was indispensable. Unlike the semi-circular arches and ribs which, unless distorted, defined the late Romanesque dome-like vaults in square bays, the pointed arch, whose height was not dictated by its width, could be freely adjusted to produce straight ridged vaults of uniform height, even over oblong nave bays repeating the divisions of the aisles.[1]

Suger began the reconstruction of his Carolingian church in 1137 with the western end (Fig. 1) – where the triangular arrangement of the openings in the façade is already in marked contrast to the former Romanesque agglomeration of parts,[2] despite the divisive buttresses. The use of rib-vaulting for the narthex, behind heavy retaining walls, is not yet truly Gothic. However, the ambulatory, to which Suger turned his attention three years later, has all the essentials of the new style with its fully pointed arcading on incredibly slender supports, aligned on axes radiating from the centre of the semi-circular choir so as to interfere as little as possible with the penetration of light. Suger's clerestory was replaced in the 1230s, and his nave project was never executed, but clues to its form are provided in the descriptive booklet he issued in connection with the consecration of the new work. His insistence there on unity and harmony is as obsessive, and as uncharacteristic of Romanesque designers (Figs. 2a and 2b), as his preoccupation with light.

A more tangible image of Suger's St-Denis is provided by the near-contemporary cathedral at Sens (c. 1140) – the first great project to be executed generally in accordance with Gothic principles, though the original clerestory was altered in the 1230s. The vaulting is sexpartite[1] after the example of St-Étienne at Caen, based on paired nave bays, though this ignores the division of the aisles which determines those bays. Each of the main support piers at Sens is a cluster of shafts rising from the ground through a triforium to the springing of the main lateral transverse arches and the diagonal ribs of the vault. Over the paired columns of the intermediate piers, shafts rise to the extra lateral arches bearing the interpolated segments of vaulting. Noyon (c. 1150), the next great church, with a tall light gallery as well as a triforium, is a more advanced expression of the Gothic ideal of integrating piers, shafts and arches into a skeleton whose visual significance matched its structural role.

The sequence of circular piers at Laon (c. 1160) represents the first significant departure from the late Romanesque accretion of paired bay units towards the High

1. Bourges facing page 112   2. Jumièges page 147

Gothic continuous sweep of single ones,[1] following the division of the aisles, but as the sexpartite vault continued to imply pairing there was an awkward discrepancy in the expression of support at upper and lower levels. The application of shafts to the later piers of the series was an unsatisfactory attempt at resolving this discrepancy, but in the choir of Notre-Dame in Paris (*c.* 1163) the incompatibility of the sexpartite vault and the regular repetition of identical piers was frankly admitted, no distinction being made in the expression of support below the springing of the vault arches. Though Bourges (*c.* 1195) retained sexpartite vaulting, the definitive solution had been reached by 1194 at Chartres, where sexpartite vaults were replaced by quadripartite ones (Fig. 4).

Notre-Dame had double aisles (Fig. 3), and this presented special buttressing problems. Normally the transverse arches of the gallery would transmit the lateral thrust of the vault to the strong outer walls. In the choir of Notre-Dame the piers between the aisles, together with the walls at ground and clerestory level, were strengthened at the expense of light. In the construction of the nave from the year 1180, exposed flying buttresses were used instead of heavy inner piers.[2] Exteriors had remained rather Romanesque in appearance until this novel development, and weighty masonry still prevailed in Notre-Dame's own early-thirteenth-century western façade, despite the delicate mouldings and the harmony of its lightly centralized compositions. In the slightly earlier exercise at Laon,[3] on the other hand, the vigorous projection and recession of the storeys, obscuring the divisive verticals of the buttresses, produces a much more dramatic contrast between solid and void.

The architects of Chartres[4] and Bourges realized the full potential of the flying buttress: the gallery, no longer needed for buttressing, could be eliminated and the enclosing wall reduced. In the double-aisled plan of Bourges, even more compact than that of Notre-Dame because there were no transepts, the nave arcade was sent up to a great height, permitting light to flood in through the upper level of the inner aisles, and triple windows filled the clerestory above the triforium.[5] At Chartres, with single aisles, the clerestory windows were brought down to a lower triforium

Fig. 4(a) Quadripartite vaulting with ridge ribs
(b) and with tiercerons
(c) and with tiercerons and liernes

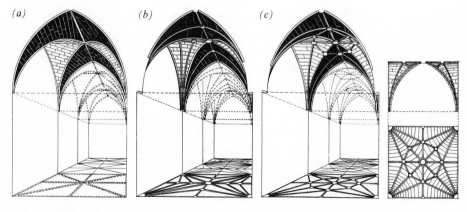

1. Bourges facing page 112   2. Notre-Dame, Paris, page 69   3. Laon page 121
4. Chartres page 221   5. Bourges facing page 112

above the relatively low main arcades. With the success of these experiments, the choir of Le Mans (1217) followed the precedent of Bourges but eliminated the triforium, the plans for Rouen were altered in the course of execution (*c.* 1200) to suppress the gallery, Reims (1210) and Amiens (1218) followed suit, and the clerestory windows at Notre-Dame were greatly enlarged (1235).

A principal concern of High Gothic architects was with the continuity of all the vertical lines of their structural frames. Their experiments at Bourges and Chartres, based on the application of slender columns to circular or octagonal piers, were furthered at Reims, perfected at Amiens. Those at Rouen, where shafts were aligned on the diagonal faces of diamond-shaped piers, provided the system for the new nave of St-Denis and most of the great later Gothic exercises. Instead of the grouped lights of the early-thirteenth-century clerestories, huge single windows subdivided by light tracery filled the upper zones of the bays at Reims, anticipating the complete elimination of the wall – as in the Ste-Chapelle, Paris (1243). At Amiens the lines of the tracery were continued down to embrace the triforium, which was now lit, moreover, paving the way for the final reduction of the internal elevation to two storeys in the late-Gothic period. The integration of clerestory and triforium was fully achieved at St-Denis (1231) and at Beauvais (1237), while the elimination of the triforium altogether followed thirty years later at St-Urbain in Troyes. At Beauvais, moreover, the aspiration to ever greater height, which obsessed the builders of the Ile-de-France, received its ultimate check. On the façades of Reims and Amiens similar aspiration to height, with the proportions revised to favour the verticals and with elements from one horizontal zone pushed up into the next, broke down the stratification still so clearly asserted at Notre-Dame.[1]

The extension of tracery in lace-like patterns, particularly after the introduction of the *lierne* and *tierceron* ribs (Fig. 4) to vaulting (Auxerre Cathedral, Solesmes Abbey near Sablé-sur-Sarthe, St-Eustache in Paris), was prolific in the late-Gothic period. The French, unlike the English and the Germans, rarely permitted such patterns actually to veil the building's frame, relying on it rather for the final obliteration of mass (Sées Cathedral, St-Ouen at Rouen, La Trinité at Vendôme, the west fronts of Strasbourg and Rouen Cathedrals, the porch of Notre-Dame at Louviers). Characteristic of their approach here was the elaboration of the ogee arch into the flamelike forms of the Flamboyant (Notre-Dame at Alençon, the west fronts of Toul Cathedral, La Trinité at Vendôme, St-Maclou at Rouen, the south portals of Sens and the porch of Albi).

Castles in the Middle Ages

Residence and military installation, seat of power in the age of feudalism, the castle long remained a rude establishment with little time for art. France was in the van of the development of both principal approaches to its design: the defensive, arranging a series of obstacles to augment a naturally secure site and permit a succession of retreats to the ultimate sanctum of a tower;[2] the offensive, providing a commanding eminence, often man-made, in a protected compound as a military base on a strategic site easy of access and egress. Naturally the development of the castle along each of these lines responded to the political context – thus, while the holders of territory from the late-Roman empire onwards concentrated their attention on the sophistication of the defensive establishment, great invaders like the Normans

1. Notre-Dame, Paris, page 69
2. Chinon jacket

developed the *motte and bailey* castle to fulfil the function of the Roman camp.

Though France had the greatest concentration of castles in western Europe in the tenth century – the legacy of localized response to the Viking incursions which decisively weakened the central power under the later Carolingians – she preserves few remains earlier than the eleventh century. Until this time, most structures were of earth and timber, rather than stone, and the *motte and bailey* type was developed elsewhere (in England and the Holy Land in particular), but Chinon,[1] Langeais,[2] Loches[3] and Beaugency preserve impressive early stone towers or keeps. The greatest of these were rectangular, but from the early twelfth century circular, multifoil and polygonal forms, less easily undermined by attackers and more easily surveilled by defenders, were preferred both for keeps and for the towers placed at intervals around perimeter walls (Houdin, Étampes and Provins). Over the next two centuries, strength was further increased by the splaying of the bases of walls, while the dominance of the defenders over the attackers – and their increasingly efficient siege machinery – was enhanced by the development of crenellation for unrestricting shelter and the projection of barbicans for the advanced protection of entrances, of bartizans for extending the range of vision, and of overhanging galleries with machicolations for dropping missiles.[4]

The Château Gaillard (Fig. 5), built by Richard Coeur-de-Lion on a spur commanding the Seine valley, made sophisticated use of curved walls – though there was no room to follow the bold example set by Henry II at Dover and ring the keep with concentric walls. With its massive bastion on the cliff edge, preceded by outer, middle and inner wards, each with its own curtain walls, its own moats and obliquely placed entrances, the Château Gaillard was the last word in defensive planning, and its fall conclusively demonstrated, if demonstration was needed, that no system of defence is proof against the despondency of the defenders. Developments in castle design thereafter are not reducible to a single formula, but certainly the most significant trend was away from successive retreats to a more aggressive concentration of strength all round the perimeter, as suggested by the concentric castle, but with the greatest weight at the principal gate rather than in a central keep (Angers, Carcassonne, Pierrefonds – Fig. 6).

With the revival of towns and monetary economies under the more stable conditions of the thirteenth century, it often suited king and vassal to substitute cash for service. With taxes to draw on – and bankers to borrow from – the great Plantagenet and Capetian kings kept paid armies, and the scope of their conflicts passed beyond the control of the individual strong-point. This, together with the increasing sophistication of artillery, led to the decline in the military importance of the castle, but it could still delay even an army and it continued to dominate local politics. During the fourteenth century its design was consolidated for smaller garrisons: around a roughly quadrangular court, accommodation was concentrated between perimeter walls similar in height to the great towers which continued to punctuate them (the Bastille in Paris, Pierrefonds – Fig. 6, Tarascon). Vincennes, with its splendid keep, is a prominent exception, devised as much to protect the King from the treachery of paid guards as from external assault.

The final product of this process of consolidation was the fortress – a gun emplacement, often sunk into the landscape for concealment and to bring the line of fire down to ground level (Rambures). Complementary to this development, the

1. Chinon jacket   2. Langeais page 231
3. Loches page 233   4. Châteaudun page 222

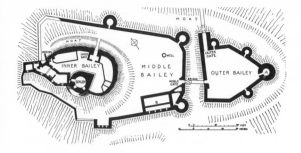

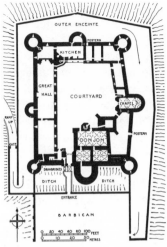

Fig. 5 Château Gaillard, Les Andelys (1196): plan

Fig. 6 Château de Pierrefonds (1390): plan

primarily residential seat emerged from the same basic forms. Hitherto the Gothic style with its light structure and large windows had not been much use for castles, but now great lords held court in Gothic halls, embellished with art inside and out, secure behind increasingly impressive town defences (Poitiers, Avignon[1]) or proof against local skirmishes in the countryside (Saumur[2]). The rulers here emulated the standards set not only by great prelates (Sens, and Cluny in Paris) but by great merchant bankers like Jacques Coeur at Bourges. Yet the palaces even of the most lavish lords hardly equalled the splendour of guild and town halls (Arras, Rouen).

As internal security waxed and waned during the Hundred Years War, until the reconsolidation of central power under the Valois, so the relaxation of the castle proceeded at an irregular pace to the late-fifteenth-century château with its large windows, open and elaborate staircases, elegant articulation, high and flamboyant roof-line, courts defined by the varied masses of *corps de logis* and *pavillons* reflecting the old ring walls punctuated with bastions (Chaumont, Rigny-Ussé, Meillant).

The Renaissance
French Renaissance architecture was the synthesis of two traditions – the French medieval and the Italian Renaissance. The former provided the basic plans of the basilican church with ambulatory and the quadrangular château with *pavillons* and *corps de logis* (Fig. 7); the quadripartite vault with *liernes* and *tiercerons*; the high pointed roof; versatile masonry and colouristic use of materials; the exuberance of Flamboyant decoration; and the symbolism of noble power in former defensive features such as the twin-towered postern, moats, and projecting wall-walks with false machicolations. From the Italian Renaissance a new repertory of decorative motifs was quickly acquired, but only gradually was the essence of its classicism – order and unity based on symmetry, the harmony of proportions with the classical orders as the framework – understood and assimilated.

The first phase of the French Renaissance, dictated by aristocratic fashion for things Italian – following the Italian campaign of Charles VIII, and continuing through the reign of Louis XII to almost the end of that of François I – was

1. Avignon page 399   2. Saumur page 209

characterized by inventiveness and structural virtuosity (the staircases of Blois[1] and Chambord, the Hôtel Pincé at Angers); agglomeration rather than coherent composition, betraying an obsession with the parts rather than the whole (Chenonceaux, Valençay[2]); the skilful, yet naïve, adaptation of imperfectly understood Italian classical detail to essentially unclassical Flamboyant forms (St-Pierre at Caen, St-Eustache in Paris, the roof of Chambord[3]). The plan of Bury was a regularization of the late-medieval courtyard, and in its principal façades, as in the garden façade of Azay-le-Rideau, the beginning of an awareness of the importance of symmetry is apparent (Fig. 7). At Gaillon perhaps the first attempt was made to unify the parts of the symbolic postern by subjecting them to elements of an order, after the pattern of the Roman triumphal arch. The Porte Dorée at Fontainebleau, among many, followed. The order of thin pilasters was essentially decorative at this stage, and it was not until the fourth decade of the century that an appreciation of columns, carefully proportioned and bearing the proper entablature, began to be apparent (the Cour de l'Ovale staircase at Fontainebleau, the court façades of the Hôtel d'Écouville at Caen). This responded to an awareness of the importance in Roman High Renaissance design of three-dimensional relief, of the contrast between solid and void, light and shade, of coherent massing and the expression of the weight of the enclosing fabric (exterior of the François I wing at Blois, the court at St-Germain, the Château de Madrid near Paris).

By the end of the reign of François I, Italian Renaissance theorists were being assiduously studied in France or, like Serlio and Primaticcio, actually came to practise in France (Ancy-le-Franc, extensions at Fontainebleau), and France began to produce theorists of her own, such as Philibert Delorme. Against this background French masters achieved their first maturity with the ability to subject the parts to the whole, to coordinate horizontals and verticals, to think in terms of mass and volume, to comprehend the importance of proportion and the symbolic meaning and compositional value of the orders.

The demolition of the medieval Louvre and the construction of a classical palace,

Fig. 7 Château de Bury (1511), southeast of Beauvais: perspective view

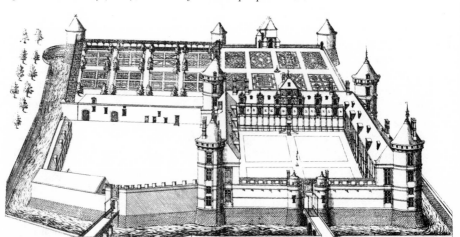

1. Blois page 217   2. Valençay page 253   3. Chambord page 204

Fig. 8 Château de Charleval (1573), east of Rouen: Court elevation

ordered towards the end of his life by François I from Pierre Lescot, was the occasion for the first full demonstration of this maturity. Lescot's work[1] still retained *pavillons* and *corps de logis*, to provide the variety which the French preferred in contrast to the Italians, and it was rich in decorative detail, but his superimposed orders, scrupulous in their observation of classical prototypes, were used in a way of crucial importance for the future, progressing from pilaster to column with the projection of the mass of the *pavillons* from the *corps de logis* to bind these disparate elements together. Philibert Delorme also experimented with the disposition of orders, not only to bind all the traditional parts of the château together along horizontal lines (St-Maur) but to cope with the exaggerated verticals of dominant central *pavillons* (Anet). Scrupulousness in the expression of the orders, if not always mastery in their handling, is apparent in contemporary works in the provinces – especially in the south, where Antique remains and recent Italian works provided more or less direct inspiration (Bournazel, La Tour d'Aigues, the Hôtel Assezat at Toulouse, the west-front gable of Rodez Cathedral).

Classical in his correctness of detail, but unclassical in scale and less interested in integration than in incident, Jean Bullant, a younger contemporary of Lescot and Delorme, announced the end of this short-lived period of maturity at Écouen, Chantilly and Fère-en-Tardenois. The architects of the later decades of the sixteenth century, inspired by the virtuoso performances of the Italian mannerists in playing with the rules, but lacking their sophistication and wit, reverted to an essentially decorative approach to articulation. Unlike early Renaissance work, this was not the result of misunderstanding but a conscious return to prolixity (Beaumesnil), often involving the wilful misuse of the orders as elements in a pattern of detail, masking rather than elucidating structural forces (Charleval – Fig. 8, the Grande Galerie of the Louvre).

Classicism, Baroque and Louis XIV
The classical values were reasserted in the second decade of the seventeenth century by Salomon de Brosse. Starting with the traditional château disposition, his

1. Louvre page 77

monumental works show a progressive coherence in massing, clarity of volume, purity of line, control of detail and coordination of articulation (Coulommiers, the Luxembourg in Paris, Blérancourt, the Palace of Justice at Rennes).

The façade of St-Gervais in Paris, usually attributed to de Brosse, well illustrates the classicizing of a still essentially Gothic form in accordance with principles derived from Delorme. The nearby, slightly later, façade of St-Paul-St-Louis by the Jesuit brother Derand, less coherently articulated, lusher in detail, offers a particularly instructive comparison. The original project for St-Paul-St-Louis by another Jesuit, Martellange, and the contemporary work of Jacques Lemercier on the Sorbonne chapel, manifested a conscious rejection of the recent French and current Flemish delight in lavish ornament and of the Roman Baroque conception of movement, both of which they considered licentious, in favour of a placid academic classicism. At much the same time François Mansart, equally bent on purifying the native tradition but intent on invigorating it as well, reverted to the more engaging example of Philibert Delorme's chapel at Anet – the first important French classical exercise in centralized planning – for inspiration in the design of his early church of the Visitation in Paris (1633) (Fig. 9).

François Mansart, in fact, had taken on the mantle of de Brosse. Such works as his châteaux of Balleroy, Blois and Maisons,[1] his projects for the churches of the Val-de-Grâce and the Minimes in Paris, have all the qualities most closely associated with the French classical spirit of the seventeenth century – concentration and clarity combined with subtlety, restraint and the elimination of inessentials with richness, obedience to a strict code of rules with flexibility within them. Yet in a way utterly characteristic of his individualism, many of his works (the plans for Blois, the Val-de-Grâce, the east wing of the Louvre, the Bourbon chapel at St-Denis) reveal a command of techniques which were soon to become the hallmarks of the Roman High Baroque – vigorous contrast in the contours of walls

Fig. 9(a) Château d'Anet, chapel (1548): plan
   (b) Church of the Visitation, Paris (1633): plan

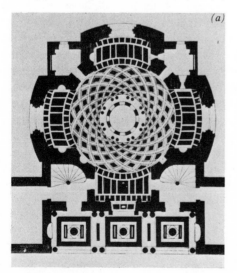

(a)

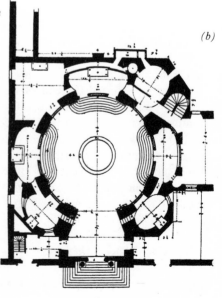

(b)

1. Maisons page 108

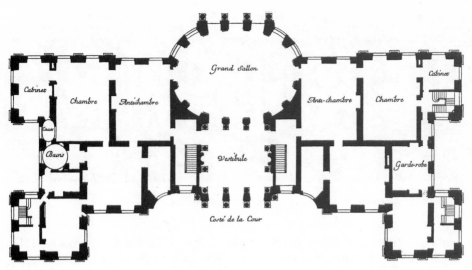

Fig. 10 Château de Vaux-le-Vicomte (1657): plan

and the profiles of masses, colossal scale, alignment of varied space shapes to provide rich vistas, vertical perspectives and dramatic lighting.

Many of the same techniques appealed to the bold imagination of Mansart's younger rival, Louis Le Vau, most of whose major works belong to the period of the minority of Louis XIV, dominated by the Baroque taste of Mazarin. In his châteaux and Parisian houses (Vaux-le-Vicomte – Fig. 10, and the Hôtel Lambert in particular) he demonstrated his skill in grouping living rooms in apartments separate from more formal reception rooms to meet new standards of comfort and convenience. But his experiments with the assimilation of Baroque techniques to the traditional French approach to composition (Vaux,[1] the Institut de France in Paris) were less happy than those of François Mansart – indeed, in his attempts to integrate disparate masses, among which a great oval central *pavillon* was usually predominant, his free combination of regular and colossal orders inhibited the production of the dramatic climax which was the aim of Baroque composition. Working with Le Brun, for the interiors, and Le Nôtre, for the landscaping, however, Le Vau was a supreme creator of spectacle (Vaux and Versailles).

Following Bernini's abortive visit to France to supplant Le Vau in the completion of the Louvre (Fig. 11), a commission composed of Le Vau, Le Brun and Claude Perrault was entrusted with the job. The result, the Colonnade, was to provide one of the principal models for French architects throughout the next century. The contemporary transformation of Versailles provided another. Betraying the influence of Bernini and his Roman contemporaries in their clear-cut lines, concealed roofs, clearly differentiated horizontal zones, sumptuous articulation and colossal scale, these works, together with Liberal Bruant's Invalides, achieved a grand compromise between the exuberant spectacle desired by the King – whose taste was formed under Mazarin and schooled by Bernini – and the disciplined order promoted by Colbert and the academies he founded. This was furthered by the founding members of the Royal Academy of Architecture, François Blondel in

1. Vaux facing page 81

Fig. 11 Louvre, Paris: Bernini's third project for the east front (1665)

particular (Portes St-Denis and St-Martin in Paris). Le Brun's approach to the decoration of the interiors at Versailles responded to the same considerations, progressively taming a rich fusion of illusionist painting and high relief stucco ornament (derived from Pietro da Cortona's work in Florence and Rome) by subjecting all to an architectural framework, clearly delineating the zones of sculpture and painting within it.

Jules Hardouin Mansart, trained by his uncle but early working in the context of 'Baroque classicism' at Versailles, was principal architect to the King for forty years from the late 1670s – at first in collaboration with Le Brun. He proved himself a consummate master in the appeasement of Louis XIV's taste for Baroque spectacle, without breaking the bounds of classical discipline, in a great series of royal works: the vast expansion of Versailles, beginning with the insertion of the Galerie des Glaces and ending with the chapel; the Grand Trianon with its coloured marble, and theatrical Marly with its painted architecture; the Dôme des Invalides,[1] based on his uncle's Bourbon chapel; the Places des Victoires and Vendôme in Paris, which set the pattern for French public squares for the next century. Yet Jules Hardouin's own personal leaning was towards a much more austere style, relying for decoration only on the orders in the centre and the frames of doors and windows (Clagny, Dampierre). This simplicity, inspired by the later Paris houses of his uncle (Hôtel Guénégaud, Rue des Archives), together with the great facility he had for planning comfortable and convenient domestic buildings, after the example of Le Vau, were to be the hallmarks of the houses produced by his younger assistants and their contemporaries (de Cotte, Lassurance, Jacques Gabriel, Boffrand, Bullet, etc.) in the first decades of the eighteenth century when royal patronage was at a low ebb (Boffrand's Hôtel Amelot – Fig. 12 in Paris, Bullet's Château de Champs).

Reason and Rococo, Romanticism and Revolution
Jules Hardouin and his office were also responsible for perhaps the most significant contribution in the period of Louis XIV's decline – the non-monumental, anti-architectural mode of interior decoration which led to the Rococo (Boffrand's oval salons at the Hôtel Soubise). This culminated in the asymmetrical, naturalistic, anti-classical, essentially flamboyant *genre pittoresque* of such decorators as Pineau and Meissonnier in the 1730s (Fig. 13). However, in Paris at least, the Rococo was

1. Invalides page 91

confined almost exclusively to the panelling of private rooms and hardly seriously affected façades – these, in their simplicity and restraint, continued to follow the rules of architectural and social propriety expounded by the members of the Royal Academy of Architecture, Jacques-François Blondel above all.

Equally in accordance with those rules, monumental architecture depended on monarchal patronage, and with a child king on a bankrupt throne from 1715 the royal builders were inactive until Louis XV reached maturity nearly a quarter of a century later. However, the French monumental tradition, continuously the subject of debate and treatise in the circle of the Academy, was furthered by leading Academicians such as Boffrand (the châteaux at Nancy and Lunéville for the Duke of Lorraine), de Cotte (the palace for the Archbishop of Strasbourg) and Jacques Gabriel (the Place Royale in Bordeaux). The competition for a Place Louis XV in Paris in 1748 proved that the monumental tradition was still vigorous.

That project (the Place de la Concorde) was carried out from 1755 by Louis XV's principal architect the fastidious Jacques-Ange Gabriel son of Jacques, who proved himself the worthy heir of all that was finest – native or imported – in that tradition. He preferred the rectilinear masses which the late-seventeenth-century French masters derived from the Romans, and the restrained approach to articulation which they learned from François Mansart's town houses, but he also shared

Fig. 12 Hôtel Amelot, Paris (1712): plan

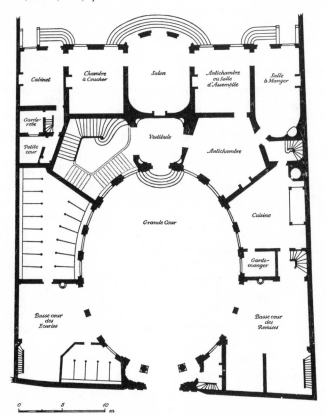

Fig. 13 Pavilion with cascade (c. 1734) – an architectural fantasy by J-A. Meissonnier

Mansart's will to unify and ability to diversify through the coordination of different masses with the application of a varied order or progressively rich articulation (early projects for rebuilding Versailles, the garden front of Compiègne). He comprehended the very different Roman conception of monumentality – that of Bernini (Fig. 11) and, beyond him, Michelangelo – Baroque in scale and based on the interpenetration or juxtaposition of forms and the confrontation of a colossal order with clear-cut austere masses (sentry boxes of Place de la Concorde, the École Militaire in Paris, the later projects for rebuilding Versailles). He was a master of the Rococo when working in its context (the council chambers at Versailles and Fontainebleau) but, in sympathy with progressive critics, when free to do so he preferred refined classical mouldings and the orders after the example of the great seventeenth-century masters (the Opéra and Library of Louis XVI at Versailles). Further, achieving a monumental expression of the academic classical ideal of 'noble simplicity', his exteriors after 1750 show a progressive strictness of line, firmness of form and simplicity of contour, complemented by a more purely architectural repertory of decorative detail (Le Butard at Vaucresson, the twin palaces on the Place de la Concorde). His younger contemporary Soufflot had set the major precedent for this in the Hôtel Dieu at Lyon. In his Panthéon[1] (Ste-Geneviève) in Paris, Soufflot's interest in geometrical forms, Gothic structure and Imperial Roman decoration (not to mention the dome of St Paul's Cathedral in London) were significant pointers to the wide-ranging eclecticism which was finally to seduce architects from the straight and narrow path of classicism delineated over the previous two hundred years.

Clarity of mass, indeed discreet geometrical blocks with plain rectangular windows, colossal orders often of grave austerity, the juxtaposition and confrontation of forms and an architectural approach to decoration, were the ingredients of the 'style-Louis XVI' (Antoine's Mint in Paris, Ledoux's Château of

1. Panthéon page 95

Bénouville and theatre at Besançon, Louis's theatre at Bordeaux). A novel interest in Greek, Etruscan, Roman and Egyptian archaeology, and in the early Italian Renaissance, was increasingly marked among the successors of Gabriel and Soufflot – variously bent on a purgative return to primitive simplicity and on evoking the aura of Antique remains, rather than simply assimilating their principles (Ledoux's Barrière de la Villette, Rousseau's Hôtel de Salm, in Paris, the apartments of Marie Antoinette at Fontainebleau). But the Academy welcomed new discoveries, and this development was an enriching of the Academic tradition.

The end of that tradition, opening the way for the new eclecticism with its free association of elements derived from widely differing sources, was in fact signalled by the breaching of the rules of propriety with the crumbling of the old order under Louis XVI. Then, in the work of the so-called revolutionary architects, the subjection of the parts to a dominant centre in a hierarchic composition gave way to the autonomous association of equal parts, usually geometric forms (Brogniart's Capucin convent in Paris, many of Ledoux's *barrières*). The academic classical ideal that the character of a building should be expressed in its order and proportions was given a new meaning in *architecture parlante* – the depiction of the purpose of a building in its decorative detail or even its forms (Ledoux's salt works at Chaux, Boullée's Newton Monument project). Many of these works, especially the ideal projects of Boullée and Ledoux (Fig. 14), demonstrate the final triumph of Geometry even over Reason in the boldly impractical conception of buildings as undecorated elementary forms – spheres, cylinders, cubes, pyramids, singly or combined – existing by and for themselves. A contemporary English development, the sentimental Picturesque, had a much more profound effect on French garden design than on architecture, and among its few surviving examples the *petits hameaux* at Versailles and Chantilly are the most seductive.

*Fig. 14 A house for a river surveyor (*c. *1785) – an architectural fantasy by C-N. Ledoux*

The Bonapartes and Restored Bourbons
Whereas the reformers before the Revolution had sought their inspiration in the
primitive forms associated with unsophisticated ages of supposed moral purity,
their survivors, reacting in revulsion to the Terror, readily enough placed
themselves at the service of the various permutations of post-Revolutionary
authority, modelled on Republic or Empire, and turned their attention to the more
or less slavish reproduction of the grandeur or luxury of late-Republican and
Imperial Rome (Legislative Assembly Chamber in the Palais Bourbon, Malmaison,
Arc du Carrousel, Colonne de Vendôme, the Madeleine). Grandiose as Napoleon's
projects were – and more diverse than those of previous regimes to meet the needs of
the bourgeois society furthered by his new order – the other preoccupations of his
short reign left most of his public utilities, and even such monuments to his glory as
the Arc de Triomphe, to be completed by his successors.

The stylistic revivalism of these works was prescribed by the *Précis des Leçons* of
J-N-L. Durand, professor of Napoleon's École Polytechnique. Far wider ranging
in eclecticism, but emptier in intellectual content, than the essays of the pre-
Revolutionary period of Durand's training, recurrent new editions of this book
under the last three Bourbons provided models for the various Renaissance (and
even medieval) revivals that were preferred to ancient Roman for the public services
and institutions of post-Napoleonic society. These were supplemented from the
1830s by especially French permutations of Renaissance, found most congenial by
builders, both public and private, under the bourgeois July Monarchy. In response
to the transition from the regime of Louis-Philippe to that of Louis-Napoleon, this
aspect of revivalism had its own contracted development – from 'François I' (the
extensions to the Hôtel-de-Ville in Paris, 1837; the Museum and Library at Le
Havre, 1845) and a hardly later 'High Renaissance' (the Foreign Ministry, 1846,
and the Gare de l'Est, 1847, in Paris) to the bombastic, somewhat Baroque 'style
Napoleon III' (the extensions to the Louvre by Visconti and Lefuel, C. Garnier's
Paris Opéra, 1861–74, the Palais Longchamps in Marseille, 1862–9). Surprisingly
enough, Gothic was relatively inconspicuous among the French gamut of stylistic
revivals, even in the ecclesiastical field. Beyond the restoration and completion of
medieval buildings, most notoriously by Viollet-le-Duc, examples of it (Gau's Ste-
Clotilde in Paris, 1846; Viollet-le-Duc's St-Denys-de-l'Estrée in St-Denis, 1860) are
less numerous than various permutations of Early Christian, Romanesque and
Renaissance, singly or combined (St-Augustin, 1860; St-François-Xavier, 1861; St-
Pierre-de-Montrouge, 1864; Sacré-Coeur,[1] 1874 – all in Paris).

Several great churches of the period (Ste-Clotilde, St-Eugène, St-Augustin) relied
considerably on the structural use of iron following precedents which went well
back into the eighteenth century (generally in roofing and usually concealed, like
Soufflot's Louvre staircase and Louis's Théâtre Français in Paris). The development
of iron and glass canopies in the spanning of large spaces (Belanger's Halle au Blé,
1809; Fontaine's Galerie d'Orléans, 1829; Labrouste's Bibliothèque Ste-Geneviève,
1839; Duquesney's Gare de l'Est, 1847 – all in Paris; and the Passage Pommeraye in
Nantes, 1843) achieved what many were to regard as the only valid contemporary
architecture, analogous to Gothic with its skeletal frame but dictated by modern
materials, with the frame exposed and expressed outside and in (Baltard's Paris
central markets). Its future for the 'cathedrals' of the Industrial Age – the great

1. Sacré-Coeur facing page 80

railway sheds and exhibition halls (Eiffel's Galerie des Machines of 1867; Contamin's Palais des Machines of 1889) – was assured, though its most notable survivor is the Eiffel Tower[1] (1887–9). Perhaps more important, because more routine and applicable to a vast range of modern building requirements, was the rectilinear frame of metal, with brick and tile in-fill, provided by J. Saulnier for the Chocolat Menier factory at Noisiel in 1871 and published by Viollet-le-Duc in his widely influential *Entretiens*.

Towards a New Architecture
Viollet-le-Duc provides the connecting link between the development of reinforced-concrete construction by his disciple J-E-A. de Baudot and the work of Saulnier, and this in turn provided one of the essential premises for the twentieth century. Meanwhile, however, the theories of the *Entretiens*, no less than the great engineering feats of Eiffel and his contemporaries, together with the aspirations of the Arts and Crafts circle of design reformers in England, inspired the attempt at forging a new architecture in the period of Art Nouveau, frank in its expression of modern structural techniques and materials and purged of eclecticism.

The exploitation of the strength and malleability of iron – usually in association with masonry – to produce a structure at once versatile and decorative, infused with the vigorous organic life of stylized plant forms, was first experimented with in the early 1890s by the Belgian V. Horta. The French, who had produced the Flamboyant and Rococo styles of free-ranging plastic decoration, proved themselves his enthusiastic disciples. Most prominent among their surviving works are the interior of the Grand Palais (1897), the core of the Samaritaine (1905) – which follows the structural precedent set at the Bon Marché by Boileau and Eiffel thirty years before – and the Métro entrances of H. Guimard. That the style depended on the malleability of metal is borne out by the earlier and later attempts of Guimard and his followers to apply it to stone: despite the elegance of their best work (Guimard's flats at Nos. 16 and 17–21 Rue La Fontaine, A. Perret's block at 119 Avenue de Wagram) the conflict between the nature of the material and the aims of the style remained unresolved.

Preoccupied as it was with elaborating decoration to mask traditional structures rather than to elucidate modern ones, Art Nouveau was disowned by the main stream of reformers in their quest for a more direct expression of advanced structural techniques. Moreover, they found exposed iron work of limited potential compared to reinforced concrete, which had been developed in France in the mid-nineteenth century. A. Perret employed reinforced concrete in the block of flats at 25*bis* Rue Franklin (1902–3) to produce a rectilinear structural skeleton which, though tile-covered, determined the appearance of the exterior and permitted a new freedom in planning. In many influential projects over the following two or three decades, he went on to realize the full potential of reinforced concrete for cantilevering and the elimination of the load-bearing wall, permitting the free flow of unrestricted space beneath thin shell vaults and galleries (Garage Ponthieu, 1905; Théâtre des Champs-Élysées, 1911; Notre-Dame at Le Raincy, 1922). Usually dispensing with applied ornament, he early exposed the concrete itself; later he exposed its pebble aggregate or expressed its wooden shuttering to provide texture and colour. While drawing novel effects from the lightness and precision of his

1. Eiffel Tower page 88

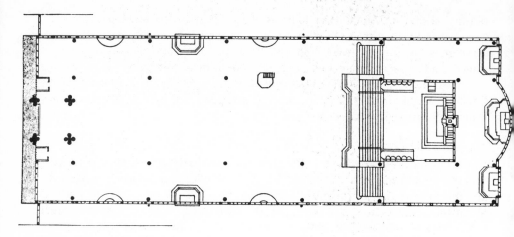

Fig. 15 Notre-Dame, Le Raincy (1922): plan

frames, his approach to the organization of their elements was determined by traditional values – generally classical in proportioning and formality. In his church at Le Raincy, moreover, with a continuous perimeter curtain of glass independent of the slender columns, which alone determined the traditional basilican plan, he achieved a complete statement of High Gothic ideals without the stylistic clichés of revivalism (Fig. 15).

Towards the end of the first decade of his career Perret was assisted by the Swiss painter and architect, C. E. Jeanneret – later 'Le Corbusier' – who went on to work for Behrens in Germany. The plain stucco walls defining rectangular blocks and the freedom in planning of his early works, reflect the influence of these fathers of the 'modern movement' as well as the ideals of other important contemporaries such as Loos in Vienna. Fired by the belief that architects should serve the community, his first important project was the Dom-ino scheme for low-cost housing (1915), which reflected an aspect of the Cité Industrielle elaborated by Tony Garnier at the beginning of the century. These social ideals, together with experiments in reinforced-concrete construction inspired by Perret's work, led to the Citrohan projects of the early 1920s: discreet concrete boxes ultimately raised from the ground on slender piers which were essential parts of the structural skeleton, like Perret's at Le Raincy. His book *Vers une Architecture* (1923) reveals that the inspiration for the smooth surfaces, mechanical precision of finish, rejection of inessential detail, came from the typical products of modern technology – cars, ships, aircraft – yet there is in his crisp geometrical ordering a striking affinity with the late-eighteenth-century idealists. Over the rest of the decade he developed this approach in a series of houses conceived as discreet rectilinear volumes, usually on stilts, whose insides were partitioned along lines and coloured in planes recalling the patterns of his earlier paintings (La Roche and Jeanneret houses, Auteuil, 1922–4; Les Terrasses, Garches, 1927; Villa Savoye, Poissy, 1929 – Fig. 16).

This 'new aesthetic' having been so well established by the early 1930s that his work was widely imitated, Le Corbusier began to develop a radically different line of approach – weightier, sculptural, no longer necessarily discreet but often rooted in the soil – based on a revised view of the nature of concrete, again inspired by Perret, as a plastic, textured material (Mandrot house, Provence, 1930). When stilts were retained they were heavy and moulded, expressing strength in support of boldly cantilevered superstructures, and when the latter were still rectilinear they were offset by free-flowing curved elements (The Swiss Hostel at the Cité Universitaire, Paris, 1931–2) and relieved by vigorous projections and recessions setting up rich contrasts of light and shade (La Tourette, at Éveux-sur-L'Arbresle, 1957–61).

The vast block of apartments in Marseille, Unité d'Habitation 1946, with its protean supports, its vigorous pattern of recessions behind the advanced sun-screening frame, its boldly coloured and textured surfaces, and above all its sculptured concrete roof garden, is the most influential example of this late mode. The fullest expression of that mode, emphatically denying the mechanical, constructional, geometrical and rational ideals promoted so assiduously in the 1920s, Notre-Dame-du-Haut at Ronchamp (1950),[1] recommended the spontaneous, the sculptural, the irregular and the emotional as the qualities of the future, but – precisely because it was such a personal testament – its example has proved elusive to would-be followers.

Fig. 16 Villa Savoye, Poissy (1929): plan

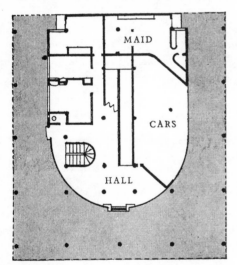 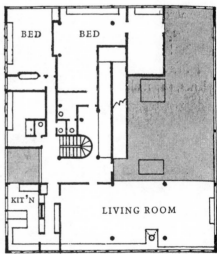

1. Ronchamp page 199

Illustration Acknowledgments

Fig. 1 from Crosby *L'Abbaye royale de Saint Denis* 1942
Fig. 2a from *Mem. Acad. Ins. et B.L. xxxviii*
Fig. 2b from *Bull. Mon.* l, *xv*
Fig. 3 after M. Aubert *Notre-Dame de Paris*
Fig. 4 from Cecil Stewart *Gothic Architecture*
    Longmans, 1961
Fig. 5 Sidney Toy
Fig. 6 Sidney Toy
Fig. 7 Anthony Blunt and R.I.B.A.
Fig. 8 Anthony Blunt and R.I.B.A.

Fig. 9a Drawing by du Cerceau. British Museum
Fig. 9b from *Petit Marot*
Fig. 10 from *Grand Marot*
Fig. 11 from *Grand Marot*
Fig. 12 from Jean Mariette *L'Architecture Française*
    1727
Fig. 13 from J-A. Meissonnier *Livre d'Ornemens* (1734)
Fig. 14 from Ramée *L'Architecture de C-N. Ledoux*
    1847
Fig. 15 © 1948 Benziger Verlag Zurich, Köln, Einsiedeln
Fig. 16 Reprinted by AMS Press, New York

Paris: Introduction

Michael Peppiatt

One can picture the Ile de la Cité as a rock cast up by the Seine and Paris as having formed in slow ripples round it. The early Gallic settlement of the Parisii spilt over on to the Left Bank under the Romans, while the marshlands of the northern bank were gradually reclaimed for building once Clovis had made Paris the capital of his Frankish kingdom. The city continued to grow in uneven waves throughout the Middle Ages. By the time of Philippe Auguste (1180–1223), it ranked as a great capital, with a cathedral, a university second to none and a vast circular wall skirting the Montagne Ste-Geneviève in the south and protected on the west by the recently erected Louvre fortress. Each of the four subsequent city walls (built under Charles V, Louis XIII, Louis XVI and Louis-Philippe) provides a graphic illustration of the way Paris continued to overflow – northwards to the Porte St-Martin, east to the Bastille, and then on every side, with increasing rapidity. The last wave was checked in the 1920s, when the present city-limits – marked by the Bois de Boulogne, the Bois de Vincennes and a ring-road – were made definitive.

The image of Paris rising out of its river is also geologically true, because the limestone with which it was built was quarried from a dried-out part of the Seine's ancient course. Now the river washes past buildings as ancient as Notre-Dame and as historically insignificant as the skyscraper flats west of the Eiffel Tower. City-planning controls have been applied to Paris for a thousand years, but they have not prevented it from changing constantly – and rarely less so than in the 1970s.

Countless individuals – monarchs and war lords, architects and churchmen – have imposed their taste on Paris. The Marais reflects the style of France's leading families in the seventeenth century as surely as the Faubourg St-Germain mirrors that of the eighteenth or the fashionable new boulevards the nineteenth. To Bishop Sully we owe the great Cathedral; to St Louis the Ste-Chapelle; to Henri IV the exquisitely shaped Place Dauphine and that model of a city square, the Place des Vosges. But three men shaped Paris above all others, and left so indelible a mark that one cannot go about the city without being drawn persistently into their vision.

Louis XIV, the first of these men, perfected so powerful a concept of national pride and desire for glory that it formed a complete epoch of French civilization. In his reign and that of his successor, Louis XV, Paris became the royal city *par excellence* and as such, in the Sun King's own estimate, an example for all other cities. The Louvre's massive Cour Carrée was completed, and in front of it Le Nôtre laid out the Tuileries Gardens, thus linking the palace to what was to become the Place de la Concorde. To one side of this majestic perspective, the significantly

Paris from the Eiffel Tower   *Anne Bolt*

named Place des Victoires and Place des Conquêtes (now Place Vendôme) were designed as elegant backgrounds to contain statues of the great king. Opposite, in architectural salute along the Left Bank, the Collège des Quatre Nations, the Invalides with its commanding dome and esplanade, and later the École Militaire rose to state the grandeur of France and her divinely appointed rulers.

The concept of glory – of military conquest, valour and pomp – was spun into the very air that Napoleon breathed. For the Emperor, Paris could be no less than an Imperial city, successor to Rome and the envy of the world. Once again work began on the long-neglected Louvre: the cumbrous north wing, with its niches for great Frenchmen, took form at last. Alongside came the Rue de Rivoli, whose massive arcades and victorious name Napoleon originally hoped to extend as far as the Bastille. More bridges – Pont d'Austerlitz, Pont de la Cité, Pont des Arts – were thrown across the Seine, and streets were opened round many existing monuments, such as the Panthéon, so that they could be shown off in proper perspective. The Triumphal Way, leading from the Louvre across the Tuileries to the Concorde, was given its great tree-lined sweep up to the new Arc de Triomphe. (It was on this Elysian vista that, in 1814–15, Prussian and British occupying forces were to encamp.) Napoleon also commissioned a colonnaded Temple de la Gloire (now the Madeleine); and to complete one more imperial axis, a columned front was superimposed on the Chambre des Députés.

However remarkable Napoleon's achievement in Paris, it was as nothing to the prospect of temple, statue and cenotaph with which he had dreamed of ennobling either side of the Seine. 'If I had only had twenty years and a little leisure,' he recounted in 1816, 'I should have changed the whole face of France . . . What I did was immense – but what I was planning to do!'

The third man, Haussmann, carried out in slightly under twenty years the greatest transformation Paris has ever known. His notorious 'Plan' resulted (to take one example) in 50 kilometres of narrow streets being razed and replaced by 160 kilometres of broad thoroughfare. The case for and against the incorruptible, humourless Préfet is still open. On the one hand, he turned a fundamentally medieval, insanitary city into a modern metropolis. On the other, his Paris tends to be precisely what lingers in the mind after the things one admires have faded. For behind the masterpieces of the Grand Siècle or the Latin Quarter's hallowed charm lie the long grey boulevards with their crusty façades and pot-bellied balconies which, if not always due to Haussmann himself, are Haussmannian in spirit.

No doubt it is idle now to bewail this hinterland of dullness and the great gashes Haussmann left in the closely-knit architectural ensemble which Paris had remained until the 1850s. Yet as one advances under the frown of the Préfecture or Palais de Justice, one finds it hard to forgive his destruction of two-thirds of the Ile de la Cité – leaving only Notre-Dame and the Place Dauphine of what had been a network of medieval streets with an ancient church or chapel at nearly every corner.

If Haussmann had not bulldozed his plan through Paris, it can be argued, the city might have forfeited its role as a capital of the modern world. Subsequent administrators have continued to accommodate the 'demands of progress', often with comparably questionable results. Large swathes of the Seine already serve as motorways, and the late President Pompidou keenly advocated another *autoberge*

The Centre Pompidou

which would have run along the Left Bank past Notre-Dame. This project was narrowly avoided, but nothing has stopped the Tour Maine-Montparnasse or the futuristic La Défense area, whose silhouette, hovering beyond the Arc de Triomphe, now completes the celebrated perspective of the Triumphal Way. 'Paris cannot remain a museum-city,' Pompidou very reasonably claimed. And if these juggernauts are devoid of the least 'Parisian' life (or often of any life, La Défense after dark being as companionable as a crater on the moon), they at least proclaim a resolute modernism infinitely preferable to the half-baked neutrality of most constructions that were erected in Paris during the 1970s.

Other aspects of contemporary Paris can be found at the Halles and the Centre Pompidou. The former provides a glaring example of how in the name of 'progress' a unique area can be reduced to a shopping complex of unredeemable banality. The graceful iron-and-glass market pavilions might have been transformed to serve new ends but they were razed, and what was once a historical and intensely human city centre is now simply a commercial convenience. Still contested as a piece of architecture, the Centre Pompidou has nevertheless given ample proof of its ability to draw vast crowds daily. Although its factory-like spaces are not ideal for exhibiting art, the Centre's range of activities and relaxed atmosphere have made it Paris's most popular institution.

These buildings jut out so controversially against the Paris landscape because they symbolize radical change in a city where tradition is instinctively revered. Yet a fast-moving, technocratic, forward-looking Paris is gaining ground against the conservative, picturesque capital with its roots in its history and its provinces. With much less preparation than his counterpart in London, the Parisian has been plunged into an American-style life which has little connection with his own social and cultural past. However much one might regret certain aspects of that change, it is clearly inevitable – and accounts, along with the density of the city's population (2·4 times that of London per square mile), for some of the tension which characterizes the atmosphere of Paris today. Accordingly, Paris seems each year less and less the legendary and romantic capital of cafés, conversation and love in the afternoon (once so favoured by the official two-hour lunch break) and more a centre for top-level conferences, big business and administrative efficiency. 'The face of a city changes,' said Baudelaire, Paris's most subtle lover, 'more quickly, alas, than a human heart.'

Yet not so far from Roissy's space-age airport (Charles de Gaulle) and the spectacularly new express-line subway (the RER) lies the old, undisturbed Paris of quiet, crumbling streets, specialist shops and people whose style and language make up a map of nineteenth-century literature. Within minutes of the blank mass of the Tour Maine-Montparnasse, one still finds more or less intact whole areas of *petites gens*, small-time artisans and tradesmen who appear to have seen, if not Louis XIV, then certainly Napoleon and Haussmann, as well as two world wars, go by. Within yards of the Centre Pompidou's massive modern-culture machine are streets which date back to medieval times and lives whose rural primitiveness is barely less ancient. These are the areas which the lover of French literature will be drawn into instinctively, for they embody the vision and respond to the voice of the Paris poets, from Villon to Verlaine to Apollinaire.

No other city interweaves daily reality and art with the same ease and profundity. The boulevards at dusk or the Seine swollen yellow under a lowering sky, a protest march at the Bastille or statues in a deserted park, instantly conjure up their counterparts in literature and painting. The imagination of Pissarro and Degas, Hugo and Baudelaire is written into the very stone of Paris, leaving a labyrinth of image and metaphor. It is infinitely suggestive, a 'city of a hundred thousand novels', as Balzac said; while painters continue to set up their easels beside the Seine or haunt the streets of Utrillo. And Paris has no more glorious moment than when a change of light or simply the repetition of the daily round recreates the lines and colours which her greatest artists have left of her.

Of course, it is never a question simply of the new and the ancient Paris, but a series of subtle contrasts, extreme contradictions and unexpected unities. At times, the metropolis gives itself over wholly to display, flaunting its advantages along the Champs-Élysées or on the café-terraces of St-Germain-des-Prés; at others, it transpires as an altogether private place, made up strictly of castes confined to the suave gardens of the seventh *arrondissement*, the coop-like apartment blocks of the fifteenth, or the mysterious cafés of the Arab, Chinese or Jewish ghettoes. Similarly, it is the capital of formality, of ceremonious *maîtres d'hôtel* and *maîtres à penser* whom no one has ever seen smile; and a mecca for snobs and the cold scrutiny of people obsessed with *chic*; but it is also one of the world's great sources of spontaneity, where directness of manner and clarity of desire are the only recommendations required.

The secrets of this protean city belong chiefly to those who go on foot, venturing down alleyways, pushing on doors, stopping to watch, with an eye for the real and a mind open to the bizarre. What walk in the world can compare in beauty, information and charm with the one which explores the Marais, crosses the Seine by one of the islands, then continues up through the Latin Quarter to the Luxembourg Gardens – unless it is the one which follows the river along either of its banks? Small wonder, perhaps, with such a background of invention and taste, that excellence – whether in mechanics, talking or swallowing fire – is still what Parisians admire most, and that this freighted vessel on a sea argent has resisted so well the worldwide advances of uniformity – 'tossed', as its heraldic motto predicts, 'but not engulfed'.

Notre-Dame

J. Allan Cash

Paris: Gazetteer

Practical and General, Right Bank,
Left Bank

Michael Peppiatt

NOTE: See map 8 for Paris. Important tourist sights have been numbered on the map and references occur in the text where relevant.

Practical and General

AIRPORTS

Paris has three airports: Orly, to the south, and Le Bourget and Charles de Gaulle (more commonly called 'Roissy') to the northeast. Air France coaches link them to each other as well as to city terminals (*aérogares*) at Porte Maillot and/or Les Invalides; a regular train service operates between Gare du Nord and Roissy-Charles de Gaulle. Taxis are available at all three airports. Orly and Roissy-Charles de Gaulle have luxury shopping centres and hotels nearby.

ART GALLERIES

Paris's commercial art galleries are grouped in three distinct areas: Rue de Seine and adjoining streets on the Left Bank; round the Centre Pompidou; and along the Faubourg St-Honoré, Avenue Matignon, Rue de la Boétie, etc. The first two tend to deal in contemporary work, the last in traditional, or established modern, art. Some of these innumerable galleries appear to have stayed unchanged since the 19th-c., others might have been shipped in entire from New York's SoHo. The difference in quality of work shown is quite as wide; the best way to form a personal opinion, perhaps, is to compare a number of gallery shows, then test one's preferences against a good museum collection. *Pariscope* lists some of the more important shows, and a complete guide can be found in *L'Officiel des Galeries*, on sale particularly in the areas mentioned above.

BOOKSHOPS AND LIBRARIES

Browsing in the *bouquinistes*' bookboxes along the Seine is as traditional a part of a stay in Paris as lounging on café terraces. Their line in erotic literature looks a little quaint now, but it was mostly from here that Anglo-Saxons smuggled the once-banned books of Genêt, Henry Miller and Sade back home. In the same area, opposite Notre-Dame on the Rue de la Bûcherie, is Shakespeare & Co – only the namesake of the long defunct bookshop which first published Joyce's *Ulysses*, but an excellent place for new and second-hand English books which one can consult in a sympathetically anarchic atmosphere. Con-

siderably more formal, Brentano's (37 Ave. de l'Opéra), Galignani (224 Rue de Rivoli) and Smith's (248 Rue de Rivoli) offer an excellent selection of English books. Smith's also has English-language newspapers (like many central kiosks) and a tea-room upstairs. On the Left Bank, the Nouveau Quartier Latin (78 Bd. St-Michel) can be highly recommended for English and American literature; while, for French publications of every kind, the Latin Quarter is one continuous bookshop. Worth visiting for the tourist with time are the new British Cultural Centre (library and reading room, 9–11 Rue de Constantine, overlooking the Esplanade des Invalides), the American Library (10 Rue du Général Camou, 7e), and the reading room at Centre Pompidou (Rue Beaubourg), which is generously stocked with the world's press, new books and records.

BUSES

Buses are considerably slower than the Métro, above all during rush hours, but they are an incomparable way of seeing the city, and on some routes the journey has been accelerated by means of special 'lanes'. Tickets are the same as for the Métro; but two are required for any trip exceeding two 'sections' of the itinerary (consult route-map inside bus or the conductor-driver). Special four- or seven-day passes, for unlimited bus and Métro travel, are obtainable at main Métro stations, which will also supply a map of Paris bus routes. Bus stops indicate route-numbers and, occasionally, each itinerary in detail. Visitors will be glad to note that the open-air platform, once a characteristic of Paris buses, has been reintroduced on some lines – though without the little gate which permitted stylish ascent and casual departure.

CAFÉS

With a few honourable exceptions, Paris cafés have become rather utilitarian, anonymous places. They allow one to eat, drink and telephone with a minimum of fuss, but not often with pleasure. This is one reason why most cafés hardly live up to their reputation as places *par excellence* to meet and talk (the other being that Parisians are increasingly pressed for time). On the other hand, they are resilient institutions and it takes only an agreeable *patronne* and a couple of witty regulars to turn a hole in the wall into a club. Worth seeking out are the cafés which offer more than the usual dubious plonk and anaemic ham or gruyère sandwiches. Among the more famous establishments one might mention the Coupole on Bd. Montparnasse for its 1930s associations and its acreage of faces, the Deux-Magots, Flore and Brasserie Lipp as focal points of St-Germain-des-Prés, and the renovated Café de la Paix, beside the Opéra, a home from home for an older, more staid generation of tourists,

ENTERTAINMENT

Paris is a great cinema-going city. A fair number of houses (especially round the Latin Quarter) show foreign films undubbed, and movie fans will hardly resist the classics offered abundantly every day at the Cinémathèque (in the east wing of the Palais de Chaillot). Theatre is more hazardous. A good production of Racine at the Comédie-Française or of Claudel at the Odéon is obviously an event not to be missed. The Théâtre de la Ville (Place du Châtelet), the Compagnie Renaud-Barrault at the Gare d'Orsay, Ariane Mnouchkine out at the Cartoucherie in Vincennes, often provide excellent theatre. The Théâtre Récamier, the Espace Pierre Cardin and the Théâtre de Chaillot are more exclusively experimental, with the occasional pitfalls that inevitably entails. The café-theatres that have sprung up by the dozen over the last few years offer a more immediate way of taking the city's pulse. All the big cafés stay open late, and an evening watching the migrations and humours of the crowd at the Coupole or the Sélect can be as entertaining as any show. For a more intimate atmosphere in Montparnasse, there is the Rosebud bar (11*bis* Rue Delambre), the American bar with its piano-player at the Closerie des Lilas (171 Bd. Montparnasse), and the jazz or dancing places scattered round the Rue St-Jacques and in the St-Germain area. The Halles have opened up in a new way at night with all kinds of restaurants and clubs, many with an agreeably fresh North or South American atmosphere. Nor is there any lack, naturally, of plush nightclubs and cabarets, such as the Crazy Horse, Régine's and Chez Castel. Lists of these – as well as of every other kind of entertainment, from music festivals to massages – are given in the various 'what's on' magazines like the *Officiel des Spectacles* and *Pariscope*.

MARKETS

Paris's great market, the Halles, has been removed to the anonymous spaces of Rungis, beside Orly airport, but a few of its vassal street-markets, such as the one in Rue du Montorgueil or in Rue Rambuteau (opposite Centre Pompidou), continue to function. Every quarter in Paris, from comfortable Passy to the poorest Arab ghetto, has a food-market of some kind; and the adventurous visitor might like to explore the profusion of comestibles and human types in one of the city's less touristic areas – e.g. at the Marché d'Aligre, off the Rue du Faubourg St-Antoine, in the 12th *arrondissement*. On the Left Bank, a stroll along Rue de Buci, off St-Germain-des-Prés, or down the lively Rue Mouffetard, followed by a glass or two of white wine, is the best preparation in the world for a good lunch.

Paris has markets of other kinds, naturally. There are pets for sale along Quai de la Mégisserie, and flowers beside the Madeleine and on Place Louis-Lépine in the Cité (where, on Sundays, flowers are replaced by birds). Quantities of clothes at low prices are sold at the Carreau du Temple, the garment district's curious covered market (near Métro Temple); and stamps change hands on Thursday morning and at weekends in the gravelled garden between the Ave. de Marigny and the Champs-Élysées. Flea-markets exist at the periphery of the city, at Montreuil and at the Porte de Clignancourt (*see* Marché aux Puces).

MÉTRO

The Métro is the quickest and cheapest form of transport in Paris. Trains run from 5.30 a.m. to around 12.30 at night; if not particularly comfortable, they are efficient and – to anyone familiar with the London Underground or the New York subway – surprisingly clean (as on buses, smoking is prohibited). Tickets may be bought singly or, more economically, in *carnets* of ten; tourist passes for four- or seven-days' unlimited travel on Métro and bus are also obtainable at main stations, such as Châtelet, Concorde, Montparnasse, etc. The only advantage of 1st-class carriages over 2nd-class is that they tend to be less crowded. The various lines are indicated by the names of their terminal stations (e.g. Vincennes – Neuilly). Connections (*Correspondances*) are marked at the interchange stations on indicators hanging above the platforms. At the entry to each platform are blue-and-white panels listing all the stations served on that particular line.

Another network, the new RER (Réseau Express Régional), stops at a few stations in Paris on the way to various suburbs. Within the city, an ordinary Métro ticket is sufficient (NB the ticket must be kept to get through the automatic turnstiles at most exit stations); beyond city limits, a higher tariff applies. The RER has immensely accelerated cross-city travel, going non-stop from Châtelet-Les Halles to the Luxembourg, or from Auber to the Étoile.

MUSEUMS

Paris has museums to attract virtually every taste and interest. It should be remembered that they charge an entry fee (with a few exceptions, such as the Louvre on Sundays) and that almost all of them are closed on Tuesdays. For visitors interested in the visual arts, the Louvre, the Jeu de Paume, the Petit Palais (excellent permanent collection of 19th- and early 20th-c. painting), the

Musée Marmottan and the Centre Pompidou are essential. The two Musées d'Art Moderne (on Ave. Président Wilson, 16e), the display of artisanal and agricultural implements preserved like enigmatic works of art at the Musée des Arts et Traditions Populaires (in the Bois de Boulogne at 6 Route du Mahatma-Gandhi), and the remarkable collections of applied art at the Musée des Arts Décoratifs (107 Rue de Rivoli, 1er) are also important. Two outstanding centres of non-European art can be found at the Musée Guimet (sculpture and objects from the Far East) and the Musée des Arts Africains et Océaniens (African masks, totems, etc., at the edge of the Bois de Vincennes: 293 Ave. Daumesnil, 12e). The Musée de l'Homme (Palais de Chaillot, 16e) offers something for everyone interested in the guises and peculiarities of his fellow man; the Musée du Cinéma is in the other, eastern wing of the same tentacular building. Beautiful weapons in a very fine *hôtel particulier* are on show in the Musée de la Chasse (60 Rue des Archives, 3e), while a little further along the Rue des Francs-Bourgeois, the Musée Carnavalet (entrance at 23 Rue de Sévigné, 3e) sets out the history of Paris by means of exhibits ranging from maps and shop signs to souvenirs of Louis XVI's imprisonment in the Temple. The Conservatoire National des Arts et Métiers (292 Rue St-Martin, 3e) offers a fascinating array of historical precision instruments and a deconsecrated church housing early aircraft and automobiles. Paris is the city of museums, and more specialized institutions – rendering homage to the Post Office or the phonograph, to Balzac or Bourdelle – abound.

RAILWAY STATIONS

Paris's main railway stations are the Gare du Nord (Lille, Calais, London, Brussels, Amsterdam, etc.); Gare de l'Est (Reims, Strasbourg, Switzerland); Gare d'Austerlitz (for the Southwest – Bordeaux, Toulouse, Barcelona, Madrid); Gare de Lyon (for the Southeast – Lyon, Nice); Gare St-Lazare (Normandy); and the new Gare Montparnasse (Brittany, La Rochelle). The French railways have made commendable efforts to improve their service over recent years; taken as a whole, they are efficient and comfortable. Restaurants are numerous round the main stations, and although they often have little else to their credit, they are used to serving meals at odd or late hours. 'Le Train Bleu', a famous station-restaurant overlooking the tracks at the Gare de Lyon, has a massive Belle-Époque décor which is a trip in itself.

RESTAURANTS

Over the last ten years, restaurants in Paris have tended to go down in quality as surely as they have gone up in price. What is fast disappearing is the good, inexpensive *restaurant du quartier* which once set high basic standards. Deterioration in raw materials and the more Americanized tempo of life are mainly to blame (vast cafeterias and fast-food shops are almost as rampant here as in any capital nowadays). Nevertheless, those little restaurants certainly still exist – and tourists are sometimes adept at nosing them out. A solid, sensible menu and a provincial family air bode well. For the more expensive restaurants there are guides aplenty, though none of them should be followed blindly; even the very best places may go through a bad patch or simply decline. Beware snacks in fashionable cafés: they may cost quite as much as a proper meal elsewhere. The sensation of having eaten well and cheaply will be rare; but many Chinese, Vietnamese and North African restaurants can be relied on for inexpensive, and sometimes very good, food (the Latin Quarter is rich in these and other relatively cheap places). Most Paris restaurants are closed on Sundays and through August. The areas round stations and the Halles are good for eating late at night.

TAXIS

Taxis can be obtained either at a rank (marked *Tête de Station*) or hailed in the street. At night, cars for hire have their sign fully lit up. A small extra charge is made for luggage stowed in the boot, and for passengers taken at stations and airports; after 10 p.m., meters are changed to the higher, night tariff. The usual tip is 10%–15% of the fare. Three passengers are the legal maximum. More and more drivers keep a dog on the front seat, as much for conversation as protection. Drivers are on the whole well informed and efficient, but only foreign journalists in search of a line of local colour need believe that they are oracular. Be prepared, too, for a new and infuriating habit: drivers will frequently stop, ask where you are going, then roar off without you if your destination does not happen to be on their route home.

Right Bank

ARC DE TRIOMPHE (8–1). This massive arch and the twelve avenues radiating from it form a most emphatic memorial to national and imperial pride – and as such a fitting conclusion to the Triumphal Way, which begins at the Louvre Palace and continues through the Tuileries, the Place de la Concorde and up the great sweep of the Champs-Élysées. Napoleon, who sought to stamp his will so lastingly on Paris, chose this site in 1806 for a triumphal arch to honour the French army. Chalgrin was made architect, and when Marie-Louise entered Paris as Empress in 1810 he mounted a *trompe-l'œil*, by means of painted canvas on a wooden framework, to give an impression of what the barely-begun Arc would look like when finished. In 1836 the project was complete, and in 1854 Haussmann brought the number of radial avenues (formerly five) to their present dozen. Chalgrin's arch is based on antique models, but it outstrips them in its size: 50m high by 45m wide. François Rude was commissioned to make monumental sculptures on the Arc's four sides, but in the end he executed only the 'Departure of the Army in 1792' (also known as 'La Marseillaise'). The groups on the other sides were carried out by Cortot and Etex. The spandrels of the archway have allegorical figures, by Pradier, representing Fame. The frieze running all the way round the Arc contains hundreds of figures larger than life. On the shields above the frieze 172 victorious battles are listed, while the 558 generals of those campaigns are listed on the inside walls (those who died in battle have their names underlined). In 1920, an unidentified soldier killed in World War I was buried under the Arc, and the flame on his tomb has been kept burning ever since. A small museum inside the Arc contains extensive information about the monument; and, at the top, an observation deck provides a panoramic view of the city.

BOIS DE BOULOGNE (8–2). Long a royal forest rich in game and a useful hideout for brigands, the Bois de Boulogne was opened to the public under Louis XIV, and soon gained a reputation for doubtful encounters (valiantly upheld today). During the Revolution, it swarmed with a wide range of fugitives. In 1815, the English and Russian encamping troops so ravaged sections of it that they had to be reforested – not with the traditional oaks, but with chestnuts, acacias and sycamores. Under Napoleon III, the forest was converted into a park for which Hyde Park – much admired by the Emperor while in London – served as model. The Avenue de l'Impératrice, now the

Avenue Foch, was completed in 1854 and provided a highly fashionable thoroughfare between the city and its 'Bois'. Restaurants and cafés sprang up, and the Bois' vogue went from strength to strength right through the century to the Belle Époque. One of its undiminished attractions is Bagatelle, a delightful pleasure-dome and garden whose owners included the Comte d'Artois (for whom, to win a wager, the house was built in a record time of sixty-four days), Napoleon and Sir Richard Wallace, who supplied Paris with graceful drinking fountains (still known as 'fontaines Wallace'). Bagatelle's rose garden and lily ponds are deservedly popular. The Pré Catelan contains a famous restaurant and a 'Jardin Shakespeare' believed to include all the plants and flowers mentioned in the plays. Boating can be found on the large Lac Inférieur, and the Jardin d'Acclimatation is a traditional haven of games and activities for children. A relatively recent addition is the Musée des Arts et Traditions Populaires (completed in 1966), which displays with unusual taste and care time-honoured agricultural tools and equipment as well as many other fascinating relics of everyday life in rural France. Set in these elegantly neutral spaces, the familiar objects reveal a truly sculptural beauty.

CENTRE POMPIDOU (Centre National d'Art Georges Pompidou) (8–3). When opened in 1977, the Centre National d'Art de Culture Georges Pompidou (more generally referred to as 'Beaubourg') met with a storm of criticism. Nothing remotely like it had been seen in Paris, above all in the city's dourly conservative museum world. Appalled by the unabashed modernity of the building (designed by the Anglo-Italian team,

The Bois de Boulogne

Rogers and Piano), many citizens fumed and foresaw the whole enterprise as being doomed to fail. Yet nowadays the Centre is not only an irreplaceable part of the city's life, it is by far the most popular cultural institution in France.

The main reason for this is that the Centre is determinedly democratic and caters for a wide range of interests. In addition to permanent and temporary exhibitions, it offers easy access to a magnificent library and a reading room where the world's press is available. The ground floor serves mainly as a huge reception area, much favoured by the kind of culturally underprivileged people (such as immigrant workers) who would rarely enter a conventional 'museum'. The auditoriums in the basement are used for lectures and plays.

Over the past couple of years, the Centre has scored several triumphs with vast, comprehensive exhibitions on such themes as *Paris – New York* and *Realisms*. By means of movable screens, the massive, girder-encased floors can accommodate this type of wide-ranging anthology successfully. But single easel-paintings are rarely seen at their best here. A traditional museum room with solid whitewashed walls is more suited to the contemplation of a Matisse.

Outside, the sloping piazza has proved a fertile ground for spontaneous 'culture' of every kind, from bongo-drumming to impromptu debate, Arab dancing and fire-swallowing. On the south (Seine) side of the piazza, the Acoustical and Musical Research Institute (IRCAM) has its impressively equipped underground headquarters. Not least of the Centre Pompidou's pleasures is the ride on the transparent escalator up the building's side. The cafeteria and restaurant at the top provide a superb view, and a good place for planning one's day in Paris.

The nearest Métro station is Hôtel-de-Ville.

CHAMPS-ÉLYSÉES (8–4). This imposing and

hyperactive thoroughfare was marshland under Henri IV (1553–1610). The gardener-architect Le Nôtre had it drained and planted with trees in 1670 as an extension to his Tuileries gardens. It was called the Grand Cours until 1709, when its bosky perspective was renamed the Elysian Fields. During the 18th-c. the avenue was extended as far as Neuilly; but even as late as the beginning of the 19th-c. only a few large houses were to be seen on this strip of landscaped country. Cossacks pitched their tents there in 1814, leaving a wilderness in their wake that took two years to repair. Pavements and gas-lighting were introduced, and under Napoleon III (1852–70) the Champs-Élysées became the very place for the elegant to cut a dash – on horseback or in the latest Tilbury. Fashionable dancing-halls, café-concerts and restaurants thrived on either side of the avenue, which became more thronged than ever when races were held at nearby Longchamp. The Belle-Époque elegance described by Marcel Proust

(admirers will be gratified to find an *allée* in the gardens near the Concorde named after him) has been almost entirely replaced by hard-nosed commerce and a fairly sleazy nightlife. A few old landmarks remain, such as the restaurant Fouquet's (pronounced, for obscure Anglomanic effect, 'Foo-ketts'), but otherwise the avenue is lined with car showrooms, airline agencies, etc. The Champs-Élysées remain nevertheless many people's idea of a real 'night out', and they can be a pleasant enough place for a stroll on a summer evening. They also constitute the obvious venue for certain national or political manifestations since the Liberation procession headed by General de Gaulle in August 1944.

DÉFENSE, La (8–5). On the west of Paris, across the Seine from the Porte Maillot, the newly constructed area of La Défense (named after a monument commemorating the defence of Paris in 1871) will attract primarily those visitors who are interested in town planning and contemporary architecture. Most of the space has been used to erect high-rise office buildings, and its daytime activity contrasts curiously with its emptiness outside office hours. The simplest way of getting there is a RER train from Étoile Métro station. All traffic passes under or round La Défense itself, which has been conceived for pedestrians in the form of a huge platform broken into squares and terraces. The oldest building is the Palais de la Défense, completed in 1959 and now established as a trade-fair centre. The Fiat Tower, designed by a Franco-American team of architects, is the highest (178m); to counteract the impression of 'shrinkage' common to buildings rising above a certain height, the windows of its forty-five floors have been enlarged towards the top. The GAN Tower is another landmark; it is constructed almost entirely in metal, while its façades are overlaid with glass. Perhaps the most highly admired building, however, is the Manhattan Tower, whose elegantly sinuous mass (formed basically of two towers joined together) is clothed in mirroring glass that creates a counterpoint to the mobile Parisian sky.

FAUBOURG ST-HONORÉ and **ÉLYSÉE PALACE** (8–7, 6). Leading out of the Halles, the ancient Rue St-Honoré becomes, as from the Rue Royale, the considerably more opulent Rue du Faubourg St-Honoré. This celebrated street came into fashion during the 18th-c., when its splendid new mansions vied in distinction with those of the Faubourg St-Germain. Today its reputation is based mainly on the excellence of its jewellers, cosmeticians, leather specialists and clothes-makers, and its windows are a source of expensive temptation. Next to the Cercle Interallié, a large club set in ample gardens, comes the British Embassy at No. 39. Formerly the Hôtel de Charost and built in 1723, this house belonged to the Princess Borghese (Pauline Bonaparte) before passing to the Duke of Wellington in 1814. Berlioz and Thackeray were both married at the Embassy, and Somerset Maugham was born there. St Michael's, the English church, stands in the Rue d'Aguesseau opposite. Further along on the same side and set back in an impressive courtyard, the Élysée Palace has served as official residence to the twenty presidents that France has had since 1873. It was built in 1718 for the Comte d'Evreux, then enlarged by a subsequent owner before being turned, during the Revolution, into a temporary dance hall. Napoleon signed his abdication here after Waterloo, and it was inhabited by Louis-Napoleon Bonaparte before he moved into the Tuileries Palace as Napoleon III.

The area also contains a large number of art galleries (particularly along the Ave. Matignon), which specialize mostly in 19th- and 20th-c. European painting and sculpture. Artcurial, on the corner of the Ave. Matignon and the Rue de Ponthieu, has the largest commercial showrooms in Paris and an excellent art bookshop.

GRANDS BOULEVARDS. Describing a broad curve from the Madeleine to the Place de la République, the *grands boulevards* were laid down at the end of the 17th-c. on the site of inner ramparts razed in the reign of Louis XIV. They remained obscure and rural for the next fifty years until Parisians took to sitting in the shade of their trees to watch riders and carriages as they journeyed to and fro. The streets round the Madeleine and the Opéra then became fashionably residential, while further east the boulevards grew famous for their theatres, cafés, dance halls and the crowds that flocked to them. Gas-light and pavements made these wide thoroughfares the ideal place to sit, stroll and be seen. A new type, the *boulevardier* (beautifully caught in Maupassant's *Bel-Ami*), came into being. Latest fashions – inspired equally by Antiquity and Anglomania – were tried out on the Boulevard des Italiens, in whose famous cafés and restaurants (Café Anglais, Café Riche, Tortoni, La Maison Dorée, etc.) the latest *bon mot* or pun was perfected. Haussmann's plan transformed the *grands boulevards*, giving them their actual, more utilitarian appearance. An area still of cafés, theatres and now cinemas, they exist nowadays by virtue of banks, newspapers and offices of every kind, just as the present-day Parisian runs more than strolls and prepares reports rather than epigrams. Foremost among their curiosities is the Musée Grevin (10 Bd. Montmartre) whose waxworks are accompanied by trick mirrors and other illusions. Opposite is the Passage des Panoramas, one of the many covered galleries of the area that seem quite unchanged – curious oases of a past age. The Rue Vivienne leads off the Bd. Montmartre to the Place de la Bourse. The Bourse itself (built 1808–26) is open for business on week-days and tends to be most busy around lunchtime and can be visited during the mornings.

GRAND and **PETIT PALAIS** (8–8). These massive stone-iron-and-glass structures, facing each other across the Avenue Winston Churchill, were built specially for the Exhibition of 1900. The Petit Palais is visited mostly for its temporary art exhibitions, which are often of outstanding interest; but it also possesses a permanent collection of paintings not as widely known as its excellence deserves. It is particularly fortunate in having a number of key pictures by Courbet (notably the 'Demoiselles des Bords de la Seine' and 'Les Amies', surely one of the most sensuous pictures ever painted), Vuillard, Bonnard (including a superb 'Dans le Bain'), Cézanne ('Portrait d'Ambroise Vollard'), Toulouse-Lautrec, Van Gogh, Monet and many other 19th-c. painters. There is also a good selection of Dutch paintings (Hobbema, Metsu, Rembrandt, Teniers, etc.) and some 18th-c. tapestry and furniture (the Edward Tuck Collection). However ornate on the outside and cavernous within, the Grand Palais is crowned with an iron-and-glass roof of impressive dimensions and intricacy. Part of this vast building is given over to such regular events as the yearly Art Fair (Foire Internationale d'Art Contemporain), while another is used for retrospective shows of major modern painters (in recent years, Picasso, Matisse, Bacon and Dubuffet) as well as for more general art exhibitions. The Palais de la Découverte, on the west side, sets out the history of scientific discovery in an easily comprehensible form and also contains a planetarium.

Linking the Avenue Winston Churchill with the Left Bank is the Pont Alexandre III, built in the same period to celebrate the Franco-Russian alliance. It consists of a single metal span, rampant with cherubs, garlands and sea-gods.

HALLES, Les (8–9). Markets have stood on this site since the 12th-c. Not only food, but every other product, from France and abroad, was put on sale, and each street specialized in a single commodity. Theft and fraud were frequent, and a specially erected pillory awaited offenders. In order to cater for Paris's growing population, the Halles began to specialize in food alone from the 16th-c. onwards. By the 19th-c. its reputation for dirt and insurgency combined with Haussmann's modernization scheme to bring about a complete renewal of the area. Between 1854 and 1866, Baltard built ten soaring metal-and-glass pavilions which in time came to symbolize a whole district and a way of life. A century later, the markets were transferred to new premises at Rungis, close to Orly airport, and Paris lost one of its great spectacles: the nightly landscape of fruit, flowers and meat, and the distinctly other world, intensified in cafés that never shut, of porters, prostitutes and people who did not want to go home. In 1971, despite protest from home and abroad, President Pompidou gave the order for the pavilions to be razed (but not before they had shown their remarkable potential as theatre spaces). The new underground Forum des Halles, which has replaced the 19th-c. market pavilions, consists of a wide variety of modish shops, as well as cinemas and restaurants. Predictably enough, it has nothing of the picturesque vitality and architectural grace that characterized the old, much-regretted Halles. Traces of that charm can still be found in the neighbouring streets, which also house some of Paris's more amusing boutiques and nightclubs.

Of the area's remaining monuments, the **Église St-Eustache** is the most imposing. Dedicated to the Roman general who was converted by the vision of a stag with a cross between its antlers, this church was begun in 1532, but not consecrated until 1637; and although its decorative elements are Renaissance, its overall plan remained Gothic. The west façade was left incomplete and replaced, in 1754, by a ponderously inapt classical colonnade. During the Revolution, St-Eustache was rebaptized the 'Temple of Agriculture'. Inside, its plan follows that of Notre-Dame, with double aisles and chapels continuing round the chancel. Of particular note are Le Brun's tomb for Colbert, a pietà attributed to Luca Giordano and, at the W end, Vouet's 'Martyrdom of St Eustache'. Across the former Halles from St-Eustache is the circular Bourse de Commerce, or Halles aux Grains (Corn Exchange), built in 1889 on a site where Blanche de Castille is believed to have died on a bed of straw, as a token of humility, in 1252.

JEU DE PAUME. Built in 1861 as a real-tennis court (Paris once had some 250 establishments for this historic racket game), the Jeu de Paume has served to exhibit the Louvre's Impressionist collection since 1947. The story of the Impressionists' long struggle against stylistic convention and the degree to which they subsequently changed the course of European art has become legendary. They took painting out of the officially consecrated platitude into which it had sunk and made real life, on streets and in fields, its subject again. Nowhere in the world can the freshness and breadth of their innovation be as fully appreciated as in these rooms. The collection contains works not only by all the Impressionists but also by a couple of their predecessors and mentors (Boudin, Jongkind), so that some idea can be gained of the movement's whole aesthetic development. Similarly, the last of the fifteen rooms indicates how Impressionism's original impetus also led to the greater, more rigorous fragmentation of form practised by the pointillists (or Post-Impressionists), Seurat and Signac.

The **Musée de l'Orangerie**, on the Seine side of the Tuileries, is used for special temporary exhibitions. On permanent display downstairs, however, are Monet's huge mural paintings of 'Water Lilies'. The Impressionist vision of form broken down into flecks of coloured light has been taken so far that these scenes frequently come within a hairsbreadth of total abstraction.

LOUVRE (Palace) (8–10). One of the great palaces of the world and for centuries a focal point of French life, the Louvre began as a fortress constructed by Philippe Auguste in 1200 to protect Paris from attack via the Seine. It occupied only a quarter of the present-day Cour Carrée, and during the 14th-c. its strategic importance was annulled by new city fortifications. Charles V, who reigned 1364–80, made the Louvre his official residence and housed his famous library of 973 volumes – the largest in the kingdom – in one of the towers. Under François I, much of the old fortress was razed, and Lescot – seconded by the sculptor, Jean Goujon – was commissioned to erect a palace in the modern, Renaissance taste. Work was continued under Henri II; his widow, Catherine de Médicis, began the Long Gallery (parallel to the Seine) in order to join the Louvre to the palace she had instructed Delorme to build her across the Tuileries. The Pavillon de Flore (designed by Jacques du Cerceau) went up under Henri IV, and the Pavillon de Marsan (by Le Vau) under Louis XIV. When the court moved to Versailles in 1682, work on the Louvre ceased, and this vast palace, suddenly emptied of its world of guards, courtiers and petitioners, fell into disrepair. A large group of artists (including Boucher, Chardin and Fragonard) moved in and set up studios in the disused galleries; the gardens then became famed for their licentiousness. In 1750, it was suggested that the dilapidated palace be pulled down; it survived to see the massacre of Louis XVI's Swiss guards, however, and from 1793 to 1796 became the headquarters of the Convention. Work was resumed under Napoleon I by Percier and Fontaine, who completed the Cour Carrée and began building the north wing (along the Rue de Rivoli). Construction was completed, after more than three centuries, under Napoleon III. During the Commune, in May 1871, the Tuileries Palace was gutted by fire; the remains were cleared to make way for a garden, and the Louvre, which had escaped serious damage, took on its present open-ended appearance.

LOUVRE (Museum) (8–11). François I, who invited Leonardo to spend his last years in France, formed a royal art collection which, enlarged by subsequent rulers, was to provide the basis of the Louvre's great treasure. In 1793, a Musée de la République was opened in the Grande Galerie of the Palace. Many of Europe's most famous works of art – booty from Napoleon's conquests – were exhibited there before being returned to their original owners in 1815. Legacies and acquisitions have brought the collection to a total of some 400,000 items. The following list indicates a few of the most interesting exhibits in each of the museum's six departments.

ORIENTAL ANTIQUITIES: Sumerian carvings including the Stele of the Vultures, which celebrates the

Dr Christopher Tadgell

The Louvre

King of Lagash's victory over a rival city, and the stele of the triumphant monarch Naram-Sin (Room 1). Numerous statues of Gudea, a later ruler of Lagash (Room 2). An alabaster statue of the Intendant Ebih-Il (Room 3). The Codex of Hammurabi, a black basalt slab inscribed with the laws of Babylon as dictated by the god Shamash (Room 4). An enamelled brick frieze showing the Archers of Darius in relief (Room 8). Bas-reliefs from the great Assyrian palaces (Room 21). And the five-legged winged bulls from the Palace of Khorsabad (Room 22).

EGYPTIAN ANTIQUITIES: the 'mastaba' or tomb of the 5th dynasty, whose walls record scenes of life in the Old Kingdom as well as of the deceased's funeral (Room 2). Limestone bas-relief of a girl smelling a flower (Room 4). The powerfully lifelike Seated Scribe (Room 5). Sesostris III offering bread to the god Montou (Room 6). Statues of Sesostris as a young and an old man (Room 7). Black granite statue of Amon protecting Tutankhamen; painted bas-relief of Seti I touching the magic necklace of the goddess Hathor (Room 11). On the staircase (named after Champollion, the first orientalist to decode Egyptian hieroglyphs) to the first floor, the great bust of Amenophis IV, who founded a new, short-lived religion, and changed his name to Akhenaton. In Room A, devoted to prehistoric and Thinite periods, a decorated knife from Gebel-el-Arak (c. 3400 BC) and naked statuettes called 'concubines of the dead'. Carvings and furniture from the Old Kingdom, including wooden sculpture of a couple (Room B). Papyri, statuettes and jewelry, notably a pectoral and rings belonging to Rameses II (Room C). Highly stylized bust of Akhenaton, bas-relief of the young king with Nefertiti, his wife, and selection of everyday objects of the Amarna period (Room E). Damas-

cened bronze statue of Queen Keramana (Room F). Between Rooms G and H, the famous black basalt 'healing statue', inscribed with magical signs.

GREEK AND ROMAN ANTIQUITIES: 5th-c. bronze Apollo, found in the sea near Piombino (Room 1). Vénus de Milo, one of the most famous of Greek sculptures, found on the island of Milos in 1820 and acquired for Louis-Philippe (Room 3). The 'Dame d'Auxerre', an extremely ancient statue, presumed Cretan in origin (Room 5). The 'Rampin Rider', of which the head is original, the body and fragment of horse a plaster cast of work in the Acropolis Museum, Athens; Hera of Samos, famous sculpture of Zeus's wife, goddess of marriage (Room 6). Metopes from the temple of Zeus at Olympia (Room 7). Fragments of the frieze of the Parthenon in Athens (Room 8). Hermes fastening his sandal, an antique copy of a work by the great 4th-c. sculptor, Lysippus (Room 9 – called the Salle des Cariatides, and the oldest room in the Louvre). Series of portrait-heads, notably of Octavius, Agrippa, and Livia (Room 15). Nike, or Victory, of Samothrace, celebrated Greek masterpiece of 1st-c. BC, found on the island of Samothrace in 1863 (Escalier Daru). Collection of silver objects found in a villa in Boscoreale covered by the notorious eruption of Vesuvius in AD 79 (Salle des Bijoux). The following nine rooms of the Galerie Campana contain an extensive display of antique pottery (10th-c. BC–4th-c. BC), including statuettes from Tanagra (Room 8). Sarcophagus from Cerveteri (Etruscan Room, or Salle Henri II). Greek, Etruscan and Roman bronzes (Salle La Caze).

SCULPTURE: Romanesque capitals, reliefs and portal from the priory of Estagel (Room 1). Beginnings of Gothic sculpture, including column-statues and a Head of St Peter from Autun (Room 2). Vierge de la Celle, a figure of the Virgin with traces of original polychromy. Tomb sculptures of Charles IV and Jeanne d'Evreux (Room 3). Tomb of the Grand Seneschal of Burgundy (Room 5). Marble relief of St George and the Dragon by Michel Colombe (Room 6). The Three Graces by Germain Pilon and sculptures by Jean Goujon, whose work decorates the Louvre's Cour Carrée (Room 7). The Isenheim Virgin, c. 1470–80; Virgin of the Annunciation, by Tilman Riemenschneider (Room 9). Bronze Nymph of Fontainebleau by Cellini; works from the Della Robbia workshop; Virgin and Child by Donatello (Room 11). Upstairs are works (not always on view) of Coysevox, Nicolas and Guillaume Coustou, and Pigalle. Room 6 contains works by Houdon, notably busts of Diderot, Rousseau, Voltaire and Washington. The Carpeaux Room contains this 19th-c. sculptor's masterpiece, 'The Dance', formerly placed against the façade of the Opéra. Downstairs, in the basement, are the two slaves by Michelangelo originally intended for the monumental tomb of Pope Julius II.

PAINTINGS (the Louvre's collection is divided according to country; it stretches from the 14th-c. to the end of the 19th-c., and is so extensive that only a very few of the most outstanding works can be signalled here): on entry through the Salles Percier et Fontaine, two frescoes by Botticelli. The Salle Duchâtel, containing 14th-c. French painting, leads into the Salon Carré, which has two portraits by Jean Fouquet, Jean Clouet's 'François I', and 'Gabrielle d'Estrées and her Sister, the Duchesse de Villars', by an artist of the Fontainebleau School (late 16th-c.). The Grande Galerie is devoted to French painting of the 17th- and 18th-c.: works by Poussin ('Echo and Narcissus'), Georges de la Tour ('The Cardsharper', 'Magdalen with Candle'), Lorrain (three 'Views of a Port'), Chardin ('The Skate'), Watteau ('Gilles'), Fragonard and Boucher. The Salle Mollien includes works by David ('Coronation of Napoleon I') and Ingres ('La Grande Odalisque'). The Salle Daru (beyond the Salle Denon) has Gros' 'Napoleon at Eylau', Géricault's 'Raft of the Medusa', Delacroix's 'Liberty leading the People', and works by Courbet ('Funeral at Ornans', 'The Artist's Studio').

The Dutch School, in the Salle des Sept Mètres, is represented, among others, by Frans Hals, van Ruysdael, Claesz, de Hooch and a score of Rembrandts (among which are 'Christ at Emmaus' and the self-portrait of the ageing artist by his easel).

The Salle des États houses 16th-c. Italian works, notably such masterpieces as Leonardo da Vinci's 'Mona Lisa' ('La Joconde' in French) and 'The Virgin of the Rocks', Raphael's 'Portrait of Baldassare Castiglione', Veronese's 'Marriage at Cana', Titian's 'Man with a Glove' and 'Pastoral

Concert' (long attributed to Giorgione). The second section of the Grande Galerie is devoted to early Italian painting, with which the Louvre is particularly well endowed, containing works by Cimabue, Giotto, Simone Martini, Pisanello, Jacopo Bellini, Uccello, Fra Angelico, Filippo Lippi, Botticelli, Mantegna, Giovanni Bellini, Signorelli, Ghirlandaio, Piero di Cosimo and Perugino.

The Salle Van Dyck contains several portraits by Van Dyck (including his famous 'Charles I of England') as well as works by Rubens, Jordaens and other Flemish artists. Rubens' 'Life of Marie de Médicis' (originally intended for the Luxembourg Palace – see entry) consists of twenty-one large allegorical scenes, hung in the Galerie Médicis. A few steps down on the Seine side are the Petits Cabinets, housing pictures by Jan van Eyck (including 'Chancellor Nicolas Rolin before the Virgin'), Rogier van der Weyden, Hans Memling, Gérard David, Quentin Massys, Patinir, Bosch, Baldung Grien, Holbein the Younger, Dürer, Cranach, Ter Borch, Rubens, Brouwer, Teniers, and 'Velvet' Bruegel.

The Pavillon de Flore presents 17th- and 18th-c. Italian paintings, notably by Caravaggio, Guido Reni, Pietro da Cortona, Salvator Rosa, Guardi, Giambattista and Domenico Tiepolo. The Beistegui Collection occupies the last part of this gallery, with works by Van Dyck, Fragonard, Rubens, Lawrence, David, Ingres and Goya. On the first floor of the Pavillon de Flore is the Cabinet des Dessins, one of the richest collections of drawings, watercolours and pastels in the world. These works (about 100,000 in number) can be seen only by special permission, because of their fragility; but numbers of them are taken out for specific exhibitions. This first floor also contains the Louvre's Spanish paintings, notably by El Greco, Ribera, Zurbarán, Murillo, Velázquez and Goya.

The remainder of the Louvre's paintings are on the second floor of the Cour Carrée (in the S wing). These works are above all by 19th-c. French artists (Gros, David, Ingres, Géricault, Delacroix, Corot, Daubigny, Daumier, Courbet, and Puvis de Chavannes); but there are sections devoted to the Dutch 17th-c. (van Honthorst, Avercamp, van Goyen) and to the English School (Gainsborough, Reynolds, Wright of Derby, Lawrence, Raeburn, Bonington, Constable, Turner and Burne-Jones).

OBJETS D'ART and FURNITURE: the collection begins in the Galerie d'Apollon (decorated by Le Brun, with a ceiling by Delacroix), which contains St Louis' crown, the Crown jewels (including the 147-carat Regent diamond) and numerous precious vessels. The Salles de la Colonnade (in the Cour Carrée) display Henri II's 'Chambre à Alcôve' (Room 2), precious carved ivory, notably the 10th-c. Byzantine Harbaville Triptych (Room 4), the ivory Virgin from the Ste-Chapelle and Limoges enamels (Room 5). Room 6 has some fine

Italian Renaissance bronzes and Room 7 more enamels and ceramic ware. Over in the N wing of the Cour Carrée, Room 8 opens the collection of French furniture and *objets d'art* (16th-c. to early 19th-c.) with a number of tapestries and the silverware donated by the David-Weill family. Room 11 has some pre-Gobelins tapestries, after cartoons by Vouet, while Room 12 contains Gobelins work after Giulio Romano. Furniture by the celebrated cabinet-makers André-Charles Boulle (Rooms 13–14) and Charles Cressent (Room 16) lead on to Vincennes and Sèvres porcelain (Room 20) and an outstanding collection of snuffboxes (Room 23). In the remaining rooms, the tapestries from the 'Chambre Rose' of the Palais Bourbon (Room 29), Marie-Antoinette's travelling-case (Room 35) and a fine 13th-c. reliquary in silver (Room 38) are especially worthy of note.

MADELEINE, La (8–12). The Madeleine's neoclassical severity contrasts curiously with the luxury restaurants (Maxim's, Lucas-Carton) and grocers (Fauchon, Hédiard) which surround it. At the end of the 18th-c. the site was occupied by an unfinished building modelled on the Panthéon. Various functions for its use – from library to Stock Exchange to Banque de France – were put forward. Napoleon solved the matter in 1806 by commissioning Vignon to build a Temple of Glory for the Grande Armée; Vignon had the site cleared and designed a building that recalled Imperial Rome. In 1816, Louis XVIII decreed that the Madeleine (Ste-Marie-Madeleine, to give the full, correct name) should become a church, but before being consecrated it narrowly escaped conversion into a railway station serving the new Paris to St-Germain-en-Laye line. Its colonnade consists of 52 Corinthian pillars, each 20m high. The pediment they carry has a massive 'Last Judgment' by Lemaire (1834), while the bronze doors contain bas-reliefs of scenes drawn from the Ten Commandments by Triqueti. Inside, the broad nave is lit by three cupolas. On either side of the vestibule stand Rude's 'Baptism of Christ' and 'The Marriage of the Virgin' by Pradier; on the high altar is Marochetti's 'Ascension of the Magdalen'. Nowadays, one way of savouring the discreet charm of the Parisian bourgeoisie is to attend a High Mass at the Madeleine, where the congregation tends to be very *comme il faut*.

Before leaving the area, it is worth visiting the Musée Cognacq-Jay at 25 Bd. des Capucines. It has a fine collection of 18th-c. painting which is hung in rooms decorated with furniture by famous cabinet-makers of the same epoch. Both the paintings and the furniture were left to the city by the original owners of the Samaritaine department store. A little further along, at No. 35, the photographer Nadar had his studio. It was there, in 1874, that the Impressionists held their first joint exhibition.

MARAIS, Le (8–13). This old aristocratic area stretches from the Place des Vosges westward to the Bd. de Sébastopol, and from the Seine up to the Rue Réaumur and the Rue de Bretagne. Covering most of the 3rd and 4th *arrondissements*, it consists essentially of 17th- and 18th-c. town houses. As its name indicates, the area was originally marshland. Templars and other religious orders settled around it during the 13th-c. and gradually turned the marsh into arable land. Having fled the Palais de la Cité after the 1358 uprising led by Étienne Marcel, Charles V had his new palace, the Hôtel St-Paul, erected here. Under Henri IV, the Place Royale (laid out in 1605–12 and later renamed Place des Vosges) became the centre of court life. Courtiers and ambassadors had their mansions built in its vicinity; and for over a century the Marais was the seat of power and the source of fashion. During the 18th-c. the Faubourg St-Germain overtook it as the new elegant residential district. Emptied by the Revolution and then confiscated by the State, the Marais' great houses were let out and converted into a honeycomb of small factories, storehouses and shops. Inevitably they deteriorated, and the whole area became so dilapidated that by the mid-20th-c. there were plans to raze it altogether. It was not until 1962, in fact, that full-scale restoration got under way. Much of the area has been renovated since then, not least as the result of intense property speculation; and while the Marais has lost the animated charm of its population of small craftsmen (forced to seek cheaper lodgings), its architectural masterpieces are out of danger.

A number of the Marais' finest houses lie on either side of the Rue des Francs-Bourgeois. On the corner of this street and Rue des Archives stands the Hôtel de Soubise, set in a magnificent colonnaded courtyard. Built in 1705–9 by Delamair for the Prince de Soubise, the palace's façade is decorated with sculptures of the Four Seasons (copies of Robert Le Lorrain's originals). The interior, richly decorated in rococo style, contains works by Boucher and Van Loo. It also houses a Museum of French History whose rare documents include one of the six known letters of Jeanne d'Arc, the Edict of Nantes, signed by Henri IV, its Revocation, Louis XVI's diary (with the entry '*rien*' under 14 July 1789!), and Napoleon's will. The Palace is linked by its gardens to the Hôtel de Rohan (entrance at 87 Rue Vieille-du-Temple), also by Delamair, which was inhabited in succession by four cardinals of the Rohan family. Its right-hand courtyard contains Le Lorrain's celebrated Horses of Apollo. The first floor leads through a Salon Doré to the Cabinet des Singes, rampant with animal paintings by Christophe Huet. Much of the Hôtels de Rohan and de Soubise is occupied by the Archives Nationales – some 6000 million documents relative to the history of France since the Merovingians.

Further down the Rue des Francs-Bourgeois is the impressive Hôtel Carnavalet (entrance at 23

Rue de Sévigné), begun in 1544, then remodelled in 1655 by François Mansart. Mansart's façade retains the original 16th-c. gate with its sculpture by Goujon; the courtyard is decorated with bas-reliefs and Coysevox's bronze statue of Louis XIV. Madame de Sévigné occupied the mansion from 1677 until her death in 1696. Carnavalet is also famous for its museum, which traces the history of Paris by means of shop signs, models, maps and paintings, from the 16th- to the 19th-c. Of particular interest are the panelling and interiors saved from other town houses and the section devoted to Revolutionary France.

Opposite the Hôtel Carnavalet is the Hôtel Lamoignon (entrance at 14 Rue Pavée), built around 1585 for Diane de France, Henri II's legitimized daughter, and now a library specializing in the history of the city. Other nearby houses of outstanding architectural merit are François Mansart's Hôtel Guénégaud, containing the Musée de la Chasse (60 Rue des Archives), the Hôtel des Ambassadeurs de Hollande (47 Rue Vieille-du-Temple), and the Hôtel Salé (5 Rue Thorigny), so named because its owner benefited from the salt tax. For a description of the remaining areas of the Marais, see Place des Vosges and St-Gervais/St-Paul.

MARCHÉ AUX PUCES (Flea Market) (8–14). Set in an otherwise desolate area just beyond the Porte de Clignancourt, the Marché aux Puces (open Saturday, Sunday and Monday) is a world unto itself where one can reasonably expect to find the most outlandish, as well as the most disinherited, objects for sale. Its enormous success originated in the 1920s when a number of valuable paintings were discovered amid the market's usual rags and bones. This lucky find turned into a myth about treasure buried out at the Puces, and dealers and public came running. Today there is not simply one market but six different sections, with over 2000 shops, dealing in everything from old clothes and spectacles to period furniture. Prices are by no means necessarily lower than those to be found in specialist shops in central Paris, but adventurous early-risers might try their luck at the 'thieves' market', held at 6–8 a.m. on Saturdays between the Paul-Bert market and the second-hand clothes.

MONTMARTRE (8–15). Even more than in Montparnasse, Montmartre's interest tends to lie in its past and the myth that has grown out of it. Ancient legend explains its name as 'Mont des Martyrs' by situating the execution of St Denis here in c. AD 250. For most of its existence, Montmartre has been a village, reputed even in the 19th-c. for its leafy gardens and provincial charm (still quite tangible in Utrillo's paintings). The Commune of 1871 was sparked off by a fatal

incident here, but Montmartre did not begin to build the reputation which continues to draw armies of tourists each year until it became popular with artists and writers. Romantics such as Berlioz, Heine and Nerval paved the way, but the real metamorphosis got under way in the last quarter of the 19th-c. and continued until World War I. Cheapness and novelty were what first attracted artists, but soon the Chat Noir, the Moulin-Rouge and the Moulin de la Galette gave the area an effervescence, as well as a pathos, that Toulouse-Lautrec, above all, was to capture.

Montmartre's other great moment came at the beginning of this century when Picasso, Braque and Gris lived in the decidedly unpicturesque, but fertile, poverty of the Bateau-Lavoir. It was in this wooden slum (burned down in 1970) that Picasso produced the 'Demoiselles d'Avignon', thus bringing Cubism into the world. Even today Montmartre has kept a certain village air in some of its streets, despite the Place du Tertre's having degenerated into a tourist trap of the most blatant sort. Traps of another kind await at the bottom of the hill or butte of Montmartre in the 'hot' streets (as they are called in French) round the Place Pigalle. Before leaving the area, two other visits can be recommended: to Montmartre Cemetery, off Rue Caulaincourt to the W, where Fragonard, Degas, Stendhal, Dumas fils, Heine, Nijinsky and others are buried; and, further S, to the Musée Gustave-Moreau (14 Rue de la Rochefoucauld), where a vast number of this painter's intricate fantasies (about 1000 paintings and 7000 drawings) are preserved in the remarkable surroundings of his studio.

MUSÉE MARMOTTAN (8–16). With its large collection of works by Claude Monet, this secluded museum forms a natural pendant to the Jeu de Paume and the artist's 'Water Lilies' downstairs at the Orangerie. The house and original collection of Renaissance sculpture and tapestry, as well as Empire painting and furniture, were left to the State in 1932 as a museum by the art historian Paul Marmottan. A subsequent donation included a number of Monet paintings, notably the much-mocked 'Impression – Sunrise' which provided the press with a nickname (that stuck) for the group of independent painters who held their first, unconventional exhibition in 1874. Michel Monet, the artist's son, gave the museum some sixty-five of his father's paintings, and a special gallery was built under the garden to accommodate them. Most of the works date from the artist's last period in his house in the Norman village of Giverny, and they reflect Monet's passion for his famous garden and lily ponds. Renoir, Sisley and Pissarro, Monet's companions-in-arms, are also represented, and their works are given perspective by a few watercolours by

Boudin, their precursor, and by the Post-Impressionist painter, Paul Signac.

OPÉRA, L' (8–17). In 1860, plans by Charles Garnier, an unknown 35-year-old, won the competition for a new Paris opera house. Garnier's ambition was to invent a style proper to the age of Napoleon III, and the Opéra remains the Second Empire's most memorable monument. Construction began in 1861, but the building was not inaugurated until 1875. The result was the largest theatre in the world (covering nearly three acres), with a stage designed to hold up to 450 actors. The huge space set aside for technical equipment and storage, however, means that only the comparatively modest number of 2150 people can be seated. Dominating the Avenue de l'Opéra, the façade is remarkable for its large arcades, surmounted by twin groups of columns, and abundant groups of sculpture. The most famous of these is Carpeaux's 'The Dance' (last group but one on the right), the original of which has been removed to escape further damage from the weather (see Louvre Museum). Medallions and statuettes of composers join with allegorical pieces to complete the façade's decoration. Equally ornate, the interior is rich in marble (brought from all the quarries in France) – particularly in the white marble steps of the Grand Staircase. The auditorium itself, in traditional plush and gilt, is surmounted by a domed ceiling redecorated in 1964 by Chagall (just as Masson was invited to decorate the Théâtre de l'Odéon at the same period, when Malraux was Minister for Culture). On the left of the building, in the Rue Scribe, is the Pavillon de l'Empereur, specially conceived so that Napoleon III could be driven straight to his box (mainly as a security precaution). This section has been turned into a library and museum containing costumes, instruments, busts and portraits of musicians (notably by Carpeaux, Delacroix and Renoir) and all the scores of the works put on at the Opéra since it opened.

The Opéra is in the middle of Paris's busiest shopping centre. Behind it are two of the city's largest department stores, the Galeries Lafayette and Au Printemps; the American Express, Café de la Paix and Harry's New York Bar are within easy walking distance, while the Avenue de l'Opéra is filled with clothes shops, and airline and travel agencies.

PALAIS DE CHAILLOT (8–18). Originally the site of a pleasure-dome built for Catherine de Médicis (and later used by the vigorous Marshal Bassompierre), this was later known for its convent, until that in turn was destroyed during the Revolution. Napoleon planned a palace here for his son, the King of Rome; but its grandiose plans (by Percier and Fontaine) were confined to

paper after the fall of Napoleon in 1812. The present Palais de Chaillot was built for the Paris Exhibition of 1937; its two great curved wings, joined to pavilions facing each other over a terrace, make it look like a great bird without a body. Both in daytime and at night, the terrace offers a splendid view of the gardens and fountains below and on across the river to the Eiffel Tower and the dignified mass of the École Militaire beyond. The Palais' grandiloquent interior houses the recently redesigned Théâtre de Chaillot (the old Théâtre National Populaire) and four museums. Its Musée de l'Homme has a fine selection of ethnological exhibits, covering all areas of the world. Its presentation is rather dated, but agreeably so, and the human diversity displayed makes the museum an ideal place for visitors to take an hour off from homo Parisiensis. The Musée de la Marine, in the same wing, is rich in models of famous ships, figureheads and maritime paintings, notably Joseph Vernet's thirteen delightful views of the 'Ports of France'. Across the terrace, the Musée des Monuments Français provides – by means of copies and reproductions – a way of studying some of France's finest architecture, sculpture and wall-painting. Lastly, the Musée du Cinéma illustrates the history of the seventh art with a splendid array of photos, posters, décors, machinery and costumes. The Cinémathèque, at the garden entrance of the same wing, shows films from its huge stock of recent and vintage works.

PALAIS-ROYAL and area (8–19). The Palais-Royal and its immediate surroundings are as historically interesting as they are agreeable to the eye. The original palace, known as Palais-Cardinal, was built (1634–9) by Lemercier for Richelieu, who willed it on his death in 1642 to Louis XIII. When Anne of Austria moved there with her son, the young Louis XIV, its name was changed to Palais-Royal. The Fronde forced Louis to flee the palace, and he never returned to live there, giving it instead to his brother, Philippe d'Orléans. The latter's son, who acted as regent during Louis XV's minority, gave such unbridled parties there that the 'soupers du Palais-Royal' have remained a synonym for licentiousness. Philippe-Égalité had arcaded houses added round the three sides of the garden in the 1780s, and commissioned the same architect, Victor Louis, to build the Comédie-Française. Already highly popular with the Paris public, the Palais-Royal gardens and the cafés in their arcades became open assemblies in the period leading up to the Revolution. It was there that Camille Desmoulins launched his call to arms, and on the following day, 14 July 1789, the Bastille fell. The arcades were subsequently occupied by some disreputable gaming houses, and when they were shut down in

Château de Vaux-le-Vicomte, Seine-et-Marne (see page 115)   *Rainbird (Carrieri)*

1838 the gardens' commercial activity declined beyond repair. All that remains today are a handful of intriguingly dusty boutiques dealing in medals, genealogies, visiting-cards, etc., and the celebrated Grand Véfour restaurant, a leading literary café during the Second Empire. The palace itself now houses the Conseil d'État and the Ministère des Affaires Culturelles. Among the famous to have lived in the much-coveted flats overlooking the gardens are Colette and Jean Cocteau (who also lived for a time in the splendid Hôtel de Biron, now the Musée Rodin).

The **Comédie-Française** was formed in 1680 when Louis XIV had Molière's troupe and actors from the Hôtel de Bourgogne (where plays had been put on since the mid-16th-c.) merge to form one company – the only one licensed to perform in Paris. Napoleon completely revised their statute, which, in certain essentials, remains unchanged today. The interior, sparkling from a recent renovation, contains several remarkable busts (Rodin's 'Mirabeau', Houdin's 'Voltaire', Carpeaux's 'Dumas fils') and the chair in which Molière was overtaken by his fatal malaise while playing 'Le Malade Imaginaire'. The Comédie-Française is devoted above all to the classics of French theatre from Molière to Claudel; in the late 1970s it added Beckett's *Waiting for Godot* to its repertory.

The other building of outstanding interest in the vicinity is the **Bibliothèque Nationale**, whose main entrance is at 58 Rue de Richelieu. Its contents originated in the private libraries of the kings of France. Under François I, the post of royal librarian was created. The 200,000 volumes which constituted the royal collection were added in 1720 to those of Cardinal Mazarin in the Hôtel Tubeuf, which now forms about one-fifth of the Bibliothèque Nationale's actual premises; adjoining buildings were added during the 19th-c. to accommodate a considerably enlarged collection. The Library now possesses around seven million volumes, including two of the original Gutenberg Bibles and first editions of Villon, Rabelais and other often unique books. Each day 4000 new periodicals, as well as every new book and gramophone record published in France, are filed away. Its print collection is the largest in the world, numbering some 12 million, and the manuscript department is exceptionally rich, whether in papyri, illuminated texts or the correspondence of France's greatest men. Also of considerable interest is the Cabinet des Médailles et des Antiques, which contains 400,000 coins and medals, as well as fine antique and medieval objects.

PALAIS DE TOKYO and MUSÉE GUIMET

(8–20, 21). Most of the modern art formerly housed in the Musée National d'Art Moderne (now called Palais de Tokyo) has been transferred to the Centre Pompidou. The museum's new role, for the foreseeable future at least, is to present temporary exhibitions of works from the Louvre. The opposite wing of this gaunt, colonnaded edifice (built for the Paris Exhibition of 1937) continues to serve as the Musée d'Art Moderne de la Ville de Paris. The Paris Biennial Exhibition (of work by artists under thirty-five chosen from all over the world) and a regular flow of other contemporary art shows, as well as concerts and poetry readings, have made this museum one of the city's liveliest cultural centres.

Opposite the two museums, set in a garden on the Avenue Président Wilson, is the Musée Galliéra, which is also used for temporary exhibitions and other events, notably during Paris's autumnal arts festival (the Festival d'Automne). A little further west on the same side, overlooking the Place d'Iéna, stands the Musée Guimet, where the city's major collections of Indian and Far Eastern art are displayed. The ground floor contains Khmer, Vietnamese, Javanese, Thai and Tibetan sculptures. On the first floor are Indian, Pakistani and Afghan carvings and objects, as well as an outstanding collection of Chinese bronzes. The third floor houses some fine examples of Chinese and Japanese porcelain. The museum has a specialist library, and it organizes talks and projects films about the Far East.

PÈRE-LACHAISE CEMETERY

(8–22). This largest and most famous of Parisian cemeteries occupies a site where the Jesuits had a country house built for them in the 17th-c. Père François de la Chaise, Louis XIV's confessor, was sufficiently involved in its construction for his name to have been attached to the estate. In 1803, under Napoleon, the land was acquired by the State and laid out as a cemetery by Brogniart (who also built the Bourse). Molière and La Fontaine were the first to be interred here. The cemetery became the scene of violent fighting in May 1871, when the last Communards took up position here. Shooting continued among the tombs until, at dawn, the 147 survivors were put up against a wall (the 'Mur des Fédérés', to the east of the cemetery) and shot by the Versaillais troops. Beside this wall stands a monument to the Frenchmen who died in German concentration camps or in the Resistance. A complete guide to the cemetery can be obtained at the entrance. Suffice it here to name the best known of the illustrious dead who make Père-Lachaise a tourist attraction: Balzac, Nerval, Musset, Oscar Wilde, Proust, Apollinaire, Éluard, Gertrude Stein and Colette, among writers; David, Ingres, Corot, Delacroix, Seurat, Modigliani, among the artists; Chopin, Cherubini, Bizet, Poulenc, among musicians; and, of those famed for other achievements, Sarah Bernhardt, Maréchal Ney, Isidora Duncan, the gastronome Brillat-Savarin, the Egyptologist Champollion, Haussmann, the historian Taine, and the philosopher Auguste Comte. Not surprisingly, it is considered a rare privilege to come to rest in Père-Lachaise; and the burial there of a 'personality' – such as Maurice Chevalier in 1972 – is definitely regarded as an event in Paris.

PLACE DE LA BASTILLE (8–23). The original massive fortress, with its eight great towers and moat, was built by Charles V as a potential place of refuge. By the time of Louis XIII (1601–43), however, it was being used almost exclusively as a political prison where a subject could be committed, without trial, simply on a letter bearing the king's seal. Its inmates included the enigmatic 'Man in the Iron Mask', Voltaire and the Marquis de Sade (who wrote several of his books while imprisoned here). As a traditional symbol of tyranny – but more precisely because of the precious gunpowder stored within – the Bastille became the first objective of the revolutionaries who seized arms from the Invalides on the morning of 14 July 1789. Having successfully stormed the fortress, they killed its governor and his garrison, and then triumphantly freed its seven prisoners (of whom two were insane). Eight hundred workers then set about razing the building, and a year later the people of Paris danced on its vestiges. Today the only traces of the Bastille are the site it occupied, outlined on the Place itself. The July column which rises in its place was erected (1831–40) under Louis-Philippe in memory of the Parisians killed in the insurrection of July 1830. Their bodies, and later those who fell in the revolution of 1848, were buried in vaults beneath the square and their names inscribed on the bronze column, which is surmounted by a figure of Liberty.

PLACE DE LA CONCORDE (8–24). Magnificent in itself, the Place de la Concorde offers a perspective of magnificence in every direction, from the Louvre to the Arc de Triomphe, and from the colonnaded Madeleine to the colonnaded Chambre des Députés across the Seine. Its history is a mixture of pomp and blood. The square was originally laid out by Gabriel around a bronze statue of Louis XV, commissioned by the city's magistrats (in an attempt to curry royal favour) and unveiled in 1763. Baptized Place Louis XV, it was octagonal in form and surrounded by ditches. During a firework display to celebrate the Dauphin's marriage to Marie-Antoinette, panic caused 133 people to be crushed to death, and the ditches lay full of corpses. In 1792, the royal statue was replaced by a statue of Liberty and the square renamed Place de la Révolution. The guillotine (familiarly known as the 'national razor') was set up in the same year. Prominent among its victims were Louis XVI, Marie-Antoinette, Philippe-Égalité, Madame Roland (who, as she faced the statue, delivered the famous remark: 'O Liberty, what crimes are committed in thy name!'), Danton and Robespierre. At the end of the Reign of Terror, in 1795, the square received its present optative name. Hittorf, who built the Gare du Nord, partially replanned the square in 1836–40.

The Egyptian obelisk, presented to Louis-Philippe by the Egyptian viceroy, Mohammed Ali, records the achievements of Rameses II and once stood in front of a temple at Thebes. Two fountains (copied from those of St Peter's in Rome) and eight statues representing the main provincial cities were also added. On the north side are Gabriel's two elegantly imposing mansions: the Ministère de la Marine is installed in the one to the right (of the Rue Royale), the Hôtel Crillon and the French Automobile Club in the one to the left. The mansion to the right of the Ministère de la Marine is the Hôtel de la Vrillière (now the United States Information Service), where the statesman Talleyrand died. Beyond the Hôtel Crillon is the US Embassy, built on the site of a town house erected for that exacting epicure, Grimod de la Reynière.

PLACE VENDÔME (8–25). This soberly majestic square was designed to hold Girardon's equestrian statue of Louis XIV (just as the Place de la Concorde was built round Louis XV's statue). Plans for an ensemble of great magnificence – with mansions for the Mint, a Library and a Residence for Ambassadors Extraordinary – were put forward. But it fell to Hardouin-Mansart, who built the Dôme des Invalides and the Place des Victoires, to draw up the definitive plans, and the result, completed well after his death in 1720, has the grandeur of simplicity and restraint. Baptized Place des Conquêtes, the square later took its name from the Duc de Vendôme, whose mansion had stood on this site. The buildings which enclose the large octagonal square have an arcaded ground floor, pilasters reaching up the next two storeys, and dormer-windows. Pediments mark each of the square's main façades, stressing the regularity of the architectural rhythm. Louis XIV's statue was destroyed during the Revolution, and in 1810 Napoleon had it replaced by the present column, based on Trajan's Column in Rome and 44m high. Its spiralling bas-relief is made of captured cannon and depicts scenes of military valour. The statue of Napoleon at the top is in fact a copy of Chaudet's original, which the Royalists destroyed in 1814. During the Commune of 1871 the column itself was pushed over by a group which included the painter Courbet (who was imprisoned as a result). Today, the Place Vendôme's serenity is disturbed only by the traffic; under the benign gaze of the Ritz Hôtel, long-established banks and jewelers discreetly continue their business.

PLACE DES VICTOIRES (8–26). This dignified square was laid out by Hardouin-Mansart in 1685 to surround a statue of Louis XIV – the whole having been financed by Maréchal de la Feuillade in a bid to secure the King's favour. The statue, by Desjardins, showed Louis on foot, crowned with laurels, while the pedestal embodied four captive figures, representing the conquered countries of

Austria, Holland, Prussia and Spain. During the Revolution, this statue was melted down; the present equestrian piece was made by Bosio in 1822. The elegance of the arcades, crowned with sculptured heads, has been impaired by shop signs (it has recently become a centre of *avant-garde* fashion designers), to say nothing of parked and mobile cars; but on Sunday mornings or in mid-August, when all is quiet, the Grand Siècle breathes again.

PLACE DES VOSGES (8–27). Considered a virtual slum earlier in the century, the Place des Vosges has resumed its rôle over the last twenty years as one of the city's noblest squares. The site was originally occupied by the Palais des Tournelles, torn down by Catherine de Médicis after Henri II died there, in 1559, of a jousting wound. Henri IV toyed with the idea of founding a silk farm in its stead, before deciding to have a new palace laid out (1605–12) in the form of a square – composed of 36 uniform pavilions with a spaciously arcaded ground floor. The King's pavilion took up the middle of the S side, over the archway, and the Queen's stood opposite on the N side. The square's name was changed from Place Royale to Place des Vosges in 1799, in recognition of the fact that the Vosges department had been first to pay its taxes. The trees (many of which were destroyed in the 1970s by blight) and the fountains were later additions, while the equestrian statue of Louis XIII replaces an original work demolished during the Revolution. Of the famous people to have lived in this solidly elegant ensemble, Madame de Sévigné was born at No. 1, Richelieu resided at No. 21, and Victor Hugo spent sixteen years at No. 6. This last house now serves as the Musée Victor-Hugo and contains, among other personal relics, a collection of the author's powerfully imaginative wash-drawings whose techniques (such as playing with the possibilities of a blob of ink or spilt coffee and cigar ash) are disturbingly *avant-garde*.

SACRÉ-CŒUR (8–28). At the end of one of the most painful and humiliating periods in French history, the Franco-Prussian war of 1870–1, a number of French Catholics put forward the idea of erecting a church by subscription as a sign of their continuing confidence in their religion and their country. The project was adopted by the National Assembly in 1873. The architect, Paul Abadie, drew inspiration from St-Front, the church he had restored in Périgueux, and produced the unhappy mixture of Romanesque and Byzantine elements that has become so famous and so ubiquitous a part of the Paris landscape. Begun in 1876, the basilica was not consecrated until 1919 (although services were held there from 1891). The bell-tower contains La Savoyarde, one of the largest bells in existence. The gallery round the large central dome offers a fine view over the city whose skyline has been transformed over recent years by the erection of skyscrapers to the west, at La Défense, by the new Montparnasse Tower, and by the colourful mass of the controversial, but often crowded, Pompidou Arts Centre.

ST-GERVAIS and **ST-PAUL** (8–29, 30). These two areas, named after the churches which dominate them, make up the whole south side of the Marais – from the Rue François-Miron in the west to the Rue du Petit-Musc, and between the Rue St-Antoine and the Seine. The Église St-Gervais-St-Protais, founded in the 6th-c., was rebuilt in successive stages between 1494 and 1657. During the Revolution, the church became a 'Temple of Youth'. The interior is notable for its original stained glass and carvings; the organ (1601) is one of the oldest in Paris, and it is also famous because eight Couperins, including François 'le Grand', succeeded each other here as organists. The adjacent Rue François-Miron displays a mixture, typical of the area, of architectural elegance and casbah exoticism (which extensive restoration will inevitably efface). Outstanding is the Hôtel de Beauvais, at No. 68, built by Lepautre in 1655: its courtyard is one of the finest in this richly endowed area. Two other *hôtels particuliers* are especially worth visiting: the Hôtel d'Aumont, at No. 7 in the nearby Rue de Jouy, which has the considerable distinction of having been built by Le Vau, enlarged by François Mansart and decorated by Le Brun and Simon Vouet; and, nearer the Seine in the Rue du Figuier, the Hôtel de Sens (1475–1507), once residence of the archbishops of Sens and now the Bibliothèque Forney, a public library devoted to fine and applied arts.

The Église St-Paul-St-Louis, overlooking the populous Rue St-Antoine, was built for the Jesuits, on land given for that purpose by Louis XIII, between 1627 and 1641. Based on Vignola's Gesù in Rome, it is the first example of Jesuit architecture in France; the lofty façade hides the dome – which was to become so prominent a feature of the new style in the Église de la Sorbonne and the Val de Grâce. On the opposite side of the Rue St-Antoine, nearer the Bastille, the Hôtel de Sully stands in a magnificent Louis XIII courtyard decorated with allegorical figures of the Elements and the Seasons. Built between 1624 and 1630 by Jean du Cerceau, the house was bought by Henri IV's minister, Sully, in 1634. The interior contains some fine painted ceilings and looks out, on the other side, on to a garden and an orangery which leads into the Place des Vosges.

ST-ROCH (8–31). The Église St-Roch is situated at an agreeable point in Rue St-Honoré where the down-to-earth atmosphere of the Halles (from which it leads) mingles easily with the more refined air of the nearby Place Vendôme and Faubourg St-Honoré. The bullet scars still visible on the church's façade recall the troops, commanded by

Bonaparte, who mowed down a party of Royalists that had come to attack the Convention, at that time lodged in the Tuileries Palace. The church (dedicated to the Italian saint who cared for plague victims) was begun under Louis XIV in 1653, but lack of funds later caused the work to stop. When building recommenced, three interlinked chapels were added on to the apse, thus extending the originally planned length for the church by half. Meanwhile, the nave remained unfinished until John Law, the Scots-born financier who had recently been converted to Rome, donated 100,000 livres for its completion. Finally, in 1736, Robert de Cotte designed its plain Jesuit-style façade. The interior contains numerous chapels and, behind the chancel, a Lady Chapel (by Hardouin-Mansart) which gives on to a Communion Chapel which in turn leads to a rectangular Calvary Chapel. The church possesses several distinguished paintings and sculptures, notably Renard's tomb for the Comte d'Harcourt (in the first chapel on the right) and Coysevox's bust of the garden-architect Le Nôtre (at the beginning of the ambulatory on the left). With Le Nôtre, the dramatist Corneille, the philosopher Diderot and Duguay-Trouin, the daring corsair, are among the illustrious men to be buried here.

TOUR ST-JACQUES (8–32). This Flamboyant Gothic bell-tower is all that remains of St-Jacques-la-Boucherie, built in 1508–22 and long an assembly-point for pilgrims setting out towards Santiago de Compostela. The top of the tower now houses a weather station, while at its base a 19th-c. statue of Pascal commemorates the experiments that the great savant made in relation to the weight of air. The rather desolate square round the tower also contains a plaque in memory of Gérard de Nerval, the poet, found hanging dead from a nearby lamp-post in 1855.

The adjoining Place du Châtelet takes its name from the former fortress (or Grand Châtelet) which guarded access to the Cité via the Pont au Change, and which was demolished in 1802. The fountain in the middle of the square, known as the Palm or Victory Fountain, was erected in honour of Napoleon's victories. The two large theatres, by Davioud, date from 1862. The Théâtre de la Ville (formerly Théâtre Sarah-Bernhardt) is one of the city's foremost centres for theatre and dance.

Slightly N of the Tour St-Jacques, the Église St-Merri (entrance in Rue de la Verrerie) is a fine example of late Flamboyant Gothic, begun in 1515 and completed in 1552. Many of the sculptures on the W façade are 19th-c. copies, but the stained glass has survived and the bell in the NW turret is believed to be the oldest in Paris (1331). Saint-Saëns was organist here.

TUILERIES (8–33). Few places make one so conscious of the planned perspectives of Paris as the Tuileries Gardens. On one hand there is the Arc du Carrousel and the solemn rhythms of the Louvre's great, three-sided courtyard; and on the

The Tuileries Gardens

A.F. Kersting

other, the Place de la Concorde and the sweep of the Champs-Élysées leading to the Rond-Point and the Arc de Triomphe. It is called the Triumphal Way, and few more explicit expressions of national pride exist anywhere in the world. The Tuileries derive their name from the tiles made of clay dug on this site in the 15th-c. The first garden was laid out for Catherine de Médicis on the Italian model, complete with labyrinth, grotto, menagerie and silkworm farm. It became a favourite parading-ground for the nobility, hitherto confined for all fashionable purposes to town house and château. Louis XIV's right-hand man, Colbert, commissioned Le Nôtre (who also designed the celebrated parks at Versailles and Vaux-le-Vicomte) to lay out a new garden. The result was a perfect example of the formally precise, balanced French gardens of which Le Nôtre was the inventor. Two outer terraces (along the Rue de Rivoli and the Seine) enclose a symmetric pattern of parterres, fountains, pools, quincunxes, geometric paths and ramps (leading to the Jeu de Paume and the Orangerie). Colbert was so impressed by Le Nôtre's design that his first reaction was to make the Tuileries a private park for the royal family; but he was persuaded in the end to leave them open to the public. The gardens' abundant sculpture dates mostly from the 17th-c. and includes works by Nicolas and Guillaume Coustou, Coysevox and Le Pautre. The Tuileries' tree-shaded, outdoor cafés are perfect places to stop on a hot, sightseeing day.

VINCENNES (8–34). A historic castle, a large wooded park with several lakes, a zoo and two museums make Vincennes an attractively varied area to visit, and on all warm weekends part of Paris emigrates there for the day. The castle (once described as the 'Versailles of the Middle Ages') was begun by Philippe VI and completed in 1370 under Charles V, who had been born there. It took until 1659, however, when Mazarin was governor and Le Vau appointed architect, for the King's and Queen's pavilions to be finished. By that time the castle had established itself as a prison rather than a royal residence; the Grand Condé, the Cardinal de Retz, Fouquet and Diderot were to be among its most illustrious inmates. Once Versailles was complete, the court abandoned Vincennes completely. In 1788, it was even put up for sale – but it found no purchaser. Accused of a plot against Napoleon, the Duc d'Enghien – last of the Condé family – was court-martialled here, then shot beside the moat, in 1804. Four years later, Napoleon converted the castle into an arsenal; all its towers except the one at the entrance were shorn to the level of the surrounding walls. Restoration of the badly damaged buildings began under Napoleon III, and work has continued until recent times. During World War II, German troops established a supply depot in the castle; before they evacuated it, an explosion blew up parts of the Pavillon de la Reine.

Inside, the square keep represents a particularly fine example of 14th-c. military architecture: 52m high, it is flanked by turrets and surrounded by its own enceinte. The Sainte-Chapelle, begun under Charles V and directly inspired by its namesake at the Palais de Justice, was not completed until nearly two centuries later in 1552; nevertheless the style has remained purely Gothic, and the Flamboyant façade with its great rose-window is exceptional.

The woods and gardens of Vincennes were closely guarded royal hunting grounds from the 12th-c. on. Under Louis XV, they were reforested and opened to the public. Among the wood's present attractions are boating on the Lac Daumesnil (named after a famous governor of the castle), a large floral garden, and France's best-stocked zoo. At the edge of the woods, at Porte Dorée, the Musée des Arts Africains et Océaniens offers a superb display of tribal and religious carvings, while the Musée des Transports (60 Ave. Ste-Marie) provides the enthusiast with a panorama of vehicles from the reign of Louis XIV to present times.

Left Bank

CLUNY, Hôtel de (8–35). One of the finest examples of domestic Gothic architecture extant in France, the Hôtel de Cluny stands on the site of Roman baths built in the early 3rd-c., possibly during the reign of Caracalla (AD 212–17). A few vestiges of these public baths, and notably of the *frigidarium*, remain in what has otherwise been turned into a garden. Backing on to these ruins, the Hôtel de Cluny was originally founded in 1330 by the Abbot of Cluny to serve as his town house and to accommodate his monks come from Burgundy to study at their college near the Sorbonne. It was rebuilt, between 1485 and 1498, and given its present form by Abbot Jacques d'Amboise. Having served as a residence for papal nuncios during the 17th-c., the Hôtel became state property during the Revolution, was sold and variously inhabited by a surgeon (who used the Chapel as a dissection theatre), a cooper and a laundress. Sufficient earth lay on the ancient Roman vaults for a vegetable garden to thrive. It was then bought by the collector Alexandre du Sommerand; on his death, both the building and his collections went to the State, and Cluny was opened as a museum in 1844. Rising over a cobbled courtyard with a 15th-c. well, the façade is remarkable above all for its cross-windows and staircase-tower. The museum is richly endowed with examples of medieval craft, from clothes to jewelry and metalwork, which give a valuable insight into the everyday life of the Middle Ages. Its 15th- and 16th-c. tapestries are justly famous,

The Conciergerie

in particular the 'Lady and the Unicorn' series. Five of these six tapestries are believed to represent the senses; but although they bear the arms of a Lyonnais family and are believed to have been given as a wedding present, no full explanation has yet been found for their elusive allegory. The Chapel, on the first floor, possesses an exceptional star-vault.

COLLÈGE DE FRANCE (8–36). This rather dour building, begun in 1610 and completed around 1778 by Chalgrin, is synonymous with a higher flight of thought in France. Guillaume Budé, the French humanist, convinced François I of the need for a more liberal education than that provided by the increasingly bigoted Sorbonne, where all 'pagan' literature was eschewed. The new college was consequently founded in 1530 (on the site of Gallo-Roman baths) to teach Latin, Greek and Hebrew. Popularly known as the Collège des Trois Langues, it received the more sonorous title of Collège Royal de France under Louis XIII, and its syllabus grew to include Arabic, medicine, canon law and astronomy. French literature was admitted as a subject for study under Louis XV. During the Revolution, the Collège's name was abbreviated to its present form, and additions (notably new laboratories) were made as late as the 1930s. Ampère, Cuvier, Renan, Bergson, Valéry and, more recently, the biologist François Jacob and Claude Lévi-Strauss, the ethnologist, are among the many illustrious minds to be associated with this ancient seat of learning.

CONCIERGERIE (8–37). The '*concierge*' was originally governor of the king's palace, and the Conciergerie the part of the residence that came directly under his authority. It was his privilege to let out the Palace's considerable number of shops, turning it into a thriving commercial centre as well as a source of profit to himself. The Conciergerie's three massively vaulted rooms were built in the 14th-c. for Philippe le Bel. The largest and most impressive is the Salle des Gens d'Armes, divided into four naves, and one of the French Gothic's outstanding achievements. The smaller Salle des Gardes (where the guided tour begins) has some noteworthy capitals on its sturdy pillars. The third room is the kitchen, monumentally installed to feed a royal household of up to 3000.

The Conciergerie had often held prisoners, but its great claim to fame as a jail came with the Revolution, when large numbers of people were kept here – in most cases, to await the guillotine. The Galerie des Prisonniers contains a sinister cell where inmates were prepared for execution: their hands were tied, their collars loosened and the hair covering their necks cut off. Then they were transported to one of Paris's three guillotines: on Place de la Concorde, Place de l'Hôtel de Ville, or Place de la Nation. Between January 1793 and July 1794, some 2600 prisoners left the Conciergerie to be executed. Among the most famous were Marie-Antoinette (whose cell can be visited), Charlotte Corday, who stabbed Marat to death, Madame du Barry, Louis XV's mistress, the poet André Chénier, Danton and Robespierre.

Before the Quai de l'Horloge was built, the Seine washed right along the Conciergerie's main façade. The best general view of its four towers is from across the river, on the Right Bank. From east to west they are the Clock Tower (Paris's first public clock, which has been working continuously for over six centuries), Caesar's Tower, the Silver Tower (so called because the Crown jewels were kept there), and Bonbec Tower (whose name illustrates the way prisoners' tongues loosened under torture).

ÉCOLE DES BEAUX-ARTS (8–38). This curious jumble of architectures and monuments was considered a Mecca by many 19th-c. artists, both French and foreign. Now that formal artistic education is less respected, the Beaux-Arts no longer enjoys the same prestige, but it continues to play a central rôle in forming France's young artists. Particularly admirable is the School's practice of offering key teaching posts to famous contemporary artists, and of sending students who show particular promise to study at the Villa Medici in Rome. The Beaux-Arts also continues to hold its own as a centre of anarchic fun, especially in early summer, when students dress up and tour the streets with brass bands in preparation for their annual ball. The site originally held a convent which was converted during the Revolution into a storehouse for works of art rescued from destroyed buildings. (This operation was supervised by the archaeologist Lenoir, who frequently risked his life to save works now at Versailles, in the Louvre or in churches. The number of masterpieces destroyed or damaged during the Revolution is nevertheless phenomenal.) From 1820 to 1862 rebuilding (by Debret and Duban) was so extensive that only the church and the cloister of the former convent remain. A part of the Château d'Anet's façade, another segment of the Renaissance Château de Gaillon in Normandy and the front of the former Hôtel de Chimay combine with numerous sculptures to give the Beaux-Arts its intriguingly heterogeneous appearance. The Library is rich in drawings and engravings. The Beaux-Arts' most famous teacher was no doubt Ingres, and Renoir its best-known pupil.

ÉCOLE MILITAIRE (8–39). Facing the Eiffel Tower across the Champ-de-Mars, this famous military academy was founded in 1751 by Louis XV (at the insistence of Madame de Pompadour) to train impoverished young men for an army career. Jacques-Ange Gabriel, who built the Petit Trianon at Versailles and laid out the Place de la Concorde, drew up the plans; considered too lavish, they had to be scaled down, but the modified building maintained a certain grandeur – especially for a barracks. A quadrangular dome dominates the façade, whose regular rhythm is broken in the middle by eight Corinthian columns carrying a decorated pediment. Two fine porticos distinguish the *cour d'honneur*. Guided tours of the interior – which contains a fine staircase and the beautifully panelled Salon des Maréchaux – can be arranged by written request. The École Militaire still functions as a military academy. Its most famous cadet will no doubt remain Napoleon, whose leaving certificate contained the remark: 'Will go far if circumstances are favourable'.

While Gabriel was building the École Militaire,

The Eiffel Tower

Peter Baker

the market-gardens leading down to the Seine were transformed into a parade ground (whence the name: Field of Mars). Later the Champ-de-Mars became a public garden and the site from which several early aeronautical attempts, such as those by the Montgolfier brothers, were launched. A number of Revolutionary festivals took place here – in particular, the Fête de la Fédération in 1790, exactly one year after the fall of the Bastille, when Louis XVI swore to abide by the new constitution; and the Fête de l'Être Suprême, at which, in the presence of Robespierre, the 'Incorruptible', revolutionary Parisians officially recognized the existence of a Supreme Being and the immortality of man's soul. From 1867 on, the Champ-de-Mars was the venue for a series of World Fairs, including the Exhibition of 1889, in honour of which the Eiffel Tower was erected.

EIFFEL TOWER (8–40). The Eiffel Tower is no doubt the most loved and least lovely of Paris's traditional monuments, with the Sacré-Cœur coming a close second. It is nevertheless there to stay, and on a fine day it does offer an incomparable view of up to 67km over the city and beyond (one hour before sunset is reckoned to be the best moment for visibility). When it was erected for the World Fair of 1889, the Tower ranked as the tallest building in the world. With its television cabin, it now measures 320m in height. Gustave Eiffel, its gifted and daring engineer, had made a name with metal pylons designed to carry viaducts but his project was strongly opposed, notably by Gounod, Charles Garnier, the architect of the Opéra, Maupassant and the poet Leconte de Lisle – but to no avail. Up the Tower went, joined bit by bit by 300 acrobatic riveters; and when its original lifespan ended in 1909, it was not demolished. Its prodigiously slight weight of 7000 tons is carried by cement piers sunk in the ground. For those with an interest in statistics, it is made up of 12,000 metal struts held by 2,500,000 rivets. The Tower's height varies up to about 15cm according to the prevailing temperature. Its first and second platforms contain restaurants, and the third a bar.

FAUBOURG ST-GERMAIN (8–41). Until the end of the 16th-c. this aristocratic residential area – stretching from the Seine roughly to Rue de Varenne, and from Rue du Bac across to Bd. des Invalides – was woodland and pasture belonging to the powerful Abbaye de St-Germain-des-Prés. A few convents sprang up over the next century, as well as a huge palace built for Marguerite de Valois, Henri IV's first wife, and, as from 1671, the Hôtel des Invalides. The new Pont-Royal made access easier, and between 1690 and 1725 fashion weaned the aristocratic and rich away from the Marais to build their mansions there. These houses, of which about a hundred survive, set a new pattern of domestic architecture: sealed off from the street by massive gates, they stand

between a formal *cour d'honneur* in front and a garden behind; the finer façade is often the one overlooking the garden – and so invisible to the general public. During the Revolution the whole Faubourg was closed; and in the 19th-c. another fashion led Parisians to build their new houses around the Champs-Élysées. The Bd. St-Germain and the Bd. Raspail, part of Haussmann's modernization, struck a lasting blow at the Faubourg's patrician calm, but the Rues de Lille, de l'Université, de Grenelle and St-Dominique still give a representative idea of its grandeur. Most of the great houses are now used as embassies or ministry buildings. The most famous is no doubt the Hôtel Matignon, at 57 Rue de Varenne, built by Courtonne around 1721 and later inhabited by Talleyrand; since 1958 it has served as the Prime Minister's residence.

GARE D'ORSAY (8–42). At the beginning of the 1970s the Gare d'Orsay would hardly have been allotted more than a passing reference in a guide book. But its rôle has changed so radically that it is much more a point of interest now than when it functioned as one of Paris's train stations. Built in 1898–1900 by Laloux, its fussily lugubrious façade swallows some 170m. of the Quai Anatole-France. Having served as the location for Orson Welles' film version of *The Trial*, this disused station narrowly escaped demolition before being converted into a highly successful new home for Madeleine Renaud, Jean-Louis Barrault (director of the Odéon until 1968) and their troupe. Over the past few years, the large and small theatres of the Compagnie Renaud-Barrault have won a reputation for putting on some of the best new productions in Paris. The huge restaurant and bar beside the theatres can be recommended for friendliness and reasonably priced food.

Another part of this cavernous space houses the ex-Hôtel Drouot, Paris's main auction-house, which organizes sales of every kind of fine art as well as more lowly merchandise. Though the salerooms have lost the Balzacian peculiarity of their former warren at Richelieu-Drouot in the 9th *arrondissement*, the same improbable range of human type and attitude wanders through the building: happiness may be a Poussin drawing or a second-hand bedstead. The latest and most exciting plan for this prestigious ex-station is a Museum of the 19th Century. As such, it would group France's great collections of 19th-c. art, notably from the Jeu de Paume and the Musée d'Art Moderne.

GOBELINS (8–43). This ancient factory at 42 Ave. des Gobelins is synonymous throughout the world with the art of tapestry-weaving. In 1440, Jean Gobelin, head of a family of dyers that had discovered a scarlet dye, settled here on the banks of the river Bièvre (which today runs unseen beneath the Rue Croulebarbe and down into the Seine). Interest in the art was consolidated under

Henri IV, when a factory named after Gobelin was installed in the present buildings. Louis XIV's minister, Colbert, brought together a number of tapestry factories (including the one that had belonged to the recently disgraced Fouquet at Vaux-le-Vicomte) at the Gobelins and so founded the Royal Factory of Tapestry-Makers to the Crown. Five years later, in 1667, the Royal Cabinet-Makers also set up here; Charles Le Brun and Pierre Mignard, both acclaimed painters and decorators, were put in charge of the whole enterprise. From Poussin to Boucher to Picasso, a number of great artists have supplied works for the factory to make into tapestries. Some of the looms used today date from Louis XIV and working methods have changed little over the centuries: the weavers still work by daylight alone, on the reverse side of the tapestry with the picture they are copying behind them and reflected in mirrors. They can choose from over 14,000 tones to create the exact shade of colour needed. Each weaver's daily production amounts to a square about the size of a large postage-stamp.

ILE DE LA CITÉ (8–44). Despite Haussmann's wholesale modernization, the Ile de la Cité has survived as the womb of Paris. It was on this largest of what were then several small islands in the Seine that Celtic fishermen of the Parisii tribe settled around 200 BC. They called it 'Lutetia', from the Celtic word for a 'dwelling in the midst of the waters', and to this day it has retained an exciting precariousness – as if it might slip its moorings of bridges and sail in state down to the sea. The Romans colonized it in 52 BC, and the native inhabitants became known for their skill in river transportation. By the 4th-c., the settlement had taken on the name of its founders: Paris.

Providentially, as Geneviève (later the city's patron saint) had predicted, Attila marched on Paris but did not attack it; and in 506 Clovis, King of the Franks, made it the capital of his realm. During the Middle Ages, the Cité (as it had become known under Clovis) extended to both banks; it became famous for its profusion of churches and chapels, and for the excellence of its theological schools. The island's close-knit medieval centre remained intact right up until the time of Napoleon III, when it was razed to make way for what are now the Hôtel-Dieu hospital and the Préfecture de Police.

Notre-Dame, the Ste-Chapelle and the Conciergerie uphold the Cité's ancient claim as the starting-point of Paris, but there are several other less august reminders of its past that should not be missed: the agreeably sleepy Place Dauphine, for instance, which still has some of its original 17th-c. houses, and the tree-shaded prow of the Square du Vert-Galant, named in honour of Henri IV's reputation as a lover.

ILE ST-LOUIS (8–45). The combination of river, fine houses and trees makes the Ile St-Louis one of the most delightful places in Paris, and one of the easiest to walk round now that traffic has been restricted. At the beginning of the 17th-c. it still consisted of two islands, the Ile aux Vaches and the Ile Notre-Dame, which were famous for the duels fought there. Under Louis XIII, they were joined (the Rue Poulletier marks the former channel which separated them) and bridges were thrown across to either bank. Large-scale building in the current classical style began, and by the second half of the 17th-c. the Ile St-Louis already looked like an extension of its aristocratic neighbour, the Marais. Its façades (many of which carry plaques commemorating former inhabitants of note) often hide magnificent or enviably peaceful courtyards. The great Louis Le Vau is responsible for two of the island's finest mansions. He built the Hôtel de Lauzun on Quai d'Anjou in 1657. The Duc de Lauzun occupied it only for a short while, and it will be remembered above all as the setting for the 'Club des Haschischins' where Théophile Gautier and Baudelaire explored the 'artificial paradises' procured by drugs. Its decorated ceilings, panelling and tapestries form a sumptuous ensemble. The Hôtel Lambert, on the Rue St-Louis-en-l'Ile, was designed by Le Vau in 1640, and was once the home of Voltaire.

The Rue St-Louis-en-l'Ile, which runs down the middle of the island, also leads to the Église St-Louis-en-l'Ile, which was begun in 1664 on Le Vau's plans but not completed until 1726; the interior is a resonant Baroque play of gold, marble and enamel-work, and it houses not only French and Flemish paintings but Italian faience and English alabaster.

INSTITUT DE FRANCE (8–46). Built on the site of the 12th-c. Tour de Nesle (from which Marguerite and Jeanne of Burgundy are said to have had their lovers tossed lifeless into the Seine), the Institut is above all famous as the seat of the 'Immortals' – or French Academy. The present building was designed by Louis Le Vau to be in harmony with the great Louvre Palace across the water. It had been provided for in Cardinal Mazarin's will: an immense sum was set aside to build a college for students from the four provinces (Piedmont, Alsace, Roussillon and Flanders) acquired by France during his ministry. Le Vau's design consists of a central colonnaded façade, surmounted by a most elegant dome, and linked by curved wings to pavilions. Inside, on the left of the octagonal courtyard, is the Bibliothèque Mazarine, which houses around 350,000 volumes as well as an extensive collection of manuscripts and incunabula; by opening his private library to scholars in 1643, Mazarin created what was in fact the prototype in France of a public library. On the right is the ceremonial hall – formerly the college chapel – where the Académie congregates under the famous Dôme: it is here, to the accompaniment of carefully wrought speeches, that newly elected members are received. The Académie is in fact one of five learned bodies comprised by the Institut, but by far the most illustrious. Its members' official function is the constant revision of the French language, in particular deciding on new entries and definitions for their Dictionary. The list of those never to have been made '*Immortals*', from Descartes and Pascal to Flaubert and Proust, shows that even the Académie is not infallible; but its present-day members at least represent a very wide spectrum of expertise, since they number – in addition to writers – diplomats, doctors, an anthropologist, a film-maker, scientists and economists. Mazarin's tomb, sculpted by Coysevox, is kept here.

Flanking the Institut on the Quai de Conti, the Hôtel des Monnaies or Mint is situated in an imposingly sober building by Antoine (1771–5). Inside, a double staircase leads to a museum which illustrates the history of medals and coins in France.

INVALIDES, Les (8–47). The ideal approach to this imposing monument is by way of the Alexandre-III Bridge and the spacious Esplanade, laid out (1704–20) by Robert de Cotte. The Hôtel des Invalides was founded by Louis XIV in 1670 to care for old and disabled soldiers, who habitually had to beg for a living. It once housed thousands of soldiers, but there are fewer than a hundred there today, and much of the former hospital space is now given over to the museum and administrative offices. Libéral Bruant's designs for this regal ensemble (completed by Hardouin-Mansart's St-Louis Church and Dôme) produced a façade nearly 200m long, broken in the middle by a great portal whose pediment contains an equestrian statue of Louis XIV flanked by Prudence and Justice. The dormer windows have been carved to resemble trophies. Eighteen pieces of captured cannon, known as the 'triumphal battery' because they were fired to mark great French victories, point out over the Esplanade. The severely elegant courtyard, arcaded on two storeys, seems to echo still with horses' hooves and gallant arrivals. Seurre's bronze statue of Napoleon (which once topped the Vendôme Column) stands above the entrance to the St-Louis Church, at the far end of the *cour d'honneur*. The simplicity of this church's interior is offset by a serried display of flags captured from the enemy, ending with a number of Nazi banners. A wall of glass behind the altar leads the eye into Hardouin-Mansart's Dôme, which he built after the St-Louis Church. It can be reached either through the *cour d'honneur* or by its main entrance on the Place Vauban, but it should be seen at sufficient distance to appreciate its fine combination of lightness and grandeur. Built between 1675 and 1706, the Dôme des Invalides rises through its motif of double columns, repeated on two floors and the drum, into a dome surmounted by a lantern and spire 107m above ground. The niches on either side of the entrance contain statues of Charlemagne and

J. Allan Cash

Les Invalides, Église du Dôme

St-Louis (by Coysevox and Coustou). Hardouin-Mansart's masterpiece was originally to have been approached through a colonnade inspired by the one Bernini had given St Peter's in Rome; eventually, only an avenue (now the Ave. de Breteuil) was cleared to reveal the church in perspective. The interior maintains the impression of effortless soaring space, though the heaviness of the decoration and the monumental tombs rather pull the other way. The Four Evangelists on the cupola are by Charles de la Fosse, also responsible for the huge scene above of St-Louis presenting Christ with his sword. Sunk in a crypt directly beneath the cupola is the red porphyry Tomb of Napoleon. The Emperor died on St Helena in 1821, but his body did not return to Paris until 1840; it was then enclosed in six successive coffins before being lowered into the sarcophagus, over which 12 'Victoires' by Pradier now keep watch.

The Army Museum, housed in the main courtyard, has one of the finest collections of arms, armour, uniforms and other items of military interest in the world. The craftsmanship alone of many of the exhibits (damascened weapons, etc.) is prodigious; and there are also such dramatic objects as the cannon-ball which killed Turenne (as well as his perforated cuirass) and a host of Napoleonic souvenirs, from his tent to the stuffed skin of Vizier, his white horse.

JARDIN DES PLANTES (8–48). These large botanical gardens were founded in 1626 by Louis XIII's doctors as the Royal Garden of Medicinal Herbs, and opened to the public in 1650. Doctors and botanists – Fagon, Tournefort and the three de Jussieu brothers – roamed far and wide to add to what was already a prestigious collection of plants; but it was above all from 1739 onwards, when the great naturalist Buffon took them in hand, that the gardens grew in size and importance. During the Revolution, the nucleus of a zoo was formed there with animals from the royal menagerie at Vincennes. For the first time in their lives, Parisians came face to face with elephants and giraffes. Later, when Paris was under siege in 1870, the animals had to be killed for food. The gardens were also endowed with a Natural History Museum which remains a tribute to the 19th-c.'s meticulous attention to the natural world; and today the Jardin still exudes the previous century's methodical, rationalist approach. Over 10,000 species of plants are classified in the various beds; and in addition to the Winter and Alpine Gardens there are numerous 'galleries' devoted to mineralogy, palaeontology, etc.

Just behind the Jardin des Plantes rises the gleaming white and green Mosque, dominated by its tiled minaret. The building encloses a patio based on the one at the Alhambra; mint tea and coffee are served in an atmosphere which is wholly North African. A few minutes' walk away, at 49 Rue Monge, is the city's ancient Roman arena – the Arènes de Lutèce. Thought to date from the 2nd- or 3rd-c. AD, the Arènes were destroyed and remained buried until they were rediscovered by chance in 1870. They were conceived as an amphitheatre for plays and games, and the foundations of the stage are still visible.

LATIN QUARTER (8–49). The area was named (by Rabelais, originally) after the Latin spoken by students who had come from different parts of Europe to study at the University. Founded in 1215 and the oldest, with Bologna, in Europe, the University was the organized result of a dissension which led a number of masters (such as Abélard) and scholars to leave the traditionalist school attached to Notre-Dame for the greater freedom of the Left Bank. The fame of its teachers – among whom were Aquinas and Bonaventura – established it internationally. Today the Quarter's natural centre is still the Sorbonne, even though the University of Paris is now scattered in several other parts of the city and its suburbs. But while it has remained an area of lycées and learned institutions, it is as one of the world's irreplaceable meeting-places for the young that the Latin Quarter continues to excel. While the 'Boul Mich' provides the big cafés, bookstores and, rather too predominantly, clothes shops, areas like the one round the Rue de la Harpe (a former Roman road) form an exciting introduction to exotic and esoteric tastes in literature, food, and cinema. The student-led uprising of May 1968, even if it had few concrete results, added a fresh dimension to the area's romantic mythology – or rather reaffirmed its reputation as a place of unrest.

LUXEMBOURG PALACE AND GARDENS (8–50). Up until the Revolution, a great Carthusian monastery stood on these famous gardens, and they did not begin to take on their present appearance until Henri IV's widow, Marie de Médicis, decided to leave the Louvre in favour of a palace which would remind her of her Tuscan birthplace. She acquired the Duc de Luxembourg's mansion in 1612, bought up the surrounding land and set Salomon de Brosse to build her an Italianate Palace. The French architect took the Pitti Palace as his model, but while the façade's heavy rustication and ringed columns are noticeably Florentine, the Palace's ground-plan remains classically French. Marie's enjoyment of her new home was short-lived; political intrigue against Richelieu brought about her downfall, and she ended her life in poverty and exile. The Palace remained in royal hands until the Revolution, when it was used to detain such famous figures as Danton, Camille Desmoulins, the painter David and Tom Paine; most prisoners then proceeded to the guillotine. From 1940 to 1944 it was occupied by the Germans, and it did

The Luxembourg Gardens

Picturepoint

not receive its present status of Senate until 1958. The Duc de Luxembourg's mansion (now called the Petit Luxembourg) still stands to the west of the Palace and serves as residence for the Senate's President. The interior of the Palace contains a number of paintings by Delacroix and Jordaens; Rubens's great allegorical suite devoted to the life of Marie de Médicis and specially commissioned by her for the Palace now hangs in a room at the Louvre. The gardens are laid out in formal French style except along the west side where the English notion of winding paths and less-disciplined foliage prevails. It is perhaps the most attractive and – because it flanks the Latin Quarter – certainly the youngest and liveliest of Paris's parks. Tennis, a Punch and Judy show, donkeys and impromptu music are some of the Gardens' characteristics; chance encounters another.

MONTPARNASSE (8–51). In terms of myth, Montparnasse shares the fate of Montmartre and St-Germain-des-Prés, dining out on a dwindling past. It gained its name of Mount Parnassus, sacred to Apollo and the muses, in the 17th-c. when students took to reciting their verses on what was then a grassy mound. The mound was later levelled, and from around the time of the Revolution Montparnasse became known as an area of cafés and dance-halls with names like the Élysée-Montparnasse, the Arc-en-Ciel and the Grande-Chaumière (later adopted by a famous art-school); here the polka and the can-can were aired before going on to take the city by storm. Haussmann drove the Boulevard Raspail and the Rue de Rennes into the area, but they did not suffice to reduce it to bourgeois orderliness. Alfred Jarry, the violently anarchic writer, and the so-called 'naive' painter, Henri 'Douanier' Rousseau, settled here and they were followed by Rilke and Whistler. Montparnasse did not really come into its own, however, until the poets Max Jacob (who had finished his stint at the picturesque slum of the Bateau-Lavoir in Montmartre) and Apollinaire arrived and began to define the new spirit that was about to sweep its otherwise rather lugubrious-looking Boulevard. In the large new cafés (whether the Rotonde or the Dôme, the Sélect or the Coupole) political exiles such as Lenin and Trotsky easily found themselves seated near musicians (Satie, Stravinsky) and certainly within hailing distance of a few painters (Chagall, Modigliani, Soutine) or writers (Fargue, Cocteau, Cendrars). Around them revolved such legendary characters as the model Kiki, who was a creation in herself, or the curious Abbé Gengenbach, who delighted in flirting furiously with *les Américaines* while still dressed in his soutane. More and more foreign artists, from Foujita to Hemingway, headed to Montparnasse as to a promised land; and the great moment of effervescence – of movements and manifestos, of inspired nonsense and radical subversion – lasted until the Civil War in Spain. Montparnasse's reputation and much-

coveted studios have meant that it still retains a fair number of artists, but commerce – symbolized as much by the Boulevard's close-packed cafés, cinemas and restaurants as by the gigantic new tower – now outstrips art as the area's speciality.

MUSÉE RODIN (8–52). One of the few great *hôtels particuliers* of the Faubourg St-Germain that visitors are likely to be able to see inside and out is the Hôtel Biron, or Musée Rodin, at the corner of Rue de Varenne and Bd. des Invalides. It was built (1728–30) by Aubert and Gabriel for a former wig-maker, then came into the hands of Marshal de Biron, whose passion for flowers led him to lay out 200,000 livres each year for tulips. The house passed to a Papal nuncio and an ambassador from the Tsar before it was converted into a convent for the daughters of the leading families. The Mother Superior, later canonized, saw fit to strip the *hôtel* of much of its magnificent panelling as symbolic of the vanity of this world; some of it has fortunately been recovered and restored. The house then went to the State, which let it out to a number of artists and writers (notably Rodin, his temporary secretary, Rilke, Proust's friend, Robert de Montesquiou, and Jean Cocteau). In exchange for bequeathing his works to the State, Rodin was given the house until his death in 1917. In 1927 the present museum was opened. Its collections fill two floors and include such famous pieces as 'The Kiss', 'The Hand of God' and the busts of Victor Hugo, as well as paintings by Van Gogh, Monet and Renoir. The magnificent gardens are enhanced by a number of Rodin's monumental works, including 'The Thinker', 'Balzac', 'The Gate of Hell' and 'The Burghers of Calais'.

NOTRE-DAME (8–53). A Roman temple, a Christian basilica, then a Romanesque church occupied this eminently central site before Pope Alexander III laid the first stone of the great new Cathedral in 1163. Work was directed by Maurice de Sully, the Bishop of Paris; but although most of the choir was complete by 1182, nearly two centuries elapsed before the army of builders, sculptors and glass-makers had carried out the original plans to the last detail. When St Louis temporarily entrusted the Crown of Thorns to the unfinished edifice in 1239, however, Notre-Dame was already established as the focal point of the city's religious life. Among its most memorable coronations were those of Henry VI of England, the Huguenot Henri of Navarre (who became Henri IV), and Napoleon, who had himself made Emperor here in 1804. Most dramatically, Notre-Dame echoed with the fire of hidden German snipers when General de Gaulle entered the Cathedral to give thanks for the Liberation of Paris on 26 August 1944. State funerals (as those held for De Gaulle and Pompidou) continue to take place here.

The exterior – considerably restored by Viollet-le-Duc and recently cleaned – can be seen at its most striking from the Square Viviani on the Left Bank or (especially for the full array of buttresses round the apse) from its own 19th-c. garden, the Square Jean–XXIII. The W façade (from which Paris road distances are measured) is made up of three distinct, though harmoniously interlinked, storeys, with the rose window (nearly 10m in diameter) like a huge, multi-coloured hub at its centre. On the ground floor, the portal in the middle depicts the Last Judgment (restored by Viollet-le-Duc); the Christ on its pier is 19th-c., and only in the upper reaches of the door has the original sculpture remained intact. The Portal of Ste-Anne, on the right, contains sculpture dating back to c. 1170 (prior to the door itself) in its tympanum, while the St Marcellus on the pier is 19th-c. The Portal of the Virgin, on the left, also has a fine tympanum (which was much copied throughout the medieval world). Running over the portals is the Gallery of the Kings of Judah, pulled down in 1793 by the revolutionary mob in the belief that they represented the Kings of France. (The reconstruction is by Viollet-le-Duc, but many of the original heads were rediscovered very recently and exhibited at the Musée de Cluny.) The two great towers (nearly 70m high) offer a fine view over Paris; Emmanuel, the Cathedral's famous bell, is housed in the S tower. The porch on the S side, overlooking the garden, has conserved some original sculpture that depicts the Life of St Étienne. A beautiful statue of the Virgin adorns the N porch, while a few yards to the E is the superbly carved Porte Rouge.

The Cathedral's interior presents an awesomely simple contrast to the decorative complexity without. Its nave is flanked by double aisles which give on to chapels; the overall dimensions are 130m long, 48m wide and 35m high. Of the two rose windows which light the transept, that on the N side is particularly fine and well preserved. The 14th-c. Virgin and Child (called 'Notre-Dame de Paris') at the crossing and Coustou's 'St Denis' by the entrance to the choir are two outstanding examples of the Cathedral's statuary.

OBSERVATOIRE, L' (8–54). The southern side of the Luxembourg Gardens gives on to the Avenue de l'Observatoire, a delightful chestnut-lined *parterre* which encloses the great Fountain of the Four Continents (1873), famous for its graceful maidens uplifting a globe sculpted by Carpeaux. To the right, beside Rude's monument to Marshal Ney, shot on this spot for treason, stands the Closerie des Lilas, a literary café once frequented by Apollinaire, Gide and Hemingway (whose name is engraved on a brass plaque at his customary place at the bar). Rising on the far side of the Bd. du Montparnasse, the Observatoire was founded on 21 June (summer solstice) 1667, by Louis XIV's minister, Colbert, and completed in 1672. Designed by Claude Perrault, the building's four sides are precisely orientated to the cardinal points of the compass, and the south side marks

the city's latitude. Among the achievements of astronomers working here are the measurement of the solar system, the first map of the moon, and the mathematical discovery of Neptune. The cupola and wings were added under Louis-Philippe. A museum of instruments is housed inside the building, where one can also see Paris's meridian line traced on the second-storey floor.

A short distance behind the Observatoire is the Place Denfert-Rochereau, with its monumental black lion, and the entrance to the Catacombs. This subterranean space began as a limestone quarry in Gallo-Roman times, and in 1785 it proved a convenient place to lodge millions of skeletons brought from several cemeteries across the city. During World War II, the French Resistance set up headquarters in the gallery which leads to the charnel-house.

ODÉON (8–55). The Odéon is an area in itself, belonging neither to St-Michel nor to St-Germain-des-Prés but blending elements of both in a more discreet, ancient atmosphere. It stretches roughly from Bd. St-Germain up to the Théâtre de France (or de l'Odéon, as it is more popularly known). All the surrounding streets – Rue de Condé, Rue de Tournon, Rue Monsieur-le-Prince, Rue de Médicis – are worth wandering down for that particular variety of pleasures (rare book and print shops, galleries, fine houses and courtyards, specialist craftsmen, etc.) which reconfirms Paris's reputation as a place where the best may still be expected in most things. The famous theatre was built on the gardens of the former Hôtel de Condé, demolished under Louis XV. It took the form of a classical temple (designed by Wailly and Peyre) and opened as the Théâtre Français in 1782. Though the actors found themselves sharply divided into aristocrats and republicans at the onset of the Revolution, the building (renamed the 'Odéon') survived unscathed – only to be destroyed later by a fire, and rebuilt, in its original form, by Chalgrin in 1807. For a long time the theatre was overshadowed by the popular success of a number of Right Bank stages, but it came into its own, after World War II, as an outlet for the *avant-garde* (Genêt, Beckett, etc.) under the guidance of Jean-Louis Barrault. Today both the small and the large theatres within the Odéon appear to be waiting for new playwrights to give them a rôle again. The ceiling of the large auditorium was decorated in 1965 by the Surrealist painter André Masson.

PALAIS-BOURBON (8–56). The mansion that originally occupied this site was built for the legitimized daughter of Louis XV and Madame de Montespan: the Duchess of Bourbon, from whom the present building derives its name. The Prince de Condé, whose house had been pulled down to make way for the Théâtre de l'Odéon, made his home here and considerably enlarged the existing mansion. He was relieved of it during the

A.F. Kersting

The interior of the Panthéon

administer justice. Philippe le Bel added the Conciergerie Palace, whose Salle des Gens d'Armes impressed àll civilized Europe by its size. In 1358, insurgents under Étienne Marcel broke into the Palace and forced the future Charles V to witness his councillors being put to death. Once he had gained control, Charles left this place of evil memory for the Louvre and his country palace at Vincennes. Parliament, which had previously shared the building with the king, occupied it entirely as from 1431. Its members, who constituted the Supreme Court of Justice, were originally appointed by the monarch; to raise money, François I allowed the offices to be bought, and thereafter they became hereditary. The building was rebaptized Palais de Justice during the Revolution, and it has served as Paris's Law Courts ever since. The main steps lead into the Salle des Pas-Perdus, a huge hall where barristers and clients meet and discuss; originally designed by Salomon de Brosse, it was burned down during the Commune and later restored.

Revolution, when it was rebaptized the Maison de la Révolution and used as a meeting-place for the Council of Five Hundred. Napoleon commissioned Poyet to build a façade (1807) that would harmonize with the Madeleine across the Seine and so complete another imperial vista. The resultant portico of twelve Corinthian columns carries a pediment sculpted with weighty allegory by Cortot. Since 1815 the Palace has functioned as the Chambre des Députés while the Palais du Luxembourg serves as the Upper House or Sénat. The interior contains paintings by Horace Vernet and Ary Scheffer and a Library decorated with Delacroix's frescoes of the History of Civilization.

Also of interest in this area are the Place du Palais-Bourbon, a square made up of uniformly built Louis-XVI town houses, and the Palais de la Légion d'Honneur, in the Rue de Lille. Originally built for the German Prince de Salm-Kyrbourg, this mansion later became the Swedish Embassy; and it was here, as the Swedish Ambassador's wife, that Madame de Staël kept her renowned salon. Burned down during the Commune, the house was rebuilt shortly afterwards to the original plans. Since 1804 it has been the headquarters of the Legion of Honour (founded by Napoleon in 1802); its museum displays related documents and insignia.

PALAIS DE JUSTICE (8–57). This name designates the group of buildings which covers the Ile de la Cité from bank to bank and includes the Ste-Chapelle, the Conciergerie and the Palais de Justice itself (that 'cathedral of chicanery', as Balzac described it). It was on this site that the Roman governors built their headquarters, and the Merovingian kings their royal palace. Clovis died there, and St Louis sat in its courtyard to

PANTHÉON (8–58). Lying seriously ill in 1744, Louis XV vowed that if his health returned he would replace the crumbling church of Ste-Geneviève by a more splendid building. He recovered, Soufflot was appointed architect, and in 1758 the foundations were laid for an exceptionally large edifice (110m long, 84m wide and 83m high) to be built in the form of a Greek cross. Lack of funds continually slowed the work down. In 1780 Soufflot died – of worry, some say, caused by rivals' criticism of superficial cracks in the Panthéon's walls; and the building was completed by one of his pupils in 1789. After Mirabeau's death in 1791, the Constituent Assembly resolved that the church become a Panthéon for eminent citizens: '*Aux grands hommes la patrie reconnaissante*' ('To its great men from a grateful fatherland') was inscribed across the pediment. Later it served again as a church before being reconverted into a secular temple, this time definitively, when Victor Hugo was buried here after a State Funeral in 1885. The coldly neoclassical exterior is particularly remarkable for its great allegorical pediment by David d'Angers (representing France distributing the laurels handed to her by Liberty), and for its dome, which springs from a drum surrounded by Corinthian columns. The equally cold interior is decorated with numerous works, including Puvis de Chavannes' 'Stories of Ste-Geneviève'. The second cupola carries a fresco by Gros. Among the famous interred in the crypt are Rousseau, Voltaire, Soufflot himself (after whom the street leading up to the Panthéon has been named), Zola, the assassinated socialist and pacifist Jean Jaurès, and Jean Moulin, the Resistance leader.

ST-ÉTIENNE-DU-MONT (8–59). Set back from the coldly classical mass of the Panthéon, this stylistically unique church was begun in 1492 and took over a century to complete. The result is an intriguing amalgam of Gothic and Renaissance elements. St-Étienne's façade consists principally of three superimposed pediments, each highly decorated and incorporating a separate order of pilasters; the exterior's overall effect is lightened by a slender bell-tower. The interior, even though it dates from the 16th-c., is predominantly Gothic: an elegant rib-vault springs from its lofty columns (so high that they replace the triforium customary in Gothic churches). Worth special notice are the opulently ornamented organ, the pulpit and, above all, the rood-screen – the only one extant in Paris. Designed to separate the nave from the chancel, this richly sinuous, Renaissance-style screen extends into spiral staircases which in turn lead to the openwork balustrade running round the chancel arcade. Beside the Lady Chapel in the ambulatory are the graves of Pascal and Racine; on the same side of the choir is a chapel containing the shrine of the city's patron saint, Ste-Geneviève, whose bones were taken out of a nearby abbey and burned by the crowd in 1793. (During the Revolution, St-Étienne was renamed the 'Temple of Filial Piety'.)

The Lycée Henri IV on the other side of the Rue Clovis reminds the visitor that this is Paris's traditional centre of learning. The École Polytechnique, the Collège Ste-Barbe (founded in 1460 for Spanish scholars) and the Lycée Louis-le-Grand lead over to the Sorbonne and the Collège de France. In their midst, the Bibliothèque Ste-Geneviève (built on the site of the former Collège de Montaigu, where Erasmus and Calvin studied) houses a vast library and an impressive collection of manuscripts, including some by Rimbaud, Baudelaire and Valéry.

ST-JULIEN-LE-PAUVRE. To one side of the Rue St-Jacques stands this small church dating from the same period (1165–1220) as Notre-Dame, which it faces across the Seine. Chapels dedicated to no less than three St-Juliens have occupied this site since the 6th-c., St Julien-le-Pauvre being a bishop of Le Mans who constantly gave away whatever his purse contained. Throughout the Middle Ages it served as church to the University, whose members also assembled here to elect their Rector; the students created such havoc within its walls, however, that the custom was dropped in 1524. The ancient Hôtel-Dieu hospital took it as their chapel in 1665. But since 1889, Melchites (Greek Catholics under papal authority) have worshipped here; and the opportunity to hear their high mass sung on Sunday mornings should not be missed. The church's structure was considerably transformed in 1651, when the present west front was built and the nave covered with a cradle-vault. The interior contains noteworthy capitals, decorated with acanthus leaves and harpies; a screen bearing icons divides the chancel.

The Square René-Viviani, which lies between St-Julien and the river, offers a magnificent view of Notre-Dame; the garden contains a false acacia brought back from North America and planted there around 1680 – which makes it the second oldest tree in Paris (the oldest being in the Jardin des Plantes). Two neighbouring streets of interest are the Rue Galande, which was the ancient Roman way to Lyon, and the Rue du Fouarre, named after the bales of straw (*fouarre*) which students sat on during the public University lectures given here.

ST-GERMAIN-DES-PRÉS (8–60). Most visitors to St-Germain-des-Prés are drawn more by its cafés and a hankering after something new or fashionable than by its ancient church. Plenty of intriguing-looking people sit and scribble, or sit and stare, at the Deux Magots and the Flore, but the St-Germain of legend – the existentialist forties and fifties, from Sartre to Juliette Greco – is a mere memory that haunts these former temples of intellectual ferment. Every stay in Paris should include a couple of hours' wandering round the famous crossroads, whether in homage to its myths or exploring the paintings, rare books and antiques that make the neighbouring streets so delightful. But the church itself need not be overlooked: it is the oldest in Paris, and the only one to have such extensive traces of its original Romanesque structure. From the 6th-c. it was the site of a Benedictine abbey – one of the 17,000 the order once controlled – which grew to such wealth and power that it existed as a state in itself. Norman raiders destroyed it several times, and the church was rebuilt over a long period: the W tower and nave in the 11th-c., and the choir in the mid-12th-c. It has since undergone several radical transformations, including the loss of two of its towers. During the Revolution, the abbey was dissolved and the church used as a saltpetre factory. The interior (extensively restored and redecorated in the 19th-c.) is above all interesting for its combination of Romanesque nave and the very early Gothic of the choir. There are some interesting tombs, including those of two Scots who died in the service of French kings.

Nearby, in the Place Fürstenberg, one can visit the house and studio of Eugène Delacroix, which is filled with paintings, documents about the artist and personal effects. In addition to the interest of its collections, this Musée Delacroix offers the peace of a delightful little garden.

ST-MÉDARD and **RUE MOUFFETARD** (8–61, 62). Adviser to the Merovingian kings, St-Médard also founded the old French custom of the *rosière*, whereby virtuous maidens are awarded a wreath of roses (and nowadays, where the custom still prevails, a sum of money). The church dedicated to him lies at the bottom of the winding, populous Rue Mouffetard. Begun in the 15th-c. and not completed until 1655, it is lit by a large Flamboyant window in its Rue Mouffetard façade; the nave is also Flamboyant Gothic, whereas the chancel, considerably later in date, shows a Renaissance influence in its rounded arches and windows. Several paintings of interest decorate the church, notably a 'Dead Christ' attributed to Philippe de Champaigne. The graveyard formerly attached to St-Médard (and now a garden) became a great centre of attraction because the tomb of Abbé Pâris, a Jansenist who died in 1727, was reputed to work miraculous cures. Sick believers (called *convulsionnaires*) screamed, imitated animals, writhed under the tombstone and even ate the earth in hysterical devotion. Their antics so troubled the peace that Louis XV had the cemetery closed. The following *mot* then appeared on the cemetery wall:

'De par le Roi, défense à Dieu
De faire miracle en ce lieu'
(The King commands that God abstain
From doing miracles on this terrain.)

The Rue Mouffetard climbs up to Place de la Contrescarpe through a huddle of narrow façades: its charm lies not in its picturesquely mean proportions but in the atmosphere created by its shops, cafés and market-stalls – of hundreds of lives lived mainly in the streets. It is at once unmistakeably Parisian and yet so village-like as to exist in no other *quartier* in quite the same way.

ST-SÉVERIN (8–63). Built on the site of an ancient oratory, St-Séverin served as parish church for the whole Left Bank around the end of the 11th-c.; it was from here, in the following century, that Foulques preached the Fourth Crusade. The present building was begun in the first half of the 13th-c. but not finished until 1530, so that it can be seen as a demonstration of the development of styles, from early Gothic to Flamboyant. In the 17th-c., pillars and arches in the apse were classicized to suit the taste of Mademoiselle de Montpensier, Louis XIV's cousin. The W door dates from the early 13th-c. and was brought from the church of St-Pierre-aux-Bœufs, pulled down in 1839 when the Cité was substantially rebuilt. The rose-window above it is pure 15th-c. Flamboyant. The surprising width of the interior (34m, but only 50m long by 17m high) was produced by a problem of land: when the church had to be enlarged in the 14th–15th-c., only lateral extension was possible. St-Séverin has double aisles but no transept. The first three bays of its nave, with their short, capital-topped columns, are the oldest (13th-c.); the following bays are Flamboyant. The apse, with its famous double ambulatory, and the rib-vaulting that gracefully welds pillar to vault, produces a dramatic impression of moving, changing volume. Some 14th- and 15th-c. stained glass remains, while the windows in the apse were designed by the contemporary French artist, Jean Bazaine. A door in the fourth bay to the right on entering leads to a small garden (formerly a cemetery), where the first

operation for removal of a stone was carried out in 1474; the patient had been previously condemned to death, but he was set free by order of the King when the operation proved successful.

ST-SULPICE (8–64). The church of St-Sulpice was originally founded by the powerful Abbaye de St-Germain-des-Prés. It had been rebuilt several times before the present building was undertaken in 1646 by Gamard; no less than six other architects succeeded him in the 134 years that elapsed before the church was completed. After Le Vau, Gittard and Oppendort, the Italian Servandoni won a competition for the church's façade: his massive, antique design was later modified by Maclaurin and Chalgrin. The result of so much time and change of mind is a double portico surmounted by two towers; the North Tower, 73m high, is decorated with seated Evangelists and remains 5m higher than the South Tower, left unfinished at the Revolution. St-Sulpice's imposing interior is 113m long, 58m wide and 34m high (only a metre short of the height of Notre-Dame's vault). The case decorating the celebrated organ (with its 6588 pipes, it is one of the largest in the world) was designed in 1776 by Chalgrin. By the entrance the two shells holding holy water were sent to François I by the Venetian Republic. Towards the end of his life, Delacroix decorated the first chapel to the right with frescoes: on the vault one sees 'St Michael Slaying the Dragon', on the right wall 'Heliodorus Driven from the Temple', and on the left 'Jacob Struggling with the Angel'. The Lady Chapel has a 'Virgin and Child' by Pigalle over the altar, pictures by Van Loo on the walls, and a fresco by Lemoyne covering its cupola.

The Place St-Sulpice is embellished by Visconti's Fontaine des Quatre Évêques, named after the statues of four bishops in its niches. The neighbouring streets (Rue des Canettes, Rue du Vieux-Colombier, Rue du Four) are worth visiting for their shops, restaurants and general atmosphere of a stylish village.

STE-CHAPELLE (8–65). This surpassingly graceful Gothic chapel was commissioned by St Louis to house the Crown of Thorns, which he had bought from the Venetians, and other relics. These and the reliquary made to contain them cost the King two and a half times the total expense of the Ste-Chapelle itself. The chapel rose in the incredibly short period of thirty-three months and was consecrated in 1248. The sheerness of its construction – slender pillars giving rise to a vault without the counterbalancing aid of buttresses – was immediately recognized as a new feat of architectural invention. The open-work spire, sheathed in lead, rises 75m high; it has been burned down three times. Each of the high windows is crowned by a sculptured gable. A porch leads into the lower chapel, which was reserved for the servants from the adjoining royal palace (*see*

The interior of Ste-Chapelle

Palais de Justice). The upper chapel is reached by a spiral staircase. The impression of great height is due not only to the chapel's outer dimensions (35m long, 17m wide, 42m high), but to the expanse and intensity of coloured light shed by the windows. They virtually replace walls, and depict over a thousand scenes from the Old and New Testaments. By the quality of their conception and their colours, they rank among the finest windows of the 13th-c. Each pillar bears aloft the statue of an Apostle holding one of the twelve crosses used during the consecration of the chapel; only six of these statues are original. The wooden baldaquin in the apse once held St Louis' precious reliquary, which was melted down during the Revolution; what was left of the relics is now in Notre-Dame.

SALPÊTRIÈRE (8–66). Partly because of its out-of-the-way situation in the 13th *arrondissement* and also, no doubt, because it continues to

function as a hospital, the Salpêtrière is one of Paris's least-visited monuments. Yet its stern and massive presence, so eloquent of France's 'Grand Siècle', invites comparison with the more glorious Invalides. Under Louis XIII, the site was occupied by an arsenal specialized in making gunpowder with saltpetre. In a general drive to clear beggars (contemporary reports estimated them at around 50,000) off the Paris streets, Louis XIV had a 'hospital for the Paris poor' set up here. Along with the poor came the physically and mentally sick, prostitutes, orphans and criminals; and all the Salpêtrière's inmates were subjected to the same prison-like treatment. As early as 1662, the hospital's population is believed to have numbered 10,000. The designs for the new buildings were entrusted to Le Vau (to whom we owe part of the Louvre and Versailles, Vaux-le-Vicomte and many town houses) and Le Muet. Libéral Bruant, while still at work on his plans for the Invalides, designed the St-Louis Chapel in the formal gardens behind the Hospital's main front. Eight aisles – to keep the various categories of inmates apart – have been ingeniously created here by means of a Greek cross with four interlocked chapels. The Chapel is crowned by an octagonal dome and a lantern; and the compact drama of its interior space has proved an excellent backdrop for contemporary theatre in recent years. In the 19th-c., the hospital's conditions were vastly improved, not least by Charcot, the neurologist whose research on hysteria drew Freud to Paris.

SEINE, The. Few rivers are as vital to their cities as the Seine is to Paris. Constantly the same, constantly changing, it is its heart and its finest 'street'. The best way to see it is by *bateau-mouche*, particularly since most of the former footpaths have been swallowed by motorways. Its bridges also provide wonderful views, particularly on a quiet Sunday morning, or at sunset.

The Pont-Neuf, which crosses the prow of the Ile de la Cité, is the oldest surviving bridge (completed in 1604). Although it was once crowded with stalls, with tooth-pullers and mountebanks doing a brisk trade, the Pont-Neuf was the first Paris bridge not to be lined with houses, as well as the first place in the whole city to have pavements. The Pont au Change, linking the Place du Châtelet to the Palais de Justice, was so named because foreigners arriving in Paris had to change their money there. A little further upstream, the Pont de l'Archevêché offers a fine view of the apse of Notre-Dame, with its great leap of buttresses. Going downstream, the Pont des Arts has perhaps the most commanding position of all. It joins the Louvre to the Institut, and offers a sweeping view both of the Ile de la Cité and of the river flowing down towards the Pont de Solférino and the Pont de la Concorde. Built in iron under Napoleon, the Pont des Arts is the only real footbridge across the Seine, and one sincerely hopes that plans to pull it down – vigorously rejected by the Institut itself – will be stopped. Looking at the hurtle of quayside cars, it is difficult to imagine that the Seine was once renowned for its beaches. Henri IV is said to have bathed frequently beneath the present Pont de Sully, which links the Left Bank to the Ile St-Louis. Although fishing rights are no longer the big affair they were during the Middle Ages, the Seine still draws a few hopeful anglers during the summer. One undiminished riverside activity is book-selling: on a fine day, the *bouquinistes* transform the banks of the Seine into an open-air library.

SORBONNE (8–67). In 1253, Robert de Sorbon, confessor to St Louis, founded a college to instruct sixteen poor students in theology. It established itself rapidly as a centre of religious learning and came to dominate the University of Paris's other colleges (of which some forty had been created by the 16th-c.). The Sorbonne also became known for its extremely independent, not to say bigoted, attitudes – notably in favouring Joan of Arc's condemnation and justifying the St Bartholomew massacre. Less illiberally, it accommodated presses brought from Mainz in 1469 and so became the first printing-shop in France. Later, the narrowness of its curriculum and outlook prompted the creation of the much freer, more humanist Collège de France (*see entry*). In 1629, Richelieu commissioned the architect Lemercier to redesign the Sorbonne's various buildings and church; only the church survived extensive rebuilding at the end of the 19th-c. The Sorbonne's reputation as a centre of turbulence was dramatically revived in May 1968, when it became the headquarters of a spontaneous revolution.

Inside, its maze of lecture-rooms and labora-tories contains numerous murals, including Puvis de Chavannes' 'Sacred Grove' (in the Grand Amphithéâtre). The elegant Baroque façade and cupola of Lemercier's church dominate the Place de la Sorbonne. It contains the white marble tomb of Cardinal Richelieu, designed by Le Brun and sculpted by Girardon in 1694; the archaeologist Alexandre Lenoir saved it from destruction by the Revolutionary mob by covering it with his body and sustaining a bayonet wound (*see* École des Beaux-Arts).

VAL-DE-GRÂCE (8–68). After twenty-three years of childless marriage, Anne of Austria vowed that she would erect a magnificent new church if her longing for an heir were fulfilled. When the future Louis XIV was born, in 1638, Mansart was commissioned to draw up plans. In 1645, the young king (he had been crowned two years previously) came up the Rue St-Jacques to lay the Val-de-Grâce's foundation stone. Finding Mansart too slow in completing the work, Anne replaced him by Jacques Lemercier; and the last stages of the work (1654–67) were carried out by yet two other architects, Le Muet and Le Duc. The church is linked behind to a noble building that originally housed a convent; since 1793, however, it has been used as a military hospital, and the gardens it looks out on provide an unexpected haven from the traffic-clogged street outside.

The Val-de-Grâce church belongs, with the Sorbonne church, to a moment when the Italian influence in France was running high; its ornately elegant façade and its dome, modelled on St Peter's, speak distinctly of Rome, as do the delightful freestanding figures placed round the base of the dome. The interior is a tempered Baroque. The barrel vault is intricately carved, and the baldaquin, with its six twisted columns, recalls the one by Bernini at St Peter's. Mignard's fresco of the 'Blessed in Glory' on the cupola contains a host of figures three times larger than life. Some forty-five royal hearts were kept in the Ste-Anne Chapel on the left-hand side – until the Revolution, when they vanished.

Paris Environs: Introduction
Ile-de-France

Edward Young

This section of the book covers the five departments which surround Paris (Essonne, Oise, Seine-et-Marne, Val-d'Oise and Yvelines), plus a number of historic places in the suburbs of the capital itself. The area coincides roughly with the region once known – and indeed still known – as the Ile-de-France, the scene of so many of the events that have played their part in the shaping of France. For many centuries it was the only region that recognized the authority of the King – it *was* France, the royal 'island' from which the kings slowly extended their power.

Today, looking at the road map, with its spider's web of trunk roads and autoroutes converging on Paris from every corner of France, it is difficult to believe that this comparatively small area centred on the capital can still find space for so many forests and such a wealth of architectural treasures. Yet there they still are, the eloquent heritage of two thousand years of turbulent history – feudal castles like Pierrefonds and Senlis; the three great royal palaces of Versailles, Fontainebleau and Compiègne; the lesser châteaux scattered everywhere like a handful of jewels (Chantilly, St-Germain, Maisons-Laffitte, Vaux-le-Vicomte, Dampierre, to mention only a few); the austere ruins of the ancient abbeys of Royaumont and Chaâlis; the soaring Gothic cathedrals of Beauvais, Noyon and, above all, St-Denis, where the Gothic style was born and where the kings were laid to rest in their tombs; the vast forests, remnants of the royal hunting forests (Compiègne, Rambouillet, Fontainebleau); and the spacious formal gardens and parklands laid out by the landscape gardening genius Le Nôtre (Versailles, Chantilly, Vaux, Dampierre, and many others).

Among all these famous buildings and green spaces are small but historic towns, hamlets bordered by forestland, riverside villages, and modest hotels and restaurants in sylvan surroundings. This is the corner of France, more than any other, that has been made familiar to us by the great French painters – Pissarro at Pontoise, Corot and Millet at Barbizon, Monet and Renoir at Bougival, Sisley at Moret-sur-Loing. Here the light is generally soft, with misty blue-grey distances, and though the weather can be uncertain it is rarely too hot or too cold. There is also an astonishing amount of agricultural land, though today the latest in technical farming equipment has made the once-familiar sight of an ox-drawn plough a thing of the past.

Through it all flow the three great rivers of the region with their innumerable tributaries: the majestic Seine, wide and navigable, moving northwest in a series of nonchalant loops towards the Channel; the Oise, approaching from the northeast through the wheatlands of the old dukedom of Valois, where the farm buildings are sometimes still the same fortified 'castle-farms' that once belonged to prosperous abbeys; and the Marne which, having risen in the east and passed through the vineyards and blood-soaked battlefields of Champagne, joins the Seine just before it enters Paris. Southwest of Paris, between the forests of Rambouillet and Orléans, rivers and woods are sparse; here the distant spires of Chartres Cathedral can be seen from afar across acres of wheat and sugar-beet, for this is the Beauce plateau where the farms are large, the land is flat, the climate fairly dry and the population a mere 30 inhabitants per square kilometre. Nearer the capital, and due south of it, the Hurepoix district has more rainfall, lush valleys lined with poplars, forests for hunting, and extensive areas of alluvial soil; here grow the vegetables, strawberries, watercress and other market-garden produce delivered daily to Rungis (the new 'Covent Garden' of France near Orly airport, replacing the old 'Halles') for distribution to the markets of Paris.

Most of the places included in this section are within a radius of about 60 kilometres from the centre of Paris, though there are a few on the perimeter, like Compiègne and Noyon, which are further out but linked historically with Paris.* For the convenience of the tourist using Paris as his base, the section has been divided into three sectors radiating from the capital: North; West and Southwest; and South and East. A note at the end of each entry tells the motorist the distance and approximate route; where there is a convenient train service (as in the case of Versailles) this information is also given.

* Strictly speaking, the Ile-de-France also used to include what is now the department of Aisne (which stretches nearly to the Belgian border and seems to belong more to The North than to the Paris Environs) and did not include the eastern part of Seine-et-Marne, which belonged to Champagne.

The gardens of Château de Compiègne

Paris Environs: Gazetteer

North of Paris, West and Southwest of Paris, South and East of Paris

Edward Young

North of Paris

BEAUVAIS, *Oise* (2–B4). The centre of this important crossroads town was wiped out by an air raid in 1940, but the Cathedral of St-Pierre, one of the tallest and most daring Gothic structures in France, somehow survived. Its choir, the highest in the world, was begun in 1247 but threatened to collapse 37 years later and was only saved by massive buttressing. The transept was not built until after the Hundred Years War. Then, instead of continuing with the nave, the builders erected over the transept crossing a huge tower and spire which, soaring over 150m above ground, collapsed four years later through inadequate structural support. The nave was never even begun. For a cathedral that consists only of a choir and a transept, it remains extraordinarily impressive. Note the famous 19th-c. astronomical clock, and the 20th-c. rose window by Max Ingrand over the N door. Adjoining the cathedral is the nave of an earlier, pre-11th-c. church. A short walk S is the church of St-Étienne, with a Romanesque nave and transept and a Gothic choir containing marvellous Renaissance stained glass.

Access from Paris: 76km N on N1.

CHANTILLY, *Oise* (2–C4). Famous for its lace, its whipped cream, its racecourse, and above all, its château, one of the most elegant in France. The domed corner turrets, the steep slate roofs and the slender spire of the chapel are reflected in the formal lake which shimmers with fish and laps the château walls on every side. Outside the ornamental gates the handsome façade of the 18th-c. Grand Stables looks out across the most beautiful of all French racecourses, on which the valuable *Prix de Diane* and *Prix du Jockey Club* are run every June. If you wish to visit the château, avoid days when the racing is on, because it will be shut; otherwise it is open every day except Tuesdays from March to mid-November, but in winter only at weekends and on bank holidays.

The present château is the fifth on the same site, the first having been built by a Roman called Cantilius. It is really two châteaux joined together. The older 'Petit Château', to the left of the chapel as you approach from the main gate, is 16th-c. and roughly square in plan; the 'Grand Château', irregular in plan, was rebuilt in the 19th-c. after the previous building was wrecked at the time of the Revolution. The whole building is now devoted to the famous **Condé Museum**, a rich collection of paintings, tapestries, stained glass and precious stones. Among its treasures are the famous 15th-c. illuminated manuscript of *Les Très Riches Heures du Duc de Berry*, a series of royal and other portraits by Jean Clouet and his son François, priceless paintings by Raphael, Sassetta, Memling, Watteau, Van Dyck, Ingres, etc., and – so precious that it is exhibited only on Saturday and Sunday afternoons – the celebrated Condé Rose Diamond, a large pink stone that was stolen in 1926 but found, hidden in an apple, several months later.

In the 16th-c. the château was the home of a remarkable figure in French history – the Baron de Montmorency, rich diplomat, brave soldier, and confidential adviser to six kings from Louis XII to Charles IX. He was known as Le Grand Connétable and for 40 years was the most important person in the kingdom after the king. (There is a fine equestrian statue of him on the raised terrace facing the main entrance into the *cour d'honneur*.) In the following century Chantilly was inherited by one of France's outstanding generals, the Great Condé, who once invited Louis XIV and the whole Court (5000 guests in all) for a three-day visit; on the second day the premier chef in France, Vatel, impaled himself on his sword because the fish he had ordered for the luncheon failed to arrive on time. After the 1789 Revolution, Condé's descendant, the Duke of Bourbon, returned from exile and set about repairing the château and restoring the grounds to their former glory; but a few years later, disheartened by the 1830 Revolution, he hanged himself. Chantilly passed to his great-nephew the Duke of Aumale, who rebuilt the present 'Grand Château' and on his death in 1897 left it all to the State, including the contents which form the core of the present Museum.

The gardens and park were laid out in 1622 by the great landscape gardener Le Nôtre. The formal ponds and fountains, the Grand Canal, the vistas enhancing the grandeur of the buildings, were a forerunner of the masterpiece he was to create a few years later at Versailles. Even the 'rustic hamlet' in a corner of the park was to be imitated at Versailles for the amusement of Marie-Antoinette. Beyond the park, S and E, extends the

Château de Chantilly: the winter garden in the 'rustic hamlet'

Forest of Chantilly, much of which is fenced off as a State forestry reserve. On the NW side of the château the informal Jardin Anglais with its wandering paths and natural lakes contrasts with the geometric patterns of Le Nôtre's formal garden.

To the N of the town, on D44, is the well-known Chantilly golf course in lovely woodland surroundings. 5km further W on the same road the attractive village of **St-Leu-d'Esserent** lies on the right bank of the Oise, close to the quarries which supplied the stone for Versailles, Chartres Cathedral, and many great churches – not least for St-Leu's own remarkable 12th-c. abbey church, whose impressive interior glows with the colours of modern stained-glass windows. Outside are the remains of a fortified cloister and a subterranean vaulted chamber that once formed part of the abbey. Well worth the extra effort when you are visiting Chantilly.
Access from Paris: 43km on N16, or 50km on N2/N17/D924.

COMPIÈGNE, *Oise* (2–B4, C4). A historic old town on the banks of the Oise, with a royal palace ranking third after Versailles and Fontainebleau, and acres of forest stretching E and S. Joan of Arc was captured here, and in a clearing in the forest nearby two armistices were signed – one in 1918, the other in 1940.

The site of the present Palace was previously occupied by a more modest château, built by Charles V in the 14th-c. This was a favourite royal hunting residence, and even Louis XIV liked to come here as a change from the formal atmosphere of Versailles. He once said: 'At Versailles I am a king, at Fontainebleau a prince, but here I am a countryman.' It was Louis XV who decided to enlarge the château into a palace. He died before it could be finished, and it was left to Louis XVI (who first met Marie-Antoinette here) to see it through to its completion in 1785 – only four years before the Revolution, when it was taken over first as a military academy and then as a technical college. However, despite its severe exterior and rather awkward triangular plan, Napoleon took a fancy to it for one of his imperial residences and had it thoroughly renovated. Its heyday came later in the 19th-c., in the reign of Napoleon III and the Empress Eugénie, when it was the scene of extravagant balls, soirées, hunting parties and all sorts of gaiety – to which the German invasion of 1870 put a sudden end.

The Palace is open to the public every day (except Tuesdays) throughout the year. The Royal and Imperial apartments are on the first floor, overlooking the great vista of parkland extending SE through the forest, and are full of First Empire furniture, fine tapestries and souvenirs of the various reigns. In the N wing is a Musée de la Voiture, a fascinating collection of horse-drawn and motorized vehicles from all periods.

To the W of the Palace is the splendid late-Gothic Hôtel-de-Ville; statues grace its façade, including a handsome equestrian Louis XII, and it has an unusual belfry from which wooden uniformed figures appear by clockwork to mark the hours and quarters. In the building is the Musée de la Figurine Historique, a celebrated collection of toy soldiers, some of them actual portraits of military figures from the great Gallic chieftain Vercingétorix onwards, together with dioramas of famous battles. Further W, near the river, the Musée Vivenel houses an important collection of Greek vases and other antiquities, archaeological finds, and *objets d'art* of all periods from the Middle Ages to the present day. Nearby is the Beauregard Tower, in which Joan of Arc is believed to have been imprisoned after her capture in 1430 (just across the river) before she was handed over to the English. (There is a statue of her in the Place de l'Hôtel-de-Ville.) There are also two interesting Gothic churches, St-Jacques and St-Antoine, and just W of the Hôtel-de-Ville are the remains of the cloisters of the ancient abbey founded by Charles the Bald in the 9th-c.

For centuries the great **Forest of Compiègne** was the venue of royal hunting expeditions, and it still has a rather grand air with its broad grassy avenues lined with majestic beech and oak trees. You can wander happily in it for hours, constantly coming upon unexpected little lakes, brooks, outcrops of rock and rustic villages. Near the Palace are a golf course and a popular race-track. On the northern edge, 7km out of Compiègne near the village of Rethondes, is the **Clairière de l'Armistice**, the clearing in the woods, marked by a monument, where the Germans signed the Armistice of 1918, and where in 1940, in a petty gesture of revenge, Hitler insisted on accepting the French surrender in the same railway carriage on the same railway siding.

To the SE, on the edge of the forest, is the pleasant little town of **Pierrefonds**, with a huge feudal château that now consists mostly of the thorough restoration and rebuilding carried out by the architect Viollet-le-Duc about 100 years ago – very impressive all the same, and well worth a visit. Further S, in the village of **Morienval**, is a beautiful 12th-c. church with three towers, one of the most perfect examples of the transition from Romanesque to Gothic, containing one of the earliest uses of ogive vaulting.
Access from Paris: 82km NNE on A1/N31.

ENGHIEN-LES-BAINS, *Val-d'Oise* (6km NW of St-Denis: 2–C4). The nearest spa to Paris, in an agreeable situation on the edge of a lake. A racecourse and a casino are handy, and there is boating on the lake. The sulphurous waters in the thermal station are claimed to relieve rheumatism and ailments of the skin and throat.
Access from Paris: 18km N on N14.

ERMENONVILLE, *Oise* (2–C4). At the western edge of the forest which bears its name is the 18th-c. château of Ermenonville, with an attractive English-style informal park laid out by the Marquis of Girardin. The château is not open to the public, but the park is open all day throughout the year. The philosopher Jean-Jacques Rousseau, whose writings helped to prepare the ground for the Revolution, died here in 1778 while visiting the

Marquis and was buried on the small 'island of poplars' at the S end of the lake; in 1794 his coffin was removed to the Panthéon in Paris.

N of the château the road leads to the romantic ruins of the former 13th-c. Cistercian abbey of **Chaâlis**, surrounded by forest and lakes, a sandy desert area turned into a 'park of attractions', and a small zoo.
Access from Paris: 47km NE, by A1 or N2/N17, then D922 through Mortefontaine.

ISLE-ADAM, L', *Val-d'Oise* (2–C3, C4). A popular weekend escape from Paris, L'Isle-Adam is a small rural town on a pretty stretch of the Oise, with two islands crossed by a picturesque old bridge. Dinghy sailing and swimming off a pleasant beach. The church of St-Martin is early 16th-c. with a Renaissance doorway and furnishings. E and SE lies an extensive forest in which you can drive, walk and picnic.
Access from Paris: 40km N on N1 (signposted to left).

NOYON, *Oise* (2–B4). An ecclesiastical town of great age. A bishopric since AD 581, it was the scene of the coronation of Charlemagne as King of Neustria (Normandy) in 768 and of Hugues Capet as King of France in 987. Calvin was born here. The Cathedral, which itself dates back to the 12th-c., is the fifth church to have been built on the same site. Completed at the end of the 13th-c., damaged in World War I but now restored, it is a remarkable example of the transition from Romanesque sobriety to soaring Gothic splendour. The façade, which was badly affected by damage, has two towers, one 13th-c. and the other a century later, both still minus the spires that were originally intended. Inside, the nave and the choir are of the same height and give an impression of great space; the sides of the nave have a four-tier elevation, including a gallery with double arches. Note the unusual rounded ends of the transept arms. A door in the N wall opens into the cloister, of which only one gallery survives; facing it across the little garden is the chapter house, containing a precious library of manuscript and early printed books. Opposite the S wall of the Cathedral the former Bishop's Palace now houses a modest archaeological museum. Among the town's 15th-c. buildings that were completely reconstructed on the original plans after wartime destruction are the town hall and, in the street named after him, the birthplace of Calvin (1509–64), now a Calvin museum.

5km due S on D165, in a lovely setting on the edge of a forest, are the romantic-looking ruins of the old Cistercian abbey of **Ourscamps**. Partly destroyed in the Revolution, then sold for use as a factory, pillaged and burned in World War I, it is now occupied by a religious order. The former infirmary, now used as a chapel, is a splendid 13th-c. monastic hall. Open to visitors.
Access from Paris: 106km NNE on A1/N31/N32.

106

PONTOISE, *Val-d'Oise* (2–C3). Despite the recent industrial developments around it, the old town remains full of character. Some of the medieval ramparts still exist, overlooking the Oise, though a garden now covers the site of the former château. It was here in 1437 that the English, under Talbot, approached the town in deep snow; camouflaged in white clothing they laid their ladders against the walls, took the town completely by surprise and were not dislodged until four years later. On the higher ground, steep and narrow streets crowd against the church of St-Maclou, a beautiful Gothic building with a 12th-c. choir and transept, 15th-c. nave and façade, and Renaissance side-aisles. From the public garden opposite, a flight of steps descends to the town's other church, Notre-Dame, which was rebuilt after its destruction during the siege of Pontoise towards the end of the 16th-c. Note the lovely 13th-c. statue of the Virgin in one of the chapels, and the 12th-c. tomb of St Gautier in the nave.

Pissarro lived in Pontoise for several years; Cézanne frequently stayed with him and painted in and around the town.
Access from Paris: 33km NW on A15 or N14.

ROYAUMONT, Abbaye de, *Val-d'Oise* (8km SW of Chantilly: 2–C4). One of the most beautiful Gothic structures of France, this Cistercian abbey was founded and richly endowed by the pious King Louis IX, who reigned from 1226 to 1270 and was canonized as St Louis 27 years after his death. It is an impressive symbol of the wealth that often accrued to the great abbeys of the Middle Ages, especially in northern France; and because the rooms have been refurnished in simple, monastic style, it enables us to glimpse something of the way of life followed by the monks of the brotherhood.

At the time of the Revolution, like all other religious institutions, it was confiscated by the State. The Order was suppressed, the huge church demolished (only fragments remain) and the abbey buildings used as a cotton factory. Nearly 100 years later it returned to private hands and has since been gradually restored. It is now an international Centre of Culture; this occupies some of the buildings and organizes concerts and exhibitions, but the public is admitted to other parts of the abbey buildings – notably the fine refectory, the very hall in which Louis IX would take his turn at serving the monks at table during his periodic self-chastising visits; the magnificent kitchens with their vaulted ceilings, pillars adorned with sculptured capitals, a 14th-c. Virgin and a chapel; and the lovely cloisters, covered in creeper and surrounding a garden. (Guided ½-hour tours, April–October, daily except Tuesdays – in winter months weekends and bank holidays only.)
Access from Paris: 40km N on N1/D909.

Abbaye de Royaumont

French Government Tourist Office

ST-DENIS, *Seine-St-Denis* (2–C4). St-Denis is a modern industrial suburb of Paris, but in the middle of it stands the solemn and impressive Basilica (now the Cathedral) of St-Denis, containing the tombs and effigies of most of the kings of France from Dagobert I to Louis XVIII – a remarkable span of twelve centuries. During the Revolution the mob ransacked the church, broke open the tombs and scattered the remains. Later, Napoleon gave orders to repair the damage and bury the remains in a common grave in the crypt.

St Denis was a 3rd-c. saint who brought Christianity to Paris and northern France. Beheaded in Montmartre ('*le mont des martyrs*') in about AD 250, he was buried on or near the site of the present Cathedral (legend has it that he walked here, carrying his head). The small chapel erected over his tomb was replaced in the 5th-c. by a large church. This again was replaced by new churches built in turn by King Dagobert I (who founded a rich and important abbey beside it) and just over 100 years later by King Pépin the Short. The present building was begun in the 12th-c. by the abbé Suger; the nave and transept were completed in the 13th-c. Misconceived restoration in the early part of the 19th-c. ruined the original concept; later efforts by the architect Viollet-le-Duc to put things right were only partially successful. Nevertheless it remains architecturally important as one of the earliest Gothic structures in France. *Access from Paris:* 10km N on A1, or by Métro.

SENLIS, *Oise* (2–C4). A very old town with a royal history going back to 987 when, in the ancient castle here, Hugues Capet was elected King of France – then a small territory consisting of little more than the Ile-de-France. All the future kings of France were his descendants, and most of them down to Henri IV resided here from time to time. Some of the castle, including the square keep, is still standing. In its grounds a former 18th-c. priory now houses a Hunting Museum.

The splendid Cathedral of Notre-Dame, just to the E of the castle, was begun in 1153, 10 years before its namesake in Paris, and its belfry still dominates the town with a spire reaching nearly 80m above the ground. The W façade is Romanesque, and has a main doorway carved with representations of the Death, Resurrection and Coronation of the Virgin. The lofty interior is remarkable especially for the great gallery which runs above the side-aisles on both sides of the nave and choir. On the E side of Place Notre-Dame stands the former 13th-c. Bishop's Palace, much altered in the 16th-c. and now the Palais de Justice. Immediately E of that is the church of St-Pierre, now used as a covered market-place. Remains of Gallo-Roman defences have been excavated around the castle perimeter, also in the Arena at the edge of the town just outside the ancient ramparts (now partly replaced by wide boulevards).

Senlis is an agreeable place for a day or two's stay. Fascinating narrow streets and alleys with handsome old houses cluster S of the Cathedral on the hill sloping down to the river Nonette. The great forests of Chantilly, Ermenonville and Halatte stretch for miles N and S of the town, and Chantilly itself (*see entry*) is only 11km to the W. *Access from Paris:* NNE, 51km on A1, or 44km on N2/N17.

West and Southwest of Paris

BOUGIVAL, *Yvelines* (18km W of Paris: 2–C4). A pretty village on the banks of the Seine. The excellent and luxurious restaurants here today are perhaps a far cry from the more informal atmosphere, immortalized in paintings by Monet and Renoir, of the boating parties and the riverside cafés where the artists used to eat, drink and dance with their girl friends in the latter half of the 19th-c., but the village certainly retains its tranquillity and charm. *Access from Paris:* 18km W on N13.

CHEVREUSE, Vallée de, *Yvelines* (17km NE of Rambouillet: 2–C3). The Chevreuse valley is well known to Parisians for excursions and walks in sylvan surroundings. It is actually the valley of the river Yvette and its many tributaries, but popularly takes its name from the little town of **Chevreuse** which lies on the N bank, dominated by the imposing ruins of the feudal château of La Madeleine on the hill behind it.

Only 4km W is the beautiful château of **Dampierre**, whose elegant façade of stone and brick stands on the S side of the main road (D91). It was built in the 16th-c. but refashioned by Hardouin-Mansart in the latter half of the 17th-c. for the Duke of Luynes, Colbert's son-in-law. With its little domed corner turrets and its moat of running water, it is an architectural jewel in a restful setting of woods, lakes and trees which extends E into a spacious park laid out by the ubiquitous Le Nôtre. The château, which still belongs to the Luynes family, can be visited, April to mid-October, every afternoon except Tuesdays; the interior is rich in 17th-c. furnishings and decoration, and there is a fine staircase with *trompe-l'œil* murals. *Access from Paris:* Chevreuse is 32km SW on N306.

MAISONS-LAFFITTE, *Yvelines* (7km N of St-Germain: 2–C3). The most important horseracing and training stables in France. The famous racecourse is close to the Seine, and the stables and rides occupy the remains of the former park of Mansart's classic Louis-XIV-style château. Often frequented in the 18th-c. by royal visitors, the château was bought in 1818 by the well-known banker Laffitte, who added his name to the

Dr Christopher Tadgell

Maisons-Laffitte: the château

original '*Maisons*'. When his political activities eventually led to disgrace and ruin, to pay off his debts he turned a large section of the park into a sort of 'housing estate'; it ruined the park but saved Laffitte; the scheme was a financial success and is still well regarded as an early example of planned urban development. The château, now State-owned, is open to the public at weekends (afternoons only, at 3.30 p.m.). The entrance hall, the dining hall and the great staircase are superbly decorated by the sculptor Sarazin and others.
Access from Paris: 20km NW on N192/N308.

MALMAISON, Château de, *Hauts-de-Seine* (15km W of Paris: 2–C4). In the suburb of Rueil-Malmaison, beyond the Bois de Boulogne, is this relatively modest château in which Napoleon and Josephine lived in the early 1800s. Domestically it was probably the happiest period of his life. When he became Emperor he had to spend more and more of his time at the Tuileries and Fontaine-bleau, and less at Malmaison. Josephine, bored, spent lavishly and ran up debts. After their divorce he gave her the château, and she lived here until her early death in 1814. It is now a Napoleonic museum, open all the year except Tuesdays. The rooms are furnished just as they were, and the house is full of fascinating souvenirs of the Emperor and the Martinique beauty he once dearly loved. The present grounds are a small fraction of the original park.
Access from Paris: 15km W on N13.

MARLY-LE-ROI, *Yvelines* (5km S of St-Germain: 2–C3). Only the park now remains of this royal residence 6km N of Versailles, used by Louis XIV and Louis XV from time to time to escape from the rigid etiquette of court life. It was designed by Hardouin-Mansart in the form of a series of *pavillons*, or small houses, with the Sun King's *pavillon* facing N down the wide avenue and twelve smaller ones (the 'signs of the Zodiac') lining the avenue on either side. The site of the King's *pavillon* is marked by stone slabs outlining the ground plan; and the formal lakes and ponds, and the long 'carpet' of lawn (the '*Tapis Vert*'), are still there. On the W side of the park is the Pavillon du Président de la République, sometimes used by the President to receive official guests.

To the W stretches the **Forest of Marly**, once part of the royal hunting forest. The A13 autoroute to Normandy now slices through it, but there are many agreeable smaller roads that wander through the forest of oaks, chestnuts and beeches and provide occasional glimpses of deer.
Access from Paris: 25km W, on A13 (turning right on to N184), or on N13 (turning left on to N184).

MONTFORT-L'AMAURY, *Yvelines* (13km N of Rambouillet: 2–C3). A very old and charming small town built on the side of a hill, N of the Forest of Rambouillet. Below the ruins of an 11th-c. fort built by Amaury de Montfort, ancestor of Simon de Montfort, is an old cemetery walled within an arcaded gallery, and a 15th-c. church with beautiful Renaissance stained glass; there are lovely glimpses of the peaceful countryside between the ancient houses.

In the Rue Maurice Ravel is the house where Ravel lived for 17 years, composed 'Daphnis and Chloë', 'Boléro' and many of his other celebrated works, and died in 1937. The house, 'Le Belvédère', is a Ravel museum.

Access from Paris. 50 km W on A13/A12/N10/N12.

POISSY, *Yvelines* (2–C3, C4). This ancient town on the Seine, at the W edge of the Forest of St-Germain, is now overshadowed by the vast Simca-Chrysler car manufacturing plant and its 80m water-tower. (If you wish to make a tour of the plant, which takes nearly 3 hours, you need to make an appointment.) Poissy has historical associations going back to the 5th-c. when it was a royal residence, and the old quarter has retained much of its charm and character, especially along the river front. The church of Notre-Dame is largely 11th–12th-c. and has two Romanesque belfries and a Flamboyant Gothic porch; St Louis (Louis IX) was baptized in 1214 in the first chapel to the right of the entrance. At the W edge of the town the ruins of a royal abbey founded in the 11th-c. contrast with the celebrated Villa Le Corbusier constructed by the famous architect in 1929.

Access from Paris: 30km WNW on N190.

RAMBOUILLET, Château de, *Yvelines* (2–C3). Since 1897 Rambouillet has been the official summer residence of the French President, but the château is open to the public when he is not there. The vast park is open all the year round from sunrise to sunset. The château has undergone many changes over the centuries, and the only vestige of the original 14th-c. building is the large tower, in which François I died in 1547. Louis XVI bought the property in 1783 – as though he did not have enough homes already – and in order to please Marie-Antoinette, who hated the place, he built the Queen's Dairy (Laiterie de la Reine) in the far corner of the park. Close by is the amusing Chaumière des Coquillages (literally, Cottage of Shells) on the edge of a *jardin anglais* surrounding an elongated lake with islands. At the NW corner of the park is the important National Sheep-Rearing Farm, started in 1786 by Louis XVI.

Close to the château the main feature of the gardens is water – a stiffly geometric fan of canals spreading outwards through a garden *à la française* and a row of cypress trees. The present château is on a right-angle plan (Napoleon, who stayed here with Marie-Louise after his divorce from Josephine, for some reason had the left wing pulled down). The construction is largely brick, with round stone towers. The interior is rich in 18th-c. panelling and tapestries, and echoes with memories of historic moments.

The little town, with its 18th-c. town hall, lies close to the château. NW and SE extends the vast **Forest of Rambouillet**, a great place for walking and picnicking, full of surprising little lakes, ponds and hamlets. On the N edge is the charming and ancient little town of Montfort-l'Amaury (*see entry*), and ENE along the N306 is an attractive

Château de Rambouillet

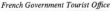

return route to Paris via Dampierre and the Chevreuse valley (*see entry*).
Access from Paris: 54km SW on N10.

ST-CLOUD, Parc de, *Hauts-de-Seine* (12km W of Paris: 2–C4). Just across the Seine from the Boulogne-Billancourt district is this fine expanse of parkland, another of those grand formal designs by Le Nôtre with long perspectives, ornamental lakes and ponds, flamboyant waterfalls and jetting fountains. The old château where Napoleon often resided was set on fire by the Prussians in 1870 and demolished soon afterwards; now only a plantation of yews marks the site. The park is best seen in the afternoon of the 2nd and 4th Sunday of each month from June to September, when the waterfalls and fountains are turned on. You can drive through much of the park, and there are authorized car parks, but many of the *allées* are reserved for walking only. S towards Sèvres is the 'Rond Point de la Balustrade', from which there is a splendid view of Paris.
Further S, at the SE corner of the park, is the world-famous National Factory of **Sèvres** Porcelain. This can be visited on certain days only (it is advisable to telephone for an appointment), but the national Museum of Ceramics is open every day except Tuesdays and bank holidays, and contains a unique collection of pottery and porcelain of every make and period.
Access from Paris: 12km W – on N307 for St-Cloud, on N10 or by Métro (line 9) for Sèvres. (NOTE: The well-known racecourse of St-Cloud is not in the park, but off N185 on the N side of the St-Cloud district.)

ST-GERMAIN-EN-LAYE, *Yvelines* (2–C3). From the 12th-c. until 1682, when Louis XIV moved the Court to Versailles, this was the summer residence of the Kings of France. It also has links with British history. Mary Stuart, whose mother was French, spent ten years of her childhood here until her marriage at the age of 16 to the Dauphin, soon to reign briefly as François II; for just over a year she was Queen of France, but after his early death she went home to reign as Queen of Scotland. A little over 100 years later, James II, deposed from the English throne in 1688, was given sanctuary by his cousin Louis XIV and lived here, intriguing constantly against William III, until he died in 1701 with the Sun King at his bedside. Louis XIV was himself born and brought up here, as were many of the French kings.
The present castle, a curiously irregular pentagon with towers at each corner and a low roof hidden behind balustrades, was by no means the first on the same site. Erected in the 16th-c. by François I, it incorporates a fine chapel (built by St Louis in about 1235) which miraculously survived the destruction of the previous castle by the Black Prince in the Hundred Years War – also the keep erected by Charles V in 1368 which stands to the left of the main gateway. Henri II found the castle

too severe and started the building of a grand new residential château, facing E with gardens and staircases descending in terraces to the river. When it was completed under Henri IV, with grottoes sheltering mythological figures moved by hydraulic power, it was one of the most celebrated *châteaux de plaisance* of its time, but after the departure of Louis XIV's Court to Versailles it fell into neglect and ruin. In 1780 it was demolished, with the exception of the Pavillon Henri IV (now a hotel) and the Pavillon Sully, whose gardens provide a glimpse of what the great terraces must have been like in their heyday.
The 'old château' remained, but was stripped of its contents after the Revolution and turned into a military prison. Later, Napoleon III came to the rescue, as Louis-Philippe did at Versailles, restoring it as a museum of French national antiquities. Open every day, and spectacularly modernized in recent years, it is well worth a visit, followed by a walk through the gardens laid out by Le Nôtre for Louis XIV – the formal garden close to the castle, the less formal Jardin Anglais, somewhat marred now by a railway cutting, and finally the magnificent Grande Terrasse, nearly 2½km long, lined with ancient lime trees and providing superb views of the Seine and the W side of Paris. Beyond, to the NW, is the **Forest of St-Germain**, once part of an unbroken royal hunting forest stretching S as far as Rambouillet, and still a delightful area of forest walks and rides.
Access from Paris: WNW, 24km on N13, or by Métro (RER).

THOIRY, *Yvelines* (14km SE of Mantes: 2–C3). A fine safari-park type of zoo, open all the year round, with a restaurant and an attractively arranged picnic area. It is set in a huge park with a 16th-c. château and extensive woodlands, in which over a thousand wild animals – lions, giraffes, elephants, etc. – roam around in comparative open-air freedom. The château is open to visitors, and a reptile museum has been well laid out in the cellars.
A good day's outing for the family.
Access from Paris: 50km W. Take N10 (or A13/A12) passing Versailles, then N12 (signposted Dreux); soon after the village of Pontchartrain turn NW on D11 for Thoiry.

VERSAILLES, *Yvelines* (2–C3, C4). The Sun King's Palace of Versailles is probably the most imposing and gracious assembly of buildings, gardens and parkland in the world. Every visitor to Paris must see it, but it is no good going there just for an hour or so – it is too vast. Ideally you need at least three days: one for the Palace itself, another for the Trianons, and a third for the gardens, the ornamental lakes and the parks with their glorious vistas. (For a note on the fountains, see end of entry.)
If you only have time for one day, take a picnic and make an early start. The gates are open from

The Palace of Versailles: the Hall of Mirrors

dawn to dusk, and the Palace opens at 10 a.m. Spend an hour or so walking through the Grand Apartments, the Chapel (Hardouin-Mansart's masterpiece), the Hall of Mirrors (where the Treaty of Versailles was signed), and the Private Apartments of the King and Queen. You won't have time for the guided tour of the museum and the other apartments. Then a stroll through the Palace Gardens to the beginning of the Park and the Grand Canal. In the afternoon cut NW across the park to the Trianons and see as much of these two exquisite mini-châteaux as you have time for. After a brief wander in the Trianon park, including perhaps a visit to Marie-Antoinette's 'hamlet', followed by the long walk back to your car or the station, you will have had a tiring but eminently rewarding day.

It was Louis XIII who first had a house here – a small château, not much more than a hunting-lodge, on a small hill surrounded by game forests and marshlands. Louis XIV loved the place as a boy and when in 1661, at the age of 23, he began to reign in his own right he determined to turn it into a great palace, large enough not only to be the seat of royal government but also to house all the nobles of the Court with their families and retainers. He hated Paris; he had unhappy memories of his childhood experiences there during the 'Fronde' (a revolt by the nobility against the centralized power of the monarchy, during the Regency when Mazarin virtually ruled the country). He wanted to move the government away from Paris as early as possible; at the same time, by having the nobles close at hand he could establish the ascendancy over them that he saw was necessary for firm management of the nation's affairs.

He commandeered the services of the three creative geniuses who had been responsible for the sumptuous Château of Vaux-le-Vicomte (*see entry*) – the architect Le Vau, the decorative arts impresario Le Brun, and the great landscape gardener Le Nôtre. With this team he set to work on the creation of his dream, personally supervising every detail and urging its progress at the greatest possible speed. The site he chose was absurdly unsuitable, but nothing daunted him. The marshlands were drained, forests were cleared, new ones planted, hills moved, water for the fountains channelled from miles away. Meanwhile Le Vau, retaining the original château of Louis XIII, enlarged it by enclosing it within an 'envelope' of surrounding extensions, making it into what now forms the centre block of the Palace, framing the so-called Marble Courtyard (its marble pavings long ago removed). But though the King took up residence at the earliest opportunity, the Palace was still too small to accommodate the Court. In 1678 a new architect, Hardouin-Mansart, was commissioned to build the two vast wings which extend N and S and include the Chapel and the Opera House – thus completing the Palace as you see it today, nearly half a kilometre from end to end.

The fame of Versailles spread abroad long before it was completed. Foreign princes and rulers came to see, to envy and to wish to emulate. The King's chief minister, Colbert, alarmed at the escalating cost of the new palace but accepting its inevitability, saw the opportunity to use it as a national shop window for the exports he was trying to encourage. He set up factories to ensure that everything in it was made in France – the carpets, the tapestries (the great enlargement of the Gobelins factory in Paris dates from this time), the furniture, the silks, the glass – and there is no doubt that Versailles, under the shrewd and tasteful guidance of both the King and Le Brun, provided a tremendous fillip to the reputation of French art and crafts. In 1682 the Court moved from the Louvre to Versailles, even though the work was not yet finished. Thousands of workmen and horses continued to labour on the site for another 30 years. The Court consisted of about 1000 nobles and 4000 servants – all resident in the Palace – not to mention the 15,000 soldiers quartered in the barracks and stables facing the main gate. The volume of traffic on the Paris road must have been enormous. To keep his nobles diverted and out of serious mischief, the King organized an endless round of balls, banquets and other amusements, against the background of a regime of the strictest etiquette.

Sumptuous revelries on this scale were not to the taste of the Sun King's successors. Louis XV altered the Royal Apartments to gain more privacy for himself and his Queen, and near the end of his reign built the Petit Trianon for his mistress Madame Dubarry, close to the Grand Trianon. Louis XVI and Marie-Antoinette also preferred the simpler life, and indeed the Queen so hated the intrigues of court life that she spent much of her time at the Petit Trianon and in the 'rustic hamlet' created for her amusement in the grounds. They were the last king and queen to live in Versailles. After their executions in 1793, the Palace was stripped of its furnishings and abandoned. Half a century later Louis-Philippe saved it from demolition by turning it into a museum dedicated to 'Toutes les Gloires de la France'. After World War I the Beaux-Arts, aided by generous contributions from J. D. Rockefeller and others, began the work of restoring and refurnishing the buildings and the rehabilitation of the gardens and fountains.

The fountains: these operate on the first and third Sunday of the summer months (May–September), afternoons only from 4.30 to 6.00 p.m. On certain Sundays in the summer there is a marvellous night display (fêtes de nuit) of illuminated fountains followed by fireworks; for up-to-date information apply to the tourist office (Syndicat d'Initiative, 7 Rue des Réservoirs, immediately N of the Palace – telephone 950.36.22).

Parking: Place d'Armes outside the main gate; for the Trianons you can drive round via Rue des Réservoirs and Bd. de la Reine and park close to the entrance to the Grand Trianon.

Access from Paris: WSW, 24km by A13, 20km by N10 or N185; frequent trains from Gare Montparnasse and Gare St-Lazare.

South and East of Paris

BARBIZON, Seine-et-Marne (9km NW of Fontainebleau: 2–D4). A delightful village on the edge of the forest, and made famous by the 19th-c. painters – Théodore Rousseau, Millet and Diaz de la Peña among them – who came to be known as the Barbizon School. They went there to paint landscapes in the open air, direct from nature, thus foreshadowing the Impressionists. The village consists virtually of one long street, in which some of the houses where the artists lived are kept in their original state. Also preserved is the auberge of Père Ganne, where the painters used to eat. Access from Paris: 58km SSE on A6 or N7.

ÉTAMPES, Essonne (2–D3, D4). An old town that has spread lengthways along the valley of the Chalouette. It has several interesting 12th-c. churches. The crenellated Notre-Dame-du-Fort, closely surrounded by ancient houses, has a slender steeple, an 11th-c. crypt and a doorway adorned with statues that were badly mutilated during the Wars of Religion. St-Martin has a leaning tower. St-Basile still has its original façade, portal, belfry and transept, the rest being 16th-c. restoration. Behind the railway station, dominating the N side of the town, is the large 12th-c. Guinette Tower in which King Philippe-Auguste kept his Danish queen Ingeborg locked up from 1201 to 1212 because she refused to divorce him. Opposite St-Basile is a fine Renaissance house that was built for Diane de Poitiers, the second

Duchess of Étampes and mistress of Henri II.
Access from Paris: 51km S on N20.

FONTAINEBLEAU, *Seine-et-Marne* (2–D4).
Versailles dazzles with its size and breathtaking
vistas, but Fontainebleau, surrounded by its great
hunting forest, is a royal palace of almost intimate
charm. All the same, it looks very impressive as
you enter the gate through Napoleon's grille and
walk across the great three-sided courtyard, the
Cour du Cheval-Blanc, towards the curving
'horseshoe' staircase that faces you at the far end.
On 20 April 1814 Napoleon walked down this
staircase to bid an emotional farewell to his Old
Guard before being taken off to exile on Elba –
hence the alternative name for this courtyard, La
Cour des Adieux. Fontainebleau was Napoleon's
favourite palace; even in his final exile on St-
Helena he spoke of it as *'la vraie demeure des rois,
la maison des siècles'*.

Certainly many kings, and their queens and
mistresses, have lived there and made their mark
on it, and many centuries have passed since it first
appeared in 12th-c. records as a small château-
fortress used by Louis VII. It was François I, that
great Renaissance man, who organized its transformation into a palace, commissioning large
numbers of artists and craftsmen from Renaissance Italy, notably Primaticcio and Rosso, to
supervise and carry out the decorations. Having
pulled down most of the original medieval fort,
except for the keep, he rebuilt it on the same site
(this is the Cour Ovale, much as we see it today); to
the W of it he laid out the present main courtyard
(enclosed on all four sides then, and scene of
jousting tournaments), and linked the two with the
long gallery still called the Galerie de François I.
His successors continued the work of enlargement,
and the palace grew by stages into the pleasantly
irregular plan which is part of its charm.

Louis XIV, who came frequently to Fontainebleau to hunt in the forest and pursue his intrigue
with Louise de la Vallière, made virtually no
alterations to the palace, apart from changing
some of the decorations – he was too busy with
Versailles – but he did get Le Nôtre to redesign
parts of the formal gardens. Louis XV, who
married Marie Leczinska in the chapel here,
offended contemporary opinion by knocking
down the S side of the main courtyard and
replacing it with the present grander, but less
gracious, wing. During the Revolution the palace
and its priceless decorations were miraculously left
unscarred, though much of the furniture was
carried off. The Empire-style furniture which is
there today was introduced by Napoleon when he
adopted Fontainebleau as his imperial palace.

If you are short of time you can follow the
arrows and helpful captions on the unaccom-
panied tour of the Grand Apartments. You enter
on the ground floor, under the 'horseshoe', and
climb a staircase to the magnificent Galerie de
François I, with its original Renaissance decoration and its view of the Fountain Court and
the 'Carp Lake' beyond. At the far end of the
gallery you pass through the Guardroom (note the
Louis XIII ceiling) and descend the King's
Staircase, flanked by stuccoes and frescoes by
Primaticcio, to the finest room in the whole palace
– the marvellous ballroom designed by Delorme
for Henri II. The octagonal pattern of its stunning
ceiling is echoed in the design of the parquet floor.
The walls are partly panelled, partly decorated
with paintings by Primaticcio and dell'Abbate, as
are the deep barrel-vaulted arches framing the
windows, which look on to the Cour Ovale on
the N side and the formal gardens on the other.
The pillared chimney-piece at the E end bears the
linked monogram of the initials of Henri II and his
favourite, Diane de Poitiers.

Returning by the King's Staircase to the first
floor, you come to the Royal Apartments in the
NW curve of the Cour Ovale: among them the
Salon du Donjon (the only remaining part of the
medieval fort) where all the kings up to Henri IV
slept; the room where Louis XIII was born; the
Queen's Apartments, on which Marie-Antoinette
left the imprint of her taste; the Salle du Trône,
formerly the bedroom of later kings but converted
into a throne room by Napoleon; the splendidly
decorated Council Room with its bow window
overlooking the Jardin de Diane; and finally
Napoleon's Grand Apartments, including the
Salon Rouge in which he signed his abdication in
April 1814.

Another tour, accompanied by a guide and
lasting about half an hour, consists largely of a
visit to the smaller, ground-floor apartments of
Napoleon and his two wives, Josephine and
Marie-Louise.

After your tour of the interior try to spare time
for a walk through the gardens – the formal garden
designed for Louis XIV by Le Nôtre; the long vista
of Henri IV's Grand Canal stretching a whole
kilometre eastward through the park; the 'Carp
Lake'; and finally the informal Jardin Anglais in
which you will find the original spring – named
after a medieval forester called variously Bliaud,
Blaud or Bleau – which as the 'Fontaine Bleau'
gave its name to what became by general consent
the most appealing of all the French royal palaces.

The **Forest of Fontainebleau** lies all around it, a
vast area of ancient oaks and beeches, full of
pockets of unexpectedly wild country – rocky
gorges, moorlands, sandy desert, rushing rivers,
and even miniature 'mountains' on which professional mountaineers practise. A drive along the
signposted 'Route Ronde' will take you through
surprising variations of scenery. Alternatively, if
you prefer to combine the pleasures of the forest

Palace and park of Fontainebleau

with a visit to an attractive village, take the short drive to Barbizon, 9½km NW, or to Moret-sur-Loing, 10km SE (*see entries*).
Access from Paris: 68km SSE on N7.

MEAUX, *Seine-et-Marne* (2–C4). An old town and agricultural market on a narrow loop of the river Marne, and centre of the district that produces Brie cheese. Every September the town still commemorates the **Battle of the Marne**, when the taxis of Paris rushed reinforcements to stem the first German onslaught in 1914; several monuments mark the site of the battle N of the town.

Meaux has been a bishopric since the 4th-c., but the massive Cathedral was built between the 12th-c. and 16th-c. in various Gothic styles. Only one of the intended two towers was completed, but this one is over 60m high. The Cathedral interior is lofty and solemnly impressive, and contains the tomb of the 'Eagle of Meaux', the illustrious orator and preacher Bossuet (1627–1704), Bishop of Meaux and one-time tutor to the Grand Dauphin. Close to the Cathedral on its N side are the former Bishop's Palace (now a Bossuet museum) and the canon's chapter house, first built in the 12th-c. The N façade of the Bishop's Palace looks across a garden created by Le Nôtre, beyond which a flight of steps climbs to a terrace laid out on part of Gallo-Roman and medieval ramparts, from which there is a lovely view of Cathedral and town.
Access from Paris: 54km E on A4, or 45km on N3.

MORET-SUR-LOING, *Seine-et-Marne* (2–D4). A lovely old village in a peaceful setting by the banks of the river Loing, E of the Forest of Fontainebleau. Very popular with Parisians at weekends. Some of the old ramparts still exist, and

a 12th-c. stone gateway stands at each end of the main street, which is lined with ancient houses. Napoleon spent a night at No. 24 after his escape from Elba. The English Impressionist painter Sisley spent the last 20 years of his life in Moret (his house was 9 Rue du Château) and painted many of his well-known landscapes in and around the village; he died here in 1899 in great poverty, and soon afterwards his canvases began to fetch high prices. The church is interesting because the choir, the first section to be built, was consecrated in 1166 by Thomas-à-Becket, while the rest, with its Flamboyant Gothic doorway, was not completed until the 15th-c. S of the church, along the river, is the site of a 12th-c. fortress once lived in by Louis VII; the only remnant is the keep, in which Fouquet was temporarily imprisoned by Louis XIV after his ejection from Vaux-le-Vicomte (*see entry*).

Every Saturday evening in the summer there is a *son-et-lumière* by the river.
Access from Paris: 76km SE on N5, 10km SE of Fontainebleau.

NEMOURS, *Seine-et-Marne* (2–D4). A pleasant little country town 15km S of Fontainebleau, straddling the river Loing. The view upstream from the bridge takes in the 16th-c. church with its elegant spire, the friendly roofs of ancient houses, and the 12th-c. castle (largely rebuilt in the 15th-c. and now a museum) with its square keep and four perimeter towers. The park on the SW edge of the town contains an unexpected 'chaos' of curious rock-formations, and in the countryside to the NW and SE are stretches of woodland with other areas of rocky outcrops.
Access from Paris: 81km S on A6 or N7.

The North: Introduction

Artois, Flanders, Picardy

Edward Young

The windy plain that stretches from the Ile-de-France to the Belgian border – the old provinces of Picardy, Artois and Flanders – can hardly be described as France's most popular tourist attraction. It is for the most part flat and bleak, and has more than its fair share of driving rain and winter fog. The landscape is dotted with slag-heaps, factory chimneys, and blast-furnaces – especially in Flanders to the northeast, where the long east–west coal-belt south of Lille has turned the area into one huge industrial zone. The flatness of this whole region has always made it vulnerable to invading armies, and even today the vast war cemeteries, the Allied memorials, the river Somme itself, the very words Picardy and Flanders – sometimes, perhaps, a name seen suddenly on a signpost – still recall the holocaust of battles ancient and modern. As you speed south from Dunkirk, Calais or Boulogne on the Autoroute du Nord or on one of the poplar-lined N-roads, there seems little reason to dally.

Yet if you could be persuaded to spend a day or two here at the end of your holiday, within comfortable reach of the Channel ferry, you would find in this most northerly corner of France many places worthy of attention. To start with, there is the marvellous coastline with its white cliffs matching those across the Channel but – unlike the shingle-bound resorts of Kent and Sussex – rejoicing in miles and miles of golden beaches and sand dunes. This sand, deposited by the up-Channel tides for thousands of years, has gradually caused the whole of the Picardy coast from Boulogne to Le Tréport to extend westward into the sea, leaving former seaside towns such as Rue and Montreuil stranded several kilometres inland. Fashionable Le Touquet is the liveliest of the many new resorts that established themselves during the nineteenth century along the fringe of this new coastline. But the inexorable march of the dunes continues, and already the little fishing port of Étaples behind Le Touquet is struggling to keep its harbour open to the sea.

Inland, the historic war-battered towns are full of unexpected interest and famous architectural treasures – Amiens (finest of all), with its glorious cathedral and its 'market-on-the-water'; pleasant, gracious, eighteenth-century St-Omer; Hesdin, with the site of Agincourt close at hand; St-Riquier, with its marvellous abbey, and nearby Crécy; Arras, with its two grand and enormous squares; St-Quentin and its great basilica with the huge belfry . . . and if you are interested in French painting and happen to be near Lille, this humming industrial capital has one of the best Fine Art museums in the whole of France outside Paris.

For those who wish to visit one or more of the World War I battlefields, a list of the principal sites is provided in the last entry of the Gazetteer which now follows.

St-Omer Church   A.F. Kersting

The North: Gazetteer

Edward Young

ABBEVILLE, *Somme* (2–B3). An important British army H.Q. in World War I, and well known to cross-Channel travellers as the first fairly large town they come to when driving S on the N1 from Calais or Boulogne. Not many stop, because the rest of France beckons them on, and indeed it has little to offer the tourist as it was virtually destroyed in 1940. It is now a thriving modern commercial and industrial centre (metallurgy, sugar, textiles). The church of St-Vulfran, though badly damaged, is still worth seeing for its superb Flamboyant Gothic façade, graced by two symmetrical towers. Just N of the church is a museum named after Jacques Boucher de Perthes, the 19th-c. 'father of pre-history'; among its other interests, the museum houses an important display of Boucher's prehistoric finds in the Somme valley.

If you are driving S on D901, note to your left as you leave the town the elegant 18th-c. house called the Château Bagatelle, in a charming setting of gardens and parkland.

8km ENE on D925, in the little town of **St-Riquier**, is a remarkable abbey church, largely Flamboyant Gothic, with a spacious nave nearly 100m long.

N of Abbeville, 19km on D928 and D10, is the village of Crécy-en-Ponthieu, close to the site of the battle of **Crécy** in which Edward III gained his resounding victory over the French in 1346 at the beginning of the Hundred Years War. The actual site is 1km N of the village on D111.

An important survivor of the Hundred Years War, the formidable castle of **Rambures**, lies about 20km SW of Abbeville (N28, then D29 through Oisement and right on D180). It was a French-occupied fortress in the centre of English-held territory. Amazingly, it is still in the hands of the same family that owned it then.

AMIENS, *Somme* (2–B4). Amiens Cathedral is the largest and most perfect cathedral in the whole of France, the prime example of northern Gothic. Miraculous survivor of two World Wars, it towers sublimely above the modern town that has replaced the rubble of thousands of destroyed buildings. The W façade, with its two towers of uneven height, its great rose-window, its three high-arched portals, its rich adornment of statues of kings, apostles and prophets, is tremendously impressive. The interior of the nave, 145m long, is

vast, solemn and luminous; 126 slender pillars soar towards the vaulted roof, lit by high windows. The choir-stalls are a celebrated masterpiece of early 16th-c. oak carving, with over 3000 biblical, homely and satirical scenes. There are rose-windows at each end of the transept, but finest of all is the majestic, lacy rose-window above the organ loft at the W end of the nave. The main vessel of the Cathedral, begun in 1220, was completed in 50 years; the façade and the towers took a further 200. The result is a superb edifice. If possible, plan your journey so as not to miss it.

A unique feature of the town is the 'market-on-the-water', E of the Cathedral and just across the river. Known as the *hortillonnages*, it is an area of market-gardens criss-crossed by a network of irrigation canals lined with fruit and vegetable stalls; shopping is done from little boats, which can be hired. S of the Cathedral the Picardy Museum includes a good collection of paintings from Chardin to Salvador Dali. At the W edge of the town centre, adjacent to a sports complex, is the fine modern Maison de la Culture, inaugurated in 1966 by André Malraux. Opposite the railway station stands the Perret Tower, another symbol of the new Amiens, commemorating the architect who helped to create it; there is a splendid view from the top. At the S of the town is the campus of the new university, founded in 1964. But the past lives on in the continuing manufacture of velvet, for which Amiens has been famous since the reign of Louis XIV.

16km due E along the Somme, in **Corbie**, are the remains of an abbey which played an important part in the spread of Christianity in northern Europe. 3km S of Corbie, outside the village of **Villers-Bretonneux**, is the Australian War Memorial and Cemetery on the site where 10,000 Australian soldiers were killed halting the German spring offensive of 1918.

ARRAS, *Pas-de-Calais* (2–A4, B4). This ancient town was virtually in the front line in World War I, but despite the devastation wrought by bombardment it has managed, by undaunted reconstruction, to preserve its 17th-c. Flemish aspect. The two great squares, La Grande Place and La Place des Héros, which on Saturdays bustle with market stalls, are framed by elegant stone-and-brick houses with Flemish ornamental gables and

A.F. Kersting

Amiens Cathedral: the carved screen in the ambulatory

covered arcades. The town hall in the Place des Héros, originally 15th-c. but reconstructed after 1918 just as it was, complete with its 75m belfry, is a splendid reminder of Flemish architecture at its best. The Cathedral is early 19th-c., with a monumental staircase leading up to a classical façade. On its S side is the former Benedictine abbey palace, now housing a mixed museum of 12th–15th-c. sculpture, Arras porcelain, and paintings from many periods, including a Corot of a scene near Arras. The museum also displays a 15th-c. Arras tapestry, reminding us of the town's ancient craft that was already flourishing in Charlemagne's day. Shakespeare's stage direction in *Hamlet* – 'Polonius hides behind the arras' – indicates how widespread the fame of Arras tapestry was, and even today tapestry is still *arazzi* in Italian.

At the SW edge of the town is one of the many great 'citadel' fortifications erected in this vulnerable frontier area by Vauban, Louis XIV's great military engineer. Close by is the Mur des Fusillés, a monument to the Resistance heroes shot there in 1942, and just N of that is a British 1914–18 Memorial. About 10km due N, to the left of the Lens road (N25), is the huge and imposing memorial on **Vimy Ridge**, a moving tribute to the 75,000 Canadians who died there in 1917.

BOULOGNE-SUR-MER, *Pas-de-Calais* (2–A3). Cross-Channel terminal for car ferries and hovercraft; seaside resort with fine sandy beaches; growing industrial centre; and the largest fishing port in France. The high-rise flats to your left as you arrive by ferry from Dover or Folkestone are a

sign of the newness of the lower town, laid flat in World War II. Only the upper town, within its rectangle of ramparts, was largely unscathed. The 13th-c. castle, surrounded by a dry moat, is not open to visitors. The Basilica of Notre-Dame is a 19th-c. replacement of an earlier church destroyed in the Revolution, but it has a fascinating crypt which has survived from the 11th-c. and contains remnants of a 3rd-c. Roman temple. The 18th-c. Hôtel Desandrouins is the house where Napoleon stayed in 1803 when he assembled an army and a fleet here for the projected invasion of England that was cancelled after Trafalgar.

CALAIS, *Pas-de-Calais* (2–A3). Edward III captured Calais in 1347 after an eight-month siege which ended with the surrender of the six burghers, commemorated in Rodin's celebrated statuary group in front of the town hall. The town remained in English hands for 210 years until it was retaken for France by the Duc de Guise in 1558. The nearest Continental port to England, Calais is often a Briton's first glimpse of 'abroad'. The port handles over 4 million passengers and about a million cars a year, quite apart from a vast tonnage of commercial goods. The town is famous for its *tulle* and machine-made lace industry – started here, incidentally, by the British in the early 19th-c.

The two World Wars (especially the second) destroyed most of the area near the docks, except for the 13th–14th-c. church of Notre-Dame and Vauban's citadel (now a sports stadium). The new post-war town is a brave and largely successful attempt to fit architectural modernity into the

'French way of life'. The sandy beaches stretching westward for miles ensure its continuing future as a popular holiday resort.

CAMBRAI, *Nord* (2–B4). Now happily by-passed by the Paris–Brussels A2 autoroute, Cambrai is an old textile-manufacturing town, famous since the 14th-c. for the fine linen known in England (and mentioned in Shakespeare) as 'cambric' – and still woven here. Like all Flanders towns, Cambrai suffered badly in both World Wars; in the Battle of Cambrai, 1917, tanks were used for the first time. In the 18th-c. Cathedral lies the tomb of the writer Fénélon who was a much-loved archbishop here from 1695 to 1715 (*see also* Carennac, *in the Southwest section*) and reprimanded by the Pope for his unorthodox mystical writings. The 17th–18th-c. church of St-Géry has a magnificent rood-screen, now positioned at the rear of the nave, and in the left arm of the transept an enormous painting of the Entombment by Rubens. Between the two churches are several streets with interesting old houses, one of which contains the municipal museum with its good collection of Dutch and Flemish paintings, canvases by Ingres, Boudin, Utrillo, Vlaminck, sculptures by Bourdelle, Rodin, etc. The 70m belfry standing alone in the Mail St-Martin is the remnant of a 15th-c. church. On the SE corner of the town are the remains of another of Vauban's 17th-c. citadels, surrounded by public gardens.

CHÂTEAU-THIERRY, *Aisne* (2, 3–C4, C5). Birthplace of La Fontaine, 17th-c. author of the celebrated *Fables* (his house is a museum), this small town on the N bank of the Marne suffered severe damage in both World Wars. It is dominated by the impressive ramparts of the ancient fort built in the 8th-c. by Charles Martel. From the ramparts is a good view of the Marne valley; 2km W can be seen the great monument on 'Hill 204' commemorating the capture of the position by the American 2nd Division and the French 39th Division in July 1918 after a bitter five-week battle which turned the tide of the last German advance in World War I.

8km W is the village of **Belleau**, scene of another American victory in 1918. Abandoned guns can still be seen lying close to the road through the wood where the battle was fought by the 4th Brigade of Marines. An American cemetery with over 2000 graves lies close to the village.

DOUAI, *Nord* (2, 3–A4, A5). An old Flanders town on the site of a Gallo-Roman fort. Surrounded by a large coalfield belt, it has suffered from the enormous growth of industry – chemicals, metallurgy, etc. – not to mention the damage from the various wars fought in the area. The present aspect of the town derives from a spate of new building in the 18th-c., and despite the severe bombardments of 1940 Douai has managed by judicious reconstruction to maintain its 18th-c.

flavour. The town hall, partly 15th-c., is celebrated for its belfry, a great square Gothic tower 65m high, embellished with 'romantic' turrets and pinnacles, and containing a famous carillon that plays tunes every quarter of an hour.

DUNKIRK (Dunkerque), *Nord* (2–A4). Gets its name from its beginnings in the 9th-c. as a tiny fishing harbour close to a church (or kirk) on the dunes. In the 17th-c., led by the great sea captain Jean Bart (commemorated by a statue in the city centre), its corsairs ranged the seas for enemy booty during the wars of Louis XIV. Despite the destruction by several wars (it was 80 % wiped out in 1940), it has nevertheless grown steadily in size. It is now the third largest port of France, with extensive docks, deep-water quays, etc., and with increasingly busy cross-Channel ferry connections to Dover and Harwich.

The story of the events of May–June 1940, which made the name of Dunkirk part of British history, is too well known to be retold here, but the long sandy beaches where the embarkation rescue of half a million British and Allied soldiers took place are still here, opposite the holiday resort of Malo-les-Bains to the E of the harbour area.

9km S on D916 is the picturesque old fortified town of **Bergues**, with Flemish-style 17th- and 18th-c. houses and one of Vauban's typically star-shaped fortresses.

HESDIN, *Pas-de-Calais* (2–A3). An attractive old town on the N39 from Le Touquet to Arras. The river Canche runs through the centre, close to the 16th-c. church of Notre-Dame with its unusual main doorway. The 16th-c. town hall faces a spacious square, the Place d'Armes; it was once a palace, and when it became the town hall the local dignitaries added over the centre doorway an amusingly ornate, square, pillared gallery – a 'folly' almost. The abbé Prévost, 18th-c. author of *Manon Lescaut*, was born at 11 Rue Daniel-Lereuil.

12km N, to the right of D928, is the village of **Azincourt**, close to the site of the battle of 1415 in which Henry V won his famous victory, killing or taking prisoner 10,000 of the French nobility.

LAON, *Aisne* (3–B5). An old town with ramparts and ancient gateways, built on a perfect defensive site – an elongated ridge of hill rising abruptly to 100m above an immense plain. In the 8th–10th-c. Laon was actually the capital of France and residence of the kings, until Hugues Capet, elected King in 987, broke the tradition and moved to Paris.

The oldest part of the town, the Cité, lies at the E end of the ridge; its old houses and narrow streets cluster round the marvellous 12th-c. Cathedral, one of the oldest and finest Gothic churches in France. It has seven towers – two on the impressive façade, surmounted by huge stone oxen in honour of the beasts of burden which hauled up the stone for building the Cathedral; a lantern tower over the transept crossing; and four other towers at the corners of the transept arms. The nave is long and high, the sides being in four tiers: an open arcade surmounted by, first, a large pillared gallery or *tribune*, then a blind arcade and finally high windows. The choir is unusually long, and there are rose-windows with superb 13th-c. stained glass. The S transept leads to the 13th-c. chapter house opening into a peaceful cloister; at the NE corner of the Cathedral stands the former Bishop's Palace, now used as the Palais de Justice, and facing it across the square is a stimulating cultural centre, the House of Art and Leisure, opened in 1971.

From the 13th-c. ramparts the fertile land below stretches SE to an apparently infinite horizon; this is the plain of Champagne, and Reims is only 45km away. Close to the SE ramparts, in the grounds of the Museum, stands a perfect little octagonal Romanesque Templar chapel with its surrounding graveyard transformed into a lovely garden.

LILLE, *Nord* (2–A4). The vast industrial urban metropolis of Lille-Roubaix-Tourcoing is the greatest economic centre of northern France. It produces cotton, linen, biscuits, sugar, chocolate; it has chemical, metal and printing works, distilleries and breweries; it makes tractors, turbines, and diesel engines; it has a celebrated International Fair every April (half a million visitors each year), a vast new hospital complex and a university; and autoroutes converge on it from Paris, Dunkirk, Antwerp, Brussels and Cologne. It is in fact an ugly, noisy, energetic

Laon Cathedral

French Government Tourist Office

conglomeration, not the place for the tourist seeking a quiet holiday.

But if you happen to be there, it has many things worth seeing, mostly in and around the old quarter centred on the Place Général de Gaulle, named after Lille's best-known native. For example, the 17th-c. Flemish Baroque building of the old Bourse with its galleried courtyard and bronze statue of Napoleon cast from guns captured at Austerlitz; the great new Cathedral, begun in 1854 and still unfinished; the grandiloquent triumphal arch of the Porte de Paris, erected to the glory of Louis XIV in 1682; and – perhaps the best thing in Lille – the Museum of Fine Arts, with one of the richest collections of paintings in France. From the museum the wide Bd. de la Liberté leads NW straight to the Vauban 'citadel', the finest and best-preserved example of that great 17th-c. military engineer's defensive monuments, now surrounded by a canal; the interior fort is an army establishment and entry is forbidden, but you can walk round the impressive battlements.

To the NE, **Roubaix** and **Tourcoing** have both grown and merged with Lille, losing their separate identities in one huge built-up industrial area. But just S of Roubaix in the village of **Hem** is a beautiful modern chapel, La Chapelle de la Ste-Face, completed in 1958, with a tapestry after a design by Rouault and a whole wall of stained glass by Manessier in the most glorious colours (well worth a diversion).

LUCHEUX, *Somme* (6km NE of Doullens: 2–B4). A village in a woodland setting just N of the Arras–Doullens road (N25) and worth a visit for its Romanesque church with decorated vaulting and most unusual and amusing capitals (the 'Seven Deadly Sins', etc.); and up on the hill the partly restored ruins of a castle in whose keep Joan of Arc was held prisoner for a while after her capture at Compiègne, before being transferred to Le Crotoy, near St-Valéry-sur-Somme, and thence to Rouen.

QUESNOY, Le, *Nord* (14km SE of Valenciennes: 3–A5). Most of Vauban's defensive citadels are on the edge of a town. Here the town is *inside* the hilltop citadel. Lakes and moats still lap the outer walls on the NW and SE sectors. The battlements first took shape in the 14th-c.; Charles V and Louis XIII both had a hand in them, but the final design with its sharply pointed embrasures bears the unmistakable stamp of Vauban. Now white-washed houses, great trees and luxuriant vege-tation have softened the military aspect of the place, and the walk round the battlements is extremely pleasant. By the postern gate on the W side is a monument to the New Zealand Rifle Brigade, marking the scene of their World War I exploit in scaling the walls in the face of enemy fire.

ST-OMER, *Pas-de-Calais* (2–A3,A4). About 25km from the Channel coast, St-Omer makes an agreeable overnight stop before catching the ferry

Le Touquet

at Calais or Dunkirk (both about 40km away). It is a peaceful town with an air of 17th–18th-c. elegance, built on rising ground above the surrounding marshlands. These cover a large area with a network of waterways which provide not only fun for fishermen and canoeists but also boat transport for the extensive market-gardens (famous for cauliflowers) and a seasonal refuge for migrating herons. At the W end of the town, overlooking the beautiful public gardens laid out among the ancient ramparts, stands the majestic Basilica of Notre-Dame, a huge edifice dating from the 12th-c., with an enormous nave, many statues and sculptured tombs, and a 16th-c. astronomical clock. There are two good museums, both housed in 18th-c. buildings: the Hôtel Sandelin Museum (Flemish and Dutch paintings, and ceramics including over 700 Delft pieces) and the Henri-Dupuis Museum (natural history). At the E end of the town are the ruins of the ancient abbey of St-Bertin.

ST-QUENTIN, *Aisne* (3–B5). A large industrial town whose traditional textile production has now been overtaken by chemicals and metalworks. The St-Quentin canal links it through the northern waterway system to the industrial capitals of Belgium and N Germany. Throughout World War I the town was surrounded by battlefields, and for four years occupied by the German army.

Yet some of its ancient past remains. The Basilica is 12th–15th-c. and enormous; its massive belfry can be seen for miles, and the nave is nearly 35m high; there is some fine though sombre stained glass, and in the 9th-c. crypt lies a tomb reputed to be that of the 4th-c. martyr St Quentin himself. The town hall has an early 16th-c. Gothic façade, an 18th-c. bell-tower with a spirited 37-bell

carillon, and in the interior a superb Renaissance chimney-piece. Highlight of the excellent Antoine Lécuyer Museum is its collection of works by the great 18th-c. pastel painter Maurice Quentin de la Tour, who was born and also died here and left a large number of his portraits of great personages to his native town. The Museum of Entomology (Rue des Canonniers) has one of the world's finest collections of butterflies and other insects.

14km N on N44*bis*, just beyond the village of **Bellicourt**, is the United States 1914–18 War Memorial; the cemetery is a short distance further N in the village of Bony.

ST-VALERY-SUR-SOMME, *Somme* (2–B3). Holiday resort with sandy beaches, a fishing port and yacht harbour. Situated on the W side of the mouth of the river Somme, it looks out across a wide estuary full of sandbanks partly covered by vegetation, on which sheep graze until the tide rises. In 1066 William of Normandy embarked part of his army here for the conquest of England, and in World War I it was an important supply port for the British army.

From the entrance of the little harbour a long promenade extends W along the seafront, overlooked by the ramparts of the upper town, which still preserves its two ancient gateways. Here on the hill, with magnificent views over the bay, are two modest churches: St-Martin, at the very edge of the ramparts, its walls a chequerboard of flint and sandstone, and a little further W (past the remains of an old abbey, down in a dip to the left) the Chapel of the Mariners, sheltered by age-old trees and containing the tomb of St Valery.

Across the bay, reached by a new road with wonderful views of sand and sea (or by the light railway which operates at weekends in summer), is the little town of **Le Crotoy**. There used to be a small castle here, where the English temporarily imprisoned Joan of Arc before taking her to Rouen. Now it is a great place for locally caught cockles, eels, prawns, etc. Beyond it is a nature reserve for over 300 species of migratory birds.

8km N of Le Crotoy is the medieval port of **Rue**, now separated from the sea by 8 kilometres of sand dunes; it is notable for its marvellous Flamboyant Gothic chapel with a unique vaulted roof carved in starry pendants.

SOISSONS, *Aisne* (2, 3–C4, C5). An important agricultural centre on the S bank of the Aisne. It has a long history, but was so badly damaged in both World Wars that it is today virtually a new town. The vast Gothic Cathedral, almost a wreck in 1918, has since been courageously restored; it is remarkable for the symmetry and proportions of its tremendous nave, the elegance of the upper gallery in the S transept, the Rubens 'Adoration of the Shepherds' in the N transept, and the glowing 13th–14th-c. stained glass above the choir. Of the abbey church of St-Jean-des-Vignes there remain only an outstandingly impressive façade, a fine refectory and cellar, and parts of the cloisters. The ruins of the 12th-c. abbey of St-Léger, wrecked by the Protestants in the Wars of Religion, now serve to house the municipal museum.

17km due N are the battlemented remains of **Coucy-le-Château**, a medieval castle with mighty walls and towers; the huge central keep was blown up by the Germans in 1917, but the castle is still well worth a visit.

TOUQUET, Le, *Pas-de-Calais* (2–A3). Well known to the English, Le Touquet-Paris-Plage is a fashionable seaside resort that has maintained its reputation of a somewhat exclusive elegance. Yet despite its expensive hotels, its two casinos, its rich villas, its racecourse, its smart yacht harbour, its nightclubs, its riding facilities, its tennis courts and golf clubs, it is still permeated by an infectious atmosphere of amiable holiday relaxation. The beaches are gorgeous stretches of sand, and behind the town are delightful walks among the scented pinewoods.

Slightly inland, on the other side of the airport and across the river Canche, is the fishing port of **Étaples**, struggling against the encroachment of the dunes; a new dam has created an artificial lake for dinghy sailing.

14km up river is **Montreuil**, a little medieval hilltop town that was once able to call itself Montreuil-sur-Mer. It has an abbey church dating back to the 11th-c., a citadel, old winding streets, and an hour-long rampart walk with extensive views over the surrounding plain. Victor Hugo loved it, and set part of *Les Misérables* here.

VALENCIENNES, *Nord* (3–A5). An industrial town in a coalfield area close to the Belgian border. Its centre was largely destroyed in World War II

and is of little interest to the tourist except for its large Museum of Fine Arts, containing paintings by Rubens, Bosch, Brueghel the younger, Watteau, etc.

WAR MEMORIALS AND CEMETERIES (1914–18)

The large-scale (1cm to 2km) Michelin road maps of Northern France towards the Belgian border (Maps 51 and 53) mark the sites of countless British and Allied memorials and cemeteries, as well as French, especially in the areas between Lille and Arras and throughout the triangle Arras–Amiens–St-Quentin. The principal sites are as follows (the map references here being to the Michelin maps mentioned above):

Vimy (between Lens and Arras: Map 51, fold 15), Canadian Memorial. (*See also* Arras entry.)

Notre-Dame-de-Lorette (6km SW of Lens: Map 51, fold 15), main French Cemetery.

Albert (28km NE of Amiens: Map 53, fold 12), starting point for tour of the Somme battlefields, including **Thiepval** (6km NNE of Albert), British Memorial, and **Beaumont-Hamel** (8km N of Albert), Canadian Memorial.

Villers-Bretonneux (16km E of Amiens: Map 53, fold 11), Australian Memorial and Cemetery, just N of the village. (*See also note at end of* Amiens *entry.*)

Bellicourt (14km N of St-Quentin: Map 53, fold 14), USA Memorial, with Cemetery in the village of Bony, 1½km NW.

Vimy: Canadian War Memorial

French Government Tourist Office

The Northwest

Normandy and Brittany

Normandy: Introduction

Gerald Barry

The ancient province of Normandy presents two utterly opposed geological faces. The eastern part was created by invasions of the sea about 6000 BC, which brought with it vast deposits of chalk and limestone that had lain in the ocean bed for some 200 million years. Later, prevailing winds spread a depth of fine soil, rich in organic debris, over the chalk base. It was this which was later to produce the prosperous farm and dairy lands of Normandy.

The western face consists of the Armorican Massif, a triangular region with its base in the Paris Basin and its apex in Brittany. It rises to its greatest height of 417 metres in the Écouves Forest and the Mont des Avaloirs in the Mancelle Alps. Consisting of hard sandstone, slate and imperishable granite, it was formed in the Carboniferous Ages, eroded and then reformed 70 million years ago. During the cataclysmic period it was often split and creviced into the wild rugged valleys typical of the Suisse Normande.

Between these two divisions lay a hybrid zone of transitional regions separating the chalklands of Upper Normandy from the *bocage*, or woodland country, of Lower Normandy. The Seine, twisting its way through almost the centre of the province, was to play a vital rôle in its development, not only as the earliest and most important means of communication, but also for its rich alluvial deposits fertilizing the surrounding countryside.

The long coastline from Le Tréport down to Mont-St-Michel shows clearly the two dominant geological features of chalk and granite: first the cliff-lines of the northeastern coast, then the Cotentin peninsula, thrusting out into the sea, its northern tip aggressively culminating in the sinister granite cliff of the Nez de Jobourg. Its western coast, rocky and often forbidding, sweeps down to neighbouring Brittany, separated only by a narrow ribbon of water – and history.

Little is known of the earliest settlers in this province. They were probably the same Mediterranean people who crossed to Britain in the sixth century BC, who had already intermarried into the various Celtic tribes. When the Romans came and conquered Gaul, they built one of their great military roads from Paris to Lillebonne and on to the harbour at Harfleur, roughly following the course of the Seine. They made Rouen the capital of the province. This was the main road link between Marseille, Lyon and Britain. Another Roman road, from the Loire valley, passed through Sées and Bayeux. Before the Romans withdrew from Gaul at the end of the fifth century, their northern province had settled very much into the political entity we know as Normandy today.

The fishing harbour, Honfleur   J. Allan Cash

That it maintained this identity was due to its widespread Christianization in the fourth and fifth centuries. Rouen had become an important Christian bishopric before the end of the fourth century. The other Roman centres of administration – Bayeux, Avranches, Évreux, Lisieux, Coutances and Sées – were all bishoprics within twenty years of the departure of the legions. This ecclesiastical pattern, based firmly on the Roman plan of civil government, was to withstand all the future devastations of the Scandinavian invasions which were to engulf the province in the ninth century.

Already in the third century, Germanic tribes of Visigoths, Vandals and Huns were making forays into Gaul. By the fifth century, another German race, the Franks, had taken control and, under their king Clovis, with the help of the Gallo-Roman bishops, unified a whole kingdom by the end of the century. His son Clothaire became king of the Western Country, or Neustria, which included two-thirds of the territory we know as Normandy, but rival tribal chiefs attempted to erode the power of the king. Again, only the power of the bishops prevented complete disintegration, and the sheer necessities of defence brought into being the feudal system.

But in the ninth century a new race of Scandinavian pirates were sailing up the Seine, laying waste to the countryside. With increasing ferocity they laid siege to Paris and overran Neustria, burning and looting churches and monasteries, and it seemed as though complete collapse was inevitable. Gradually these wild Northmen became known as 'Normans'. One of their most intrepid leaders was a Norwegian called Rolf, later known as Rollo or Rollon. By 911, Charles of the Franks came to terms with him and, on condition of his accepting baptism, offered him lands for himself and his followers in Neustria. From the date of this meeting at Clair-sur-Epte begins the story of modern Normandy, and Rollo became its first Dux or Duke.

For some time at least Rollo seems to have taken his baptism seriously, and set about making some reparation to the churches and monasteries he had destroyed. This process continued throughout the tenth century, which saw the foundation of the great Norman abbeys that were to play an important historic rôle in Britain after the Conquest. The civilizing force of Benedictine culture, interplaying with the older Gallo-Celtic monasticism, made an amazing impact on a people as savage as the Vikings. Slowly they became integrated with the Gallo-Franks – though Norse, the Viking language, survived until quite late in Bayeux. Most of Normandy was speaking the latinized Gallo-Frankish tongue by the following century.

Although there was still much fighting between rival leaders, a certain feudal cohesion enabled them to take possession of the remainder of Neustria, including the peninsula of Cotentin with its frontier bordering the Celtic province of Brittany. Mont-St-Michel, on the furthest western point of the province, had already been founded by a bishop of Avranches in 709. Within seventeen years of the new century, the Normans were building the great abbey church on its summit. In 1035 the great-great-great-great grandson of Rollo, William the Bastard, was born. Thirty-one years later he had so consolidated his position as Duke of Normandy that he was able to set sail and conquer England, and so change the whole face of medieval history. Building, learning, the arts, law and new patterns of civilized behaviour were to thrive under the patronage of the Norman Dukes.

J. Allan Cash

Mont-St-Michel

The particular characteristics of the Normans were to survive the integration of Normandy into France under Philippe-Auguste in 1204. The Viking traits are still recognizable, even after centuries of intermarriage. They are taller than their Celtic neighbours in Brittany. Ruddy complexions may glow beneath incongruous dark brown hair, but the clear blue eyes of the Scandinavian still have the penetrating power of a sea-faring people. Stolid, with tremendous self-confidence, they have a passionate belief in individual liberty. They are kindly, cautious yet generous, hard working yet ready to make much of a ceremonial occasion. Not for nothing was worldwide maritime law based considerably on the ancient '*droit Normand*', and this profound respect for law was to flow easily into the English judicial system. The vicissitudes of their history have made them cool in the face of danger, with an indomitable will to survive, a quality which made them invaluable allies during the devastating bombing and invasion of their country in World War II.

The climate is particularly mild, especially in the coastal areas. Between Le Tréport and Le Havre the prevailing winds tend to bestow a bracing quality, which extends along the Calvados coast. Near to the bay of Mont-St-Michel there are warmer streams of air, with pockets affected by the Gulf Stream, which produce semi-tropical foliage. The rainfall is similar to that of the south coast of England, though perhaps greater during parts of October. It can, however, frequently occur that while the interior is rainy and gusty the coast is sunny and warm. Uncertainty in prediction of sudden squalls was one of the factors complicating the Normandy landings in 1944.

Château Gaillard, at Les Andelys

In a province so rich in agricultural land and dairy produce, and with some of the finest orchard country in Europe, good food and drink are naturally basic to the way of life. All the raw material for the somewhat rich Norman cooking is of excellent quality. The dairy produce in butter and cream and the wide variety of cheeses is world famous. Camembert is perhaps the best-known cheese, though Pont l'Évêque and Livarot have been famous since the days when the Plantagenets laid in great stocks of these products in their castle-cellars in both England and Normandy. It is quite usual to be offered a choice of at least a dozen cheeses on an ordinary cheeseboard. From the Auge valley comes the best of the many Norman ciders, which is drunk with seafood, poultry or a *gigot* of succulent lamb from the same area. Calvados, the distilled spirit of cider, requires at least twelve to fifteen years to mature. It is drunk not only after a meal but frequently in the middle of it, and on a cold winter morning agricultural workers will nip into a café and order a '*calva*' with their black coffee. In industrial Upper Normandy wine is more often drunk with a meal.

The seafood of Normandy is rightly renowned – from the fresh soles of Dieppe cooked in a rich velvety cream sauce, or the mussels *à la marinière* of Villerville, to the lobsters of the Cotentin peninsula or the oysters of Courseulles. Certain towns have their own specialities. Caen is renowned for its tripe cooked with calves-foot in cider and Calvados; Rouen for its inimitable preparation of duckling.

Normandy: Gazetteer

Gerald Barry

ALENÇON, *Orne* (2–D2). Lying in the centre of fertile countryside well watered by the Upper Sarthe, Alençon is a natural agricultural as well as departmental capital. Its history was linked for centuries with the powerful (and later tragic) Dukes of Alençon, whose turreted 14th-c. fortress stands at the edge of a park in the centre of town. It is now a prison. Nearby, the elegant curved façade of the 18th-c. Hôtel-de-Ville is finely proportioned. Inside is an interesting collection of paintings as well as examples of rare Alençon lace. Together with the Palais de Justice, it stands on the vast Place Foch, which is a major solution to the town's parking problems.

The 14th-c. Flamboyant church of Notre-Dame was completed in 1444 except for the unusual three-sided porch on the W front which was finished in 1506. The carving of the Transfiguration group at the centre has St John standing with his back to the street. The young Carmelite, Thérèse of Lisieux, who was born at 50 Rue St-Blaise close by, was baptized in a chapel now surrounded by an iron grille and dedicated to the saint. Almost next to Notre-Dame is a well-restored town house, the Maison d'Ozé, built by a wealthy 15th-c. merchant and now a museum. By the Pont Neuf is the School of Lace, where among many fine exhibits is a veil worn by Marie-Antoinette.

To the N of the city lies the deeply gladed Forest of Écouves where deer and roebuck roam freely. Within the forest is a granite crest rising to over 400m. The Forest of Perseigne to the SE of the town has an interesting ruined abbey. To the W are the gorse- and heather-covered hills of the Mancelle Alps rising above the winding river Sarthe.

ANDELYS, Les, *Eure* (2–C3). The twin villages of Petit Andely and Grand Andely. The former, nearest the river Seine looping its way through tall chalk cliffs, is dominated by the massive chalky white ruins of Richard Cœur de Lion's formidable **Château Gaillard**. Built with the military expertise he had learned during his Crusade in the East, Richard used it effectively to keep out any inroads of the French King Philippe-Auguste into Normandy. A 15m-deep moat separated the five-towered redoubt (one of which still stands) from the three-storeyed keep with walls 5m thick. Three years after Richard's death in 1199, the French attacked again. King John put his Constable of Chester in charge of defence; he withstood a siege of nearly a year until, it is said, a soldier climbing through the latrines let down the drawbridge, and the famished and weakened Normans were quickly defeated. The whole dukedom surrendered, and Normandy became part of France. The castle was finally dismantled by Henri IV during the Wars of Religion. It should be explored with caution, especially in wet weather. The views to the left of the village, the Gothic church of St-Saviour and the graceful suspension bridge below, are rewarding. To the right is Grand Andely, which was almost completely destroyed in 1940 and has been rebuilt to house small industries. Almost miraculously the splendid church of Notre-Dame, with its lofty Gothic nave and 13th-c. twin towers, survived. Its grand Renaissance organ loft and organ, as well as 16th-c. stained glass, make it well worth visiting.

ARGENTAN, *Orne* (2–C2). In and around this small but historic town, built mainly on the W bank of the river Orne, was fought the final battle for Normandy in August 1944. Badly damaged, it has been almost entirely rebuilt, though the splendid Flamboyant churches of St-Germain and St-Martin are both still undergoing restoration.

Near St-Germain are the feudal remains of a 14th-c. castle built by a Duke d'Alençon.

A happy rediscovery in the last century of original 18th-c. patterns enabled the beautiful Argentan lace to be made again. Good examples can be seen in the Benedictine abbey on the Rue de l'Abbaye.

ARQUES-LA-BATAILLE, *Seine-Maritime* (6km SE of Dieppe: 2–B3). Dominant on a steep hilltop overlooking this historic town are the ruins of one of Normandy's oldest stone castles. Built by the Counts of Arques, it was wrested from them by Duke William six years before his conquest of England. Only one wall tower and the ramparts remain as witness to its sturdy strength. The town, famed for the ingenuity of its iron-smiths, gets its hyphenated name from a great battle fought here in 1589, when the then still Protestant Henri IV with 7000 men defeated the 30,000 strong army of the Catholic League. An obelisk stands as a memorial of the battle on a mound above the river. The church of Notre-Dame has a delicate 17th-c. rood-screen with fluted columns separating the Flamboyant chancel from the nave. To the E of Arques is the now sadly diminished ancient Forest of Arques, used as camouflage by the Germans in World War II for launching the flying bombs against England.

10km N is the very typical Norman market town of **Envermeu** situated on important cross-roads. It has a fine Gothic church with a long history stretching back to 1066 when two brothers, Hugues and Turold of Envermeu, set out with Duke William to fight by his side at the Battle of Hastings. Later Turold, through the influence of Archbishop Anselm of Canterbury, was rewarded with the Bishopric of Bayeux.

AVRANCHES, *Manche* (1–B4). Perched 100m above the Sée estuary, Avranches benefits from the many panoramic views across the bay to the fairy-tale mass of Mont-St-Michel. The best view is from the edge of the colourful Botanical Gardens. It was from this town in the 8th-c. that Aubert, monk and bishop, was reputed to have been physically impelled by the Archangel Michael to build an oratory on the top of the now world-famous rock. Another good view can be had from the top of the opposite hill, where once stood the ancient Cathedral which collapsed in 1790 and was never rebuilt; within a quiet square there are only a few excavated foundations, a broken column and a paving stone to mark the spot. This paving stone, incised with a chalice and

La Tour Donjon at Avranches

known as '*la plate-forme*', is part of the cathedral square where in 1172 Henry II knelt to do penance and receive absolution from the Pope's Legate for the murder of Thomas-à-Becket two years earlier. A bronze plaque records the incident. Across the square is the 15th-c. Episcopal Palace, now the Law Courts.

In the Avranchin Museum is a remarkable collection of early manuscripts dating from the 8th-c. They are mostly from the Abbey of Mont-St-Michel.

Halfway down the hill on the wall of the restored Norman keep, an inscription recalls that a certain Hugues Goz, nicknamed 'The Wolf' and one-time counsellor to William the Conqueror, lived in this fortress, was made Earl of Chester in 1071, and died in 1101.

At the end of the long Rue de la Constitution is a wide open square named after General Patton. A tall monument marks the actual spot of his H.Q. where he prepared his big breakthrough in 1944. The surrounding trees, and the earth in which they are planted, were brought specially from America.

BAGNOLES-DE-L'ORNE, *Orne* (2–C1, D1). In a glorious setting of fir woods this once fashionable Edwardian spa, built around a lake formed by the river Vée, has taken on a new lease of life. Perhaps a three-centuries-old tradition of the rejuvenating properties of its waters has become a magnet for tired executives. The first patient to be cured here was a horse – however, the sulphuric and radioactive baths are highly recommended by the medical profession for human diseases of the circulation.

Casinos and a clutch of luxury hotels assure its present renaissance.

BALLEROY, Château de, *Calvados* (14km SW of Bayeux: 2–C1). A short distance off the main road between Bayeux and St-Lô, almost on the edge of the pretty woodlands of the Forest of Cerisy, is the celebrated Château de Balleroy. It was built in 1626 in the austerely classical style by Louis XIII's master architect, François Mansart. The grounds were laid out by Le Nôtre; the geometrical beds flanking the drive, which is a continuation of the village street, are masterpieces of the great French landscape gardener.

The interior, in marked contrast to the simplicity of line of the front elevation, is richly ornate. The State Reception Room has panelled walls filled with some of Mignard's finest portraits of the then reigning royal family, while the colouring of the allegorical scenes on the painted ceiling seems so fresh that it might have been painted yesterday.

The château is now owned by an American Advisory Institute, whose president has installed a unique balloon museum. Exhibits cover the history of ballooning from the days of Montgolfier to the present day, and balloonists from all over the world gather here once a year.

A short drive NW through the forest leads to the remarkable Romanesque ruins of the 11th-c. Abbey of Cerisy-la-Forêt. The massive tower and turreted apse are particularly beautiful when floodlit. In the summer there are *son et lumière* performances. (*See entry.*)

BARFLEUR, *Manche* (1–A4). In the summer, this sleepy little fishing port becomes animated as the harbour fills with colourful pleasure craft. In the 11th- and 12th-c. it was the principal port of entry and exit for the Norman and Plantagenet kings. From behind the W end of the church with its fortress-like tower is a good view up the coast to the 3km-distant **Gatteville lighthouse**, one of the tallest in France and open to the public. The waters here are shallow with swift currents, and it was off this coast that the famous White Ship carrying William, son of Henry I, foundered, drowning the heir to the English throne and all his companions.

BARNEVILLE-CARTERET, *Manche* (4km E of Carteret: 1–A3). Situated on the estuary of the river Gerfleur and with all the climatic advantages of being on the Gulf Stream, this twin town centred on its lively harbour attracts large numbers of holiday-makers. It is the nearest French port to Gorey on the Isle of Jersey, which can be seen plainly from the Cap de Carteret. Barneville, just S of the cliffs, has fine white sandy beaches extending for about 40km. Its 11th-c. church has good Romanesque arches and capitals with delightful animal carvings. On the other side of the port is the first of Carteret's two sandy beaches. Along the top of the rocky headland the Sentier des Douaniers, a winding path with ever-changing views and passing the lighthouse, leads down to a second beach where the dunes of white sand stretch away for miles to the N.

BAYEUX, *Calvados* (2–C1). Few travellers in Normandy would dispute that Bayeux is one of the best preserved and most interesting of its many historic towns. Pliny the Elder was already writing about this Gaulish city of the 'Bajocasse' tribe around AD 50. By the third century it was a walled town with a wealth of temples, baths and public buildings. The poet Ausonius wrote of its renowned Druidic College on the banks of the little river Aure. A hundred years later saw the establishment of its first bishopric. Captured as a much-prized city by Bretons and Saxons, it finally fell to the Viking Rollo, who married the Governor's daughter, Popa, and founded the strong dynastic line of Norman dukes. It was in Bayeux that the Saxon Harold swore his ill-fated oath to Duke William which was to lead to the Norman Conquest of England. Nearly a thousand years later, history was to be reversed, when on 7 June 1944 the 50th Northumbrian Division of the British Armed Forces took Bayeux almost without inflicting any material damage; it was the

French Government Tourist Office

The Bayeux Tapestry: detail

first town in France to be liberated in World War II. On the outskirts of the town, off the Bd. Fabian Ware, is the British Military Cemetery where 6000 combatants lie buried.

Although it possesses one of the finest French cathedrals and a wealth of beautiful old houses, Bayeux owes its worldwide fame to a strip of linen 70m long and 50cm wide, embroidered in a stitchwork of coloured wools – the remarkable 'Bayeux Tapestry' which vividly tells the story of events leading up to and including the Norman Conquest. It might reasonably be called a 'strip-cartoon in 58 scenes'. Commissioned almost certainly in England by the Conqueror's half-brother Odo, who was both Bishop of Bayeux and Count of Kent, it seems likely to have been worked by a Saxon School of Embroidery in England over a period of ten years. It was destined to be hung round the apse of the Cathedral somewhere about 1077.

A unique work of art, it can be seen expertly exhibited on the first floor of the splendid 17th-c. former residence of the Dean. Admirably lit, the restrained colourings of reds, blues, greys and neutral-tinted wools have withstood the centuries of exposure. Although the wide central strip relates the main story, the upper and lower bands are also worth close examination. The latter, depicting everyday scenes of rural life, are often curiously erotic. Visitors can hire a listening device with a recorded commentary in English or French. The entrance ticket also provides right of entry to the excellent Baron Gérard Museum housed in the old Bishop's Palace, across the adjoining square which is dominated by the 'Liberty' plane-tree planted in 1797. The museum has a good collection of Impressionist and modern paintings, some good porcelain and fine examples of old and new Bayeux lace.

As you come out from the Tapestry Exhibition,

the S porch of the Cathedral is immediately opposite. The somewhat weather-worn tympanum tells the story of Thomas-à-Becket's martyrdom (from right to left working up from the bottom panel, and culminating in the murder at the high altar, at the top). One of the best ways of appreciating the Gothic exterior of the Cathedral is to go past the twin-towered W front, much praised by John Ruskin in *The Seven Lamps of Architecture*, through an archway and down an alleyway called Passage Flachat after the 19th-c. engineer who saved the 15th-c. bonneted central lantern-tower from collapse.

The interior is a perfect marriage between late Romanesque and Gothic. The sturdy pillars of the nave contrast with the light-hearted carvings, particularly in the spandrels of the decorated arches. These consist of humorous little scenes of bishops and apes, dragons and jugglers, all in delightfully primitive designs. The chancel, which was rebuilt about 1230, follows the lines of the earlier apse, and is a soaring vision of slender columns with light filtering down from the inset rose-windows above the richly decorated triforium. The 16th-c. carved choir-stalls set against the arches of the ambulatory are ornate but aesthetically pleasing. The chapter house has its tiled floor set out as a maze, and the crypt has fine 13th-c. frescoes.

Outstanding among the many old houses is the turreted manor house at 5 Rue Franche, followed by a long row of well-preserved buildings dating from the 15th-c. to the 18th-c. At 10 Rue Bourbesneur, beside a low arch, rises the 15th-c. tower of the Governor's House.

Approximately 10km W, off D12, is the feudal **Château de Creully**, the earliest part of which was built by Robert Fitz Haymon whom the Conqueror made Earl of Bristol and Gloucester. Nearby is **Creullet Castle** where General Montgomery parked his caravan H.Q. in June 1944 to direct the Normandy Offensive.

BEAUMESNIL, Château de, *Eure* (12km SE of Bernay: 2–C2). Situated on the main road between Bernay and Conches, the 17th-c. Château de Beaumesnil is widely regarded as the finest example of Louis XIII architecture in France. Its richly ornamented façade, an expression of restrained Baroque, is mirrored in the water of the wide surrounding moat. The gardens on the other side of the château are laid out somewhat formally, but by nature of their planning offer a series of surprises. The château, owned by the Furstenberg Foundation, opens its grounds to the public except in August.

BEC-HELLOUIN, Le, *Eure* (4km N of Brionne: 2–C2). It would hardly be an exaggeration to call this peaceful monastic settlement, situated by the tree-lined rivulet of the Bec, the cradle of Anglo-Norman culture and religious development. Bec-Hellouin produced three of the greatest Arch-

bishops of Canterbury, three Bishops of Rochester, one of whom was the architect of the Tower of London, as well as numerous scholars and clerics who have left their seal on many of today's institutions throughout Europe. Its name is even enshrined in London's populous district of Tooting Bec.

In 1034 a young knight from the nearby town of Brionne renounced his military life. Determined to become a hermit, he took the name Herluin and a year later, with a few companions, made the first simple wooden foundation. After five years they moved to a spot near the present monastery; by now their numbers had grown to 32. It was then that a brilliant young Italian scholar called Lanfranc joined the community and lent lustre to its growing fame for learning.

About this time the emerging figure of Duke William the Bastard laid siege to Brionne, then occupied by a son of the Duke of Burgundy. Somehow the man destined to become Conqueror of England met the scholar-monk and a lifetime bond was forged. From the peace and tranquillity of Bec, Lanfranc became both spiritual and political adviser to the fiery Duke. In 1059 another young Italian philosopher called Anselm came from Aosta to pursue his studies. By now the monastery was recognized as one of the great intellectual centres of Europe, its students becoming popes and counsellors to kings and

The abbey at Le Bec-Hellouin

French Government Tourist Office

refashioning the face of the whole medieval world. Lanfranc went on to build, and become Abbot of, St-Étienne de Caen, and was finally appointed Archbishop of Canterbury by one of his earlier students, Pope Alexander II. Meanwhile the Abbey had moved to its present position, and Anselm became its Abbot on the death of Herluin in 1078. Fifteen years later, following the death of Lanfranc, he too became Archbishop of Canterbury. In sixteen years, under the influence of the Benedictine tradition and culture, he shaped the church in England for the centuries to come.

The splendid buildings seen today are part of a great restoration, undertaken between 1948 and 1959, of the mainly 17th-c. abbey. This had been erected over various semi-ruined parts of the monastery dating back to the disaster of 1150 when the Norman abbey was all but destroyed by fire. Only the isolated 15th-c. St-Nicolas Tower is witness to the splendour of the medieval monastic church; a plaque inside reminds the visitor of the close ties between Bec and England.

Tribute must be paid to the present community who, with the Ministry of Education and the Department of Historic Monuments, have restored not only the buildings but the intellectual and religious life of Bec-Hellouin.

Thus the magnificent façade of the Cour de France is to be seen in all its 18th-c. graciousness, together with the elegant lodges of the Commendatory Abbots and the grand Prior's staircase with the superb new ironwork of its curving banisters. The cradle-vaulted refectory of 1747 has been converted into the abbey church. Its austere lines are particularly suited to the simplicity of today's Benedictine worship. The unadorned green marble altar was a gift of the town of Aosta in 1959 to commemorate the birth of St Anselm; before it lies the 11th-c. sarcophagus of Herluin the founder.

Among the multifarious activities of the monks is a pottery which helps to provide funds for the restoration work.

Curiously, just outside the Abbey gates is an automobile museum. The village with its pretty green is quite unspoilt.

BELLÊME, *Orne* (2–D2). Capital of the beautiful Perche region renowned for the famous Percheron horses, Bellême is built on ancient crossroads on a high spur, overlooking miles of unrivalled forest scenery. The little town has retained much of its medieval character. The formidable 13th-c. city gate called 'La Porche' is flanked by two towers erected over the remains of the 11th-c. fortress of the powerful Counts of Bellême. Several fine houses were built over the citadel during the 17th- and 18th-c. Outstanding is 26 Rue Ville-Close, whose façade is reflected in the waters of what was once the castle moat.

About 8km due W on the far edge of the forest is La Perrière, a spectacular viewing point over the Perche country.

BERNAY, *Eure* (2–C2). This typical small Norman town in the very heart of the province owes its existence to an important abbey founded in 1013 by Judith, grandmother of William the Conqueror. The church, noted for the purity of its Romanesque architecture, has recently been restored with considerable success, preserving the fine arcades, triforium and clerestory. The domed vaulting was restored in the 17th-c. The abbey buildings now form part of the Hôtel-de-Ville, the grounds being laid out as a public garden.

Halfway up the hill on the nearby Rue Thier is the 14th-c. church of Ste-Croix with altar and statues saved from the medieval abbey of Bec, also the imposing tombstones of various Abbots of Bec of the same period.

Several ancient half-timbered houses survive, particularly Nos. 6 and 9 in the same street. The Bernay Museum housed in the 17th-c. Abbot's Lodge is worth visiting; among its treasures is a charming small painting by Bonington.

One of the pleasures of Bernay is to walk on the Promenade des Monts, a fine beech avenue on the hillside with views over the town and the river Charentonne.

At the other end of the town is the rather gloomy 15th-c. church of Notre-Dame-de-la-Couture, where a famous 16th-c. statue of the Virgin (replacing a much older one) draws huge crowds of pilgrims on Whit Monday. It has some good 16th- and 17th-c. stained glass.

Bernay was once a capital of wandering troubadours and it was Alexandre de Bernay who gave the world the poetic form of Alexandrines.

BRICQUEBEC, *Manche* (18km S of Cherbourg: 1–A3). Situated amid the wooded hills of the beautiful interior of the Cotentin Peninsula, Bricquebec boasts one of the best examples of medieval military architecture in the Manche. Towers and walls are well preserved, with a 23m-high 14th-c. polygonal keep in the centre. From an upper platform, reached by 160 steps, is a superb view of the surrounding countryside. Below is a 13th-c. vaulted crypt with sturdy pillars. Part of the 14th-c. buildings are incorporated into the Hôtel du Château. The clock tower houses a regional museum. 2km N is the strict Trappist monastery of Notre-Dame-de-Grâce which may be visited at certain times; it is renowned for its Gregorian chant.

CABOURG, *Calvados* (2–C1, C2). Invoking the spacious days of the Second Empire, Cabourg still retains a flavour of *chic* and elegance and has a wide beach of fine golden sand. It miraculously escaped damage in World War II. Wide avenues, which look much as they did in 1907 when they were built, fan out from the hub of the Grand Hotel and Casino on the Bd. des Anglais. Marcel Proust, who lends his name to part of the promenade, wrote *Within a Budding Grove* during his stay here and records much that is still recognizable in the town. An enlarged marina is being built at the mouth of the Dives.

From Dives-sur-Mer on the other side of the estuary, Duke William in 1066 assembled his fleet for the conquest of England, before sailing up the coast to join forces with reinforcements from St-Valéry-sur-Somme. Dives was even then a large and busy port, and today it is an ever-expanding industrial centre. Its 15th-c. timber-covered market has been well preserved as has the ancient pilgrimage church of Notre-Dame. In 1862 the names of the Conqueror's companions were inscribed on a wall of the church. The 16th-c. Hostellerie de Guillaume le Conquérant is an attractive focal point in the town.

The countryside through the valley of the Dives is particularly pretty.

CAEN, *Calvados* (2–C1). The story of this now almost completely rebuilt city, the capital of Lower Normandy, begins when, as a small cluster of dwellings at the confluence of the rivers Orne and Odon, it was chosen by Duke William and the French King Henri I for the signing in 1047 of the curious 'Truce of God'. This extraordinary document permitted warfare only on certain days of the week and seasons of the year. From this time on, the future Conqueror enlarged and fortified the town until it became his favourite residence.

It was precisely the passage of these rivers, the Odon and the Orne, that prompted General Montgomery to launch his grim offensive in June 1944 for the capture of the city, having first heavily bombed it on D-Day. Only after more than two-thirds of Caen lay in ruins, were the British and Canadian forces able to take possession of this vital sea-port town on 9 July.

The replanning and rebuilding of Caen over a period of fifteen years has been one of the great successes of post-war France. Splendid wide avenues were laid out, flanked by dignified yet functional new buildings. Many of them are faced with the mellow local stone which has worn so well over the centuries on the Tower of London and Canterbury Cathedral. Pleasant tree-lined riverside walks now border long straight stretches of the river Orne.

With the tremendous growth of steel production and many new industries, the port has been enlarged. The 19th-c. canal, linking the port with Ouistreham on the coast, has been deepened and enlarged to take ships of ever-increasing tonnage.

The rebuilt University, founded by Henry VI in 1432, nine years before he built King's College, Cambridge, England, is an imaginatively conceived modern complex covering some 80 acres and using wide-open spaces set off by contemporary sculpture to good effect. It lies to the N, just behind the massive ramparts of William the Conqueror's Castle. This keep is now proudly exposed on its hilltop, uncluttered by the buildings which previously obscured it.

Photo Alfa

Caen University Campus

Within the castle walls is the Hall of the Exchequer built by Henry I. Nearby is the chapel of St-George, now a memorial to those who fell in the Battle of Normandy. Also within the grounds is the Modern Museum of Fine Arts. The 17th-c. Governor's House serves as a *folklorique* museum of Norman crafts. There are sweeping views over the whole city from the castle terrace.

Fortunately some historic buildings and churches escaped grave damage during World War II. Among them were Caen's two most important monuments, the Abbaye aux Hommes and the Abbaye aux Dames. To understand the importance of these two great conventual churches, a brief historical note may be useful.

The future William the Conqueror, having united the whole of his duchy, decided to enlarge his sphere of influence by proposing marriage to his cousin Matilda of Flanders. Her reply was less than ladylike. The Duke in a fury rode off to Flanders and, bursting in on his chosen fiancée, gave her a merciless beating. The tactic paid off and the marriage was celebrated at Eu about 1052. It promptly brought both of them under a papal interdict on the grounds of their blood relationship. Seven years later their friend Abbot Lanfranc went to Rome and succeeded in getting the excommunication lifted on condition that William would found and endow an abbey for men and that Matilda would do likewise for women.

The church of William's Abbaye aux Hommes, under the patronage of St-Étienne, was designed and built by the same Abbot Lanfranc. Its graceful lofty lines, and the austerely restrained decoration of the interior, place it well in the forefront of the Romanesque buildings of the period. Beneath the sweep of the high chancel arch, and within the sanctuary, is William's tomb. It is marked by a plain stone with a simple inscription. His body was pillaged during the French Revolution and only a thigh bone was recovered. The exterior of the church is also beautiful, with a simple gabled façade buttressed on each side. The two soaring towers flanking these had their finely proportioned spires added in the 13th-c. An imposing view is seen from the rear of the church, looking up to the three-tiered apse with rounded, interlaced and early Gothic arches, the top tier being supported by flying buttresses and slender towers. These, together with the octagonal lantern-tower, make a quite unforgettable silhouette. An old legend says that as long as St-Étienne remains intact the English throne will never fall. This took on an added significance during the War. The abbey has close links with St Alban's, whose first Norman abbot was Paul of Caen. The elegant monastic buildings joined to the abbey were reconstructed in the 18th-c. and now form part of the town hall.

Some distance away, just off the wide Ave. Georges Clemenceau, is the church of Matilda's Abbaye aux Dames, the Church of the Holy Trinity. Outwardly it is less imposing than St-Étienne. The twin towers flanking the W door seem somewhat squat in spite of some fine Romanesque arcading. Each of two storeys of the apse contains five rounded arches with good geometrical carvings. They frame windows of excellent modern glass shedding crimsons, blues, purples and yellows over the stonework of the chancel. Matilda's actual tomb is covered with a dark slab surmounted by glass and bears a touching epitaph. The crypt, dedicated to St Nicolas, is very similar to that of Hexham Abbey.

The Abbaye aux Hommes, Caen

French Government Tourist Office

Other historic churches which have been restored are those of St-Pierre, St-Ouen, St-Nicolas and St-Sauveur. In the district of St-Sauveur, just off the fashionable Rue St-Pierre, are some outstanding Renaissance houses. At No. 1 is the superb mansion of the Escovilles, now the main tourist office. The Théâtre Municipale, near the Place Gambetta, was rebuilt in 1963 and is a classic piece of modern architecture.

CAP DE LA HAGUE, *Manche* (1–A3). This NW extremity of the Cotentin Peninsula facing Alderney and Guernsey is a completely untamed 'land's-end' of truly savage grandeur. From the signalling station on the tip, the coast swings dramatically southward along the Baie d'Écalgrain, edged with fine sands, up to the immense granite cliffs of the **Nez de Jobourg**, the highest in Europe (126m), their awesome appearance only slightly mitigated by brilliant golden patches of gorse. The old Customs Patrol paths follow the contours of the cliffs. Below, the tidal waters of the perilous Alderney Race, running at terrifying speeds, churn and spray over tall splinters of granite rising above the waves.

From the hinterland of this wild region came the men who followed the three sons of Tancred de Hauteville to conquer Sicily and for a while to control the destinies of the whole Byzantine Empire, at a time when Duke William and his sons were consolidating the conquest of England.

CARENTAN, *Manche* (1–A4). The rich alluvial soil of the surrounding countryside attracted marauders and settlers early in the history of the Cotentin, and it is certain that there was a town here by the 5th-c. Today it is a thriving butter and cattle market showing little signs of the fierce fighting which took place as the US troops from Utah Beach drove out the occupying forces in June 1944. The museum of the American 101st Parachutists tells the story vividly. The huge market-place with ancient houses built over 15th-c. arcades seems to ignore all the turbulences of the past. The mostly 13th-c. Gothic church has later additions and a beautiful central tower with a soaring slender spire. The chancel is spanned by a fine wooden rood. The atmosphere of Carentan is enhanced by the long stretch of tree-lined water-way which extends from the port to the open sea.

CAROLLES, *Manche* (10km S of Granville: 1–B3). Situated at the base of a 70m-high cliff on the Bay of Mont-St-Michel, this sheltered floral resort has retained all the atmosphere of the small tranquil watering places beloved by the Edwardians. Endless sweeps of fine sand make it a paradise for children. The town is really divided into two parts with the Bourg built high on the spur of the cliff. There is an infinite variety of woodland walks. 1km N is a spectacular viewing point called Pignon-Butor looking across to the Brittany coast.

CARROUGES, Château de, *Orne* (22km NW of Alençon: 2–D2). Just 1km S of the hilltop village of Carrouges, stands this massive rose-red brick and stone four-square château, built in the late 16th-c. by the powerful Tillières family to replace the ancestral 12th-c. fortress. Surrounded by a moat, it is reached through a most elegant gatehouse with the lines of its steeply pitched roof broken by an elaborate Renaissance window; flanked by four circular towers, each capped by a tall pewter-coloured pepperpot roof, its symmetry is enhanced by a high pink-brick chimney which rises over all.

Now owned by the State, the château with its rich furnishings is open to the public. The formal gardens are beautifully kept and are typical of their period. The classical formalism is relieved by splendid avenues of chestnut trees.

CAUDEBEC-EN-CAUX, *Seine-Maritime* (2–B2). Built on a wide majestic loop of the Seine, roughly halfway between Rouen and Le Havre. So well laid out are its riverside promenade, gardens and quaysides flanked by elegant hotels and restaurants, it is hard to realize that, with the exception of its fine church and three very old houses, the whole town was practically burned to the ground in June 1940.

The ogival Flamboyant Gothic church of Notre-Dame was built during the English occupation of the town in the 15th-c. Over the N door is a stained-glass window which was brought from England as a gift from the last of the English captains commanding the garrison sometime between 1436 and 1448. The great organ with its splendid loft and 2300 pipes was built during the reign of François I and has an international renown. Rich in wood and stone carving, the church has much 16th-c. stained glass of an infinite variety of subjects and depth of colour. The Lady Chapel has a remarkable keystone pendentive, weighing 7 tons and only supported by the lateral arches. It has a drop of some 6m. This was the achievement of the architect Guillaume Le Tellier, who is buried in the chapel. Among the interesting statuary is a very English-looking St George and an 'Ecce Homo' over the sacristy door which conveys a sense of utter desolation. Many of these statues came from the ancient abbey of Jumièges. Outside on the W front the details of the statuary can be studied at eye level; they provide a feast of medieval costumes.

Nearby are the three ancient houses mentioned above, of which the 13th-c. Templars House is the most interesting.

It is, however, the river itself with its busy passing traffic of tankers and pleasure boats which is Caudebec's real magnet. The unique quality of the light attracted artists from Turner to Boudin to come here to paint. On the opposite bank across the river is the forest and national park of Brotonne. Up river eastwards the Seine is spanned by the Brotonne Bridge, opened in 1977, which rivals in grace the famous Tancarville Bridge downstream; seen from the riverside its huge span seems hung on threads of gossamer.

CERISY-LA-FORÊT, *Manche* (14km NE of St-Lô: 1–A4). On the northern edge of a deep forest of beech and oak the Abbey of Cerisy-la-Forêt is a near-perfect expression of Norman Romanesque architecture. The earliest part was built by Duke Robert, father of the Conqueror. The apse with three storeys of fine windows gives a harmony of line perhaps unique in this 11th-c. style. Only three bays of the nave remain of the original seven. Coming out of the church a short tree-lined path links up with the monk's living quarters. The Abbot's Chapel, a gift of St-Louis in the 13th-c., has much of the Gothic grace found in the Ste-Chapelle in Paris. The Monks' Parlour has some interesting graffiti on the remains of the walls.

CHAMP-DE-BATAILLE, Château du, *Eure* (4km NW of Le Neubourg: 2–C2, C3). One of the 'stateliest houses' in Normandy, this superb château was built between 1696 and 1702 and is owned by the Duc d'Harcourt. It is reached by the road linking Brionne with the nearby market town of Le Neubourg. Set on a richly wooded plain and bordering the road, its sheer size comes as something of a surprise. It consists of two 85m-long elegant wings of rose-coloured brick and stone, facing each other and linked by balustraded arms forming a splendid courtyard. The balconied centre *pavillon* of white stone has a beautifully proportioned pediment surmounted by a towered dome. The visitor is likely to enter by the S gate, a huge broken-pedimented Baroque portico, giving a splendid vista through the pilastered archway opposite and the extended avenue crossing a leafy deer park.

Richly furnished with rare *objets d'art*, the panelled rooms give the same impression of spaciousness as the exterior. There are some fine paintings, particularly by Fragonard, and some outstanding sculpture by Canova and Pigalle.

A short distance from the château is the pretty but small village of Ecaquelon in the heart of the woods. Its church contains an altarpiece in alabaster brought from England in the 15th-c.

CHERBOURG, *Manche* (1–A3). Used by traders in the Bronze Age, a key port during the Hundred Years War, it was not until the mid 19th-c. that Cherbourg became an important naval base and arsenal. 1869 saw a Hamburg–America liner dock here and from then on it was as a major transatlantic port that it established its fame. Watching the movements of liners from the Quai de Normandie or the Quai de France is still its great tourist attraction.

Mined and smashed by the retreating Germans in June 1944, the port was rapidly restored to order by the US invading forces. With Pluto, the undersea oil pipeline, fully functioning some weeks later, Cherbourg was to become the principal port of supplies for the Allied Armies. On the summit of the hill overlooking the harbour is the Fort du Roule, once a German stronghold and now the War and Liberation Museum. From the terrace there are striking views across the rebuilt town, the harbour and all its complex installations. During the summer there is the added stimulation of watching the increasingly important Anglo-French yacht races.

7km NW along the coast road to La Hague at **Querqueville** is a miniature shamrock-shaped chapel dedicated to the Celtic St-Germain. From the unprepossessing cemetery are views of entrancing coastal scenery.

CLÉCY, *Calvados* (8km NE of Condé: 2–C1). Although often called the capital of 'Swiss Normandy', Clécy has much more in common with some of the Cumbrian Lake District centres than lofty alpine resorts. It serves as a tourist hub for walkers, climbers and fishermen who come to explore the verdant charms of the delightful Orne Valley. This extends from the ancient town of Putanges-Pont-Ecrepin in the S, to Thury-Harcourt in the N. In both directions from Clécy, the Orne cuts its way through cliffs golden with yellow broom in springtime, through deep gorges and the rocky escarpments of the Armorican Massif. The most dramatic of these overhangs the serpentine tributary river Rouvre at Oëtre Rock. From a café built on the cliff edge there is a spectacular view of the whole wild valley below. It is easily accessible by a route S of the town.

Nearer to hand is the Sugar Loaf Rock. From the summit is a good view of a wide sweeping curve of the Orne. About 2km W is the 260m-high Eminence Rock providing a panoramic view of the Normandy *bocage*. 1km E of the town is the Vey Bridge with an old mill now converted into an inn; its grinding water-wheels make a great splash and noise.

The 16th-c. Placy Manor houses an interesting *folklorique* museum. The ticket to visit the cider cellar includes free cider tasting, and there is a miniature railway in the leisure park much appreciated by children.

CLÈRES, *Seine-Maritime* (10km SE of Tôtes: 2–B3). Just 10km northwards on the main Rouen–Dieppe route at Malaunay, a minor road is clearly signposted to the small town of Clères with its weathered timber-covered market. A few yards away is the somewhat unpretentious entrance to a remarkable wild-life park, a splendid if over-restored Renaissance château, ruins of a feudal castle and a half-timbered manor house dating from the 15th- and 16th-c. The park, though specializing in pink flamingoes, white peacocks, storks, crested cranes, rare oriental geese and ducks and some 120 different species of water fowl, is so interestingly laid out that the antics of large numbers of kangaroos, antelopes and deer can also be enjoyed, and on the little islets which dot the lake Indo-Chinese gibbons can be seen at play high up in the trees. Some rooms of the château are open to the public.

Almost opposite the timbered market is the third largest automobile museum in France. A whole range of machines can be seen at close quarters, from a steam fire-engine of 1878 to some of the most famous racing cars of today.

CONCHES-EN-OUCHE, *Eure* (2–C2). In a pleasantly wooded valley on a curve of the river Rouloir, at the northern limit of the Ouche Region, is this interesting and typically Norman market town. Only 18km from Évreux, it was surprisingly almost undamaged in World War II. The creeper-clad ruin of its 12th-c. castle is reached through the Gothic gateway of the Hôtel-de-Ville leading to a public garden. Its small motte-and-bailey is surrounded by a wide moat, and several ruined towers survive.

Nearby is the town's chief glory, the church of Ste-Foy. An elegant Gothic structure stands on the site of the original church built by Roger de Tosney in the early 11th-c. This Norman warrior had been fighting the Moors in Spain; returning to his hometown of Douves, he passed through Conques in SW France (*see entry in the* Southwest *section*) to pray at the shrine of a child saint called Foy; his zeal seems to have prompted him to filch part of the child's body, and he renamed the town Conches and built a shrine to house the young martyr's relics. Today they lie under the modern high altar. In the N and S aisles is some of the finest stained glass ever made in the 16th-c. The modern tapestry of Christ in Majesty is reminiscent of that of Coventry Cathedral. Three alabasters forming a triptych of the Passion exemplify some of the best work of English carvers of the 15th-c. and can be seen at the end of the S aisle. The alabaster carving in the N aisle is almost as fine, and also of English provenance. A walk on to the terrace on the S side provides lovely views across the peaceful valley.

It is interesting to recall that modern meteorologists owe much to the 13th-c. observer and scholar William of Conches, whose accurate predictions still have power to astound.

COUTAINVILLE, *Manche* (1–A3, B3). 12km W of Coutances, this is perhaps the most forward-looking of the resorts on the W coast of the Cotentin Peninsula. Not only does it have 7km of fine sandy beach, but the influence of the Gulf Stream encourages the growth of semi-tropical foliage on the hills backing the long stretch of dunes. The tropical illusion is heightened by the proliferation of 'South Sea Island' straw huts which have replaced the old bathing cabins. A nine-hole golf course, casino, theatre and race-track are added attractions. The adjoining parish of Agon has a 13th–15th-c. church, and all the surrounding countryside is very pretty with some characteristic old manor houses sheltered in the valleys.

COUTANCES, *Manche* (1–A4, B4). Mentioned as Cosedia in AD 161 by the Roman travel writer Antoninus, by the year 300 the city covered an area roughly the same as Coutances today. It was then called Constantia. By the 5th-c. a church had been built on the site of a Roman temple on the summit of a low hill, and on that same site the present Cathedral soars in all its Norman-Gothic majesty. After centuries of sackings and pillage Coutances became an important bishopric. Under Duke William, the see was given to Geoffrey de Montbray, one of his bishop-knights who later accompanied him on his conquest of England. With funds flowing in from the sons of Tancred de Hauteville from their conquest of Sicily, Geoffrey continued the construction of an impressive Romanesque Cathedral. The work was accelerated by rich rewards pouring in from England. Two of his beautiful Romanesque towers on the W front survived the terrible fire of 1218 which gutted the town. So too did the two enormous pillars of the transept, though these were overlaid with slender, lofty Gothic pillaring when the present church was rebuilt in the ogival style of the 13th-c. The erection of this vast church on the foundations of the earlier building presented a massive challenge to the architects employed by Bishop Hugh de Morville. With no fussy ornamentation to distract the eye, the functional beauty of pure

The Cathedral, Coutances

upswept lines of endless soaring columns is completely satisfying. To stand in the centre of the transept and look up at the domed elegance of the 41m-high octagonal lantern is to look on one of the marvels of Norman-Gothic construction. The blind triforium windows allow the light from the high clerestory above to flood over its own superbly carved balustrade. The chapels radiating from the apse were added in the 14th-c. The central chapel has a serene statue of Our Lady of Coutances of the same period. One of the chapels in the N transept is dedicated to St Thomas-à-Becket with a richly stained-glass window illustrating scenes from his life; it dates from about 1220.

The impact of the sky-piercing pinnacles and spires of the exterior of the Cathedral, capped by the tall domed and balustraded lantern tower, is a miracle of lightness and grace unexcelled by any other church in Normandy.

The Cathedral was fortunately spared during the Battle of Normandy, but the town was mostly destroyed and has been rebuilt with excellent shops and restaurants. It has a particularly fine public garden laid out in the 17th-c. manner on different levels with pools, unusual flower-beds and many rare and beautiful trees.

Just outside the town and dominating the green valley, are the ruins of a 13th-c. aqueduct built on the site of an earlier Roman aqueduct.

DEAUVILLE, *Calvados* (2–C1, C2). Built by the Duc de Morny in the 1860s on the aptly-named Côte Fleurie, this resort, in spite of changing modes and fashions, has remained what he intended it to be: the most elegant watering-place in northern Europe. The rich, the famous, and the merely notorious still flock to Deauville in the high season. On the famous board-walk 'Les Planches' the glamorous models of the great Parisian couturiers parade the newest fashions while competing with stars of theatre, television and films for attention. The long balustraded white casino flanked by opulent hotels remains the main magnet, but the world of sport draws its devotees in almost equal numbers. The yacht club is extending the harbour into a huge marina for the ever-growing numbers of yachts berthing in the estuary of the Toques.

The racing season attracts top jockeys and trainers from all over the world while the polo-grounds have been given a royal cachet.

Colourful bars, restaurants and swimming pools extend down the long promenade fronting wide stretches of golden sand. A world thought dead at the end of the 1920s has survived.

DIÉLETTE, *Manche* (6km NW of Les Pieux: 1–A3). A tiny yacht harbour built within a small 17th-c. port under a rugged mass of granite. Apart from its attraction as a resort, it is a sightseeing centre for wild granite cliff scenery of almost unparalleled grandeur. The cliffs extend for several kilometres in each direction and rise to nearly 100m by Flamanville. The granite has been fissured by gigantic forces of nature into deep crevices. From the top of awesome precipices can be seen enormous boulders torn from the face of the rock and hurled into the sea millions of years ago. The area was once a Druidic centre, of which one dolmen called 'La Pierre au Rey' remains.

DIEPPE, *Seine-Maritime* (2–B2, B3). A bustling, many-faceted port through which more than half a million passengers pass each year. Perched high above the port, dramatically etched against the eastern skyline, is the fishermen's chapel of Notre-Dame-de-Bon-Secours. From this clifftop is a splendid panoramic view of the whole town below. Stretching westward, almost as far as the eye can see, is the long sea-fronted Bd. du Maréchal Foch with its English-looking wide expanses of lawn, dividing it from the busy dual carriageway of the Bd. de Verdun. Hotels, casino, swimming pool and sports complex all contribute vitality to this popular seaside resort. At the far end of the esplanade another chalk cliff rises steeply from the sea, crowned by the formidable mass of Dieppe Castle. Its medieval turrets are linked by strong 17th-c. curtain walls of flint and sandstone. Constructed in 1435, it replaced an earlier fortress built during the reign of the Plantagenet Henry II. It houses a museum with a unique collection of carved ivories, a craft that was established in the Middle Ages and continued well into the 19th-c. Some of the finest examples are model battleships carved by French prisoners of war during the Napoleonic struggles with England. Other galleries have good examples of work by 19th-c. Impressionist painters such as Pissarro, Sisley and Sickert for whom Normandy, and Dieppe especially, had particular appeal because of its unusual qualities of light and colour. From the ramparts there is a good view of the old town.

Dieppe was first colonized by Vikings. From the time of the Norman Dukes, its shipbuilding yards assured its prosperity, and by the end of the 15th-c. Dieppe shipbuilders were renowned throughout Europe. One of these was Jehan Ango, a moneylender to François I who was so rich and powerful that he was able to wage an independent war on the King of Portugal and win (*see also* Varengeville-sur-Mer). Another was Samuel Champlain, who founded his Norman colony in Quebec in 1608. In 1695 the English reduced Dieppe almost to rubble by naval bombardment. Most of the old town still standing is 18th-c.

On 19 August 1942 the town again faced fierce bombardment, as its 1½km of shingle beach became the centre of a landing operation, extending from the little resort of Ste-Marguerite, W of the town, to Berneval 9km to the E. This historic 'Operation Jubilee' was carried out, under extreme difficulties, by a mainly Canadian Commando force of nearly 7000 men. Just behind the rather dilapidated church of St-Rémy, near the centre of the town, is a small stone inscribed 'Two Canadians fell here on 19 August 1942' – sadly commemorating just two of over a thousand Canadians who died that day on this narrow strip of coast together with many of their supporting troops. This terrible experience was to provide invaluable information two years later in the Normandy landings. Canadian flags still fly everywhere and Canadian memorials abound.

At the heart of Dieppe is the famous Café des Tribunaux, its clock-towered gable and its romantic wrought-iron-covered well, the Puits-Salé. Both contrive to give a curiously theatrical Swiss appearance to the square from which radiate all the main shopping streets. At the end of the Grande Rue is the fish market, and on the quayside are excellent and often very cheap fish restaurants. Just off the Place du Puits-Salé is the Rue St-Jacques leading to the cathedral-like Flamboyant Gothic church of St-Jacques, a mixture of 14th-, 15th- and 16th-c. architecture; its early rose-window above the central doorway is particularly fine, as is its flanking 15th-c. tower. Much painted by Pissarro, it is well worth visiting. Look for an interesting modern stained-glass window in St-Anthony's Chapel, evocative of stormy sea turbulence. The artist has used the leading to express a sense of unrest. Also modern is a huge hand-beaten iron candelabra with seventeen branches, standing by the high altar.

The new casino and a well-designed modern hotel are linked by a pepperpot-towered medieval gateway called Les Tourelles, witnessing perhaps Dieppe's indestructibility. Generous parking facilities are free and traffic flows easily with a simple one-way system, despite crowds of visitors in the high season.

DOMFRONT, *Orne* (2–C1). Once a fiercely contested fortified border-town, Domfront is built on a long ridge of rock, high above the river Varenne in the heart of the Normandy *bocage*. Of the castle, which at various times sheltered seven of the Anglo-Norman kings, only two great walls of the keep remain. It was dismantled in the 17th-c. Remains of the ramparts now form a back-drop to a well-laid-out terrace with fine views across the countryside. Many of the 13 original towers still look out over the narrow streets, gateways and ancient rooftops.

Down below on the riverbank is the original 11th-c. Romanesque cruciform church of Notre-Dame-sur-l'Eau, where Henry II's daughter Eleanor was baptized and where Thomas-à-Becket said mass.

Within a radius of less than 10km are some 40 picturesque manor houses dating from the 15th- and 16th-c. in pretty farmland settings.

EAWY, Forêt d', *Seine-Maritime* (12km W of Neufchâtel: 2–B3). One of the three principal forests of Upper Normandy, this beautiful beech woodland, lying in the undulating country between the valleys of the Varenne and the Béthune, was even recently famed for its boar-hunt. On the NE side of the forest the Béthune follows closely the main road between Dieppe and Neufchâtel-en-Bray. On the W side, the trout-filled Varenne follows the D154 Dieppe to St-Saëns road.

The most rewarding way to enjoy the peaceful serenity of Eawy is to enter it from the village of Les Grandes Ventes on the D915, whence a quiet road, the D22, leads SW to join the D154. At the junction with D154 turn left up the valley and follow the signs for the crossroads called Carrefour de la Réformation. The road to the E enters the dense forest of huge beech trees and leads to the Carrefour du Châtelet, then SE to the Carrefour de la Heuze, near a pilgrim chapel dedicated to the patron saint of travellers, St Christopher. This is the centre of the forest, and soon the Allée des Limousins opens up into a fine wide avenue and continues SE in a straight line for some 6km, passing a number of secluded picnic spots provided by the Forestry Administration. Eventually a road to the right emerges from the forest at St-Saëns – but take your choice, for all round the forest are scattered little hamlets and villages, often with old manor houses or interesting churches.

ÉTRETAT, *Seine-Maritime* (2–B2). Straddled between two fantastic cliff formations, Étretat is one of the most popular of the Alabaster Coast resorts. Retaining an almost indefinable elegance, it still has much of the character which attracted so many writers and painters of the last century. The old timber covered market has been happily reconstructed in the Place Maréchal Foch. Much of the church of Notre-Dame dates from the 11th-c., and the sturdy incised pillars of the nave are pure Romanesque – as is the portal, though spoilt by an over-enthusiastic restorer who added a tympanum in the 19th-c. The lantern and other parts of the church are 12th-c. The main attraction of the town lies, however, in the physical grandeur of the two great cliffs, the Amont and the Aval at either end of the shingle beach. The Amont is surmounted by a little chapel, and it was from here that the tragic first attempt to fly the Atlantic was made in 1927. The Aval ends in a huge natural arch caused by sea erosion and faces a 70m-high needle rock. When the sea is rough it presents a truly awesome spectacle.

EU, *Seine-Maritime* (2–B3). This quiet unpretentious town boasted a royal residence from the time of the first Dukes of Normandy until the end of the reign of Louis-Philippe in the mid-19th-c. Only just inside the NE boundary of Normandy, it lies between the sea, some 4km away, and the forest which comes up to the edge of the town. It was here that William the Conqueror received Harold before the latter made his ill-fated promises at Bayeux, and where William married the Count of Flanders' daughter, Matilda. Lawrence O'Toole, 12th-c. Primate and last canonized saint of Ireland, came here and died here, and shares in the dedication of the much restored but still beautifully proportioned collegiate church of Notre-Dame et St-Laurent. The interior, which is endowed with some splendid 15th-c. sculpture, gives a remarkable effect of spaciousness. Below, in the crypt, is the late-12th- or early-13th-c. recumbent sculpture of St Lawrence O'Toole himself, odd man out among the effigies of the Artois Counts of Eu. Near the church and in complete contrast is the 17th-c. Renaissance college chapel with a rather Flemish-looking façade of brick and stone and two flanking domed towers. It was built by Catherine of Clèves, widow of the murdered Duc de Guise who had founded the college in 1573. Their magnificent marble mausoleums are much admired.

The Château d'Eu was rebuilt by the Duc de Guise on the site of earlier royal residences dating back to AD 922. Much restored by the Orleanist Louis-Philippe, it became his favourite palace until he was forced to flee to a refuge in Surrey. It still bears all the marks of his occupation and the décor of Viollet-le-Duc. Understandably, it was much admired by Queen Victoria, who spent two holidays here with the Prince Consort. The fine park laid out by landscapist Le Nôtre blends harmoniously into the surrounding countryside. Inside the grounds is a vigorous equestrian statue of Louis-Philippe.

The **Forest of Eu** is one of the three ancient forests of Upper Normandy. Its three sections extend for about 30km from Eu to the little town of Aumale, from whose early Counts the English family of Albemarle descend. Lying between the rivers Bresle and Yères, it is often 5–6km across. It was jealously preserved by the Dukes of Normandy until it passed successively to the Counts of Eu, to the Orléans family, and finally to the Forestry Administration who are responsible for laying out many of the excellent forest drives and walks. To enjoy to the full this wonderland of tall beeches and great oaks it is essential to stop frequently and explore on foot. From the Ste-Catherine Post, a short walk past a forest warden's house leads to a rewarding viewpoint on the edge of the forest, overlooking the Yères valley. Within the area of the forest are many small hamlets and villages, often with unrestored churches.

ÉVREUX, *Eure* (2–C2, C3). The cathedral town of Évreux on the river Iton gives its name to the whole surrounding region of rich fertile plains. The Romans built here, as did the Gauls and later the marauding Goths and Vikings. On numerous occasions, it has been fired, sacked and rebuilt, by Normans, English and French. In the last war it blazed for a whole week in the German *blitzkrieg* raids of 1940, and in 1944 one whole quarter was practically razed to the ground by the Allied aerial bombardments.

From each of these many disasters some integral part of its splendid Cathedral of Notre-Dame escaped total ruin, as the majestic 12th-c. arcades of the nave bear witness. The resultant mixtures of styles throughout the centuries, culminating in the traceried Flamboyant glory of the N door, have produced a rich expression of French Gothic. Fortunately only the roof was severely damaged in the last war, though the lead spire surmounting the lantern melted in the heat of the 1940 conflagration.

The lofty cool interior has a wealth of stained glass, particularly beautiful in the apse and the great rose-window of Paradise in the S transept. Interesting historical records are depicted in the 15th-c. windows of the Lady Chapel. The fine octagonal 15th-c. lantern and the apsidal windows suffuse the whole of the dignified tessellated chancel with light. The carvings on capitals and choir-stalls are worthy of close inspection. The wrought-iron grille enclosing the chancel is an outstanding piece of 18th-c. craftsmanship. So, too, are those round the Treasury Chapel. Equally interesting are the Renaissance wood-carvings on screens and doors in the many chapels radiating from the ambulatory.

Outside the Cathedral, a path banked by lawns leads to the old Bishop's Palace, a fine example of a 15th-c. partly fortified domestic building. It now houses a museum mostly devoted to the Gallo-Roman epoch. Pleasant little streams from the dividing arms of the river Iton, crossed by stone bridges, make walking a pleasure in this part of the town. The nearby tall 15th-c. bell-tower was once part of an old city gate; the slender stonework capped by a spire rises from a path beside the Iton, and its tocsin bell of 1406 still rings out the hours.

Some way from the Cathedral, at the end of the junction of the Rue de Verdun and the Rue Joséphine, is the former Benedictine abbey church of St-Taurin. It has a beautiful Romanesque arcade and three inspiring stained-glass windows, as well as some amusing misericords rich in medieval humour. Its real treasure, however, is the chiselled and enamelled silver-gilt reliquary of St-Taurin, fashioned in the shape of a miniature Ste-Chapelle. It was presented in the 13th-c. by King Louis IX, better known as St Louis. Taurinus was one of the first bishops of Évreux.

The modern buildings erected since World War II avoid harshness by being set in tree-lined avenues and squares. The town's numerous hotels make it a good centre for touring, and it has an unusually attractive shopping centre.

FALAISE, *Calvados* (2–C1, C2). Birthplace of William the Conqueror, this small market town is dominated physically and historically by the massive fortress built high up on an escarpment overlooking the rocky valley of the river Ante. Almost certainly one of the earliest stone castles in Normandy, it was the home of the 17-year-old Duke Robert when he fell in love with a local

Equestrian statue of William the Conqueror, Falaise

tanner's teenage daughter Herlève, or Arlette in modern French. He took her to live with him in 1027. The following year William was born. Seven years later Robert died on a Crusade to the Holy Land, having first married off Herlève to one of his nobles, to whom she bore the notorious Odo. William the Bastard became Duke of Normandy.

The castle is reached by a steepish incline from the cobblestoned Place Guillaume le Conquérant with its magnificent equestrian statue of William rearing into battle in full panoply of war, raised high on a pedestal and guarded by the bronze statues of his six ducal ancestors. Although the whole town was practically reduced to rubble in Montgomery's great push against Rommel's 7th German Army from June to August 1944, the statue of England's only conqueror emerged from the battle of Falaise unscratched.

The great keep, with strong buttresses soaring to its full height, is slightly mellowed by the six Romanesque arched windows at the top. Henry I had considerably strengthened its defences, and by the time Henry II had taken possession it was all but impregnable. Yet it is easy to imagine the splendour of the court he and his Queen Eleanor of Aquitaine set up here. In 1159 troubadours from all over Europe came to take part in the pageantry of a Court of Love within the vast area of the castle walls.

There is much of interest to see inside the castle. The great hall has its fine chimney and original 12th-c. windows. The dungeon, in which King John's nephew Arthur was imprisoned, can be visited. King William the Lion of Scotland was also incarcerated here during the same period. In a side tower between the main keep and the Talbot

Tower, note the uncomfortable-looking stone seat of one of the latrines.

The round 35m-high Talbot Tower gives a fairy-tale quality to the castle. Though it is named after Henry V's intrepid governor, there is considerable evidence that it may have been built in the 13th-c. and was merely strengthened and enlarged by Henry V. It was even used by the Germans in World War II as an observation post until they were dislodged by Canadian artillery fire. The damage has been expertly repaired.

On the SE angle of the keep is the site of the chapel of St-Prix, badly restored in 1870 and practically destroyed by Allied bombing. The modern bronze memorial bearing the names of 315 companions of the Conqueror survived. A staircase leads down to the crypt where, it is said, the Plantagenet kings hid their treasure.

The two main churches, St-Gervais and Holy Trinity, though badly damaged in the war, have been almost completely restored. Below the castle grounds, between two turrets, is a large stone relief plaque set above a well. The inscription tells the story that this was the spot where Arlette first met her ducal lover. Beyond, the 15th-c. wash-house is well preserved.

At the end of the Rue du Camp Ferme is the picturesque 13th-c. Cordeliers' Gate with its long flight of well-worn steps. It opens out to a lovely view of the Ante valley.

During the summer the whole town is imaginatively floodlit.

FÉCAMP, *Seine-Maritime* (2–B2). Several factors have established the fame of this resort on the Alabaster Coast. The first was the creation of its fishing port, which achieved importance as far back as the 6th-c.; today it is the fourth largest in France and by far the most important for the vast volume of its cod-landings. Fleets of trawlers make regular sailings to the Newfoundland fishing banks. The visitor driving in from the E by way of the picturesque resort of Senneville will have a splendid panoramic view of the town cradled between two chalk cliffs. Its animated harbour stretches right into the very centre of Fécamp. The Freycinet Quay is nearly always crowded with spectators watching the huge daily landings of fish. The many associated industries of fish-processing provide almost complete economic stability for a population of nearly 22,000.

Already by the 7th-c. a pious legend was to lend lustre and lasting fame to Fécamp and a powerful stimulant to its development. The legend ran that Joseph of Arimathea stanched some of the Precious Blood at the time of the Crucifixion and placed it in the care of a nephew, Isaac. He, in turn, hid the relic in the trunk of a fig-tree and entrusted it to the waves of the sea. It was finally cast up on the Normandy coast and came to rest by a spring of water in the town, where it was discovered by a missionary of St-Denis of Paris. A monastery was built and the shrine became the most important place of pilgrimage in France until the building of Mont-St-Michel.

The next development was the establishment of a great Benedictine abbey by the Conqueror's great-grandfather Duke Richard I. Nordic myth and Christian tradition provided a mystic knife, a footprint of an angel, and yet another miracle for good measure. The real achievement, however, was to be found in its schools and library and in a rare standard of scholarship under the reforming Abbot William of Dijon. Richly endowed, it was given the flourishing port of Steyning and other lands in Sussex by Edward the Confessor. Nothing is now left of the abbey since the last vestiges of the monastery were incorporated into the town hall after the Revolution.

The present abbey church of the Holy Trinity is one of the largest in all France. It was built on the site of the original church called the 'Heavenly Gate to Paradise' because of the richness of its gold and silver ornaments. This was destroyed by lightning in 1168. Henri de Sully, kinsman of Henry II, immediately set about rebuilding it. Today, the Renaissance W façade masks a magnificent Norman Gothic interior of noble austerity. A sense of soaring loftiness is heightened by the light diffused from its 40m-high lantern. There are surprising contrasts too. The graceful 18th-c. gilded, wooden, half-domed canopy above the high altar enhances rather than distracts from the fine vaulted proportions of the chancel. Two interesting radiating chapels survive from the earlier church built by Duke Richard I in AD 990. He and his son are buried nearby. The 15th-c. polychrome carving of 'The Falling Asleep of Our Lady' is worth studying for the exquisite details of the heads of the apostles. Just behind the high altar is the Sanctuary of the Precious Blood. Huge pilgrimages still take place on the Tuesday and Thursday after Trinity Sunday.

Finally, perhaps the greatest contribution to Fécamp's claim to world renown lies in its manufacture of the golden nectar called Bene-dictine, said to have been first distilled by a monk called Vincelli in the year 1510. The secret recipe was lost in the French Revolution, but rediscovered in the 19th-c. by Alexandre le Grand, whose name is still on every bottle. In 1892 a vast

The abbey church, Fécamp

French Government Tourist Office

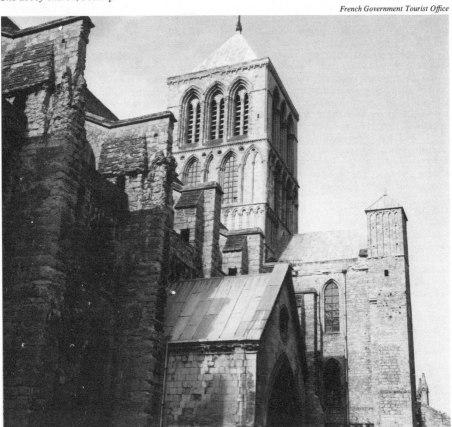

neo-Renaissance building was erected to house the distillery, as well as an interesting museum which contains many works of art from the former monastery. During the season the tour of the distillery is a great tourist attraction.

FONTAINE-HENRY, *Calvados* (10km NW of Caen: 2–C1). Built in a pleasantly wooded valley, the Château Fontaine-Henry is an outstandingly impressive and imposing building. Erected on the site of a 13th-c. keep, it shows the transition from the Gothic ornamentation of the late 15th-c. into the classical style of the 16th-c. The enormously steep roof surmounting one wing is taller than the whole building it covers. The château has some splendid furnishings and a staircase in the grand 16th-c. manner. In the grounds is a 13th-c. chapel.
2km S is a gem of a small 12th-c. church at Thaon, now unused. A key can be obtained for entry.

FORGES-LES-EAUX, *Seine-Maritime* (2–B3). One of the nearest spas to Paris, and made popular by Louis XIII and Cardinal Richelieu, whose massive reclining bronze statue stands at the entrance to the park. 42km NW of Rouen, the town lies in a green geological fault of the Bray region called 'the buttonhole', between the rivers Andelle and Epte. There are some eight different medicinal waters containing many curative minerals which can be taken in a small pavilion, below the imposing white pedimented Casino with its balconied gallery. Just beyond the pavilion is the grotto where Louis and his wife Anne of Austria often came to drink the waters. The park is pleasantly laid out with amenities for boating and tennis. There are two richly decorated 17th-c. façades standing at the park gates. The one nearest the Casino was taken from a hunting-lodge at Versailles, the other, on the opposite side of the road, was part of the Carmelite Convent of Gisors. The town, although rather dull, has some good colour-washed half-timbered houses.

GISORS, *Eure* (2–C3). The capital of the richly fertile lands of the Norman Vexin region. This territory, lying in the valley of the Epte between the Epte and Andelle rivers, was for centuries a turbulent border country between France and Normandy. Today it is a popular and much promoted tourist route linked by the imaginatively landscaped autoroute between Paris and Rouen. Dotted prolifically throughout the region are the ruins of castles and strongholds of the Norman dukes, the Norman and Plantagenet kings and those of the Kings of France. Of all these the Château Gaillard on the Andelle (*see* Les Andelys), and Gisors here on the Epte, are the most important.
The castle stands high on a hill dominating the town. Carefully preserved, it spells out dramatically three centuries of military techniques in building.

In 1096, to protect this strategic gateway into Normandy from three nearby threatening towns in France, William Rufus entrusted the building operations to Robert de Bellême, a renowned military engineer whom he later made Earl of Shrewsbury. Henry I made it almost impregnable by surrounding it with walls and tall fortified towers. Under Henry II, William Earl of Arundel spent much money making the castle more habitable as a royal residence. Among other things he provisioned it with vast amounts of cheeses, imported from England. He also built a chapel dedicated to St Thomas of Canterbury. King John lost Gisors to Philippe-Auguste of France, who built the great surrounding wall and enlarged the keep and probably erected the three-storey Prisoner's Tower. Surprisingly, though it changed hands frequently by treaty (the English again controlled it between 1419 and 1449), the castle never actually fell by assault.
The vast area within the walls has been laid out as a most attractive garden, though the great circular keep on a high mound, with its tall buttressed tower, loses something of its dramatic impact as a consequence. The Prisoner's Tower, entered on the third floor, has a vaulted hall whose chimney, ovens and well are built into the thickness of the walls. Below in the dungeon is a wealth of graffiti, some depicting religious scenes, dancing, and tournaments, mostly dating from the 14th- and 15th-c. A later one on the right of the doorway is dated 1575, inscribed 'Mother of God remember me' and signed N.P. The four-storeyed crenellated Governor's Tower overlooking the town is also worth a visit.
Descending from the castle ramparts the visitor passes the imposing church of St-Gervais-et-St-Protais. The most interesting part is the chancel completed in 1249. Seen from the outside, the rose-window of the E end of the church is almost hidden by a group of ambulatory chapels with pointed gables and amusing gargoyles.
The town was badly damaged in 1940, but much survived to allow it to retain its character, like the timbered 17th-c. wash-house of the rich Guild of Tanners built on a curve of the river.

GRANVILLE, *Manche* (1–B3). Granite-built and presenting a somewhat austere appearance in its upper town Granville has an interesting historical past. It was built by the English in 1439 to consolidate their position against the threat of the French-held Mont-St-Michel. The citadel stood on the site of the present ramparts. From here there are superb views, though an even better panorama can be obtained from the Place de l'Isthone, where on a fine day the Brittany coast can be clearly seen. In the lower town, now the commercial and resort centre, the English dug a large defensive ditch, still called the 'Tranchée aux Anglais', but by 1442 they had been driven out by the Knights of Mont-St-Michel. In World War II the Germans realized the strategic value of this rocky promontory and made it into a fortified stronghold. In early August a Breton-like 'Pardon of the Sea' (*see introduction essay to the Northwest: Brittany section*) draws large crowds to the harbour.

HARAS-DU-PIN, Le, *Orne* (12km E of Argentan: 2–C2). Set in the heart of rich forestlands, the Haras-du-Pin, founded by Colbert, is one of the most important studs in the country. Aptly named the 'Horses' Versailles', the graceful château and stables were planned and designed by Mansart, architect to Louis XIV. The stud was opened 15 years after the King's death. Today the *haras* houses about 200 stallions, many with famous names in the world of horse-breeding.

One can visit the stables accompanied by a groom, and the daily exercise through woods or on training ground is eagerly watched by visitors.

HARCOURT, *Eure* (6km SE of Brionne: 2–C2). This splendid example of a feudal castle somewhat tamed by the elegant living of the 17th- and 18th-c. stands in the centre of the second most important arboretum in France. The double-moated and turreted edifice is reached through a long avenue of trees, with specimens carefully labelled. The medieval gateway over a bridge (originally a drawbridge) leads to an inner courtyard with a well over 70m deep. The ground floor containing the kitchen gives the best idea of its medieval appearance. The grand staircase was built in the early part of the 17th-c. The rooms on the first floor have all been furnished in the more flamboyant style of Louis XIV. During the Hundred Years War the English held the castle for over 30 years. The great family of Harcourt (a name as well known in England as in Normandy) still own the property. A path leads round the 20m-wide outer moat, following the old perimeter wall and enabling the visitor to get a good perspective of the keep and the contrasting towers. During the year various exhibitions are held both inside the castle and in the grounds.

HAVRE, Le, *Seine-Maritime* (2–B1, B2). An important ocean gateway to North America, Le Havre is a relatively modern port by European standards. It was founded by François I in 1517 to replace the silted-up medieval port of Harfleur; by dint of brilliant engineering skill the marshes were drained and the new harbour (Le Havre) opened to sea traffic in the following year. It grew steadily in importance; in the American War of Independence a gamble to supply and buy from the 'rebels' paid off, and its later prosperity was assured by its shipping, banking and international commercial facilities. Today it is the second port of France.

Though by-passed by the actual battle of Normandy, during eight days in September 1944 it was almost completely flattened by continuous Allied bombing. Any port installations left standing were destroyed by the remaining Germans prior to the town's liberation soon after Paris had fallen to the Allied Forces. It took two years just to clear away the rubble.

In 1946 Auguste Perret, Belgian-born French architect and a contemporary of Le Corbusier, was given a free hand to reconstruct the town. He succeeded in building a splendid new city, curiously un-French in atmosphere.

From the Porte-Océane on the front of the Avenue Foch, a wide boulevard flanked by enormous beige-coloured vertical and horizontal buildings in concrete, extends down to the huge open Place de l'Hôtel-de-Ville, one of the largest city squares in Europe. The lines of the surrounding flat-roofed three-storey buildings are broken by six tall ten-storey towers. The town hall, simple in design, is fronted by formal, well-proportioned gardens and typifies the best of Perret's town planning.

One of his outstanding buildings is the church of St-Joseph on the Bd. François I with its impressive steepled tower over 100m high. Inside is a dazzling kaleidoscope of colour from over 12,000 pieces of glass set into concrete-framed panes, with a dominant tone of gold. Four great square pillars support an 80m-high lantern. In spite of its size, the church seems to relate to human values and never overawes.

Nearby on the sea front is the Fine Arts Museum. Built almost entirely of glass and steel, it has a brilliantly conceived roof of glass covered by aluminium slats contrived to filter daylight and artificial light into the various galleries, which are on different levels and reached by gangways. The collection of paintings reflect both the wealth and artistic sensibilities of the Havrais. Not surprisingly, two of the town's eminent 'sons', Eugène Boudin, born across the water at Honfleur, and Raoul Dufy, are well represented.

Since the establishment of the pipeline to Paris, oil forms 80 % of all the commodities handled by the port. The best way to see all the different installations is by the ordinary harbour boat trips. Most of the big liners can be visited by application to the Transatlantic Shipping Company at 89 Bd. de Strasbourg.

Just to the E of the town is the seaside resort of **Ste-Adresse**, which was very fashionable in the 19th-c. and today is making a bid to regain some of its earlier fame. From the grassy terrace of its ancient fort there is a splendid panoramic vista of the whole of Le Havre, the port, the Seine estuary and right across to Honfleur and the Côte de Grâce.

Almost lost at the E edge of Le Havre in a maze of fly-overs and underpasses connecting with the oil-refineries and industrial suburbs, the medieval town of **Harfleur** still has a good deal of character, and its 15th-c. steeple rising 83m remains an important landmark. There are some tombs in the church which must have been there when Henry V landed here in 1415.

HONFLEUR, *Calvados* (2–B2, C2). Even the most cursory visit to this old French port on the W bank of the Seine estuary makes it easy to understand why it became the inspiration of world-renowned poets and painters. Sauntering along the old dockside and watching the colourful sails of yachts and fishing craft, or gazing up to the steep slate roofs of houses often seven storeys high, one is confronted at almost every turn with something to please the eye or some historic building to stimulate interest.

On a wall of the broken pedimented arch of La Lieutenance, a twin-turreted house capped by heather-coloured tiles, is a plaque recording that Samuel Champlain made the first of his many voyages to Canada from here and founded the province of Quebec in 1608. The building is what remains of the Governor's house. The cobblestone streets, lined by partly restored half-timbered houses with overhangs, give a good idea of what 16th-c. Honfleur really looked like.

Dominating the central square, and opposite a delightful old inn, is Honfleur's unique, huge timber-built church of Ste-Catherine. Constructed in 1468 by the port's ship-carpenters on a stone foundation, using oak from the Forest of Touques, it was a thanksgiving offering for the expulsion of the English two years earlier. A S nave was added nearly 30 years later. The roof, like an inverted ship's hull, is supported on massive wooden pillars, and the 16th-c. organ loft has a balustrade with panel carvings of many of the musical instruments of the period. Standing apart from the church is its weatherboarded belfry.

It was the superb light on this part of the Seine estuary that attracted Impressionist painters such as Corot, Monet, Boudin, Bonington and later Jongkind, to form an artists' colony here. They lived at the farmhouse hotel of St-Siméon, built on the site of an ancient lepers' chapel, about 2km down the river, and still a hotel. Many of their paintings are in the Musée Eugène Boudin in Honfleur.

From the summit of the Côte-de-Grâce hill NW of the town are panoramic views of the surrounding countryside, the estuary and the great bridge of Tancarville upstream. Nearby is a famous chapel which attracts large numbers of seafaring pilgrims at Whitsuntide.

HOULGATE, *Calvados* (2km E of Cabourg: 2–C1, C2). Just above Dives-sur-Mer, and right on the coast, is the resort of Houlgate, sheltered by wooded hills. It owes its popularity to the splendid stretches of fine sand. The promenade extends up to the foot of the cliffs, Les Falaises des Vaches Noires, so-called from the seaweed patterns below. From the top are wide panoramic views. On the beach, patient anglers, active shrimpers and seekers after succulent shellfish compete with young geologists looking for rare fossils in the lower strata of clay. It is a pleasant tree-shaded

town set in the pretty countryside of the Drochon Valley.

JUMIÈGES, Abbaye de, *Seine-Maritime* (15km W of Rouen: 2–B3). France has few monastic ruins to compare with Fountains Abbey or Rievaulx Abbey in England, but Jumièges, built on the banks of one of the dramatic loops of the Seine, is an outstanding exception. No one seeing for the first time the two octagonal towers soaring to 43m on either side of the W front can fail to be impressed by the grandiose ruins of the abbey church of Notre-Dame. The massive pillars and Romanesque arches of the long nave sweep up to a height of 27m. Much of the transept is a ruin but one massive wall of the lantern-tower is still supported by a huge rounded arch rising spectacularly above the groin-vaulted galleries. To stand in the centre of the base of the tower and look westward gives some idea of the original vastness of this church. Eastward, the outlines of the enlarged chancel are clearly visible, as well as an ambulatory, with two of the seven radiating chapels still preserved. Most of this is the original building of AD 1040 undertaken by the Benedictine Abbot Robert Champart. Elected Archbishop of Canterbury in 1051 under Edward the Confessor, he became known as Robert the Norman. Showering generous gifts on his Abbey of Jumièges, he saw most of the work completed before his death in 1052. He was buried beneath the chancel. Fifteen years later the Abbey was consecrated with great pomp in the presence of William the Conqueror. Hayling Island, in Hampshire, was given to the Abbey as a gift to mark the occasion.

Its history, however, had started 400 years earlier when St Philibert had settled a brotherhood of monks on the site of an old Roman military camp guarding the Seine. His monks rapidly transformed a tract of marshy land backed by dense forest into a thriving and fertile area. They built their church probably on the site of the present one, as well as two oratories, one of which survives in the ruins of the church of St-Pierre, separated from the main building by the 12th-c. chapterhouse. It was repeatedly pillaged and burned by marauding Vikings sailing up the Seine during the 8th- and 9th-c. Monastic life was not resumed until about 930, and it took another 100 years before the foundations were laid on which Robert the Norman was to build.

The Hundred Years War took its toll, and the following centuries brought fluctuating fortunes. In 1791 the Revolutionary Constitution decreed the suppression of the monasteries, and the last 15 monks left. Most of the precious manuscripts, deeds and books were saved, but the buildings were sold off for the value of the stone. The choir was destroyed and the lantern-tower blown up, demolishing three walls. In 1853 a new owner set about preserving the ruins and later acquired the 17th-c. Abbot's Lodge which had escaped the

Abbaye de Jumièges

original sale. This is now an interesting museum. In 1947 Jumièges became national property.

A little way beyond the monastery is a car ferry across the Seine, and from the hillside on the opposite bank a fine view can be obtained of the Abbey and its tree-shaded grounds.

LESSAY, *Manche* (1–A3). Situated at the mouth of the river Ay, this lively little town is built around its magnificent Romanesque abbey church. In a country so rich in early Norman monastic churches this is still an outstanding example. Constructed in a mellow golden stone, it was founded in 1056 by the neighbouring barons of La Haye du Puits and was completed in the 12th-c. The façade of its W front is deceptively simple, with a single central doorway surmounted by two rounded lights topped by a tall single arched window connected to the triforium, with another small light set into the gable. The whole effect of the church is a tribute to harmony of design and perfect proportion. Badly damaged in 1944, it has been restored with the existing original materials and the beauty of its interior is enhanced by the austerity of its furnishings.

For four days from 9 September the ancient Holy Cross Fair, the most important in Normandy, is held in the town; colourful tents are erected in the immediate countryside, preparing for the vast horse and sheepdog sales which take place each day. Sheep and geese are roasted in the open air, and dancing and music go on far into the night.

Away to the S, extending almost to Coutances, is a sandy wasteland of scrub and gorse called Lande de Lessay; a sort of northern Camargue.

LISIEUX, *Calvados* (2–C2). The long history of Lisieux, centre of the rich and fertile Auge region, has been almost obscured by the phenomenal fame of a young nun from the local Carmelite convent who was canonized in 1925 as Ste Thérèse of the Infant Jesus. Little is left of the old town where she grew up. It was a principal target of aerial bombardment by the Allied Forces on 6 and 7 June 1944. However, the ancient cathedral where she worshipped, the convent where she took her vows, and 'Les Buissonnets', the comfortable middle-class home of her devout family, the Martins, have survived.

Some way out of the town rises the vast neo-Byzantine basilica which bears Ste Thérèse's name. It was built to accommodate the tens of thousands of pilgrims who come here throughout the year from every corner of the earth. The wide esplanade fronting the church was constructed as a processional way. From the top of the dome there is a splendid view of the surrounding countryside. Within its lofty interior, mosaics and stained glass tell the story of this extraordinary young religious who said she would spend her heaven doing good on earth. Although sentimentalized sometimes by her devotees, she led a deeply spiritual life in face of much hardship, and died of tuberculosis in 1897 at the age of 24. She was certainly 'a saint for her times'.

The Carmelite Convent is just across the way from the main tourist office. In the simple austere chapel of the nuns, Ste Thérèse's remains are enshrined in a glass casket enclosing her wax effigy clothed in the coarse brown habit of her order.

In contrast to the basilica, the historic Cathedral of St-Pierre is a jewel of early Transitional architecture. It was built by Bishop Arnoult in 1170 on the site of the earlier Romanesque church which had been consecrated six years before the Conquest. A lantern-tower, completed in 1452, rises above the transept crossing; the proportions between nave and chancel, with solid round pillars sweeping upwards to soaring arches, give a pleasing effect of harmony. It claims, perhaps rightly, to be the first Norman Gothic church of France. The apse, ambulatory and radiating

chapels were completed by 1233, and the enlarged chapel was the work of Bishop Cauchon, a notorious judge in the trial of Joan of Arc. The 12th-c. S doorway, called the Door of Paradise, is flanked by massive buttresses; the gallery over the pinnacled arch was added in the 15th-c. Thomas-à-Becket fled here during his quarrel with Henry II, and his vestments are still kept in the war-damaged church of St-Jacques in the Rue au Char.

The old Bishop's Palace adjoining the Cathedral is now the Palais de Justice. Typical of the triumphalist ecclesiastical pomp of the 17th-c. is the ornate golden robing chamber, with its magnificent coffered painted ceiling, richly gilded.

LOUVIERS, *Eure* (2–C2, C3). Louviers is known for its splendid Flamboyant Gothic church of

The basilica at Lisieux

Notre-Dame. Perhaps the most interesting feature is the contrast between the early 13th-c. chancel and nave and the later, quite extraordinary, embellishment in the 16th-c. The S porch has been described as the highest expression of the art of the silversmith, interpreted in stone. Certainly no masons have ever surpassed the craftsmen of Louviers in the moulding and shaping of stone into a fantasy of intricate swirls, festoons and openwork capped by crocketed pinnacles. The interior is rich in treasures, accumulated during the years of its great wool-weaving prosperity. Among them is some fine sculpture in English alabaster. The E window, filled with brilliant modern glass, filters its colours throughout the church and blends well with the 16th-c. stained glass in the nave.

The town, a centre of light industry, is criss-crossed by the many arms of the river Eure. It has some well-preserved half-timbered houses and an almost Italianate 14th-c. Convent of the Penitents, with the broken arches of its one-time cloisters bordering the placid waters of the river.

LYONS-LA-FORÊT, *Eure* (2–C3). Nestling in the centre of the 100 square kilometres of a vast oak and beech forest, this small town is full of atmosphere and a delight to the eye, with its colour-washed, half-timbered houses and very old inns. The covered market-hall has a sturdy 18th-c. timber roof, hewn from the ancient oaks of the forest. The 15th-c. church, built on older foundations, has a timber belfry and some imposing wooden statues. Henry I died here in 1135, having the previous day eaten his historic 'surfeit' of eel-like lampreys at the nearby Abbey of Mortemer.

Jealously preserved hunting-ground of all the Dukes of Normandy, the forest may well have provided a precedent for the harsh forest laws enacted in England after the Conquest. It is too large to permit any detailed description, but the 42m-tall Bunodière Beech near Gourney-en-Bray and the massive 300-year-old oaks just S of Lyons-La-Forêt are worth seeing. Between the ruined Abbey of Mortemer, and Menesqueville with its beautiful little 12th-c. church, stands the mighty 'God's Beech' ('Hêtre à Dieu') which is nearly 300 years old with a circumference of 4·5m. Trees grow to enormous size in the chalky soil of the forest.

MONT-ST-MICHEL, *Manche* (1–B3). Rising starkly out of the sea at high tide, this pyramidal granite island rock has a fortress, a town, ramparts and a monastery clinging to its sides. It is surmounted by the 11th-c. abbey church whose slender 19th-c. spire is tipped by a gilded statue of St Michael brandishing his sword. The whole complex rises to a height of 150m above sea-level.

Its situation, at the dividing point between Brittany and Normandy where the river Couesnon flows into a 22km-wide estuary, assured its place in history. Already a shrine in Celtic and Roman times, it was sought out by Christian hermits.

Early in the 8th-c. a series of gigantic tidal waves submerged the vast surrounding forest and completely isolated this granite outcrop from the mainland. The violent changes in the ebb and flow of the tides left immense deposits of mud and dangerous quicksands. The tides still flow in with surprising rapidity and at low tide reveal vast stretches of silt and sandbanks rich in colouring. At spring-tides the rise and fall can be as much as 15m.

Roughly at the time of the sea's invasion, St Aubert, a Bishop of Avranches, had a vision of St Michael the Archangel in which, according to legend, he was commanded to build an oratory on the rock. He called it 'St Michael at Peril from the Sea' and it was consecrated on 16 October AD 709. It was, however, under Duke Richard, great-grandfather of the Conqueror, that Benedictine monks began building the abbey in 966. Gifts were showered on the abbey by popes, emperors and kings, not least by Edward the Confessor, who gave the monks title to the Priory of St Michael's Mount in Cornwall. Multitudes of pilgrims thronged to the rock, and the buildings developed and expanded, reaching their culmination by the end of the 15th-c.

Mont-St-Michel is reached from the mainland by a long three-lane causeway, and all cars have to be parked at the base of the rock. The visitor enters the town through the 15th-c. emblazoned 'King's Gate' which leads to the long, winding and steeply up-hill Grande Rue. Immediately on the right is the arcaded lodging of the Abbot's Guard. The ground floors of the medieval granite or half-timbered houses lining the street are used as souvenir shops or restaurants. To the right are the ramparts, mostly built during the Hundred Years War and strengthened in the 15th-c. Of the five great defence towers, the Tour du Nord is the loftiest. The cobbled street becomes stepped as it gets steeper near the parish church of St-Pierre. Some of the columns in here date from the 11th-c. Finally the 90 great steps, or Grand Degré, come into view, leading up to the abbey church. Terrace after terrace is built into the rock, the tall cliff of granite giving the monastic buildings a dizzying verticality.

The interior of the abbey church can hardly fail to impress as the visitor looks down the Romanesque nave and realizes that it is only the transept crossing that stands on the actual level of the rock summit, a few square metres of flat surface; the rest, including church, cloisters and refectory, is on foundations built up from the steep slopes of the granite pinnacle. The chancel was rebuilt in 1421 in decorated Gothic with light granite shafts soaring up to the vault. The superb cloisters, with 277 graceful columns supporting the arches, give the impression of being suspended in mid-air, and there are glorious views of the sea far below. The sense of space and light in the vast refectory can only be described in superlatives. All of these stand above great halls and crypts built into the rock, buttressed and supported by huge blocks of granite. The Knight's Hall, 26m by 18m, is a reminder of the Military Order of St Michael founded in 1469 and whose motto was 'Terror of Immense Ocean'. The 35m-long Guest Chamber evokes the memory of the long list of kings and princes who enjoyed the hospitality of Mont-St-Michel.

At a lower level again are the remains of that first church of Duke Richard, the crypt of Our Lady of the Thirty Tapers, and St Stephen's Chapel built in the 12th-c. for sick pilgrims.

Either by boat or on foot a wonderful impression of the Mont can be gained by looking up at the N side of the rock at a distance. The dramatic impact of that silhouette is never likely to be forgotten.

MORTAIN, *Manche* (1–B4 or 2–C1). Situated halfway up a rocky hillside in undulating country, watered by spuming cascades of the river Cance, this historic small town had to be completely rebuilt after the violent German counter-attack of August 1944. Because of the beauty of its surroundings with deep forestlands, it has become a popular tourist centre. From Mortain came Robert, the half-brother of William the Conqueror, to lead the cavalry attack at Hastings in 1066. The rather severe collegiate church, originally built by the same Count Robert, has a wealth of carved misericords on the choir-stalls. In the sacristy is an early Byzantine pyx with inscriptions in Anglo-Saxon runes.

Just N of the town, past the 25m-high Grande Cascade in a rock-strewn setting, is the 12th- and 13th-c. former Cistercian Abbaye Blanche. It has a large and beautifully proportioned Romanesque cloister.

NEUFCHÂTEL-EN-BRAY, *Seine-Maritime* (2–B3). A cheese distribution centre and a pleasant town set in the heart of the verdant Bray region which contrasts dramatically with the bareness of the surrounding Caux plateau. Right at the centre of the town is the vast, mostly Gothic church of Notre-Dame, still undergoing restoration after severe war damage. A new Civic Centre has been built with an excellent small round theatre constructed of reddish brick and set in spacious green lawns. A few picturesque old houses survived World War II. The Mathon Museum has an interesting *folklorique* collection of Bray arts and crafts. 11km NW at Croixdalle off the D56, the first flying bombs were launched against England.

THE NORMANDY INVASION BEACHES, *Calvados* (From 13km S of Quettehou: 1–A4 to Ouistreham: 2–C1). Along some 80km of the Calvados coast extending to the Cotentin peninsula in the department of Manche, was enacted the greatest military epic in history. Code-named 'Operation Overlord', the mighty cross-

Channel invasion by the Allied Forces to free Europe in World War II was launched on its D-Day, the unforgettable 6 June 1944, during the early hours of the morning.

Long top-secret preparations had included the building of huge artificial ports, called Mulberry Harbours, to be towed across the Channel by a vast fleet of tugs once the initial landings had been effected. Code-named 'Pluto', an undersea fuel pipeline had been laid from the Isle of Wight to emerge at Cherbourg once that port had been captured. They were the vital keys to mobility ensuring the continuous landing of supplies, and fuel to feed the immense number of vehicles involved in this mammoth undertaking. 185,000 men, 20,000 vehicles in more than 4000 craft were landed in spite of adverse weather and ferocious enemy opposition. 20,000 airborne troops were carried in over 1000 planes and gliders to support the landing troops, while 10,000 aircraft bombed, destroyed or disrupted the German lines of communication. All this activity was backed up by the now legendary British 79th Armoured Division with ingenious armoured weaponry never before seen in any war.

There were five main groups of landing beaches. Listing them from E to W, they were code-named 'Sword', 'Juno' and 'Gold' under the command of General Montgomery, and 'Omaha' and 'Utah' under the command of General Bradley.

'**Sword**' extended from Ouistreham to Langrune and was mainly a British operation, assisted by Franco-British Commandos and supported by the 6th Airborne Division of Paratroopers who landed a little to the S of Bénouville.

'**Juno**' took over from 'Sword' at St-Aubin and extended up to Courseulles. This was mainly the responsibility of the Canadian 3rd Division assisted by the 4th Royal Marine Commandos. One month later the Canadians were to be the first troops to enter Caen.

'**Gold**' Beach was a much longer stretch. Here the British 50th Infantry Division landed at Ver-sur-mer and Asnelles, captured and held Arromanches so that the all-important Mulberry Harbours could be brought into position. Meanwhile on this same stretch the 47th Royal Marine Commandos advanced 20km through enemy lines, reaching their objective at the cliff-dominated harbour of Port-en-Bessin the following day.

Here they linked up with the American forces at '**Omaha**' Beach. This was the longest and most difficult landing terrain of all. It extended from just E of Colleville up to Isigny-sur-Mer. The 1st US Infantry Division reinforced by the 116th Infantry Regiment of the 29th Division had to contend with atrocious coastal currents, storms, great walls of barren cliff and the ceaseless bombardment and shelling from the German batteries. In spite of this severe resistance and with casualties running into many thousands, by the following day they were

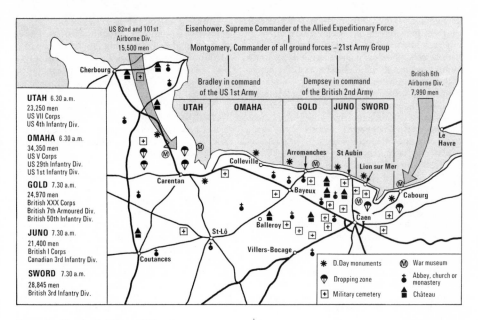

Operation Overlord: 6 June 1944

able to force their way inland. After the capture of Isigny, links were made with the American Divisions landed on 'Utah' Beach.

'**Utah**' stretched from just E of La Madeleine and N of Carentin up to Ravenoville. Four Divisions of Infantry were assisted by the 82nd and 101st Airborne Divisions. 23,250 men were landed on this beach, together with 1700 vehicles and 1695 tons of supplies. By midday enemy resistance had been crushed and American parachutists dropped around Ste-Mère-Église were able to link up with the tanks advancing from the beach-head. The American goal was the liberation of Cherbourg while the British offensive was concentrated on the taking of Caen.

The following is a simple outline of the beaches holding the most interest for visitors who try to re-live, however briefly, some of the heroic hours of that historic day. For simplicity the names of the towns and villages are given in an E to W direction.

Between Caen and the sea, the Ranville–Bénouville Bridge crosses the River Orne and its flanking canal. This was the first Allied objective in the Normandy Campaign. Captured by the British 5th Paratroop Brigade, the section over the canal has been renamed **Pegasus Bridge** after the paratroopers' famous insignia. An excellent museum records the story of that first night and day visually and in great detail. A monument marks the spot of the landings. In **Bénouville** both church and château are worth visiting.

Ouistreham, bordering the Caen canal, is a well-known yachting centre. The adjoining **Riva-Bella**, with its fine sandy beach, has still one blockhouse standing near the Casino and a war memorial to remind the holiday-maker of the important part it played in the invasion.

Colleville-Montgomery, which saw the landing of the Franco-British Commandos, has a statue erected to the memory of the British Commander and has officially hyphenated his name to that of the town.

Lion-sur-Mer is a popular little seaside resort, many of whose villas fronting the sea were fortified by the Germans and saw heavy fighting when enemy reinforcements were sent in to support their defenders on D-Day.

Luc-sur-Mer is a noted, if small, health resort with a spa. Its interesting church has a renowned Romanesque tower and some fine capitals. **Langrune-sur-Mer** is so called from a type of prolific seaweed covering the rocks at low tide. Both these resorts saw heavy fighting on D-Day. Fortified villas, minefields and anti-invasion devices took a heavy toll of the Royal Marine Commandos.

St-Aubin is a bracing, modest seaside town where the remains of a German blockhouse, still containing its gun facing inland, can be seen. A memorial records the landing of the Canadian troops and the Royal Marine Commandos.

Bernières-sur-Mer saw the landing of the French Canadian 'Chaudière' Regiment, supported by the Royal Berkshires, after whom a street has been named. It was here that press and radio reporters were first allowed to land. The village has a beautiful 13th-c. Romanesque church in which the vaulting has been reconstructed. Its impressive belfry and spire stand 67m high.

Courseulles-sur-Mer is a somewhat larger resort famous for its oysters. Its little port at the mouth of the river Seulles to the E of the town was used by British and Canadian forces until the Mulberry Harbour was in service at Arromanches. There is a memorial to the Canadians who landed here, together with a converted Sherman 'swimming tank', a gun and its emplacement. Other memorials have been erected to the Regina Royal Regiment and the Canadian 1st Scottish. Nearby, in the village of **Graye-sur-Mer**, is a plaque commemorating the first visits of George VI and Winston Churchill to the Normandy Beaches. A row of German pillboxes are still in good repair.

Arromanches-les-Bains has a special place in the history of the Normandy landings. Just offshore from the wide curving sandy beach between two cliffs can be seen the remains of the remarkable Mulberry Harbour which was fully operational for the British Forces within 12 days of the initial landing. To understand how this immense artificial harbour, with its breakwater, pierheads and floating piers contained within a 12km semicircular arc, was built and towed into position, a visit is recommended to the excellent Invasion Museum situated at the E end of the beach. It has two cinemas, one showing the Royal Navy film of the landing, the other giving fascinating details of

every aspect of the Mulberry Harbour from its earliest conception to the daily landing of 9000 tons of materials, building up to over half a million tons by the following August. Uniforms, weapons, blow-ups of military photographs, plans, maps and autographs are all superbly displayed.

Port-en-Bessin, cradled between tall cliffs, marked the eastern boundary of the American 'Omaha' Beach. It is once again the animated and colourful fishing port painted by the Post-Impressionate Seurat in the last century. Taken by British Commandos on the day after D-Day, it saw the link-up with American forces whose desperate fighting with tragic losses continued against terrifying odds for 14km westward.

A short distance to the N of **St-Laurent-sur-Mer**, on a high plateau overlooking the sea and above the beach where the first casualties of D-Day were temporarily buried, are nearly 10,000 graves of American servicemen. In a setting of moving simplicity, and radiating in all directions against long sweeps of lawn, the white marble gravestones are each marked with a cross or a Star of David with the combatant's name incised – except for 307 marked 'Known but to God'. An impressive semi-circular colonnaded monument stands near the entrance, with a loggia at each end containing huge marble relief-maps to tell the story of the liberation of France. Centred between the middle columns is a herculean bronze statue

Mulberry Harbour, Arromanches

Douglas Dickins

depicting the 'Spirit of American Youth' by the sculptor Donald de Luc. The statue is impressively reflected in the blue water of a large rectangular pool facing the colonnade.

Nowhere is there a more vivid witness to the seemingly insuperable difficulties encountered on 'Omaha' Beach than at the **Pointe-du-Hoc**. Spectacular needlepointed rocks rise up steeply from the sea against a sheer face of almost impregnable cliff; yet three companies of the 2nd Rangers Battalion scaled these heights with ropes and ladders and succeeded in taking the enemy batteries, aided by supporting fire from a British and an American destroyer. A tall granite stele near the edge of the cliff bears an inscription in French and English. Otherwise this battlefield has been left as it was after D-Day, with shell and bomb craters all round and smashed gun emplacements, which give some idea of the tough opposition the Americans encountered from the German Atlantic defence. Two days later the 29th Infantry Division had stormed their way into **Isigny** and linked up with the forces from 'Utah' Beach.

Within the Commune of **Ste-Marie-du-Mont**, where there is a fine mostly 12th-c. church, about 6km to the N is a boundary of the main 'Utah' landing beach at **La Madeleine**. On the outskirts is a monument to the 1st Brigade of US Engineers whose work in the weeks following the landing enabled 836,000 men, 220,000 vehicles and 750,000 tons of war material to be brought ashore. Nearby in a German blockhouse is a memorial crypt dedicated to the Americans who died in this most successful of the US assaults. Beyond this is the impressive American Commemorative Monument reached by a long flight of steps. Here too is yet another German blockhouse converted into an important museum housing many unique exhibits, including a huge model of the whole area of the landings, with lighted dioramas to illustrate the story of the campaign. Windows on one side of the building look out on to the actual beach. Some idea of what the battlefield looked like can be gained by walking over the dunes where landing craft, guns, a tank and many pillboxes are still half submerged in the sand.

At **Ste-Mère-Église**, a little inland to the W where 15,500 American Paratroopers of the 82nd and 101st Airborne Division were dropped to protect 'Utah' Beach, is another excellent museum. Under a domed roof representing a parachute is a collection of some of the finest military photographs to come out of the war. Weapons, models, documents and even a 'Waco' glider are all well displayed.

The first of the commemorative kilometre stones along the Liberty Highway, which stretches from 'Utah' Beach right across northern France to Metz, can be seen nearby.

PONT-AUDEMER, *Eure* (2–C2). The principal town on the river Risle, this one-time port played a strategic part in William the Conqueror's plans for the invasion of England. In the Middle Ages it became an important centre for the tanning industry and remains so today in spite of the large expansion of other enterprises.

The town seems built on endless little waterways deriving from the Risle. Its many half-timbered and stone-façaded buildings have charming wrought-iron balconies overhanging the water, giving it some resemblance to Bruges. One of these houses is the ancient Vieux Puits Inn near the 'port'; it is still a hostelry and has retained its old Norman interior.

The church of St-Ouen has an austere early Romanesque chancel. The later nave with a coffered vault has a balustraded triforium as well as a clerestory above the richly decorated Flamboyant arches. Renaissance side chapels are lit with some magnificent glass. Through the Renaissance arch to the baptistry can be found a very ancient font with curious early carving. The two alabaster relief panels, one of St George, were both imported from England in the 15th-c.

ROUEN, *Seine-Maritime* (2–B3). Capital of Upper Normandy, cradled in a valley of protective wooded hills on a sweeping curve of the river Seine, Rouen is the fifth largest port in France, with a population (including suburbs) fast climbing towards the half-million mark. Its history is a rich tapestry of stirring events. Under the Roman Emperor Diocletian, as Rotomagus it became the capital of a Gallo-Roman province, and its first bishopric was established. After the Roman withdrawal it survived centuries of violence by Franks and Northmen until Rollo, ancestor of William the Conqueror, made it the capital of the new Norman Duchy in AD 911. From the time of the Conquest in 1066 its close links with England were firmly forged.

After Henry II's marriage to Eleanor of Aquitaine in 1152 Rouen became the administrative centre of a vast Anglo-Norman territory extending from the Pyrenees to the Cheviots of Scotland. Throughout the 12th-c. the Kings of England were solemnly invested as Dukes of Normandy in Rouen Cathedral after their coronation in Westminster Abbey. Even after the French had wrested province and city from King John in 1204, the privileged trade with England continued to be its main source of prosperity. If the disasters of the Hundred Years War struck cruelly, worse was to come with the bitter siege of Rouen by Henry V. In 1419 the city surrendered to the English. Under Henry's brother the Duke of Bedford, Regent for the infant Henry VI, the town was rapidly rebuilt with great Gothic splendour. The vacillation of their Burgundian allies, the trial and execution of Joan of Arc in 1431 and the death of the Duke four years later, all contributed to the defeat and expulsion of the English by Charles VII in 1449. Thereafter the city's destinies were bound up with France.

By 1460 its wealth and influence were restored,

and for the next hundred years were manifested in superb Renaissance and Flamboyant Gothic buildings. The Wars of Religion once again caused havoc and destruction. The French Revolution halted for a while a new spate of classical building and promotion of industry. The 19th-c. brought a mixed bag of industrial progress and many disasters of planning. The latter were mostly wiped out by the terrible bombardments of 1940 and (especially) June 1944 which destroyed most of the old quarter of the town, its bridges and a vast area of the industrialized left bank.

With the end of the war Rouen again asserted its capacity to survive. Rapidly the Ministry of Historic Buildings set about restoring the badly damaged Cathedral, the churches of St-Ouen, St-Maclou and many others, as well as a large number of ancient houses whose immensely strong wooden frames had withstood the blast of bombs. The two old bridges, the Pont Boïeldieu and the Pont Corneille, were rebuilt and two fine new bridges, the Pont Jeanne d'Arc and the Pont Guillaume-le-Conquérant, constructed to enable the ever-growing volume of traffic to flow easily between left and right banks. The deepening of channels in the river, the reconstruction of port and quays, the establishment of vast new industries, have all contributed to restore and increase Rouen's economic vitality.

Amid its prolific wealth of historic buildings, the two indisputable principal monuments of Rouen are its Cathedral and the Great Clock or Gros-Horloge.

The impressive CATHEDRAL OF NOTRE-DAME is a history lesson in stone of the long development of Gothic architecture. It is the third cathedral to stand on its present site. Of the Romanesque cathedral consecrated in the presence of Duke William three years before the Conquest only the crypt and three tiers of the NW tower of St-Romain have survived; the choir and transept were burned to the ground in 1200. With the financial aid of King John and the labour of the town's citizens, the Cathedral was rapidly rebuilt. Between the St-Romain Tower and the elaborate Butter Tower, so called from an indulgence allowing butter to be eaten in Lent, four centuries of flowing Gothic art can be seen, culminating in the Cathedral's dominant Flamboyant style. The façade is such an exuberant riot of crockets, lattices and pinnacled niches, that the eye can hardly take in the detail as it looks upwards to the 151m-high open ironwork spire above the lantern-tower – the tallest spire in France. First erected in the 19th-c., it was reinforced with stainless steel after being damaged in World War II. The great W door is flanked by the two exquisite early doorways of St John and St Stephen. The

Rouen

French Government Tourist Office

imaginative medallions sculpted on the doors of the S and N transept are worthy of close inspection for their amusing fantasies. The S wall had to be totally rebuilt after the war, but its reconstruction has perfectly reproduced the 14th-c. original.

The interior is surprisingly austere, depending on the soaring pillars for effect. The lantern tower over the transept crossing rises to a height of 50m from the ground to the keystone of the vault. A wealth of fine 13th-c. and 14th-c. stained glass was preserved from destruction during World War II, some of it signed by the master craftsman Clément of Chartres. The splendid window of St-Julian-the-Hospitaller was erected by the Fishmongers' Guild in the 13th-c. on the N side of the ambulatory. Here are some of the tombs of the early Dukes as well as that of Henry Plantagenet, son of Henry II and elder brother of Richard-Cœur-de-Lion. Richard's tomb is on the S side to the right of the high altar; only his heart is buried here – his other remains are interred in the Abbey of Fontevrault. The beautiful Lady Chapel was reconstructed in the 14th-c. as an expression of the townsfolk's marital devotion. Against its Gothic background is the truly splendid early 16th-c. Lombardian Renaissance tomb of the immensely powerful minister of Louis XII, Cardinal Arch-bishop Georges d'Amboise and his nephew, also Georges, who succeeded him and had the tomb altered so that his praying effigy might be included with that of his uncle. Close by is another Renaissance tomb of different character, that of the Seneschal Louis de Brézé, husband of the remarkable Diane de Poitiers.

Across the square facing the Cathedral's W door is another Renaissance building, once the Treasury and now the tourist office. In contrast is the nearby modern Palais des Congrès, housing exhibitions, conference halls and a museum.

The GROS HORLOGE, magnet of all visitors to Rouen, is a huge ornate and colourful clock with a single hand pointing the hours over a gilded oriflamme. The whole is mounted on a back-ground of brilliant scarlets and blues, where classical gods and goddesses mark the ever-changing days. It was taken from the adjoining Gothic belfry and placed on the present Renais-sance arch in 1529. Within the belfry still hangs a bell cast in 1260 which rings the Conqueror's 'curfew' each night at 9 p.m. In one corner of the arch, angled between the belfry and some timber-framed houses, is an elegant Louis XV 'rocaille' fountain of 1732. All these different styles blend in perfect harmony.

The long cobbled street which passes under the arch extends from the Place du Vieux-Marché, where Joan of Arc was burned, to the Cathedral Square, whose crowded shops and cafés have an added vitality now that it is a pedestrian precinct. Half-timbered houses showing changing styles from the end of the 15th-c. up to the beginning of the 17th-c. can still be seen in the streets around the

Cathedral, particularly in the Rue Damiette, the Place Barthélémy and the Rue St-Romain, opposite the archiepiscopal palace, which leads to the church of ST-MACLOU, a jewel of Rouen's Flamboyant Gothic. Note the charming 'cherubim-pissant' fountain on the N side. Nearby is the celebrated Cloister of St-Maclou, once a charnel house, whose timbered houses have macabre carvings of a Dance of Death; it is now the centre of the School of Fine Arts and is open to the public.

A short walk away is the abbey church of ST-OUEN, the largest church in Rouen and one of the finest in France. Its chancel and nave together are 134m long. A wealth of 14th-c. stained glass above the delicate clerestory was saved from the iconoclastic fury of the Huguenots in the 16th-c.; its choir-grille is a masterpiece of 18th-c. Rouenais ironsmiths' art. The adjoining classical Hôtel-de-Ville was once part of the abbey. In the centre of its vast square is a hatless equestrian statue of Napoleon.

Much damaged during the war, the Flamboyant Gothic PALAIS DE JUSTICE is being meticulously restored. Once the Exchequer of Normandy, it became the Parliament under François I. Its sheer opulence is heightened at night when the whole building is floodlit. Nearby, towards the river, is a remarkable part-Gothic, part-Renaissance early-16th-c. house, the Bourgtheroulds (pronounced 'Boortrood') Mansion. Built by a Counsellor to the Exchequer, it now houses a well-known bank. One of the lower friezes above the arches on the S side records the story of the Field of Cloth of Gold when Henry VIII of England met François I amid scenes of unprecedented splendour.

The church of St Patrick, with fine stained glass, is a reminder of the direct commerce held with Ireland in the 10th-c., later expanded under Henry II to a monopoly in fish, leather and sables, thus establishing a thriving Irish colony in the city.

Museums and art galleries abound. The Musée des Beaux-Arts houses many world-renowned paint-ings; the Secq des Tournelles Museum has a unique collection of the ironsmith's art; the antiques museum in the old Visitandines Convent exhibits fine ivories and gold and silver objets d'art. The small Joan of Arc Museum in the Place du Vieux-Marché has interesting relics. The latter square is being completely rebuilt with a new cantilevered church, a national monument cover-ing the site where Joan of Arc was burned. The monument, a huge cross, church and market are being planned as one complex with a vast car park beneath. The fine timber-framed houses surround-ing the old market place will fortunately remain untouched. Another grim reminder of Joan's persecution is the pepperpot-roofed tower called La Tour Jeanne d'Arc, in the Rue du Donjon, just N of the Musée des Beaux-Arts; it is all that remains of Philippe-Auguste's massive medieval castle. Here Joan was imprisoned and threatened with torture; some documents of the trial are exhibited. Across the river, soaring above the Pont Boïeldieu, a skyscraper tower has been built to house the archives department; linked to the graceful horizontal curves of the Préfecture, it is a new and not unpleasing landmark.

ST-GERMAIN-DE-LIVET, Château de, *Calvados* (6km S of Lisieux: 2–C2). A delightful 16th-c. moated château just S of Lisieux in the rich Auge countryside. With its façade patterned in a chequerwork of brick and stone it is one of the best examples of 15th-c. half-timbered Norman manor houses in the duchy. Both house and gardens are open on most days except during the Christmas and New Year season.

ST-LÔ, *Manche* (1–A4). Looking up from the tree-lined banks of the river Vire to the massive round machicolated tower and the ramparts built high on the spur of a rock, it is hard to realize that St-Lô, capital of the department of Manche, was almost completely destroyed in one of the bitterest operations against the Germans in the summer of 1944. It took 20 years to rebuild. Fortunately, care has been taken to preserve the dramatic outlines of the oldest quarter, the medieval 'Enclos' in the upper part of the town.

The new town has been conceived with imagination. Its Civic Centre is dominated by a lofty open-work concrete tower, contrasting with the remains of the old prison porch, preserved within a war memorial which lists hundreds of names of those executed and deported from St-Lô during World War II.

Restoration of the fine 14th- and 15th-c. church of Notre-Dame continues with sensitive understanding. The two mutilated towers of the W front, though reinforced, have been preserved as a perpetual reminder of the town's ordeal. The 18th-c. rood-screen survived the terrible devastation. This is vividly illustrated by photographs exhibited on the S side of the church. A graceful 14th-c. statue of the Blessed Virgin is set back between soaring slender columns. By the N wall is an unusual open-air pulpit which also escaped damage. At the end of the Champ de Mars, one of the many planned open spaces which are a feature of the new town, the old Romanesque church of Ste-Croix has been similarly and successfully restored.

The Hôtel-de-Ville houses an excellent art collection, including some priceless tapestries. Mosaics by Fernand Léger are incorporated into the façade of the Franco-American Memorial Hospital on the road towards Villedieu.

At the other end of the town, it is possible to visit the famous St-Lô Stud, which has some 250 thoroughbred stallions of English, Norman and Percheron origin.

ST-SAUVEUR-LE-VICOMTE, *Manche* (14km S of Valognes: 1–A3, A4). Rebuilt after the bombardments of 1944, this little town in the granite heart of the Cotentin peninsula still manages to evoke its historic past. The remains of the feudal fortress with its massive square keep and towers are a reminder of its importance during the Hundred Years War. The 13th-c. Benedictine abbey, with its Romanesque nave, was restored in the 19th-c. by the foundress of the worldwide Order of the Sisters of Mercy. She is buried in the church. Nearby, river fishing is popular, and there are many attractive picnicking sites in the forest of St-Sauveur.

ST-SEVER-CALVADOS, *Calvados* (12km W of Vire: 1–B4). On the edge of the richly wooded forest of St-Sever, this small market town grew up around an ancient Benedictine abbey, rebuilt in the 11th-c. on the site of a hermitage 500 years older. The granite church just below the main street was, however, mostly built between the 13th- and 14th-c. Its interior is impressive, with arches soaring from earlier Romanesque bases, corbels carved to represent various reptilian creatures from dragons to scorpions, and it has a pleasantly austere lantern-tower. An 18th-c. belfry stands isolated from the church.

ST-VAAST-LA-HOUGUE, *Manche* (2km E of Quettehou: 1–A4). An attractive little fishing port on the E coast of the Cotentin peninsula. Edward III landed his troops here before the battle of Crécy. Here too Louis XIV assembled a fleet to help James II regain his throne, but it was quickly dispersed by the English off the nearby Ile de Tatihou.

The apse of the 11th-c. fishermen's chapel at the end of the harbour is painted white as a navigational marker for incoming yachts and fishing-boats. A causeway now leads to the fortified island of La Hougue where it is possible to walk round the 17th-c. granite walls. The oysters from St-Vaast are good, plentiful and cheap.

ST-VALERY-EN-CAUX, *Seine-Maritime* (2–B2). Prior to its almost total destruction in 1940 St-Valery was a fishing and coastal trading port. After the collapse of the Somme front, the British 10th Army fought a desperate rearguard action here as they were driven towards the sea and the 51st Highland Division was almost wiped out. Their surrender was accepted by General Rommel. A monument to the British Army stands high on the chalk cliff, La Falaise d'Amont, to the right of the harbour, and on the opposite cliff is the memorial to their comrades of the 2nd French Cavalry. Rebuilding their town from scratch, the inhabitants used initiative and ingenuity to turn it into a popular resort and yachting centre. Beneath its alabaster cliffs is a safe beach with sand at low tide. On the quayside the Renaissance house visited by Henri IV has been restored and an impressive and lofty church built in the market-place.

ST-WANDRILLE, *Seine-Maritime* (3km E of Caudebec: 2–B2). A small village which takes its name from the monastery founded in AD 649 by Count Wandrille, a man possessed of great physical beauty and a yearning for the religious life who became known as 'God's True Athlete'. After he and his wife renounced their married state, Wandrille and his followers came to settle in this wooded valley watered by a stream called La Fontenelle. Under this name and the Benedictine rule, the abbey, school and library became famous. The Emperor Charlemagne appointed the author of his great law reforms to be its abbot. *The Epic of the Abbots of Fontenelle*, written in 831, was the very first history of a western monastery. Within a few years the peace of the 'Valley of the Saints' was shattered by the terrifying invasion of the Vikings, and monastery, church and school were destroyed. With Christianity restored by the Norman Dukes, the monastery was rebuilt. Again it flourished, and by the 13th-c. a great Gothic church soared above the woodlands of the valley. With the end of the Wars of Religion, the abbey became wealthy again. The building activity of this period has firmly left its stamp of French Classical architecture on much of the present monastery and is exemplified by the imposing Jarente Gate linking two elegant pavilions. With the French Revolution, the monks were dispersed and the abbey church allowed to fall into ruin. In the mid-19th-c. the abbey was bought by the English Marquis of Stacpool. He built another gateway and helped to preserve the 14th-c. S gallery of the original cloisters and the three remaining 15th-c. galleries as well as the exquisite Flamboyant lavabo with its grinning jester set above the ornate carving, warning against intemperance. In 1894 the Benedictines returned, until they were expelled from France under the anti-clerical laws of 1901. For some years Maurice Maeterlinck, author of *The Blue Bird*, lived here. In 1931 the abbey was restored to the monks.

The 33m-long refectory, with the original Norman intersecting arches and earlier 11th-c. herringbone wall, has been returned to its original use, as have the cloisters and 17th-c. chapter house. Although the lofty springing of the ruined transept arches against the open sky make the greatest romantic appeal, it is the present monastic church that excites the admiration of all visitors. In 1966 the monks acquired a 15th-c. tithe barn at La Neuville du Bosc some 50km away. It was 48m long and 16m wide and 12m high. Stone by stone and timber by timber it was transported to its present site. Its stark simplicity conveys a sense of breathtaking beauty with its plain altar set on the raised white stone of the sanctuary. It depends for decoration on the massive 15th-c. timber posts, supports and beams. Every piece of wood is wooden-pegged. A splendid new organ has been installed to provide accompaniment to the Gregorian chant. Before leaving the grounds, visit the little 10th-c. Oratory of St-Saturninus, with its three apsidal chapels and primitive carving of grotesques.

SÉES, *Orne* (2–C2). Time seems to stand still in the ancient city of Sées. Its bishopric was old long before early Norman marauders came and destroyed the Cathedral of St-Latrium. Centuries later reparation was made, and the present lofty fane is a remarkable achievement of the 12th- and 13th-c. Norman-Gothic. The chancel has a splendid upsweep of columns to the fine vaulted roof and is lit by a vast expanse of glass. The triforium windows of the transept still glow with the rich colouring given them by the 13th-c. craftsmen. The serenely beautiful marble 'Madonna and Child' facing the high altar is 14th-c. and escaped damage in the Wars of Religion and the Revolution.

An air of dilapidation seems to hang over the surrounding streets, with the faded façades of convents and community houses which still manage to witness to their important ecclesiastical past.

7km W is the curiously named **Château d'O**. Originally built in the late 15th-c., it shows a steady transition from Gothic to early Renaissance. Chequerboard ornamentation, highly decorated turrets beneath steeply pitched roofs, and the whole château reflected in the waters of a wide moat, make a visually pleasing and romantic impression.

TANCARVILLE, *Seine-Maritime* (2–B2). The village, once the seat of the proud Norman family of Tancarville, descendants of the almost mythical Tancred of the Vikings, is now dwarfed by the mighty suspension bridge which bears its name. Linking Le Havre and the Caux promontory with the S side of the widening estuary of the Seine, it gives access to western Normandy. Built in 1959, it is a miracle of grace and brilliant engineering skill. 58,000 tons of concrete and 18,000 tons of steel went into its making. It is 1410m long, 608m spanning the distance between its two 124m-high pylons. Soaring 50m above the river at high tide it allows large tonnage ships clear passage up to Rouen. It is perhaps seen at its best when floodlit at night.

On a spur of the wooded chalk cliff above the village is the Eagle Tower, the only part of the feudal castle built by Henry I of England that remains intact. This remained in the hands of the Tancarville family until 1320. The modern castle was built in the 18th-c. The views from the terrace are quite spectacular.

TRÉPORT, Le, *Seine-Maritime* (2–B3). This picturesque fishing port and lively seaside resort is situated at the mouth of the river Bresle. Once a major maritime port, it was burned down several times by the English in the Hundred Years War. Its importance diminished as the river silted up.

The suspension bridge at Tancarville

Hotels, colourful shops and fish restaurants line the harbour quay, and a popular broadwalk stretches down to the white lighthouse. Across the river dividing the provinces of Normandy and Picardy lies its twin town of Les Mers-les-Bains.

At a right angle to the new casino the Digue Promenade runs the length of the long grey shingle beach. The sheer white chalk cliffs that rise steeply behind give their name to the Alabaster Coast which extends SW for some 150km to Le Havre. A telecabin car takes visitors up from the beach to the summit of the cliff crowned by a large Calvary. From the terraces there is a good view of the coastline and the harbour below. Queen Victoria recorded two enthusiastic visits she made to the town.

TROUVILLE, *Calvados* (2–C1, C2). On the E side of the Toques estuary, Trouville is a lively fishing port and popular seaside resort. Made famous by the Empress Eugénie at the beginning of the Third Empire, the town has retained much of the flavour of its early opulence without degenerating into seediness. Its somewhat flamboyant casino backing on to the harbour has made the concession to changing modes by allowing a large Olympic-sized swimming pool to be built almost on its doorstep. Like its somewhat more fashionable neighbour Deauville, it has a boardwalk stretching the whole length of its beach. The lovely wide sands with safe bathing make it still one of the most favoured family resorts of France. In spite of the crowds, it is easy to imagine why the Impressionists were so concerned to capture on canvas the illimitable

light and space conjured by sea, sky and sand. While all sporting amenities are available to the visitor, it is still the bustle and colour of the fishing harbour, quite unspoilt by tourism, which draws the crowds to the quayside.

The airport at St-Gatien, with fast links between London, Paris, Lyon and the Channel Islands, is only 6km S of the town.

VALOGNES, *Manche* (1–A3, A4). Only 20km from Cherbourg, Valognes, a pleasant butter-market town, inevitably suffered near annihilation in the American advance of 1944. Rebuilt, it has regained much of its earlier charm. Many of its numerous 17th- and 18th-c. town houses are now restored to the elegance which had caused it to be called the 'Norman Versailles', particularly the Hôtel de Beaumont and the house from which the unpopular French King Charles X fled to England after the revolt of 1830.

On the NE outskirts is the ancient Roman city of Alléaume where archaeologists have uncovered the remains of important thermal baths. The nearby church, part of which dates from the 11th-c., amazingly escaped war damage.

VARENGEVILLE-SUR-MER, *Seine-Maritime* (5km W of Dieppe: 2–B2, B3). A somewhat scattered village with some Norman farmhouses. It is on the main coast road towards St-Valery-en-Caux.

Just before you enter the village, a signpost to the left points the way down a narrow lane, a double beech-lined driveway to the Manoir d'Ango. It was built in 1530 by the astute Dieppe shipbuilder Jehan Ango, appropriately named the Médici of Dieppe (he was moneylender to François I). He decided to build his country home in the prevailing style of Florence. Surrounding a quadrangle, the steeply roofed house is constructed in black with white stones forming pleasing geometric patterns. Above the raised arched galleries runs a frieze spaced with medallions, bearing the monogram of François I and his Queen who were frequent guests at the house. The Queen, jealous of the opulence and wealth of her host, eventually brought about his downfall and near ruin. At one corner of the courtyard is what must be one of the most imposing of all dovecots, with a vast almost oriental dome surmounting a round tower of intricately blended stone and brick with niches for 1600 pairs of doves; Ango, who had just won a war against Portugal, was determined that his *colombier* should outshine all in Normandy. The house, well restored, is privately owned but open to the public.

Back on the main road, a short drive through the village leads to a fork by a café with a cul-de-sac sign and a signpost pointing towards the church of Varengeville. Reached by a twisting narrow lane, the church is dramatically situated almost on the cliff edge overlooking the sea. Its stone-and-flint construction, patterned with brick, stands out boldly against the sea, with sweeping vistas of high chalk cliffs stretching northward to a distant view of Dieppe. Mostly 14th-c., the church still retains many 12th-c. Romanesque features. It has an unusual 'Tree of Jesse' window in blues and ambers designed by Georges Braque. The simple tomb recording his death in 1963 lies in the churchyard.

Halfway between the village and church a noticeboard at the entrance to a driveway records that 'the famous British architect of New Delhi, Sir Edwin Lutyens, built the house known as Le Bois des Moutiers in 1898'. The real glory of the house lies in the beautiful gardens laid out by the *fin-de-siècle* English landscape gardener, the remarkable Miss Jekyll. The gardens, which are always open to the public, are a joy of sweeping vistas of sloping lawns broken by a progression of vivid colours from flowering shrubs; rhododendrons, azaleas and rare camellias massed for their colour effect. Tall cedars lend their shade to open spaces; trees from the Himalayas, Japan, Brazil, etc. abound and flourish. Paths and alleys lead to unexpected finds of rare plants, while roses, hydrangeas and unusual clematis all lend colour around the mellowed house. A new arboretum is being planned.

3km W at Ste-Marguerite-sur-Mer is a completely unspoilt small Romanesque church of great beauty.

VASCOEUIL, Château de, *Eure* (9km NW of Lyons-la-Forêt: 2–C3). Not far from the Forest of Lyons at a spot where the river Crevon flows into

the Andelle, the Château de Vascoeuil, perhaps more a fortified manor than castle, is set in beautiful surroundings of gardens and waterways. Attractive half-timbered cottages have been reconstructed in the grounds. Built in the 14th-c. and completed by the 16th-c., it has been well restored by the present owners and is often used for modern art exhibitions. Its tall octagon tower, with a tiled pepperpot dome, is an interesting feature, so too is a fine *colombier* or brick dovecot. The rooms of the château, with splendid furniture, tapestries and a fine private art collection, are open to the public for several months of the year. Michelet, the French historian and a contemporary of Macaulay, lived and wrote here.

A drive of 8km up the little Crevon Valley reveals the fresh beauty of this part of the countryside.

VERNEUIL-SUR-AVRE, *Eure* (2–C2). The interesting thing about this southerly Norman town is that it was entirely the creation of Henry I of England. He built it to link up with the frontier fortifications of Tillières and Nonancourt, a river defence line along the Avre to keep out the French. It suffered terrible afflictions during the Hundred Years War. In 1424, with the aid of 5000 Scottish archers, 2000 wild Highland axe-men and other traditional enemies of the English, Charles VII of France tried in vain to penetrate the town. Not for another 25 years, and only after serious seditions in the English camp, did Verneuil finally fall to the French.

Rich in artistic and architectural treasures, the town has much to offer the sightseer. At one end, its wide, open and colourful market-place is dominated by the magnificent Gothic tower of the church of La Madeleine that soars up into the sky like some intricate medieval skyscraper. There is more than a chance resemblance to Rouen Cathedral's Butter Tower in the graceful double octagonal lantern which surmounts its three tiers of arches and traceried stonework; the 24 statues that grace the niches are by general consent even more beautiful than those of Rouen. The church, by contrast with its splendid tower, is something of an anticlimax. Reconstructed time and time again, it was badly restored in the last century. Notwithstanding this disappointment, it has some of the finest 16th-c. statuary in the country and some even earlier, like the statue of St Giles and the polychrome statue of Our Lady of the Apple.

The 12th-c. church of Notre-Dame, though somewhat impaired by the disfigurement of later building, still presents a devotional and cared-for appearance. Here, too, the visitor can admire the creative imagination of the local master carvers of the 16th-c. Outstanding is the wooden polychrome 13th-c. statue of Our Lady of Sorrows. On the N side of the nave is a very early and curious holy-water stoup with two primitive faces entwined by serpents. Among many other works of art are the gigantesque St Christopher and the neighbouring

St Denis, cupping his ears as though to keep out the noise but in reality holding on to his cranium which has been struck by the executioner. They stand on either side of the gates leading to the vaulted and dignified sanctuary. The robust columns at the apsidal end are late 12th-c.

Just to the S of Notre-Dame is the Convent of the Benedictines. It has some beautiful examples of silversmith craftsmanship created during the Middle Ages. Of particular interest are three remarkable reliquaries of repoussé work in silver, silver-gilt and enamel. Adjoining the church is one of the best early timber houses in the town, and to the E is the circular redstone Tour Grise, built by Henry I to defend his new town.

VERNON, *Eure* (2–C3). There is an embracing view of this ancient gateway town into Normandy from the modern bridge crossing the Seine. Beyond the wooded islands, up on the hillside of Vernonnet which forms part of the Forest of Vernon, can be seen the remains of the Château de Tourelles, a fortress built by Henry I of England to protect the bridge immediately below. Many of the wooden piles of the old bridge are still visible. On the opposite bank he constructed another fortress, the keep of which survives in the much-restored Tour des Archives. Vernon seems to have been a favourite place of relaxation for both English and French kings in the Middle Ages. It is still a much-frequented river-haunt for Parisians who come to enjoy its invigorating air.

After suffering considerable damage in World War II, the town now has splendidly laid-out residential avenues and all the amenities of a popular resort. During hostilities it lost many of its ancient timbered houses but one particularly fine 15th-c. example still stands near the church of Notre-Dame. This partly 12th-c. church has a tall and graceful 15th-c. nave and a beautiful rose-window.

VILLEQUIER, *Seine-Maritime* (4km W of Caudebec: 2–B2). A historic small village on the right bank of the Seine below wooded foothills. Here from the quayside you can watch the marine pilots taking over from the river pilots, and vice versa. It was between here and Caudebec that in 1843 Victor Hugo's young daughter and her husband on a boating expedition were engulfed by a phenomenal tidal bore and drowned. Their tombs are in the village churchyard only a stone's throw from the site of the tragedy. Nearby is the Victor Hugo Museum, once the house of his son-in-law's family.

The church, parts of which date back to the 12th-c., has a fascinating 16th-c. stained-glass window depicting a naval battle in 1522 in which English flags are clearly discernible.

On the hill above the village is the Château de Villequier, with superb panoramic views of the Seine valley and the Forest of Brotonne. Its history goes back to early Norman times. Badly

damaged by fire in 1763, it was restored before the Revolution and somehow escaped the Terror, preserving its fine domed dovecot, its Louis XIII stables and even its own miniature Petit Trianon. It has recently been converted into a hotel.

VIRE, *Calvados* (1–B4). Built on a rise in the undulating wooded countryside called the 'Bocage Virois', the ancient town of Vire has a curious claim to fame. In the 14th-c. a local clothworker called Olivier Basselin, known as the 'Vaux de Vire', became renowned for his bawdy tavern songs and sketches; the collection of songs became known as the 'Vaudevire' and, corrupted into 'vaudeville', entered the language of many nations.

Vire, overlooking a wide expanse of forests, rivers and deep ravines, and standing on an important crossroad between Brittany and eastern Normandy, held a strategic value in World War II. As a consequence, it suffered near obliteration. Even so, some ancient key buildings survived or were able to be restored. Among these was the sturdy granite twin-towered and machicolated 13th-c. gateway, surmounted by a tall and rather ugly clock-tower. Off the main square, overlooking the valley, are the remains of a square tower built by Henry I. The granite Gothic Church of Our Lady had only a part of its E end left standing, but has now been completely restored.

All around, the beautiful scenery of the enchanting river Vire region provides a background to mellow manor houses, peaceful farm cottages, old churches, strange Calvaries, and dolmens more reminiscent of nearby Brittany.

YVETOT, *Seine-Maritime* (2–B2). This populous market town in the centre of the Caux region lies strategically on the main road between Le Havre and Amiens. Proud of its Viking origin, it likes to remind visitors of its link with the town of Yvetofta on Lake Ivo in Sweden. Almost obliterated by the bombing of 1940, Yvetot has been entirely rebuilt. Its focal point is the astonishing modern round church of St Peter, built entirely in concrete and glass by the architect Yves Marchand. A huge panel placed above the central doorway depicts St Peter standing against a gigantic fisherman's net stretching upwards to the full height of the building. To one side, and linked by a small circular baptistry, a tall slender campanile rises to over 30m. Inside, the eye is dazzled by the glowing colours of the cylindrical wall of stained glass by Max Ingrand. With pale blues intensifying to rich purples and vivid reds, the windows tell an episodic story of the religious history of the archdiocese of Rouen, culminating in the almost blinding brilliance of the yellow and gold background to a red crucifixion encircled in blue. In the Lady Chapel greens merge with pale mauves to contrast with the deep blue of the Virgin's mantle. The impact of this modern glass is tremendous.

Brittany: Introduction

Gerald Barry

The whole of Brittany's 3500-kilometre coastline is jagged, with many deep indentations and gorges where wide rivers have carved their way through tall granite cliffs to the sea, particularly on the northwest coast where a whole group of these 'abers', or deep river valleys, disgorge their waters over foam-drenched rocks between Aber Wrac'h and Aber Benoît. Between the inlets are the long stretches of fine sand which make this province a paradise for the holiday-maker. From earliest times it has been known by its Celtic appellation 'Armor' or 'Armorica' – the land of the sea. The interior is the 'Argoat', or land of the woods.

The province is mainly composed of the western extremity of the triangular geological formation known as the Armorican Massif, the base of which lies in the Paris Basin. There are two main sections – the highlands of the Arrée and Menez in the north, and the Montagnes Noires and Lanvaux moorland in the south – divided by the lowland basin of Châteaulin and Rennes. Over millions of years, erosion has reduced the one-time great peaks of mountains from heights of over 4000 metres to just under 400 metres, and many considerably less. However, they give an impression of some height, as they dominate wide plateaux of fields and pasturelands, criss-crossed by low boundary walls of rough granite chips.

The wild moorland country, apart from the Lanvaux district, gives that sense of strange isolation often found in the highlands of Northwest Scotland, where a brooding atmosphere of curious melancholy lends credence to Celtic myth and legend. This entire area of Brittany was once dense forest; now, after centuries of ruthless clearing, there are only wastes of gorse, with sparse survivals of beech and oak.

The climate of Brittany, though generally mild, is mainly affected by the vagaries of Atlantic weather. As in southern Ireland, they have a good many 'soft' days when a fine misty rain falls for longish spells. As soon as the sun breaks through, it diffuses that rare quality of light which attracted so many of the Impressionist painters. The south tends to be warmer than the north, with warm streams in the Atlantic enabling much of the Mediterranean-type flora to flourish on the coast. There are, however, parts of the north affected by the Gulf Stream and producing the same semi-tropical vegetation. Although winters are mild, the late autumn can bring rough squalls and fierce gales, providing a spectacle of savage grandeur as mountainous seas lash the apparently impervious granite coastline. Even when northern Europe is experiencing a summer heat wave, it is always tempered on the Brittany coast by gentle sea breezes.

The earliest known inhabitants were certainly an Iberian people, similar to those who occupied the British Isles at the same period. They left an archaeological wealth of mysterious standing stones, dolmens and cromlechs. Those of Carnac and Stonehenge are of approximately the same date. In the sixth century BC a new migration of Celts swept across Europe. Those who settled in Armorica were kinsmen to the Irish, Scots and British settlers. They divided the territory between five tribes, and these areas retained their separate identities through the Roman occupation and right down to the post-Revolution period.

Rome left little mark on the province, nor did early Gallo-Christianity make much headway against the Celtic druidism, which adapted many of the old menhirs for their own religion. Only towards the end of the fifth and early part of the sixth century, when their kinsmen from Britain, probably driven out by the Anglo-Saxons, emigrated in large numbers and brought with them Irish and Welsh missionaries, did Armorica accept Christianity, with a fervour it has never lost. They also changed the name of their newly adopted country, first to Little Britain and then simply Bretagne or, in its anglicized form, Brittany. Although French is the common tongue of the province, the Breton Gaelic is still spoken in Lower Brittany and follows very closely the linguistic patterns of Welsh.

By AD 799 Charlemagne had organized the province into a fortified outpost of empire, governed first by tribal overlords, then by the Dukes of Brittany. In 919 the Viking Normans invaded Brittany and devastated the country, but twenty years later the legitimate duke, Alain Barbe Torte, managed to unite all the Breton nobles and drive out the Normans. Later, with the rise to power of the Plantagenets in the twelfth century, Brittany became a fief of the Anglo-Norman kings. But King John's murder of his nephew Arthur provided the excuse for Philippe-Auguste's seizure of his French possessions. The Dukes of Brittany became vassals of the French crown, and through marriage a line of French dukes was established. Only when Duke John III died childless in 1341 did the English succeed in opposing the claims of the French-backed Charles de Blois, by supporting the dead duke's brother, John de Montfort. This led to the long War of Succession, terminated by de Montfort's victory in 1364. From this date, a long period of prosperity was established by the now almost completely independent dukes. Building, the arts and the native Breton religious expression all flourished.

In 1488 Anne of Brittany, a daughter of Duke François II, inherited the dukedom; three years later she married Charles VIII of France, thus uniting Brittany with France but at the same time securing all the independent rights of her dukedom. This independence was recognized until the French Revolution, when the intensely individualistic province reluctantly became absorbed into modern France.

Like the Welsh and the Cornish, to whom he is closely related, the Breton has never lost his Celtic identity. His temperament is mercurial, quickly transported from joy to melancholy. The Bretons are a deeply religious people, and the most obvious outward expression of their fervour is to be found in the Breton 'Pardons', held all over the province. Hundreds of pilgrims will assemble at innumerable shrines; every village and town has its own venerated patron saint. Mass, processions and singing by candle-bearing devotees are made a colourful spectacle by the traditional costumes, the women especially conspicuous by the variety of the starched lace head-dresses or coifs. Once the religious rites have been observed, there is dancing

A Breton lace-seller

and wrestling, followed by local songs harking back to ancient legend and myth.

Brittany's destiny has been shaped by the sea, and the majority of France's Navy and fishing fleets are manned by Breton sailors. The sea, too, provides most of the Breton gastronomic delicacies. Lobsters, oysters, crayfish, prawns, shrimps, clams, mussels and scallops are abundant. The rivers of the Argoat provide salmon from the Aulne and Elorn and superb trout from the Montagnes Noires. Perch and pike, cooked simply *au beurre blanc*, are specialities. The *gigot* of lamb from the salt-pasture sheep of the coastlands and prepared with *haricots blancs*, as eaten in the ordinary Breton restaurants, becomes an expensive gastronomic delight in Paris. Vegetables and fruit are of high quality. Breton onions are known to most British housewives, and since the Common Market so too are artichokes from St-Pol and strawberries from Plougastel.

The most usual drink is good rough cider, but the dry crisp Breton Muscadet is the perfect accompaniment to seafood. There is a local and powerful brandy distilled on the Rhuys peninsula, but according to the Bretons it should be drunk with great caution and a handrail to hold on to.

Brittany: Gazetteer

Gerald Barry

AURAY, *Morbihan* (1–C2). An ancient town on the banks of the river Loch where it widens into the river Auray and flows into the almost enclosed island-strewn Gulf of Morbihan. Its strategic value was recognized even before the Romans built a military camp on the hilly rises of the old St-Goustan quarter.

On the marshy ground of Kerso, just N of the city, an important battle was fought in 1364 that ended in a decisive victory for John de Montfort, backed by Edward III against the French-supported Charles de Blois and his captain, the indomitable Breton knight Du Guesclin. Charles was killed and Du Guesclin taken prisoner for a time. It brought to an end the 23-year-old War of Succession for the dukedom of Brittany, in which the English and French fought almost continuously.

In 1776, along the wide stone quay of St-Goustan, Benjamin Franklin disembarked on a mission to sign a treaty with France during the American War of Independence. The old house where he lodged, near the large square which now bears his name, has a plaque on the wall commemorating the event.

This part of the town is full of character, with a maze of narrow streets and alleyways, all lined with story-book 15th-c. houses that seem on the verge of tumbling down the slopes towards the port.

An excellent view of the St-Goustan quarter can be obtained from the Promenade du Loch on the other side of the river, which is crossed by a pretty stone bridge. The promenade skirts the vestiges of the old ducal castle, and there are good views over the harbour and out to the famous oyster-beds which line the banks of the estuary.

2km N, on the site of the 1364 battle, an old one-time Carthusian monastery was badly damaged by fire a few years ago and with it a chapel, which commemorated the Chouans and *émigrés* who sought to restore the monarchy after the Revolution. They were defeated after a huge rising in Quiberon in 1795. At least 350 were shot on the nearby Champ des Martyrs. Over a burial vault in the funeral chapel is a marble mausoleum still intact, bearing the names of 953 exiles, many of whom had fled at one time to England.

6km NNE of the town is **Ste-Anne-d'Auray**, site of Brittany's biggest annual pilgrimage. From 7 March onwards there are many parish pilgrimages, but they reach a climax of devotional fervour for the Great 'Pardon' on the Feast of Ste-Anne, which starts on 25 July and lasts for two days. The night ceremonies are particularly impressive. The Breton cult of the mother of the Blessed Virgin Mary goes back to very ancient times. The ornate 19th-c. basilica replaces an earlier church built to commemorate a vision of Ste-Anne vouchsafed to a local peasant in 1623.

BELLE-ILE, *Morbihan* (1–C2, D2). 15km S of Quiberon, out in the Atlantic, is Brittany's largest island, well-named Belle-Ile. 20km long and about 10km across at its widest point, it has a much indented coastline with numerous little coves, ports and sheltered beaches. The regular steamship service takes 45 minutes to do the crossing from Port Maria on the Quiberon peninsula to Le Palais, the island's principal town and port.

Belle-Ile has always attracted poets, painters, philosophers, prelates, and actresses like the great Sarah Bernhardt, who were all drawn to it by its infinite variety and mild climate.

It has had a turbulent history over the ages. Invaded by Saxons and Normans, it was later given to the Abbey of Redon in 1006. During the next 500 years, it was many times attacked by the English, who effected a landing in 1572 and held the island for three weeks. The French king then decided on strong measures for its defence and gave it to the powerful Retz family. They eventually sold it to the notorious Fouquet, Louis XIV's Minister of Finance, who was arrested for fraud before he could complete the huge fortifications in Le Palais, which he hoped would give him security against all intruders. (*See also* Vaux-le-Vicomte *in the* Paris Environs *section.*)

After an attempted Dutch invasion, Louis XIV sent Vauban, the greatest military engineer of his time, to strengthen and complete the ramparts and redoubts of the Citadel, which can still be admired.

Nearly 200 years after the first short English occupation, George III's fleet, following a long blockade, forced the island to surrender in 1761; it was held until 1763, when the French, having captured Minorca, agreed to exchange it for the island of Belle-Ile.

At the time the English left, many French-Canadian settlers, described vividly in

Longfellow's poem 'Evangeline', were driven out of Nova Scotia and, after wandering in New England, resettled on Belle-Ile. Some of the oldest families on the island pride themselves on their Arcadian blood.

Many interesting documents concerning all these events can be seen in the 17th-c. museum in Le Palais.

There is much to see and do on the island. Sauzon, to the NW, is famous for its lobsters and sardine fishing. As its name implies, it was a Saxon settlement. Still further NW, on the Pointe des Poulains, in an almost Mediterranean atmosphere, Sarah Bernhardt built a sumptuous villa. It was destroyed by the Germans during their occupation in World War II and replaced with a small fort, overlooking a rock-framed creek. From here can be seen much of the grandiose scenery of the Côte Sauvage and its fantastically shaped rocks, and a sweeping vista right across the Quiberon Bay to the islands of Houat and Hoedic.

SW of the Pointe des Poulains is a remarkable cave called the Apothecary's Grotto, from the numerous cormorants who once nested here on rock ledges, looking like so many bottles on a chemist's shelves. Port Donnant has a fine sandy beach, sheltered by tall cliffs, but the sea can be treacherous here. Just S of this small resort is the Great Lighthouse, built on to rock in 1835 and rising to a height of 84m above the sea. Its beam can be seen for a distance of 120km, and there are splendid views from its lantern balcony. The long line of needlepointed rocks at Port Coton is quite spectacular as the foaming sea surges around and through them. Below this is Port du Goulphar, built on an inlet resembling a small Norwegian fjord, protected by steep cliffs. On the opposite side of the island is its finest stretch of safe sandy beach, Les Grands Sables. Inland is the oldest village on the island, with the Celtic name of Bangor and a parish church dating from 1071.

BREST, *Finistère* (1–B1). The vast port and arsenal of Brest, capital of NW Finistère, is situated on a huge sheltered roadstead fed by the rivers Elorn and Aulne.

From 1940 it was one of the most important of the German submarine bases and of such strategic value that it was bombed repeatedly by the Allies until its capitulation, which was not effected until the German defenders had blown up all the port and military installations in September 1944. The city then lay in ruins.

But pride in its long history, from the time when it was a fortified Roman settlement to the founding of its great arsenal, naval schools and shipyards by Colbert in the 17th-c., strengthened the determination of post-war Brittany that a great new city should rise rapidly from the rubble. Looking from the splendid Place de la Liberté, with its imposing vertical cenotaph, across the formal gardens fronting the municipal buildings, down the seemingly endless Rue Jean Jaurès, it

must be granted that the planners and architects succeeded in creating a fine modern city.

Although strict security is maintained in the dockyards, views over these and the rest of the port can be had from the Pont de Recouvrance, claimed to be the highest drawbridge in Europe, or from the further Pont de l'Harteloire, both spanning the Penfeld estuary.

The 15th-c. castle, built on the site of an early Roman fort, was considerably enlarged between the 16th- and 18th-c. Damaged during World War II, the precincts have been restored, and it is now the Préfecture Maritime, with a fascinating naval museum in the Paradise Tower.

The Tour Tanguy, opposite the castle on the W bank of the Penfeld, with yachts and rivercraft moored alongside its medieval walls, now houses an interesting museum unfolding Brest's long history.

An observation table in the hilltop park at the end of the Promenade of the Cours Dajot, enables visitors to get their bearings and affords wide panoramic views over the whole roadstead.

CANCALE, *Ille-et-Vilaine* (1–B3). First of the popular seaside resorts on the Brittany side of the Emerald Coast, Cancale is particularly famed for its oysters. The long Fenêtre Jetty separates the attractively sited port beneath the cliffs from the oyster beds which are clearly visible at low tide. Beyond the beds is a curving stretch of clean shingle beach. Above the cliffs, the Customs Patrol Path leads over the Pointe du Hock with splendid views over the Cancale Rock and across the bay to Mont-St-Michel. The parish church of St-Méen has remarkable views from its clock-tower, reached by 189 steps. Nearby is a museum displaying unusual local wood-carving.

4½km N is the 40m-high Grouin Pointe, where the typical jagged Breton coastline can be seen in a great sweep from Cap Fréhel in the W across to Mont-St-Michel in the E. A path down the cliff leads at low tide to a huge cave. The long island opposite is a bird sanctuary.

CARNAC, *Morbihan* (1–C2). The great standing stones or megaliths of Carnac have excited the curiosity of students of prehistory throughout the ages. More than 4000 stones arranged in parallel lines, often terminating in a semi-circle and appearing to be set with amazing astronomical accuracy, are to be seen in three major areas, all a little to the N of the town. Nothing is known of their original purpose, though they would appear to have had a religious significance. They are dated by archaeologists as having been erected between 3500 and 1800 BC, the generally accepted date for Stonehenge. The mystery still remains how these stones, some weighing up to 350 tons and some standing over 6m high, could have been placed with such precision. Like those in Britain, they are often incised with strange symbols.

The principal Menec alignment is a kilometre

The prehistoric standing stones at Carnac

long and 100m wide and consists of over 1000 stones, some 4m high. The lines of Kermario are the next group, a little to the N, on the road to Auray. Beyond these are the alignments of Kerlescan, ending with a semi-circle of 39 huge menhirs.

Just E of the town centre is the vast tumulus St-Michel, with its great central chamber and connecting galleries leading off to smaller rooms. Most of the prehistoric finds from here are now in the remarkable museum, founded by a Scot, James Miln, about 1875. The museum is right in the town centre, near the 17th-c. church of St-Cornély and the 20th-c. town hall.

To the S of the town is a splendid long stretch of sandy beach, which has turned Carnac into a very popular seaside resort.

CHÂTEAULIN, *Finistère* (1–B1). Built along both sides of a quay-lined and canalized stretch of the peaceful river Aulne and crossed by two bridges, Châteaulin is renowned as a salmon fisherman's paradise. Hundreds of fish can be seen leaping the weir-falls as they come upstream to spawn. Built on a rocky spur of the town's wooded hillside is a 15th-c. oratory dedicated to Notre-Dame which was once the chapel of a feudal fortress. From this spur there is a lovely view of the long verdant Aulne valley.

COMBOURG, *Ille-et-Vilaine* (1–B3). Surrounded by wooded countryside, dotted with many small lakes, Combourg has a great four-square granite feudal castle rising above its own tranquil sheet of water edged with old houses and inns. The imposing fortress was built in the 11th-c. by an Archbishop of Dol and considerably enlarged during the 14th- and 15th-c. Here lived the almost legendary knight Bertrand du Guesclin, who after an initial defeat by John of Gaunt in Spain, practically drove the English out of France towards the end of the Hundred Years War.

In 1761 the castle was bought by Count Chateaubriand, father of the illustrious French writer, whose *Memoirs from Beyond the Tomb* was inspired by recollections of part of his childhood spent here, when he slept up in the haunted 'Tower of the Cat'. This has now been converted into a museum, and from the rooftop are some fine views. Each angle of the castle has a sturdy round crenellated and machicolated tower surmounted by a conical roof, giving the austere fortress a romantic medieval appearance. It is still owned by a member of the Chateaubriand family and is open to the public in spring and summer.

CONCARNEAU, *Finistère* (1–C1). Apart from being the second largest fishing port in France, Concarneau is also a delightful seaside resort with good sandy beaches.

Protected within the Baie de la Forêt, on the estuary of the river Moros, huge fleets of fishing trawlers often shelter from winter Atlantic storms within the wide harbour. Most mornings provide a colourful and animated scene as the famous blue fishing nets are taken on board before the trawlers put out to sea. On the penultimate weekend in August, the harbour and town are crowded for the exciting Fête des Filets Bleus when some of the infinite variety of Breton costumes can be seen, the best bagpipe music heard and some of the best folk-dancing watched.

Concarneau derives its unusual character from its sturdy granite-walled town or Ville Close, sited like an island within the harbour. Already fortified before the Conquest, by the 14th-c. it was regarded as almost impregnable. During the War of Succession under John de Montfort the English held it for thirty years and greatly strengthened the fortifications. It withstood two sieges by the famous Du Guesclin and fell to him at the third when the English occupiers were finally driven out. Under Louis XIV, Vauban completed the ramparts and other installations. Although some restoration was undertaken in the last century, everything is as Vauban built it. Access by ticket is made over a narrow bridge.

CROZON Peninsula, *Finistère* (14km S of Brest: 1–B1). Possessing some of the most spectacular coastal scenery in Brittany, this jagged peninsula between Brest and Douarnenez takes its name from the little inland town of Crozon, its geographical and commercial centre. The fairly modern parish church is dominated by a tall round tower, a clearly visible landmark for miles around.

Concarneau: the entrance to the Ville Close

The church has a curious early 17th-c. polychromatic carved reredos depicting the story of the Emperor Hadrian's slaughter of the whole Theban Legion, said to have been 10,000 Christian converts.

8km NW is **Camaret**, the principal lobster port of France. On a little arm jutting into the bay is the ancient but restored chapel of Notre-Dame-de-Roc'h-Amadour, where every year on the first Sunday of September a 'Pardon' is held, following the Blessing of the Sea. Votive model sailing ships and steamers decorate its interior.

On the S side of the cape is the Pointe de Penhir looking over a perilous range of rocks and across to the equally dramatic scenic beauty of the Pointe de Dinan. This promontory has a curious natural arch linking its fortress-like rock to the mainland.

DINAN, *Côtes-du-Nord* (1–B3). A fine medieval town with much character, Dinan is built high up on a rocky crag some 75m above the winding river Rance. Much of the sturdy granite wall of the ramparts, together with the bastions, the Constable's Tower and the massive 14th-c. castle, are well preserved. The Duchess Anne de Bretagne, who became Queen of France when she married Charles VIII in 1491, often resided in the castle. The little chapel where she worshipped is an architectural jewel. Many of the English troops taken prisoner in the American War of Independence were interred in the keep, which now houses a historical museum.

The Old Town, with tortuous twisting cobbled streets, such as the steeply descending Rue du Jerzual, is rich in tall, slate-roofed, half-timbered houses, mostly of the 15th- and 16th-c. Particularly interesting is the 15th-c. Governor's House on the road down towards the river. In the steepled 15th-c. clock tower, off the Place des Merciers, hangs the bell presented by the Duchess Anne in 1507 but later recast.

Near the Clock Tower is the famous Place du Champ Clos. On this spot in 1359 an extraordinary chivalric event took place. Bertrand du Guesclin, who was to become Constable, of France, was defending the city, together with his brother Olivier, against the Duke of Lancaster. Du Guesclin asked for a forty-day truce which was granted. It was broken by an English knight, Canterbury, who took Olivier prisoner and demanded a huge ransom. Du Guesclin challenged him to single combat under Lancaster's presidency. Canterbury, defeated in the combat, released the brother and actually paid Du Guesclin the sum of the ransom he had himself demanded. Some 20 years later Du Guesclin died and at his request his heart was buried in the nearby church of St-Sauveur; it lies behind a heart-shaped cenotaph in the N transept. Beyond the church with its many mixed architectural styles is an English Garden, with splendidly laid-out walks and views over the river and the great viaduct carrying the main road to Paris.

DINARD, *Ille-et-Vilaine* (1–B3). Set in impressive rock scenery, by emerald seas and golden sands on the W side of the river Rance opposite St-Malo, Dinard lives up to its title of 'Queen of the Brittany Resorts'. It still attracts its smart clientèle, though they are no longer exclusively British and American. It was founded in the mid-19th-c. by a rich American on the site of a small fishing hamlet by the little port of St-Énogat. He quickly realized the advantages of the natural amphitheatre of tall cliffs which shelters the splendid beaches, as well as the equable climate which encouraged the growth of semi-tropical foliage. He was joined by a wealthy English colony, who set a seal of opulence on the new town which has never been broken. It still has its English church of St- Bartholomew and the sort of smart tea-rooms which are mostly a memory in England today.

There are three main beaches. At the E end of the Plage de St-Énogat is the Pointe des Etetés, with good views of the islands beyond. Just inland is the old parish church and a very old turreted house in the Grande Rue, called the Lodge of the Black Prince. The Grande Plage, also called the Plage de l'Écluse, provides an animated spectacle both on land and sea during the season. It fronts the magnificent new Casino and Olympic swimming pool. Behind are the main shopping and residential areas. Just past the Palais des Congrès

begins the terraced path up to the Pointe du Moulinet where the Rance flows into the sea. A great sweep of glorious seascape opens to the view, stretching from Cap Fréhel across to St-Malo. The path rounding the headland leads to the famous Promenade du Clair de Lune which runs the full length of the sea-wall. There are beautiful lighting effects at night providing a colourful setting for numerous open-air concerts. The Promenade ends beside the extensive third beach, the Plage du Prieuré, which takes its name from the nearby picturesque ruins of a 14th-c. priory founded by two crusaders, Oliver and Geoffrey de Montfort, after they had been ransomed from the Turks in 1324.

An International Horse Show, golf tournaments and regattas draw huge crowds during the summer.

4km SE is the Rance Dam and the world's first tidal power station. Permission to visit can be obtained through the Dinard Tourist Office.

DOL-DE-BRETAGNE, *Ille-et-Vilaine* (1–B3). Dol, when founded by the British missionary St Samson in AD 548, was built on a cliff which towered above a vast forest stretching beyond the Bay of Mont-St-Michel. The phenomenal tidal waves which turned Mont-St-Michel into an island, in about the 8th-c., swept up as far as Dol and surrounded it. As the waters slowly retreated they left wide marshlands which could only gradually be drained and reclaimed. The town, now 8km from the coast, is still known as the Capital of the Marshes.

In the Grande-Rue-des-Stuarts are many fine old houses and in particular a unique 12th-c. example of domestic Romanesque called La Maison des Plaids. At the top of the street stands the vast and imposing granite Cathedral, built over the ruins of a Romanesque church burned down by King John in 1203. It was constructed mainly with funds sent by him from England as an act of reparation. Its somewhat severe nave is lined with three tiers of Gothic arches and presents an appearance more Norman than Breton. Within the rectangular chancel are 80 choir-stalls of the 14th-c. The carvings are a fascinating expression of the wit and humour of the medieval wood-workers. Above are some well-restored 13th-c. stained-glass medallion windows. In the N arm of the transept is a splendid tomb of the late-15th-c. Oxford theologian, Bishop Thomas James. The exterior shows a harmonious mixture of styles over the centuries. The squat lantern-tower seems to accent the Norman influence. Perhaps the most interesting feature is to be found in the 13th-c. S porch which was modified to the present perfect proportions two centuries later.

Just beyond the Cathedral is the pedestrian-only Promenade des Douves (or moats), with an inspiring view across the now fertile marshes to the remarkable 65m-high Mont Dol, 3km to the N. This strange geological mound retains a curiously eerie atmosphere. Holy wells, grottoes and ruined chapels abound, reminders of how pagan altars of Roman invaders were overthrown by Druids, who in turn saw their sanctuaries taken over by Christian hermits and mystics. Archaeologists have excavated the remains of prehistoric mammoth elephants and even rhinoceros together with Stone Age tools and weapons. The mound is capped by the chapel of Notre-Dame-de-l'Espérance, a popular centre of pilgrimage.

1½km S of Dol is one of Brittany's finest menhirs, standing 9m high.

DOUARNENEZ, *Finistère* (1–C1). Already old when the Romans came to Gaul, Douarnenez, now an important harbour for its large fleet of sardine, lobster and deep-sea fishing-boats, inevitably has its origins misted by legend. Here, it is said, King Mark of Cornouaille had his palace and held court, and here was the background to the story of his betrothed Iseult and his nephew Tristan immortalized in Wagner's opera. The mythical town of King Gradlon's Ys, too, is supposedly buried beneath the sands and waves of the Bay of Douarnenez.

The town is now linked with **Tréboul** across Port-Rhu by a 24m-high bridge, making it an important seaside resort. To the W of Tréboul, the popular Sables Blancs beach has fine views across the bay, made colourful in summer by the yachts and fishing-boats coasting around the Ile Tristan or heading out to sea.

2km E of Douarnenez is another splendid stretch of sand, sheltered beneath pine-topped cliffs, called La Plage du Ris, and beyond this, miles of sandy beaches at Kervel and at Ste-Anne-la-Palud, where on the last Sunday of August the most brilliant of all the Breton 'Pardons' takes place.

Each morning, on the Rosmeur quays, freshly caught fish is sold or auctioned. Countrywomen mingling in the crowds display amazing variations of the traditional Breton starched lace coifs.

Among the many festivals held in and around Douarnenez, the 'Fête of the Seagulls' (*mouettes*) and the 'Blessing of the Sea' on the third Sunday of July, and the 'Fest-Noz' or Night Festival at Ploaré in early August, are outstanding.

FAOUËT, Le, *Morbihan* (1–C2). Situated in pretty countryside watered by the river Inan and the Ellé, which comes cascading down from the Montagnes Noires, the village of Le Faouët is a haven of tranquillity. Its vast carved timber market-hall dates from the 16th-c.

There are three outstandingly beautiful chapels, all within easy reach of the town. That of the 15th-c. St-Fiacre lies 2km W and has a most elaborately carved wooden rood-screen, separating the chancel from the aisle. It is one of the best examples in Brittany. Some of the finest of the carved figures can be seen from the chancel side.

The chapel of Ste-Barbe is 2km in the opposite

direction. Built in 1489 in Flamboyant Gothic, it stands within a rocky cleft, 100m up on the hillside and overlooking the Ellé valley. There is a splendid Renaissance stairway, with elegant balustrading and a terrace, where a colourful 'Pardon' takes place on the last Sunday in June. From the terrace, an immense panorama opens up, stretching away to the jagged crests of the Black Mountains. Perched on an adjoining spur of rock is the little Oratory of St Michael.

The third chapel, dedicated to St-Nicolas, lies a little further to the W and is set in pine-scented woodlands. There is some fine carving to be seen, particularly on the Renaissance rood-screen. The story of St-Nicolas is depicted in nine separate panels.

FOUGÈRES, *Ille-et-Vilaine* (1–B4). Built high on a promontory above the winding river Nançon with a fine beech forest on its N perimeter, Fougères for centuries guarded the frontier between Brittany and Normandy. Its immensely strong medieval fortress was called by the Duchess Anne de Bretagne 'the key to my royal treasure'.

The original curtain walls of Fougères Castle (once surrounded by a loop in the river) are broken by 13 towers and encircle some 5 acres of enclosure. The foundations of the once lofty keep, demolished during the destruction of the fortress by Henry II in 1166, can still be seen within these wooded precincts. The fortress was almost immediately rebuilt by a powerful Breton baron, Raoul II. It then passed to the Lusignan family, who built the picture-book 14th-c. tower called 'La Mélusine', after an Arthurian fairy from whom they claimed descent. Its walls are 3½m thick and 13m in diameter, and it rises to over 30m above ground. The view from the parapet of this tower gives an indication of the vastness of the castle against the panoramic background of the Nançon valley. The oldest of the towers is the Cadran or Sundial Tower, dating from the 13th-c.

Just S of the castle is the high spire of the mostly 15th-c. church of St-Sulpice. The chancel has some excellent examples of Louis XV wood-carving. Preserved in the sacristy is a Bull of the Borgian pope, Alexander VI.

Although it still has many 14th-c. and 15th-c. houses, Fougères is a modern industrial town, renowned for its traditional manufacture of shoes. Every summer there is an interesting exhibition in the castle of the shoemaker's craft over the centuries.

FRÉHEL, Cap, *Côtes-du-Nord* (1–B3). One of the natural marvels of the Breton coast, and certainly the most spectacular, is the multi-coloured sheer cliffs of Cap Fréhel. They thrust their spur out to sea at a height of 70m above the often turbulent waters below. If the weather is rough, the spray from waves crashing over the deeply fissured rocks of the 'Grande Fauçonnière' below can rise well above the cliff edge. These rocks are sanctuaries

The Calvary at Guéhenno

for gulls, cormorants and some rare sea birds. During the nesting season, it is fascinating to watch their movements, and it is possible by taking a steeply descending path to watch more closely from a special platform.

On a clear evening the distant horizon sweeps far round the Emerald Coast from Normandy's Cotentin peninsula in the E to the Ile de Bréhat in the NW. Occasionally the Channel Islands can be seen. The brilliant colours change continually as the late sunlight turns to twilight.

Centrally placed on the tip of the promontory is the modern tall square granite tower of the lighthouse, whose beam in clear weather can carry over 100km. A lift takes sightseers up the 30m tower to the lantern platform.

Good paths enable the walker to cover the whole cape easily. During the season there are motorboat trips from Dinard. If anything, the view from the sea is even more spectacular.

GUÉHENNO, *Morbihan* (10km SW of Josselin: 1–C2, C3). Among the many famous Calvaries in Brittany one of the most interesting is that of Guéhenno. Erected in 1550 in a parish close (*see next entry*), it is a remarkable piece of studied sculpture, in spite of certain restorations. The ossuary behind is designed as Christ's tomb, with the two soldiers guarding the door. Above is a statue of the risen Saviour. In front of all, mounted on a tall column, a cock is crowing.

GUIMILIAU, *Finistère* (6km SW of St-Thégonnec: 1–B1). Perhaps the most vivid expression of Brittany's religious fervour can be found in the architectural groupings within the parish close. These enclosures are usually set up

between the cemetery and the parish church and mostly consist of a Calvary, a Triumphal Arch and a Charnel House, all intricately sculptured in stone. Of them all, the Calvary at Guimiliau is probably the largest and certainly the most ornate. Carved between 1581 and 1588, great clusters of figures tell the story of the Passion of Christ on a platform beneath a column of thorn which supports the Cross, with the figures of St John and the Virgin on a pedestal at one side and St Peter and the Breton St-Yves on the other. In common with several Calvaries in Lower Brittany, one part of the Passion group tells the story of Catell-Gollet with a pointed moral; she was a servant-girl who, withholding her wrongdoing in confession, found her lover had become the devil, who clawed her down to hell. Below the platform is a frieze supported at each corner by an Evangelist, and depicting scenes from the life of Jesus. Altogether 200 figures make up this remarkable Calvary.

The 16th-c. church rebuilt in the Flamboyant Renaissance style has an equally richly carved interior and a beautiful S porch. Above its classical pediment is a statue of St-Miliau, King of Cornouaille. Among the church's 'Treasure' is a magnificent carved-oak canopy supported by twisted columns covering the balustraded baptismal font.

Just over 3km W across country roads is **Lampaul-Guimiliau,** which has another fine parish close with a splendid arch of 1699 and a mortuary chapel built two years earlier. The church has a wealth of remarkably fine woodcarving. The 16th-c. rood-beam crossing the chancel is particularly impressive; so too are the baptismal font and a lovely polychromatic panel, portraying the Birth of the Virgin, with Ste-Anne in a four-poster bed. Gothic and Renaissance art succeed here in blending into one harmonious whole.

GUINGAMP, *Côtes-du-Nord* (1–B2). Centred between the Armor, or sea-country, and the Argoat, the inland wooded country, Guingamp has always been of geographical importance and a lively agricultural market town.

It is, however, because of its huge pilgrimage or 'Pardon', which takes place on the Saturday before the first Sunday of July, that it is particularly renowned. Thousands of pilgrims, mostly in national dress, the women wearing their differing local coifs or head-dresses, pour into the town and make for the Sanctuary of the Black Virgin, in the 14th–16th-c. Basilica of Notre-Dame-de-Bon-Secours. The church was probably the first in Brittany to accept the innovations of the Renaissance when a section had to be rebuilt.

The great candle-lit procession on the night of the 'Pardon' is most impressive as the bishop, surrounded by the pilgrims, lights three separate braziers from a flaming torch. The ritual is carried out in the Place du Centre, near the Renaissance three-tiered fountain called 'La Plomée', on which angels, sea-horses and pagan figures supporting the basins are surmounted by a statue of the Blessed Virgin. Around the square are many good corbelled and gabled houses, mostly dating from the 15th-c.

HENNEBONT, *Morbihan* (1–C2). Because of its proximity to Lorient, the once proud feudal town of Hennebont, built on the steep banks of the wide river Blavet, lost much of its medieval splendour in the intense bombardments of World War II. Its sturdy 14th-c. Bro-Erec fortified city gate and some of the ramparts, which saw amazing scenes of chivalry during the Hundred Years War, still stand, though damaged. The vast Place du Maréchal Foch is dominated by the 16th-c. Gothic Notre-Dame-du-Paradis. Its large W tower is surmounted by a steeple over 70m high.

The town boasts one of the famous Breton stud farms, with 230 stallions.

HUELGOAT, *Finistère* (1–B1). Situated within the Parc Régional d'Armorique, between the wild barren hill country of the Monts d'Arrée and the reforested sandstone and quartz Montagnes Noires, Huelgoat is in the heart of an untamed part of Brittany. It is thus an ideal centre for walkers and fishermen who seek solitude in a setting of savage grandeur.

The town, with an old fountain in the middle of its central square, has a 16th-c. church with a delightful if rather squat piece of statuary showing the integrity of St-Yves, the Breton lawyer, refusing the rich man's bribe while accepting the poor client's petition.

The hilly countryside around is a wonderland of strangely shaped rocks and boulders of granite and sandstone set in a forestland with mysterious pools, underground rivers, rushing streams and waterfalls. All the groupings of rocks are given imaginative names. At 'Le Gouffre', or 'The Chasm', the river Argent, flowing from Huelgoat Pool, disappears as it falls into a deep cleft, reappearing some yards away. To see the extraordinary 'Devil's Grotto' requires some agility, as both stone steps and an iron ladder have to be negotiated. One of the prettiest spots is the 'Pool of the Wild Boars' ('La Mare aux Sangliers'), where two waterfalls crossed by a bridge cascade into a pool.

From the top of the Cintrée Rock, just out of the town, is a wonderful view of the two ranges of high hills and the strange landscape around.

JOSSELIN, *Morbihan* (1–C2, C3). One of the best preserved feudal towns in Brittany, Josselin basks, as it has done for nearly 1000 years, in the reflected glory of its magnificent riverside castle. The first

The castle at Josselin

fortress was built by Guthenoc de Porhoït about the year AD 1000 and it was his son Josselin who completed his father's work and built the city which bears his name.

Entering by the lower road and crossing the river Oust, you see the three great circular towers rising up sheer from the granite rock washed by the river, each capped with high pepperpot roofs and linked by tall machicolated curtain-walls. It makes an unforgettably romantic impression and stirs the imagination to thoughts of the High Middle Ages.

There have been many romantic stories about Josselin over the centuries and some with sinister undertones. It was many times razed to the ground and immediately rebuilt. During the long War of Succession, Josselin took the side of the French pretender Charles de Blois, against the English-supported John de Montfort, who was garrisoned at nearby Ploërmel. His captain, John Bamborough, and the French captain, Jean de Beaumanoir, both wearying of the long indecisive skirmishes which brought misery to the countryside, proposed that each side should choose 30 knights led by its leader. They would engage in combat on foot armed with axes, swords, daggers and pikes. Whichever pretender's side prevailed would be proclaimed victor. All the knights passed the eve of the fight in prayer. The combat, which lasted all day, took place in March 1351, at a spot exactly halfway between the contenders' camps. The place can be seen today off the main road, marked by a stone obelisk. Bamborough was killed with eight of his knights, the rest were taken prisoner and the victory went to Josselin.

Of the original nine towers built after 1371 by Olivier de Clisson, one-time knight companion to the redoubtable Du Guesclin whom he succeeded as Constable of France, only four survive. Of these, one is the now isolated Prison Tower. Believing himself secure in the friendship of the King of France, de Clisson married Marguerite de Rohan, widow of Beaumanoir, whose family still own and live in the castle. When Charles VI was struck by insanity during an assault against the Duke of Brittany, de Clisson was banished to Josselin, where he died in 1407.

Thereafter, the castle saw many changes of fortune, but the de Rohans held fast and under the great Duchess Anne were restored to power and affluence when she became Queen of France. It was during this period, between 1490 and 1510, that the superb Flamboyant Gothic façade was built in the inner Court of Honour. It is probably the finest 'jewel' of domestic Gothic architecture in the country. The sculptured monogram 'A' surmounted by a crown appears frequently in the lavish decoration, and on one of the balustrades linking two of the gables the motto of the de Rohans, 'A Plus', can be seen intricately carved into the hard granite.

The aftermath of the Revolution saw the château at its lowest ebb. Then, from the middle to the end of the 19th-c., the de Rohans undertook a vast restoration. Much of the interior was decorated in the 'Troubadour style', a French expression of 'baronial Gothic'. Except in winter, the castle is open to the public.

There is much of interest in the often-restored Basilica of Notre-Dame-du-Roncier, founded at the same time as the castle. Its name comes from a pious legend of a statue, found among wild-rose brambles in the 9th-c. Many old houses of considerable character surround the church.

LAMBALLE, *Côtes-du-Nord* (1–B3). Once the capital of the powerful Counts and later Dukes of Penthièvre, historic Lamballe is built on the side of a hill and situated at an important crossroads.

The lofty Gothic church of Notre-Dame has an interesting 11th-c. N portal. It was strongly fortified during the lengthy War of Succession when English- and French-supported contenders fought for dominance. There is a pleasing view from its terrace overlooking the Lower Town and the Gouessant valley.

The central Place du Martray has some fine old houses, today mostly shops or boutiques. The ancient 15th-c. Executioner's House is now the tourist office.

There has been a large and important stud in Lamballe since before the Revolution. One can watch the horses being exercised, and at certain times of the year visitors are welcome during the afternoons.

LANNION, *Côtes-du-Nord* (1–B2). The port founded in the 11th-c. on the banks of the river Léguer gives movement and colour to the little rose-granite town of Lannion that has grown up round it. With many roads radiating to the N Lannion is handy for all the famous beaches of the Trégor coast.

To the N of the town, high on a rocky spur, 142 steps lead to the church of Brélévenez, built by the Knights Templar in the 13th-c. and remodelled in Gothic style. The bell-tower, with double balcony and spire, is 15th-c. There is a sweeping panoramic view over the countryside from the church terrace.

3km N is a remarkable research training centre for the French telecommunications and electronics industry. Not far to the S of the town is the prettily sited 15th-c. Chapel of Kerfons, which has an interesting rood-screen. A short drive leads to the impressive 15th-c. ruins of the Fortress of Tonquédec, torn down on the orders of Cardinal Richelieu. Still further to the S the Château de Kergrist opens its beautiful gardens to visitors.

LOCRONAN, *Finistère* (1–C1). A Breton version of a typical English Cotswold village, built in granite instead of sandstone, on a steeply wooded hillside, Locronan is perhaps the most picturesque small town in Brittany. It derived its wealth from weaving sailcloth for the ever-expanding French Navy in the 17th-c., and it is no wonder that its

Lannion

splendid Renaissance houses, clustered around a wide cobbled square, contrive to look like miniature manors. In the centre of the square is the ancient town-well, with wrought-iron fittings, facing a fine Ogival Flamboyant 15th-c. church dedicated to St-Ronan. The church was built on the site of an earlier priory church which preserved the relics of the Irish missionary who converted much of this corner of Cornouaille to Christianity. The name of Ronan is as popular throughout the countryside as it is in Ireland.

The Pénity Chapel, close to the right of the church, was built about 1505 to house the beautiful 15th-c. tomb of St-Ronan. His recumbent effigy was carved in granite-like Kersanton lava, much used for the Breton Calvaries, by a master mason of Quimper Cathedral. It is gracefully supported on the wings of six kneeling angels. A stained-glass window relates episodes from the life and death of the hermit-bishop.

From early times, Locronan was a famous centre of pilgrimage. Kings and queens, and even the great Breton St-Yves, mingled with the devout crowds who came on foot from long distances to pay homage at the 'holy place of Ronan'.

Even today, the 'Little Pardon' or '*Petite*

Troménie', still takes place on the second Sunday of July and wends its way up the Locronan Mountain where St Ronan had his hermitage; the pilgrims following the traditional route the hermit is reputed to have taken each day, barefooted and fasting. From the top, in front of the Kergoat chapel, is a magnificent view across Douarnenez Bay.

LORIENT, *Morbihan* (1–C2). A naval base designed to support the activities of France's India Company trading in the East (*l'Orient*), Lorient was created by Colbert in 1666 under Louis XIV to elude the English ships patrolling the Channel. Within 50 years John Law, the astute Scotsman and financier who became Controller General of the French Treasury, had made it into a flourishing commercial centre, with a rapidly expanding population.

Between September 1940 and August 1944, the town and port installations were repeatedly bombed, and only about 15 % of Lorient remained standing by the end of the war. But the huge submarine base by the harbour of Keroman, built by the Germans under enormously thick concrete, withstood every aerial attack, and at the time of the Liberation fell into the hands of the French

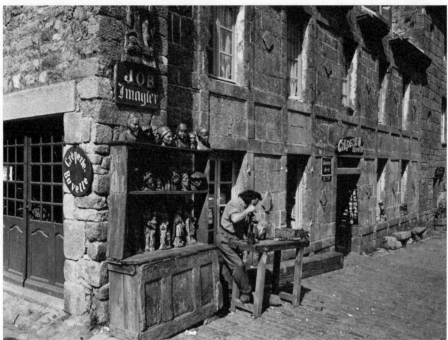

A corner in the town of Locronan

practically unscathed; it is still used as a submarine base – by the French.

A vast new city has risen on the rubble of the old, with gleaming white buildings lining well-planned spacious boulevards, the exciting new church of Notre-Dame-de-Victoire with its tall campanile, and a new Hôtel-de-Ville and Palais de Congrès. The fishing port of Keroman is as lively and colourful as ever.

There are splendid sandy beaches and picturesque little fishing harbours, all within easy reach of the city centre.

MALESTROIT, *Morbihan* (1–C3). An ancient, unhurried baronial town situated on important crossroads, and a good centre for exploring the heart of Brittany. Many old houses, both Gothic and Renaissance, survive from the late Middle Ages. Some have amusing carvings: one house in the Place Bouffay near the parish church shows a citizen in his nightshirt beating his wife. The 12th–16th-c. church of St-Giles is full of interest, and there are pretty walks along the banks of the canal before it flows back into the river Oust.

It was in Malestroit that Edward III and Philip VI of France signed a truce which gave the English a foothold in Brittany that lasted 40 years.

MOINES, L'Ile-aux-, *Morbihan* (8km SW of Vannes: 1–C2). Out in the almost enclosed Gulf of Morbihan are some 40 inhabited islands and

another 300 occupied only by sea birds. Of these islands, the largest and most popular with holiday-makers is the Ile-aux-Moines, or Monks Island; a reference to the days of ownership by the wealthy Abbey of Redon. 6km long, the island is reached in 5 minutes by regular crossings from Port Blanc, at the extreme end of D101, just SW of Vannes. A haven of tranquillity, it is noted for the excellence of its fresh seafood. While sailing and bathing are the principal attractions, there are interesting short excursions to be made to prehistoric sites. 1km S from the landing stage in the village of Kergonan is a large semi-circle of standing stones. 3km further on is the fine dolmen of Boglieux, where a wonderful view stretches out beyond the islands to the Atlantic; the sunsets are often spectacular.

Another pretty but smaller island called Arz, only 3km long, can be reached by boat from Vannes by the Conleau Channel; it too is rich in megalithic monuments.

MORGAT, *Finistère* (1–B1). With one of the finest sandy beaches in Finistère, and sheltered by the N arm of the Bay of Douarnenez, Morgat is a popular resort. It is only 3km from Crozon, capital of the peninsula. There is a lively harbour protected by a jetty, from which tunny-boats still go out, though it is now used mostly for sailing craft. The clifftop paths make for interesting walks; one leads up to the lighthouse, from which there are sweeping views across the bay. At low tide it is possible to walk out to small caves at the foot of the rocky spur dividing the Morgat beach from Le Portzic. There are motorboat trips to a number of big caves beyond Beg-ar-Gador. The most impressive is a grotto called 'l'Autel', or 'The Altar', 80m deep and 15m high, with curious mineral colourings on its roof and walls.

MORLAIX, *Finistère* (1–B1). Where the deep valleys of the Jarlot and the Queffleuth merge and their rivers join to form the Dossen, historic Morlaix, capital of Northern Finistère, is crossed by a monumental two-storey railway viaduct, nearly 300m long and almost 60m high. It was built in 1864 and towers above the portside quays which extend down to the estuary flowing out to the Bay of Morlaix. Early in its history, the Romans made it a military base, but it seems that the first stone fortress around which the town grew up was not built until *c.* AD 1000. Fief of the Counts of Léon, it was absorbed into Brittany in 1277. Its strong defences paradoxically led to many attacks over the centuries. In 1522, as a consequence of a violent foray into Bristol by Breton pirates, 80 English ships sailed into the Bay of Morlaix to uphold the honour of Henry VIII. Finding most of the townsfolk had gone off to festivities as far afield as Guingamp and Noyal-Pontivy, the English ransacked the town, looting (among other things) quantities of wine, which they imprudently drank. The returning men of Morlaix, shocked to find their town pillaged, sought out and found most of the invaders, dazed or asleep in nearby woods. Slaughter and defeat for the English followed. Morlaix celebrated by adding to its coat of arms a Lion of France confronting the Leopard of England, with the motto 'If they bite you, bite them back'. Shortly after this, the Château de Taureau was built to defend the narrow arm of the estuary.

Anne de Bretagne stayed in Morlaix in 1505. The corbelled house in which she is said to have resided is a beautiful example of early 16th-c. domestic architecture. With three overhanging storeys, this richly decorated half-timbered mansion in the Rue du Mur has a closed court with a lantern roof and an exquisite staircase. The town has many other 16th-c. examples, particularly in the Grande Rue and the Place des Halles.

In the restored church of St-Mathieu there is a curious 15th-c. statue of the Blessed Virgin which opens out on hinges to reveal a carving of the Trinity. High up to the right of the viaduct is the 15th-c. Flamboyant Gothic church of St-Melaine, with good modern stained glass, and a new spire to replace the one that was damaged in the bombing of 1943.

10km due N, on a peninsula at the E side of the Morlaix estuary, at Barnenez, is a great tumulus, covering 11 dolmens and still being excavated; it constitutes one of the most important megalithic groupings in Europe.

PAIMPOL, *Côtes-du-Nord* (1–B2). Once a deep-sea cod-fishing port with its trawlers a familiar sight off the banks of Iceland, Paimpol is now a pleasant little resort well known to yachtsmen. Oyster cultivation has replaced cod-fishing and brought prosperity back to the town. The fishermen's 'Pardon' of Our-Lady-of-Good-News takes place on the second Sunday of December.

A short boat trip round the shores of the bay makes it easy to understand how at the time of the Revolution Paimpol became a safe retreat for pirates and smugglers.

PAIMPONT, Forêt de, *Ille-et-Vilaine* (15km NE of Ploërmel: 1–C2, C3). It is curious that the small hamlet of Paimpont, which only came into being at the time of the Revolution, should have given its name to the 40 square kilometres of woodland once known as the Forest of Brocéliande. It is the only surviving eastern part of the ancient Breton 'Argoat' or land of the woods. There was an early 7th-c. monastery beside Paimpont's tranquil little lake. In the late 12th-c. a more ambitious and larger abbey was built on this site, but only the later 13th-c. church and a restored N wing remain today.

The village is a good centre for exploring an enchanted land of mysterious pools and lakes (there are 14 of them) where half-forgotten legends still have power to cast their spells. At many points where the forest diminishes to open wasteland it can strongly remind you of parts of Cornwall. As such it will come as no surprise to learn that this is the legendary country of King Arthur, Merlin, Morgane, Sir Launcelot and the other Knights of the Round Table. Away to the SW, Le Val Sans Retour (Valley of No Return) is a narrow, wild valley threatened by sinister-looking overhanging rocks where, they say, Morgane practised her magic to ensnare faithless lovers and wicked boys. A little to the N from here is the Fountain of Baronton, where water spilling over the stone called Merlin's Step can be used to unleash savage storms and conjure up a dreaded Black Knight, omen of ill. Further NW is the strange Fontaine de Jouvenance with its waters of magical power, and near this the reputed tomb of the wizard Merlin.

Quiet but good roads cross the forest in many directions, but it is on the well-marked footpaths leading into the forest depths that the solitude and unique atmosphere of the Brocéliande can be best enjoyed.

PERROS-GUIREC, *Côtes-du-Nord* (1–B2). Although the resort of Perros-Guirec on the northern section of the Rose Granite Coast draws enormous numbers of holiday-makers, there is never a sense of being overcrowded. This is partly due to the deeply serrated shoreline, making many self-contained beaches. The 18km stretch of road aptly called the Corniche Bretonne overlooks a magical coastline of pools, caves, lagoons, creeks and huge strangely sea-sculpted rocks.

Pleumeur-Bodou Space Telecommunications Centre

The well-protected little port, with fishing-boats, and pleasure craft jostling for mooring space, lies on the SE side of the peninsula. The wide Bd. de la Mer swings N, skirts the sea and passes two beaches. Soon a narrow road branches right and leads to the Pointe du Château on the tip of the peninsula; immediately W of this is a lovely sandy cove, the Plage Trestrignel. Back on the boulevard, the road climbs, turns NW, becomes the Bd. Clemenceau, then turns again SW into the town. On this last turn is a splendid viewing-table with vistas of a wide seascape dotted with islands, while below an agglomerate of curious rocks can be seen. The other main road from the port leads steeply uphill to the town centre.

The old squat-looking granite parish church is partly Romanesque and partly Gothic and is topped by a low tower with an odd little spire shooting up from a small dome surrounded by a balcony. Inside is a holy water stoup which was once the legal measurement for selling corn.

On the W side of the town is the wide, curving, fashionable Trestraou Beach. Well sheltered, with an expanse of white-gold sand, it is lined by large hotels, a casino and an imposing new conference centre overlooking the Bay of the Seven Islands.

At the extreme W end is a popular sailing school. From here, steps lead up to the Customs Patrol Path (Sentier des Douaniers) which runs right round the Ploumanach Peninsula. At first it follows the cliff-line, with splendid views of the Seven Islands, then slopes down to the rock-strewn shore. These granite rocks take on rich

hues, shading from vermilion to pink and then to grey; sometimes they look like the huge heads of Polynesian gods, sometimes like petrified sea-monsters.

Les Sept Iles, or Seven Islands, are a sanctuary for myriads of cormorants, gannets, puffins, gulls and oyster-catchers. More than 4000 pairs nest on the rocky slopes of the distant Ile Rouzic alone. During the summer there are frequent boat trips out to the islands from the Trestraou beach. Landing is forbidden, but the boatmen make it possible to film the birds and record their cries.

PLEUMEUR-BODOU, *Côtes-du-Nord* (5km NW of Lannion: 1–B2). Set in lonely countryside – near the ancient castle of Kerduel, haunted by the ghosts of King Arthur and his court, and near the even older Celtic chapel of St-Duzec and its strangely Christianized menhir – an enormous white dacron sphere 50m high has made the little village of Pleumeur world-famous. It forms part of the extensive Pleumeur-Bodou Space Telecom-munications Centre.

With Andover in the USA and Goonhilly in Cornwall it enables permanent telephone and television links to be maintained between Europe and America by satellites, with liaisons around the world. The historic first intercommunication was made here through Telstar in 1962. The station, with its giant saucer-shaped antenna, covers a huge area and employs a vast number of technicians, scientists and engineers.

Guided visits to the spherical 'Radôme' can be

made all through the summer. There is an animated model and a film; the visit lasts about an hour. During other seasons visiting days are somewhat reduced.

PLOUGASTEL-DAOULAS, *Finistère* (7km SE of Brest: 1–B1). The Plougastel peninsula, jutting out into the Brest roadstead, is a corner of Brittany quite impervious to change, despite the main highway which crosses it. Old Breton customs survive here as nowhere else, and the local costumes are among the most colourful in the province. Around its coast are many small resorts with shingle beaches, offering the visitor a variety of fresh, succulent seafood.

Plougastel-Daoulas, principal town of the peninsula, is the centre of a 2000-acre area devoted to strawberry growing. It is also renowned for its famous Calvary in the parish close. Built in 1602 as a thanksgiving for the ending of a plague four years earlier, it has 180 figures grouped around the base of the cross. Like so many others, it depicts the awful end of the servant-girl Catell-Gollet (*see* Guimiliau). The 19th-c. church, badly damaged in World War II, has been rebuilt in granite and reinforced concrete, with a brilliantly painted interior.

Two 'Pardons' are held here each year – one at the end of June and the other in mid-August.

PLOUMANACH, *Côtes-du-Nord* (1–B1, B2). Once a sleepy fishing port, Ploumanach, 6km NW of Perros-Guirec, has become a popular resort. The little harbour has become somewhat vulgarized, but just beyond the Promenade de la Bastille in the Bay of St-Guirec is a delightful and sheltered beach. A path uphill joins the Customs Patrol Path, which overlooks fabulously shaped rocks caused by centuries of erosion. The square granite lighthouse can be visited during the season and has splendid sea views from the lantern platform. A little further on, towards the Pointe du Squewel, a municipal park preserves some of the fantastic rocks in their original setting; particularly curious is the 'Devil's Castle' below on the seashore.

PONT-AVEN, *Finistère* (12km E of Concarneau: 1–C1). At the mouth of the tidal river Aven, the small town of Pont-Aven has attracted painters ever since Gauguin. Many of its picturesque old mills still survive. The museum has excellent art exhibitions during the season, often showing the work of Gauguin.

PONTIVY, *Morbihan* (1–C2). On the junction of the wide river Blavet and the Nantes–Brest Canal, Pontivy is an important market town. It grew to prosperity around the curiously squat-looking fortress, with its two huge bastion towers built in 1485. It has recently been restored and its deep moat lined with grass. The Old Town, with narrow cobbled streets and half-timbered houses surrounding the Place du Martray, contrasts

strangely with the New Town built by Napoleon in 1807. This was to have been a strongly defended strategic point on his new canal, linking Brest with Nantes to circumvent the English naval supremacy off the Atlantic coast. The town was laid out in long wide avenues on the grid-iron plan and renamed Napoléonville. After Napoleon's defeat, all building stopped and it reverted to its former name, changing back again for a short period during the Second Empire.

17km N, just over the department border, is Mur-de-Bretagne, a lively little town close to the long and sinuous reservoir of Lac de Guerlédan, in one of the most picturesque areas of inland Brittany.

QUIBERON, *Morbihan* (1–C2). On the S tip of the narrow 15km-long peninsula to which it gives its name, Quiberon is a lively and popular resort, with a huge, curving, safe, sandy beach. It has a consistently mild climate, and a reputation for seawater cures of nervous disorders.

The W end of the beach is bounded by Port Maria, where boats and ferries ply to and from Belle-Ile. From the Pointe du Conguel at the other end is a splendid view across the bay and of the many neighbouring islands. From the viewing point, the road turns sharply N to Port Haliguen.

In 1795 a small army of French exiles from England landed here, hoping to join forces with the Breton Chouans to restore the monarchy after the Revolution. The revolutionary General Hoche attacked and defeated them on the isthmus to the N. Many were killed in battle, others tried in vain to regain the English ships anchored off-shore in a dangerous swell. The survivors were taken prisoner and many of them were shot later by the Revolutionary Convention.

The W coast of the peninsula is well named the Côte Sauvage. The cliff path overlooks a wild grandeur of rocky grottoes, crevices and coves, lashed by tormented seas. There are tempting little sandy beaches below the cliffs which should be resisted, as powerful undercurrents make bathing extremely dangerous.

QUIMPER, *Finistère* (1–C1). A stone equestrian statue of the half-legendary 6th-c. King Gradlon, above the gabled W door of Quimper's cathedral, looks out over the graceful city he made his capital of Cornouaille.

Situated in a pretty valley where the sedate river Odet, flowing between tall hills, meets the lively river Steir, Quimper has the advantage of a long stretch of wide quayside along the Odet, bordering its central shopping district. All the most interesting parts of the city lie to the N side of the quay. The old lay-capital, with its Law Courts and main market, was built on the W side of the Steir, its streets still lined with many 15th-c. houses, built on foundations of indestructible Breton granite. Across the bridge on the E side of the Steir, the Rue Kéréon, with shops tumbled beneath

178

THE NORTHWEST: BRITTANY

Topham (Walter)

The Cathedral, Quimper

perilous-looking overhangs, opens up an imposing
view of the town's splendid twin-towered Cathedral of St-Corentin, named after King Gradlon's
first bishop.

Probably the earliest example of Gothic
architecture in Brittany, it is built throughout in
the hard granite of the province, but tamed by the
master masons and sculptors who fashioned the
soaring arches of the buttressed nave in the
15th-c., giving the church a rather sophisticated
Norman appearance. The chancel is 13th-c. and
somewhat out of alignment with the nave. The
upper windows of the nave have fine 15th-c. glass.
Surmounting the twin towers are remarkable
stone spires, added in 1852; so excellent was their
design and so quickly did the sea air tone down
their colour, that today they merge effortlessly
with the original fabric of the church.

The former Bishop's Palace, mostly early
16th-c., houses an excellent historical and folklore
museum, with a gallery devoted to Breton
costumes. Beyond this is a Pottery Gallery
showing how ceramics of the 16th-c., originating
in Rouen, gradually assumed Breton characteristics and became famous as Quimper ware. Nearby,
the Fine Arts Museum has one of the best art
collections in NW France.

For three days, ending on the fourth Sunday in
July each year, Quimper holds one of the biggest
Folk Festivals in Europe.

QUIMPERLÉ, *Finistère* (1–C2). At the junction
of the rivers Ellé and Isole, Quimperlé is a pleasant
and convenient centre for exploring the forest
country of Carnoët, rich in the ancient legends of
Cornouaille.

Once ruled by a strong English garrison until
liberated by Du Guesclin in 1373, it is divided
between the Upper Town, dominated by the
square tower of the Church of the Assumption,
and the Lower Town built around the ancient
abbey church of Ste-Croix, with a rotunda based
on the design of the Holy Sepulchre in Jerusalem.

REDON, *Ille-et-Vilaine* (1–C3). This small but
flourishing town on the crossing of the wide river
Vilaine and the Nantes–Brest Canal owes its
origin to a 9th-c. Benedictine abbey. The town
rapidly grew up around the monastery, and by the
14th-c. it was surrounded by ramparts; the
remains of these can be seen down by the Quai St-
Jacques.

The front of the abbey church of St-Sauveur
presents a strange sight with an isolated 13th-c.
Gothic tower and its tall octagonal stone spire
sweeping up from the centre of the Place de
l'Hôtel-de-Ville. It was separated from the main
body of the church by a disastrous fire in 1782. The
most interesting part of the church is its triple-
arcaded 12th-c. Romanesque tower over the
transept crossing, in alternate granite and sandstone. Under the vault of the tower a 13th-c.
fresco was recently cleaned to reveal a face of
Christ set in a geometric design. The elaborate
high altar, erected by Cardinal Richelieu when he
was Commendatory Abbot, somewhat detracts
from the beauty of the Gothic chancel.

Several characteristic 15th- and 16th-c. half-
timbered houses can be seen in the Grande-Rue.

RENNES, *Ille-et-Vilaine* (1–C3). Presenting a
generally 18th-c. classical appearance, with
impressive public buildings of granite and sandstone, spacious open squares and wide rectangular streets, this administrative centre of the
province of Brittany was already an ancient Celtic
town when the Romans gave the city its first wall.
Though contested by its rival town Nantes,
residence of the early Dukes of Brittany, Rennes
became the recognized capital of the Duchy in
1213 and the Dukes came here to be crowned. Its
situation near the French frontier gave it a
political and military importance which was
strengthened rather than diminished when the
popular Duchess Anne married Charles VIII of
France in 1491 and united the Duchy with France.
Despite this union, Breton privilege and pre-
rogative were jealously safeguarded, and in 1561
the Parliament of Brittany was established in the
city. Except for a troubled 19 years in the 17th-c., it
continued to meet until its final suppression during
the Revolution.

In 1720 Rennes experienced a great fire similar
to that of London some fifty years earlier. The

La Porte Mordelaise, Rennes

conflagration raged for a week, fanned by strong winds, and burned out the major part of the town. Over a thousand houses were destroyed. Such was the extent of the catastrophe that responsibility for rebuilding had to be left to the Crown. Under the young Louis XV, the architect Jacques Gabriel (father of Jacques-Ange who built the Place de la Concorde in Paris) set to work to restore the burned-out town. To him Rennes owes its layout and design in the Louis-Quinze manner. Tall buildings in severe classical style, beautifully proportioned, became flats or apartments, so that the citizens could be quickly rehoused. This may well have been the origin of the urban French custom of buying apartments rather than houses.

The magnificent PALAIS DE JUSTICE, formerly Parliament of Brittany, built between 1618 and 1655 by the architect of the Luxembourg Palace in Paris, fortunately escaped destruction in the great fire. However, its splendid pedimented and balustraded façade was damaged. Its restoration was undertaken by Gabriel while he laid out the harmonious rectangular Place du Palais. The visitor enters through the imposing Salle de Gros Piliers, leading to the Salle des Pas Perdus which extends the full length of the façade. Its wooden vaulted ceiling painted in blue and gold has the arms of France and Brittany centred conspicuously. A majestic double staircase sweeps up to the first floor where in numerous rooms some of the greatest artists employed by Louis XIV have left a rich heritage. The Grande Chambre highlights the importance and prestige of the Parliament. This former debating hall has an incomparable splendour of decoration. Predominantly crimson and gold in colour, its beautiful painted, carved and panelled ceiling covers the full 20m length of the chamber. The walls, 7m high, are hung with ten modern Gobelin tapestries which depict episodes from Brittany's historic past. An added theatricality is given by the finely decorated loggias from which important visitors could listen to the debates.

The restrained Baroque TOWN HALL, with its great clock 'Le Gros', was also the work of Jacques Gabriel. The Banqueting Hall is particularly impressive.

Except for its Renaissance façade and flanking towers the CATHEDRAL OF ST-PIERRE is comparatively modern, being the third church to be built on the site. It resembles one of the larger Roman churches of the time of Pope Pius IX. There is an exuberant 15th-c. Flemish altarpiece in a chapel before the S transept.

The MUSÉE DES BEAUX ARTS, severely damaged during the air raids of 1944, has been restored and has a large collection of paintings perhaps unrivalled in provincial France.

A part of Old Rennes survived the great fire and has preserved in its cobbled streets beyond the Cathedral some picturesque half-timbered houses with overhangs, dating from the 15th- and 16th-c. Some were obviously built by wealthy citizens. The Hôtel de Blossac in the Rue du Chapitre has a lovely curving staircase leading off from a courtyard. Nearby in the Rue St-Guillaume is perhaps the most visually satisfying of them all. It is now a restaurant called 'Ti-Koz' and specializes in that Breton delicacy – the pancake. Unfortunately the legend that the famous Breton knight Du Guesclin lived here must be discredited, since the house was certainly built more than a hundred years after his death.

Another survivor from the fire was the old city gate, called LA PORTE MORDELAISE, through which the Dukes and Duchesses of Brittany passed on their way to be crowned in the Cathedral. It is all that remains of the 15th-c. ramparts.

On the E side of the town are the famous THABOR GARDENS, covering 25 acres and once part of the monastery garden of the Benedictine abbey of St-Melaine. It comprises a grand formal French garden, a landscaped garden, a botanical garden and, in season, a wealth of rare rhododendrons and roses. There is even a children's garden, with a miniature zoo. The nearby abbey church has a partly 11th-c. tower and transept but was mostly rebuilt during the 14th- and 17th-c. To the left of the Place St-Melaine is the former 18th-c. Bishop's Palace. On the far side of the gardens lies the University city.

In the highly industrialized suburbs to the SW of the town are huge oil refineries and chemical and electronic works. SW, near the airport, is the important Rennes-La Janais Citroën car works.

ROCHEFORT-EN-TERRE, *Morbihan* (20km W of Redon: 1–C3). One of the best-kept villages in Morbihan, Rochefort-en-Terre is built on a rocky spur, surrounded on all sides by deep wooded valleys. It has a wealth of attractive old granite houses made bright by a profusion of well-tended window-boxes. The remains of the 12th-c. feudal castle were incorporated with taste into the present château by an American artist in the early part of the 20th-c. It is still occupied by his family, though open to the public. The view over the Gueuzon Valley from the terrace shows the full beauty of this countryside, which continues to attract painters from many parts of the world.

The 12th–16th-c. church has a well-cared-for look and possesses some fine Renaissance choirstalls and a skilfully wrought 18th-c. grille. A 'Pardon' is held here on the Sunday after 15 August each year, when a very ancient statue of the Blessed Virgin is venerated.

ROCHERS, Château des, *Ille-et-Vilaine* (7km SE of Vitré: 1–C4). This 14th-c. château was the home of the remarkable 17th-c. woman of letters, Madame de Sévigné. It has changed little since it was remodelled in her time. It consists of a modest two wings; its tall roofs, broken by round gables and pinnacled turrets, make an interesting skyline. It is linked by an iron grille to what appears to be an impressive octagonal and domed dovecot surmounted by a small belfry and cross. It is in fact the private chapel where she normally worshipped. The quiet garden was laid out by the celebrated Le Nôtre.

Madame de Sévigné's vivid letters, written to her daughter about simple country happenings and the foibles of the minor nobility in this corner of Brittany, have provided a valuable insight into life in France under Louis XIV.

The castle is still owned by the same family. Open to the public are the Green Room – containing the desk at which she wrote her 267 letters and many of her personal treasures – and the chapel.

ROSCOFF, *Finistère* (1–B1). Loading point for the familiar Breton onion-sellers and ferry-port connecting Brittany with Plymouth, Roscoff has always had important historical links with England. In 1387 the English burned the small town to the ground. Seventeen years later the Bretons had their revenge by defeating the English fleet off the Cape of St-Matthieu and capturing 40 ships. In 1548 the five-year-old Queen of Scots landed here for her engagement to the French Dauphin. The house in which she is said to have stayed can still be seen, with Tudor-like arched windows and door. It is near the parish church. Two hundred years later, Bonnie Prince Charlie landed here after his defeat at Culloden.

Roscoff's attractive port looks across to the rugged Ile de Batz, dominated by its tall lighthouse. The island can be reached by a regular motor-ferry which takes 15 minutes. There are some good sheltered sandy beaches out in the Gulf Stream. Those around Roscoff are mostly shingle.

The town owes its once considerable prosperity to its successful pirate adventurers. Today it is renowned as a huge distribution centre for vegetables, for its remarkable sea-cures and its important scientific research station in the field of marine biology.

A superb Renaissance tower, built up on three stages of supporting pillars, graces the Flamboyant church of Notre-Dame-de-Kroaz-Baz. In the former garden of the Capucin friars at the S edge of the town is an enormous fig-tree, planted by them around 1625 and, although propped up, still producing abundant fruit.

ROTHENEUF, *Ille-et-Vilaine* (5km NE of St-Malo: 1–B3). This family seaside resort has two excellent beaches, one open to the Channel and the other set in a cove, within what is almost a lagoon. There are interesting views from its clifftop, with tall pines and curving sweeps of dunes. The sheltered bay attracts large numbers of water skiers. Nearby are some rocks sculpted by a retired priest.

ST-BRIAC, *Ille-et-Vilaine* (6km W of Dinard: 1–B3). In one of the many indentations along the Emerald Coast is the pretty resort of St-Briac, named after a 6th-c. Irish monk. On the E bank of the wide estuary of the river Frémur, it has a lively fishing and yachting harbour and several pinelined beaches. Not least of its attractions is the beautifully laid-out golf course.

The town is linked by a 300m-long bridge crossing the river to Lancieux, which has a long sandy beach and westward views across the bay as far as St-Cast and the distant Cap Fréhel.

ST-BRIEUC, *Côtes-du-Nord* ((1–B2). Busy commercial and administrative capital of the department, St-Brieuc is a city of wide boulevards, tall skyscrapers with a nub of very old streets and ancient houses abutting its massive fortress-like Cathedral of St-Stephen. Built on a plateau between the two waterways of the Gouédic and the Gouët, their valleys crossed by impressive viaducts, it is just 4km from the sea.

The 13th- and 14th-c. Cathedral, built on the site chosen for the 5th-c. foundation by the Cardiganshire monk Brieuc and his companions, has a long history of sack and pillage. Turrets and towers with pepperpot roofs give variety to its otherwise rather grim outline. The interior has been happily restored to its former austerity. The nearby Rue Fardel has many old houses on its hillside, among them the Hôtel des Ducs de Bretagne which once sheltered James II after he was deposed from the English throne in 1688. Not

St-Briac

far from here is a lovely 15th-c. Flamboyant Gothic portico sheltering the ancient Fontaine de Notre-Dame, built out from the restored chapel which stands over the reputed site of the first oratory of St-Brieuc.

There are interesting walks in almost every direction from the town centre, with extensive views over the countryside and out to sea. The best view is from the high mound called the Tertre Aubé with its sight of the dormitory town and port of Légué; to the right are the romantic ruins of the Tour de Cesson built over the site of a Roman camp and demolished by Henri IV at the request of the townsfolk.

The 'Pardon' of Notre-Dame-d'Espérance takes place on the night of 31 May, and there is a lively Michaelmas Fair on 29 September.

ST-CAST-LE-GUILDO, *Côtes-du-Nord* (1–B3). A very popular resort on a peninsula, with one of the largest beaches in Brittany, St-Cast incorporates four main areas. Les Mielles is the main hotel and shopping centre. L'Isle, to the N of the 2km-long sandy beach, has a lively fishing and yacht harbour. Le Bourg is the administrative centre and has an interesting modern church with a window depicting the defeat of the English in the battle of St-Cast during the Seven Years War. La Garde is a well-wooded residential quarter, laid out like a garden-city; from the Pointe de la Garde is a good view across the bay and down to the beach of Pen-Guen and the Arguenon estuary.

The tall monument in the Rue de la Colonne commemorates that same battle of St-Cast and is surmounted by the French greyhound trampling the English leopard.

From the N tip on the Pointe de St-Cast there is a fine view of the Emerald Coast to the E and W. The rugged Forte la Latte with its massive circular keep can be seen away to the NW; strengthened by Vauban in the 17th-c., it has stood on its rocky promontory for over a thousand years.

ST-LUNAIRE, *Ille-et-Vilaine* (4km W of Dinard: 1–B3). A fashionable small resort situated on a peninsula, with beaches on both sides of its northern tip, the Pointe du Décollé. This is joined to the mainland by a natural granite bridge crossing a fissure in the rock, called the 'Cat's Leap'. There are splendid views of long stretches of the Emerald Coast from the promenades. Seen from the bridge above, a fascinating grotto known as the 'Siren's Cave' is spectacular at high tide.

ST-MALO, *Ille-et-Vilaine* (1–B3). One of the most interesting and popular resorts in France, with access to miles of sandy beaches, St-Malo is built on a rocky promontory surrounded by impressive ramparts, and looks as though it is hundreds of years old. In fact it is almost entirely new.

During the first two weeks of August 1944 the ancient city, which had been the pivot of a powerful German resistance, was pounded to ruin by the American forces. Only the strong medieval ramparts and a few granite houses survived the bombardment. With remarkable energy and skill the post-war restorers have rebuilt the town and the Cathedral. St-Malo today looks almost exactly as it did before the war, down to the most humble twisted cobbled streets.

Its history begins in the late 6th-c. with the coming of a Welsh missionary bishop called Malo, who settled in the Gallo-Roman town of Aleth, now part of St-Servan, the suburb to the S of St-Malo. After the colony was sacked and pillaged, first by the troops of the Emperor Charlemagne and later by Norman invaders, the town and bishopric moved to the more easily defended rocky promontory to the N, the site of the present town. From early times the bishops claimed sole sovereignty, and it was they who built the strong ramparts and led the town into prosperity. The Dukes of Brittany, envious of St-Malo's power and wealth, never succeeded in crushing the independent spirit of the fortified city.

During the Hundred Years War St-Malo took the side of France; in 1378 the Breton knight Du Guesclin came to the aid of the town by defeating the besieging Duke of Lancaster. Some time later, through papal intervention, St-Malo was declared a free port, to the considerable enrichment of the sea-orientated inhabitants, aided by an addiction to piracy that was silently encouraged by the French kings (when the Bretons were on their side). Perhaps the title 'Corsair City' dates from the successful pirate raid on Yarmouth in the Isle of Wight in 1405.

When one of its famous sons, Jacques Cartier, discovered the mouth of the St Lawrence in 1534 and called the region Canada, St-Malo's sea traders were not slow to seize the opportunity of widening their commercial horizon. The town's overseas ventures helped to increase its spirit of independence, so much so that during the Wars of Religion it declared – and for four years actually maintained – its political independence, declaring in its motto, 'I am neither a Frenchman nor a Breton, I am a man of St-Malo.'

Such a history, together with the wealth and power of its merchants and ship-owners (among whom must be counted Chateaubriand, the great 18th–19th-c. writer and one-time ambassador to England), has left its imprint on much of the town's characteristic architecture.

To appreciate the variety of St-Malo there is no better way than by simply walking round the ramparts, starting at the Port St-Vincent near the car-ferry terminal and the new Olympic pool. Turning left, almost immediately there are good views across the busy commercial and yacht harbours, and the modern suburbs of Paramé and St-Servan. Between the bastions of St-Louis and St-Philippe the view opens out to the sea; here, facing out across the ramparts, are some of the best examples of the elegant town houses owned by the rich privateers of the past. On the next stretch, along the western ramparts leading to the

St-Malo

J. Schweisthal

Tour Bidouaine, the sea-view extends right across the estuary to Dinard and the Emerald Coast beyond. Close inshore is the islet of Grand Bé, which can be reached on foot at low tide; Chateaubriand was buried here in a lonely tomb, on his own instructions.

As the wall swings E, the Fort National, built on a little island of rock in 1689, comes into view, and finally, at the NE corner of the town, stands the square castle (now housing the town hall) with its formidable keep, built in 1424 and containing a historical museum. On the NW wing of the castle Anne de Bretagne built a tower, despite protests from the bishop. It is called the Quic-en-Groigne, from the first words ('Who complains . . .') of the motto carved on the tower, forming part of the rough retort made by the Duchess to the complaining bishop. It is now a fascinating museum-cum-waxworks vividly portraying the highlights of St-Malo's history. Close by is an unusual aquarium of fish mostly native to the Emerald Coast.

At frequent intervals along the ramparts, stone steps and ramps lead back into the town. Dominating the centre of it is the impressive Gothic Cathedral of St-Vincent, rebuilt in typical Breton granite and incorporating the remains of the 12th–18th-c. building. A long flight of steps leads down into the nave, which is lit by fine modern stained-glass windows by Max Ingrand. In a side chapel is a simple black marble slab covering a tomb, incised only with the name, Jacques Cartier.

ST-MICHEL-EN-GRÈVE, *Côtes-du-Nord* (10km SW of Lannion: 1–B2). Lying at the E extremity of a spectacular piece of highway called the Armorican Corniche, St-Michel-en-Grève is an attractive little resort, commanding a vast stretch of flat sand extending 5km W, called the Lieu de Grève. At a halfway point, a huge rock rises 80m from the sand; the view from the top, reached by a steep path, is very rewarding. At extremely low tides the sea recedes to the far horizon, revealing fossilized tree trunks, remains of a vast forest which once covered the bay.

Near here, an Irish monk called Efflam with seven companions set up a hermitage in AD 470. His name was given to the next little village resort, where every year pilgrims gather at an ancient domed fountain. At the far W end of the Corniche, in the next bay, is the little fishing and sailing resort of Locquirec.

ST-POL-DE-LÉON, *Finistère* (1–B1). Situated in the rather flat countryside bordering the Bay of Morlaix, St-Pol-de-Léon, a busy vegetable market town famous for its artichokes, has two remarkable churches.

The 14th–15th-c. former cathedral, dedicated to its Welsh founder-saint, Paul the Aurelian, replaced an earlier Romanesque building. Looking surprisingly Norman in appearance, its perfect

A.F. Kersting

The Cathedral, St-Pol-de-Léon

proportions throughout have always excited the admiration of architects. The W front has three great windows surmounting a fine porch, topped by another storey with four graceful arches set back from a finely carved balustrade. The whole granite façade is set between two elegantly spired towers. The nave is built entirely of Norman sandstone. The S transept has a huge, beautiful rose-window. Just behind the high altar, and curving over it, is a carved and gilded palm tree, shaped like a crozier. The 16th-c. Gothic carved choir-stalls, with 68 places for canons, attendants and singers, witness the church's earlier episcopal importance.

Not far from the old cathedral, and now used by an adjoining college, is the 14th–15th-c. Kreisker Chapel, with one of the most splendid spired belfry towers in France. The granite stonework of the steeple, begun in 1350, is so delicately carved that it appears as a miracle of grace and balance. It soars over 75m into the sky. It has been several times copied, but never equalled.

ST-THÉGONNEC, *Finistère* (1–B1). A massive Triumphal Arch, built in 1587 and representing the Gateway to Paradise, leads into one of the finest parish closes in Brittany and reflects the wealth amassed by St-Thégonnec's once-important linen industry. Its Calvary, though having fewer figures at its base than its rival at Guimiliau, has unusual two-tiered pedestal arms beneath the central cross and is a piece of unsurpassed early-17th-c. Breton sculpture. In a niche, it shows the founder Thégonnec with the wolf he tamed.

In the crypt of the elaborate ossuary of 1676, later transformed into a splendid chapel supported by elegant Corinthian columns, is an imposing group vividly portraying the Entombment of Christ.

The parish church is so ornately carved that it has almost the appearance of an Indian temple. The Renaissance tower is probably the finest in the province, with a graceful lantern dome. The tower almost masks an early piece of Gothic survival in a gabled belfry. Inside the church, the pulpit is an amazing example of Breton wood-carving, achieved by two brothers in 1683. The canopy, finished later in 1732, rises to a crescendo of triumph with the Angel of Judgment, shown with almost Baroque gusto, sounding a final fanfare.

TRÉBEURDEN, *Côtes-du-Nord* (1–B1, B2). Particularly noted for its many crescent-shaped beaches of fine sand, each separated by narrow arms of rock jutting out to sea, Trébeurden has always held an attraction for French families with children.

An isthmus leading to a rocky mound called Le Castel divides the two main beaches. From the top of the Castel the distant coast of Finistère can be seen in clear weather. At the S end of the long, sweeping Tresmeur beach, the Pointe de Bahit looks out over islands dotting a sea made colourful in summer by the sails of small yachts.

TRÉGASTEL, *Côtes-du-Nord* (2km W of Ploumanach: 1–B1, B2). Whether inland, on its beaches, or off-shore, Trégastel looks as though it had once been the scene of a titanic struggle between prehistoric giants. Everywhere are huge boulders and rocks of pinky-grey granite moulded over the ages by the forces of nature into fantastic

shapes, and trivialized by man with fanciful names like 'The Tortoises', 'The Corkscrew', 'The Death Head' and so on. The little town of Trégastel, 3km inland, has a 12th–13th-c. parish church, also a good Breton Calvary standing on a knoll with fine views out to sea.

TRÉGUIER, *Côtes-du-Nord* (1–B2). Terraced up the side of a hill overlooking the junction of the rivers Guindy and Jaudy, where the latter opens out into a wide estuary, Tréguier was at one time the capital of the whole Trégor region.

Its magnificent granite Gothic Cathedral, dedicated to its founder the Welsh monk Tugdual, is one of the finest in Brittany. Originally the seat of an important bishopric, it has three towers, all of them over the transept. From the central Place du Martray, the intricate open-slatted spire over the S arm soars up well over 60m. Over the N arm is a Romanesque tower which is all that remains of the original 13th-c. church. The Sanctus Tower above the transept crossing, though somewhat squat, rises over 30m. The Cathedral's interior has a splendour matching the grace of its external 15th-c. walls and buttresses. It is lit by 68 windows, whose medieval glass was destroyed in the Revolution and has been replaced by modern stained glass. Just off the chancel, through the Porte St-Jean, are beautiful cloisters built in 1461 with 42 delicate ogival arcades, supported by slender little columns. From an angle at the far end, there is a superb view of the triple-towered Cathedral.

In the finest of the 13 chapels, known as the Chœur du Duc, is a modern reproduction of the 15th-c. tomb of St Yves, also destroyed in the Revolution. St Yves, a 13th-c. priest and magis-

St-Thégonnec: the Entombment of Christ in the crypt of the chapel

A.F. Kersting

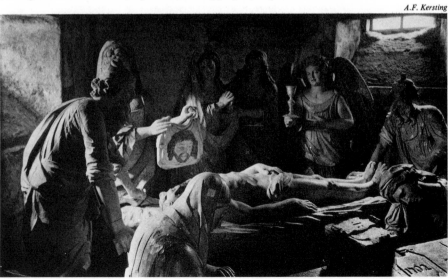

Trébeurden

trate, is not only the patron saint of Brittany but of lawyers all over the world. Yves Hélori was born in the Manor of Kermartin in Minihy-Tréguier, 2km S of the town centre. Such was his fame as a 'righter of wrongs' that he was canonized only 45 years after his death in 1303. One of the greatest of all the Breton 'Pardons' is held on 19 May and draws thousands of pilgrims to assist at 'the ceremony in honour of Monsieur St-Yves' and the blessing of the poor. The huge procession, often including world-famous men of law, goes from the Cathedral to the church built over the house where Yves lived and died. In the centre of the cemetery is a low 13th-c. stone table, possibly an altar, where the relics of the saint are placed during the festival. The Breton costumes, the bagpipe music, the sound of bombards, the candles and banners, and later the dancing, make this one of the most colourful of the 'Pardons'.

Paradoxically, the statue of one of France's greatest rationalist writers, Ernest Renan, stands in the square in front of the Cathedral. The 17th-c. half-timbered house where he was born in 1823 is now a Renan museum.

TRINITÉ-SUR-MER, La, *Morbihan* (1–C2). On the W bank of the Crac'h Estuary, which flows into Quiberon Bay, La Trinité-sur-Mer is a paradise for yachtsmen, with a sheltered harbour and moorings for 700 boats. A good choice of

hotels and restaurants and a long sweep of sandy beach have made it a popular resort. Trinité is also an important centre for the flat Belon oyster culture. The long Kerisper Bridge crossing the estuary makes easy access to the renowned megaliths and dolmens of Locmariaquer.

VAL-ANDRÉ, Le, *Côtes-du-Nord* (13km N of Lamballe: 1–B3). Most westerly resort of the Emerald Coast, Le Val-André is fringed by a splendid sheltered beach of golden sand. Its long promenade extends for 2km, from the Pointe de Pléneuf in the NE as far as the Pointe des Murs Blancs in the SW. With every amenity for the holiday-maker, it gets very crowded in summer. The town is linked to the village of Pléneuf, where a tumulus, dolmen and cromlechs are evidence of its antiquity.

At the SW end of the promenade is a little port; here a path signposted 'La Guette' leads to a walk with sweeping views over the whole of St-Brieuc Bay with its long and dramatic coastline. From the far end of this walk the once important fishing port of Dahouët can be seen lying in a creek between high cliffs.

VANNES, *Morbihan* (1–C2). A flourishing agri-cultural and industrial centre, Vannes is a town of great dignity, with a long and distinguished past. A Celtic chieftain, descendant of the ancient British emigrants driven from their homeland in the 5th-c. by the invading Anglo-Saxons, was made Count of Vannes by the Emperor Charlemagne, and in AD 826 became the first Duke of Brittany. Within ten years he had unified the whole province under his rule and made Vannes its capital. It was to hold this position until the time of the French Revolution.

Escaping major damage in World War II, the town has retained all its charm and much of its unhurried vitality. The little Place Henri IV in the centre of the Old Town is lined with 15th–16th-c. half-timbered overhanging houses with tall roofs. At one corner the 13th-c. Romanesque belfry of the Cathedral of St-Pierre rises majestically above the rooftops.

Quite the most interesting part of the many-times restored Cathedral is the fine circular granite Renaissance chapel built on to the N side of the church in 1537. It catches the classical spirit of the Renaissance as perhaps no other building in Brittany. It has two storeys, with a conical roof dating only from 1829. The first storey has charming pedimented niches divided by Doric columns. The second storey, separated by a Latin inscription encircling the tower, depends for its decoration on rounded arches and Ionic columns. Inside the main church, the Chapel of the Blessed Sacrament shows the same classical purity and houses the tomb of the influential Spanish Dominican friar, St Vincent Ferrer. An eloquent preacher, he was instrumental in ending the papal schism between Rome and Avignon which had

Vannes: the old walls and ancient wash-houses

divided loyalties all over Europe for so long. A 17th-c. tapestry depicts scenes from his life. The house where he lived for two years, and in which he died in 1419, can be seen and visited in the nearby Place Valencia, which is part of the Rue des Orfèvres.

Still in this quarter of narrow cobbled streets is the Rue Noé where, on a corner just S of the Cathedral, is a 15th-c. house with one of its timber beam-ends carved humorously with two figures called 'Vannes and his wife.' No one quite knows their origin, but they are worth searching out. This leads on to the Place des Lices, scene of many medieval tournaments.

Also within this area is the 15th-c. residence of Bishop Jean de Malestroit, which in troubled times became Brittany's first Parliament building. Known as Château Gaillard, it now houses a comprehensive museum of prehistoric antiquities. The ramparts are remarkably well preserved, with little obvious restoration. The granite Constable's Tower, built after the town had suffered four sieges during the War of Succession, presents a striking picture when the whole town is floodlit at night during the season. The great moat, built for its defence, is now filled in and laid out as a garden. From a parapet, the visitor can obtain a view of the long-roofed 'wash-houses' bordering a pretty stream, where in earlier times the women of

Vannes in their flat starched lace head-dresses came to do their communal laundry and to gossip.

The proximity of Vannes to the Gulf of Morbihan makes it a popular centre for excursions, with a wide choice of steamer services during the summer season.

VITRÉ, *Ille-et-Vilaine* (1–C4). Built high on a spur above the cleft valley of the river Vilaine, the walled border-town of Vitré is dominated by its formidable triangular granite fortress. It is probably the best preserved and most characteristic of Brittany's many medieval cities.

The pepperpot-capped bastions, massive curtain-walls and machicolated towers of the feudal castle date from the strengthening and rebuilding activities of the 14th- and 15th-c. The impressive entrance, flanked by two massive towers supporting a redoubt, was strong enough to give confidence to defenders garrisoned inside. Indeed, during the Hundred Years War it was attacked many times without success by the English, who had occupied the N part of the town. After some years they were paid off by the disgruntled townsfolk. The area is still called 'Rachapt', meaning 'bought back'. Inside the castle walls, the town hall now occupies the former seignorial lodgings. Nearby is a gallery leading to the chapel, which has an elegant little early-16th-c.

apsidal loggia emblazoned with arms and the inscription 'After the darkness, I hope for light'. Three of the towers have been converted into an interesting museum.

The view over the town from the castle-wall walk reveals Vitré's wealth of old houses. Due to its proximity to France (in the days when Brittany was an independent province), the town was also protected by strong ramparts, which still survive intact on the N and S sides. On the S side is the sturdy Porte d'Embas, once a city gate through the ramparts. It leads to the Rue Beaudrairie, a hilly street leading up to the castle and lined with medieval houses, many half-timbered and slate-roofed and some with curiously shaped gables. This is only one of many streets where 15th- and 16th-c. houses are perfectly preserved.

The 15th-c. Flamboyant church of Notre-Dame affords an unusual silhouette on the S side, with seven pinnacled and sculpted gables. On the exterior below is a finely chiselled stone pulpit, from which the Catholics debated publicly with the Calvinist followers of the Coligny family who owned the town. In the sacristy is a 16th-c. triptych embellished by Limoges enamels.

From a path high up on the W extremity of Vitré, called 'Le Chemin des Tertres Noirs', there is an extensive panorama of city and fortress below.

Château des Rochers, Vitré

A.F. Kersting

The Northeast: Introduction

Champagne, Alsace, Lorraine, Franche-Comté

Edward Young

The old province of Champagne stretches due north from Burgundy to the Ardennes on the Belgian border. Most of it is a chalky plain – cold, wet and windy in winter – but not all of it is as flat as the wheat-growing area centred on Troyes. The very north, the Ardennes, is heavily wooded, and in Haute-Marne, towards the Jura, the ground rises gradually to pleasant hills and valleys with lively rivers. For the tourist, however, the most interesting and scenically attractive corner of the province is undoubtedly the small area of gently rolling hills known as the Montagne de Reims between Reims and Épernay, the two rival 'capitals' of the champagne wine district.

Épernay is the smaller town, but it is closer to the vineyards themselves. It lies on the Marne, a surprisingly modest river which wanders westward along a gentle valley, where on the south-facing slopes of the 'montagne' acres of sun-warmed vineyards stretch as far as the eye can see. Immediately south of Épernay are the other champagne vineyards of the Côte des Blancs and the valley of the little Cubry. On the eastern and northern slopes of the 'montagne' the vineyards curve round towards Reims, a historic city that has the advantage of possessing one of the most famous cathedrals in the world.

The whole of this area has a subsoil of solid chalk – part of the same chalk stratum which emerges further north as the white cliffs of the Pas-de-Calais and the southeast coast of England. The chalk was used by the Romans to make roads, Reims Cathedral was built of it, the trenches of World War I were dug out of it, and a rabbit-warren of champagne cellars burrows into it. In these cellars, some of which extend for twenty kilometres or more, millions of bottles lie stacked, undergoing the various stages of fermentation, ageing, *remuage*, *dégorgement*, etc. at a constant temperature of 10–12°C. In both Reims and Épernay the tourist office will arrange a visit to one of the champagne cellars (an unforgettable experience) and provide a map of routes through exquisite vineyard scenery.

Eastward from Champagne lie the former provinces of Alsace and Lorraine. Surprisingly, this is the only part of France to have a common frontier with Germany. It has frequently suffered enemy invasion. For nearly fifty years, from the defeat of France in 1870 to the Allied victory in 1918, the whole of Alsace and the northeast corner of Lorraine belonged by treaty to Germany, yet – despite the German-sounding names of some of the towns, and the German (or perhaps Austrian) look of many of the villages – the population remained and still remains passionately French.

Farming scene in the Vosges mountains   A.F. Kersting

The soil of Lorraine is stubborn, the climate somewhat harsh, yet there are not only thick forests dotted with lakes but large areas of undulating cornfields, orchards of cherries and plums to be distilled into delicious liqueurs such as *kirsch*, *mirabelle and quetsche* (and they also make a *framboise* liqueur which 'goes down like firewater and comes back like raspberries') – and near Hohneck on the high ridge of the thickly-forested Vosges mountains is an unexpected stretch of pastureland where graze the cows that produce the milk for the cheeses of Munster and Géromé. From Lorraine's soil, too, come iron ore and coal, mineral springs (Vittel and Contrexéville) and something like half the salt produced in France.

Alsace, the most easterly of these northeast provinces, is a narrow strip running north and south and consisting of just two departments, Haut-Rhin and Bas-Rhin, each of which has the Vosges mountains to the west, the Rhine to the east and the plain of Alsace in the centre. Of its three main towns, Mulhouse is mainly industrial, Colmar has a charming old quarter of houses with carved wooden façades, and Strasbourg, the capital (and the seat of the Council of Europe), is a historic and lively city with an outstanding cathedral whose tower looks across the Rhine into Germany. Most tourists will want to follow the Route du Vin and drink the cool, light and 'grapey' Alsatian white wines. This well-posted route along the eastern slopes of the Vosges follows quiet roads through vineyards and sleepy wine towns and villages – Riquewihr, Obernai, Molsheim and dozens of others – with their modest Romanesque churches, their old town gateways, their fountains, their gabled houses and twisting alleyways – and their inevitable storks' nests.

Franche-Comté runs south from Lorraine almost to Geneva, its eastern boundary following the crests and western slopes of the Jura. It is a region relatively unfrequented by tourists, partly because its towns – apart from Besançon and Belfort – are not particularly interesting, and partly because of its high rainfall. Yet it is this rain that is the source of its beauty, especially in the late spring when, after a long severe winter, the snows in the valleys melt, the air is soft, and the green slopes are a carpet of crocus, narcissus, orchid and the yellow gentian. The swollen rivers roar and tumble over waterfalls, and the lakes behind the hydro-electric dams are brim-full. The summers can be very hot, often with little rain, except when sudden storms refill the rivers and send grey squalls sweeping across the emerald lakes. The mountain slopes echo with the whine of the mechanical saw and the musical notes of cowbells. The cows here are the colour of cream, with patches of reddish brown, and their milk will go to the cheese factories to be made into Gruyère. In September the vineyards north of Lons-le-Saunier are busy with the grape-harvest; some of these grapes will become the dry, fragrant, nutty *vin jaune* called Château-Châlon, rarely met with outside Franche-Comté. Too soon snow will start falling in the higher valleys, the skiers will come, and the isolated farmhouses with their wide overhanging roofs will settle down to their long winter.

The Northeast: Gazetteer

Edward Young

AMMERSCHWIHR, *Haut-Rhin* (5km NW of Colmar: 3–D8). Small wine town on the vine-clad eastern slopes of the Vosges mountains. Except for the church, the façade of the Hôtel-de-Ville, the town gateway with its tower, sundial and storks' nest, and two other old defence towers, the town was virtually destroyed in World War II (including half a million gallons of wine). It has now been completely rebuilt in the true Alsatian style, including the restaurant of M. Gaertner which under its new name, 'Aux Armes de France', has maintained its reputation as one of the hundred best restaurants in the country.

BAR-LE-DUC, *Meuse* (3–C6, C7). A busy industrial town (metallurgy, textiles, etc.) and famous for its redcurrant jam. During World War I it was the S end of the only road left open by which supplies and reinforcements could get through to beleaguered Verdun (56km N – *see entry*); even today the road – the 'Sacred Way' – has no number, appearing on the maps simply as 'N (Voie Sacrée)'. At the summit of the old part of the town, which still has many elegant 16th-c. houses, stands the Gothic church of St-Pierre, containing the curious 16th-c. 'Skeleton' statue of René de Châlon, a Prince of Orange; it was made in accordance with his dying wish as he lay mortally wounded in battle.

BELFORT, *Territoire de Belfort* (3–D8, E8). The 'Belfort Gap' between the Vosges and Jura ranges has long been a traditional route for invaders from the E – from the Celts to the Germans. Vauban was commanded by Louis XIV to make Belfort impregnable, and he succeeded so well that in 1870 the town, with a garrison of 16,000 men, withstood a siege by 40,000 Germans for over 100 days until the French government ordered it to surrender. Belfort's courage was recognized in the peace treaty which handed Alsace and Lorraine to the Germans, for though until then part of Alsace it was allowed to remain French as the capital of a small autonomous *territoire* (and has remained so ever since). Economically it benefited from the influx of hundreds of skilled Alsatian refugees; with renewed industrial activity it grew from a population of 8000 in 1870 to nearly 60,000 at the present time. Today its industries include metallurgy, textiles, plastics, electric locomotives, and electric typewriters and calculators. It has also become an important tourist centre for skiing, climbing and walking.

The Vauban fortifications are well worth a visit,

The statue of the Lion of Belfort

French Government Tourist Office

if only for the magnificent views of the Vosges and Juras. Within the ramparts is an interesting museum illustrating Belfort's military past. Below, at the foot of the rock, is the famous, enormous statue of the Lion of Belfort (11m high, 22m long) carved in 1880 by the sculptor Bartholdi (*see also* Colmar) to symbolize the heroism of the town's defenders in the siege of ten years earlier.

BESANÇON, *Doubs* (3–E7). Largest town and the capital of the old province of Franche-Comté, situated on the NW flank of the Jura mountains. Its unusual setting, within a huge loop of the river Doubs and ringed by hills, has made it a natural strategic site since Gallo-Roman times. In recent times Besançon has overflowed on to the further bank, but the old town slopes up from river level towards the Citadel on its high rock at the neck of the loop, 120m above the river.

The visitor is advised to enter the old town by the Pont Battant, park near the river and walk up the Grande-Rue, which has been the main street ever since the Romans built it. It climbs in a roughly straight line for over half a kilometre, past a Renaissance palace with a cloistered courtyard, decent 16th–17th-c. houses, including the house where Victor Hugo was born (No. 140) and, near the top of the town on the corner of Place Victor Hugo, the birthplace of the Lumière brothers who invented the cinematograph. Nearby to the left is an attractive garden with a grotto and a row of antique columns; directly opposite to the right stands the old Bishop's Palace, today occupied by a branch of the University. At the top of the Grande-Rue the road passes through a 2nd-c. Roman archway, known as the Porte Noire, and comes to the modest Cathedral of St-Jean, mostly 12th-c. but with an 18th-c. belfry replacing the original tower which had collapsed. In the interior is a fine painting, 'The Virgin with Saints' by Fra Bartolomeo (*c.* 1474–1517). In an adjoining building there is a remarkable astronomical clock, best seen between the hours of 12 a.m. and 3 p.m.

Beyond the Cathedral a path zigzags upward to the summit of the rock. The present fortress, the Citadel, was erected by Vauban in the 17th-c.; the outer walls are still much as they were then, but the area within the walls is now occupied by some attractive little museums of local interest and a small zoo park. From the watch-path on the walls there are splendid views of town and valley.

Down by the river, facing the Place de la Révolution near the Pont Battant, the Musée des Beaux-Arts is well worth a visit. The interior, designed by a pupil of Le Corbusier, is arranged on a series of ramps and gentle gradients. The collection contains works by painters such as Bellini, Giorgione, Renoir and Bonnard; also landscape sketches by Courbet, who was born at Ornans (25km SE – *see entry*) and studied in Besançon. There is also an absorbing collection of clocks and watches, a reminder that watchmaking is one of the town's principal industries.

Another important local industry is the manufacture of artificial silk. The process was first perfected here in 1884 by the Comte de Chardonnet, a civil engineer, and the first factory in the world to make artificial fibres was set up in Besançon six years later.

CHÂLONS-SUR-MARNE, *Marne* (3–C6). A large city crossed by the river Marne and several canals. Administrative centre of the Marne department, it lies in the centre of the great plain of Champagne, with main roads coming into it like the spokes of a wheel. It is an important agricultural market and food distribution centre, and it makes a little champagne and a good deal of high-quality beer. St-Étienne Cathedral is a huge Gothic edifice with a wealth of stained glass from the 12th- to the 13th-c. The church of Notre-Dame-en-Vaux, is 12th-c. and a mixture of Romanesque and Gothic styles; it is rich in stained glass and has a famous carillon of 56 bells.

CHARLEVILLE-MÉZIÈRES, *Ardennes* (3–B6). Originally two independent towns, this capital of the Ardennes department lies within two loops of the river Meuse. Charleville, the northern half, where the French poet Rimbaud was born in 1854, was laid out in the 17th-c. on a regular grid plan, centred on the spacious Place Ducale. Unfortunately the Ducal Palace itself was pulled down in the mid-19th-c. to make way for the present Hôtel-de-Ville, but the square is still imposingly grand and makes a fine sight on market day. The southern part of the town, Mézières, is older, with

The Church of Notre-Dame-en-Vaux, Chalons-sur-Marne

remains of medieval ramparts. Throughout World War I Charleville-Mézières was in the hands of the Germans, and the Kaiser sometimes resided there. A few hours before the Armistice the German troops opened fire on the town, causing much damage. In World War II the town suffered further damage during the German advance of 1940.

CHAUMONT, *Haute-Marne* (3–D6, D7). Situated in a picturesque setting in gently undulating country between the rivers Marne and Suize, which join just N of the town. The chief local industry is glove-making. The Basilica of St-Jean, surrounded by an old quarter that has preserved many old houses with corner staircase turrets, is a twin-spired church of different periods from simple Gothic to elegant Renaissance. A plaque on the Hôtel-de-Ville records the fact that the American General Pershing set up his headquarters here in 1917.

27km NW, on the main road to Bar-sur-Aube (N19), is the village of **Colombey-les-Deux-Églises,** home of General de Gaulle, the former President of France. He retired here after the election defeat of 1969 and died here in the following year. His grave is in the village cemetery, and there is a memorial to him on a nearby hill in the form of a huge Cross of Lorraine, the double-barred cross which he used as the Free French symbol during World War II.

COLMAR, *Haut-Rhin* (3–D8). Capital of the department, and an Alsatian town of immense charm, with an old quarter of narrow streets and carved wooden houses (notably the Maison Pfister in Rue Mercière and the Maison des Têtes in the street named after it) and a picturesque 'Little Venice' area bordering the modest river Lauch.

It also contains two famous masterpieces of painting. The earliest of them is the entrancing 'Virgin and the Rosebush' by Martin Schongauer, the 15th-c. painter who was born and lived in Colmar. Normally it is to be found in the 13th–14th-c. Gothic church of St-Martin, but at the time of writing this church was in course of restoration and the painting was on display in the nearby Church of the Dominicans (which has some fine 14th–15th-c. stained glass).

The other painting is the great Issenheim Altarpiece, painted early in the 16th-c. by Mathias Grünewald. The monastery for which it was painted was suppressed at the time of the Revolution, and the painting, with its hinged panels unfolding scenes from the New Testament, was brought to Colmar in 1793. It is now in the former chapel of the Musée d'Unterlinden, a collection of paintings, local history and folklore housed in a 13th-c. monastery – whose cloisters, an oasis of tranquil serenity, are the setting for widely celebrated Thursday evening musical *soirées* during the summer.

Colmar is well known for its various summer folklore events, including a Wine Fair in the middle of August and a *Fête de la Choucroute* in September. It was also the birthplace of Bartholdi, the 19th-c. sculptor of New York's Statue of Liberty and the Lion of Belfort (*see entry*), and of Baron Haussmann, who transformed the face of Paris with his grand boulevards but happily left his native Colmar untouched.

DOLE, *Jura* (3–E7). Charming little town on the river Doubs SE of Dijon. Pasteur was born here in 1822, the son of a tanner; his birthplace, situated between the Canal des Tanneurs and the Rue Pasteur, has been turned into a fascinating Pasteur museum. The high belfry of the 16th-c. church of Notre-Dame stands at the centre of the old quarter of the town, with its narrow streets twisting and climbing up from the river, its remarkable old houses of all periods from the 15th- to the 18th-c., and its glimpses of arcaded courtyards, outside staircases, fountains and wrought-iron grilles. A pleasant view over the roofs of the old town can be had from the delightful Place aux Fleurs.

DOMRÉMY-LA-PUCELLE, *Vosges* (3–D7). On the river Meuse, 10km N of Neufchâteau, lies this village in which Joan of Arc (*La Pucelle,* the Maid) was born in 1412. Her birthplace can be visited; it is a small house, and next door to it is a museum devoted to her history. The church has been considerably altered since her day, but the medieval font at which she was baptized can be seen in the N transept. 1½km S is the modern Basilica of Bois-Chenu, built on the supposed spot where at the age of 13 she first heard the 'voices' urging her to liberate France from the English yoke.

EGUISHEIM, *Haut-Rhin* (5km SW of Colmar: 3–D8). Time seems to have stopped still in this small wine town surrounded by vineyards, with little streets and alleyways bordered by old houses and Renaissance fountains. It is dominated by the three red-sandstone towers of the old hilltop castle, whose rampart walls date back as far as the 8th-c. The church is modern, with stained-glass windows representing scenes from the life of Pope Leo IX, who was born near Strasbourg in the year 1002.

ÉPERNAY, *Marne* (3–C5). Vies with Reims as one of the two wine capitals of Champagne. It has paid the penalty for its strategic position on the river Marne by having been destroyed so many times in its history – by sacking, burning and bombardment – that it has virtually nothing left of historic or architectural interest. But it is an agreeable small town, nicely laid out with green open spaces, and devotes most of its energies to the production of champagne.

In the chalk subsoil, at a constant temperature of 10–12 °C., are over 100km of cellars. Most of the big firms have offices in the Avenue de Champagne and are prepared to receive visitors, but some, like Moët & Chandon and Mercier in particular, organize guided tours and explain the whole process of manufacture. Full information on visiting champagne cellars can be obtained from the tourist office in Place Thiers. On the N side of the Avenue is a fascinating museum devoted largely to champagne and its history and partly to local prehistory and archaeology.

There are many good excursions to be made in the beautiful countryside around: S on D10 through the gently undulating vineyard area of the **Côte des Blancs**, where some of the champagne grapes are grown; SW on N51 up the valley of the Cubry, taking in the châteaux of **Brugny** and **Montmort** (the latter 18km from Épernay) and returning via St-Martin-d'Ablois to complete the circuit through the Forest of Épernay; or N from Épernay through the champagne vineyards on the slopes of the **Montagne de Reims**, not forgetting to visit the Benedictine abbey of Hautvillers (*see entry*) where champagne was invented.

ÉPINAL, *Vosges* (3–D8). A pleasant town built largely of pink sandstone, straddling the upper Moselle in a setting of woods and hills. Capital of the Vosges department, it lives by cotton weaving and other light industries. The oldest part of the town is on the right bank, where the Basilica of St Maurice (parts of which date from the 13th-c.), the Palais de Justice, the Hôtel-de-Ville and the covered market are all grouped close to the Place des Vosges, an attractive square bordered by 16th-c. houses with arcades at street level. Behind this part of the town rises a wooded hill where a castle used to stand; a plateau of forested parkland and deer reserve, known as the Parc du Château, extends eastward. Opposite, on the left bank of the river, is an interesting church, built in 1958; the choir is illuminated by a remarkable modern stained-glass window of large dimensions.

In the middle of the town the Moselle divides round an elongated island, at the S end of which stands an unusual museum. Part of it consists of the usual collections of local archaeology, coins, medals, paintings, drawings, etc., but its unique feature is a constantly changing exhibition of popular prints, engravings and woodcuts of many nations, reflecting the modest specialist industry for which Épinal has been widely known from the 18th-c. onward – namely the production of prints. Those interested should visit the 'Imagerie Pellerin' works, named after the man who founded it in 1796; it is to be found less than a kilometre downstream on the right bank, at 42 Quai de Dogneville.

GUEBWILLER, *Haut-Rhin* (3–D8). A small elongated industrial town on the river Lauch, at the entrance to one of the highest valleys in the Vosges. The terraced vineyards were originally planted by the monks of the nearby abbey of Murbach. The Hôtel-de-Ville is a fine early-16th-c. building with an unusual and very handsome five-sided *loggia*. The church of Notre-Dame is 18th-c., adorned with much sculpture and carving in stone and wood. More interesting perhaps is the now secularized Church of the Dominicans, which forms the setting for a well-known festival of classical music, on the first Saturday of each month from June to September.

HAUTVILLERS, *Marne* (5km N of Épernay: 3–C5). Charming village on the S slope of the Montagne de Reims, with an ancient Benedictine abbey which played an important rôle in the history of champagne. In about 1670 a monk called Dom Pérignon was appointed chief cellarer to the abbey. Up to this time the wines of Champagne had been unblended still wines, though sometimes they would be slightly *pétillant* (tongue-tingling); Dom Pérignon, by careful study and experiment, discovered the way to make a blended, fully sparkling wine very similar to the wine we know as champagne today. A new industry was born.

HOHNECK, *Vosges* (11km E of Gérardmer: 3–D8). A famous beauty-spot and one of the highest points (1360m) in the Vosges mountains, with tremendous views; in clear weather the Alps can be seen on the southern horizon. It is the summit of the spectacular **Routes des Crêtes**, which runs through forest country from crest to crest up the spine of the southern Vosges, from Thann (*see entry*) in the S as far as the Col de Bonhomme, SE of Ste-Marie. Between Thann and Hohneck it passes close to the highest summit of the whole Vosges range – the 'Grand Ballon' at 1425m (*ballon* is a rounded peak). The whole route, which is well signposted, was actually the frontier between France and Germany from 1871 to 1914, and the road was built by the French during World War I as a line of military communication. Though extremely sinuous and steep in places, it provides stirring views of forested peaks and valleys and of the plain of Alsace.

KAYSERSBERG, *Haut-Rhin* (10km NW of Colmar: 3–D8). One of the most charming of the small wine towns on the Route du Vin (*see entry*). Its ancient castle, whose ruins still dominate the town, once guarded the entrance to the narrow valley of the Weiss. The main street, the Rue du Général de Gaulle, crosses a 15th-c. fortified bridge, on which a small chapel is wedged in the crenellations, then wanders past medieval and 16th-c. houses and a 13th–15th-c. church containing a remarkable altarpiece. In the courtyard at No. 54 Grand'Rue a Renaissance fountain bears the inscription: 'Too much water at table chills the stomach; better to drink an old and subtle wine and leave my water to me.' Albert Schweitzer (1875–1965), the famous organist, doctor and missionary, was born in Kaysersberg; a small museum has been devoted to him.

LANGRES, *Haute-Marne* (3–D6, D7). One of the northern gateways into Burgundy, this very old city surrounded by 5km of ramparts stands high on the edge of a plateau. Its history starts before the Romans, when it was already an independent Gaulish town; it was a bishopric by the end of the 2nd-c. AD, and it became one of the most important sees in France.

The road from below winds up to an open space in front of the 17th-c. gateway called the Porte des Moulins; immediately inside the gate a turn to the right leads to one of the towers on the ramparts, where the views embrace the Vosges and Jura ranges and sometimes the snow-capped summits of the Swiss Alps. A short walk northwards along the ramparts leads to the early-13th-c. Cathedral of St-Mammès; its architecture is a happy marriage between Burgundian Romanesque and early Gothic, though the original W front was replaced in the 18th-c. by a somewhat pompous classical façade; the interior is well proportioned, with a nave rising to ogive vaulting, a triforium, and – the oldest part of the structure – a 12th-c. choir and apse with radiating chapels. The tour of the ramparts includes a Roman gateway, several 14th- and 15th-c. towers, and an orientation table. Within the town are delightful narrow streets with old houses, and there are two interesting museums.

LUNÉVILLE, *Meurthe-et-Moselle* (3–C8). Former home of the Dukes of Lorraine, where in the early part of the 18th-c. Duke Léopold built a château in imitation of Versailles, though on a much smaller scale; he even laid out a Le Nôtre type of park, with fountains, long alleyways to suggest infinite perspective, and a canal, fed from the river Vézouse, diverted along the N edge of the park to add a glimpse of running water to the landscape. Later, the château became a frequent residence of Stanislas (*see also* Nancy), who added further embellishments, entertained nobles and intellectuals, and died there in 1766. After his death the château and park were taken over by the army and went to rack and ruin. Since World War II, however, it has all been restored to something like its original condition. The château now contains a museum of Lunéville history, and in summer months forms the setting for a *son-et-lumière*.

METZ, *Moselle* (3–C7). A historic old town of nearly 200,000 inhabitants, straddling the Moselle near the German border at a point where the river divides into several branches and is joined by the Seille. Metz has been a strategic focus of crossroads for over 2000 years, and is surrounded by strongly defended forts. The German defence of Metz in 1944 held up Eisenhower's advance for nearly 2½ months.

The town is especially notable for its soaring Gothic Cathedral, third only to Beauvais and Amiens in height and full of light and colour from its astounding windows – an amazing wall of stained glass at each end of the transept, a glorious rose-window at the W end measuring 11½m in diameter, and a wealth of other stained glass throughout the building, both ancient and modern. The Mutte tower on the S side is nearly 100m high and well worth climbing for the view at the top; though part of the Cathedral fabric it belongs to the town and serves as the municipal belfry; it contains a famous bell, cast in 1605 and weighing over 10,000kg, which is rung on historic occasions.

Metz has a large number of churches, ranging from St-Pierre-aux-Nonnains, the oldest basilica in France (it belonged to a 7th-c. abbey and stands on the foundations of a 4th-c. Roman basilica), to the Église Ste-Thérèse, consecrated in 1954 and shaped rather like an airship hangar with an immensely tall needle-like spire erected to one side of it.

At the E side of the town a picturesque 13th-c. château-fort, known as the Porte des Allemands, guards the narrow river Seille and the old road to Saarbrucken; its name is a reminder that Metz was in German hands from 1870 to 1918. The Museum, just N of the Cathedral, occupies a former Carmelite monastery and is devoted to French, Flemish and Italian painting, natural history, and a remarkable collection of Gallo-Roman archaeology.

MOLSHEIM, *Bas-Rhin* (3–C8). Despite its closeness to Strasbourg and the presence of the Bugatti works on its outskirts, this delightful little town on the W bank of the river Bruche has managed to preserve its old-world charm, its ancient fortified gateway and some of its ramparts. In the centre, on the triangular Place de l'Hôtel-de-Ville, stands a remarkable Renaissance building called the 'Metzig'. It was built in the 16th-c. by the butchers' corporation, with huge ornamental gables, a double staircase going up to the first-floor entrance – an elaborate *loggia* on pillars and surmounted by a fine belfry, with two angels to strike the hours – and a very solid-looking balcony on three sides of the building, supported on arched pillars which frame what used to be shop windows on the ground floor. Now the upper floor is a museum, while the ground floor is devoted to the promotion of the local wines.

MULHOUSE, *Haut-Rhin* (3–D8). A large industrial city with little attraction for the tourist apart from the paintings in the Musée des Beaux-Arts, the medieval stained glass in the Protestant church of St-Étienne, and a fine 16th-c. Hôtel-de-Ville with a painted façade, an imposing entrance staircase and a council chamber with a coffered ceiling and stained-glass windows. In the past the city has changed allegiance several times: having

been a Free City for 200 years, it was Swiss from
1515 to 1648, an independent republic until 1798
when it voted to become French, unwillingly
German from 1871 to 1918, and French ever since.
Its industries include weaving and spinning of
linen, printed fabrics, dyes, machinery, chemicals,
and car manufacture (Peugeot). In the SW
suburbs is a vast complex of university buildings,
technical colleges and research centres.

NANCY, *Meurthe-et-Moselle* (3–C7). The most
elegant provincial town in France, designed in the
18th-c. not by a Frenchman but by a Polish exile.
Stanislas Leczinski was not only the dethroned
king of Poland but father of Marie Leczinski, wife
of Louis XV. Louis installed his father-in-law as
Duke of Lorraine, on condition that the province
would revert to France on his death. Stanislas,
with the help of two French geniuses – the
architect Héré and the master ironworker Lamour
– set to work to create in the centre of Nancy a

masterpiece of 18th-c. planning worthy of comparison with Versailles.

Most of the sights of interest to the tourist are
conveniently placed within easy reach of the
magnificent square now known as Place Stanislas,
an impressive assembly of dignified palaces,
fountains and wrought-iron archways. The largest
of the palaces, filling the whole S side of the square,
is now the town hall; a monumental staircase leads
to the upper floor, whose windows have a thrilling
view of the square; and from mid-July to mid-
September guided evening tours, accompanied by
commentary and floodlighting, provide a wonderful spectacle. In the centre of the square a statue of
Stanislas himself looks N to the triumphal arch he
erected in honour of his son-in-law, and beyond it
to the vast Place de la Carrière, lined with trees and
handsome 18th-c. terraced houses, which ends in
an oval space with a graceful colonnade in front of
the old Palais du Gouvernement. Behind, to the
left, is the former Ducal Palace, a 13th-c. building,

The Fountain of Neptune in the Place Stanislas, Nancy

Ornans

largely restored in the 19th-c. It has a superb Renaissance doorway with a rich Flamboyant gable over an equestrian statue of one of the dukes, and now houses a museum of Lorraine history. Next to the Palace is the Église des Cordeliers, where all the dukes lie buried; it is full of splendid tombs carved in stone. A little further N stands the 14th-c. Porte de la Craffe with two imposing round towers, remnants of the ancient fortifications.

To the E lies an extensive park, La Pépinière, containing not only a tree nursery but a beautiful rose garden, a zoo, and a statue by Rodin of the painter Claude Gellée, better known as Claude Lorrain, who was born near Nancy in 1600.

Nancy has many other facets of interest. The Cathedral is 18th-c. with twin towers, imposing Baroque monuments and fine wrought-iron grilles. Well served by gourmet restaurants, the town has a famous vegetable market and is celebrated for its *quiche lorraine*, a delicious flan made with bacon, eggs and cream. Among its several museums are the Musée des Beaux-Arts in one of the former palaces on the Place Stanislas, devoted largely to European painting from the 14th-c. onwards, and the Zoological Museum (Rue Ste-Catherine) which has a tropical aquarium and a botanical garden with over 3000 specimens.

OBERNAI, *Bas-Rhin* (3–C8). A small peaceful town 25km SW of Strasbourg. It has managed to preserve its medieval ramparts; shaded by lime-trees, they make a delightful promenade, with extensive views over the surrounding orchards to the forest-clad slopes of the Vosges and the plain of Alsace. Around the large central market-place, with its ornamental fountain, are many lovely houses and other buildings: a 13th-c. belfry with four corner turrets and an elegant spire, a Renaissance Hôtel-de-Ville with an open-work stone balcony, and a 16th-c. corn market surmounted by a stork's nest. Opposite the Hôtel-de-Ville is a curious municipal well, dated 1579,

with three wheels, each lifting two buckets. The church is 19th-c. Gothic, but has stained glass and other items from earlier periods – including a 16th-c. casket containing the heart of a bishop of Angers who, when he died in 1891, expressed a wish that it should be placed in the church of his native town – but only when Alsace had been returned to France.

ORNANS, *Doubs* (3–E7). The river Loue flows straight through the middle of this attractive small town where the painter Courbet was born in 1819. His birthplace, now a Courbet museum, is one of the many old houses that line both sides of the river standing at the very edge of the water. Ornans is a good starting-off point for exploring the beautiful **Loue Valley** (W from Ornans on D103) where Courbet found inspiration for many of his paintings.

REIMS, *Marne* (3–C5). Famous for its superb Gothic Cathedral and its champagne cellars. Situated on the river Marne in low-lying country, the ancient town has suffered the ravages of war for many centuries. In World War I it lay for four years in the centre of the battle zone; over three-quarters of the town was obliterated by bombardment. That the Cathedral survived, though severely damaged by shellfire, is a miracle. In World War II General Eisenhower had his headquarters in a technical college just N of the railway station, and it was here, in the SALLE DE GUERRE (the 'war room'), that he received the German surrender in 1945; the room has been preserved, complete with its wall maps, and is open to the public.

Today Reims (pronounced 'Răns') is an energetic, thriving city, with animated cafés, wide boulevards, fashionable shopping-streets, a university, up-to-date hospitals. The oldest industry is not champagne but textiles, deriving from Roman times. Some of its tapestry workshops were acquired by Louis XIV's minister Colbert (who was born in Reims, son of a draper) and transferred to the Gobelins factory in Paris to help weave the tapestries for Versailles. The Reims textile industry still survives, but on a reduced scale, and it is now overshadowed by champagne and the new industries in the three industrial zones to W and SE of the city – chemicals, metallurgy, building, and wholesale grocery (supplying supermarkets all over France). There are also modern stained-glass workshops, where artists of the calibre of Braque and Chagall have been able to put their designs into effect.

The extent of the CHAMPAGNE CELLARS is amazing, the largest in Reims itself being those of Mumm and Pommery with 18km each. Tourists wishing to visit one of the celebrated firms and see the fascinating process by which champagne is made should contact the tourist office (Syndicat d'Initiative) at 3 Bd. de la Paix (NE of the Cathedral).

Reims was capital of a Gallic tribe when Paris was a mere village. Under the Romans, as Durocortorum, it became an important centre of the wool trade and had a population of 80,000. The subsoil chalk provided ready building material for its temples, forums and baths; Emperor Hadrian called it the 'Athens of the North'. In AD 406 the city was razed to the ground by the invading Vandals; its Christian bishop, Nicasius, was slaughtered in the forecourt of the first Reims cathedral, which had just been completed only to be destroyed in the holocaust. The only building to survive from the Roman city is the PORTE DE MARS, the 3rd-c. triumphal arch which, later incorporated into the now vanished medieval ramparts, today stands in isolation facing the Place de la République; it is 13½m high, with three arches decorated with bas-relief carving.

Undaunted by the destruction of their cathedral and the martyrdom of their bishop, the Christian community built a new cathedral and for the remainder of the 5th-c. made Reims the centre of their struggle to convert the heathen northerners. Their efforts were rewarded in 496 when Clovis, King of the Franks and the first true King of France, knelt at the altar steps to be baptized and anointed by Archbishop St-Remi. Nearly all the subsequent French kings (37 in all) were consecrated and crowned in Reims Cathedral, the last being Charles X in 1825.

Over the next 700 years the 5th-c. cathedral was enlarged, pulled down and rebuilt, and in 1210 completely gutted by fire. The building of the present CATHEDRAL was begun at once and completed within 100 years (though the two W towers were not finished until 1428). To provide a worthy setting for the coronation of kings it was planned as the largest church in Christendom – 138m long, 30m wide and 37m high, longer and taller than Notre-Dame in Paris but less broad – and it happened to be designed at a time when the Gothic style had reached the summit of perfection.

The result is one of the greatest Gothic structures ever built. The W façade dazzles with its array of statuary and wrought stone; three doorways, deeply set within richly sculptured pointed arches, are surmounted by a sublime rose-window almost as wide as the nave itself; above, a high gallery of royal statues occupies the full width of the façade, and twin towers soar like organ-pipes to a height of 82m.

The interior is austere and majestic; the vaulted nave, narrow in relation to its length and height, gives a tremendous effect of lofty splendour. Over 100 statues stand in niches on the W wall, but otherwise there is a remarkable absence of religious statuary and painting, emphasizing the simple harmony of the structure and the glowing colours of the remaining 13th-c. stained glass, restored by the Jacques Simon workshops. Recently, modern glass by Chagall has been incorporated into the central chapel beyond the altar. The whole Cathedral impresses with the unity and purity of its design. Despite another serious fire in 1481, the vandalism of the Revolution and the grievous damage suffered in two World Wars, thanks to patient restoration it stands today much as it was on the day when Joan of Arc witnessed the consecration of Charles VII in 1429.

Close to the S side of the Cathedral is the old PALAIS DE TAU, built at various periods from the 12th-c. onwards and much restored since its battering in 1914. Formerly used as the royal residence at the time of a coronation, it is now a museum of monumental statues, tapestries and ecclesiastical treasures. From the Cours Anatole-France just behind it there is a fine view of the Cathedral's E end, bristling with pinnacles and flying buttresses.

The oldest church in Reims, two centuries older than the Cathedral, is the BASILICA OF ST-REMI, about 1km to the SE. Built in the first half of the 11th-c., it is largely Romanesque in style and immensely long (122m) but narrow (28m), with two square towers 56m high. The nave and transept are 11th-c., but the choir, completed a century later, is early Gothic; it still retains its original 12th-c. stained glass and is surrounded by a colonnade separating it from the radiating chapels. The nave is somewhat sombre, with lovely capitals carved with designs of animals and foliage. Behind the altar lies the tomb of St-Remi, the archbishop who anointed King Clovis in the Cathedral. Like the Cathedral, the church was damaged in World War I but has been well restored. Attached to it on the N side are the buildings of the former 12th-c. abbey, now used as a museum of medieval art and archaeology. Both church and abbey form the setting for a *musique et lumière* every evening in July, August and September.

Another church of great interest, though small and 20th-c., is Notre-Dame de la Paix, known as the CHAPELLE FOUJITA, in the Rue de Champ de

Feast day in Ribeauvillé

Mars opposite the main entrance to the Mumm champagne *caves*. It was designed and decorated by the Japanese painter Léonard Foujita (1886–1968), who was schooled in the École de Paris; stained glass and frescoes depict biblical scenes.

Immediately W of the Cathedral is one of the best Fine Art museums in France, the MUSÉE ST-DENIS; it is especially rich in French painting from the 17th-c. to the present day, and most of the great painters from Poussin to Matisse are represented.

RIBEAUVILLÉ, *Haut-Rhin* (3–D8). Small Alsatian wine town, renowned for its storks' nests and its Traminer and Riesling wines. It is an elongated town, squeezed into a narrow valley, and the Grand'Rue straggles between old houses to the central square, the Place de l'Hôtel-de-Ville; here is a Renaissance fountain which on the great annual feast day ('Pfifferday', on the last Sunday in August) dispenses free wine to all comers. NW of the square the Grand'Rue continues through the arch of the 13th-c. belfry known as the Butcher's Tower. Immediately W of the town a road climbs the hill to the well-preserved ruins of the Château de St-Ulrich; the keep dates from the 12th-c. and rewards those prepared to climb to the top with glorious views.

RIQUEWIHR, *Haut-Rhin* (10km NW of Colmar: 3–D8). Fairytale Alsatian wine village, luckily undamaged by war and preserved as it must have been in the 16th- and 17th-c. The cobbled main

street, closed to traffic in summer, slopes gently upwards between ancient houses with gables, bow windows or flower-covered balconies, to the tall 13th-c. 'Dolder' gateway (which contains a wine museum) and through its arch to the upper town gateway dating from 1500. The vineyards of Riesling and Muscat grapes, crowding the E-facing slopes of the Vosges, come right up to the walls of the village, which lives entirely for and by wine.

RONCHAMP, *Haute-Saône* (3–D8). A small industrial town which has become famous on account of the hilltop chapel of Notre-Dame-du-Haut just outside it. It was built by Le Corbusier in 1955 as a war memorial to the soldiers who died here in heavy fighting in 1944. Set against a background of trees and hills, its daring design of irregularly curved white walls and roof has aroused much controversy; it is considered by Le Corbusier's admirers to be among his finest achievements.

ROSHEIM, *Bas-Rhin* (5km S of Molsheim: 3–C8). Wine village containing very old houses, one of which, the 12th-c. so-called 'House of the Pagans', is believed to be the oldest house in Alsace. The church is a beautiful example of Alsatian Romanesque, with a 16th-c. octagonal tower over the transept crossing and interesting carved capitals on the nave pillars. Four town gateways and parts of the ramparts still stand.

The chapel of Notre-Dame-du-Haut, Ronchamp

ROUTE DU VIN D'ALSACE. Perhaps the best way of seeing the true Alsace is to follow this well-signed route through the vineyards down the eastern flank of the Vosges mountains. It starts just N of Molsheim (map 3–C8) at Marlenheim, 20km W of Strasbourg on N4, and ends at Thann (*see entry*) W of Mulhouse (map 3–D8). In all it covers about 180km of road distance (though you can take short-cuts in places if your time is limited), and it passes through dozens of peaceful wine towns and villages, many of which have changed little over the centuries. Some are of great repute among connoisseurs, but there are others less well known which nevertheless produce excellent wines. It is a gentle, welcoming country-side, with vineyards everywhere crowding the villages and climbing the eastern and southern slopes of the Vosges, whose rounded summits fill the western horizon. To the E lies the Alsatian plain, stretching all the way to the Rhine.

Many of the places on the wine road have entries devoted to them in this section of the book – Molsheim, Rosheim, Obernai, Ribeauvillé, Riquewihr, Kaysersberg, Ammerschwihr, Turck-heim, Eguisheim, Guebwiller, Thann – but there are other little towns and villages where it is well worth stopping for a stroll and a cool glass of local wine. Here is a selection of them:

Wangen, with its old houses, courtyards and winding streets; **Avolsheim**, which has an ancient Romanesque baptistry and the oldest church in Alsace; **Boersch**, with its three old gateways and central square surrounded by old houses; **Ottrott**, which produces one of the few red wines of Alsace and has not just one but two medieval châteaux; **Barr**, where there is an annual wine fair in mid-July in the splendid 17th-c. town hall, and at the beginning of October a harvest fair during which the town fountain runs with free wine; **Andlau**, which has a church dating partly from the 11th-c. and the remains of an ancient monastery; **Dambach**, a walled town with three gateways and many ancient houses; **Bergheim**, with a 14th-c. fortified gateway and remains of medieval ramparts; **Hunawihr**, whose fortified church at one time served both Catholics and Protestants; **Bennwihr**, whose modern church has a remarkable stained-glass window extending the full length of the S wall, with intense colours; **Kientzheim**, a small fortified town, with a gateway carrying a sculptured head which puts its tongue out at tourists; **Husseren-les-Châteaux**, highest point of the Route du Vin (380m), with panoramic views and the ruins of three ancient hilltop defence towers; **Rouffach**, with its Renaissance town hall, corn market and other buildings.

STE-ODILE, *Bas-Rhin* (3–D8). Ste Odile is the Patron Saint of Alsace, and the hilltop convent she founded over 1200 years ago, with its panoramic views, is the most popular tourist site in the whole of Alsace, especially on her saint's-day in December when pilgrims come from far and wide.

According to the legend, Odile was born blind at Obernai in the year 670, and her father, who had wanted a son, gave orders for her to be killed. Her nurse fled with her to a convent, where she was brought up; at her baptism she suddenly recovered her sight, and when, several years later, her father saw she had grown into a lovely young girl he wanted to marry her off to a rich merchant. Wishing to remain a nun, she fled, hotly pursued by her father. A fall of rock saved her from capture; recognizing this as a miraculous sign her father repented, and gave her the castle of Hohenburg, which she converted into a convent. It soon became a pilgrim centre, and daughters of noble families entered the nunnery. In 1546 the convent was destroyed by fire, except for the chapel; a century was to pass before it was rebuilt and re-inhabited. In the Revolution it was declared national property, and it was not until 1853 that the Bishop of Strasbourg was able to recover it and restore it to its original purpose. Now every summer the isolated site is a magnet for thousands of pilgrims and tourists. The relics of Ste Odile herself are preserved in her chapel in an 8th-c. stone tomb.

Below the convent a short walk S leads to a view of the mysterious 'Pagan Wall', a rough wall of heaped unhewn stones extending in a wide loop for a distance of about 10km. Whether it was built by prehistoric man or by the Celts is not known; it remains an enigma.

SAVERNE, *Bas-Rhin* (3–C8). Pleasant small town on the river Zorn, notable for its imposing pink-sandstone château which until the Revolution had belonged to the prince-bishops of Strasbourg for 500 years. After the previous château had been destroyed by fire in the 18th-c., it was rebuilt in its present grandiose form by the celebrated Cardinal Louis de Rohan (*see also* Strasbourg), who proceeded to live there in princely style. It now belongs to the state and houses a museum of local history and archaeology. The N façade, with its immense row of tall pillars, high windows and balustraded terrace, looks out across a park limited on two sides by a canal. W of the château, at the river end of the Route de Paris, is a famous rose garden, containing over 1000 varieties and open every day from June to September.

SEDAN, *Ardennes* (3–B6). Small industrial town on a bend of the river Meuse, not far from the Luxembourg frontier. It was the scene of the disastrous French defeat of 1870 which led to the surrender of Napoleon III and his army to the victorious Prussians, and so to the siege and eventual capitulation of Paris in the following year. Throughout World War I Sedan was behind the German lines, and suffered severe damage early in World War II. The town is dominated by its huge fortress, one of the largest in Europe, built originally in the 15th-c. around a 13th-c. keep (which is still there), and enlarged a century later with 30m-high ramparts, moats, bastions, etc. Though never taken by storm, the presence of this mighty fortress has failed nevertheless three times to prevent the surrender of the town. It is well worth visiting, however; it also contains the ancient Palace of the Princes of Sedan, where the great Général Turenne was born in 1611, and there is an interesting historical museum. Fine views from the ramparts.

SÉLESTAT, *Bas-Rhin* (3–D8). An old town in the Alsatian plain, situated on the left bank of the river Ill and on the main road between Colmar and Strasbourg. Around the old quarter the town has spread into busy industrial areas, but in the centre there are remains of medieval ramparts, elegant Renaissance houses, and two fine churches – one 12th-c. Romanesque, the other 13th–15th-c. Gothic with a carved stone Renaissance pulpit and a good deal of beautiful stained glass, some 15th-c. and some modern by Max Ingrand. In the 15th-c. Sélestat was a centre of Humanism, and the Humanist Library in the Rue de l'Église was founded at that time; it is a library of considerable repute, containing a wealth of precious manuscript books, and the nucleus of it is the unique private library of 2000 books that belonged to Beatus Rhenanus, a well-known Humanist scholar who was a citizen of Sélestat and a friend of Erasmus.

STRASBOURG, *Bas-Rhin* (3–C8). Capital of Alsace and one of the largest and most attractive cities of France, with a population of about 260,000 (excluding suburbs). The only French city on the Rhine, it is also the terminus of the Marne–Rhine and Rhône–Rhine canals. Its autonomous river port, handling a vast tonnage of commerce, is the largest on the upper Rhine. Strasbourg is also the seat of the Council of Europe and the European Parliament; the building where they meet, the MAISON DE L'EUROPE near the Orangery NE of the city centre, is open to the public from April to October by guided tour.

Most of the tourist sights of this lively city, with its wide choice of hotels and restaurants, are concentrated within the island formed by the two branches of the river Ill. Dominating them all is the soaring tower and spire (142m) of the great red-sandstone Gothic CATHEDRAL. Its tremendous façade of three portals, carved with hundreds of biblical scenes and figures and surmounted by a rose-window 15m in diameter, rises finally to a level platform 66m from the ground. The huge tower with its spire rises from the left side of the platform; the right tower was never built. If you are fit and do not suffer from vertigo, it is worth climbing the external spiral staircase (about 330 steps) for the tremendous view from the façade platform at the foot of the tower – as Goethe used to do regularly when he was a student in Strasbourg, to exercise will-power over his fear of heights.

The vast Cathedral interior, with its broad nave and wealth of stained-glass windows – some dating from the 12th-c. and 13th-c., some, like those by Max Ingrand in the choir, as recent as 1956 – is rich in interest: the Flamboyant Gothic pulpit, the 17th-c. tapestries, the 15th-c. baptistry and the sculpture of Christ on the Mount of Olives (both in the N transept), and in the S transept the carved 'Pillar of Angels' and – most popular tourist attraction of all – the remarkable ASTRONOMICAL CLOCK which goes into action at noon every day with a procession of mechanical figures representing Death, striking the hour, and Christ blessing the Apostles. The crypt, whose apse is the sole survivor from the previous Romanesque cathedral, is entered down a flight of steps to the left of the choir.

Opposite the NW corner of the Cathedral is one of the oldest houses in Strasbourg, now a restaurant – the MAISON KAMMERZELL, a typically Alsatian house with elaborately carved exterior timbers, original leaded windows and a doorway dating from 1467. On the other side of the Cathedral stands the 18th-c. CHÂTEAU DES ROHAN, former residence of the Cardinal-Bishops of the Rohan family, now a museum of painting, decorative arts, ceramics and Alsatian archaeology. The CATHEDRAL MUSEUM next door contains statuary, stained glass and other relics from the previous cathedral, also engraving and documents illustrating the history of the Cathedral.

Other museums within easy reach are the HISTORY MUSEUM (close to the 'Square of the Sucking-Pig Market'), the MUSEUM OF MODERN ART, housed in a former customs house nearby

The astronomical clock in Strasbourg Cathedral

and containing an outstanding collection of Impressionist and Modern painting, sculpture and stained glass, and, just across the river in three handsome 16th-c. houses, the ALSACE MUSEUM of local history and folklore.

Opposite the Cathedral entrance the Rue Mercière leads into PLACE GUTENBERG, where a statue of Gutenberg recalls the 14 years he spent in Strasbourg as a political refugee from his native Mainz; during this time he perfected his invention of printing, returning to Mainz in 1448 to reveal his work to the world. A short distance N is PLACE KLÉBER, the animated centre of the city. A short walk SW leads to the point where the river Ill divides. Here, in the area known as LA PETITE FRANCE, is a charming quarter of old Strasbourg with 16th-c. houses reflecting their wooden balconies and gables in the calm waters of broad canals.

In the summer there are regular sightseeing boat tours on the river Ill, the canals and the docks; up-to-date information is available from the tourist office (Syndicat d'Initiative) in Place Gutenberg or opposite the railway station; the boats leave from the Promenade Dauphine near the Cathedral.

THANN, *Haut-Rhin* (3–D8). Situated at the S end of both the Route du Vin (*see entry*) and the Route des Crêtes (*see* Hohneck), this old town along the banks of the river Thur, W of Mulhouse, is close to the long-famous Rangen 'mountain' whose vineyards once belonged to Strasbourg Cathedral, and of which an anonymous 18th-c. chronicler wrote: 'Take note no one can drink a tankard of

The Cathedral, Troyes

French Government Tourist Office

this generous nectar without getting roaring drunk and falling to the ground.' Thann is also renowned for its large collegiate church of St-Thiébaut, known locally as the Cathedral. Tradition has it that red wine was mixed with the mortar in order to blend with the red sandstone of which the church is built. With its fine W and N portals, adorned with realistic carvings and statues, its 15th-c. stained glass and above all its choir-stalls superbly carved with vivacious comic characters, it must count as one of the finest Flamboyant Gothic structures in the whole of Alsace. In the town are many old houses and fountains. At its NW corner are the dismantled ruins of the 17th-c. castle of Engelbourg.

TOUL, *Meurthe-et-Moselle* (3–C7). The old part of this ancient episcopal city on the left bank of the Moselle lies within the massive fortifications erected by Louis XIV's military architect Vauban. Unfortunately considerable damage was caused in World War II to the Cathedral, the old episcopal palace nearby (now used as the Hôtel-de-Ville) and an area to the S of the old city. Restoration work still continues on the Cathedral, which was built from the 13th-c. to the 16th-c., with twin octagonal towers, a splendid Flamboyant façade of stone tracery, and a beautiful 13th-c. cloister with fine capitals. Another notable church is St-Gengoult, by the market-place; it too was begun in the 13th-c. and has a short nave, a large transept, the original 13th-c. stained glass, and a superb Flamboyant Gothic cloister with elegant stone-work.

TROYES, *Aube* (3–D5, D6). Situated on the Seine, about 150km SE of Paris, Troyes has been a city of importance from Gallo-Roman days onward. Though nearly at the S limit of the old province of Champagne, it was once its capital. Now, capital of the Aube department, and still a traditional centre of the hosiery trade, it preserves in the old centre within its ring of boulevards an astonishing number of churches and a network of narrow streets and alleyways twisting between ancient houses with narrow gables.

The Cathedral of St-Peter and St-Paul, though it was four centuries in the building, from 1208 onward (and the second tower has never been completed to this day), is nevertheless a splendid Gothic edifice, rich in sculpture and stained glass. Both the 15th-c. façade and the 13th-c. portal of the N transept have fine rose-windows and a wealth of statuary and carving, much of it unfortunately damaged at the time of the Revolution. The interior has impressive dimensions and proportions and strikes a satisfying balance between strength and lightness. The stained glass – 13th-c. in the choir, 16th-c. in the nave – depicts portraits of popes and emperors and scenes from the Bible, and is remarkable for the intensity of its colours. Note especially the famous but rather macabre window in the fourth

Denis Hughes-Gilbey

Turckheim

chapel on the left, representing Christ and the Wine Press, in which a vine grows from his breast and blood issues from his wounded side into a wine chalice. The Cathedral 'Treasure', on view in a 13th-c. vaulted hall, includes a wonderful collection of enamels and goldwork.

Other notable stained glass can be seen in the 13th-c. church of St-Urbain and the 16th-c. church of Ste-Madeleine. The latter also possesses a fine, intricately carved rood-screen and a superb statue of Ste-Martha, regarded as a masterpiece of 16th-c. sculpture.

The Musée des Beaux-Arts, housed in a former abbey close to the Cathedral, has departments of natural history, local archaeology, 15th–20th-c. painting, and an outstanding library of some 300,000 books and manuscripts dating back to the 7th-c.

TURCKHEIM, *Bas-Rhin* (5km W of Colmar: 3–C8). An attractive little walled town, with the river Fecht flowing along its southern flank. On the other side, vineyards slope upwards to an impressive background of mountains. A sturdy 14th-c. gateway, topped by a stork's nest, opens immediately into a delightful main square with a fountain in the middle and gracious Renaissance houses all round it. This square is named after the celebrated Général Turenne, who in 1675 won a famous victory near Turckheim, defeating a German army against odds of three-to-one and gaining Alsace for France.

Paper is made here, and the vineyards produce a well-known wine called 'Brand'.

VERDUN, *Meuse* (3–C6, C7). Situated on the Meuse in a position of such strategic importance

that by the beginning of World War I it had been built up into the strongest fortress in France. Between 1916 and 1918 it was the pivot of a bitter and crucial struggle in which half a million French soldiers died in its defence; the German losses were about the same. The site of the battlefields, with their monuments and cemeteries, lies to N and NE of the town. Much of Verdun was destroyed by shellfire, but the 12th-c. Romanesque Cathedral, well restored, still stands, with its early-16th-c. cloisters and its famous 'Lion Door'. The 18th-c. Bishop's Palace adjoins it on the W side, and just beyond that is the Citadel, part of which has underground sleeping quarters in which the troops took turns to rest and sleep during the long-drawn-out battle which saved the town and held the line.

VESOUL, *Haute-Saône* (3–E7). Capital of the department, built in a curve round the foot of a hill called 'La Motte' which rises steeply to 160m above the town. From the summit of the hill, where prehistoric man once lived, are far-reaching views of both the Vosges and Jura mountains and, on exceptionally clear days, the Alps as well. Vesoul itself has many attractive old houses and a classic 18th-c. church.

VITTEL, *Vosges* (3–D7). Well-known health resort, with a large thermal establishment set in extensive parkland. The mineral waters of both Vittel and the neighbouring health resort of **Contrexéville** (beneficial for sufferers from arthritis, migraine, and liver and kidney complaints) are among the most popular of the bottled waters sold throughout France. The bottling factory in Vittel is open to the public.

The Loire Valley and Poitou-Charentes: Introduction

Anjou, Maine, Orléanais, Touraine, Poitou-Charentes

Pauline Devaney and Edwin Apps

Stretching from Normandy to the Dordogne, from the Atlantic to the Ile-de-France, this vast tract of France, composed of so many different landscapes and peoples, is a land of transition, bridging north and south. Since the Revolution, maps have shown the area partitioned into fifteen departments, all named after the rivers that flow through them, but even today the old provincial boundaries reflect a much truer division of the region, and for an understanding of the people, their customs, loyalties, traditions – and their cooking – it is essential to grasp them.

These provinces, whose names ring through French history and find echo in the plays of Shakespeare, begin in the north with Maine, whose capital Le Mans is today an industrial city famous for '*Les Vingt-Quatre Heures*', the annual 24-hour motor race. Maine is a country of woods, grazing land, thick hedges, rivers, lakes and cider orchards. It is at its best in May when the blossom of apple and hawthorn, the wild flowers, and the woods just coming into leaf, make it a beguiling place. Here you may eat delicious freshwater fish, bream and tench, cooked in wine, and the *rillette* and *pâtisseries* of Le Mans.

Below Maine lies the Loire Valley with its wide, lazy river which, 'serving no purpose except beauty', its appearance changing almost daily as its sandbanks shift and reform, flows through some of the richest and most beautiful country in France. Born in the Massif Central, it is already a large river when it reaches Orléans and turns west for its long run to the Atlantic. Orléans, once capital of the Orléanais, city of roses and vinegar, is a busy, commercial town where the visitor, even if he cannot find many authentic reminders of 'the Maid', can comfort himself with the excellent local *pâtés* and the apple tart known as *tatin*. On flows the river, through Touraine, the 'garden of France', richest of all these rich provinces, past gardens and vineyards, orchards of peaches, pears and apples – to Tours, most dignified yet most lively of cities – to Saumur with its sparkling wines and great Military Riding School – to Angers, old capital of Anjou and home of the Plantagenets, as well as of a delectable soft cheese called *crémets d'Anjou* – and so on to Nantes, the edge of Brittany and the sea.

On the banks of the river, and throughout the surrounding region, lie the châteaux, those pattern books of French architecture and taste with their memories of courts and kings. They range from medieval fortresses to fairy-tale palaces and *châteaux de plaisance*, and there are literally dozens of them. For the tourist with limited time to spare, the choice is far from easy. There is the great palace of the Dukes of Brittany at Nantes; or the dark stronghold at Angers, with its unique

Château de Chambord   Rainbird (Jeremy Whitaker)

'Apocalypse' tapestry; Saumur's 'castle of love'; the ruins of Chinon, where Joan of Arc first met the Dauphin; Amboise, where Leonardo da Vinci is buried; Loches with its fearful dungeons and memories of Agnès Sorel, 'La Dame de Beauté', the first royal mistress to be granted official status; or Blois, where you can stand in the courtyard and follow the whole development of the Renaissance style. Or you can settle for the sheer loveliness of Azay-le-Rideau; or Chenonceaux, effortlessly straddling the Cher; or Villandry and its gardens; or the staggering magnificence of François I's 'hunting-lodge' at Chambord.

Beyond the Loire Valley is the great plain of Poitou where the warm Atlantic winds blow, and where the squat stone farmhouses no longer have slate roofs but red tiles, heralding the approach of the Midi. Poitou is a land of goats and figs, fresh vegetables and salt mutton from the marshes, fat poultry, good butter, fish from the coast, in fact 'everything except money', as the Poitevin peasants say – a boast which does not seem far off the mark to anyone lucky enough to be invited into a farmhouse, to sit beneath blackened rafters round a huge table with the family and eat *bouilliture d'anguille* (eels cooked with garlic and wine), a plate of *jambon de pays* (the excellent dry-cured ham made each year when the pig is killed), or best of all – and smelling glorious as they are ladled on to the plate – the *mojettes*, the beans for which Poitou is justly famous, followed by home-made goat's cheese and washed down with a '*bon coup de rouge*' made from last year's grapes.

Southwest of Poitou lies the smallest of these old provinces, Aunis. Its former capital, La Rochelle, which defended itself so gallantly but in vain against the forces of Richelieu, is today an elegant and stylish place full of fish restaurants, young people and boats. Below Aunis are Saintonge and Angoumois, the three together known as 'Les Charentes', now the departments of Charente and Charente-Maritime. It is an area rich in butter and other dairy products, and the centre of it is Cognac, whose vineyards stretching as far as the eye can see are devoted to the grapes for the celebrated brandy, as well as for an aperitif much appreciated locally, Pineau des Charentes. Here, for the most part, the land is still flat: the same plain, in fact, as Poitou. But the light is more luminous, more southern, so that worries seem to recede and even the most bustling of northerners begins to feel there is more to life than work and perhaps tomorrow will do after all. . . .

Further east is Berry, the heart of France; a plateau of grazing land; home of the writer George Sand (her château at Nohant is an evocative museum). Bourges, the old capital, is the very essence of a French provincial town with its beautiful cathedral and the extraordinary 'palace' or mansion of Jacques Cœur, a sort of fifteenth-century 'ideal home'. The cooking of Berry, like the cooking of Poitou, is simple, rustic even; it is the quality of the ingredients that makes it exceptional. The mutton, and the game from the Solange region, are first-class, but the two specialities are their soups (which in Berry take on a gastronomic importance not usually associated with such a humble dish) and their *clafoutis*, a sweet batter cooked with cherries. The wines of the district are very good; the *vin du pays*, or *vin de culture*, drawn from a barrel, as so often in these regions, is often more rewarding than anything in a labelled bottle.

To wander through these old provinces is to see and feel the history of France, for history is everywhere – not least in the straight roads, a legacy of the Romans who

Château de Chenonceaux

were here for nearly five centuries and have left their mark on the region. With the Romans came Christianity, which put down strong roots, especially in Poitiers where the baptistry of St-Jean, perhaps the earliest ecclesiastical building in France, is only one of nearly seventy churches in the city which Rabelais – who knew it well – said had 'surrendered to priests and monks'.

Christianity, however, was wearing a bit thin towards the end of the first millennium, when a series of terrifying raids by marauding Norsemen completely destroyed Saintes and Angoulême and reduced the people to such a state of alarm that they were an easy prey to fears that the world would end in the year 1000. When that year came and went without the expected catastrophe, the consequent wave of relief led to a great renewal of faith and a frenzy of church building, in the course of which hundreds of Romanesque churches were built throughout France, and especially in the southwest where the soft limestone is easy to work. These churches, of which a great many have survived, are the chief glory of the region below the river Loire. Many of them are of outstanding beauty with their façades covered in remarkable sculptures; standing white and clear in the sunlight, their arcading and carvings etched with shadow, they are like an open page in a medieval *Book of Hours*.

Another expression of the renewal of faith at this time was the pilgrimage, a major bourn of which was the shrine of St-Jacques, or Sant'Iago, at Compostella in Spain. There were four pilgrim routes, the most important of which ran from Paris through Chartres, Tours, Poitiers, Aulnay, Saintes and Bordeaux. Along this road some half a million pilgrims set out each year. Going on a pilgrimage in the Middle Ages was a major undertaking: something between a public act of faith, a down payment on the Next World, and the holiday of a lifetime. The Benedictines of Cluny in Burgundy acted as travel agents, organizing departures and guides, and the routes were policed by the Knights Templar, who also acted as bankers. Along the route, abbeys and churches competed for religious relics to attract the pilgrims and their gifts of money, precious stones, and gold and silver.

Of all the historical events affecting the region none was more far-reaching than the marriage in 1152 between Henri Plantagenêt and Eleanor of Aquitaine, divorced wife of Louis VII. Their combined territories exceeded those of the King himself, and when two years later Henri Plantagenêt unexpectedly became Henry II of England nearly the whole of western France became English territory (*see* the map on page 37) and remained so for three hundred years. It has to be remembered that the Plantagenets were French counts before they were English kings. Henry II, and after him Richard Cœur-de-Lion and the Black Prince, spent more time in France, fighting, fortifying towns, building castles and besieging them, than they ever spent in England. It should not surprise us when we find two English kings and two English queens buried in France at Fontevrault Abbey.

When the English were driven out by the resurgence of national spirit inspired by Joan of Arc, culminating in the French victory at Castillon in 1453, the peace that followed lasted barely a century before Calvin preached at Poitiers and the Wars of Religion plunged the area once more into a bitter struggle. The Protestants, or 'Huguenots', were strong in such centres as La Rochelle and Saumur. Later, on the Revocation of the Edict of Nantes in 1685, most of them emigrated, leaving the region seriously depopulated. They were mainly middle-class tradesmen and skilled workers, and their departure dealt a mortal blow to the industries that were developing. More and more the west fell back on agriculture, beginning a long siesta from which they only awoke briefly but violently at the Revolution, when the peasants of the Vendée, traditionally staunch Catholics and Royalists, incensed at the persecution of their priests, rose against the newly formed Republic. Led by the heroic 21-year-old Henri de Rochejacquelin – 'Monsieur Henri' – and armed only with pitchforks and scythes, they reached Le Mans before they were finally put down by the 'Colonnes Infernales' with a brutality reminiscent of the reprisals in Scotland after the '45 Rebellion. The marks of this repression are still visible in Vendée, and the memory of it has given the people a sense of separateness that has made it perhaps the one department in the region where a real sense of identity remains.

Today this long sleep is ending with a rush as industry moves in and modern farming methods replace the old. But for the visitor with time to go off the main roads and wander through the countryside, that old world of the peasant can still be found; the horse and the ox can still be seen working in the fields, or an old man in smock and wooden sabots patiently hoeing his vineyard, so that suddenly one loses sense of time and the medieval world seems extraordinarily close.

For this is a region which does not yield its secrets easily or quickly, and certainly gives nothing to those who rush through it in search of the sun – though they too might do well to turn aside and make for the coast here, where the long, clean sandy beaches backed by pines, and the beautiful offshore islands, can produce annual figures for sunshine normally associated with areas much further south, and where the delicious seafood, the oysters, mussels, fresh tunny-fish and sardines, accompanied by the dry white wines of the Pays Nantais, are a cogent argument in favour of a more leisurely exploration.

The château and old town of Saumur

Douglas Dickins

The Loire Valley and Poitou-Charentes: Gazetteer

Pauline Devaney and Edwin Apps

AIX, Ile d', *Charente-Maritime* (17km NW of Rochefort: 4–B2, B3). Fortified by Vauban in the 17th-c. for its strategic position at the approach to La Rochelle, the island today is a peaceful, car-less holiday resort with an almost Mediterranean feel. The vineyards produce a pleasant dry white wine and the main industries are shrimping and working in mother-of-pearl. The mother-of-pearl craftsmen can be watched in their workshop opposite the church (crypt 11th-c.).

The Maison de L'Empereur, one of the few two-storey houses on the island, was built at Napoleon's orders when he visited the defences at the height of his power in 1808. Seven years later, as he prepared to flee to America after Waterloo, the appearance of an English fleet caused him to stay there during the four days of 12–15 July 1815 before he decided, dressed in the green uniform of a Colonel des Chasseurs de la Garde which he had worn at Austerlitz, to throw himself on the mercy of the English. The house is today a museum with many fascinating relics of Napoleon, including the letter he wrote to George IV claiming asylum from 'the most powerful, the most constant and the most generous' of his enemies.

The island is reached by a motorboat from La Pointe de la Fumée NW of Fouras (20 minutes).

AMBOISE, *Indre-et-Loire* (2–E2, E3). The remains of the Château d'Amboise, the first royal residence built in France, stand above the town on the left bank of the Loire.

During the Hundred Years War and up to the death of Charles VII in 1461, it served only as a royal fortress. Louis XI had it rebuilt as a dwelling for his wife; their son, the future Charles VIII, was born there. When Charles became king he set about building Amboise into the palace of his dreams. Eager to see it completed, he urged the work forward at all possible speed. The builders worked at night by torchlight, and in winter the stones were heated so that they could be handled. In 1491 he began the exquisite Chapelle St-Hubert, which stands on the ramparts and is of the purest French Gothic style, the interior richly carved to suggest the forest home of St Hubert, the patron saint of huntsmen. Besides the chapel several buildings since destroyed were completed then; also the wing facing the Loire known as the Logis du Roi. This too is in the French Gothic

style and the entire first floor comprises a vast Salle des États. Work was also begun on the two great towers, the Tour des Minimes and the Tour Hurtault. These remain unique in France, consisting of a tower within a tower, the inner forming the central column of support for a spiralling ramp which, in the case of the Tour Hurtault, is so gently sloped and so wide that horses, carriages and now automobiles can go up it without difficulty, enabling it to serve as the main entrance to the château.

In 1493 Charles embarked on an expedition to conquer Naples, to which he believed the House of Valois had a claim. On the outward journey all went well, Naples was captured without a struggle and Charles, who was bowled over by the Italian style and especially the gardens of Italy, assembled an army of Italian masons and a great baggage train of treasures to bring home. But the return journey was a very different affair, and by the time the King reached France nearly every gain he had made in Italy had been lost, the Venetian troops had captured the baggage train and, far more seriously, his beloved son, the Dauphin, had been killed.

After this the King and Queen shut themselves up in Amboise, and two years later Charles died. However, nothing could stop the new taste for Italy and Italian objects which the expedition had imported, and the new king, Louis XII, who married Charles's widow, continued the work at Amboise (although he preferred Blois), adding the wing which stands at right angles to the Logis du Roi and continuing the work of landscape gardening begun by his predecessor. It is said that orange-trees were first seen in France at Amboise.

The next king, François I, was far too busy with Blois, Chambord and Fontainebleau to do much building at Amboise, but he did bring Leonardo da Vinci here and install him at the Manoir du Clos Lucé, which is today a Leonardo museum (E end of Rue Victor Hugo). Da Vinci was buried, at his own wish, in the church of the château, but this was destroyed and sold in the Revolution without anyone thinking of the great Italian interred there. However, in 1863 a search was undertaken, and what are believed to be his remains have been reburied in the Chapelle St-Hubert.

In 1560, the château became the scene of the aftermath of a plot launched unsuccessfully by some Protestants against the Guises: a horrifying mass public execution, which the royal family was obliged to witness.

After that, Amboise was never again popular as a royal dwelling. It pursued a chequered career until in 1872 the National Assembly presented it to the Orléans family, in whose hands it remains.

The town of Amboise is picturesque, with many old houses of the 15th-, 16th- and 18th-c. The Tour d'Horloge was built by Charles VIII, and the Hôtel-de-Ville, which is 1505 but restored, houses the municipal museum. In the 16th-c. Hôtel de Joyeuse there is a Musée de la Poste, with some fascinating exhibits recalling the history of the post and stage-coaching in France. On the Promenade du Mail is a fountain (1968) by Max

Ernst. The island in the middle of the river, the Ile St-Jean, is a well-equipped municipal camping site with an excellent view of the castle.

3km S the 18th-c. Pagode de Chanteloupe is all that remains of the great château built by the Duc de Choiseul in imitation of Versailles. From the top there is a fine view.

6½km NE of Amboise the church of Limeray has Angevin vaulting (*see* Angers) and some lovely old statues.

ANET, Château d', *Eure-et-Loir* (2–C3). First the great fortress of Charles le Mauvais, Comte d'Évreux, then the glorious Renaissance château built in about 1550 by Philibert Delorme for Diane de Poitiers. All the great artists of the day

Château d'Amboise

Dr Christopher Tadgell

The chapel of Château d'Anet

contributed their skills, and it was said to have been the first building of the Renaissance where the French and Italian styles were fully integrated. Anet was a victim first of the Revolution and then of predatory speculators, until in 1840 what was left of it was acquired by the Moreau family, who have tended it ever since. The buildings that remain include: the Portail d'Entrée, with its tympanum sculpted by Benvenuto Cellini; the left wing, which has been handsomely restored and furnished; Delorme's beautiful Chapelle, with its two pyramidal towers finished in 1582, and its bas-reliefs by Pierre Bontemps and Jean Goujon; and the Chapelle Funéraire of Diane de Poitiers, built by Claude de Foucques in 1566 to house her remains, and from which they were ejected in the Revolution when her tomb was used as a horse trough. In this chapel is a lovely kneeling statue of her, said to be by Bontemps.

ANGERS, *Maine-et-Loire* (2–E1). Angers lies on the banks of the Maine and is a large and prosperous town, the centre of the Anjou wine trade, the home of the celebrated liqueur Cointreau, and site of a major electrical industry.

From the 10th-c. it was owned by the Comtes d'Anjou, and rose to great importance in the 12th-c. as a result of two marriages. The first of these took place in 1129, when Foulques, Comte d'Anjou, married his 16-year-old son Geoffroi to Matilda, the 29-year-old grand-daughter of

William the Conqueror. Geoffroi habitually wore a sprig of broom in his cap; the French for broom is *genêt*, and this led to his being called Plantagenêt. The second important marriage occurred when the son of Geoffroi and Matilda, Henri Plantagenêt, married Eleanor of Aquitaine in 1152. Two years later he succeeded to the throne of England, becoming Henry II.

The Cathedral of St-Maurice dates from this time. It is 12th–13th-c. Gothic. The great doorway, which was damaged in the Wars of Religion and in the Revolution, is surrounded by some fine statues. Three towers soar above it, the outer ones surmounted by pinnacled spires, the centre one by a modest belfry and lantern-tower. Below the belfry, and high above the main doorway, is a row of niches containing bearded figures in military costume. The nave is enormous and dates from the mid-12th-c. It is the first example of the so-called Angevin style of vaulting, in which the central crossed arch is higher than the side arches, giving a lofty effect. On the N side is some 12th-c. stained glass and in the chancel some of the 13th-c. The rose-window in the transept is 15th-c., the side windows of the N transept 16th-c. The Cathedral 'Treasure' contains superb gifts made by René le Bon (1409–80), the last of the Ducs d'Anjou and titular King of Sicily, a man of great culture and learning. The 12th-c. Bishop's Palace is beside the Cathedral.

The Angevin style can be seen again in the church of St-Serge in the Rue Tussieu, with its magnificent choir. Note the delicacy of the columns and the 12th-c. monochrome glass. The collegiate church of St-Martin in the Bd. Maréchal Foch is a good example of the Carolingian style and has a Plantagenet chancel.

Angers was taken for the French by Philippe-Auguste in 1205; Louis IX (St Louis) gave it to his brother, who became the first Duc d'Anjou.

Under St Louis, between 1230 and 1240, the château was rebuilt; it is a magnificent pentagonal fortress, with a kilometre of outer wall flanked by 17 great towers (all once pointed and tiled), making it one of the best examples of French defensive architecture of this period. Today it houses a world-famous collection of tapestries, including the great Apocalypse Tapestry made between 1375 and 1380. Although not complete, it is 168m long. Considered of small value, it was bought for the Cathedral in the mid-19th-c. by the then bishop for 300 francs. Now displayed in a room built specially for it, this oldest surviving medieval tapestry can be seen in all its incomparable beauty. In the grounds of the château is the early 15th-c. Chapelle Ste-Geneviève, built by Yolande d'Aragon, the protectress of Joan of Arc.

To prove that the art of tapestry making is very much alive in Angers, the beautiful Musée St-Jean in the old hospital (1180–1210), on the W side of the river, houses the work of Jean Lurçat (1892–1966) who did much to revive the art. The

THE LOIRE VALLEY AND POITOU-CHARENTES

building itself is remarkable; the great Salle de Malades has Angevin vaulting supported by 14 great pillars.

The Musée des Beaux-Arts in the 15th-c. Logis Barrault in the Rue Toussaint (S of the Cathedral) has an important collection of the work of the early-19th-c. sculptor David d'Angers. In the Rue Lenepveu the graceful Renaissance Hôtel Pincé, built between 1523 and 1535, contains the Turpin de Crissé collection, with fine pictures, Greek and Etruscan vases, and a set of prints tracing the history of fashion in France.

Of the many fine old houses in the city, perhaps the most picturesque is the Maison d'Adam with its half-timbering (Place Ste-Croix behind the Cathedral). Nearby, in the Rue des Lices, is the 12th-c. Tour St-Aubin, all that remains of the former abbey.

A feature of Angers is its flowers and streets planted with magnolia and camellia trees. The Jardin des Plantes, off the Place du Pélican, established 150 years ago, is of great botanical interest.

In the vicinity of Angers are four châteaux of interest: 20km N is the moated 15th-c. **Plessis-Bourré**, built by Jean Bourré, Treasurer to Louis XI and Charles VIII; the guardroom has an amusing painted ceiling of the 15th-c. depicting fables and proverbs, and there is some fine 18th-c. furniture. The **Château de Plessis-Macé**, 12km NW, is also moated, but dates from the 12th-c.; it was largely rebuilt in the 15th-c. and has a notable

The Apocalypse Tapestry in Château d'Angers
French Government Tourist Office

Renaissance chapel. 24km E is the exquisite 18th-c. **Château de Montgeoffroy**, which is not only still owned and occupied by the family of that name but retains all the furniture made for the château when it was built. The **Château de Brissac** 8km S of Angers was built for the ancestor of the present owner in 1614–21 on the half-demolished shell of an earlier building; the beautiful furniture is 17th-c.

ANGOULÊME, *Charente* (4–B4). Angoulême – or Iculisma, as it was called under the Romans, when it was already an important city – stands behind its ramparts high above the river Charente. The ramparts (which you can drive round) give such a splendid view across the plain that they have been called 'the balcony of the Southwest'.

In the Middle Ages, Angoulême, then the capital of the old province of Angoumois, was the hereditary property of the Princes of the Blood. Traces of its rich past may be seen in the upper town, known locally as '*le plateau*', and especially in the beautiful Cathedral of St-Pierre, which dates from the 12th-c. and has a magnificent façade which is like a page from a medieval illuminated book in sculptured stone. It depicts the Last Judgment and has a superb figure of Christ in Majesty. The building was badly damaged by the Calvinists, restored in the 17th-c., and then again more fully in the 19th-c. by the locally born architect Paul Abadie, who built Sacré Cœur in Paris. The interior, as in his restoration of St-Front in Périgueux (*see entry in the* Southwest *section*), appears a little too coldly classical.

The Hôtel-de-Ville was also built by Abadie; it is on the site of the old château of which it incorporates some parts, notably the 13th-c. keep and a round tower of the 15th-c., where Marguerite d'Angoulême (1492–1549) was born, one of the distinguished figures of the French Renaissance. Her brother François inherited the throne of France from his uncle, Louis XII, and became the great King François I, to whose reign (1515–47) we owe so many of the châteaux of the Loire.

There are many fine houses in the surrounding narrow streets, once the homes of aristocratic families, of which the Hôtel St-Simon in the Rue de la Cloche-Verte is a good example with its lovely Renaissance courtyard.

The Musée Municipal is in the Bishop's Palace by the Cathedral; it dates from the 12th-c., although altered in the 15th-c.

The lower town, which is the commercial and industrial quarter, has an equally long history. Angoulême has been famous since the Middle Ages for the manufacture of watermarked paper. In the 17th-c. there were almost 100 mills making paper for Holland. Although the industry received a severe check when many of the workers, who were for the most part Huguenots, left the country at the Revocation of the Edict of Nantes (1685), it never wholly died out and still today several factories make stationery and cigarette paper. The other traditional industry is the manufacture of felt slippers, *pantoufles charentaises*.

Recent industrial expansion, with the introduction of heavy engineering, has led to a scheme known as 'le Grand Angoulême', whereby factories have been sited in country areas to give the workers a healthier and more balanced life. The scheme, a pilot scheme for the rest of France, is being watched with interest.

ARGENTON-CHÂTEAU, *Deux-Sèvres* (2–E1). On the beautiful site above the valley of the Argenton and the Ouère, this once fortified hill town has preserved part of the Château and its collegiate church of the 12th–15th-c. The Château was the home of Philippe de Commynes (1464–98), Sénéchal of Poitou and the chronicler of the reigns of Louis XI and Charles VIII. The church of St-Gilles has a notable Romanesque doorway with a 13th-c. square tower and a nave of the 11th-c.

ARGENTON-SUR-CREUSE, *Indre* (5–A5). Known as Argentomagus under the Romans, this picturesque town on the Creuse, whose old mills and galleried houses hang, Venice-like, over the river on both sides, joined by the lovely Pont Vieux, is best explored on foot. The church of St-Sauveur, on the right bank, is 15th-c. and the chapel of St-Benoît, on the opposite bank, 15th–16th-c. with a 15th-c. stone Virgin. The chapel of Notre-Dame-des-Bancs, which is surmounted by a huge statue of the Virgin, contains a statue called the 'Bonne Dame d'Argenton' which is believed to have protected the town from the plague in 1632.

Adjoining the town to the N is St-Marcel with its priory church dating from the 12th-c. The crypt is the oldest part of the church; the choir-stalls are 15th-c. and the 'Treasure' contains two shrines, one of them 13th-c. The Roman city of Argentomagus is currently being excavated, and a small archaeological museum has been opened by the church.

ASNIÈRES-SUR-VÈGRE, *Sarthe* (9km NE of Sablé: 2–D1). The small town lies snugly at the bottom of the valley of the Vègre, with its old houses and lovely saddle-backed bridge. From the bridge there is a view of a picturesque old mill with the 17th–18th-c. Château du Moulin Vieux beside it. Near the church is a curious Gothic building known as the Cour d'Asnières, where the canons of Le Mans came to receive their feudal dues. In the nave of the church are some 13th-c. painted murals; others in the choir date from the 15th-c.

5km NE is the delightful late 15th-c. **Château de Verdelles,** part fortress, part Renaissance *château de plaisance*.

AUBETERRE, *Charente* (10km E of Chalais: 4–B3, B4). At the S of the department of Charente,

Aubeterre (*alba terra*: white earth) owes its name to the amphitheatre of chalk cliffs against which it is built, high above the river Dronne with a fine view over the surrounding country.

The 'Église Monolithe', the church of St-Jean, is by definition a church cut out of a single piece of rock. It was hollowed out of the cliff in the 12th-c. to house the relics which the local lord had brought back from a Crusade. At the Revolution it suffered the same fate as the monolithic church in St-Émilion (*see entry in the* Southwest *section*) – it was turned into a saltpetre factory. At the end of the nave is a primitive chapel of the 6th-c., later transformed into a burial place.

The church of St-Jacques was a Benedictine abbey and then a college of canons. In the carvings on the Romanesque façade, with its triple doorway, it is easy to see the Moorish influence which is often a feature of the decoration of the churches on the pilgrim routes to Compostella.

AULNAY, *Charente-Maritime* (4–B3). Set in the middle of a very old cemetery, surrounded by cypresses and neglected tombstones, is the remarkable pilgrim church of St-Pierre-de-la-Tour, one of the most perfect examples of Poitevin Romanesque, amazingly rich in early-12th-c. sculpture, both inside and out, some of it suggesting an eastern influence. In the cemetery is an interesting 15th-c. 'Croix Hosannière', an elaborate cross which featured in Palm Sunday processions, with a pulpit and statues of saints.

AZAY-LE-FERRON, Château d', *Indre* (17km SW of Châtillon: 2–E3). The façade of the château, set in a great park and looking out on to formal gardens, resembles a pattern book of architectural styles. On the left, the 15th-c. Tour Ronde with machicolations, then the 17th-c. Humières wing which joins the tower to the Pavillon François I, built in the 16th-c., and finally the elegant 18th-c. Pavillon Breteuil. The interior is a veritable museum of furniture, carpets, tapestries, chinaware and precious objects from periods ranging from the 16th- to the 19th-c.

AZAY-LE-RIDEAU, Château d', *Indre-et-Loire* (2–E2). Taking its name from an early owner, Ridel or Rideau, the château as we see it today dates from the early 16th-c. when Gilles Berthelot, a grandson of a former mayor of Tours who had bought the property in 1450 when it was a ruin (having been brutally sacked and burned by Charles VII), rose to be one of the four Généraux des Finances of France. Berthelot set about rebuilding it in the early Renaissance style, only to fall out of favour with François I and die in exile. Although the château is lapped by the river Indre, the surrounding water and woods have never, it is clear, had any purpose beyond being decorative. The whole beautiful Renaissance structure shows clearly the change in purpose that took place in château building at that time, when defence ceased

La Baule

to be the main consideration. Inside there are some fine carved chimney-pieces and a splendid stairway. The whole of the interior, with contemporary furnishings, is in effect a Renaissance museum. There is a *son-et-lumière* every evening during the summer months, and on certain public holidays.

The nearby village church is 12th–15th-c. although the façade incorporates parts of an earlier church dating from the 5th- and 6th-c.

BARBEZIEUX, *Charente* (4–B3). The capital of the Petit Champagne district of Cognac and renowned for its *marron glacé*. In the centre, the winding streets and old houses surround the twin-towered gateway which is all that remains of the 12th-c. hilltop castle. The towers house a small theatre and a museum.

10km ESE is the small Romanesque church of Conzac, and 15km due E the church of St-Arthémy de Blanzac is surrounded by the ruins of a 12th-c. castle.

BASSAC, Abbaye de, *Charente* (3km SE of Jarnac: 4–B3). This former Benedictine abbey was founded just after the year 1000; among the precious relics treasured there were the cords said to have been used for the flagellation of Christ. Severely damaged during the Hundred Years War and again during the Wars of Religion, the abbey church was deconsecrated in the Revolution and only reconsecrated in recent years. The façade is Romanesque, and was altered in the 15th-c. for defensive purposes. Inside there is an early statue of St Nicolas (probably 13th-c.); its feet were traditionally kissed by girls looking for husbands. The convent buildings were rebuilt in the 17th- and 18th-c.

BATZ-SUR-MER, *Loire-Atlantique* (7km W of La Baule: 1–C3). Once an important salt town, now a pleasant fishing and seaside resort on the Croisic peninsula just W of La Baule. Batz-sur-

Mer has a fine granite church, St-Guénolé (15th–16th-c.) with a high tower affording a splendid view of the coast and across the Loire estuary. Inside, the keystones of the arches have unusual carvings, and there is a good statue of the Virgin. Close by the church is a ruined 15th–16th-c. chapel, Notre-Dame-du-Mûrier.

BAUGÉ, *Maine-et-Loire* (2–E1, E2). A small agricultural town on the river Couasnon. The château facing the central square and some fine old houses are reminders of the days when it was the favourite seat of Joan of Arc's supporter, Yolande d'Aragon, and her son René le Bon, Comte d'Anjou.

The château – today housing both the Hôtel-de-Ville and a museum – was built under the personal direction of King René, both as an escape from the grander châteaux of Angers and Saumur and as a hunting-lodge from which to hunt the wild boar in the magnificent forest of Chandelais (5km SE). On the rear watch-tower, the masons have carved some amusing self-portraits.

The Hôpital St-Joseph in the Rue Dr Zamenhof was founded in 1643 and has a remarkable 17th-c. *pharmacie* which is beautifully preserved and well worth a visit.

In the Chapelle des Filles du Cœur de Marie, in the Rue Girouardière, is the famous Croix d'Anjou, reputed to have been made from a piece of the True Cross brought back from the Holy Land in the mid 13th-c. and later decorated with pearls and jewels. Formerly in the 12th-c. Abbaye de la Boissière (22km E), where the chapel that housed it may be seen, it has a second shorter cross-bar above the normal one, and figures in the arms of Anjou. In the 17th-c. it was adopted by the Ducs de Lorraine; today it is perhaps better known as the Croix de Lorraine.

At 9km W is the Flamboyant church of Jarzé, with 16th-c. murals of prophets and an appealing statue of the infant martyr St Cyr, holding a pear.

The Château de Durtal, which lies 18km NW, is late 16th- and early 17th-c.; to the S of it stretches the beautiful forest of Chambiers.

BAULE, La, *Loire-Atlantique* (1–C3). With so many superb beaches on this coast, it is perhaps invidious to suggest that La Baule is the best, but it certainly has a strong claim to be so. Sheltered from the N by pine forests planted to settle the sand dunes (between the 15th- and 18th-c. a nearby village disappeared under blown sand), facing S and sheltered on either side by the arms of the bay, it has an 8km stretch of fine clean sand. The town, with its parks and casino, is smart and lively.

La-Baule-les-Pins, a neighbouring spa with houses built among pine-trees, has now joined up with the town. On the other side, to the W, the old fishing port of Le Pouliguen has a picturesque quayside and an attractive woodland park.

BEAUGENCY, *Loiret* (2–D3). A picturesque medieval town 25km SW of Orléans on the right bank of the Loire. It was here, in 1152, that the Council of Beaugency was held at which the marriage between Louis VII and Eleanor of Aquitaine was annulled; her subsequent marriage to Henry II of England in the same year led to the 300-year presence of the English in France. During the Hundred Years War, Beaugency, which possessed the only bridge over the Loire between Blois and Orléans, was often fought over before being finally taken for the French in 1429 by Joan of Arc.

Immediately S of the bridge is the old quarter (very attractively lit at night) with several impressive monuments of the town's history. First are the old abbey buildings close to the river, with the Devil's Tower which formed part of the bridge defences and was at that time lapped by the river; the former abbey church was built in the 12th-c., burned by Protestants in 1567, rebuilt in the 17th-c. The Château de Dunois, built in the 15th-c. by the celebrated Bastard of Orléans, companion-in-arms of Joan of Arc, now contains a regional folk museum; in June the courtyard is the setting of drama performances during the annual Theatre Festival. At the W corner of the church stands the great square keep, the Tour de César, built in the 11th-c.; its exterior is still formidable, but the interior, alas, is a wreck. Nearby is another tower, the Tour St-Firmin, all that is left of a 16th-c. church, also destroyed by Protestants. At the other end of the Rue de la Sirène is the Maison des Templiers with an interesting Romanesque façade. Beyond that again, in a fine Renaissance building in the Rue du Change, is the Hôtel-de-Ville, whose council room, decorated with some splendid 17th-c. embroidered hangings from the old abbey, can be visited.

BEAUMONT-SUR-SARTHE, *Sarthe* (22km S of Alençon: 2–D2). An attractive old town with narrow streets whose ruined château, standing above the river on the old route from Le Mans to Alençon, bears witness to its former importance. The French and English fought over it many times. The church has a 12th-c. Romanesque doorway, and the Hôtel des Gouverneurs is 16th-c. No trace of the former ramparts exists. From the Motte à Madame, which was part of the old defences, there is a fine view over the valley.

BEAUREGARD, Château de, *Loir-et-Cher* (8km SE of Blois: 2–E3). Famous for its Galerie de Portraits, which contains 363 historical portraits, including 15 kings of France, and with a remarkable floor of Delft tiles, this handsome Renaissance château was built in the 16th-c. and enlarged in the 17th-c. The Cabinet des Grelots is a pretty room with fine carved panelling and a coffered ceiling.

BELLEGARDE, *Loiret* (2–D4). The château, which has a 14th-c. moated keep, passed at the end of the 17th-c. to the Duc d'Antin, legitimate son of Madame de Montespan, Louis XIV's mistress. D'Antin put in hand the construction of a number of brick buildings, including the Pavillon de la Salamandre and the Tour Capitaine. There are also some fine stables.

The church of Bellegarde has a beautiful Romanesque façade, with pillars whose capitals are carved with designs of foliage and mythological animals. The broad nave contains some unusual paintings.

14km SE is the agreeable riverside resort of Olivet, with a Renaissance Hôtel-de-Ville, a 12th–13th-c. church and a timbered market hall. A popular place for fishing and canoeing.

BERCÉ, Forêt de, *Sarthe* (SE of Le Grand-Lucé: 2–D2). This beautiful forest, part of the once vast forest of Le Mans, is full of unexpected little valleys, springs and streams. The Futaie des Clos is an extensive plantation of ancient oaks, several of which are 300 years old. Here and there one comes across a little church, like the priory church of St-Vincent-du-Loroeür, or the odd château – the Château de Jaille, for example, with its spreading lawns, or the Château de Bénéhart, with its long, white façade and great grey roofs, which once belonged to the Maillé family, one of whom was beheaded by Henri III for treason.

BLOIS, *Loir-et-Cher* (2–E3). When, in 1498, Charles VIII hit his head on a doorpost at Amboise on his way to watch a tennis match and died some hours later, the crown of France passed to the Duc d'Orléans, Louis XII. The court moved to Blois, where the Château became the focus of national events for almost 200 years.

Blois was built originally as a fort to withstand the Vikings, but the only buildings surviving from that time are the Tour du Foix and the beautiful 13th-c. Salles d'États. From the accession of Louis

J. Allan Cash

Château de Blois: the spiral staircase

XII onward, the Château was to undergo a number of transformations.

The new king, whose father had been a prisoner in the Tower of London for 25 years after he was captured at the battle of Agincourt, began his reign by marrying Anne of Brittany, the widow of his predecessor; he brought her to Blois, where they built the Chapelle St-Calais and the Louis XII wing. This enchanting building, part brick, part stone, although almost completely rebuilt during the 19th-c. restoration – even the equestrian statue of the King over the main entrance is a copy of the original – manages nevertheless to give a vivid impression of the first exuberance of the French Renaissance style, before the more formal Italian influence began to be felt. This shows itself very happily in the lack of symmetry and the arbitrary placing of door and window openings. The first floor contains the Musée des Beaux-Arts with paintings of the French school.

The Italian influence is more in evidence in the wing built by Louis's successor, François I, which lies to the right as one enters the courtyard. The magnificent spiral staircase, which it has been suggested may have been designed by Leonardo da Vinci while he was living at Amboise, is uniquely beautiful.

A century later, it was in the King's Apartments, in this wing, that the weak and vicious King Henri III had the Duc de Guise murdered, and where his mother, the formidable and scheming Catherine de Médicis, died later. In her Cabinet de Travail one may still see the secret cupboards worked by concealed pedals where she is said to have hidden her poisons.

The last phase of building at Blois was in the 17th-c., when Louis XIII, anxious to keep his brother, Gaston d'Orléans, out of mischief, persuaded him to rebuild the château. François Mansart (1598–1666) was engaged, and it was he who designed the austere and rather chilly wing which completes the quadrangle.

The town of Blois, which today is the capital of Loir-et-Cher, centre of a thriving agricultural community and also a producer of shoes and chocolate (the Chocolaterie Poulain, to the W of the Château at 6 Rue Gambetta, may be visited), was badly damaged in June 1940, when many old houses were destroyed. These have been replaced and care has been taken to ensure that the new roof-line does not spoil the panoramic view which can be enjoyed from the Place du Château, the spot where Joan of Arc made her soldiers take communion before going to relieve Orléans.

The extremely beautiful former abbey church of St-Nicolas in the Rue St-Laumer which is part Romanesque, part Gothic, manages a successful harmony between these two styles. The Cathedral of St-Louis, in the Place St-Louis, although mostly 17th-c. Gothic, has a fine crypt of the 10th–11th-c. Behind it the Hôtel-de-Ville occupies the former 18th-c. Bishop's Palace with its splendid garden. In the old streets running down to the Loire from the Cathedral there are some very picturesque houses.

Two famous men born here are remembered in the city: Robert Houdin (1805–71), the conjurer, whose museum is at 5 Rue de la Voûte-du-Château; and Denis Papin (1647–1714), the inventor of an early form of pressure-cooker; he was a Huguenot who was driven from France by the Revocation of the Edict of Nantes and spent much of his life in England; there is a statue to him, and the street which runs from it down to the bridge is named after him. In the Rue St-Honoré are two fine Renaissance buildings, the Hôtel d'Alluye and the Hôtel Denis-Dupont.

9km NE is the **Château de Ménars**. Built in the 17th-c., it became the home of Madame de Pompadour, favourite of Louis XV, and was enlarged by her in the 18th-c. It has charming gardens and terraces overlooking the Loire.

BOCAGE VENDÉEN, Le, *Vendée* (E and W of La Roche-sur-Yon: 1–D3, D4). An old word meaning 'woods', the Bocage covers most of the Vendée (roughly E of a line drawn between Nantes and La Roche-sur-Yon) and consists of high ground broken into tiny fields by tall hedges. (In recent years the Government-sponsored re-apportionment of land, known as *les remembrements*, has greatly increased the size of these fields.) It was here in 1793 that the Vendéen peasants, Les Chouans, traditionally conservative and Catholic, joined with the old nobility, the Whites, to rebel against the Revolution and fight a guerilla war against the Republican Army, the Blues.

Successful at first, the Chouans with their pitchforks and scythes reached Le Mans before being driven back by the 'Colonnes Infernales', who burned and slaughtered everything in their path. Even so it was long before the Vendéens were subdued, and many a detachment of Blues was decimated by unseen marksmen sheltering behind the tall hedges.

Always poor, the Bocage with its granite churches and plain houses has a slightly Scottish feel, and the quality of secretiveness which made it difficult to conquer is equally hampering to the tourist.

Mont des Alouettes (231m), a highpoint of the Bocage (just N of Les Herbiers on N160, 40km NE of La Roche-sur-Yon), has a splendid panorama which gives an impression of the small fields and the hidden *logis*, the manor houses where the Rebellion was planned. The windmills were used by the Chouans during the war: the position of their sails, clearly visible to all, transmitting messages.

BONNEVAL, *Eure-et-Loir* (2–D3). On the left bank of the Loir, this once fortified town was built round the Benedictine abbey of St-Florentin. Today the abbey is a psychiatric hospital, and the interior is not open to the public, but the exterior is very handsome and has a 15th-c. gateway with two machicolated towers. There is a fine 13th-c. Gothic church. Of the town's original ramparts only a couple of towers and gateways remain, but the moat still has water in it.

BOURGES, *Cher* (2–E4). Once the capital of Berry, now the capital of the Cher department. 'Surrounded' – according to Stendhal – 'by plains of bitter ugliness', the city stands on raised ground dominated by its Cathedral at the junction of the rivers Yèvre and Auron.

Its history stretches back long before the Romans, who occupied it for nearly five centuries. As Avaricum it shared with Bordeaux the administration of Aquitaine. Part of the Roman ramparts, built from materials already old, may still be traced in the city, though they are mostly hidden by houses. However, the Musée de Berry, in the elegant Hôtel Cujas, 6 Rue des Arènes, which was built in 1515 for a rich Florentine merchant, contains many things which have survived from the Roman occupation.

Christianity was introduced by St-Ursin in the 3rd-c., and four churches have preceded the present Cathedral on the same site. The last of these, which was 11th-c. Romanesque, saw the coronation in 1137 of Louis VII. The decision of the Chapter to rebuild in the new Gothic style then coming into vogue in the Ile-de-France, owed much to the Archbishop Henri de Sully.

The resulting Cathédrale St-Étienne, begun at the end of the 12th-c. and finished in the middle of the 13th-c., although it has been altered and added to many times, is acknowledged to be one of the most beautiful ecclesiastical buildings in France. It is 125m long, 40m wide and 37m high below the vaulting. The incomparable W front is approached by steps and has five deeply recessed doorways with the most varied and lively sculpture, the subject of each doorway being different. Particularly fine is the Last Judgment above the central door with, below it, St Michael weighing souls above a host of extremely sprightly devils. The left tower was built in the 15th-c. and promptly collapsed. Rebuilt with the help of money raised from the sale of Indulgences allowing people to eat fat during Lent, it is known as the Tour Beurre (the Butter Tower). The tower on the right, which also threatened to collapse and so was stopped at its present height without its bell-tower being added, is known as the Tour Sourd (the Deaf Tower). Curiously, their unequal height seems to enhance the effect by varying the outline. They are divided by an immense 14th-c. window.

The S side of the building has a great line of flying buttresses with three storeys of glass. The two side doors of the Cathedral, which survive from the Romanesque predecessor, have 15th-c. porches with beautiful open tracery.

Inside there is a central nave with double aisles on each side. Because there is no transept, or cross aisle, the effect of the four rows of parallel columns stretching to the choir in unbroken lines makes what is in fact one of the shortest cathedrals in France seem one of the longest: a majestic vista of grey and brown, lit by gleams of colour from the 13th-c. stained glass in the choir and chapel. The W window, seen to full effect at sunset, was presented in 1390 by Jean Duc de Berry, whose strikingly life-like effigy is in the 11th-c. crypt under the choir; some of the remarkable *pleurants*, hooded figures in white marble and alabaster which once surrounded his tomb, may be seen in several of the city's museums.

Near the Cathedral, in the Rue Molière, is a 13th-c. Grange aux Dîmes (tithe barn), where the canons kept those of their tithes paid in kind. Of the other churches, Notre-Dame in the Place de la Barre is 15th–16th-c. with a Renaissance tower; St-Pierre-le-Guillard, in the Rue des Trois Bourses, is 13th-c. Romanesque; and St-Bonnet, where the painter François Boucher is buried, is 15th-c.

During the Hundred Years War, Bourges was the headquarters of the Dauphin, derisively called 'the King of Bourges' until Joan of Arc persuaded him to be crowned at Reims and lead his armies to victory. This campaign was made possible by the help of a remarkable man, Jacques Cœur, the King's silversmith, who was born in Bourges the son of a furrier, and who through an extraordinary gift for business amassed a vast fortune which he put at the service of the King. For a whole year he provided the funds for the maintenance of four armies. Sadly, Charles VII proved as ungrateful to this friend as he had been to Joan of Arc, and when in 1451 Cœur was arraigned by jealous courtiers on a trumped-up charge and condemned, Charles merely commuted the death sentence to banishment for life, with the seizure of all his goods and wealth.

The great mansion he built for himself but scarcely lived in, the Palais Jacques Cœur in the Rue Jacques Cœur, was built between 1443 and 1450 and is one of the finest examples of Gothic domestic architecture in France. In fact it was greatly ahead of its time in matters of comfort, even having running water. The façade is typically Flamboyant, achieving a wonderful balance without any attempt at symmetry. The figures on each side of the entrance are said to represent the welcoming host and hostess. The courtyard is surrounded on three sides by an open cloister; on the fourth rise three turrets, the central one richly carved with palm-, olive- and orange-trees, a reference to Cœur's trade with the East. Inside, the house is extraordinarily decorated with carvings, many of the owner and his wife, playing chess, eating oranges, etc. In the chapel, their seats have each their own window and fireplace. Cœur's arms appear everywhere, and also his motto: 'To the valiant heart nothing is impossible.'

The Hôtel-de-Ville was formerly the Archbishop's Palace. It is 17th-c., and the garden, which has an impressive view of the Cathedral, was laid out by Le Nôtre.

Explored on foot, Bourges is full of rewards for the tourist: the many Renaissance houses, the typically French provincial Place George Sand, the old butcher's shop in the Place Planchet, or just the little Rue Guichet, with its lovely glimpse of the Cathedral.

10km S of Bourges lies the ruined abbey of **Plaimpied** with its 15th-c. abbey buildings and fine Romanesque church with notable capitals.

BOURGONNIÈRE, Château de, *Maine-et-Loire* (8km SE of Ancenis: 1–C4). An early 19th-c. château standing in a large park with the remains of a 15th-c. keep and an exquisite Renaissance chapel containing a remarkable reredos with Christ in Majesty.

18km W at **Champtoceaux** are the remains of a feudal château, with a superb view from a promenade to the left of the church. The local white wine is excellent.

BOURGUEIL, *Indre-et-Loire* (14km N of Chinon: 2–E2). A small town famous for its red wine, produced from a local grape known as the 'Breton'. Bourgueil once had a powerful Benedictine abbey, founded in the 10th-c., of which only the 18th-c. priory, part of the 15th-c. cloisters and a few other vestiges remain. The parish church is 12th-c., though much restored.

2km N, on a well signposted route, lies the Cave de la Dive Bouteille, where one may visit the wine museum and taste the local wine.

BRENNE, La, *Indre* (6km NE of Le Blanc: 4,5–A4, A5). A curious area of lakes and scrub

dotted with the occasional sheep farm which is not without charm and contains several places of interest, such as the imposing medieval Château de Bouchet-en-Brenne, with its round towers and square bastion overlooking the Mer Rouge – a lake which takes its name from a crusading Seigneur de Bouchet, who was made a prisoner on the shores of the Red Sea. On an island in the lake is the Chapelle de Notre-Dame de la Mer Rouge, rebuilt in the 19th-c. and containing a 16th-c. copy of a miraculous 13th-c. Virgin, the original of which was destroyed during the Wars of Religion.

To the N at Mezière-en-Brenne is the 14th-c. church of Ste-Madeleine with its glorious mid-16th-c. Renaissance Chapelle d'Anjou containing some fine 16th-c. stained glass.

BRESSUIRE, *Deux-Sèvres* (4–A3). The capital of the Bocage Vendéen (although technically in Deux-Sèvres). In March 1794 Bressuire was burned and the population massacred by the Republican Army during the Vendéen uprising (*see entry* Bocage Vendéen). The church of Notre-Dame has a 12th-c. nave, a large choir of the 16th-c. and a Renaissance steeple some 55m high. The remains of the château, which dates from the 11th-c. form a romantic ruin.

26km NW, at St-Aubin-de-Baubigné, is the 15th–17th-c. Château de la Durbelière, the birthplace of Henri de la Rochejacquelin (1772–94), 'Monsieur Henri', the 21-year-old hero of the Vendéen uprising. It was here, under the gateway, that he addressed 2000 peasants, saying: 'If I advance, follow me! If I retreat, kill me! If I die, avenge me!'

BRINAY, *Cher* (8km NW of Mehun: 2–E4). A village whose Romanesque church of St-Aignan has a choir entirely covered with remarkable 12th-c. frescoes showing scenes from the life of Christ. Well worth going out of your way to see them. The village is close to the river Cher, 6km SE of Vierzon on the D27.

BROUAGE, *Charente-Maritime* (4–B2, B3). A curious fortified port standing high and dry on salt marshes from which the sea has receded. The birthplace of Samuel Champlain (1567–1635), founder of Quebec, whose monument (1970) stands beside the church of St-Pierre (16th–17th-c.), Brouage was fortified by Cardinal Richelieu after the siege of La Rochelle. For a time it was the most powerful arsenal on this coast, with 6000 men. Today there are barely 200 inhabitants and it is slowly sinking into the mud.

6½km S is **Marennes**, famous for its green oysters; the 15th-c. tower of St-Pierre-de-Sales gives a panoramic view of the marshes, and there is a fine Renaissance house at 182 Rue de la République.

CANDES-ST-MARTIN, *Indre-et-Loire* (14km NW of Chinon: 2–E2). The beautiful 13th-c.

church, which was fortified in the 15th-c., is built on the site of the house where St Martin, the great Bishop of Tours, died in AD 397. His body was carried to Tours on a barge; tradition has it that as the barge passed, although it was November, the banks burst into flower, the trees into green leaf, and the birds into song – hence 'St Martin's summer', the French equivalent for the English 'Indian summer'.

The setting is particularly lovely, and from a spot a little to the right of the church, along a path, there is a superb view of the point where the Vienne and the Loire come together. The little château dates from the end of the 15th-c.

CHAMBORD, Château de, *Loir-et-Cher* (2–E3). Few visitors today are likely to agree with Louis XIV, who found Chambord too small. The one great impression it gives is of space, vast limitless space. As you wander among its 440 rooms or up and down its 50 staircases, it is impossible to believe that anyone should have built it just as a hunting-lodge, yet that is precisely what François I did build it for and the only use to which he ever put it.

In a sense Chambord is the apogee of the châteaux of the Loire, the point to which the others lead, the fantastic utterance of a society in decadence. Yet it is quite unlike the others, indeed it is unlike anything else in the world.

It lies in a vast deer park at the end of an avenue and seems suddenly to appear as you approach, a great mass of white stone with a unique roof-line, where chimneys, turrets and pinnacles intermingle in such fantastic profusion that it is unimaginable they can ever have been designed. The designer was in fact Trinqueau, the architect of Chenonceaux and Blois, and the plan of the building is a huge rectangle flanked by massive corner towers, which still suggests the layout of the feudal castlefortress. The work was begun in 1519, but though 1800 workmen were employed at the King's death 28 years later. His successor Henri II added a wing, but it remains unfinished to this day.

François had wanted the Loire to pass in front of it, but the architect baulked at this (it is 5km away) and the little river Cosson was diverted instead. The great feature of the place is the famous staircase rising from floor to roof, formed of two spirals starting from different points and at different elevations, yet winding up the same hollow shaft, so that two people may pass up and down for ever without meeting, but continually catching tantalizing glimpses of each other.

In spite of his criticism, Louis XIV came often to Chambord with his court. It was here that Molière wrote *Le Bourgeois Gentilhomme*, and was present at its first performance here before the King in 1670.

CHAMPIGNY-SUR-VEUDE, *Indre-et-Loire* (6km N of Richelieu: 2–E2). A small town with a number of 16th-c. houses. It once had a great château, built by Louis de Bourbon between 1508 and 1543, but it was later pulled down on the orders of Cardinal Richelieu who disliked the competition it offered to the château he was building for himself at Richelieu, 6km to the S.

The remaining outbuildings give some idea of the vanished magnificence of the place. The chief interest lies in the Ste-Chapelle which was saved from destruction by Pope Urban VIII. It is a superb example of the French Renaissance just at the moment when the Italian influence was beginning to make itself felt (Louis de Bourbon had accompanied Charles VIII to Italy) and it has retained all its beautiful stained-glass windows illustrating the life of St Louis.

4½km N the 13th–15th-c. **Château du Rivau** lies in a romantic park and has a drawbridge, a keep, and all its original 15th-c. floors and ceilings.

CHARROUX, *Vienne* (11km NE of Ruffec: 4–B4). A once-powerful abbey, built at the end of the 10th-c. under the patronage of Charlemagne. Possessor of such remarkable relics as a piece of the True Cross and some of the Blood and Flesh of Christ, Charroux became enormously rich from the endowments and gifts of thousands of pilgrims (even, it is said, owning land in England). It was almost totally destroyed in the Wars of Religion.

Intelligent restoration over the last 30 years has achieved remarkable results. The remains include the massive 11th-c. Tour Charlemagne, the 12th-c. abbey door – and, in the chapter house, a collection of objects found on the site, including 14th-c. reliquaries and some notable 13th-c. statues which were once on the façade.

In the village are two 15th-c. houses and a covered market dating from the 16th-c. 9km W is the beautiful Romanesque church of St-Nicolas at Civray.

CHARTRES, *Eure-et-Loir* (2–D3). The capital town of Eure-et-Loir, Chartres lies on the left bank of the Eure and is an important agricultural centre and wheat market. For the tourist, the chief interest of the place is the Cathedral of Notre-Dame, which can be seen from miles away across the plain of La Beauce and has been called the most beautiful church in the world.

The present building stands on an ancient place of worship dating back to Druidical times and is a mixture of Romanesque and Gothic, being the result of the rebuilding of the Romanesque Cathedral, burned down before it was barely completed in 1194. The Gothic contribution, which is the bulk of the structure, was built within the space of 30 years and so has a remarkable unity of style and execution, making it almost a copybook example of early French Gothic architecture.

At the W end stand the two great towers surmounted by spires. The Clocher Vieux on the right, saved intact from the earlier cathedral, is considered a masterpiece of the Romanesque style. The Clocher Neuf on the left, which at its base pre-dates the other, had its slightly taller spire added in 1506 by Jehan de Beauce. The fine triple doorway, with its series of sharply observed sculptured figures, dates from the middle of the 12th-c.; the rose-window and upper part of the façade are early 13th-c.

Even more striking, however, are the portals of the transept, the most splendid specimens of 13th-c. decoration in France. The S façade in particular has a projecting porch with three Gothic arches and is covered with hundreds of statues of kings, saints and martyrs. Originally both portals and their statues would have been painted and gilded.

The interior is vast, 130m long, 37m high, and with the broadest nave of all the cathedrals in France. The light is impressively sombre, setting

Chartres Cathedral

A.F. Kersting

off the rich, glowing colours of the famous windows made some 700 years ago. Below the rose-window at the W end are three windows depicting the Passion and the Tree of Jesse. The magnificent choir-screen, with its series of 40 groups of sculpture illustrating the life of Christ, was begun in 1514 by the same Jehan de Beauce who was responsible for the spire of the Clocher Neuf on the W façade. The 11th-c. crypt is the largest in France (over 200m long), and contains a Gallo-Roman well. Among the Cathedral 'Treasure' is a famous relic, the veil said to have been worn by the Virgin at the time of the Annunciation, presented to Chartres by Charles the Bald in the year AD 876.

The Cathedral Close contains several old houses, including at No. 7 a canonry dating from the 13th-c. There are remains of the cloisters and a fine 13th-c. crypt, the Celliers de Loëns at 5 Rue du Cardinal-Pie, with a spacious hall divided by two rows of imposing pillars.

The municipal museum, in the former 16th–18th-c. Episcopal Palace, shows the famous enamels of the apostles made by Léonard Limosin in 1545–7; also some good Flemish paintings, including a portrait of Erasmus by Holbein.

The town of Chartres was badly damaged in 1944 but has retained many delightful streets of old houses, such as the Place de la Poissonnerie with its 15th-c. Maison du Saumon, the Rue au Lait and the Rue des Écuyers and, the oldest house in Chartres, 29 Rue Chantault. The 11th–13th-c. abbey church of St-Pierre-en-Vallée, near the river to the SE, is a three-aisled basilica, with a long choir ending in a semi-circular apse and rectangular side chapels; there is some fine 13th–15th-c. stained glass.

The area immediately surrounding the Cathedral has been declared a conservation area and much has been done to clean up and preserve the buildings.

CHÂTEAUBRIANT, Château de, *Loire-Atlantique* (1–C3, C4). An old once-fortified town in the beautiful valley of the Chère. Overlooking the river is an imposing château in two parts – one 11th-c. with a large square keep at the angle of two wings; the other, across what used to be the *cour d'honneur*, a handsome 16th-c. Renaissance Palais Seigneurial. This was built by one Jean de Laval, whose wife became a mistress of François I; when she was ousted from royal favour by the Duchess of Étampes he dragged her from the court and locked her up here in a room draped with black, where she died ten years later, possibly murdered by her husband.

CHÂTEAUDUN, *Eure-et-Loir* (2–D3). Few towns can claim to have been as unlucky or brave as Châteaudun. Ravaged by fire several times over the centuries, sometimes by accident, more often by the action of enemies, it achieved renown for its heroic resistance in the Franco-Prussian War,

Rainbird (M.A. Norbury)

Châteaudun: interior courtyard of the château

when it kept the Prussian 22nd Division at bay for the whole of 18 October 1870.

The splendid château was the home of Joan of Arc's companion-in-arms, Dunois. It has a massive round 12th-c. keep and two long wings with high, forbidding exterior walls rearing above the river Loir. But the aspect from the interior courtyard is more gracious, and there is a lovely chapel, the Ste-Chapelle, built in the Flamboyant style and containing a number of 15th-c. religious statues made by sculptors of the Loire region. The Gothic W wing was built by Dunois, but the N wing in the Renaissance style was built by his descendants around 1510. The staircase at the angle of the wings is Gothic; the staircase on the right is rich with Renaissance decoration. The château was carefully restored in recent years and has been well furnished.

Although the town was almost rebuilt after the last fire, some old houses have managed to survive; in the Rue St-Lubin, for instance, and in the little square at the end of it. The church of La Madeleine is 12th-c. Romanesque; so is the church of St-Valérien, but it has a 15th-c. bell-tower. By the cemetery, a lovely Flamboyant façade is all that remains of the old chapel of Notre-Dame-de-Champdé.

CHÂTEAU-GONTIER, *Mayenne* (2–D1). On the banks of the Mayenne, where the river flows through a narrow valley, the town has the largest calf market in France, where an average of 4000 are sold each week. Foulques Nerra, Comte d'Anjou, built a château here in the 11th-c., of which nothing remains except the former collegiate church of St-Jean. Writing in the 19th-c., Augustus Hare found this 'a valuable though over-restored specimen of the 11th-c.', since when it has been damaged (in 1940) and further restored. This latest restoration has revealed vestiges of 11th-c. wall painting. The crypt has a fine triple nave.

The museum in the Rue Jean-Bourré has examples of Greek, Roman and medieval art and some good pictures and sculpture. In the garden of the old Priory, the Promenade du-Bout-du-Monde has pleasant views of the river and a small zoo.

8¼km SE is the picturesque 15th-c. moated Château d'Écoublère.

CHÂTEAUROUX, *Indre* (5–A5). Capital of the Indre department, the town takes its name from a 10th-c. château built by Raoul, the Seigneur of Déols. The 15th-c. château which stands on the site today used as the Préfecture.

Châteauroux is the home-town of Général Bertrand, one of Napoleon's closest and most loyal lieutenants. When the Emperor fell, Bertrand accompanied him to Elba, then to St-Helena and was with him when he died. A statue of him stands in the Place Ste-Hélène, and his house is now the town museum; it contains an evocative collection of Napoleonic memorabilia.

2km N is the site of the once enormously powerful abbey of **Déols**, founded in AD 917. A beautiful Romanesque tower with carved capitals at its base is all that survives. The parish church is 12th–15th-c. and the crypt, which is much earlier, contains the tomb of a 5th-c. saint.

10km E of Châteauroux on the D925, in the bombed-out castle of **Diors**, is a museum devoted to the three wars: 1870, 1914, and 1939.

CHÂTELLERAULT, *Vienne* (4–A4). Although this well-kept and thriving town on the river Vienne consists chiefly of well-laid-out modern buildings surrounded by lawns and flower-beds, it is an ancient place and has been renowned for the manufacture of cutlery since the 11th-c. In recent years it has diversified into metallurgy and electronics.

The church of St-Jacques in the Rue Sully dates from the year 1008 and was consecrated in 1066 by Isembert II, the Bishop of Poitiers. Though somewhat spoiled by 19th-c. restoration, it is an interesting church, with 13th-c. Angevin vaulting in the nave, a 17th-c. wooden effigy of St-Jacques de Compostella in the left transept, and a N tower with a carillon of 52 bells.

The Pont Henri-IV, with its fine twin towers, once joined by a lodge, was begun with the support of Catherine de Médicis in 1572 on the site of an 11th-c. wooden bridge destroyed by flood. It was not completed until 1609. In the centre of the bridge is a mariner's cross embellished with anchors, recalling the considerable part Châtellerault's position on the navigable Vienne played in its prosperity before the days of metalled roads.

Witness to this prosperity may be seen in the many fine houses of that period (often built by prosperous boat-owners), such as the Hôtel de Sully in the Rue Sully, the House of the Sibyls at 153–5 Bd. Blossac, and Le Châtelet in the Place Ste-Catherine. Especially worthy of note is the Maison Descartes (162 Rue Bourbon) where the 17th-c. philosopher Descartes passed his youth; it is now a Descartes museum.

The former château (12. Rue Gaudeau-Lerpinière), built in 1423, now houses a museum of local interest. Across the river, to the left of the Pont Henri-IV in the old arsenal buildings (where small arms were manufactured from 1819 to 1968), is an interesting automobile museum.

CHÂTILLON-SUR-INDRE, *Indre* (2–E3). The first sight of the enormous circular wall which surrounds the keep is a reminder of the town's defensive origins. It has picturesque winding streets and an 11th–12th-c. church full of marvellous stone carvings. The château, apart from the 13th-c. keep, is 15th-c. and was a favourite home of Anne of Brittany.

CHAUMONT, Château de, *Loir-et-Cher* (2–E3). This was the château with which Henri II's widow, Catherine de Médicis, gained revenge on his mistress, Diane de Poitiers, by making her accept it in place of Chenonceaux (*see entry*). Although built as late as 1465–1510, when the Renaissance style was well established, Chaumont is still very much a medieval fortress. No doubt this is due to the fact that the first owners, the powerful family of Chaumont-Amboise, having fallen foul of Louis XI, had had their previous château razed by his orders and were therefore still concerned with defence. In fact, Louis relented sufficiently to allow them to rebuild at the Crown's expense, and it is clear they did not skimp the job. The massive walls, towers, machicolations, battlements, moat and drawbridge, make it a formidable construction. Too formidable for Diane de Poitiers, who retired to her more elegant Château d'Anet (*see entry*).

In the 18th-c. it was owned by the financier Le Ray, a keen supporter of American Independence. Benjamin Franklin was a guest here, and at Le Ray's house in Paris, over a period of nine years and was entertained in royal style. He urged Le Ray, who owned ships at Nantes, to support the Scottish-born freebooter, John Paul Jones – which he did, thus becoming a founder of the American Navy.

The château later became a refuge for Madame de Staël when Napoleon I exiled her from Paris.

The enormous stables, which can house 100 horses, were built in the 19th-c. From the terrace, there is a fine view over the river.

CHAUVIGNY, *Vienne* (4–A4). On a spur above the Vienne, the town of Chauvigny clusters picturesquely round the ruins of three great castles: the Château des Évêques, the Château d'Harcourt and the Château de Gouzon (of which only the keep remains). The church of St-Pierre is a fine example of Poitevin Romanesque and was built in the 12th-c. The church of Notre-Dame, in the lower town, is 11th-c. and has 16th-c. frescoes.

7km NW on the W bank of the Vienne is the impressive **Château de Touffou**, with its two 12th-c. *donjons* joined by elegant Renaissance buildings, set off by a beautiful garden.

CHENONCEAUX, Château de, *Indre-et-Loire* (2–E2, E3). Approached by a beautiful avenue of plane-trees, the château, which is built across the river Cher, is an almost perfect example of the French Renaissance before the Italian influence had arrived to check its exuberance.

It was built by Thomas Bohier and his wife Catherine Briçonnet. He was collector of taxes under Charles VIII, Louis XII and François I and he bought the property over many years, piece by piece, from a family called Marques who, because

of financial difficulties, were grudgingly forced to sell.

Once it was all in his hands, Bohier pulled down everything except the 15th-c. *donjon*, which now stands alone to the right of the entrance, and conceived the bold design of converting what had been the mill into an elegant dwelling house built over the water. As he was often away on business, it was his wife who in the main directed the work which, begun in 1515, continued until his death in 1524, when the King seized the property to pay for Bohier's supposed debts to the Crown.

When Henri II came to the throne he gave Chenonceaux to his mistress, Diane de Poitiers. She created the gardens to the left of the entrance and employed Philibert Delorme to throw a bridge across the Cher and build the famous Grande Galerie over it. Unhappily for her, in 1559 Henri II was killed in a jousting accident, and his widow, Catherine de Médicis, took revenge on her rival by making her exchange the Château of Chenonceaux for that of Chaumont (*see entry*).

Catherine now took possession of Chenonceaux, which she had always wanted, and proceeded to give a series of elaborate pageants and fêtes there in an attempt to revive the waning popularity of the monarchy. For this purpose she kept a bevy of beautiful young women, who lived in the attics, to provide diversion for the guests. It was at one of these pageants, it is believed, that fireworks were seen for the first time in France.

Château de Chaumont

J. Allan Cash

Perhaps the most extravagant of these fêtes was that given in 1574 for her third son, Henri III, who received his guests in the garden dressed as a woman.

After Henri III's death, his widow, Louise de Lorraine, lived in mourning at Chenonceaux and devoted herself to good works. The attics, where lately the beautiful girls had been housed, became the refuge of a group of nuns, who were given a drawbridge which they could pull up at night to cut themselves off from the other residents.

In the 18th-c. the château became the property of Claude Dupin, a Fermier Général under Louis XV. Jean-Jacques Rousseau was for a short time engaged as tutor to the son and has recorded how happy he was at Chenonceaux, where he became 'as fat as a monk'. Madame Dupin established a brilliant *salon*, frequented by many notable people of the day, including Voltaire, Montesquieu and Lord Chesterfield. This lady was held in such general esteem that when the Revolution came she was allowed to finish her days at the château, where she died in peace in 1799 aged 93.

The last *châtelaine* of note was the wife of a chemist, Madame Pelouze, who in the late 19th-c. did much to restore the buildings and gardens, so that today the visitor sees them much as they were in their heyday. Among the elegant furnishings are some superb paintings and tapestries.

There is a splendid *son-et-lumière* every night from June to September.

CHEVERNY, Château de, *Loir-et-Cher* (14km SE of Blois: 2–E3). Unlike many of its neighbours which are rich in stirring events but relatively poor in surviving furniture, Cheverny, which was built in 1634 in a soberly classical style for the son of Philippe Hurault, minister to Henri IV, has retained all its original furnishings. So tranquil has its history been that it is still lived in by the family that built it.

In the outbuildings are the kennels and a Musée de Vénerie showing the history of hunting; both may be visited.

CHINON, *Indre-et-Loire* (2–E2). A light red wine that smells faintly of raspberries; the birthplace of Rabelais; the place where Joan of Arc first met the Dauphin – Chinon is famous on all three counts. It also has three châteaux, all built on the same spur above the river Vienne and all more or less in ruins.

Of the Château du Milieu, the 'castle in the middle', where the historic meeting took place in May 1429, only a few steps and the W gable of the Grand Logis remain, but one may look up at the huge chimney-piece of the former throne-room on the first floor and imagine the scene: the 18-year-old girl entering the room crowded with courtiers and going without hesitation to kneel before the future Charles VII, who had hoped to confuse her by dressing someone else in his robes. Today there is a Joan of Arc Museum in the 12th–14th-c. Pavillon de l'Horloge over the entrance. To the

left, separated by a deep moat crossed by a stone bridge, replacing the former wooden drawbridge, is the Château du Coudray where, in a round *donjon* of the 13th-c., the Maid stayed, and where over 100 Knights Templar had been imprisoned a century earlier. The most easterly of the three châteaux, the Fort St-George, was built in the 12th-c. by Henry II of England; it was here that he died, alone, his sons having rebelled against him.

The town of Chinon has many old houses, especially in the Rue Voltaire. The Grand Carroi, or 'crossroads', the centre of the medieval town, is a remarkably preserved group of houses dating from that time; it is said that Richard Cœur-de-Lion died in one of them, after being wounded at the siege of Châlus. Rabelais (d. 1553), who was the son of a lawyer, lived for a time in the Rue de la Lamproie, off the Rue Jean-Jacques Rousseau, a continuation of the Rue Voltaire, but he was born outside the town, 1½km SW at La Devinière, where his birthplace is a museum.

Two churches are of interest: St-Maurice, built by Henry II in the 12th-c. and a good example of the pure Angevin style, and St-Étienne (1480) which preserves the Cope of St-Mexme, a relic associated with the Crusades.

11km NW, on the S bank of the Loire, is the Avoine-Chinon Centrale Nucléaire, which was the first nuclear power station in France to generate electricity.

CHOLET, *Maine-et-Loire* (1–D4). Famous for shoes and handkerchiefs and the scene of a huge Saturday cattle market. The town was largely destroyed at the time of the Vendéen counter-revolution (1793), when after much bloody fighting it was burned by the Republican Army. The Musée des Guerres de Vendée, 50 Avenue Gambetta, records these events.

37km NNW at St-Florent-le-Vieil is a church with a moving statue of the Vendéen hero Bonchamps by David d'Angers, whose father was among Republican Army prisoners to whom Bonchamps granted clemency with his dying breath.

CINQ-MARS-LA-PILE, *Indre-et-Loire* (5km E of Langeais: 2–E2). A curious lofty tower, from which the village takes its name, surmounted by four little pyramids. Its purpose is unknown, but it was perhaps some kind of Roman beacon.

Near the village are the remains of the feudal château of Cinq-Mars, which once belonged to an unfortunate Marquis of that name, a youth whom Richelieu introduced to Louis XIII, hoping to counteract the influence of Mlle de Hautefort. The move was so successful that in six months Mlle de Hautefort had been sent away and Cinq-Mars was in high favour; though he was only 18, Louis even made him Grand Écuyer (Master of the Horse) of France. Richelieu, however, refused to take 'Monsieur le Grand's' new dignities seriously: he treated him like a schoolboy and scolded him sharply when he meddled in politics. It was never hard to find enemies of the Cardinal, and the Marquis, much offended, hatched a plot against him. It failed conspicuously, for the conspirators were no match for the Cardinal. Incontrovertible proofs of the plot were shown to the King, who was powerless to save his favourite, and in 1642 Cinq-Mars and his friend Auguste de Thou were beheaded. After the execution the château was razed, except for two towers of the 12th–13th-c. The moats are exceptionally beautiful, and in the towers is a collection of armour.

CIVAUX, *Vienne* (7km NW of Lussac: 4–A4). On the left bank of the Vienne, Civaux has a notable cemetery on the site of a Merovingian burial ground. It contains piles of Merovingian sarcophagi; the walls are actually made of them. In the centre is a ruined 15th-c. chapel.
   The parish church is Romanesque 11th-c. with a 9th-c. apse. This, too, is surrounded by sarcophagi. Recent excavations have revealed the existence of a Gallo-Roman temple.

CLÉRY-ST-ANDRÉ, Basilique de, *Loiret* (10km NE of Beaugency: 2–D3). Notre-Dame-de-Cléry was the object of 13th-c. pilgrimage and later the seat of a college of canons. The original church was destroyed by the English under Salisbury on his march to Orléans. Charles VII and Jean Dunois began the work of restoration, but it was Louis XI who carried out the main part of it and Charles VIII who completed it. Only the 14th-c. tower remains of the early church, the rest of the building being 15th-c. Louis XI's tomb is in the nave, surmounted by a 17th-c. kneeling statue by Bourdin. The skulls of Louis and his wife, sawn open for embalming, are exposed in a glass case.
   The Chapelle St-Jacques is Renaissance and the chapter house 15th-c. Jean Dunois, companion-in-arms to Joan of Arc, is buried in the Dunois family chapel.

COGNAC, *Charente* (4–B3). Famous for its *eau-de-vie*, over three-quarters of which is exported, notably to Britain and the United States. The method of distillation has barely changed in 400 years, as may be seen by visiting one of the fascinating *chais* (or cellars) situated along the quays and streets near the river. The exportation to northern Europe of distilled wines began in the 17th-c. This *vin brûlé*, or 'burnt wine' – which the Dutch pronounced 'brandewijn' and the English corrupted to 'brandy' – had the merit of keeping indefinitely. Brandy does not mature in bottle, only in cask; the casks used for cognac are made from the oak grown in the forests of Limousin, and it is this that gives the spirit its pale amber tint. (*See also the essay on* 'Wines of France' *at the beginning of this book.*)
   Cognac is a bustling town, with its old quarter clustered round the 12th-c. church of St-Léger and towards the river Charente. The old ramparts have

long since disappeared. Near the brandy establishments the buildings take on a curious brown tinge, caused by a fungus that flourishes on the vapour of distillation. At right angles to the river the Rue Saulnier, the street of the salt-traders, is a reminder that Cognac has been in the exporting business for a very long time. St-Léger has also seen the passing of many centuries, and has a 15th-c. rose-window set into its Romanesque façade. The Porte St-Jacques, the old gateway to the town, with its twin towers, is 16th-c. Close to it stands the Château, where François I was born and spent much of his youth; though most of it was rebuilt in the 19th-c. it still retains vestiges of earlier building. Since 1795 it has housed the *chais* of the Otard company.

CONFOLENS, *Charente* (4–B4). An attractive small town at the confluence (hence its name) of two rivers: the Vienne, crossed by two bridges, one of which is 15th-c. and slightly hump-backed and used to have three towers and a drawbridge, and the smaller but swifter Goire. In the angle between the rivers are the ruins of a castle and a number of picturesque old houses. The monument near the new bridge honours the memory of the native-born Dr Émile Roux (1853–1933), Pasteur's successor, who discovered the treatment for diphtheria.

CRAON, Château de, *Mayenne* (1–C4). An elegant white-stone 18th-c. château, built on the site of a 9th-c. fortress that had been destroyed by order of Henri IV. The English-style park and French formal garden make an attractive setting and are open to the public. To visit the interior of the château, written application is necessary.
   10km SE, just to the E of the D25, is the fine moated **Château de Mortiercrolles,** late 15th-c. and recently restored. The interior is not open to visitors, but the grounds are.

CROISIC, Le, *Loire-Atlantique* (1–C2, C3). A small white town on the end of the peninsula that sticks out from La Baule (*see also* Batz-sur-Mer). It has a busy fishing and sailing harbour and is a great place for oysters and other shellfish. It faces NE across the salt-marshes; the S-facing beaches on the other side of the peninsula at Port-Lion are only 1km away. Le Croisic was once entirely surrounded by sea. In 1759 there was a naval battle here in which the French were beaten by Admiral Hawke and ran aground; the local diving club has been looking at the wrecks. There is a naval museum in the Hôtel-de-Ville (a 17th-c. château). The town has many 17th-c. houses, an interesting little 15th-c. church with a high lantern-tower, and an aquarium.

CUNAULT, *Maine-et-Loire* (12km NW of Saumur: 2–E1). A group of monks fleeing from the Vikings built a priory here in AD 857 which quickly found support among the local nobility. The church, which is all that remains, was built in the 12th-c. and is perhaps the finest example of the Romanesque style in the Loire Valley.

The W end is fortified, and there is a superb bell-tower and a very beautiful nave with some Angevin vaulting. Some medieval wall-paintings remain and the sculptures, especially of the capitals, are extremely beautiful.

1km SE along the Loire, close to a sturdy round tower (sole remnant of a 15th-c. castle), is the attractive little Romanesque church of **Trèves**; in it is the tomb of Robert Le Maczon, a chancellor of France and a friend of Joan of Arc.

DAMPIERRE-SUR-BOUTONNE, Château de, *Charente-Maritime* (7km NE of Aulnay: 4–B3). Built at the beginning of the 16th-c. this Renaissance château stands on an island and is notable for its two galleries, one on top of the other, the top one having a splendid coffered ceiling with rich and unusual carvings. At each end of these galleries are two round towers with machicolations.

DOUÉ-LA-FONTAINE, *Maine-et-Loire* (2–E1). Famous for its roses, the town takes its name from the abundance of its spring water (the word *doué* meaning gifted or endowed). The romantic ruin of the former collegiate church of St-Denis is in the Angevin style. Slightly S of the town is a curious medieval arena or open-air theatre (still in use), in the underground vaults of which people once lived. The Zoo des Minières, on the road toward Cholet, specializes in snakes.

DREUX, *Eure-et-Loir* (2–C3). Standing in the valley of the Blaise on the edge of the Ile-de-France, this former frontier town has in its time suffered a number of gruelling sieges, notably in 1421, when it was besieged and taken by Henry V of England, and in 1593 when it was besieged by Henri IV of France during the Wars of Religion. On the second occasion the siege lasted three years, and when the town finally surrendered the King had part of the town set on fire and the château demolished.

In the remains of the château, on the wooded rising ground W of the town, is the early-19th-c. Doric chapel of St-Louis, built by Louis-Philippe as a burial place for the Orléans family: the unusual stained glass in the crypt was made at Sèvres.

The great belfry in the Place Métézeau is part Flamboyant, part Renaissance, and dates from about 1530; the campanile is a 17th-c. addition. Inside is fine timbering, excellent carving and a beautiful staircase. The church of St-Pierre, which dominates the town centre, dates from the 13th-c., with later restorations, and has some good stained glass of the 15th–16th-c. A short walk to the S is the museum, installed in a deconsecrated chapel, and containing documents and other souvenirs of local interest.

ÉVRON, *Mayenne* (2–D1). The Basilica of Notre-Dame is one of the most beautiful churches in this part of France. It was founded, according to tradition, because a 7th-c. pilgrim returning from Palestine brought with him a phial containing drops of milk reputed to be from the breast of the Virgin. Lying down to sleep in the forest, he hung this unusual relic in a thornbush. When he awoke, the bush had grown so much he could no longer reach it. He tried cutting it down, but his hatchet remained fixed in the trunk. The Bishop of Le Mans was summoned, who promptly knelt before the relic, whereupon the thornbush shrank to its normal size. The Bishop, seeing this as a clear indication that the Virgin wished to be honoured on this spot, built a church and founded a monastery of monks to guard the relic.

The 11th-c. square buttressed tower of the Basilica is joined to the 18th-c. Benedictine abbey buildings. Part of the nave is 12th-c. Romanesque and the rest of the building is 14th-c. In the nave are vestiges of an ancient fresco of the Virgin suckling the Holy Child, an allusion to the legend. The choir, which contains 14th-c. stained glass illustrating the legend, is a delightful example of the lightness and grace of the best period of French Gothic. The 12th-c. chapel of Notre-Dame-de-l'Épine, at the N corner of the choir, contains murals, Aubusson tapestries and a celebrated 13th-c. statue of the Virgin in silvered wood.

4km SW is the 17th-c. moated **Château de Montecler** with a drawbridge operated from an unusual and handsome *pavillon* porch.

FERTÉ-BERNARD, La, *Sarthe* (2–D2). An old market town on the main road (N23) from Paris to Le Mans, now by-passed by the A11 autoroute. The Porte St-Julien is a splendidly preserved fortified gateway, with two round towers, machicolations, arrow-slits, a wagon-gate and a postern. There are several interesting old houses in the Rue de l'Huisne, the Rue Carnot and elsewhere, and in the Place de la Lice is a fine old market hall dating from the early 16th-c.

The outstanding monument of this little town is its church of Notre-Dame-des-Marais, a remarkable example of Flamboyant Gothic and Renaissance styles, built at the very time of transition – the tower, nave and transept being 1450–1500, while the choir and the three apsidal chapels, with their stained glass and their astonishing ceilings dripping with hanging ogives, were completed during the subsequent century. Outside, the charming lower galleries on the S façade have sculptures depicting the King of France, Louis XI, and his 12 peers.

FLÈCHE, La, *Sarthe* (2–D1). An agreeable town on the Loir, famous for its military college, the Prytanée Militaire, in a former 17th-c. Jesuit college founded by Henri IV, which counted Descartes among its pupils. The military college (founded in 1808) has turned out many of France's most famous generals, Davoust, Junot, Jourdan, Bertrand, Galliéni, etc.

On the edge of the river, the Château des Carmes, today the Hôtel-de-Ville, was built in the 15th-c. but much altered in the 19th-c. At the W edge of the town is a delightful little Romanesque chapel with a wealth of Renaissance carved woodwork and a vaulted ceiling covered in decoration.

4½km SE is the Parc Zoologique du Tertre-Rouge which has some 700 live animals, with another 700 (stuffed) in a museum.

FONTENAY-LE-COMTE, *Vendée* (4–A3). On both banks of the Vendée, this quiet provincial town, which was once the capital of Bas-Poitou, was a distinguished intellectual centre of Renaissance France when François I gave it the motto: '*Fontanacum felicium ingeniorum fons et scaturigo*' ('Fountain and source of bright spirits'). This motto may be seen on the lovely Fontaine des Quatre-Tias in the Rue du Château, built in 1542 and inscribed with the names of the town's magistrates, including Nicolas Rapin, father of the poet, who built the Château de Terre Neuve (SW of the Place Viète) with its richly ornamented Renaissance chimney-pieces and ceilings.

Among the 'bright spirits' who gathered here was Rabelais, who was a monk at the monastery which stood near the present Hôtel-de-Ville until he was expelled for owning books which favoured reform, and took refuge at nearby Maillezais (*see entry*).

The church of Notre-Dame (15th–16th-c.), with its steeple rebuilt in 1700, has an 11th-c. crypt and a Flamboyant doorway with sculptures representing the wise and foolish virgins. The old streets near the church have several Renaissance buildings. The Place Belliard, with the birthplace and statue of Général Belliard, who saved the life of Napoleon I at Arcole, has five arcaded houses of the time of Henri IV, and in the Rue du Pont-aux-Chèvres are several fine *hôtels* or mansions. No. 6 has a Louis XIII gateway with a statue of the Laocoön between Hercules and Diana. No. 9 was once the town house of the Bishop of Maillezais.

In 1648, Molière, aged 26, acted at the theatre here. La Rochefoucauld, author of *The Maxims*, spent much of his childhood here while his father was the governor of the town. In the 18th-c. the Marquis de Sade, stationed at the garrison, wrote his novel *Justine* before leaving the town in a hurry after fighting a duel with a magistrate.

In more recent times, Fontenay has maintained its literary connection: Georges Simenon spent the Occupation here and used the town as the scene of more than one of Maigret's adventures.

FONTEVRAULT, L'Abbaye de, *Maine-et-Loire* (12km SE of Saumur: 2–E1). Once the principal seat of a religious order of the same name, the abbey was founded by an erstwhile hermit towards the end of the 11th-c. The Plantagenets took an

French Government Tourist Office

L'Abbaye de Fontevrault: effigies of Henry II and (right) Eleanor of Aquitaine

early interest in it, showered it with gifts and chose it to be their mausoleum.

The Order of Fontevrault, which had separate buildings for monks, nuns, lepers, and ladies who for whatever reason wished to retire from the world, was traditionally run by an abbess of good family. Between its foundation and its suppression in 1789, the abbey was managed by a total of 36 abbesses, many of whom were remarkable women.

Damaged by the Huguenots in 1562 and plundered during the Revolution, the abbey was turned by Napoleon into a State prison, and it actually remained a prison until 1963.

Today it is still undergoing restoration, but the public is now admitted all the year round. The great Romanesque abbey church itself is 80m long and dates from the first half of the 12th-c. The nave, with its finely carved capitals and curious domed roof, typical of some of the Romanesque churches further S, shelters the remarkable recumbent effigies of two kings and two queens of England. Those of Henry II, his wife Eleanor of Aquitaine and their son Richard Cœur-de-Lion are carved in local chalkstone and date from the early 13th-c. The fourth, that of Isabelle d'Angoulême, third wife of King John, dates from the middle of the 13th-c. and is made of wood.

The cloisters, refectory and chapter house are part Gothic, part Renaissance, but the most remarkable building is the kitchen, an amusingly ingenious 12th-c. structure topped by 20 pepper-pot chimneys to enable five wood fires to be used simultaneously.

FONTGOMBAULT, L' Abbaye de, *Indre* (7km NW of Le Blanc: 4,5–A4, A5). Named after a nobleman called Gombault who joined a colony of hermits here on the banks of the Creuse in the 11th-c. Led by one of the hermits, Pierre de l'Étoile, the colony put themselves under Benedictine rule and began the building of this vast abbey, which grew and prospered so well that in the 13th–14th-c. it contained nearly 90 Benedictine monks. At the time of the Revolution the State suppressed the order and sold off the buildings, which were then quarried for stone. A change of heart and policy led to the start of restoration work about the middle of the 19th-c. Since 1945 the abbey buildings and the cloisters, which date from the 15th-c., have been reoccupied by the Benedictine order. The splendid church is open for services, and the public is admitted. Despite the rebuilding and restoration, it remains a stirring Romanesque edifice; the choir especially, with its tall windows, is soaring and majestic. In the nave lies the recumbent effigy of Pierre de l'Étoile, who started it all and died over eight centuries ago.

FOUGÈRES-SUR-BIÈVRE, *Loir-et-Cher* (16km S of Blois: 2–E3). The man who rebuilt this castle in the late 15th-c., Pierre de Refuge, the King's Treasurer, would have no truck with the new-fangled foreign Renaissance ideas that were transforming Blois, Chambord, Chenonceaux and other castles into palaces for elegant living. For him, a castle was a castle, built for defence.

Retaining the 11th-c. square keep, he built round it a conventional feudal fortress, complete with moat, drawbridge, arrow-slits and other means of keeping out potential enemies. He would not have approved of the modifications that were made later in the 16th-c.

FOURAS, *Charente-Maritime* (11km NW of Rochefort: 4–B2, B3). Opposite the Ile d'Aix, at the mouth of the Charente, a pleasant leafy seaside resort with sandy beaches. Boats leave from here for the Ile d'Aix and Ile d'Oléron. It has a château with a 15th-c. keep and ramparts by Vauban. A monument on one of the beaches marks the spot from which Napoleon left the mainland of France for the last time, in July 1815.

GALLARDON, *Eure-et-Loir* (11km SE of Maintenon: 2–D3). A once-fortified little town standing at the junction of the rivers Voise and Ocre. The 12th–13th-c. parish church, part of a former great priory, has a Gothic choir that is a masterpiece of the period. In the Rue Porte-Mouton there is a lovely 16th-c. wooden house. The Épaule de Gallardon is a solitary round *donjon* from an old fortress captured from the English in 1443 and afterwards dismantled.

GIEN, *Loiret* (2–D4, E4). Lying along the right bank of the Loire, and joined to the opposite side by a splendid 15th-c. bridge with formidable cutwaters, this most attractive little town was badly bombed both in 1940 and in 1944 but has been carefully rebuilt in the regional style. The church dedicated to Joan of Arc was completely destroyed except for its 15th-c. tower; its reconstruction in 1954, in pink and black brick, has been highly successful, blending well with the 15th-c. château, which dominates the town and contains a fine hunting museum. The Faiencerie, where the famous Gien porcelain has been made since 1820, lies by the river on the W edge of the town, close to the railway bridge.

GOULAINE, Château de, *Loire-Atlantique* (11km NW of Vallet: 1–D4). Still inhabited by the family who built it at the end of the 15th-c., this splendid moated château contains traces of an earlier fortress. The Tour de Yolande celebrates Yolande de Goulaine who, left alone in command of the château and surrounded by the English, put a dagger to her breast and threatened to kill herself if the soldiers of the château surrendered. There are superb rooms of the 17th-c. built for a royal visit.

Nearby is Vallet, a centre of the Muscadet wine district.

GRANDE BRIÈRE, La, *Loire-Atlantique* (N of St-Nazaire: 1–C3). Now designated the Parc Régional de Brière, this is a fascinating region of swamps where a special way of life has evolved. It is dotted with small white thatched houses, and the inhabitants live by fishing and marsh farming. The soil is an alluvial deposit and consequently very rich.

GRAND-PRESSIGNY, Le, *Indre-et-Loire* (15km N of La Roche-Posay: 4–A4). Situated in a beautiful valley where the Aigronne joins the Claise, this village lies below an old castle which now houses an excellent museum of prehistory, with a remarkable collection of Stone Age exhibits found locally.

During the Hundred Years War this was one of the most redoubtable fortresses in Touraine. The ruins of the castle include the doorway and two 13th-c. crenellated towers, the keep, ramparts and moat, and part of the Renaissance additions, with a curious minaret.

7km SW, overlooking the river Creuse, stands the imposing Château de la Guerche, built by Charles VII for a cousin of his mistress Agnès Sorel; it has an unusual and enormous basement vaulted granary.

GUÉRANDE, *Loire-Atlantique* (6km N of La Baule: 1–C3). A remarkably well-preserved medieval fortified town, overlooking the salt marshes that once brought great prosperity to the region. In these days of deep-freezing, it is hard to realize the importance of salt as a preservative in the Middle Ages, an importance which the Government was not slow to exploit by means of a swingeing tax, known as the 'Gabelle', from which, due to a legal quirk, Guérande was exempt.

Today the salt is increasingly processed in a factory at nearby Batz.

The 15th-c. ramparts and gateways are all remarkably intact. The main gate on the E side, La Porte St-Michel, houses a museum illustrating the town's history, including regional furniture and costumes and a display showing the workings of a salt pan. The interesting granite church of St-Aubin (15th-c.), in the centre of the town, has a 15th-c. outdoor pulpit.

ILE-BOUCHARD, L', *Indre-et-Loire* (14km W of Ste-Maure: 2–E2). The double bridge across the Vienne rests on an island from which the town takes its name and where a 9th-c. fort once stood. Today it is a pleasant place with houses standing among orchards. S of the town are the remains of the 11th-c. priory church of St-Léonard with its beautifully carved capitals representing the life of Christ; and, standing on the left bank of the river, the 14th–15th-c. church of St-Maurice with an octagonal bell-tower of 1480. Across the river, on the N bank, is the 11th–12th-c. church of St-Gilles.

3km W, in the crypt of the church of Tavant, there are some interesting 12th-c. wall-paintings in a style unusually realistic for the period.

ILLIERS-COMBRAY, *Eure-et-Loir* (12km N of Brou: 2–D2, D3). The home-town of the novelist Marcel Proust (1871–1922). Lying in the valley where the Loir rises, it is today a place of literary pilgrimage. The house of his aunt, Madame Amiot, where he spent much of his adolescence, is a museum (4 Rue Docteur Proust). The 14th-c. church has a large nave covered with a painted wooden vaulting.

INDRE, Vallée de l', *Indre-et-Loire* (S of Tours: 2–E2). This charming valley, which stretches from Azay-le-Rideau to Loches (*see entries*) and beyond, contains many places of interest: the basket-making village of **Villaines-les-Rochers**; **Montbazon** with its enormous 12th-c. *donjon*; the remains of the 8th-c. Benedictine abbey of **Cormery**, a town famous for its delicious macaroons; and **Bridoré** with its 15th-c. church and the château of the same date where, legend has it, Gilles de Rais, the notorious 'Bluebeard', shut up his wives.

ISSOUDUN, *Indre* (2–E3 and 5–A5). A thriving town before Caesar conquered Gaul, then a military barracks under the Roman occupation, Issoudun became in the Middle Ages a frontier town between the French and English and was by turn sacked, burned, and decimated by plague.

It stands on the edge of a huge plain and is dominated by the 33m Tour Blanche, a lovely round late-12th-c. keep, believed to have been built by Richard Cœur-de-Lion; in it is a main hall with an impressive ogive-vaulted ceiling. The church of St-Cyr has retained some good stained glass of the 14th–15th-c. The belfry, flanked by its

Château de Langeais

two round towers, was once the main gateway.

The early 16th-c. Hospice ·St-Roch, the medieval hospital, has a chapel with two finely carved 'Trees of Jesse', also a pharmaceutical museum containing a 17th-c. apothecary's shop and a large collection of faience from Nevers. Balzac (1799–1850) was a frequent visitor to the nearby Château de Frapesle, where he wrote his novel *César Birotteau* in 1837.

LANGEAIS, Château de, *Indre-et-Loire* (2–E2). Standing at the junction of the Loire and the river Roumer, at the very heart of the little town of Langeais, this 15th-c. château is remarkable for its period unity, having been built in the space of four or five years and barely altered since.

It was built between 1465 and 1469 by Jean Bourré, Minister of Finance to Louis XI, on the orders of the King, who told him to 'go to Paris and find the money in a magician's box'.

The building consists of a formidable wing facing on to the town and terminating at either end in a massive tower, another wing set at right angles, and the *donjon* to which, in the event of attack, the defenders could retire for a last stand. This was shut off from the rest of the building by a thick wall (now pierced by a passageway) and could only be reached from the battlements. Along the roof, on the side towards the town, runs a *chemin de ronde*, a covered gallery over the machicolations; as it partially overhung the walls it allowed missiles, boiling oil, etc. to be dropped through conveniently placed traps on to the heads of assailants.

The château is no longer moated, and the entrance is reached from the street by steps leading up to the drawbridge and through a doorway into the courtyard. Beyond is the park with the remains of the *donjon* from an earlier castle on this site. From the courtyard, entry is made to the Salle des Gardes and the Grand Salon, where in 1491 Charles VIII was married to Anne of Brittany and so united that independent province with the Crown. These rooms with their splendid chimney-pieces are furnished with period furniture and Flemish tapestries and give a vivid, if somewhat scholarly, impression of the interiors of the 15th-c.

LASSAY, Château de, *Mayenne* (22km W of Pré-en-Pail: 2–D1). Built on an earlier site in 1458 by Jehan de Vendôme, in a feudal style that was already out of fashion, the château is a quadrilateral building with machicolated towers topped by pepperpot roofs. Two of these towers flank the entrance with its drawbridge and are connected to the residential quarters, which contain furniture and arms of a later period.

LAVAL, *Mayenne* (1–C4 and 2–D1). A pretty old town straddling the river Mayenne, grouped round its cathedral and its château near the old 13th-c. saddleback bridge. Looking downstream from the other bridge, the Pont Neuf, there is a good view of the old quarter on the right bank.

The château is in fact two châteaux, one in front of the other. The Château Neuf, which faces on to the Place de la Trémoille and houses the Palais de Justice, is a Renaissance building that was considerably altered in the 19th-c. Behind it, across a lovely courtyard, is the Vieux Château, consisting of two wings at right angles, the one overlooking the river being the older and dating from the 13th-c., the other being 15th–16th-c. with richly carved Renaissance windows. In the angle is the oldest part of the château, the round medieval keep with walls 5m thick and a roof of fine oak timbering. A staircase leads down to an 11th-c. crypt that was used as a chapel; look out for the interesting carvings on the capitals. The first floor of the riverside wing contains an impressive Hall of Honour, over 30m long, with sculptures and frescoes; the ground floor houses the town museum, which includes a fine collection of monuments and funerary sculpture from the region and, unexpectedly, a small museum of primitive painting, including a picture by 'Le Douanier' Rousseau – Henri Rousseau (1844–1910), who was born in Laval and is buried in the lovely terraced garden, the Jardin de la Perrine, just S of the château. (Another famous native of Laval was Alain Gerbault, the single-handed circumnavigator who died in the South Seas in 1941.)

On the W side of the Place de la Trémoille is the church of La Trinité, which has been a cathedral since 1855. It is Romanesque and dates from the 11th-c. but has been much altered. The NE façade, largely 16th-c., is decorated with a number of terracotta figures and has a doorway flanked by

232

THE LOIRE VALLEY AND POITOU-CHARENTES

Corinthian pillars. Inside are some Aubusson tapestries and a fine 14th-c. tomb of a bishop of Rennes who was born in Laval.

Most of the old ramparts have disappeared, but one comes across the occasional fragment, notably in the Porte Beucheresse with its twin towers (in one of which Henri Rousseau was born), and the Tour Renaise to the NW of the Cathedral.

Across the old bridge is the 15th–16th-c. church of St-Vénérand with some fine Renaissance stained glass; note particularly the window in the left wall depicting the Passion. Other churches of interest in the town are Notre-Dame-des-Cordeliers in the Rue de Bretagne, which dates from the 14th-c. and was the chapel of a convent; the little Romanesque church of St-Martin in the street of the same name; and, close to the river beyond the Jardin de la Perrine, the beautiful Romanesque church of Notre-Dame-d'Avénières, in which are an unusual polychrome statue of Christ on tiptoe, about to ascend into Heaven, a fine 15th-c. triptych of the Pietà, painted on wood, and modern stained glass by Max Ingrand.

2km N is the curious little church of Notre-Dame of Pritz. Chains of bricks introduced into the masonry indicate where the present early 11th-c. building was built on to the the ruins of an earlier church; inside are many treasures, notably some very early murals, a 13th-c. calendar of the months, and two tombs of the same date.

15km NW is **Clermont Abbey**, a former Cistercian abbey founded by St Bernard in the 11th-c. The impressive, large, plain church is typical of Cistercian buildings in its simplicity and sobriety.

LAVARDIN, *Loir-et-Cher* (16km SW of Vendôme: 2–D3). Looking extremely picturesque on a rocky promontory above the right bank of the Loire, the ruins of this medieval château of the Comtes de Vendôme include an 11th–12th-c. keep and other later buildings up to the 15th-c. In the village, the church of St-Genest has murals of different periods ranging from the 12th- to the 16th-c.

LEVROUX, *Indre* (2–E3). Famous since the Middle Ages for its goat's cheese and for its parchment made from goatskins. The town stands on the site of the Roman town of Gabbatum, and the 13th-c. collegiate church of St-Sylvain is built on the ruins of the Roman governor's palace. The construction of the chancel is especially interesting, being an example of the transition from Romanesque to Gothic; the roof, with its large central key, is supported by ribs which descend on to the statues of the disciples below. The stalls are 15th-c. and amusingly carved with heads of laity and clergy.

9½km NE is the elegant 18th-c. **Château de Bouges**, with unusually handsome stables and harness room and an important collection of 18th-c. furniture.

LIGNIÈRES, *Cher* (5–A6). Once an active centre of Calvinism. The church is 12th-c. but much altered in the 16th-c. The château, built in 1657, once belonged to Louis XIV's chief minister, Colbert. Only the grounds are open to the public, from November to May.

LOCHES, *Indre-et-Loire* (2–E2, E3). A small town on the banks of the Indre, Loches was for many centuries a name that struck terror because it contained the prison where the kings of France kept those they wished to be forgotten.

The château, which overlooks the river from the summit of a hill in the centre of the town, came into the possession of the Comtes d'Anjou in AD 886 and was used by Foulques Nerra (973–1040) as a base from which to conquer Touraine. It was he who built the present *donjon*. The site was still more strongly fortified by his descendant Henry Plantagenet after he succeeded to the English throne in 1154. Henry's son, Richard Cœur-de-Lion, also lived at Loches. When he came back from his captivity in Austria in 1194 and heard that the French King, Philippe-Auguste, had sequestered it, he was so angry that he rushed there and retook it in three hours – although it was supposed to be impregnable. After his death Philippe-Auguste took it again, but only after a siege lasting a year in which the defences were almost totally destroyed.

Philippe-Auguste repaired the defences, but by the 15th-c. these had become out of date, so the Martelet tower and the Tour Ronde were built. A guardhouse was added to the *donjon* and the *tours-à-bec* (round towers with a sharp edge at the front to deflect cannon-balls) were also built. Later, as feudal times gave place to the Renaissance and the need for defence diminished, an elegant new Renaissance palace was built for the Royal family to live in.

Entrance to the medieval city, surrounded by its formidable ramparts, is by the 13th-c. Porte Royale with its twin towers. The road turns to the left past two museums of local interest and leads to the most unusual 12th-c. church of St-Ours, now the parish church and once the collegiate church of Notre-Dame. It has a square tower at each end, each with an octagonal pyramid spire; the nave which joins them is itself surmounted by two octagonal pyramids, much shorter than the others. Immediately N of the church is the château, whose Logis Royal, which dates from the end of the 14th-c., shows clearly the change in emphasis in the purpose of building which took place during the Renaissance. The older part (identifiable by its higher roof-line) with its turrets, watch towers and crenellations is clearly built for defence, while the new part has no purpose beyond the domestic.

It was to the old part that Joan of Arc came in June 1429, after her victory at Orléans, to urge the Dauphin to be crowned at Reims, but the Logis Royal is above all associated with the other and

A.F. Kersting

The church and château at Loches

very different woman in Charles VII's life, the beautiful Agnès Sorel, his mistress. Known as the Dame de Beauté (a pun which the King himself provoked by giving her the estate of Beauté-sur-Marne) she spent much time at Loches, where a tower is still named after her. Her tomb is in the Logis Royal; the sarcophagus is of black marble surmounted by a full-length reclining figure in an attitude of prayer; at the feet are two lambs in allusion to the name Agnès, while whispering angels support the pillow on which the head rests. The Logis Royal also contains the oratory of Anne of Brittany and a beautiful triptych of the Passion by Jean Fouquet.

Chief of the older fortress buildings, which stand together at the S of the plateau, is the Tour Ronde in which is the torture chamber where, it is believed, hung the wooden cages in which Louis XI delighted to keep his prisoners suspended. Here, where the natural defences of the château are weakest, stands Foulques Nerra's massive *donjon* with an inner and outer wall of defence, between which stands the Martelet tower containing the dungeons which gave Loches its evil reputation. Here can be seen the cell where Ludovic Sforza, Duke of Milan, known as 'the Moor', was for so long a prisoner after his capture in 1499, and the frescoes he painted on the walls. To fully appreciate the defences of the château it is best to walk round the ramparts.

The attractive town has a Renaissance Hôtel-de-Ville and two 15th-c. gateways, the Porte Picoys and the Porte des Cordeliers, several houses

of that period and a 16th-c. belfry, the Tour Antoine.

1km SE at Beaulieu-les-Loches are the remains of the abbey built by Foulques Nerra as a penance when he was under threat of excommunication for having committed a murder. The church has a fine Romanesque tower, and there is an exterior pulpit attached to one of the abbey buildings.

LOUDUN, *Vienne* (2–E2). A once-prosperous medieval walled town. The walls have been replaced by wide, tree-lined boulevards, and only the twin-towered 13th-c. Porte du Martray serves to remind one of the former importance of the place. But there are still many old tortuous streets with half-timbered houses and some stately mansions built in the 17th-c. when the population was over 20,000; at the Revocation of the Edict of Nantes in 1685, the mainly Protestant town lost a large proportion of its inhabitants.

The Place Ste-Croix, with its church converted to a covered market (though retaining its 11th-c. choir), was the scene in 1634 of the burning alive of Urbain Grandier, a 27-year-old priest found guilty of bewitching the nuns in the nearby convent; Aldous Huxley used these events as the basis of his book, *The Devils of Loudun.*

LUÇON, *Vendée* (4–A2). A small cathedral town and former port from which the sea has receded, Luçon is a lively commercial and agricultural centre, renowned for its pears. The Cathedral is largely Gothic; it was given a classical façade at the end of the 17th-c., and the slender steeple, soaring to 85m above the ground, was rebuilt in the early 19th-c. Richelieu was bishop here between 1608 and 1624. It was a tough assignment, for when he arrived to take up his appointment he was only 23, and the town, the Cathedral and the Bishop's Palace were all in a poor state after the violence of the Wars of Religion; moreover, fever was rampant in the surrounding marshlands. It was a good test of character for the man who eventually became the most powerful Cardinal France has ever had.

The old Bishop's Palace is adjacent to the Cathedral on the S side; its cloister is worth visiting.

The road across the marshes to the present coastline, 21km away to the S, passes the remains of the Benedictine abbey of St-Michel-en-l'Herm and arrives at the small seaside resort of L'Aiguillon-sur-Mer on the estuary of the river Lay. The road continues across the bridge to another small resort, La Faute-sur-Mer. 11km beyond that to the W is La Tranche-sur-Mer, famous for its spring flowers. Good sandy beaches backed by pines.

LUDE, Le, *Sarthe* (2–D2, E2). A small town on the left bank of the Loir, famous for its castle and the *son-et-lumière* which takes place below it by the river on certain evenings in the summer (for days and times see local announcements).

At first sight a Renaissance château, on closer inspection Le Lude is seen to be made of sterner stuff. The angle towers, which are built of solid dressed stone, were erected in 1457 for defence; the Renaissance decoration was added in the 16th-c. by way of a face-lift. The wing overlooking the Loir is classical. The château is beautifully cared for and the interior magnificently furnished. The room where Henri IV slept has retained its original furniture.

MAILLEZAIS, *Vendée* (12km S of Fontenay-le-Comte: 4–A3). Today little more than a village, from the 10th- to the 17th-c. this once-island fortress of the Ducs d'Aquitaine was one of the major centres of the region, with a powerful Benedictine abbey, a cathedral and a bishop.

Here Rabelais was sheltered in 1523, after his expulsion from Fontenay-le-Comte (*see entry*), by the enlightened Bishop d'Estissac, and here, as the Bishop's secretary, he did much of his writing. In the abbey ruins you can see the 'cachot de Rabelais', in which the monks are believed to have locked him up when they grew weary of his jokes. Later, in Rome, he smuggled seeds from the Pope's private garden to his friends at Maillezais, making this the place where the tomato, the melon and the 'romaine' lettuce were first grown in France.

The ruins of the Abbaye de St-Pierre and the once magnificent cathedral date from the 11th-c. The monastic buildings are 14th-c. and the outer fortifications are 16th-c. The church of St-Nicolas in the village is 12th-c. but restored, and has a fine Romanesque doorway.

Beside the abbey is an embarkation point for trips on the canals of the marshland region known as the Marais Poitevin (*see entry*).

8km NE is the beautiful 11th-c. cloister of Nieul-sur-l'Autise, where Eleanor of Aquitaine is said to have been born.

MAINTENON, Château de, *Eure-et-Loir* (2–D3). Louis XIV bought this château for his mistress, Madame de Maintenon, with whom he later went through a form of marriage. It is an early Renaissance château, built on the river Eure on the site of a 12th-c. castle. The original keep is still part of the present edifice. Madame de Maintenon added the wing joining the Gothic chapel to the main Renaissance façade, and Le Nôtre laid out the vast park. She left the château to her niece, whose descendants, the de Noailles family, still live in it – but it is open to the public at stated times and remains furnished as it was in her day.

Close by, to the S, is the ruin of the unfinished aqueduct constructed for Louis XIV by Vauban to convey the waters of the Eure to the fountains of Versailles. For four years 30,000 workmen were employed on the construction, but an outbreak of malaria killed so many of them that the enterprise was abandoned in 1688 after only a kilometre had been built.

MANS, Le, *Sarthe* (2–D1, D2). The ancient capital of Maine, now capital of the Sarthe department. When Charlemagne passed through Le Mans on his way to Spain he described it as one of the most important and industrious cities in his kingdom. Today it is still important and certainly still industrious as a commercial and industrial centre, including a big Renault factory in the SW suburbs. It has in fact been associated with the motor industry for over 100 years. Since 1923 it has also been renowned for its '*Vingt-Quatre Heures du Mans*', the annual 24-hour motor race which brings great numbers of enthusiasts from many countries to the road track on the S edge of the city. Yet in the centre of this active and thriving city, close to the E bank of the Sarthe river, is an old quarter bristling with history.

As the Gallic Oppidum Suindinum it was fortified by the Romans in the 3rd–4th-c. The Roman wall, the best preserved of any in France, may be seen at several points, especially from the stairway of the 'Grande-Poterne' which pierces the wall on the W side, and from the Rues St-Hilaire and Denfert-Rochereau near the river. The three aqueducts which brought water to the Roman city are still traceable in different cellars, but nothing remains of an amphitheatre whose site was discovered in the 18th-c. It was during this Roman epoch, in the 4th-c., that Christianity was first preached here by St Julien, to whom the present Cathedral is dedicated.

In the 11th-c. the town was taken by William the Conqueror when he seized Maine. His grand-daughter Matilda married Geoffroi Plantagenêt (father of Henry II of England), who was buried in the Cathedral; his tomb no longer exists because it was destroyed when Huguenots pillaged the Cathedral in 1562, but an enamelled portrait of him that used to hang above the tomb was saved and is now in the Tessé Museum at the far end of the gardens to the E of the Cathedral. This museum, incidentally, has a fine collection of French painting up to the end of the 19th-c.

It was in Le Mans in 1793 that the Chouans met their heaviest defeat in the Vendéen uprising (see Bocage Vendéen), and in 1871 it was here that the Prussians gained a victory which made the relief of beleaguered Paris impossible.

The splendid Cathedral of St-Julien is not only very beautiful but of great architectural interest, combining both the Romanesque and the Gothic styles. It is best approached from the huge Place des Jacobins, which is on a lower level; from here there is a splendid view of the SE end with its forest of flying buttresses supporting the great 13th-c. choir. To make space for this choir the builders had to breach the Roman wall, whose foundations still exist below the ambulatory. Steps lead up from the square to the quiet Place St-Michel which skirts the SW side of the Cathedral and is bordered by old canons' dwellings (one of which, No. 1, was once the home of the 17th-c. poet Paul Scarron, first husband of Madame de Maintenon who later married Louis XIV). Facing on to this peaceful alleyway, below the 64m tower, is the fine 12th-c. South Porch, sumptuously ornamented with statues and reminiscent of Chartres. Round the corner, the W façade of the Cathedral, dominating the Place Cardinal Grente and its beautiful Renaissance houses, is 12th-c., Romanesque and very plain.

The interior displays a striking contrast between the sober lines of the Romanesque nave (11th–12th-c.), where the decoration is confined to the impressive capitals, and the breathtaking splendour of the choir (early 13th-c.), surrounded by a double aisle and 12 radiating chapels, and soaring to a height of 34m. Prosper Mérimée, the 19th-c. writer who was appointed Inspector of Historic Monuments under Napoleon III, re-ported that going from the nave to the choir was like 'passing from a temple of an old religion to that of a new. The capitals in the nave, covered in monsters, fantastic animals and hideous masks, seem like ornaments of a barbarous cult, while in the choir the richly varied foliage and harmonious colours of the stained glass give a sense of faith which is gentle and benevolent.' The transept, built a century later, is high and full of light, with a rose-window of 15th-c. stained glass and a 16th-c. organ loft. In the baptistry chapel near to the N arm of the transept are two beautiful white marble Renaissance tombs. In the transept itself is the 13th-c. tomb of Queen Berengaria, wife of Richard Cœur-de-Lion; she is represented lying open-eyed, with a small dog at her feet.

The city has two other churches of great interest, both to the S of the Cathedral. Notre-Dame-de-la-Couture, next to the Prefecture, is a former abbey church dating from the 11th-c. and containing a lovely 16th-c. white marble Virgin and Child. St-Jeanne-d'Arc, in the Place George Washington, was built by Henry II of England to expiate, it is believed, the murder of Thomas-à-Becket; it was originally intended as a hospital for the poor, and was used as such all through the Middle Ages, with the sick lying in the aisles.

There are many medieval streets in the old quarter with fascinating old houses. The Hôtel-de-Ville, on the site of the old palace of the Counts of Maine, is 18th-c. Close by it is a stairway leading to the 'Gros-Piliers', a square 14th-c. tower which is another vantage point for seeing part of the Roman walls.

MARAIS POITEVIN, Le, (W of Niort: 4–A3). A vast area of marshland criss-crossed by canals and dykes, covering a roughly triangular area stretch-ing along the coast from just S of Les Sables d'Olonne to Esnandes (N of La Rochelle) and narrowing inland almost as far as Niort. The canal system is the result of an imaginative joint enterprise of land reclamation begun by the five great abbeys of the district when they built the Canal des Cinq Abbés in 1218. The Hundred Years War and the Wars of Religion interrupted the work, but it was continued by François I and, more especially, by Henri IV who had the sensible idea of importing Dutch engineers. The main part of the work was done between 1607 and 1658.

There are two distinctive types of marsh; the Marais Déséché near the coast, a conventional flat open landscape intersected by dykes, and the Marais Mouillé which consists of tiny fields each surrounded by narrow canals with banks lined by poplars and willows. There are few roads in the area; the peasants, known as 'Les Maraichins', live in houses served by punts in which they transport everything from cattle to wedding guests; the area is sometimes called 'La Venise Verte'. In summer, these canals make a cool green sanctuary, where one may punt for miles under a tunnel of green leaves. Of the several points of embarkation, the best known are Arçais, Coulon, Sansais, La Ga-rette, St-Hilaire-le-Palud, Damvix and Maillezais.

MAYENNE, *Mayenne* (2–D1). Occupying the slope of two hills on either side of the river of the same name, the town underwent a famous siege by William the Conqueror in 1064. It was taken by the stratagem of throwing burning material over the town walls thus setting light to the wooden houses. It was again almost totally destroyed during the Allied advance in 1944; its bridge, the only one across the Mayenne still intact, was heroically captured by an American army sergeant.

Today Mayenne has little to show the tourist. Large open spaces have taken the place of some of the destroyed houses. The Basilique de Notre-Dame, which is early Gothic, has been very much restored. From the remains of the once formidable 11th-c. château there is a good view of the town. Cardinal Cherverus, the first Bishop of Boston, Mass., USA, was born here.

10km SE (through Aron, then on the D7) is the 3rd-c. Gallo-Roman fort of Jublains with its excavated foundations of streets, shops, houses and thermal baths.

MEHUN-SUR-YÈVRE, *Cher* (2–E4). On the Canal de Berry, this little town famous for the manufacture of porcelain has only preserved two towers of its once great 'fairy-castle' château, home of the Duc Jean de Berry, the great 14th-c. patron of the arts. Among the miniaturists who worked for him here were the Limbourg brothers, painters of the celebrated illuminated manuscript, *Les Très Riches Heures du Duc de Berry*, now in the Condé Museum in Chantilly (*see entry in the Paris Environs section*). In that manuscript an illustration shows what the château of Mehun was like in its heyday. In one of the two remaining towers is a small ceramics museum. The church is 11th–12th-c. and the Porte de l'Horloge, by which you enter the town, is 14th-c.

MEILLANT, Château de, *Cher* (6km N of St-Amand-Mont-Rond: 5–A6). Standing beside the Hyvernin, and hidden among the trees of its park, this late 15th-c. château is a fine example of the early French Renaissance. It was started by Charles I of Amboise, then completed by his son, who was Governor of Milan for a time and returned full of Italian Renaissance ideas. The E façade, though richly decorated itself, is overshadowed by the intricately carved exterior of the extraordinary Tour de Lion, an octagonal tower which stands by itself in front of it and takes its name from a lead lion at its top. Inside, the château (which is inhabited but open to the public) is beautifully furnished; the chapel contains stained glass of the 16th-c.

MELLE, *Deux-Sèvres* (4–A3). Overlooking the valley of the Beronne, Melle was a mining town in Roman times, when silver-bearing lead was found in the Jurassic formation of the valley. Money was minted here from the 7th to the 10th-c. The mines are still there in the hills W of the river to the SW of the town, and may be visited. Later Melle became famous for breeding donkeys, the 'Baudets du Poitou', noted for their size, perversity and lasciviousness. Today its most important economic activity centres on the large chemical works E of the town.

The town itself is well known for its 'Horse and Rider', a curious relief statue over the N door of the beautiful pilgrim church of St-Hilaire (12th-c.). It shows a man on horseback, with a seated figure

at the horse's feet, but no one is certain what the group represents. The interior of the church has three naves and much fine carving, especially on the capitals of the pillars.

Melle has two other 12th-c. churches, St-Pierre and St-Savinien. The church of St-Savinien was deconsecrated after the Revolution and for a long time served as the local prison, but it has now been restored.

MESCHERS-SUR-GIRONDE, *Charente-Maritime* (10km SE of Royan: 4–B2,B3). An attractive seaside resort with a fine beach, Les Conches des Nonnes. It is notable for the curious 'Trous des Meschers', caves in the face of the cliff which were decorated with shells in prehistoric times, and have been used as a refuge by pirates and refugees from religious persecution. Some of them are now arranged as restaurants, with fine views over the Gironde.

MEUNG-SUR-LOIRE, *Loiret* (7km NE of Beaugency: 2–D3). An attractive small town on the right bank of the Loire, with beaches and pleasant walks shaded by lime-trees.

The Romanesque church of St-Liphard has an 11th-c. tower and a transept with curved extremities. Beside it, the Tour Manasses de Garland, a ruined 12th-c. *donjon* in which the 15th-c. vagabond poet Villon was imprisoned and tortured. The château, once the seat of the bishops of Orléans, was rebuilt in the 18th-c. The old gateway, the Porte d'Amonte, and some of the ramparts remain. The statue on the wall is to a local 14th-c. poet, Jehan de Meung.

MONTARGIS, *Loiret* (2–D4). Founded by the Gauls, conquered by the Romans, besieged by the English in 1427, Montargis now lies peacefully with its town centre nestling in a bend of the Loing, surrounded by ramparts and below the walls of its château of the 12th–15th-c. The town is full of bridges, because at this point the river divides into separate parallel channels and, at the SE corner of the town, spills over into a large lake.

The church of La Madeleine has a 12th-c. nave and an elegant choir of the 16th-c. with pillars rising up to the very vaulting. In the Hôtel-de-Ville there is a small local museum. Since 1966, Montargis has been the twin town of Crowborough in Sussex, England.

MONTENDRE, *Charente-Maritime* (16km SE of Mirambeau: 4–B3). Scene of a historic battle in 1402 between seven English and seven French knights. (The French won.) The château stands on a hill and is approached by a fortified gateway at street level. At the summit, which has a good view, the ruins of a 17th-c. façade serve as the backdrop to a romantic open-air theatre. The Halles in the central square, recently cleaned, was designed by a nephew of Eiffel (1883), and has a unique roof structure.

MONTMORILLON, *Vienne* (4, 5–A4, A5). An endearing little town on the banks of the Gartempe. The church of Notre-Dame, built in the 11th-, 12th- and 14th-c., has an 11th-c. crypt containing frescoes of the life of Ste Catherine of Alexandria. The chapel of St-Laurent, which has a fine carved frieze depicting the childhood of Christ on its (restored) 12th-c. front, and the Octogone, a 12th-c. burial chapel, are both in the grounds of the Maison Dieu, a former Augustine convent.

MONTOIRE-SUR-LE-LOIR, *Loir-et-Cher* (16km W of Vendôme: 2–D3). A pleasant town straddling the river. The older part is on the left bank, between the river and the old castle on its hill with a medieval square keep. Near the bridge, beyond a gracious Renaissance town house and surrounded by a lovely garden, is the Romanesque chapel of St-Gilles, containing some exceptional frescoes of the 12th–13th-c. Two other fine Renaissance houses are across the river in the NW corner of the large Place Clemenceau, facing obliquely across to the Hôtel-de-Ville – in which, by the way, there is a fascinating model of the château as it was in medieval times.

MONTRÉSOR, *Indre-et-Loire* (16km E of Loches: 2–E2, E3). The original 11th-c. fortress, added to, rebuilt and restored in successive centuries, has developed into the attractive château which stands today reflected in the waters of the Indrois. Inside is a collection of paintings and objects in gold and silver, many of which have been brought from Poland by the family of the present owners. Near the château is the former collegiate church, founded in 1520. It has a fine Renaissance doorway and contains the tomb of the Bastarnay family, the ancient lords of Montrésor, as well as the original glass and choir-stalls.

8km E, in the 13th-c. church of **Nouans-les-Fontaines**, is an early French masterpiece, a large and beautiful painting on wood of the Descent from the Cross, attributed to Jean Fouquet (*c.* 1420–*c.* 1480).

MONTREUIL-BELLAY, *Maine-et-Loire* (11km SE of Doué: 2–E1). An attractive town built in terraces above the river Thouet. A considerable part of the ancient ramparts remain, including three fortified gateways. The château is beautifully sited and was once considered impregnable, so much so that in the mid-12th-c. its owner, the turbulent Du Bellay, felt safe in rebelling against his liege lord, the Comte d'Anjou. However, Geoffroi Plantagenêt, Comte d'Anjou and father of Henry II of England, starved him into submission and forced him to dismantle the fortifications. Since that time, the château has become increasingly a dwelling rather than a fortress. Most of it is 15th-c., with an attractive gatehouse and a *petit château* which has a kitchen modelled on that at Fontevrault (*see entry*). The

Château Neuf was built in 1485 and is extremely elegant; so too are the collegiate church, the canon's house, and the oratory with its frescoes of angels making music.

6km NW are the romantic ruins of the 12th-c. **Abbaye d'Asnières** with its beautiful choir in the Gothic Angevin style, and 7km W, the 13th-c. Angevin church of **Le-Puy-Notre-Dame** has a belt said to have belonged to the Virgin which was brought from Jerusalem in the 12th-c.

MONTRICHARD, *Loir-et-Cher* (9km E of Chenonceaux: 2–E2, E3). This pleasant town on the river Cher has several old houses, notably the 16th-c. Maison de l'Avé-Maria and the 12th-c. Maison du Prêche in the Rue Nationale. The ruined castle was built in the 12th-c. but dismantled by Henri IV in the 16th; it contains a folk museum.

12km E is the **Château du Gué Péan**, one of the loveliest in Touraine. It is furnished and lived in, and gives a vivid impression of château life in the 17th–18th-c. (8km E on N76, then left on D21.)

9km W is Chenonceaux (*see entry*).

MORTAGNE-SUR-GIRONDE, *Charente-Maritime* (23km SE of Royan: 4–B2, B3). A village on a high cliff, inland from its port, on the right bank of the Gironde estuary. 1km S is the curious monolithic hermitage of St-Martial which was hewn out of the cliff rock by the monks in the course of six centuries, from the 4th-c. onward. It contains several rooms, a chapel, and a staircase giving access to a terrace at the top of the cliff with a tremendous view over the Gironde. At one time the monks used to operate the only ferry service across the estuary. Today the port provides shelter for yachts, has an active boatyard, and is celebrated for sturgeon fishing.

NANTES, *Loire-Atlantique* (1–D3, D4). Although it is very much a modern city, Nantes has retained much of its past, and even the losses sustained in World War II have been admirably repaired.

Historically, the city has suffered from the dichotomy of its geographical position. Though it was for a long time the capital of Brittany, it was situated on the river Loire at the southern extremity of the province. This made it for centuries an area of contention between the powerful Dukes of Brittany and the French Crown, only resolved in 1491 when the daughter of Duke François II, Anne of Brittany, married King Charles VIII – though even then the province retained a large measure of independence. When the old provinces of France were broken up into departments after the Revolution, Nantes found itself capital of the newly created department of Loire-Atlantique and officially no longer part of the province with which all its earlier history had been associated.

The formidable Château des Ducs was begun by Duke François II in 1466 on the site of an earlier fortress, and the work was continued by Anne of Brittany. Approached from the Rue du Château, the forbidding exterior with its moat and its massive towers hardly prepares the visitor for the delicacy and lightness of the inner court. Just inside the entrance is the 17th-c. 'Grand Gouvernement' building containing the former living quarters, guardrooms and prisons, now used as a museum. Immediately S is the Grand Logis with its five carved dormer windows and a corner tower with Italian-style loggias, overlooking the ornate wrought-iron of a once-gilded 15th-c. well. On the far side of the courtyard is a Renaissance building erected during the reign of François I, and to its left the large 18th-c. Harness Room with another museum.

A little way to the N of the castle stands the Gothic Cathedral of St-Pierre-et-St-Paul, which presents more of a unity than might be expected of an edifice begun in 1434 and not completed until the end of the 19th-c. It was also badly damaged in 1943 and again in a fire in 1972. Built in white stone, as opposed to the granite used for so many of the Breton churches, it has a breathtakingly lofty interior, over 35m high. In the S transept is the magnificent tomb of Duke François II, commissioned in 1488 by his daughter; it is a major work of its period.

It was at Nantes in 1598 that Henri IV signed the Edict which gave freedom of worship to the Protestants of France. When this enlightened act was revoked by Louis XIV in 1685, hundreds of thousands of Huguenots fled the country, many of them seeking refuge in England. In the 18th-c. Nantes became rich, both from the sugar trade with the West Indies and from the slave trade (the 'ebony trade') with the coast of Guinea. At this time it became the largest port in France, even though it was 50km from the mouth of the river. The area near the port still gives a good idea of this 18th-c. prosperity: the Ile Feydeau (no longer an island), notably the houses in the Rue Kervégan; the Place Royale, damaged in World War II but restored; the Place Graslin with its 1788 theatre.

At the time of the Revolution the population included a large number of Royalist sympathizers; nevertheless, the anti-Revolutionary army from the Vendée to the S failed to take the city. Under the Terror, the Convention's hatchet man, Carrier, finding the prisons choked with priests, Vendéen prisoners and Royalist suspects, and needing more room, had them all put in barges, towed out into the middle of the Loire and then sunk – an act of brutality for which he was guillotined by the Convention.

The introduction of sugar-beet, the abolition of the slave trade and the effect of Napoleon's wars led to a severe decline in the city's fortunes which was not arrested until the construction in 1856 of the deep-water port of St-Nazaire at the mouth of the river. More recent dredging has enabled Nantes to regain much of its former importance, and it has become one of the largest ports in

France. The Quai des Fosses gives a good view of the port area, with its forest of cranes, its floating docks, its cargo ships, its grain silos, warehouses and wharfs, and its five kilometres of quayside.

The Palais Dobrée (in the Rue Dobrée) and, beside it, the Manoir de Jean V, which is 15th-c. and was once the country house of the Bishops of Nantes, are both museums full of local interest, including relics of the Vendéen wars. The Musée des Beaux-Arts, E of the Cathedral in the Rue Clemenceau has works ranging from the primitives to the moderns. Also in the Rue Clemenceau is the Jardin des Plantes with a statue of Jules Verne (1828–1905), who was born in Nantes; a museum in his honour has recently been opened.

NIORT, *Deux-Sèvres* (4–A3). The capital of the department, Niort dates from the end of the Celtic period. By AD 817 it was already a flourishing port doing substantial trade with England and able to defend itself against the marauding Danes. Eleanor of Aquitaine gave Niort its first charter in 1203, by which time it was one of the principal markets of the kingdom.

The *donjon*, which stands beside the river, was once the inner keep of the great Château de Niort, supposed to have been built by Henry II and his son Richard Cœur-de-Lion. It consists of two square towers of the 12th- and 13th-c. connected by a central building of the 16th-c., and houses a collection of Poitevin costumes.

Niort reverted to France in 1244, but became English again in 1360 following the Treaty of Brétigny. It was finally recaptured for France by Du Guesclin in 1369. During the Wars of Religion there were many Protestants in Niort and their departure after the Revocation of the Edict of Nantes was a disaster for the population of the town and the local economy.

Two interesting buildings of the late 15th- and early 16th-c. are the church of Notre-Dame in the Rue de la Curé (off the Rue du Général Largeau) with its 75m steeple and notable N doorway in the Flamboyant Gothic style, and the former Hôtel-de-Ville in the Place du Pilori, housing an interesting collection of carved stones, including some from the former abbey of nearby Maillezais.

The vast Place de la Brèche was laid out in the 18th-c. and it was here that the guillotine was erected during the Revolution. Today it is the scene each May of an important Agricultural Show. The church of St-André, which with its twin spires dominates the town and river, is 19th-c. Gothic and of little interest, though the streets round it have some interesting old houses. Two notable old houses are the Hôtel d'Estissac, a fine Renaissance building in the Rue de Rabot, near the present-day Hôtel-de-Ville, and the old house on the Rue du Pont (N of the *donjon*) which was the birthplace in 1635 of Madame de Maintenon, the morganatic wife of Louis XIV; at the time of her birth her father was imprisoned for debt in the *donjon*.

In the 18th-c. the tanning of pelts imported from Canada became a major industry; the leather breeches worn by the Cavalry in the American Civil War were made in Niort. Today it is best known as the headquarters of the Mutual Assurance Companies of France – and for the growing of angelica, from which a local liqueur is made.

NOGENT-LE-ROTROU, *Eure-et-Loir* (2–D2). A market town strung out along the old main road from Paris to Le Mans (N23). It is a cattle centre, supplying meat for the Paris region, and is supported by a good deal of new light industry. Above the main road on the S side stands the great square 11th-c. keep of the Château St-Jean, fortress of the once powerful Comtes du Perche, recalling the region whose name lives on in the *percheron* horses still bred in the locality. In the 15th-c. the castle was dismantled and the town virtually destroyed by Charles VII to prevent them from becoming an English stronghold, and most of the old houses date from soon after this period. The 17th-c. Hôtel Dieu, next to the church of Notre-Dame on the main street, contains the statue and (empty) tomb of Sully, Henri IV's chief minister. The church of St-Hilaire, down by the river just off the Rue St-Hilaire, has an unusual 13th-c. polygonal choir.

NOHANT, Château de, *Indre* (5km N of La Châtre: 5–A5). This lovely 18th-c. mansion was the home of Aurore Dupin, la Baronne Dudevant, better known as George Sand, the novelist (1804–76), who grew up here with her grandmother and never ceased to return in the more stressful moments of her turbulent life. Here she entertained distinguished friends and lovers. One may see the bedroom and the study where she worked, and the dining table is laid for dinner; among the guests expected are Chopin and Alexandre Dumas. The charming puppet theatre made by her son is also preserved.

Several places in the neighbourhood are associated with the writer, such as the superb fortified Manoir de Sarzay (6km SW) which was the inspiration for one of her novels. At the neighbouring hilltop town of **La Châtre** (5km S) there is a George Sand museum, 71 Rue Venoise. 2km NW is the little village of Vic (*see entry*), where George Sand and Prosper Mérimée discovered some remarkable medieval frescoes.

NOIRLAC, Abbaye de, *Cher* (4km NW of St-Amand-Mont-Rond: 5–A6). Founded in 1150 by a cousin of St Bernard, Noirlac is the only abbey in Berry to have been lived in from its foundation. Built on the usual Cistercian plan, the monastic buildings range round the Gothic cloister. Though they have been altered and rebuilt at various times, in general they remain as they were in the 12th–13th-c., and give a vivid impression of monastic life at that period.

NOIRMOUTIER, Ile de, *Vendée* (1–D3). To the S of the estuary of the Loire, the island, 19km by 7km, is reached from Fromentine by a viaduct toll-bridge. Flat and bare, except for the wooded Bois de la Chaise, it has a gentle climate which encourages market-gardening, the principal occupation beyond fishing. In Noirmoutier-en-l'Ile, the tiny capital, is the church of St-Philibert, with the remains of a monastery founded by St Philibert in AD 680; the magnificent crypt under the choir (11th-c.) is a remake of an earlier one of the Merovingian period.

OIRON, *Deux-Sèvres* (10km SE of Thouars: 2–E1). This small village, just S of the Thouars–Loudun road, has two unusual buildings: the collegiate church and the château. In 1518 Artus Gouffier, Chamberlain to François I, accompanied the King to Italy. Returning full of enthusiasm for the Italian style, he built the church, which has the Gouffier arms on the Renaissance façade, and several Gouffier family tombs in the interior, and laid the foundations of the château. His son, Claude Gouffier, the Comte de Caravas, completed the château; the result is one of the finest Renaissance buildings in France. Note especially the left wing (1544–9) and the arcaded gallery, on the walls of which Claude Gouffier, who was Master of the Horse, has had inscribed the names of his best horses. His extravagant style of life led to his becoming the model for the 'Marquis de Carabas' in Perrault's tale of *Le Chat Botté* (*Puss in Boots*). The château was later owned by Madame de Montespan (1640–1707), mistress of Louis XIV; she lived here after her fall from favour and built the Hospice in 1704.

9km SE is the notable Romanesque fortified church of **St-Jouin-de-Marnes**, with a tremendously spacious interior and a façade rich in carved decoration.

OLÉRON, Ile d', *Charente-Maritime* (4–B2). Reached from the mainland by a superb modern toll-bridge, L'Ile d'Oléron, 30km long, is France's second largest off-shore island after Corsica. The main industry is oyster farming (Portuguese oysters) and to the tourist it offers, besides an exceptionally mild climate, good fishing, beaches and a pleasant dry wine which goes well with seafood.

There are two main towns: Le Château-d'Oléron, the chief port with its 17th-c. fortifications, and St-Pierre-d'Oléron, the administrative and commercial centre, with its 13th-c. Lanterne des Morts and the Maison des Aïeules (13 Rue Pierre Loti) where the writer and traveller Pierre Loti (1850–1923) spent his youth and where he is buried (standing) in the garden.

ORLÉANS, *Loiret* (2–D3, D4). Orléans has suffered more than most towns from the ravages of war, and not least in World War II when the centre

Orléans: statue of Joan of Arc

of the city was tragically burned and so many interesting buildings and museums destroyed. Because of this, and in spite of heroic restoration and rebuilding, it must be admitted that today it can show very little relating to its historic past. Nevertheless, it remains the place above all others associated with Joan of Arc, 'The Maid of Orléans', who raised the English siege here on 8 May 1429 and turned the tide of French defeat (an event celebrated each year by the largest fête in France). The tourist may still, with the help of a little imagination, catch something of the atmosphere of that time.

The centre of the city is the Place du Martroi with its statue of Joan of Arc (1855). The Maison de Jeanne d'Arc, in the Place du Général de Gaulle, is a reconstruction on the site of the house where she stayed after the siege as the guest of Jacques Boudier, treasurer to the Duc d'Orléans. It contains some relics and documents relating to the Maid. The modern church of Notre-Dame-des-Miracles, on the W side of the Rue Cheval-Rouge, is on the site of a chapel to which Joan went with the burghers of Orléans to give thanks after the siege before a statue of the Virgin dating from the 5th-c. This precious relic, which it was believed had itself miraculously caused the defeat of the English on a previous occasion, was sawn up and used as firewood to roast a piece of mutton by Huguenot soldiers during the Wars of Religion. The present statue is a copy donated by Henri IV.

The Cathedral of Ste-Croix is a 17th–19th-c.

replacement in the Gothic style of the 13th-c. Cathedral destroyed by the Protestants in 1568. The choir has some fine 18th-c. woodwork. Of the 16th-c. church of St-Aignan in the Rue de l'Oriflamme only the choir and transept remain above ground, but the crypt is 11th-c. The 16th-c. church of Notre-Dame-de-Recouvrance has three Gothic naves and some 16th-c. glass above the altar.

The Musée des Beaux-Arts, which has a collection of French paintings from the 15th- to 20th-c., is in the Hôtel des Créneaux, the former Hôtel-de-Ville, which is a mixture of Flamboyant and Renaissance and has a 15th-c. tower. The present Hôtel-de-Ville, in the Place de l'Étape, is also Renaissance, but heavily restored. The finest Renaissance building in Orléans is the Hôtel Cabu (1548, but restored after fire damage in 1940) in the Rue Ste-Catherine, which contains the Musée Historique et Archéologique, including a remarkable treasure-trove of Roman statuary found at Neuvy-en-Sullias, about 30km E of the city. Two more Renaissance houses are the Maison d'Alibert, 6 Place de Châtelet, and the Maison de la Coquille in the quiet little Impasse de la Pierre-Percée close to the Pont George V. This 18th-c. bridge over the Loire, 300m wide at this point, replaces an earlier one; when it was opened in 1760, the Orléanais, who are renowned for their waspish humour, having seen Madame de Pompadour, the King's extravagant mistress, drive over it in her coach, said that they now knew it was strong as they had seen it support France's heaviest burden.

28km N, Patay was the scene of a victory by Joan of Arc over the English (18 June 1429); so too was Jargeau, 18km E of the city (22 May 1429). In the latter engagement, the Maid was wounded.

PALLUAU-SUR-INDRE, *Indre* (12km SE of Châtillon: 2–E3). An attractive little town on an escarpment above the Indre, where the old houses and streets reach up to the old château with its 11th-c. keep. In the 14th-c. it was attacked and all but destroyed by the Black Prince. The Flamboyant chapel built later is decorated with Italianate Renaissance murals, and the living quarters are in the pure French Gothic style and well furnished. From the Philippe-Auguste tower there is a fine view across the valley. The old collegiate church has 15th-c. choir-stalls and some unusual painted statues of saints made about the same period. In the church of St-Laurent in the Rue Basse are some very old wall-paintings, probably 12th-c.

12km E the grim exterior of the 12th-c. **Château d'Argy** contrasts with its delicate Renaissance courtyard.

PARTHENAY, *Deux-Sèvres* (4–A3). Parthenay stands on a promontory overlooking the valley of the Thouet and has one of the largest weekly cattle markets in France. In the Middle Ages it was a

THE LOIRE VALLEY AND POITOU-CHARENTES

fortified town and an important halting place on the pilgrim route to Compostella in Spain.

The medieval part of the town, which is well preserved, lies to the W and is entered from the N by the Pont et Porte St-Jacques (1202), a narrow stone bridge over the river and a massive twin-towered gateway. Harassed pilgrims who had just crossed the 'Gâtine', the wasteland of which the town is the capital, must have entered this gate with considerable relief, safe in the knowledge that the town was considered absolutely impregnable. Leading immediately S, the Rue de la Vaux-St-Jacques with its half-timbered houses was the former main street and has changed little since medieval times. The 13th-c. ramparts which surround this end of the town, and of which a full kilometre survives, give an excellent view of valley and town.

The Château de Parthenay, once the home of the aggressive family of Parthenay-Larchévêque, dominates the sharp bend in the river and is approached by the Porte de l'Horloge, a Gothic gateway which has an old bell of 1454 and once served as the bell-tower. Like the Gothic part of the Porte-St-Jacques, this gateway was built by an English architect when the Vicomte de Parthenay was a vassal of King John of England. Of the château itself, only three 13th-c. rampart towers remain, and a lawn marks the site of the original ground-plan.

The church of Ste-Croix was built in the 11th-c. to house a fragment of the 'True Cross'. It was altered in the 12th-c. and the square tower was built in 1457. Behind the altar are the recently discovered recumbent effigies of Guillaume VII de Parthenay and his wife. The original colouring is remarkably preserved.

The collegiate church of Notre-Dame-de-la-Couldre (11th-c.) is a sad monument, for its magnificent sculptures, considered one of the glories of Romanesque art in Poitou, having escaped the ravages of the Protestants in 1562 and again in 1568, are now in museums in Paris and America; only the beautiful doorway remains.

In Parthenay-le-Vieux (1km S) is the old priory church of St-Pierre (12th-c.), with a notable façade including a figure representing a mounted fal-coner, believed by some to be Constantine crushing the heresies. Inside the church are tombs of the family of Parthenay-Larchévêque.

POITIERS, *Vienne* (4–A4). Two vital battles affecting the whole future of France, and perhaps of Europe too, took place to the N of Poitiers – the first in AD 507 when Clovis, King of the Franks, defeated Alaric and the Visigoths, and the second when Charles Martel turned the Saracen tide in 732 in a historic victory.

Poitiers fell twice under English domination, first as a result of the marriage of Eleanor of Aquitaine to Henry II of England, and again in 1356 when the Black Prince, though greatly out-numbered, won his famous victory over Jean le

Bon, the King of France, at Nouaillé-Maupertuis, 10km SE of the town, destroying his army and taking him prisoner. Retaken by Du Guesclin 13 years later, Poitiers remained French thereafter.

Once capital of the ancient province of Poitou, now the capital town of the Vienne department and surrounded by rather ugly suburbs, the old Poitiers stands on a promontory overlooking the river Clain. It is rich in history and Christian monuments. Here, in the Roman city of Limonum, early Christians gathered, and the Baptistère St-Jean (S of the Cathedral in the Rue Jean-Jaurès) is considered the earliest Christian building in France, dating from the 4th-c.; it is now a museum and includes a collection of Merovingian sar-cophagi. The church of Ste-Radegonde, between the Cathedral and the river, was built at the end of the 6th-c. to house the remains of the queen of that name, patron saint of the town; it was rebuilt in the 11th-c., but the saint's tomb still lies in the crypt and remains an object of pilgrimage.

The Cathedral, St-Pierre, is an impressive Gothic edifice with three naves of almost equal height, ending in a vast apse whose wall when viewed from the exterior soars to nearly 50m above the sloping ground. The choir, most unusually, still has its original 13th-c. stalls, and there is some 13th-c. stained glass, notably a Crucifixion in the apse dating from 1170. NW of the Cathedral, in the Place de Gaulle, is the famous church of Notre-Dame-de-la-Grande. Built in the 11th–12th-c., the façade is the apogee of the Romanesque Poitevin style, being so perfectly proportioned that, though covered in sculptures and carvings (once brightly coloured), and flanked by two slender *tourelles* capped by 'pine-cone' pepperpot roofs, which give it a distinctly Byzantine air, it never appears in the least fussy; inside, it is rich and dark like a jewel-box. Among other interesting churches (there were once over 50 of them) is St-Hilaire-le-Grand in the SW sector of the town: it is 11th–12th-c., and its unusual layout on different levels, with a central nave and three aisles on either side, and the roof supported by ranks of soaring pillars, gives an extraordinary impression of space; the saint is buried in the crypt.

During the Renaissance, Poitiers grew swiftly in importance under the enlightened governorship of Jean Duc de Berry, which lasted from 1368 to 1416. The Palais de Justice in the Place Lepetit hides behind its 19th-c. façade the splendid old Ducal Palace. At one end of the vast Grande Salle, with its fine beamed roof, a flight of steps the full width of the hall leads up to a remarkable gable wall; this consists of a triple sculptured chimney-piece under Flamboyant lancet windows and a filigreed gallery, and was built for Jean Duc de Berry in the 14th-c. The *donjon* of the Palace, known as the Tour Maubergeon, was built earlier, in the 12th-c., and altered for the Duke to live in during the 14th-c. It was to this Ducal Palace in 1429 that Joan of Arc was sent by Charles VII to be examined by learned theologians before he accepted her story that voices had called her to lead the army of France against the English. The examination lasted three weeks. When the moment came to leave, mounting her horse before a great crowd of well-wishers, the Maid took advantage of a nearby stone to give herself a leg-up. The stone, known as the *'montoir de Jeanne'*, stands in the garden of the Palace.

Between 1423 and 1436 the French Parliament sat at Poitiers. The University was founded in 1432, and quickly became the third most important in France after Paris and Lyon.

The Hôtel Fumé in the Rue de la Chaîne, which once housed the Faculté de Lettres, has a late-Gothic façade and courtyard dating from the 16th-c. Francis Bacon (1561–1626) and René Descartes (1596–1650) were students here, and Rabelais came here often with his patron, Geoffroi d'Estissac, the Bishop of Maillezais (*see entry*) and Dean of Poitiers. The house where they stayed, the 'Doyenne', is close to the church of St-Hilaire-le-Grand.

The Wars of Religion ruined Poitiers. The town sank into a lethargy from which it has only recently emerged, the University regaining much of its importance and modern industry bringing prosperity to the town. The Musée Ste-Croix, in a newly opened building opposite the Baptistère St-Jean, has a good collection of art and archaeology, including many carvings and fragments found in or near Poitiers itself.

E of the town, over the Pont Neuf in the Rue de la Pierre-Levée, is an early Christian cemetery with a 7th-c. underground chapel. The Pierre-Levée itself is a dolmen, now broken in several pieces, recorded by Rabelais as a place where the students of his day went to picnic, cutting their names on the stone and arguing at length over pâtés, hams and flagons of wine.

PONCÉ-SUR-LE-LOIR, *Sarthe* (7km NE of La Chartre: 2–D2). This Renaissance château which was built in 1542 is worth going to see if only for its magnificent sculptured staircase. The church is 11th–12th-c. and contains paintings of the 12th-c.

PONS, *Charente-Maritime* (4–B3). On a hill above the river Seugne at a point where it divides into two and sometimes three branches, Pons was an important place on the pilgrim route to Compostella in the Middle Ages. It is a rare instance of a town still having its pilgrim hospice extant. Set outside the walls to receive latecomers after the town gates were shut, it has a sick ward, the Salle des Malades, and outside it a covered way with stone benches where the pilgrims sheltered in bad weather. It also had a small chapel, but of that only the doorway remains.

The formidable rectangular keep is 12th-c. and has a good view from the top, but the 15th–16th-c. buildings of the château are occupied by the *mairie*. The church of St-Vivian has an 11th-c. façade.

There are a number of 12th-c. churches in the neighbourhood, especially to the S and E, including Echebrune, Pérignac, Fléac-sur-Seugne, Marignac and Chadenac. 1km SE is the picturesque Renaissance Château d'Ussons, and 12km SE is Jonzac with its 15th-c. château.

PORNIC, *Loire-Atlantique* (1–D3). Built in a natural creek, S of St-Nazaire, opposite the Ile de Noirmoutier, Pornic is a fishing port dominated by the 13th-c. château that once belonged to Gilles de Rais, the notorious 'Bluebeard'. The old port, which fights a constant battle against being silted up, provides shelter for a fair-sized fishing fleet. There is a series of small beaches along the wooded coast.

POUZAUGES, *Vendée* (17km SW of Mauléon: 1–D4). In the very heart of the Bocage Vendéen (*see entry*), Pouzauges is typical of the closed, secret places of the area. The old feudal castle, yet another fortress belonging to 'Bluebeard' Gilles de Rais, has a vast keep covered with ivy. There is a memorial to 50 Vendéens shot during the Royalist rebellion at the time of the Revolution. The church of St-Jacques has a 12th-c. transept and an unusually large choir with three naves.

1km SE, the church at Pouzauges-le-Vieux has some interesting 12th-c. murals. The Puy-Crapaud, 3km E, is the highest point (270m) of the Bocage and has a superb view across the plains of the Vendée towards the Atlantic.

RÉ, Ile de, *Charente-Maritime* (4–A2). This large island off La Rochelle, 28km by 5km of flat terrain, though not visually striking, has a quality of light that gives to its beaches, vineyards and market-gardens (famous for asparagus) a sparkle and refulgence that lift the spirits.

The Phare des Baleines, the lighthouse at the NW tip of the island, is 50m high, can be visited and has an outstanding view from the platform. St-Martin, the old fortified port with its charming wet-dock formed round an island of houses, has two gateways in the fortifications which have retained their portcullises. One of these, the Porte Toiras, carries the name of the governor who withstood an English siege in 1625. Renowned as a wit, he is said to have told an officer who asked if he could go and see his sick father on the eve of a battle, 'Go, honour thy Father and Mother that thy days may be long . . .'

The *quichenotte*, a white head-dress worn to protect the women against the sun, may still be seen. Once it was a sign of respectability and is supposed to have been a defence against the English soldiers – 'kiss not'.

Frequent car ferries from La Pallice (15 minutes).

RETZ, Pays de, *Loire-Atlantique* (SE of St-Nazaire: 1–C3). South of the estuary of the Loire, and SE from St-Nazaire, this stretch of marshland between Brittany and the Vendée, with its immense beaches on which the vines that produce the wine Gros-Plant grow almost to the water's edge, has a strange haunting atmosphere. The village of Bourgneuf-en-Retz, SE of Pornic (*see entry*), has a small museum of the district. Some 30km further SE is the 17th-c. **Château du Bois Chevalier**, about 4km NE of Legé. This château is a charming arrangement of high-roofed *pavillons* reflected in water. During the Vendéen wars it was the hiding place of the Vendéen hero François de Charette.

RICHELIEU, *Indre-et-Loire* (2–E2). Described by La Fontaine in 1663 as 'the most beautiful village in the Universe', this little town on the left bank of the river Mable was built in 1631 by Jacques Lemercier, architect of the Sorbonne, for Cardinal Richelieu, who wanted somewhere to house his court near the great château he was building.

Covering an area of 700m by 500m, it is a precisely rectangular design surrounded by ramparts and moats. The Grande Rue, which is bordered by fine houses, in particular No. 17, the Maison du Sénéchal, stretches from one end of the town to the other. In the Place du Marché, the roof of the covered market has some beautiful 17th-c. timbering. The Hôtel-de-Ville houses a museum of the Richelieu family.

At the S end of the Grande Rue is a statue of the great but unloved Cardinal and the gates of the vast park, now open to the populace, where one may see the remains of the once extensive château; sequestered by the Revolution, it was gradually broken up for building material during the first half of the 19th-c.

ROCHE COURBON, La, Château de, *Charente-Maritime* (16km NW of Saintes: 4–B3). Romantic 15th-c. château in a superb setting and reflected in a vast *miroir d'eau*, with formal gardens full of statues, sculptured yew-trees and perspective walks.

Richelieu

French Government Tourist Office

La Tour de la Lanterne in the harbour at La Rochelle

ROCHEFORT, *Charente-Maritime* (4–B2, B3). Standing on the right bank of the Charente in a great loop of the river, this pleasant if somewhat formal town was Colbert's great arsenal and shipyard, built between 1666 and 1668 and rivalling Toulon in power. The naval museum in the Hôtel de Cheusses, beside the Porte du Soleil, which was once the gateway to the Arsenal, has models of ships built at Rochefort. There is a museum devoted to the writer Pierre Loti (1850–1923) at 141 Rue Pierre-Loti. The municipal museum in the Avenue Général de Gaulle has a collection of drawings and paintings, and a section specializing in Polynesian masks.

3km SW is Moëze, with its Gothic tower and high spire and, in the cemetery there is a 'Croix Hosannière', the finest of these unusual monuments.

ROCHEFOUCAULD, La, *Charente* (20km NE of Angoulême: 4–B4). A quiet, dignified little town on the river Tardoire, the seat of the great French family of that name, whose eldest son has always been baptized François since the reign of François I, who honoured the family by acting as godfather. In 1622 La Rochefoucauld was raised to the status of a duchy during the lifetime of the most celebrated of the family, François VI de la Rochefoucauld, the pessimistic and cynical author of *The Maxims*. The huge château, which still belongs to the family, is not open to the public, but is worth looking at from the outside. It is a good example of fortification giving way to elegance as Italian Renaissance ideas gradually spread. Here the massive square 12th-c. keep is incorporated in a beautiful Renaissance building with a *cour d'honneur* which has three storeys of open arcaded galleries.

The town is on the opposite bank of the river. Inside the Hôpital (17th-c.) the old pharmacy is

preserved and may be visited. The former Carmelite convent, now a school, has a large 15th-c. cloister; the parish church of St-Cybard is a rare example in the province of 13th-c. Gothic.

ROCHELLE, La, *Charente-Maritime* (4–A2, A3). Bright and lively, with its famous twin-towered harbour, arcaded streets, excellent shops and restaurants, La Rochelle combines old stones with young people in a way that makes it by far the most stylish marine centre on the Atlantic coast.

Founded as a fishing village in the 10th-c., it rapidly became a major port for salt and wine. The citizens cleverly exploited the quarrels between France and England to increase their wealth, and in the 16th-c. were quick to embrace the new Protestant faith. The opening of the New World brought new commercial opportunities, notably through the sugar trade with the West Indies and the fur trade with Canada. It was from La Rochelle that the founders of Montreal and the first Canadian settlers embarked. The Rue de l'Escale is still paved with Canadian stones that came over in ships as ballast for cargoes of furs.

In the early 17th-c. the combination of wealth, independence and Protestantism brought the town into conflict with Cardinal Richelieu, who was trying to unite a Catholic France under the Crown. In 1627, from his headquarters at Brouage, he laid siege to La Rochelle by land and sea. Despite a heroic resistance under the leadership of the mayor, Jean Guiton, the town was finally starved into submission after 15 months with only 5000 of the 28,000 inhabitants surviving.

The loss of Canada in 1763 and the British naval blockade during the Napoleonic wars further reduced the fortunes of the Rochelais. But their pirates continued to plunder English shipping and their fishing fleets continued to fish. La Rochelle, which had the luck to escape damage during World War II, now ranks as France's fifth largest fishing port, and today many industrial activities – shipbuilding, car-manufacture, chemicals, etc. – contribute to the town's commercial prosperity.

Every other year the bay is a brave sight with over a thousand yachts from many nations competing in the Plymouth to La Rochelle race.

The port itself, which may be comfortably studied from a table outside any of the cafés that line the Quai Duperré, is busy with fishing and pleasure craft. The tower on the left of the basin entrance is the Tour St-Nicolas; that on the right is the Tour de la Chaîne, so called because of the great chain that used to be stretched between the two towers to close the port to shipping; they date from the 14th–15th-c. and can be visited. To the right of the Tour de la Chaîne is the Gothic spire of a third tower, the Tour de la Lanterne, the former lighthouse; oldest of the three, it has a fine view of port and town. Beyond it is the pleasant Promenade du Mail with its beach and casino.

Returning to the port area, facing the quayside by the Place Barentin stands the medieval gateway, the Porte de la Grosse Horloge, that once separated the walled town from the port. It dates from the 13th-c., though much altered since, and marks the entrance to the Rue du Palais, the main street of the old town. But the road to the right leads to the Hôtel-de-Ville, a handsome old building behind heavily battlemented walls dating from the 14th-c. The courtyard has a fine staircase and a statue of Henri IV. The Italian Renaissance façade has a gallery with medallions bearing the monogram of the initials of Henri IV and Marie de Médicis. Inside are souvenirs of Richelieu's 1627 siege. In a turning to the left after the Hôtel-de-Ville, the Rue des Augustins, is the Maison Henri II, an interesting 16th-c. house with fine sculptures; and the nearby Rue Merciers and Rue des Gentilshommes are lined with beautiful old houses of the same period, giving a vivid impression of the town at that time. The Palais de Justice and the Hôtel de la Bourse, both in the Rue du Palais, are 18th-c. The Cathedral of St-Louis facing the Place de Verdun is also 18th-c. but retains a 15th-c. bell-tower; architecturally the church is severe and rather dull.

Three museums of interest are: the Musée d'Orbigny (Rue St-Côme) with its regional collection; the Musée des Beaux-Arts in the old Bishop's Palace (Rue Gargoulleau); and the Muséum Lafaille (28 Rue Albert I) which is a fascinating natural history museum in a fine 18th-c. house with a Jardin des Plantes.

The modern port of La Pallice, built in 1900, 6km NW, operates a car ferry service to the Ile de Ré (*see entry*); the crossing takes 15 minutes.

ROCHE-SUR-YON, La, *Vendée* (1–D3, D4 and 4–A2). In 1808, after the suppression of the Vendéen uprising (*see* Bocage Vendéen), Napoleon decided for strategic reasons to build a new capital town in the geographical centre of the department. He is said to have looked at the map and chosen La Roche-sur-Yon, then a village on a plateau overlooking the Yon valley, because of the 'rock' of the title, which led him to suppose there would be building material at hand. The town, laid out as a copy of Washington, with a great square surrounded by neoclassical churches and public buildings, was renamed Napoléon-Vendée, which was swiftly changed to Bourbon-Vendée after his fall. Today, once more La Roche-sur-Yon, it has a faintly unsatisfactory air due to the fact that it has never grown to match the grandiose intentions of the emperor whose equestrian statue stands in the Place Napoléon.

ROMORANTIN-LANTHENAY, *Loir-et-Cher* (2–E3). The town where the future King François I spent much of his turbulent youth. It straddles the Sauldre at a point where the river divides and forms several islands. Today the town is busy with a variety of light industries, but on the right bank of the river the old quarter retains a number of fine buildings from the past. The Château Royal is 15th–16th-c. and in the Rue de la Résistance are three 16th-c. houses. There is a well-presented folk museum in the Hôtel-de-Ville.

10km W is the **Château du Moulin**, a late-15th-c. manor house with red-brick battlements and large moat fed by the river Croisne. The original kitchens, now the Salle des Gardes, still have their splendid chimney-piece, and the Salon has its original painted ceiling of the 16th-c. The rest of the building was well restored in 1900.

ROYAN, *Charente-Maritime* (4–B2, B3). Sheltered by forests, on the estuary of the Gironde yet open to the sea, with 12km of magnificent beaches of fine clean sand and provided with every comfort and amenity, Royan has transformed itself into a highly popular ultra-modern seaside resort since its destruction by appalling bombing in 1945.

The sea-front promenade, bordered by the Bd. Botton with its excellent shops, looks out across the bay. To its right are the port and the casino. Below it are 3km of fine beach. Across the Gironde estuary is the low-lying Pointe de Grave, and to the right of it, well out to sea, the 17th-c. Cordouan lighthouse, built on the site of the Black Prince's 14th-c. lighthouse (trips in fine weather).

The new church of Notre-Dame (1955–8), built in reinforced concrete to a highly original design by Guillaume Gillet, dominates the town with its soaring 65m belfry.

The D25 coast road NW from Royan goes through the middle of the **Coubre Forest**, a coastal strip of pine forest bordered by the Côte Sauvage with its wild seas. The **Phare de la Coubre**, 60m high, is one of the most powerful lighthouses on this coast and an important navigational guide for ships approaching the Gironde estuary. It may be visited; there are 300 steps to climb, but the view from the top is tremendous.

SABLES-D'OLONNE, Les, *Vendée* (1–D3 and 4–A2). The kind of seaside resort the French themselves like. Famous for sardines and tunny fish (the fishing port lies behind the town and has a daily fish market in the early morning) it has a magnificent beach over a kilometre long, with an embankment behind it over which bathers can wander to do their shopping or have lunch without bothering to dress. The Musée de l'Abbaye Ste-Croix in the Rue de Verdun is an interesting museum of regional prehistory and folklore in a restored Benedictine abbey.

SABLÉ-SUR-SARTHE, *Sarthe* (2–D1). The town is dominated by the vast, gloomy château built on the opposite bank of the river by a nephew of Colbert in 1711. It is not open to the public. The 19th-c. church of Notre-Dame has some 15th-c. glass. Upstream, on the right bank of the river, are some old workings which once produced a black marble grained with white, used in the construction of Versailles.

3km NE on the D138 there is an impressive view of the formidable, rather gaunt 19th-c. Gothic **Abbaye de Solesmes.** The order is Benedictine and admission is only to services.

SACHÉ, Château de, *Indre-et-Loire* (6km E of Azay-le Rideau: 2–E2). Lying in the valley of the Indre, this little manor house, which was built in the 16th-c. and altered in the 18th-c., was the home of a M. de Margonne who was a close friend of the Balzac family. Balzac often stayed and worked here. He wrote *Le Père Goriot* (1834–5) here, also *Le Lys dans la Vallée* (1835), which is set in the district. The house is now a Balzac museum, where you can see his study, left exactly as it was, and rooms full of objects which Balzac knew and used.

ST-AMAND-MONT-ROND, *Cher* (5–A6). Built round a 9th-c. monastery, this centre of a thriving dairy farming area has a 12th-c. Romanesque church and a small folk museum in the former Hôtel St-Vic, 10 Rue Philibert-Audeband.

22km SE is the well-preserved medieval castle of **Ainay-le-Vieil** with a splendid postern gate and a portcullis worked by a winch. Seen from the outside it seems a somewhat dour fortress, but the interior façade on to the courtyard is Renaissance and richly sculptured. (Open all the year except December and January.)

ST-AMANT-DE-BOIXE, *Charente* (18km N of Angoulême: 4–B4). Former sanctuary of a Benedictine monastery, the church is about 70m long with an impressive Romanesque nave, a dome over the transept crossing, and a Gothic choir. It was rebuilt after the Hundred Years War. There are some remnants of cloisters.

1½km SW, the ruin of the 12th-c. château of Montignac-Charentes, with its great medieval keep, overlooks the village and the meandering Charente valley.

French Government Tourist Office

Abbaye de St-Benoît-sur-Loire

ST-BENOÎT-SUR-LOIRE, Abbaye de, *Loiret* (9km SE of Châteauneuf: 2–D4). Founded in AD 651, this Benedictine abbey quickly became a major centre of religious life, but suffered greatly from the Norman incursions of the 9th-c. The present Basilica dates from the early 11th-c. Its W tower, known as the Tour Gauzlin, is regarded as being among the finest examples of a Romanesque *clocher-porche*, famous for its beautiful carved capitals. The crypt, which houses the remains of the saint, was begun in 1067. The apse and great colonnaded sanctuary, built in 1108, mark a high point in Romanesque art. The nave, also Romanesque, was completed a century later. Nearby, the old port has a sandy beach for children on the edge of the river.

5½km NW is the church of **Germigny-des-Prés**, one of the oldest in France. It has a remarkable mosaic of the Ravenna school, dating from the 9th-c. For a long time this church was left to rack and ruin; an attempt to repair it in the 15th-c. actually destroyed one of the apses. In the last hundred years a more informed restoration has taken place, and it is clear that the 1000-year-old mosaic which has survived is a mere portion of what was once a richly decorated church in the Byzantine style.

ST-CALAIS, *Sarthe* (2–D2). Lying on both sides of the river Anille, this little agricultural market town has the remains of a medieval castle up on the hill to the E. Nothing remains of the 6th-c. Benedictine abbey sacked during the Revolution, except some 17th-c. buildings which now house the Hôtel-de-Ville and a small museum. The church, partly Flamboyant, partly Renaissance, has a beautiful Italianate façade of the 16th-c.

18km S, the 15th–16th-c. **Château de Courtanvaux**, approached by an avenue of plane-trees, greets the visitor with a handsome Renaissance gateway flanked by two domed towers. From the interior courtyard there are lovely views of the gentle countryside.

ST-JEAN-D'ANGÉLY, *Charente-Maritime* (4–B3). A grey town on a hill overlooking the Boutonne, with narrow winding streets full of picturesque old houses. The Roman town of Angeriacum, it was renamed in AD 817 when the Duke of Aquitaine received from a monk in Alexandria the supposed head of John the Baptist (another is at Amiens). A Benedictine abbey was built to house it, and the town became one of the stopping places on the pilgrim route to Compostella. In the 12th-c. it came under the English crown, and King John gave it a charter in 1199. During the Wars of Religion, when it was a Protestant stronghold, it was almost destroyed, along with its abbey.

A new abbey church was begun in 1741, but when the Revolution brought the work to a halt nearly half a century later only part of the nave and part of the ambitious façade had been erected. These are still standing, together with three towers, one of which was used as a prison during the Revolution. The former abbey buildings nearby are now occupied by a school.

In the Rue Grosse Horloge is a late-14th-c. gateway with a clock-tower; the same street leads to an elegant Renaissance fountain bearing the date 1546; originally a well in a nearby château, it was removed to the present site in 1819 to replace an old pillory.

8km SW the Romanesque church of **Fenioux** has a notable façade, a celebrated clock-tower, and a most unusual *lanterne des morts*. There are several other interesting Romanesque churches in the neighbourhood, including those at Varaize (8½km E), Landes (8km NW) and Matha (18km SE).

ST-JEAN-DE-MONTS, *Vendée* (1–D3). A smart little seaside resort with good beaches backed by pines in which summer houses nestle, in various styles of seaside-fantastic. The beaches extend for miles in either direction. 16km NE is the market town of **Challans** which has a picturesque Tuesday duck market.

ST-NAZAIRE, *Loire-Atlantique* (1–C3). Originally the deep-water port for Nantes (*see entry*). Largely destroyed in World War II and rebuilt after it, St-Nazaire is today an important centre of shipbuilding.

During the War the Germans built a powerful submarine base here, an enormous structure in reinforced concrete which housed 20 U-boats and emerged intact from the War despite hundreds of bombing attacks; a covered lock enabled the submarines to come in and out undetected from the air. In March 1942 the docks were the object of a heroic raid by the Royal Navy and British and Canadian Commandos; the troops fought in the streets for two days, causing immense damage to installations, while the old destroyer *Campbeltown*, packed with explosives, was rammed into the eastern (Joubert) dock gates and exploded, putting the port out of action for a considerable time. A small monument recording the action faces the beach from the Bd. de Verdun, just W of the jetty of the *avant-port*.

Today the submarine base is used for a number of industrial factories.

ST-SAVIN, *Vienne* (4–A4). The abbey church, all that remains of the great Benedictine abbey over which the Black Prince once fought, is not only an important example of 11th–12th-c. Romanesque – basically untouched since it was built, apart from the tall, slender spire added in the 14th-c. – but it contains the finest surviving 12th-c. murals in France. They portray a sequence of scenes from both the Old and New Testaments, from the Creation to the Resurrection and culminating in Christ in Majesty. Time and damage have taken their toll, and restoration has been carried out at various times, not always with happy results. Work still continues. Nevertheless, the whole sequence of frescoes, particularly those in the nave and the crypt, forms one of the great treasures of Christian art. (For illumination of the frescoes and entry to the crypt, apply to the bookshop in the square outside the church.)

18km NNE is the pretty village with imposing ruins of the medieval castle of **Angles-sur-l'Anglin**, which owes its name to the Saxon tribe, the Angles, who conquered the ancient Britons. The inhabitants are known as 'les Anglais'.

STE-CATHERINE-DE-FIERBOIS, *Indre-et-Loire* (6km NE of Ste-Maure: 2–E2). Joan of Arc stayed here on 5 March 1429 in the old Aumônerie which is now the Presbytère. According to legend, it was here that she found, and buckled on, a sword marked with five crosses, reputed to be the sword that Charles Martel had placed in the chapel after his victory over the Saracens at Poitiers in AD 732.

The church is in the Flamboyant style and has a fine steeple reaching to 40m. Inside is a statue of Ste Catherine above an altar carved with another representation of the saint. Both are 15th-c. Beside the church is a 15th-c. house, the so-called Maison du Dauphin.

STE-MAURE-DE-TOURAINE, *Indre-et-Loire* (2–E2). Attractively situated above the valley of the Manse and renowned for its goat's cheese, this ancient little town was in the hands of the same family of Rohan Montbazon from 1419 until the Revolution. The keep of the château is 15th-c. with a 14th-c. tower and remains of an earlier keep. The 12th-c. church has been completely spoiled by 19th-c. restoration.

STE-SUZANNE, *Mayenne* (7km SE of Évron: 2–D1). On a rocky promontory above the river Erve, this once impregnable town, which William the Conqueror failed to take even after a siege lasting more than two years, is surrounded by walls with round towers and square bastions placed at intervals. A second – triangular – range of fortifications enclosing the château has a medieval gateway and a 12th-c. keep. The view from this point is magnificent. The 17th-c. château has picture exhibitions, plays and concerts during the summer.

2km NE, at the village of Erves, are several dolmens and two entrenched enclosures known as Les Camps des Anglais, probably occupied by the English when the Earl of Salisbury besieged the town in 1424. Lying to the E of Ste-Suzanne is the forest of La Grande Charnie, with lovely picnic spots and one or two rocky eminences providing unexpected views of the forest, with the Coëvrons hills to the N.

SAINTES, *Charente-Maritime* (4–B3). At first sight unremarkable, the ancient capital of Saintonge is one of the most interesting towns in SW France. It was already a great city (Mediolanum

Santonum) under the Romans, and reminders of their occupation are still to be seen. The Arch of Germanicus, moved to its present site in the Place Bassompierre in the 19th-c. when the Roman bridge on which it stood was destroyed, is early 1st-c. and inscribed to the Emperor Tiberius; the great Roman Amphitheatre to the W of the old town is also 1st-c., measures 126m by 102m and seated a huge audience of 20,000 spectators; and in the Musée Archéologique is one of the finest and best-displayed Roman collections in France.

In the Middle Ages the town's key position on the pilgrim route to Compostella in Spain brought it the wealth to build the magnificent Romanesque churches of which there are some 500 in the province. In Saintes itself, the 12th-c. church of the Abbaye aux Dames has a remarkable bell-tower and portico, and is one of the most beautiful in the region. The crypt of the church of St-Eutrope, also 12th-c. and in size and magnificence second only to the crypt of Chartres, was cleaned and reconsecrated in 1843 when the remains of the saint were found there after having been, with what seems extraordinary carelessness, lost for the second time; the tower was added in the 15th-c. by Louis XI in gratitude for being cured of the dropsy after visiting the church.

The Cathedral of St-Pierre (15th–16th-c.) is vast, Gothic and built on partly visible remains. The bell-tower, never finished, rises to over 75m; it was meant to have a 40m spire on top.

The old town on the left bank of the Charente, set back from the river by broad quays, is full of interesting 18th-c. houses. In the Rue Monconseil,

Saintes: the Roman Amphitheatre

the Musée Dupuy-Mestreau displays local costumes and furniture, and the Musée des Beaux-Arts in the Rue Victor Hugo has a good collection of Flemish, Dutch and French paintings. Across the bridge, in the Ave. Gambetta, the Musée Éducatif de Préhistoire imaginatively illustrates prehistoric life and skills.

Among the many remarkable 12th-c. churches around Saintes are: Corme-Royal, Rioux, Rétaud, Chaniers, Chermignac, Colombiers, Écurat, Thaims, and the ruined abbeys of Sablonceaux and Fontduce. 12km NE is the Château du Douhet, built in the 17th-c. to designs by Hardouin-Mansart, with a fine copse of ancient box-trees. 12km NNW is Taillebourg, where the English King Henry III was defeated by Louis IX in 1242; today there are only ruins of a 15th-c. château. Close by is the Château de Crazannes, with its outstanding Flamboyant doorway.

SANCERRE, *Cher* (2–E4). Well known for its delicate, slightly 'flinty', dry white wine, this former Protestant stronghold is perched above vine-covered slopes overlooking the Loire and surrounded by staggering views. The round 15th-c. keep is all that remains of the old fortress of the Comtes de Sancerre. The church tower, the old 'Beffroi', was erected in 1509. The little town is extremely attractive, with many narrow, winding, climbing streets lined with old houses, and offering something to catch the eye at every turn.

SAUMUR, *Maine-et-Loire* (2–E1). Saumur, celebrated for its sparkling wines and its cavalry school, lies between the Loire, where an island in the centre makes it seem like two rivers, and its tributary, the river Thouet. It was a Protestant stronghold during the Wars of Religion, and was so gravely depopulated after the Revocation of the Edict of Nantes that even today it has several thousand fewer inhabitants than it had in the 17th-c. Nevertheless, a thriving wine trade, the production of over half the cultivated mushrooms produced in France, a traditional manufacture of religious and lay medals, and a modern electrical and mechanical industry, make it a lively, prosperous and interesting place.

The centre of the town is the Place de la Bilange, next to the Pont Cessart, the main bridge over the Loire. The château on the hill dominates the town and is interesting both for itself and for what it contains. Built by Louis, the first Duc d'Anjou, at the end of the 14th-c. on the site of an earlier fortress, it was richly decorated with bell-turrets, gilded weathercocks and finely sculptured gable windows. The poet Duke of Anjou, René le Bon (1409–80), thought it so beautiful that he called it the 'castle of love'. From a contemporary miniature in *Les Très Riches Heures du Duc de Berry* (*see entry* Mehun-sur-Yèvre) it can be seen to have looked much as it does today, in spite of its having been fortified in 1590 by the famous Protestant Governor, Duplessis-Mornay, and

used as a prison during the 19th-c. Since 1908 it has belonged to the town. There has been a good deal of careful restoration, and the NW wing has given place to a terrace with a fine view of town and valley; the SW wing remains as it was during its time as a prison. Inside the château are two important museums, the Musée des Arts Décoratifs, which houses a collection of furniture, ceramics and tapestries, and the Musée du Cheval, a fascinating assembly of everything appertaining to the horse through the centuries. Other interesting tapestries may be seen in the Romanesque church of St-Pierre and in the beautiful Notre-Dame de Nantilly which dates from the first half of the 12th-c.

Saumur's illustrious cavalry school in the Avenue Foch, whose officers and cadets put up a heroic defence against the Germans for three days in June 1940, is now an Armoured Vehicle training college. The days of its cavalry glory are not forgotten, for it also runs the National Riding School, founded in 1789 and celebrated for its Cadre Noir riding team which gives frequent public displays. The riding school houses the Barbet-de-Vaux cavalry museum (to visit this advance written permission from the Commanding General is necessary). Nearer the river, on the other side of the Place du Chardonnet, is a remarkable historical tank museum (Musée des Blindés) which includes French, Russian, German, British and American tanks from World War II (open every day).

The wine of Saumur has been known since the 12th-c., when Henry II introduced it to the English court. It is white, dry and yet fruity, and tends to be *pétillant* – tongue-tingling – and today much of the Saumur wine is made by the *méthode champenoise* and has a true sparkle. At **Dampierre-sur-Loire**, 4km E along the river, where there is an interesting troglodyte cave, they make a *rosé* wine called Cabernet de Saumur and a red wine called Saumur Champigny.

At **Bagneux** just to the S of Saumur is a remarkable megalithic monument – the 'Dolmen', actually a group of massive stones arranged as a covered way 20m in length.

7km NW, on the N bank of the river, is the **Château de Boumois**, which dates from the 16th-c. The moat and the round machicolated towers give the exterior a somewhat feudal appearance, but within is a Renaissance *château de plaisance* of great charm.

SERRANT, Château de, *Maine-et-Loire* (15km SW of Angers: 2–E1). In spite of having been built over a period of nearly 200 years, this château with its round domed towers is remarkable for the unity of its Renaissance style. Surrounded by a wide moat and standing by a lake, it contains some beautiful furniture and has a fine library. The chapel was designed by Hardouin-Mansart, and in it is a white marble tomb by the sculptor Coysevox, last resting-place of one of Louis XIV's generals, the Marquis of Vaubrun (not to be confused with the great military engineer Vauban). The château is shut from 1 November to 31 March.

The local white wine is considered one of the best of Anjou.

SÈVRE, Vallée de la, *Deux-Sèvres* (NE of Niort: 4–A3). Lying to the NE of Niort is this beautiful valley of the Sèvre-Niortaise (the other Sèvre is further N and flows into the Loire at Nantes). Full of poplars and goats, it is a peaceful stretch of country and holds many things of interest.

In the centre is the market town of **St-Maixent-l'École**, whose abbey was founded in the 5th-c. by the hermit Agapit; its fine church, destroyed in the 16th-c. by the Protestants, was rebuilt in the 17th-c. in the Flamboyant style. Today the town is best known for its great Military Academy for non-commissioned officers, founded in 1879. No one can travel through this part of France without being struck by the long lists of dead on the World War I memorials and that of St-Maixent is the longest of all. It was unveiled by Marshal Foch, whose own son's name is on it.

To the SE lies **La Mothe-St-Héray** with its beautiful Orangerie (remnant of a 17th-c. château) and famous goat market. Nearby, 2km N of La Mothe, is the impressive 15th-c. château of **La Villedieu-de-Comblé**, where Charles VII once hid from the English; it lies on the river Pamproux and is known for its swans.

SILLÉ-LE-GUILLAUME, *Sarthe* (2–D1, D2). The original medieval château here was captured by William the Conqueror in the 11th-c. Dismantled by the English in 1434, it was rebuilt in 1459 after they had been thrown out of France. It has three towers and a keep, laid out in a rough crescent. The church of Notre-Dame in the village has a sculptured doorway and a 13th-c. crypt.

4km N, the Étang du Defais is a huge lake with sailing and water-skiing, in the centre of the beautiful **Forest of Sillé**, which extends from Montreuil-le-Chétif in the NE to the eastern ridge of the Coëvrons hills in the SW.

SULLY-SUR-LOIRE, *Loiret* (2–D4). Both town and château were badly damaged in World War II. Nevertheless, the town, which lies on the S bank of the Loire beside a large sandy beach, has retained some fine old buildings, notably the Maison d'Henri IV in the Place de la Halle.

The château is a medieval fortress, completely surrounded by water and facing across the Loire. It has a square keep, with round towers at the corners, and living quarters added in the 16th–17th-c. Maurice de Sully, the Bishop of Paris who built Notre-Dame, was born here in 1120; Charles VII sheltered here in 1429 as the guest of his favourite, Georges de la Trémoille, while Joan of Arc was fighting against the English on his behalf. But above all the château is famous for the

Duc de Sully (1560–1641), Henri IV's great minister who made France rich. He bought the château in 1602 and lived here in great splendour. In 1719 the young Voltaire, temporarily exiled from Paris for his irreverent epigrams, stayed here as a guest of a later Duc de Sully and wrote his plays, *Les Nuits Galantes* and *Artémise*, which were first performed in the great hall. The chestnut timbering of this hall is said to be the finest that has survived from the Middle Ages in France. Just before the Revolution Lafayette came here seeking financial support for the American War of Independence.

TALCY, Château de, *Loir-et-Cher* (14km W of Beaugency: 2–D3). A 16th-c. building with a deceptively medieval appearance. The courtyard has a lovely well and a huge *pigeonnier*, and the interior of the château has a nice lived-in feeling with its 17th–18th-c. furnishings.

TALMONT, *Charente-Maritime* (14km SE of Royan: 4–B2, B3). A village famous for its little streets of flowers on a cliff above the Gironde. The church of Ste-Radegonde, in an extraordinary situation on the very edge of the estuary, is one of the finest of the Romanesque churches of Saintonge.

THOUARS, *Deux-Sèvres* (2–E1). Situated on high ground above the river Thouet, at the meeting point of Anjou, Touraine and Poitou, Thouars was a fortified town of considerable importance in the Middle Ages and for long a cause of dispute between the French and the English, being only finally won for France in 1372 by Du Guesclin after a notable siege. In the 15th-c. it was given by Charles VIII to the family of La Trémoille, who held it until the Revolution. Strongly Protestant, at the Revocation of the Edict of Nantes in 1685 Thouars lost half its inhabitants.

Enough of the ramparts have survived to give a good idea of the original appearance of the town. The Porte du Prévost is the original main gate with twin towers through which Du Guesclin rode after the siege. The church of St-Médard (12th–15th-c.) has a façade which is basically Romanesque but decorated with a wealth of unusually ornate carving. The N door shows a distinctly Moorish influence. The Ste-Chapelle on the corner of château is Italian Renaissance and was built in the 16th-c. Beneath is a crypt with tombs of the La Trémoille family. The château was rebuilt in the 17th-c. and is today occupied by a boys' school and therefore not open to the public.

In the Rue du Château are several old houses including the Hôtel des Trois Rois where Louis XI stayed. The former abbey church of St-Laon has a fine Romanesque tower and was built by Margaret Stuart, daughter of James I of Scotland and wife of Louis XI. She is buried here. Also of interest are the Hôtel de Président Tyndo (15th-c.) and the

Peter Baker

Sully-sur-Loire: the château

Tour du Prince de Galles (12th–13th-c.), which contains 17th-c. wooden cages where counterfeiters of salt were incarcerated.

TIFFAUGES, *Vendée* (18km W of Cholet: 1–D4). Overlooking the valley of the Sèvre-Nantaise are the spectacular ruins of the château of the notorious 'Bluebeard' – Gilles de Rais (1404–40), half brilliant soldier and companion-in-arms to Joan of Arc, and half murderous pederast. After Joan's death the villainous half gained control; de Rais, having wasted his fortune, shut himself in the château and tried to make a compact with the Devil by offering him daily sacrifices of small boys. The terrorized neighbourhood finally brought him to justice, and he was hanged and burned at Nantes. It is said that the bones of small boys may still be found in the vicinity of the ruins.

The ruins cover a large area. Best preserved is the 12th-c. keep. The chapel is 13th-c., built on an 11th-c. crypt.

TOURS, *Indre-et-Loire* (2–E2). The capital of Touraine and a convenient centre for exploring the châteaux of the Loire, with many good hotels and several excellent restaurants. Tours is an old but lively University city where, it is claimed, the French language is spoken better than anywhere else in France. Now fully recovered from the severe war damage of 1940 and 1944, it has developed a vigorous industrial zone on the N bank of the Loire between the river and the airport. Metallurgy, plastics, electronics and many other new industries are now as important to the economic life of the city as the older agricultural and wine-making activities. Yet somehow Tours has so far managed to prevent the pressures of industrial life from spoiling its traditional leisurely atmosphere.

The original city grew up around the tomb of St-Martin, and even today this part of Tours, lying W of the Rue Nationale, remains in many ways distinct from the rest of the city. St Martin, third Bishop of Tours, died in AD 397 about 50km downstream at Candes-St-Martin (*see entry*); after his death his body was brought back to Tours and miracles quickly became associated with him. His tomb became an important focus of pilgrimage. In

252 THE LOIRE VALLEY AND POITOU-CHARENTES

the 11th–12th-c. an enormous basilica was built to cover his shrine and house the great treasure that had accumulated round it. Damaged by the Huguenots in 1562, violated by the Revolutionaries in 1790, it was finally demolished in 1808 to make way for new streets and buildings. Today all that remains of the once mighty edifice are two towers in the Rue des Halles – the Tour Charlemagne with its 11th-c. frescoes, and the Tour de l'Horloge – together with the little cloister of St-Martin at 3 Rue Descartes with its 16th-c. gallery. The site of the saint's tomb was rediscovered in 1860 and the present BASILICA OF ST-MARTIN built over it.

In the Middle Ages Tours was often fought over by French and English. A castle was built by Henry II of England near the present Quai d'Orléans, but all that remains of it is the 12th-c. Tour de Guise, so called after the daring escape of a Duc de Guise who was imprisoned there. It was at this castle that Charles VII received Joan of Arc after her victory at Orléans in 1429.

In the same eastern quarter of the city stands the CATHEDRAL OF ST-GATIEN, a fine example of the evolution of the Gothic style, having been begun in 1125 and finished in 1547. The choir and the apse with its three chapels were built first, and they have preserved their glowing windows. The transept is 14th-c. and it, too, has fine original glass in its rose-windows. The nave was built during the 14th- and 15th-c. The Huguenots did much damage to the carvings in the interior, but there remains the beautiful Renaissance tomb of the infant children of Anne of Brittany and Charles VIII. The façade

Tours Cathedral

Rainbird (R. Arsicaud et Fils)

was erected between 1426 and 1547, the work being completed by the two magnificent towers which flank it, dazzling the viewer with the intricate tracery of their stonework – topped off, not with Gothic spires, but with the *lanternes* in the Renaissance style then just coming into vogue. The effect of this façade when floodlit at night is stunning.

The picturesque Cathedral close, with its old canons' houses, was the setting for Balzac's novel *The Curé of Tours* (1832). On the N side of the Cathedral, beneath the great flying buttresses, lies the cloister, which has been restored but dates from the 15th–16th-c. By it is the Psallette, or song-school, where the minor-canons lived. It has a beautiful Renaissance staircase and some 13th–14th-c. frescoes. S of the Cathedral is the old ARCHBISHOP'S PALACE where the ecclesiastical dignitaries of the Middle Ages lived in such style that at their feasts they were served by local noblemen. One may still see the outside pulpit from which decisions of the ecclesiastical court were announced. The tower which rises above the walls of the garden is Roman (3rd–4th-c.) and the magnificent cedar of Lebanon in the courtyard was planted in 1808. The building is now occupied by the Musée des Beaux-Arts, which has a fine collection of sculpture and painting, including two important Mantegnas, 'Christ in the Garden of Olives' and 'The Resurrection'.

An interesting museum of the wines of Touraine has been arranged in a vaulted cellar in the remains of the abbey of St-Julien with its 12th-c. chapter house and dormitory. It stands beside the former abbey church on the corner of the Rue Nationale and the Rue Colbert. The church is mainly Gothic but has a Romanesque bell-tower. In the garden nearby is the beautifully sculptured Fontaine de Beaune (16th-c.).

The centre of the former ecclesiastical city in the western part of Tours, where almost every building depended on the now vanished basilica, is the Place Plumereau with its half-timbered houses and adjoining medieval streets. Note the 15th-c. Maison Tristan at 16 Rue Briçonnet with its ornamental doorway and fine courtyard; the Place des Carmes, a charming small square; the Rue de Change with several picturesque houses; the Place Foire-le-Roi, typical of a medieval alley where one would not have walked safely at night; and the Renaissance Hôtel Gouin which houses a local archaeological museum. On the E side of the Rue Nationale, at 19 Rue Émile Zola, the 18th-c. Hôtel Mame has a museum of silk, an industry for which Tours was famous after it was introduced on the instigation of Louis XI.

There is another silk museum at the Château de Plessis-lès-Tours in the parish of La Riche, W of the city; this was Louis XI's favourite home and the place where he died. Nearby, close to the railway-bridge over the Loire, is the ancient priory of St-Cosme, with the sadly romantic ruins of its 11th-c. church.

French Government Tourist Office

Château de Valençay

TRÔO, *Loir-et-Cher* (16km S of St-Calais: 2–D2). An odd little fortified town of troglodyte houses which has preserved much of its 11th–13th-c. defences, especially to the W. The chalk cliffs are honeycombed with passages which have often served to protect the citizens in the past. The former collegiate church of St-Martin, founded in 1050, has an unusual square tower in the Angevin style. The choir was rebuilt in the 14th-c. Just to the N is the 'Grand Puits', a well with a remarkable echo. On the opposite bank of the Loir is the 12th-c. church of St-Jacques-Guérets, with some good murals.

USSÉ, Château d', *Indre-et-Loire* (10km NE of Chinon: 2–E2). Grim, white and mysterious, a bristling superstructure of turrets, roofs and chimneys – a castle where you might expect to find the 'Sleeping Beauty'. Indeed it is said that Perrault did take it as his model for the story.

It stands between the river Indre and the forest of Chinon. The outside walls date from the second half of the 15th-c. and are strengthened with towers and other defensive features like *chemins de ronde*, those overhanging galleries with traps through which boiling oil and lead could be poured on the heads of assailants. The keep at the SW corner is also 15th-c.; the *cour d'honneur* is framed by Gothic and Renaissance façades, heavily restored. The 16th-c. chapel which stands in the park is marvellously preserved and has a beautiful *arc de triomphe* on the façade. Inside

hangs a 17th-c. Aubusson tapestry telling the story of Joan of Arc.

VALENÇAY, Château de, *Indre* (2–E3). Rebuilt in the mid-16th-c. to designs by Philippe Delorme, the Château de Valençay, with its domed towers and two wings at right angles framing a terrace overlooking the park, is a handsome example of the classical Renaissance. It was owned briefly by John Law, the Scots financier who first introduced a credit system to France and whose speculations led to a sensational bankruptcy in 1720. Talleyrand bought it in 1803 and entertained there in princely fashion.

The W wing (17th-c.) contains furniture of the Louis XVI, Regency and Empire periods, including the table used at the Congress of Vienna when the heads of State met to reapportion the map of Europe after the fall of Napoleon. In an outbuilding there is a museum devoted to Talleyrand. The park contains flamingoes and other birds and animals, kept in relative freedom.

VENDÔME, *Loir-et-Cher* (2–D3). Built on the Loir, at a point where the river divides into several streams under a cliff surmounted by a château, Vendôme has had an eventful history. It was fought over by French and English, almost completely razed in 1589 by Henri IV, and again badly burned in 1940.

The Renaissance Porte St-George, with its two big towers and archway, which was specially

A.F. Kersting

Vendôme: the ambulatory of the church of La Trinité

enlarged to let Napoleon's artillery pass through on its way to Spain, guards the bridge from the S. A short walk NE leads to the Place St-Martin, where the Tour St-Martin is all that remains of the 15th-c. church, this whole quarter having been rebuilt after 1940.

In the Rue de l'Abbaye is the beautiful church of La Trinité with its magnificent detached 12th-c. Romanesque bell-tower and steeple rising to 80m. This church was almost the only building in the town to survive in 1589. The lovely Flamboyant façade is by Jehan de Beauce, the architect of the Clocher Neuf at Chartres; in the transept there are some fine carved capitals surmounted by curious painted statues; and in the central chapel of the apse, beyond the choir-screen, is a famous stained-glass window of the Virgin and Child (*c.* 1150).

To the S of the church is the former Benedictine abbey with its 11th-c. chapel and 14th-c. chapter house and cloister. Part of the abbey buildings has been turned into a museum containing paintings, statues, a harp that once belonged to Marie-Antoinette, and local folklore items.

The fine old Collège des Oratoriens founded in 1623, now a school, counted among its pupils Marshal Rochambeau (1725-1807), commander of the French army in the American War of Independence, who was born here. Another pupil was Honoré de Balzac (1799–1850), who was sent here as a boarder from his home town of Tours; it is said that he used to take refuge in the little corner

tower of the nearby Hôtel de Saillant when school life became too much for him.

The ruins of the 14th–15th-c. château, once the home of the Comtes de Vendôme, stand on the hill to the S of the town. There are fine views from the terrace.

VIC, *Indre* (6km NW of La Châtre: 2–D2). The village of Vic contains the modest Romanesque church of St-Martin, which has inside it a most remarkable series of frescoes. They were discovered in 1849 by George Sand (who lived at nearby Nohant) and Prosper Mérimée. The theme appears to be that of Redemption through Christ, and there is a well-preserved Christ in Majesty. It seems likely that these frescoes, with their vigorous style and attention to detail, were the inspiration of much of the church pictorial art in SW France during the Romanesque era.

VILLANDRY, Château de, *Indre-et-Loire* (2–E2). Completed in 1536 by Jean le Breton, Secretary of State to François I, the château of Villandry incorporates a square keep of the 14th-c. and consists of three wings framing a *cour d'honneur* open to the N which looks across to the valley where the Cher flows into the Loire.

Inside the château is a museum of Spanish paintings, but the unique feature of the place is the garden. This is a remarkable re-creation of the original 16th-c. garden undertaken earlier this century by the former owner, Dr Carvallo. Laid out in terraces on three levels, with the water garden at the top, covering an area of 7000 square metres, it descends first to the ornamental garden and then to the kitchen garden, both laid out in geometrical beds bordered with hedges of box and yew. The style of the garden was introduced here by the landscape gardeners brought from Italy by Charles VIII.

The little church incorporated in the château grounds to the W is 11th–12th-c. and contains some 16th-c. stained glass.

2¼km E are the Caves-Gouttières of **Savonnières,** with stalactites and stalagmites extending for about 1km. The temperature inside is 14°c., which alone can make them worth a visit at the end of a hot afternoon in summer.

VILLEBOIS-LAVALETTE, *Charente* (20km SE of Angoulême: 4–B4). In a marvellous setting high above wooded countryside. At first a Roman town, then a medieval city, Villebois-Lavalette has ramparts with six towers, a 13th-c. covered market, and a château. The château was rebuilt in the 17th-c. but retained the original chapel. The road below, over which the town once stood guard, is the Roman road between Blanzac and Rochebeaucourt.

On the slope of a hill 4km NW stands the extraordinary Château de la Mercerie, a massive edifice in the Louis XIV style with gardens on a scale to match. It was built in 1930.

Château de Villandry

VILLEGONGIS, Château de, *Indre* (7km S of Levroux: 2–E3). The style, though not the size, of this château, built in 1530 on the site of a medieval fortress, is reminiscent of Chambord and thought to be the work of a Chambord architect. It has beautiful Renaissance chimney-pieces and a fine sculptured staircase. The furniture is 18th-c.

VILLESAVIN, Château de, *Loir-et-Cher* (17km SE of Blois: 2–E3). Built in 1537 by Jean Breton, the surveyor to Chambord, this is one of the most attractive of the smaller châteaux. In the chapel are some 16th-c. murals and in the courtyard a beautiful Italianate marble vase. There is also a small museum of horse-drawn carriages.

VOUVANT, *Vendée* (11km N of Fontenay-le-Comte: 4–A3). A small fortified medieval town perched on a promontory above the river Mère. The 13th-c. Tour Mélusine, with walls 3m thick, is all that remains of the former château of the Seigneurs de Lusignan – which, according to legend, was built by the fairy Mélusine in the course of a single night. The town has kept its ramparts and a postern gate. The 11th–12th-c. church has a richly carved façade on the N arm of the transept.

To the S is the forest of Mervent, in the middle of which is a long winding lake formed by a dam. There is sailing on the lake, and at the S end of it a small zoo with a children's playground.

VOUVRAY, *Indre-et-Loire* (8km NE of Tours: 2–E2). A small town close to Tours on the N bank of the Loire, and centre of one of the most celebrated wine areas of the Loire region. Most of the wine-growers' *caves,* some of them dug deep into limestone cliffs, may be visited, and if you are lucky you will be invited to taste a sip or two of their delicious white wine.

YEU, Ile d', *Vendée* (1–D3). 20km off the Atlantic coast of France, some 60km S of St-Nazaire, this peaceful island has a gentle climate and smiling villages. The S coast, well called the Côte Sauvage, lives up to its name in rough weather, when the sea pounding on the rocks provides a magnificent spectacle. The little harbour on this side, Port-de-la-Meule, set in a sheltered cove, has a lobster-fishing fleet. To the W of it is the ruin of an old castle, and it is worth climbing to the top of the keep for the view.

The island, 10km long and 4km wide, is reached by car ferry from the mainland resort of Fromentine, near Beauvoir. The trip across takes 1¼ hours, and it is advisable to book well in advance by writing to the Bureau Régie, 85350 Ile d'Yeu. Port-Joinville, the port of arrival, is small, lively and dedicated to tunny fishing. Marshal Pétain was imprisoned here after World War II until his death in 1951 at the age of 96; he is buried in the cemetery nearby, and there is a memorial museum.

The Southwest: Introduction

Aquitaine, Gascony, Guyenne, Limousin, Périgord, Pyrénées

Edward Young

Until the late 1950s this large region of France, stretching from the western foothills of the Massif Central to the Pyrenees and the Atlantic, could justifiably be described as 'the undiscovered provinces'. Today, with new industries, road improvements, the construction of the Paris–Bordeaux–Toulouse autoroutes, and the ever-increasing number of tourists, this description no longer holds true.

In fact it was Prehistoric Man who first 'discovered' this fertile region. Ample evidence of his presence is to be seen in the numerous cave dwellings in the valleys of the Vézère and the Lot and in the foothills of the Pyrenees. Recorded history begins with Gaulish tribes already installed in large settlements in Bordeaux, Toulouse, Périgueux, Limoges and Cahors. The Romans came, built cities in all these places, made roads to link them together, planted vines near Bordeaux and called the province Aquitaine on account of its plentiful rivers. After the Roman collapse, a succession of invaders wrought havoc throughout the region – Barbarians and Visigoths from the north, Saracens by way of Spain, and Norsemen who sailed up the Gironde estuary and penetrated inland along the river valleys. By the year AD 1000 things were settling down, trade was reviving, the pilgrim routes were well established (*see* Introduction *to* The Loire Valley), and the hundreds of Romanesque churches we see today were being built.

Then, in 1152 came the famous marriage between Eleanor of Aquitaine and the young Henri Plantagenêt, who two years later found himself on the throne of England as Henry II. The resulting struggle between France and England is too well known to bear repetition here (*but see the gazetteer entry for* Bordeaux). At first it was merely a matter of Henry trying to maintain authority over what he – and his successors – regarded as their rightful territory. Henry was after all French by origin; his father was Geoffroi Plantagenêt, his mother was grand-daughter of William the Conqueror, and he himself was Duke of Normandy. Later, the struggle intensified into what came to be known as the Hundred Years War. This was the period of the fortification of churches (see St-Amand-de-Coly, for example) and the building, by both sides, of the *bastides*, small towns surrounded by ramparts, with fortified gateways, streets arranged on a grid pattern (for quick reinforcement of points under attack) around a fortified church and a central square with arcades. Monpazier, built by the English, is one of the best surviving examples. Older towns and villages lived under the protection of great castle-châteaux. Castles and *bastides* marked the frontier between the opposing sides, and much of the 'war' consisted of sporadic raids (sporting events, almost) by the troops of one stronghold against

The Dordogne below Domme   Photo YAN

another. Two such opposing strongholds are the castles of Beynac (French) and Castelnaud (English), scarcely two kilometres apart on opposite banks of the Dordogne. The further from Bordeaux, the less effect the war had on local life, and many larger towns, like Cahors, were able to develop their trade virtually unhindered. Others – Bordeaux and Bayonne, for example – prospered contentedly under the English yoke, and suffered when the English defeat at Castillon in 1453 led to the loss of their best market.

The extreme southeast of the region, less affected by the English incursions, saw the enactment between 1210 and 1229 of one of the most disgraceful episodes in religious history – the Papal crusade, led by the brutal Simon de Montfort (father of the English statesman), against the 'cathares' or Albigensian heretics. The grim story is told briefly in the entries for Albi and Toulouse. It was a foretaste of the bitterness that was to attend the Wars of Religion 350 years later, when both Catholics and Huguenots (Protestants) were equally guilty of appalling atrocities and wanton damage to cathedrals and churches, evidence of which is still plain to see throughout the region. A ray of hope came when Henri IV issued the Edict of Nantes, granting freedom of worship to Protestants, but it was revoked in 1685 by Louis XIV and many thousands of Protestants fled the country. A century later the Revolution caused yet another wave of brutality throughout the land – not least here in the southwest – leading to widespread destruction and defacement of ancient buildings, this time not only of cathedrals and churches but castles and châteaux as well. Despite the intelligent restoration work of the Beaux-Arts, the scars remain.

The waters of all the rivers of Aquitaine, with a few exceptions, arrive eventually in the Gironde estuary. One exception is the Vienne, which rises on the northern edge of the cold Limousin plateau that is the watershed between the Loire basin and the Dordogne; after flowing through Limoges, the Vienne turns north towards the Loire. The Vézère, on the other hand, which rises a bare two kilometres from the source of the Vienne, flows southwest, past the prehistoric sites of Lascaux and Les Eyzies, and eventually into the Dordogne.

The Dordogne rises in the highest part of the Massif Central. After traversing a series of gorges and hydro-electric dams (of which the largest is Bort-les-Orgues), at Argentat the river emerges placidly into the wider valley. South of Beaulieu it turns west and meanders gently through a wide, alluvial, fertile valley bordered by dramatic walls of ochre cliff. Presently the river leaves the limestone hills and cliffs behind and proceeds majestically through open valley country, past Bergerac and its vineyards, until at last the high ground of St-Émilion comes into view on the right bank. Now the Bordeaux vineyards are in profusion on both sides of the river as it describes a final series of bends, lapping the ancient wine quays of Libourne and hastening on to join the Garonne just north of Bordeaux.

The Lot (pronounced as in English) flows south of the Dordogne and must be the most tortuous river in France. It rises in the Languedoc, just east of Mende, and in the course of its wanderings passes through some of the wildest scenery likely to be found anywhere – deep thundering gorges, long winding lakes dammed by *barrages*, hilltop villages, grim fortresses on rocky pinnacles, ancient towns like Cahors built within the loops of the river. South of the Lot again are two other dramatic rivers, the Aveyron and the Tarn; they too fight their way through rugged gorges to the

Garonne plains, then join together north of Montauban and flow quietly into the Garonne by Moissac, whose church is something not to be missed.

Unlike all these rivers, the Garonne rises high in the Pyrenees, in Spain. Crossing the border near Luchon, it bounces down the boulder-strewn valleys through the foothills, to be confronted by the ancient *bastide* of Montréjeau, high up on its plateau. Here, swollen by the cold waters of the Neste, the river swings right, following the wide valley at the foot of the Pyrenees as though aiming for the Mediterranean. But soon after St-Gaudens it turns away from the mountains and flows quietly northeast through the plain towards the great pink-brick city of Toulouse. After Toulouse it follows a generally northwesterly course all the way to Bordeaux, winding sedately through the wide Garonne plain, a fertile area rich with plums, peaches, melons and tomatoes for the markets of Agen and Marmande. From Langon onward, famous Bordeaux vineyards are on both banks – Sauternes, Barsac and Graves to the left, Côtes de Bordeaux and Entre-Deux-Mers to the right. Presently the historic city of Bordeaux, with its lofty spires and its wine quays dating from medieval times, lies along the left bank, facing the vast new industrial zone on the opposite side. Twenty kilometres north, the Dordogne comes in from the east, and the two great rivers lose their separate identities in the broad estuary of the Gironde. Westward is the low-lying area of the illustrious Médoc vineyards.

Until the coming of the railways, the rivers were busy highways, important trade routes for the varied produce of the Aquitaine basin and the early fruit and

The Pyrenees: the Cirque de Gavarnie

Denis Hughes-Gilbey

vegetables from Provence and Roussillon. On the Dordogne, for example, there were active river ports at Souillac, Domme, Lalinde and Bergerac. Upstream, the Argentat boatyards built flat-bottomed sailing-barges from logs floated down through the gorges from the Auvergne forests. Laden with vine-poles, planks, sweet chestnuts, walnuts, cheeses from the Cantal, barrels of wine, and sometimes cattle and poultry (and human passengers as well), the barges would set off on a perilous downstream voyage to Bergerac or Libourne or Bordeaux – liable at any time to be shipwrecked in the rapid current or attacked by lurking river pirates. They were one-way trips, for at the journey's end the barges would be broken up and used for building materials.

West and south of Bordeaux lies that unique Atlantic region of sand dunes and pine forest known as the Landes (*see the entry in the gazetteer*). Over the centuries the Atlantic rollers had piled up a long coastline of dunes – the highest in Europe – and westerly gales had whipped the sand inshore, creating a treeless desert that was increasing every year, even threatening the Bordeaux wine districts. Early in the nineteenth century the dunes were stabilized by the sowing of gorse and broom interspersed with seedlings of pine; protected by the gorse and broom, the seedlings flourished. Today the Landes is probably the richest timber area of France. The long straight roads through seemingly endless pine forests are rather monotonous for the motorist, but the area is a remarkable achievement in reclamation.

South of the Landes is the Basque country, a small area bounded by the Gulf of Gascony, the Pyrenees and the river Adour, with Bayonne the capital. This unique, homogeneous race of people, who live partly in Spain and partly in France (about 15% of all Basques live on the French side), have succeeded in preserving their unity, customs and language. They live largely by fishing and mountain farming. At *fête* times they express their emotions in dancing, singing and improvising poetry, and the national game of pelota is played and watched with passionate interest. The typical Basque is lean and weathered, and wears the traditional beret and rope-soled *espadrilles*. He is dignified, taciturn, and believes in ruling his family. He is as much of a gourmet as any Frenchman: he eats a delicious *ragoût* of *palombes* (wood-pigeon trapped by nets spread across the mountain passes), *piperade* (a sort of scrambled egg with pimento sauce), smoked ham from Bayonne, mountain cheese, fish from the sea, trout and salmon from the mountain streams. He also produces some very drinkable wines and a well-known liqueur called *izarra*.

But of course the whole of Southwest France is renowned for its culinary specialities, from the *cassoulet* of Toulouse and Castelnaudary, oysters and fish from Arcachon, melons, peaches and plums from the Garonne plain, to the gourmet delights of the *périgordine* menus: *pâté de foie gras, confit d'oie, rillettes de porc, pintades* (guinea-fowl), truffles, cheeses from the Pyrenees and from Roquefort in the Aveyron. I have to say that the average level of restaurant food is not quite what it used to be (with honourable exceptions), and these rich *périgordine* menus are all very well occasionally but not all the time. As for the wines, my friend George Rainbird has written eloquently about them elsewhere in this book, and I need say no more – except to recommend the brandy called Armagnac, produced near Condom and to my mind superior to any but the finest Cognacs, and the sweet, golden dessert wine called Monbazillac, which comes from south of Bergerac.

Denis Hughes-Gilbey

Najac: the château perched high above the river Aveyron

The area covered in this section of the book is a large one, with an immense variety of marvellous landscapes. I must confess that my own favourite is that long stretch of the Dordogne between Carennac and Trémolat where the river meanders from cliff to cliff, through patchwork farmlands of tobacco and maize, between banks lined with poplars, past old stone barns golden in the sun, orchards of walnut trees, villages huddled between river and cliff, and château after château perched dizzily on cliff edge or dominating clearings in the extensive woodlands. It was surely this corner of Périgord that Edmond Rostand had in mind when in *Cyrano de Bergerac* he wrote of '*la verte douceur des soirs sur la Dordogne*'.

The Southwest: Gazetteer

Edward Young

AGEN, *Lot-et-Garonne* (4–D4). Capital of the Lot-et-Garonne department, situated on the right bank of the Garonne in the long valley which connects Toulouse with Bordeaux. It is an important road and rail junction, and at the NW corner of the town a 23-arched aqueduct carries the Garonne Lateral Canal over the river. To the N and NW, in the angle between the Garonne and the Lot, is the fertile plateau of the Agenais district where the mild climate encourages the production of orchard fruit of all kinds, and especially the uniquely delicious plums and prunes for which Agen is famous.

Although it is a busy modern town with broad tree-shaded avenues, it has a long history going back to Roman times. Only recently, roadworks near the prefecture have unearthed the foundations of a large Roman amphitheatre comparable in size to the ones at Saintes and Arles. Agen's strategic situation made it inevitable that it would be fought over by the English and the French, and it changed hands many times until the English were thrown out of France in 1453.

The past is reflected in the huddle of narrow streets in the old quarter surrounding the Place de l'Hôtel de Ville. Here four Renaissance mansions have been merged to house a splendid Museum containing, as well as many ceramic treasures, paintings by Goya (including a fine self-portrait), Sisley and Boudin, and an exquisite Greek marble sculpture of Venus unearthed a century ago by a farmer near Le Mas d'Agenais, just S of Marmande. Towards the railway station is the Cathedral of St-Caprais, a collegiate church founded in the 11th-c. but restored and promoted to the rank of cathedral after the town's ancient Cathedral of St-Étienne was destroyed at the time of the Revolution.

AIRE-SUR-L'ADOUR, *Landes* (4–D3). Nothing very remarkable about this little town at the juncture of the N124 and N134, except for the cathedral, a former Benedictine abbey church from the 12th-c., but if you are driving towards Pau it is worth stopping at Le Mas at the SW corner of the town to look at the 5th-c. marble sarcophagus in the crypt of the church of Ste-Quitterie. Carved with biblical scenes, it is one of the few extant examples of early Christian sculpture.

ALBI, *Tarn* (5–D5). Not to be missed, chiefly for its extraordinary cathedral and its important Toulouse-Lautrec collection. Like the Cathedral which towers massively over the surrounding streets, the old part of the town is built of faded red brick. Prosperous and bustling today, with steelworks and other industry in the outskirts, in the 13th-c. Albi was the scene of grim events.

These events arose from Pope Innocent III's determination to suppress the 'Albigensian heresy' – a view of religion, then widely held in Toulouse and most of the south of France, based on the belief that the world was created by the devil and that salvation could be achieved only by denying this world and concentrating on the heavenly life to come; the Church of Rome was itself an invention of the devil. Simon de Montfort headed a particularly vicious crusade against the

Albi: Cathedral interior

heretics, known as the 'Cathares', but it took an Inquisition and the burning of many martyrs at the stake before the sect was finally suppressed in 1244. When Bernard de Castanet was appointed bishop of Albi in 1276 he revived the Inquisition; surrounded by a sullen and resentful populace he set about building a cathedral that was also to be a fortress. After many years of terror, the harshness of his rule came to the ears of the Pope, and he was removed.

Hence the severity of the exterior of this formidable Cathedral of Ste-Cécile even today, despite the 60m tower added in the 15th-c. and the Flamboyant white-stone S porch added in the 16th-c. None of this prepares you for the extravagance of the vast interior. Pillars, walls and roof are everywhere adorned with coloured designs created in a furore of exuberance by artists from Renaissance Italy. At the W end is a huge painting of the Last Judgment by an unknown French artist, reputed to be the largest painting in France; unfortunately the organ, introduced at a later period, has vandalized the picture by blotting out the central figure of Christ himself. Halfway down the nave is a remarkable rood-screen (the *jubé*), elaborately carved in stone; but of the hundred or so statues which once adorned it only a few remain, the rest having been destroyed at the time of the Revolution. Behind it is the great choir, occupying half the length of the Cathedral and surrounded by an enclosure of exquisitely chiselled stone, rich in ornament and sensitive representations of angels, saints and prophets. The total effect of the cathedral interior is overwhelming.

Before you visit the Toulouse-Lautrec Collection, leave the cathedral square by the Rue Ste-Cécile and follow the signs through the old quarter to the birthplace (*maison natale*) of the artist. The house is still in the family, but you can see the room where he was born, family photographs, the salon where he had the first fall which contributed to his deformity, and early efforts at drawing and painting. The visit makes a moving prelude to the tour of the famous collection of his work, given to Albi by his mother after his death. It is housed in the Palais de la Berbie, the episcopal palace built in the 13th-c. and designed, like the neighbouring cathedral, as a fortress.

In the summer months Albi puts on a splendid *son et lumière* recalling the events of the Albigensian crusade.

AMBAZAC, *Haute-Vienne* (15km NE of Limoges: 5–B5). A small town set in an area of high hills and pleasant valleys with lakes and reservoirs. The thing to see here is the 'Treasure', which came from the now ruined Grandmont Abbey just N of Ambazac. It consists of a superb 12th-c. Limousin reliquary shrine in beaten copper, adorned with a rich design in jewels and enamels, and a precious silk dalmatic (an ecclesiastical vestment) from the 13th-c. Apply to the presbytery in the Rue J.-B. Landon.

Just after World War II, uranium was discovered in the Ambazac Hills to the NW of the town. Exploration northward revealed the existence of further extensive deposits and led to the construction at **Bessines** (35km N of Limoges on the N20) of the largest uranium processing plant in western Europe.

ARCACHON, *Gironde* (4–C2). Popular summer and winter Atlantic resort 60km W of Bordeaux, with golden beaches, tamarisk-lined boulevards, and a marina with berths for over 1000 yachts. It sits on the S side of a great triangular basin sheltered to the W by a narrow arm of land which ends in the point of Cap Ferret. The town itself, something of an architect's nightmare, is a gay hotch-potch of tourist shops, restaurants, oyster bars, expensive balconied hotels and apartment blocks for Bordeaux weekenders. There are two casinos, an aquarium and a local museum.

At low tide the bay is dotted with the stakes of the vast oyster beds for which Arcachon is famous. The native oysters praised by Rabelais were virtually wiped out by disease in the 1920s. Although the beds were restocked with *portugaise* oysters, in the early 1970s these too fell prey to disease, and have now been replaced by Canadian and Japanese stock. Arcachon remains one of the most important oyster producers in France, employing 25,000 people.

At the W end of the town, facing the peninsula of Cap Ferret and the surf rollers of the Atlantic, the ocean boulevard curves between sand dunes, smart villas and tall pine woods, the advance guard of the great pine forests of the Landes (*see entry*), planted in the late 18th-c. against the encroachment of the sea. One of the dunes, the **Dune du Pilat** 7km S of Arcachon, is claimed to be the highest in Europe, over 114m high and still growing; from its summit is a fine panorama of sand, sea and pines.

To the E and N the bay is ringed with several smaller resorts: notably **Audenge**, where the receding tide uncovers the large *réservoirs à poissons;* **Andernos-les-Bains,** a lively spa with casino and sandy beaches; and Cap Ferret (*see entry*).

ARGELÈS-GAZOST, *Hautes-Pyrénées* (4–E3). To judge by the number of its hotels, an extremely popular watering-place. 13km S of Lourdes on the route to Cauterets, Luz and Gavarnie (*see entries*), it is surrounded by magnificent scenery; the view from the terrace in front of the Mendaigne tower, looking out across the park of the thermal centre to the mountains, is superb.

4km due S is the tiny village of **St-Savin,** well worth a visit for its 12th-c. abbey church with an unusual tympanum on the Romanesque doorway and, inside, a remarkably life-like Christ by a 12th-c. Spanish wood-carver. A little further S, just along the road from St-Savin, there is a wonderful view from the terrace of the Chapelle de Piétat.

Argentat

ARGENTAT, *Corrèze* (22km SE of Tulle: 5–B5). A peaceful old town on both banks of the Dordogne in an area of great natural beauty, at the point where the river emerges from the confines of its gorges into the broader valley. On the N bank the closely packed houses with their stone and slate roofs are separated from the river by a wide quay. A hundred years ago flat-bottomed barges were built here and set off on a hazardous downstream journey laden with local produce for delivery to the river ports of Bergerac and Libourne.

Seen from across the river, with the roofs, turrets, gables and spires mirrored in the swift-flowing water, the town has a most inviting air of old-age serenity. On the S bank, stone houses come right to the water's edge, with wooden balconies and terraced gardens.

If you like dramatic scenery, Argentat is a good place to stay for a few days' exploring: up the river gorge to the Argentat dam (with the square-towered château of Le Gibanel reflected in the lake above it) and to the larger, 80m-high Le Chastang dam; to the Towers of Merle (which the English understandably failed to capture), giddily situated on a bend of the river Maronne, SE of Argentat; or NW to the Murel waterfall and the Roche du Vic, which is 636m high and has a tremendous view with an orientation table; and many other fascinating places in a region full of wooded ravines, tumbling water and precipitous cliffs.

AUBAZINES, *Corrèze* (10km E of Brive: 5–C5). About 8km E of Brive on the Tulle road, which follows the upstream course of the restless Corrèze, a right turn across a bridge over the river soon brings you to this little village in a picturesque setting close to the gorges of the tributary Coiroux. The former abbey church, built in the 12th-c. but altered in the 18th-c., is severely plain in the Cistercian manner, but the magnificent tomb of its founder, St-Étienne d'Aubazines, is richly decorated with beautifully carved scenes of the saint and his flock of monks and nuns. The church also contains four of the original grey-glass windows (with the design formed solely by the lead armature), some entertaining wood carvings on the 18th-c. choir-stalls, and in the N transept a unique 12th-c. ecclesiastical oak cupboard.

Immediately NW of the village is a prominent hill, the Puy de Pauliac, which has a cromlech and a remarkable all-round view of the Corrèze valley and the surrounding hills.

AUBUSSON, *Creuse* (5–B6). If you want to see something of the world-famous tapestries and carpets which have been made here for 500 years or more, the best time to visit is July, August or September. During these months the town hall puts on a fascinating annual exhibition of tapestries and carpets made to designs of all periods, including those of the celebrated contemporary French tapestry designer Jean Lurçat; there is also a demonstration by local craftsmen. In the Maison du Vieux Tapissier, a 15th-c. house just off the Grande Rue, an old workshop is on display, together with examples of stitching, documents, and other items of technical and historical interest. In the church is an 18th-c. tapestry worth looking at. If you are interested in visiting one of the local factories, enquire at the tourist office (Syndicat d'Initiative).

Wander through the old quarter near the 16th-c. Pont de la Terrade, and climb up to the ruins of the castle on top of the hill for a fine view of the wooded hills and the river Creuse winding its way through the town.

10km S is the small town of **Felletin**, which made tapestries even before Aubusson. Felletin tapestries form part of the treasure of the church in Conques, and it was in Felletin that the Graham Sutherland tapestry for Coventry Cathedral was woven. Felletin also specializes in diamond-cutting, and is worth visiting for its monastery church, part 12th-c., part 15th-c.

AUCH, *Gers* (4–D4). This ancient city, once capital of Gascony, straddles the river Gers. The old quarter stands on a high bluff on the W bank and is dominated by the 16th-c. pale-ochre stone Cathedral of Ste-Marie, with its twin bell-towers and its somewhat pompous 'Renaissance Classical' façade (added in the 17th-c.) facing towards the spacious Place de la Libération. Behind the façade-is a huge porch which bears the weight of the famous organ, built in 1694 and provider of popular recitals during the June music festival.

The nave is rather disappointing, with ornately furnished side-chapels and banal windows, but one's eyes are drawn forward to the glorious colours of the 18 stained-glass windows above the ambulatory behind the choir. These windows, the work of a 16th-c. Gascon painter, Arnaut de Moles, are a masterpiece of vivid colouring, lively facial characterization and engaging little everyday scenes. It is a pity that their effect is marred by the high enclosure surrounding the huge choir. This you cannot enter, or even look into, without a guide, but it should not be missed, for here is the second masterpiece of the Cathedral: an amazing array of choir-stalls (over 100 of them) profusely embellished with biblical, mythological and legendary scenes, carved in oak in the first half of the 16th-c., and comparable only with the contemporary carvings in Amiens Cathedral.

On the N side of the Cathedral is the 18th-c. Archbishop's Palace, now occupied by the prefecture. On the S side, alongside the 14th-c. Tour d'Armagnac, the Place Salinis stands at the top of a monumental staircase of over 200 steps descending to the river; on a lower landing a statue of d'Artagnan reminds us that he was a real person, born near Auch in 1615, whose name and exuberant personality were immortalized by Dumas in *The Three Musketeers*.

AX-LES-THERMES, *Ariège* (5–E5). Well-known Pyrenean spa and wintersport centre. Sixty mineral springs of greatly varying temperatures are fed into the thermal establishments and are helpful for respiratory ailments. The casino has a cosmopolitan and friendly, almost family, atmosphere. In front of the hospital in the Place du Breilh is the curious 'bassin des Ladres', placed there in the 13th-c. on the instructions of Louis IX

(St Louis) for the benefit of returned Crusader soldiers suffering from leprosy. Ax-les-Thermes is on the route from Toulouse to Andorra or to the frontier post at Bourg-Madame, and is a splendid centre for exhilarating mountain excursions.

BAGNÈRES-DE-BIGORRE, *Hautes-Pyrénées* (4–E3, E4). A busy, picturesque health resort set in an amphitheatre of hills to the E of Lourdes. The river Adour flows swiftly past it on its way from the mountains which ring the southern horizon. People have been coming here for its mineral waters and healthy climate ever since the Romans discovered it. Besides taking the waters you will find plenty to do. There is a 16th-c. church, a museum, a casino, and a wide choice of excursions:

The nearby Mont du Bédat, with a splendid view high above the town; the Grotte de Médous, where you take a subterranean boat trip through illuminated galleries of stalactites, stalagmites and weird calcite concretions; the Blue Lake beyond it, at the head of the Lesponne valley; or, for the more adventurous, the great **Pic du Midi de Bigorre**, a tremendous mountain peak 2865m above sea level, with a world-famous observatory, a TV transmitter sending programmes to the whole of SW France, an orientation table, and a truly awe-inspiring panorama of mountain landscape. (This last excursion is possible only in July, August and September; for up-to-date details of access, get local information.)

BAGNÈRES-DE-LUCHON, *Haute-Garonne* (4–E4). Luchon (to give it its abbreviated name) is the most fashionable watering-place and ski resort in the Pyrenees. The road to it from the north climbs easily through the valleys of, first, the Garonne and then its burbling tributary the Pique, with the thickly wooded mountain slopes closing in on both sides and the snowy peaks of the Spanish frontier barring the way ahead.

Around Luchon itself (630m above sea-level) the mountains are so close that they blot out the further views, but if you wish you can now drive 19km to the top of the 1800m peak of Super-bagnères, where there is an orientation table and the mountain views are terrific. This is the place where in winter the ski runs begin, and this is the mountain from whose interior spring the hot, sulphurous, radio-active waters which have made Luchon famous from Roman times onward. They are good for the treatment of rheumatic and respiratory ailments, and leading opera singers, actors and barristers have come here from all over the world to restore their flagging vocal chords.

The main street of the town, the Allées d'Étigny (named after the baron who was responsible for establishing it as a popular resort in the 18th-c.) is lined with hotels, some a good deal more expensive than others. The thermal station is in the Parc des Quinconces at its southern end. There is a casino, and a museum illustrating the local history and geography. And it hardly needs saying that Luchon is a natural centre for innumerable excursions and mountain walks.

BAYONNE, *Pyrénées-Atlantiques* (4–D2). The capital of the Basque country, a busy port 6km from the sea, and an animated city with a long history from Roman times. In mid-summer the city goes wild, enjoying a week's festival of Basque games, singing and dancing, bull-fighting and night-long revelries.

Park your car near the Place de la Libération, a fine open space on the quayside at the point where the river Nive runs under the Pont Mayou and into the much wider Adour. Walk up the tree-lined Rue Thiers towards the cathedral, passing the CHÂTEAU VIEUX on your right – a medieval fortress that has been the scene of many events in French history, was altered in the 16th-c., and is now let off as apartments.

The building of the Cathedral of STE-MARIE was begun in the 13th-c. On the N door still hangs the 13th-c. door knocker, the 'ring of sanctuary' from the times when a fugitive from justice could claim sanctuary from his pursuers once his hand had touched it, and there is a stone-carved 13th-c. doorway, mercifully spared at the time of the Revolution, at the S arm of the transept. The interior has noble proportions. There are some Renaissance stained-glass windows, one particularly fine example dated 1531, others restored in the last century. The cloisters on the S side have

Bayonne: Cathedral of Ste-Marie

Topham

been much restored, but the colonnades gracefully echo the design of the Cathedral windows, as can be seen from the S gallery: here is a splendid view of the Cathedral with its flying buttresses and the soaring twin-spired towers that were only completed in the 19th-c.

Leaving the Cathedral, walk down the celebrated RUE DU PORT NEUF with its low arcades, its *patisseries* and its elegant cafés serving the chocolate for which Bayonne is as much renowned as for its hams. Here you are in the heart of the old Gascon city, whose history goes back at least to the 1st century before Christ, when it was already an important Roman town. In the middle of the 12th-c. Gascony became a possession of the English crown; for 300 years, to the very end of the Hundred Years War, Bayonne (like Bordeaux) was a prosperous English port with a thriving overseas trade. But in 1451, when the English fortunes in France were rapidly declining, the town was attacked by French forces. At the height of the battle, a 'miracle' (celebrated by a modern plaque in the Cathedral) is said to have appeared in the sky – a white cross which the defenders took to signify that their cause was lost (or perhaps to excuse their surrender).

Becoming French instead of English did not do the Bayonnais much good. They had lost the valuable English market, the channel to the sea was allowed to silt up, and they had to pay taxes to the French king. It was not until over 100 years later that work was put in hand to re-open the sea channel. Slowly prosperity returned. In the 1680s the great military engineer Vauban, who in the reign of the 'Sun King' was responsible for establishing a great chain of frontier strongholds, built the CITADEL on the N bank of the Adour and the southern ring of battlements around the city.

In the 18th-c. Bayonne was granted the status of a free port. A flourishing trade had been established with many countries, its great fishing fleets were collecting rich harvests off the Newfoundland banks, and its privateers were bringing in from the Atlantic trade-routes prize ships laden with enormous wealth. Its iron-foundries prospered through the manufacture of 'bayonettes' and other weapons of war. But the century ended with the Revolution and Napoleon's wars; the English blockade strangled the town's foreign trade and brought the port to a standstill. In 1814 Bayonne successfully resisted a siege by Wellington's forces, but that did not prevent the English from pressing on to victory.

Today the port is thriving again. At the river mouth a massive new breakwater extending over a kilometre into the Atlantic has stopped the sanding-up of the channel and so enabled deep-draught ships to enter. The post-war exploitation of natural gas and its by-products along the foothills of the Pyrenees has brought new prosperity to the whole area. In particular, Bayonne is now a major exporter of sulphur – over a million tons a year.

Do not leave Bayonne without visiting the MUSÉE BASQUE on the E side of the river Nive. This is a fascinating exhibition of everything that makes the Basque people, whether in France or in Spain, unique in the world: their history, seafaring traditions, costumes, handicrafts and art; and there is a special section devoted to the great national game, pelota.

Another museum well worth visiting is the nearby MUSÉE BONNAT. Léon Bonnat was a 19th-c. portrait painter who had a class at the École des Beaux-Arts in Paris and taught many of the Post-Impressionist painters their groundwork – among them Toulouse-Lautrec, Munch, Braque and Dufy. When he died he bequeathed his art collection to his native town. It contains some of his own work, but more important are the paintings and drawings by Dürer, Goya, Michelangelo, Leonardo, Murillo, El Greco, Ingres, Rembrandt, Rubens and others.

5½km SE is a hill called the **Croix de Mouguerre** with an orientation table and a magnificent view of Bayonne, the Landes to the N, Biarritz to the W, the western Pyrenees and the Basque coastline.

BAZAS, *Gironde* (4–C3). Because of its situation, high up on a rocky promontory overlooking the Beuve valley, Bazas has been a town of importance from Roman times onward. The Roman poet Ausonius, whose father was born here, knew it well in the 4th-c. and extolled its beauties in verse. From the 5th-c. it was a bishopric under the aegis of Bordeaux, and the bishops ruled the town.

The present Cathedral is not the first. Earlier churches on the site were destroyed in turn by the Normans in the 9th-c. and by the English at the end of the 12th. The imposing building you see today, facing down the great arcaded square in the centre of the ancient town, was begun in the middle of the 13th-c., but shortage of funds (and, no doubt, the continuing presence of English troops in the region) delayed its completion for about 200 years. A century later, in the Wars of Religion, Protestants destroyed a large part of it by fire, and only spared the wonderful Romanesque portals on payment of a huge ransom. Rebuilding started shortly afterwards, and by 1635 it was ready for reconsecration, and widely regarded as the finest Gothic edifice in SW France.

With its nine-bay nave and no transept, the interior is unusually long; viewed from the W end towards the choir, it gives a powerful sensation of lofty space. The façade, though an ᴖmalgam of different periods, is agreeably impressive, but it is the three 13th-c. portals, with their richness of sculpture and bas-relief carvings, which excite one's admiration – and one's gratitude to the 16th-c. citizens of Bazas who paid the ransom to save them.

From the terrace garden to the right of the cathedral and from the tree-shaded Allées Clemenceau there are lovely views of the Beuve valley. The town's 13th-c. ramparts, no longer in a condition to defend it, still retain one of its ancient gateways, the Porte de Gisquet flanked by twin towers.

About 10km NW is the imposing château of **Roquetaillade**, built in 1306 by Cardinal Gaillard de la Mothe, a nephew of Pope Clement V. Smaller than his uncle's fortress at Villandraut (*see entry*), it nevertheless has a massive central keep and six large round towers. It is in good repair, thanks to the 19th-c. restoration by Viollet-le-Duc, and inhabited, and is open every day during the summer months. It is well worth a visit. Walking round, one cannot help thinking that these medieval high-up ecclesiastics did themselves rather well – even in those days castle-building must have been a fairly expensive indulgence.

BEAULIEU-SUR-DORDOGNE, *Corrèze* (14km N of St-Céré: 5–C5). Eleven hundred years ago, about 840, the Archbishop of Bourges was so struck by the beauty of this spot (he gave it its name) that he founded a community of Cluniac monks here. The monastery soon became famous, and at the beginning of the 12th-c. the monks began building the Romanesque abbey church of St-Pierre which, surrounded by ancient narrow streets, today forms the centre of this lively little town on the right bank of the Dordogne.

The interior of the church is surprisingly spacious, but the nave is dark, with wide gloomy side-aisles and no windows, which has the intended effect of drawing the eye towards the better lit chancel. The chief glory of the church is the elaborately sculptured S porch, carved in 1125 by craftsmen of the same School of Toulouse which carried out similar work in other Périgord churches (*see entries for* Carennac, Moissac, Souillac). It is crowned by a large semi-circle (the tympanum) representing the Last Judgment, and below it are two rows of winged beasts and sundry monsters. The supporting pillars are adorned with prophets, and to each side are somewhat damaged scenes of Daniel in the Lion's Den and the Temptation of Christ. The whole is one of the finest extant examples of Romanesque sculpture.

The Wars of Religion forced the monks to abandon the monastery. Later their place was taken by other Dominican monks, but after a long period of relative peace they too were thrown out at the time of the Revolution. The abbey church alone remains as eloquent witness of the monastic devotion which created it.

BEAUMONT, *Dordogne* (4–C4). One of the first of the English *bastides*, built in 1272. The spacious church is still there, with its four defensive corner towers, but it was much restored in the last century. Otherwise only the remaining arcades in the attractive market square and the gateway of the western ramparts bear witness today to the character of the original town.

4km N on the D660 is the 15th-c. château of **Bannes**. It is not open to the public, but it looks

Anne Bolt

Château de Beynac

rather good perched up on a rocky spur above the road to the left; a satisfactory blend of feudal severity and Renaissance elegance. Further N on the same road, in the hamlet of Couze-et-St-Front (where they make filter-paper), a left turn brings you to the 16th-c. château of **Lanquais**, which *is* open; mainly residential on a grand scale, it nevertheless has very solid machicolated towers for defence – just in case.

BELVÈS, *Dordogne* (20km E of Beaumont: 4–C4). This quiet hilltop town, just S of the Dordogne river, once guarded the ancient route from Périgueux to Cahors. There was a Benedictine monastery here at least as early as the 9th-c., but the present building, which now forms part of the parish church, dates from the early 14th-c. The porch, the clock-tower and the reconstructed nave were added later. On the edge of the market square is a simple stone tower; the lower part was a defence post from about 1100 onwards, but when the Hundred Years War was over the four square pillars and the roof were added to make it a belfry and town clock. One of the pillars of the covered market-place still has the pillory chain by which wrongdoers were displayed for public derision.

BERGERAC, *Dordogne* (4–C4). The largest town on the Dordogne river, and an important centre for wine, tobacco, agriculture and light industry. Its best red wine is Pécharmant, its famous sweet white wines come from nearby Monbazillac (*see entry*).

As you cross the bridge to enter the town from the S, you get a pleasing view of the low profile of red-roofed buildings clustered along the river bank. A hundred yards downstream from the bridge is the old port – a busy scene in the old days when Bergerac wines were shipped by river to Libourne – and behind the port is a restored monastery with a galleried courtyard which used to be the cloister; it is now a *Maison du Vin*, and local wines can be sampled in the huge vaulted cellars. Nearby, in the main street, the Rue Neuve d'Argenson, the Hôtel-de-Ville houses the fascinating and world-famous tobacco museum, unique in France.

The town suffered much in the Hundred Years War (it was captured by the Earl of Derby in 1345) and the Wars of Religion, and most of it is relatively modern, but there is a warren of narrow streets in the old quarter around the covered market-place, and the best fish shop in the whole of the Dordogne.

The celebrated Cyrano de Bergerac (of the big nose) was a real person, a 17th-c. soldier, notorious duellist and romantic writer, who achieved posthumous fame as the hero of the well-known play by Edmond Rostand (1868–1918).

BEYNAC-et-CAZENAC, *Dordogne* (7km SW of Sarlat: 5–C5). Here the Dordogne valley road runs close to a sharp bend in the river, with the village squeezed between the road and the towering ochre cliff above it. On the very edge of the cliff, dominating the countryside for miles around, stands the formidable Château de Beynac, which simply must be visited, not only for its panoramic view of the valley but for the splendour of the castle itself. If you don't feel up to the steep walk through the village and by the cliff path, you can drive round by the road opposite the car park; signposts direct you to the château (3km).

The original castle was seized in 1189 in the name of Richard Cœur-de-Lion by a notorious thug called Mercadier, who proceeded to ravage the surrounding country. In 1214, during the Albigensian crusade (*see* Albi), Simon de Montfort took the castle and demolished it. Before the century was out, the Baron of Beynac began rebuilding it in the form in which we see it today. During the Hundred Years War the Treaty of Brétigny of 1360 ceded the whole of Aquitaine to the English, but eight years later Beynac was retaken by the forces of the French king. Clearly visible across the valley, the fortress of Castelnaud (*see entry*) remained in English hands until the end of the war in 1453, with raids and skirmishes taking place intermittently between the opposing sides.

Beynac was one of the four powerful baronies of Périgord, the others being Biron, Bourdeilles (*see entries*), and Mareuil and the castle remained in possession of the barons of Beynac until the middle of this century. It is still privately owned, but the State is gradually restoring it, and most of it is open to the public.

It is a castle to stir the imagination, with its double perimeter wall protecting it from the high ground to the N, its crenellated keep, its winding stairs, its massive stone walls plunging 150m towards the village roofs below, and its great Hall of State where the barons and their lieutenants assembled in council (and where you must not miss, in the adjoining oratory, the remains of a naive but vigorously outlined 15th-c. fresco of the Last Supper). And from the battlements the landscape of the river winding through fields of tobacco and maize, bounded by limestone cliffs and wooded hills, with the castles of Castelnaud, Fayrac and Marqueyssac in full view, must be one of the finest in the whole of the Dordogne.

BIARRITZ, *Pyrénées-Atlantiques* (4–D2). Until the early years of the 19th-c. Biarritz was a small fishing port flanked by magnificent, empty, sandy beaches on which the citizens of nearby Bayonne came to bathe. Then it was discovered by the Empress Eugénie; in 1854 she persuaded her husband Napoleon III to spend a holiday here, and it became fashionable overnight. Other royal personages followed, and streets with names like Avenue de la Reine Victoria, Boulevard Prince-de-Galles and Avenue Édouard VII commemorate the frequent visits of the British royal family. 'La Belle Époque' ended in 1914, but its memory lingers on in the sumptuous elegance of its rather expensive hotels and restaurants.

There are two casinos, four golf courses, tennis courts, several indoor heated swimming pools. Close to the ocean, on a promontory, stands the splendid museum of the sea, with a huge aquarium, an aviary, a sea lion pool, and a terrace with wonderful panoramic views of coast and mountain. A small footbridge connects with the famous Rocher de la Vierge, surrounded by foaming breakers and glorious prospects of rocks interspersed with sandy coves. Beyond, the marvellous beaches stretch N along the Côte d'Argent and curve S along the Côte Basque. To the N, on Pointe St-Martin, is a lighthouse open to daytime visitors and affording more panoramic coastal views.

BIRON, Château de, *Dordogne* (17km SE of Beaumont: 4–C4). From the level of the surrounding countryside the château looks very impressive on top of its little hill. Towers, high walls, battlements, and imposing buildings of every period from the 12th- to the 17th-c., dominate the gently rolling pastoral landscape. Inside the main gateway you find yourself in a large grassy courtyard, big enough to take all the village inhabitants (and their cattle) in times of trouble. To the right are the 12th-c. guard tower and the recently repaired funerary chapel, the lower part of which, accessible only from the village below, is still in use as the parish church. In the chapel are the fine 16th-c. tombs of two brothers of the Gontaut-Biron family, but the guide will tell you, with justifiable indignation, that two of the chapel's former treasures, though classified as historic monuments, were sold by the last duke, just before he died, and are now in the Metropolitan Museum in New York.

As you leave the courtyard and ascend the steps into the main part of the castle, you are at once aware of the dilapidation of the interior, the result of vandalism during the Revolution, a disastrous fire, and years of neglect. State-aided restoration has begun, though there is still much to be done. But it is all very romantic in a melancholy way, especially the inner courtyard with its unexpected view of the Dropt valley seen through an elegant colonnade. And don't miss the great kitchens.

The barony of Biron, created in 1598, was one of the four baronies of the province (*see* Beynac-et-Cazenac). The first baron, Charles de Gontaut, sullied the family name by intriguing against his king, Henri IV, and was beheaded in 1602. Nevertheless the castle was owned continuously by fourteen generations of the Gontaut-Biron family. It has now passed out of their hands, but it is still privately owned (though open to the public).

BLAYE, *Gironde* (4–C3). Below Blaye the Gironde opens out into an estuary 10km wide, but any tide-borne invader aiming to attack Bordeaux would have found the channel opposite Blaye narrowing to no more than 2km between the banks, and further constricted by a chain of islands and shoals. So Blaye, perched on a high cliff on the E bank, has always been an important defensive post and, inevitably, often changed hands in the long medieval struggle between the English and the French.

Apart from the ruins of the 12th-c. Château des Rudel, little remains from those days, for in 1689 Vauban, Louis XIV's great military engineer, cleared the town to make way for the imposing walled and moated Citadel you see today. The present town to the SE of it is therefore relatively modern. A deep-water basin accommodates small cargo ships and the fishing vessels which bring in sturgeon and lampreys and other marine delicacies.

From the Tour de l'Aiguillette at the N end of the citadel there is a splendid view of the busy estuary, now dredged to allow the passage of deep-water tankers. Downstream are two large refineries on islands. The two other bastions which completed Vauban's defensive barrier are the Fort Paté on the small island opposite Blaye and the Fort Médoc on the far bank. And across the river is the low-lying land of the richest wine area in the world, the Médoc. Behind Blaye lies the prolific rolling country which grows the Côtes de Blaye wines, inferior to those of the Médoc but very good all the same.

A car ferry connects Blaye with **Lamarque** on the opposite bank.

BONAGUIL, Château de, *Lot-et-Garonne* (6km NE of Fumel: 4–C4). In spite of the damage done to it during the Revolution, this towering fortress still stands impressively on its rocky hill as a remarkable example of late-15th-c. military architecture. It was carefully designed to withstand artillery attack and a long siege, with three lines of defence – an outer wall with embrasures to facilitate cross-fire and an enormous barbican, a minor fortress in itself; an inner wall containing the living quarters, with immensely strong round towers at each corner; and finally the central keep, tall and proud, pointed and narrow to reduce its target silhouette against cannon fire from the most dangerous northern sector, and with a secure water supply from a well sunk in the rock.

Bonaguil is an impressive anachronistic folly, built by Bérenger de Roquefeuil to defend himself against potential enemies (his behaviour had created many) at a time when his baronial contemporaries in Périgord were building châteaux designed more for elegant living than for defence. In fact Bonaguil never had a chance to prove itself in action – it was never attacked – perhaps for very good reasons.

Visits (in spring, summer and autumn) are by guided tours at roughly hourly intervals.

BORDEAUX, *Gironde* (4–C3). One of the great cities of France and – according to Samuel Chamberlain in his book *Bouquet de France* – its third gastronomic capital after Paris and Lyon. An important wine centre and commercial port since Gallo-Roman times, and once under English rule for 300 years, it was the temporary seat of the French government in 1870, 1914 and 1940.

The motoring tourist can soon get lost trying to park in the busy maze of one-way streets. The best plan is to make for the vast car park in the Esplanade des Quinconces adjoining the riverside Quai Louis XVIII, leave the car there and enjoy the city on foot. On the SW corner of the esplanade, at 10 Cours du 30-Juillet, is the Tourist Office (Syndicat d'Initiative) where they will give you a map of the city. Here also is the Maison du Vin, where you can inquire about the possibility of visits to wine-cellars in Bordeaux or at the wine châteaux of the region.

Bordeaux's left-bank waterfront, facing the derricks and funnels of the ships loading alongside the quays and warehouses, must be one of the most elegant in the world. The tall houses of the wine-merchants' offices along the ancient wine quarter of the QUAI DES CHARTRONS, the great open space of the tree-lined ESPLANADE DES QUINCONCES, the classical 18th-c. façades surrounding the garden and fountain of the PLACE DE LA BOURSE, and the early-19th-c. Pont de Pierre whose 17 arches span the broad Garonne, make a striking contrast with the industrial zone on the opposite bank.

To reach the heart of Bordeaux, turn away from the river into the Cours Chapeau-Rouge which goes uphill from the Bourse. It leads to the PLACE DE LA COMÉDIE, a fine open square with a gay fountain, at the corner of a triangle of broad boulevards – the Allées de Tourny, the Cours Clemenceau and the Cours Intendance – which are at the centre of the Bordeaux created in the 18th-c. period of boom and prosperity. Here are the classical rich-bourgeois terraced houses with iron balconies overlooking the plane-trees lining the boulevards, the colonnaded splendour of the GRAND THÉÂTRE (whose staircase and interior were imitated for the Opéra in Paris), the luxury shops in the Cours 'Intendance and the Rue Ste-Catherine, and the Place Gambetta with the old archway of the Porte Dijeaux in the corner. This is the part of Bordeaux to be in at *midi*, to take an aperitif at one of the elegant sidewalk cafés and afterwards lunch at one of the many excellent restaurants.

Of the many churches in Bordeaux there are two you certainly ought to visit. First, the great Cathedral of ST-ANDRÉ, nearly as long and as broad as Notre-Dame in Paris. Begun in the 11th-c., it was altered, added to, and restored many times during the next 400 years, so that it is part-Romanesque and part-Gothic; later, buttresses were added to the exterior when the roof of the nave threatened to collapse. The S door, the Porte Royale, is celebrated for its 13th-c. sculptures, including a tympanum in three tiers representing the Last Supper, the Ascension, and the Triumph of Christ. At the E end is the 15th-c. belfry, separate from the body of the Cathedral, and called the TOUR PEY BERLAND after the archbishop who had it built; it is a massive structure, ornately decorated; its tall spire had to be rebuilt after storm damage in the 18th-c. and is surmounted by a statue of the Virgin.

Opposite the W façade is the CITY HALL, occupying the former 18th-c. episcopal palace; behind that is the MUSÉE DES BEAUX-ARTS containing paintings and sculpture from the 15th- to the 20th-c., with works by Veronese, Titian, Rubens, Delacroix, Zadkine, Rodin, etc.

The other notable church is the BASILIQUE ST-MICHEL, near the waterfront just S of the Pont de Pierre. This great 14th–15th-c. edifice was badly damaged by bombardment in 1940, but it has been well repaired, and behind the high altar are beautiful modern windows by Max Ingrand, the celebrated French stained-glass designer who was also responsible for the new windows in the Église des Jacobins in Toulouse (see entry). The belfry, the TOUR ST-MICHEL, standing apart at the W end of the church, with its spire reaching a height of 114m, is the highest in the S of France; if you have the energy to climb the 228 steps to the viewing platform half way up, the magnificent view of the city, river and surrounding country is well worth the effort. In the crypt below the tower is a macabre collection of mummified corpses.

Other churches of interest are the 12th–13th-c. STE-CROIX (SE of St-Michel along the Rue C. Savageau) with a remarkable Romanesque façade, and ST-SEURIN (in the Rue de la Croix Blanche) with its 11th-c. crypt containing 6th-c. tombs.

Besides the Musée des Beaux-Arts already mentioned, there are several other good museums: notably the MARITIME MUSEUM near the river, by the Place de la Bourse; the NATURAL HISTORY MUSEUM in the 18th-c. public gardens N of the city centre; the MUSEUM OF DECORATIVE ARTS, just N of the City Hall; and for veteran car enthusiasts the MUSÉE BONNAL-RENAULAC (about 3½km S in the suburb of Bègles at 80 Rue Ferdinand-Buisson), where all the cars shown are in working order, including an 1896 Dietrich made for and personally driven by Tsar Nicholas II.

Surprisingly little remains in Bordeaux today as evidence of the city's earlier history, in which the Romans and the English played so large a part. Even before the Romans came, Bordeaux's situation as an inland port, commanding the

Bordeaux

Jean Feuille

shortest route between the Atlantic and the Mediterranean, made it a natural trading centre. The Greek geographer Strabo, writing at the time of Christ, certainly mentions it – not as a wine centre but as a stage in the tin trade between Britain and the Mediterranean. Under the Romans, the first wine shipped from here was not local wine but Midi wine brought down the Garonne.

It was not until the 1st century AD that the Romans instituted the planting of local vines – an innovation that proved more lasting than any of their forums and temples, for the only Roman remains in Bordeaux are a few arcades of a 3rd-c. arena on the site known as the PALAIS GALLIEN. The town was sacked by Barbarian invaders in 276, but the Romans threw them out and civilized life continued for a while. The Roman poet Ausonius was born here in 310, grew vines at his villa near Loupiac a few miles upstream, and – happily for him – died at the age of 85 only a few years before the town fell to the Visigoths.

The next 500 years were Dark Ages indeed. The withdrawal of the Roman legions left a vacuum soon filled by sporadic struggles between warring barons and by devastating attacks on town and countryside by foreign invaders – the Saracens in 731, the Vikings in 848. Not until the early Middle Ages did Bordeaux enjoy a period of relative prosperity, based largely on the growing trade in wine.

For the English tourist the most interesting era began when Henry II of England shrewdly married Eleanor of Aquitaine in 1152. With their combined territories the English crown could now claim ownership of the whole of western France from the Channel to the Pyrenees. Bordeaux became the English base for the next 300 years, and it was during these years that the 'English connection' with the Bordeaux wine trade, which continues to this day, was firmly established.

The city prospered, the population increased threefold, and the English crown profited greatly from its monopoly of the wine exports. English kings and princes – especially Edward I, Edward III and the Black Prince – spent a lot of time in Bordeaux, with headquarters in the Château de l'Ombrière, of which the only vestige now is the PORTE CAILHAU in the Place du Palais (off the Quai Richelieu, just N of the Pont de Pierre round-about).

English fortunes in France waxed and waned. From 1400 onwards the kings were too pre-occupied with problems at home to devote proper attention to the deteriorating situation in their French territories. The defeat, in 1453, of the English army under Talbot at Castillon led to the withdrawal of English forces from Bordeaux and virtually the whole of France. The Bordeaux merchants were dismayed. With their special tax privileges they had prospered under English rule; now they had not only lost their principal market but had to pay heavy taxes to the French king.

Time passed, the taxes were relaxed, the wine trade with England revived. Louis XI granted Bordeaux a self-governing parliament. This increased the importance of the office of mayor of Bordeaux, a post held from 1581 to 1585 by the writer Montaigne during the Wars of Religion, when Bordeaux remained staunchly Catholic; though there was little local trouble it was an anxious time, and Montaigne was glad when he could retire to his château beyond St-Émilion and write his essays (*see* Montaigne, Château de). His tomb is in Bordeaux, and can be found in the vestibule of the University Faculty of Science and Letters near the Cathedral.

The 17th-c. saw an important extension of the wine-growing area through the draining of the marshlands in the Médoc, N of the city. In the 18th-c., with the new markets provided by the acquisition of French colonies in the West Indies and West Africa, Bordeaux reached new levels of prosperity and created the fine municipal buildings, wide boulevards and elegant private houses which, as we have seen, give the city its particular character today.

The Revolution brought this prosperity to an abrupt end. The new government's economic policies, Napoleon's wars, and a series of bad harvests, ruined Bordeaux's trade. Nelson's blockade ground the port to a standstill. Even the end of the war brought little relief, and Bordeaux's economy remained depressed throughout the 19th-c., and indeed until after World War II.

Today, across the Garonne (some 400m wide at this point), a humming new industrial zone stretches 20km northward along the right bank, with deep-water quays for oil tankers, a graving-dock, aircraft factories, ship-building yards, chemical works and oil refineries – the result of a vigorous policy of heavy industrial development initiated by the mayor of Bordeaux, M. Jacques Chaban-Delmas. In the last 20 years this policy has revived the prosperity of the city and provided a much-needed 'shot in the arm' for the commercial activity of the whole of Aquitaine.

On the N edge of the city a new suspension bridge, the Pont d'Aquitaine high above the river, links the A10 Paris autoroute with a new ring road swinging west around the city, connecting with the busy international Mérignac airport, and joining up S of the city with the A61 Toulouse autoroute. Immediately W of the Pont d'Aquitaine the road crosses a huge lake bordered by the halls of a new Exhibition Park for commercial fairs. A lively University campus in the SW suburbs of Pessac-Talence, a teaching hospital of international renown, and a sports stadium seating 35,000 spectators under an audacious single-span roof, complete the picture of a great city port that is no longer resting on the laurels of a historic past.

BORT-LES-ORGUES, *Corrèze* (5–B6). This small town on the right bank of the Dordogne owes the second part of its name to the curious rock-formation which dominates it from the SW – a great cliff of volcanic basalt, 3km long and 100m high, weathered into the shape of gigantic columns reminiscent of organ-pipes. But today the town is dominated to the N by an even higher, man-made cliff – the great white concave wall, 120m high and nearly 400m across at the top, of the formidable barrage with its hydro-electric power station at the foot.

At one time the Dordogne used to flow swiftly through the narrow gorges here, often rising to a raging torrent in the rainy season, but now it has been tamed by a series of huge dams, of which the Bort barrage is the first and largest. When the water behind the barrage rises to a dangerous level, the great double chute in the centre of the wall is opened, and a spectacular torrent of foaming water cascades into the river channel below. When the water level falls too low, additional water is taken, by a 12km tunnel, from an upper level of the river Rhue which, flowing in from the E, actually joins the Dordogne downstream of the town. From June to September the public is allowed to visit the power station, where an audio-visual model of the whole hydro-electric system of the Massif Central and Dordogne is on exhibition.

8km N is the **Château de Val**, once high on the hillside above the river, now lapped and surrounded by the man-made lake behind the dam, and reached by a narrow jetty. With its slender pepperpot turrets reflected in the water, the 15th-c. château makes a splendidly romantic picture. From mid-June to mid-September guided tours of the interior are available, and you can take an hour's boat trip on the lake amid beautiful scenery.

BOURDEILLES, Château de, *Dordogne* (7km SW of Brantôme: 4–B4). A few miles downstream from Brantôme, perched on an abrupt rocky promontory on the left bank of the Dronne, stands this imposing castle with its soaring keep. Bourdeilles, once one of the four baronies of Périgord, actually has two castles within its ramparts. The older castle was built by a member of the Bourdeille family in the second half of the 13th-c. on the foundations of an earlier stronghold. It consists of a mass of fortifications and living quarters grouped round the immensely tall octagonal keep. The walls of the keep are nearly 3m thick and contain a vaulted room on each floor with a spiral staircase leading to the upper platform. Here is a fine view of the castle layout, of the village huddled below the walls, a curious boat-shaped mill, and the river flowing under a hump-back bridge. The English captured this castle in 1369, only to be thrown out six years later by the energetic French royalist Du Guesclin. Later it was held by the notorious counts of Périgord, who for some years terrorized the countryside far and wide.

The later part of the castle was built in the 16th-c., again using the foundations of an earlier fortification. The construction of this handsome Renaissance mansion was organized by Jaquette de Montbron, widow of the lord of Bourdeilles whose younger brother was the celebrated chronicler Pierre de Brantôme (*see* Brantôme). The story goes that the building was put in hand in expectation of a visit from Catherine de Médicis, the Queen Mother regent, and that when the royal visit was cancelled the work was stopped and has never been completed to this day.

The castle remained in the family until this century, but faced with the soaring costs of urgent repairs they ceded it to the State. In the 1960s it was leased to a wealthy art patron to house his collection of furniture and works of art – on condition that the rooms remained open to the public. He bequeathed his collection to the State, and it has remained *in situ* in the Renaissance mansion.

It is a remarkable assembly, much of it Spanish, of ornate travelling chests, armour, paintings, tapestries, a handsome Renaissance table and some beautiful 16th-c. wood-carvings of religious subjects. On the second floor is a great four-poster bed, elaborately carved and gilded, and reputed to have belonged to the Emperor Charles V. The finest room is the Salon Doré on the first floor, which remains virtually as it was when Jaquette de Montbron commissioned it, with walls and ceiling (including every face of the main beams) painted by Ambroise Le Noble in rich and complicated designs whose colours are still fresh and glowing; and there is a splendid tapestry of François I on horseback with his falconers.

BRANTÔME, *Dordogne* (4–B4). Set on an island site between two branches of the gentle river Dronne, which everywhere mirrors its brown-red roofs and riverside gardens, this is one of the most beautiful small towns in the whole of SW France. On the N bank, seen across the river from the town against a rising background of trees, stand the imposing buildings of the ancient Benedictine abbey around which the town grew up. Here the river flows quietly under stone bridges and between balustraded embankments bordered by spacious tree-shaded promenades. A long, curving weir, noisily spilling its shallow cascade, holds the upper level calm and deep to reflect the long façade of the former monastery building, the severe Gothic church and the lofty belfry-tower. To the left, an irregular dog-leg stone bridge leads from a Renaissance pavilion to a public garden with summerhouses, cypresses and formal rose-beds which in June are a sight to be seen.

The abbey has been rebuilt several times since it was founded, reputedly by Charlemagne, in about 780. The present building is the result of a major reconstruction in the 18th-c., though the elegance of the façade has suffered from the recent removal of the central portal with its broken semi-circle of

Brantôme: the former monastery and the weir on the river Dronne

roof gable. Today, what was once the monastery is occupied by the *mairie*, the school, and a museum containing local prehistoric finds and some rather odd paintings done by a local 19th-c. painter under the influence of a medium. But you can still climb the magnificent white-stone staircase and see the monks' refectory and dormitory; the exposed timber ceiling is as good as the day it was built.

The church, linked to the monastery by remnants of the old cloisters, is an uninspired building, with a plain nave and a flat wall at the E end. The best thing in it is in the baptistry, a 14th-c. russet-coloured bas-relief depicting the Baptism of Christ, with a smiling Christ awaiting the pitcher of water from a laughing St John – small and exquisite in its simplicity. Above the font is another bas-relief, a 13th-c. Massacre of the Innocents. The other artistic treasure of the church, a 16th-c. wooden statue of the Virgin and Child, known as Notre-Dame de Reclus, was stolen in April 1977 and at the time of writing had not been recovered.

The belfry, alongside but separate from the church, is an architectural gem. It is 11th-c. and the oldest example of a gabled belfry in the Limousin region. Soaring above the other abbey buildings, it consists of four square storeys, each a little smaller than the one below. High up on each face of the tower, occupying almost the full height of the last two storeys, is a sharply pointed gable enclosing a deep rounded arch, similar to those at St-Léonard-de-Noblat. Topping it all is a pyramid roof tiled with stone slates.

Under the foundations of the belfry, and in the cliff behind the abbey, is a series of caves, some of which had been put to use by the monks as domestic offices, including a wine cellar and a bakery. In one of the caves are some remarkable bas-reliefs carved in the 16th-c. in the solid rock walls; one huge group represents the Last Judgment, brooded over by a rather daunting God; the other depicts the Crucifixion. Another cave has, surprisingly, been turned into a trout-hatchery, whose pools and connecting channels look for all the world like the excavations of a Roman villa with underfloor heating.

A famous son of Brantôme was the 16th-c. soldier, adventurer and courtier Pierre de Bourdeille, younger brother of the lord of Bourdeilles whose castle is only 10km downstream (*see entry*). It was Pierre de Bourdeille who escorted Mary Queen of Scots on her sad journey from France to Leith after the death of her husband, the short-

lived French king François II. For one of his
military exploits Bourdeille was awarded the lay
abbacy of Brantôme, and after a fall from a horse
which crippled him and rendered him impotent he
spent the rest of his life here. Under the name of
'Brantôme' he wrote his chronicles of the *dames
galantes* he had known at the court of Valois and
of the *grands capitaines* he had fought alongside.
His simple, direct style and the often scandalous
nature of the tales have won him a lasting place in
French literature.

BRIVE-LA-GAILLARDE, *Corrèze* (5–C5). A
busy, thriving town on the river Corrèze, at
the junction of the road and rail routes from
Paris to Toulouse and from Bordeaux to
Clermont-Ferrand, and an important centre for
fruit-growing and market-gardening. The older
quarters are ringed by tree-lined boulevards (site
of the former ramparts, so successfully defended in
medieval sieges that Brive earned its sobriquet 'the
gallant'). In the centre stands the lofty church of
St-Martin, somewhat altered since it was built in
the 12th-c. but containing much skilful restoration. The lively Saturday market takes place in
the open space outside the church.

The most interesting buildings are the 17th-c.
Ernest Rupin Museum, the 16th-c. Hôtel de
Labenche (of which you can only see the elegant
façade and the inner courtyard), and the 16th-c.
Tour des Échevins (Alderman's Tower).

BRUNIQUEL, *Tarn-et-Garonne* (15km SE of
Caussade: 5–D5). The ancient castle stands above
the picturesque town in a superb setting on a sharp
bend of the Aveyron. Here the river emerges from
its gorges and, joined by the Vère, flows on into the
Montauban plain. According to the 6th-c.
historian Gregory of Tours, a fortress was first
built on this site by Brunhilda, daughter of the
King of the Visigoths. The great square tower is
still named after her, and indeed some of the
foundations of the later 12th–13th-c. castle may
well be contemporary with that wild, cruel
princess who met a suitably violent end strapped
to the tail of a bucking horse. Precipitous views of
the river continually startle you as you explore the
castle, with its Knights' Hall, chapel, guardroom,
and an elegant Renaissance gallery with a pillared
arcade.

8km E, the ancient village and castle of **Penne-
du-Tarn** perch frighteningly over the Aveyron
gorge on a great pillar of rock that bends outward
into space at the top. Well worth a visit if you don't
mind heights.

CABRERETS, *Lot* (18km E of Cahors: 5–C5). A
village on the right bank of the river Célé, just
before it joins the Lot. Its situation is extremely
picturesque, with two castles. One, perched
alarmingly over the village, is the ruined 8th-c.
feudal castle known generally as the Château du
Diable and sometimes (a reminder of the Hundred

Years War) as the Château des Anglais. The other
is the Renaissance Château Gontaut-Biron, not
open to visitors.

The importance of Cabrerets for the tourist lies
in the **Grottes du Pech-Merle,** 3km W of the
village. These remarkable prehistoric caves,
accidentally discovered in 1922, were explored and
studied in detail by a Cabrerets priest and
prehistorian, the Abbé Lemozi. Open to the public
are over 3km of linked galleries containing some of
the best known examples of prehistoric painting,
drawing and engraving: bison, mammoths, horses,
outlined hands and even an actual footprint. The
caves are also full of weirdly shaped limestone
formations.

2km upstream, close to the road, is the Fontaine
de la Pescalerie, an underground river emerging
from the rock as a waterfall, flanked by an old mill.

CADILLAC, *Gironde* (10km N of Langon: 4–C3).
For a 14th-c. *bastide* town on the banks of the
Garonne, Cadillac is curiously disappointing.
Perhaps this is due to the barrack-like aspect of the
early 17th-c. château of the dukes of Épernon
which, from its central position, broods over the
town. Ransacked at the time of the Revolution, it
was later turned into a State prison. It contains
some monumental fireplaces with rich carving,
reputed to be remarkably fine. The town still
preserves part of its 14th-c. ramparts.

CADOUIN, *Dordogne* (10km NE of Beaumont:
4–C4). The village square is dominated by the
imposing west façade of the 12th-c. abbey church.
Austere simplicity ruled the lives of the Cistercian
monks who, in about 1100, made a clearing in the
forest here, and monastic austerity is the keynote
of the large Romanesque church they built. Even
before it was completed in 1154, the community
came into possession of a piece of cloth brought
back from the Holy Land, believed to be the
shroud that had wrapped the head of Christ at his
entombment. Pilgrims came from all over Europe
to worship the relic, and the monastery became
renowned and prosperous.

During the Hundred Years War the shroud was
removed to Toulouse for safety, but when the war
ended the monks at Toulouse refused to hand
back this valuable pilgrim attraction, despite
threats of excommunication by the Pope. Finally
four monks from Cadouin travelled to Toulouse
in the guise of religious students, removed the
shroud during the night and brought it back in
triumph to Cadouin. In the 16th-c., during the
Wars of Religion, the church became a defensive
bastion – witness the scars of enemy shot still
visible on the façade – but it was eventually
captured by the Huguenots, who then mag-
nanimously forbore to destroy it. In 1792 revolutionary vandals broke into the monastery,
ransacked the furnishings and wrecked the library,
but the holy relic was saved by the local mayor and
hidden under the floor of his house.

In the latter half of the last century the pilgrimages revived, and every September the village was crowded with worshippers from far and wide. Alas for Cadouin, in 1933 the shroud was subjected to a careful analysis which proved that it had been woven in Egypt in about the 10th-c. The pilgrimages abruptly ceased.

The adjoining cloisters, built in the 15th- and 16th-c. to replace the primitive original, suffered much damage at the time of the Revolution. The W gallery was entirely reconstructed in 1908, and patient restoration work by skilled craftsmen is still going on. The fine doorways at each corner, and the marvellous carvings and sculptures of monks in procession or at confession, of biblical scenes and various allegories, make a visit eminently rewarding. (Entry by a door to the right of the church.)

CAHORS, *Lot* (5–C5). If you arrive from the north by the N20, the last big town you have come through is Brive, 100km behind you. Entering Cahors through the 14th-c. ramparts and descending the broad main street, with its plane-trees dappling the sunlight and giving welcome shade to the pavement cafés, you feel an extra warmth in the air – your first real hint of the Midi. Cahors was once the proud capital of the old region of Quercy; now it is a genial southern provincial town which still dreams of its former glory as a thriving medieval commercial and university city. But its past goes back further than that, even to pre-Roman times.

It occupies a marvellously natural defensive site. The river Lot here makes a long loop to the S and back, providing a wide 'moat' on three sides of a peninsula with only a narrow neck of land to be defended at its northern end. What is more, on the river's W bank, just upstream from the Valentré bridge, is a prolific natural spring, the Fontaine des Chartreux, which even today provides the town with drinking water. The ancient Gauls worshipped this spring, and so did the Romans after them. Of the Roman city built within the loop of the river nothing now remains except the archway known as the PORTE DE DIANE close to the Place Thiers.

As trade slowly recovered in the early Middle Ages, a modern town grew up around the new Cathedral built in the 12th-c. on the E bank of the peninsula. The former cloth trade had faded out, but the fame of Cahors wine brought gradually increasing prosperity. When Henry II married Eleanor of Aquitaine in 1152, this part of France fell into the hands of the English, but except for a brief spell in 1160, when Henry temporarily occupied the town, Cahors managed to remain independent. Indeed, it is an indication of the sporadic nature of the long struggle between the English and the French that the 13th-c. was the city's golden age. The Lombards came here and developed it into an important banking centre, with branches in many parts of France. In 1332 a

Douglas Dickins

Pont de Valentré, Cahors

university was founded here by Jacques Duèse, a famous native of Cahors who had become Pope John XXII in succession to Clement V. Unfortunately for Cahors, the Treaty of Brétigny of 1360 ceded the whole of Quercy to the English. Under their occupation, which lasted over 50 years, trade declined and the population drained away. Later, in the Wars of Religion, Cahors was sacked by the Huguenots under Henry of Navarre in 1580. The town never recovered its former importance.

The main street, named Boulevard Gambetta after the famous statesman who was born here and in 1870 led a spirited resistance against the Prussians, runs N and S and is part of the N20. Most of the old part of the town lies to the E of it, and is not much changed from what it was in medieval times. The Cathedral of ST-ÉTIENNE (St-Stephen), with its severe Gothic façade, still retains much of its 12th-c. fabric, including its remarkable Byzantine domed roof and its frescoes – and above all the marvellous N doorway (once part of the original W façade), whose tympanum of the Ascension is a masterpiece of Romanesque sculpture to be compared with those of Moissac, Beaulieu-sur-Dordogne and elsewhere. Unfortunately the cloisters were badly mutilated by the Huguenots in 1580.

Other buildings well worth seeing are: the MAISON DE ROALDÈS, a grand 15th-c. house facing the river, near the Cathedral; the COLLÈGE PELLÉGRI, part of the 14th-c. University established by Pope John XXII, with the neighbouring massive TOUR DU CHÂTEAU DU ROI, once part of the Governor's quarters and now a prison; a short walk to the N are the church of St-Barthélmy, where Pope John was baptized, and the last remaining tower of the old Bishop's Palace.

On the W side of the town is the great PONT DE VALENTRÉ, a remarkable bridge which from medieval times guarded the river as an armed fortress, with its central observation tower and its outer towers closed by portcullises – and was never taken. It is now a road bridge, and it is worth going across for the splendid view of the bridge with the weir below it and the roofs of the town behind it.

CAMBO-LES-BAINS, *Pyrénées-Atlantiques* (4–E2). A good centre for exploring the French Basque region. Cambo is a hill town 20km SE of Bayonne, enjoying a gentle climate all the year round, with a delightful park along the bank of the river Nive, good restaurants which provide Basque menus (including salmon and trout from local mountain streams), the usual pelota *fronton*, and wonderful views towards the Basque coast and the Atlantic foothills of the Pyrenees. Edmond Rostand, poet and dramatist, author of *Cyrano de Bergerac*, lived here; a short drive NW on the Bayonne road is his house 'Arnaga', now a Rostand museum with beautiful gardens.

CAP FERRET, *Gironde* (4–C2). Atlantic seaside resort and watering-place on the end of the peninsula which forms the western side of the Arcachon basin (*see* Arcachon). Sand dunes, pine woods, swimming, sailing, and plenty of oysters. The lighthouse is well worth a visit. From the platform at the top there is a splendid view of the Arcachon basin (with its expanse of oyster beds at low tide), the pine forests, the ocean surf, and the famous Dune du Pilat to the S of Arcachon.

CARENNAC, *Lot* (8km N of Padirac: 5–C5). A quiet village of lovely old brown-tiled houses on the S bank of the Dordogne, and renowned for the W doorway of its 12th-c. church. Carennac was once the seat of an important priory founded in the 10th-c. In the late 17th-c. the senior prior was François de Salignac de la Mothe-Fénélon (more conveniently known simply as Fénélon), who later became Archbishop of Cambrai but achieved more lasting fame in French literature as the author of a romance called *Télémaque*, written while he was in office here. Of the original priory, abolished and much damaged at the time of the Revolution, only a small castle (of not much interest), the priory tower and a fortified gateway remain.

Park under the trees by the river and walk through the fortified gateway into a narrow street where, at the top of a short flight of steps, stands the beautiful doorway of the church of St-Pierre.

Carennac: west doorway of the church

Jean Feuille

The vigorous white-stone carving of the tympanum over the door, representing Christ in Majesty, is better preserved than the one at Beaulieu-sur-Dordogne (across the river to the NE – *see entry*) but in the style of the same 'Toulouse School'. The interior of the church is rather dimly lit but pleasantly simple, with a painted ceiling and a 16th-c. Entombment (*mise au tombeau*) in the S transept, close to a door leading into the partially restored but dreamily peaceful cloisters.

CASTELNAU, Château de, *Lot* (7km NW of St-Céré: 5–C5). Visible for miles around, this massive red-sandstone castle occupies a dominating site overlooking the confluence of three rivers – the Cère, the Bave and the Dordogne. It began life in the 11th-c. as a single keep, the same round tower that still exists today, but by the end of the Hundred Years War it had grown into one of the largest fortresses in the south of France, with a garrison of over a thousand men. From the 17th-c. onwards it suffered from neglect, then from the vandalism of the Revolution, and finally in 1851 from a fire that swept through the interior. However, about the turn of the century it was acquired by Jean Mouliérat, a tenor of the Opéra-Comique, who restored and furnished it, and left it to the State on his death in 1932.

The site is roughly triangular, with a sturdy round tower at each corner. Within the walls, close to the ruins of the original keep, stands the huge square 60m-high 'Saracen's Tower'. The restored residential quarters now contain a remarkable collection of furnishings, tapestries from Aubusson and Beauvais, and various other art treasures. The views from the tower and the extensive ramparts are panoramic – the Dordogne valley to the N towards Beaulieu and W towards the Cirque de Montvalent, the Cère valley to the NE, the Bave valley SE towards St-Céré, Loubressac on its hill to the SW, and, silhouetted on the NW horizon, the ruins of Turenne castle (*see entry*).

This last landmark is a reminder of the days when Castelnau was under the suzerainty of Turenne. After a baronial dispute, settled by Louis VIII with a humorous 13th-c. equivalent of 'farthing damages', the fief payable by Castelnau to its overlord was ordained to be one new-laid egg per annum. This was duly delivered all the way to Turenne – 25km away as the crow flies, and a good deal further by bumpy 13th-c. roads – on a bed of straw in a ceremonial cart solemnly drawn by four oxen.

CASTELNAUD, Château de, *Dordogne* (9km SW of Sarlat: 5–C5). Once the most formidable castle in the area, Castelnaud perches on a rocky pinnacle commanding a remarkable prospect of the Dordogne and Céou valleys.

In his Albigensian crusade Simon de Montfort only captured it with difficulty; he was so impressed with its strategic situation that instead of dismantling it, like his other fortress prizes, he installed a garrison and increased its defences. During the Hundred Years War, with the connivance of its pro-Plantagenet lord, it was occupied by the English. From its battlements they could clearly see the enemy-held castle of Beynac (*see entry*) only 2km to the N. In the Wars of Religion in the 16th-c. the castle withstood sieges and attacks by the Catholics. But in the 150 years of peace after the Revolution, Castelnaud suffered more damage than in all the wars of previous centuries – through neglect and the plundering of the stonework for building material. Restoration is in progress; the huge square keep has been reconstructed (with a peaked stone-tiled roof that surely was not there originally), and work has begun on repairing the massive, rounded walls facing SE, overlooking the beautiful village whose old stone houses climb steeply up from river level.

The walk up is well worth while. The view from the castle watch-path is one of the best in the Dordogne. The ground falls away in a sheer cliff; immediately below is the road, with the bridge crossing the river. The Dordogne here approaches from the E in a wide loop, then swings away northwards to Beynac, whose dramatic castle stands equally high on a cliff, facing towards its old enemy. To the right, between high wooded slopes, lies the long valley of the Céou, a bubbling little river which can be seen emptying itself into the Dordogne a few yards upstream of the bridge.

To the left, half-hidden in the trees, is the turreted *manoir*, or residential château, of **Fayrac**, privately owned and not open to the public, though the road along the river gives a splendid view of it. If you continue on the same road you come to the château of **Les Milandes**, which has a historical connection with Castelnaud. In 1489 the lord of Castelnaud, to pacify his wife, who found the austere castle on the rock too bleak for civilized living, built Les Milandes as a *château de plaisance* on an agreeable site sloping down to the river; even so, its walls are so strong that it withstood a siege in the Wars of Religion. It remained in the family until the Revolution. More recently, it was for some years the residence of the famous singer and cabaret artiste Josephine Baker, and it was here that she set up home for her large family of adopted children of all nationalities and colours. The château is now open to the public all the year round.

CASTILLON, *Gironde* (9km SE of St-Émilion: 4–C3). This busy little town on the Bordeaux–Bergerac road is also known as Castillon-la-Bataille because it was here in 1453 that the English, under the aged Sir John Talbot, were routed in battle by the French king's army. This defeat led to the evacuation of the English from the whole of France except Calais, and so marked the end of the Hundred Years War. After the battle the town, not at all pleased at being rescued from the English 'yoke', was ransacked by the French army. Talbot was killed at the height of the battle, the spot being marked by a small monument by the river, 2km E from the town along a minor road; he is also remembered in the name of a renowned Bordeaux wine.

CASTILLONÈS, *Lot-et-Garonne* (23km S of Bergerac: 4–C4). A former hilltop *bastide* with a modest square surrounded by arcades. Worth a visit if only for the beautiful modern abstract stained-glass windows in the little church on the corner of the square.

CASTRES, *Tarn* (5–D6). A busy industrial town that has been a centre of cloth-weaving for over 500 years. The river Agout flows under several bridges connecting the two sides of the town, and there are some attractive old houses whose balconies overhang the water. The old quarter is on the W bank, centred on the huge 17th–18th-c. Baroque Cathedral of St-Benoît. Facing it is the former episcopal palace, now the town hall, which still maintains along the river bank the formal gardens laid out by the great gardener Le Nôtre, with an intricate pattern of topiary which must be a hedge-cutter's nightmare. Also in the same building is the Musée Goya, containing a remarkable collection of Spanish painting bequeathed to the town at the end of the last century by a local painter.

A 15km drive on the N622 takes you E and NE into the strange region of the **Sidobre**, an area of wild ravines and huge granite rocks tumbled one on another in an awesome 'chaos', sometimes precariously balanced, sometimes in bizarre shapes, sometimes completely covering the river bed, the water gurgling invisibly beneath.

CAUTERETS, *Hautes-Pyrénées* (4–E3). A popular spa and a centre for wintersports, climbing and camping, with many hotels, a casino, a theatre, a cinema and an indoor swimming pool. The absinthe-green river, the Gave de Cauterets, hurries through the town on its way from the mountains to Lourdes 20km N. Out of the surrounding hills flow a dozen springs of sulphurated water which from Roman times have brought illustrious visitors here – among them Victor Hugo and George Sand – seeking relief from respiratory ailments.

In the 16th-c. the childless princess Jeanne d'Albret was brought here by her mother, Marguerite of Navarre, because the waters were supposed to cure sterility in women; whether it was as a result of taking the waters, or because her husband was inspired by his mother-in-law's bawdy tales, the *Heptameron*, some of which she wrote here, is not known – but there is no doubt that in due course the princess was delivered of a child, which was fortunate for France because he grew up to be the great King Henri IV.

From the esplanade by the casino there are tremendous views of the mountainous country-side, which can be explored in many stimulating excursions – notably S on N21c to the waterfalls of Cerisey, Lutour and Pont d'Espagne, and beyond to the deep blue Lac de Gaube in a bowl closely surrounded by mountains.

CHÂLUS, *Haute-Vienne* (4–B4). An old town with the ruins of an 11th-c. hilltop castle which played a fateful part in English history. Richard Cœur-de-Lion laid siege to it in 1199 – legend has it that his vassal, the Vicomte de Limoges, had discovered a fabulous gold treasure and refused to hand over the share claimed by the king as his overlord. During the siege a bolt from a crossbowman stationed on the tall granite keep (which is still there today) struck the king a mortal blow in the shoulder. The archer, captured in the fighting, was pardoned by the king from his deathbed, but flayed alive soon afterwards.

CHAMBON-SUR-VOUEIZE, *Creuse* (5–A6). Approaching Chambon from the north along the D917, you travel for a while alongside the Voueize as it flows through a series of ravines. The river then emerges into a green valley, joins the Tardes and provides a delightful setting for this peaceful little town, which boasts one of the largest and most interesting Limousin churches in the region.

Ste-Valérie is an abbey church dating from the 11th–12th-c., built in granite, with two square towers; one a 13th-c. clock tower over the porch, the other of a later date with a shingle roof in the form of a double pyramid surmounted by a *lanterne* and a short spire. This second tower is not over the transept crossing as you might expect, but immediately W of it, over the last two bays of the nave. The interior of the church is long and lofty, with a nave of nine bays. The first seven bays are well lit from windows above as well as from those in the side-aisles. The pillars, each in four columns, are elegant and slender, without capitals, and lift the eye to the soaring vaulted roof. This vaulting, added in 1852, conceals 15th-c. wood framework resembling an inverted boat-hull, and judging from photographs it seems a pity it can't be revealed in its original state. An odd thing about this church is that after the first seven bays of the nave the whole building does a slight kink to the left, so that the eastern end, from the sombre choir to the triple chevet, is on a slightly different axis.

The simple severity and loftiness of the church are especially apparent as you walk up the side-aisles and behind the choir to the ambulatory at the rear of the altar. The S arm of the transept has two apsidal chapels, and the SW corner of it abuts on to the curved wall of a tower that was the Charter Room of the original abbey. The N arm was entirely rebuilt in the 13th-c., with no apsidal chapels; instead, the N extremity is divided into two storeys, with a chapel below and a gallery above, probably designed to hide and protect the relics of Ste-Valérie in troubled times; access to the gallery is only possible by two narrow staircases, one from the ambulatory and one indirectly from the S arm of the transept.

Ste-Valérie was a medieval martyred saint, and a pilgrimage still takes place here every year. A 15th-c. painted panel depicting her martyrdom is in one of the S side-aisles, and her silver reliquary bust can be seen on application to the presbytery.

CHANCELADE, Ancienne Abbaye de, *Dordogne* (3km NW of Périgueux: 4–C4). Just off the road to Ribérac, this once wealthy abbey could scarcely have hoped to escape the vandalism of the Hundred Years War and the later wars of religion. Much of the original 12th-c. buildings and their subsequent restorations were destroyed; the abbey living quarters we see today are 15th-c., while the cruciform church and its square tower, with a mixture of blind and open arcading, were largely rebuilt in the 17th-c. Restoration work about ten years ago uncovered two good 14th-c. frescoes in the choir – one of them depicting St-Thomas-à-Becket. In one of the rooms in the former residential building is a remarkable collection of religious art. Close by, looking over a village green, stands a little gem of a 12th-c. church, the chapel of St-Jean.

See also Merlande, a priory established about 8km N by the monks of Chancelade.

COLLONGES-LA-ROUGE, *Corrèze* (14km SE of Brive: 5–C5). It is easy to miss Collonges. It nestles in its bowl just off the D38 Brive–Meyssac road, and is one of the more endearing oddities of the Corrèze. A few years ago it had lapsed into a state of some neglect, but it is now being lovingly restored. Built mostly in the 16th–17th-c., and constructed entirely of the unusual local purplish-red stone, this miniature rose-red city was a sort of weekend retreat for the nobles and courtiers of the 'great Turenne', famous lord of the region. Turenne (*see entry*) is a bare 6km canter to the W, and one can imagine what a relief this little haven must have been from the rigours of that stark fortress. Each family built its small-scale castle or palace according to its taste and station, with turrets, mullioned windows and ornaments in profusion, creating an exclusive 'garden city'.

Cars are not allowed to enter, so you must park just off the main road and walk. The first house you come to is the Maison de la Sirène, a rather grandiose title perhaps for such a little mermaid holding her lute and regarding you at eye-level from the porch. A covered passage through what was once part of a defensive wall leads to the little square, where there is a 12th-c. Limousin-style church with a fine tympanum of the Ascension above the entrance. Close by stands the old Penitents' Chapel, and on one side of the square is the beautiful covered market whose roof also shelters the communal bread oven.

Behind the church, the Rue de la Garde brings you to the fortified Castel de Vassignac, originally the home of the captain-general of Turenne and

lord of Collonges; you can just get a glimpse of its lovely garden. In the opposite direction is the Château de Benges with its pepperpot turret and stone 'fish-scale' roof.

We are told that the best way to see Collonges is to arrange to have dinner there and see it after dark – by moonlight if you are lucky, or romantically illuminated by floodlights.

3km SW of Collonges, in the village of **Saillac**, is an enchanting little 12th-c. fortified church. Dark and secret, it guards its ancient peace and simple faith. Its tympanum is no august Christ in Majesty but a happy scene in painted stone of the Three Kings arriving with gifts for the infant in his mother's arms, their tired horses' heads snorting from a corner. This is supported on a twisted column carved with a continuous procession of animals and flowers.

CONDOM, *Gers* (4–D4). A busy town on the river Baise (a tributary of the Garonne) and centre of the Armagnac industry. Armagnac is a brandy, made in much the same way as Cognac but matured in black oak which gives it a slightly different flavour. Many prefer it to Cognac, finding it smoother than any but the very top-class Cognac. Apply to the tourist office (Syndicat d'Initiative) opposite the W end of the Cathedral for admission to the Musée d'Armagnac or a visit to one of the Armagnac plants.

The large Cathedral of St-Pierre is early 16th-c., with a Flamboyant Gothic S door and some 19th- and 20th-c. stained glass. The huge cloister adjoining its N wall was badly damaged at the time of the Revolution.

5km W, surrounded by Armagnac vineyards, is the sleepy village of **Larressingle**, which gives its name to one of the popular Armagnac brands. It is really a miniature 13th-c. fortified city, relatively unspoilt, with its gateway and some of its outer walls still intact.

CONQUES, *Aveyron* (5–C6). A 'must' for any tourist in the area of the upper Lot and Aveyron valleys. Those medieval 'tourists', the pilgrims, found Conques more than just a welcome staging post between Le Puy and Moissac on their arduous journey to Santiago de Compostella; it was a place of pilgrimage in its own right. Not only is its very position startlingly beautiful – like Rocamadour it clings to steep slopes above a gorge – but it also contains one of the finest of all Romanesque churches, with a famous tympanum on the W doorway, and perhaps the richest ecclesiastical treasure outside Rome.

You will probably approach Conques on the D601 which runs N from Rodez. To follow the pilgrim route into the town from the valley, park near the bridge at the bottom; a short walk up the Rue Charlemagne will bring you to the church. If you prefer to drive up, follow the winding D42 into the middle of the village, which is full of carefully restored old houses with steep-pitched

Conques: the nave of the church of Ste-Foy

roofs of rounded slates. But it is the church of Ste-Foy that is the glory of Conques.

It seems surprisingly large for such a small place until one remembers that it was built when the pilgrimage fever was at its height. There had been chapels here ever since the 4th-c., destroyed in turn by the Franks and the Saracens, and rebuilt again by the monks. But it was not until the 9th-c. that the abbey came into possession of the relics of the young Christian girl saint, Ste Foy, martyred at Agen at the beginning of the 4th-c. – a monk from Conques actually went to Agen and *stole* the relics. A spate of reported miracles soon afterwards happily confirmed their importance; the pilgrimages increased, kings and princes came with gifts of gold and silver and precious stones, and the abbey prospered.

In the 11th-c. the building of the present church began, and by the middle of the 12th-c. it stood virtually as we see it today. In the Wars of Religion the monastery buildings were destroyed by Huguenots; though the treasure was saved, the church was partially burned, and remained in a state of neglect for nearly 300 years until the Beaux-Arts restored it about the middle of the last century.

The ground plan is cruciform. Over the transept crossing rises an octagonal tower with an octagonal spire; at the W end the façade is flanked by two shorter square towers, each with a pyramid spire. The W doorway is one of the great masterpieces of Romanesque stone-carving. Two stout doors are separated by a wide, flat column of bare stonework; above them, framed by a simple semi-circular arch supported on twin pillars, is the magnificent tympanum, the more effective because it is the only area of carving on the whole doorway.

It represents the Last Judgment, with God in the centre raising his right hand in blessing; on the left, turning towards him, are the Virgin Mary and St Peter followed by saints, abbots and other worthies, while Ste Foy herself kneels below them in supplication; underneath, Abraham welcomes the elect into a celestial Jerusalem. The whole of the right-hand side is devoted to the horrors of damnation, and one grisly little scene shows demons shoving sinners into the 'throat' of hell to be welcomed by Satan himself. It is a busy, rich, complicated design, held together by rigid horizontal lines bearing Latin inscriptions.

Inside the church, the first impression is of great space, created by the loftiness of the nave and the severity of the architecture, relieved only by the richly varied designs of the capitals. The choir, too, is immensely high, with an ambulatory which allowed the pilgrims to walk behind the altar and pay homage to the reliquary treasure, which in those days was exposed there to public view.

Today that treasure, the finest collection in France of 9th-c. to 16th-c. goldsmiths' and silversmiths' work, is guarded in the presbytery on the S side of the church, and is open to view, for a modest fee, from Easter to the end of October. The oldest piece is a 9th-c. gold casket adorned with gold filigree and inset with precious stones, but the major item is the crowned, seated, and coldly-staring reliquary statue of Ste-Foy. It was made in the 10th-c. of wood covered in beaten gold and studded with a dazzling assembly of the precious stones donated by the crowned heads and other wealthy pilgrims of medieval Europe.

CORDES, *Tarn* (5–D5). Sometimes known as 'Cordes-in-the-Sky', this dramatically situated fortified village stands high up on the edge of a steep spur that rises out of the Cérou valley, 25km NW of Albi. It was built in the early 13th-c. by one of the counts of Toulouse as a defensive refuge against Simon de Montfort's crusade against the Albigensian heretics (*see* Albi). When that vicious campaign and the subsequent Inquisition were over, the inhabitants settled down as traders in cloth, linen-weaving, leather and dyeing. A century of prosperity was ended by the quarrels of fighting bishops, attacks by Huguenots, and finally plague. The little town, which owed its origin to its isolated site, now nearly died of it. Happily, during World War II, while this part of France was still unoccupied by the Germans, Cordes was 'discovered' by a painter called Yves Brayer. Attracted by its romantic situation and the decaying beauty of its medieval houses, he founded here a community of artists and craftsmen. The 14th- and 15th-c. houses were gradually restored, and the 20th-c. tourists came.

When first built, the town had two circles, or rather ovals, of ramparts, each with a defended gateway to the E and to the W. Attackers who breached the outer gateway were dismayed to find themselves faced with a second. Later a third and yet a fourth line of ramparts were added, though not much of these is now left. The best of the medieval houses, like the handsome House of the Great Falconer (now the *mairie*) and the House of the Huntsman with its sculpted hunting scenes, are at the top end of the steep Grand'-Rue which climbs through the middle of the town. The church, though much altered, retains the original 13th-c. transept, chancel and tower; the interior wall decorations are a 19th-c. attempt to imitate those of Albi cathedral.

It is worth climbing the stairs to the top of the church tower, for this was the old watching post when the inhabitants were expecting trouble. It has splendid views of the hills and valleys of the wild plateau where the Cérou flows NW to join the Aveyron, and you can see for yourself that the look-outs were able to give plenty of warning.

CÔTE D'ARGENT (From Soulac: 4–B2 to Hendaye: 4–E1, E2). The long, straight Atlantic coastline stretching 250km from the mouth of the Gironde in the north to Hendaye in the south. Except for the basin of Arcachon (*see entry*), it is a virtually unbroken line of sandy beaches, surf rollers, high dunes and lakes – and at the back of it lies the flat country of the Landes with its vast areas of pine forest (*see* Landes). If you are looking for a holiday with swimming and sunbathing on gorgeous beaches, and you don't mind sharing them with thousands of like-minded French families, the Côte d'Argent is the place – though you should be warned that the Atlantic weather and the coastal currents can be uncertain.

See entries for Cap Ferret, Arcachon, Biarritz, St-Jean-de-Luz and Hendaye. Other resorts are **Soulac, Montalivet, Mimizan, Hossegor** (and **Cap Breton** next door to it).

DAX, *Landes* (4–D2). A well-known watering-place on the left bank of the river Adour, at the S limit of the Landes forest region. Its hot springs and mud baths have brought relief to rheumatic sufferers ever since Roman times. One of the principal sights of the town is the Fontaine Chaude, a huge pool surrounded by arcades at the SE corner of the Place Borda, where the natural spring has been disgorging its hot mineral water at a temperature of 64°C for over 2000 years.

Dax came into English possession when Henry Plantagenet married Eleanor of Aquitaine in 1152, and did not become French again until 300 years later, two years before the English were finally thrown out of Aquitaine. The cathedral built during the English occupation was pulled down to make way for the present 17th-c. classical building, but the original richly decorated 13th-c.

doorway was preserved and adorns the interior of the N arm of the transept.

The town is well equipped with hotels, restaurants and a casino, and there are pleasant walks beside the river and in the riverside Parc Théodore-Denis, where the only Roman fragments are to be seen. Across the bridge, in the closely neighbouring town of St-Paul-lès-Dax, is an interesting little 11th-c. church; on the exterior wall at the E end is a charming series of bas-reliefs depicting biblical scenes.

DOMME, *Dordogne* (9km S of Sarlat: 5–C5). A hilltop *bastide*, and perhaps the best-preserved and most beautiful small town on the Dordogne. The road winds uphill from the village of Cénac and enters through the Porte del Bos, one of the three remaining original gateways. A little one-way street curves under an arch and into the bottom square. It is best to park there, near the war memorial. From here the narrow streets climb steeply past lovely old houses to the top square, a fine open space set in a frame of perfect ochre-stone houses of great variety, with the church on one corner, the turreted Maison du Gouverneur dominating the E side, and in the centre the ancient Halle with its little balcony on round stone pillars.

Just N of the square, past the church and through an arbour of trees, is the *barre*, a stone balustrade on the edge of a precipitous drop to the river and with a breathtaking view. The Dordogne winds in a tremendous loop through fields of maize and tobacco, the banks lined with poplars and willows. On the opposite side of the valley, extending E and W for 40km or more, are the rolling, wooded hills of Périgord Noir, broken here and there by great walls of ochre cliff, like those behind La Roque-Gageac clearly visible to the NW. The top of Château Montfort can just be seen behind trees to the NE. An even better view, including the castle of Beynac, can be obtained from the new garden on the W edge of the town, reached by the clifftop path which slopes down from the *barre*. This path was the scene of a famous exploit during the Wars of Religion: the inhabitants of Domme thought the cliff was impregnable and so left it unguarded, but one night the redoubtable Protestant captain Geoffroi de Vivans scaled it with 30 men and took the town by surprise.

Domme was built in about 1280 on the orders of King Philip the Bold (see the inscription on the Hôtel de la Monnaie in the bottom square – the oldest house in Domme). In 1347 the town was captured by an English army of Edward III and occupied for 22 years. The old castle which used to guard the steep western edge of the ridge is no longer there; the foundations exist, but are not accessible to the public.

The eastern gateway, the 13th-c. Porte des Tours, has two round guardhouse towers flanking the archway. Recent deciphering of the graffiti engraved on the interior walls showed that from 1307 they housed prisoners from the suppressed order of Templars. One of the inscriptions, 'Clement V, destroyer of the Temple', echoes the dying curse of the Grand Master at the stake, correctly prophesying the early deaths of Philip the Fair and Pope Clement. The towers, now roofless, are not open to the public – only to the wind and the rain which, sad to relate, are fast eroding the historic inscriptions.

The Halle in the top square is also the entrance to the Grottes, an interesting series of caves with stalactites, etc. which extend for about ½km and bring you out at the W end to a startling view of the valley and a steep climb up a long flight of steps (*not* for the infirm). The walk back into the centre of the town takes you past many delightful ancient houses and walled gardens.

DORAT, Le, *Haute-Vienne* (4, 5–A4, A5). An attractive little town 50km N of Limoges, with one of the finest churches in Limousin. The 12th-c. collegiate church of St-Pierre, built of pink granite, has two belfries – one, rather squat, over the W door, and the other over the transept crossing, three-tiered, surmounted by a soaring spire and topped by a 13th-c. copper angel – from which (when it was gilded) the town probably took its name. The W doorway is set within a rippling, receding archway of four scalloped covings – a suggestion here of Moorish influence. Inside the door you find yourself at the top of a wide flight of a dozen steps; the effect, as you look down into the sombre nave towards the brightly lit transept dome and chancel, is noble and spacious. The font, carved with a design of lions, is older than the church, and very beautiful. The crypt, too, below the chancel, dates from the 11th-c.; it is sturdily simple, almost primitive, and remarkably well lit from low, deep, barrel-vaulted windows.

EAUX-BONNES, *Pyrénées-Atlantiques* (4–E3). An attractive spa and ski resort 40km S of Pau, in beautiful mountain surroundings. The climate is temperate, and the waters are renowned for the treatment of respiratory and rheumatic ailments. There is a casino. A good centre for excursions and local walks, one of which takes you a short distance SE along the N618 to the impressive twin waterfall of Le Gros Hêtre.

ENTRAYGUES, *Aveyron* (5–C6). A small town situated at the junction of the Lot and the Truyère, in the centre of a region of great beauty. An undistinguished château stands on the point where the rivers meet; a church and several medieval houses group close behind it, and a little way upstream a simple 13th-c. bridge spans the Truyère.

The area, full of rivers, streams, dams and lakes, is a fisherman's paradise, and everything in the way of equipment can be obtained in the town. The surrounding country is spectacularly beauti-

ful, with any number of high viewpoints – e.g. the Puy de l'Arbre to the NW, and the Puy de Montabes to the E. Motorists should be warned that many of the roads here are tortuous; seemingly endless *virages*, corniche-type zigzags and steep hills can make driving hard work, but the rewards in terms of scenery are tremendous. Upstream from Entraygues, both the Lot and the Truyère hurtle through dramatic gorges; some of the hydro-electric dams, too, are exciting, beautiful in their own way; the easiest one to get to is the **Barrage de Couesque**, about 8km up the Truyère, with a height of 60m and a width across the curving top of some 275m.

Altogether a good centre for excursions. Conques, Rodez, Estaing and Espalion are all within easy reach (*see entries*).

ENTRE-DEUX-MERS, *Gironde* (SE of Bordeaux: 4–C3). A well-known wine district producing mostly dryish white wine of good but not great quality. The 'two seas' of the title are in fact the rivers Garonne and Dordogne. The area is a rough triangle starting from the junction of the two rivers and spreading outwards to near Langon on the Garonne and to Ste-Foy-la-Grande on the Dordogne.

The countryside is the most beautiful of all the Bordeaux wine districts – gently undulating hills with woods, streams and private little châteaux, interspersed with sloping fields where the vines are often grown in strips alongside other crops. At **St-Ferme** and **Blasimon** (E and N of Sauveterre respectively) are sad but impressive remains of two medieval abbey churches, and on the extreme edge of the area, 22km due S of Ste-Foy-la-Grande, is the ruined but romantic hilltop castle of **Duras**, ransacked at the time of the Revolution but now being restored and well worth a visit if you are in the neighbourhood.

The only section of this area that does not qualify as Entre-Deux-Mers is a narrow strip along the right bank of the Garonne, north of Langon, where the wines (mostly red) are classified as Premières Côtes de Bordeaux. Opposite Langon, on a rocky eminence close to the river, stands the ancient wine town of **St-Macaire**; 2km N is **Verdelais**, where the writer François Mauriac lived and where the painter Toulouse-Lautrec lies buried; 3km N again is **Ste-Croix-du-Mont**, another hilltop wine town, followed quickly by **Loupiac**, where the Roman poet Ausonius had a villa and grew vines; then the fortified towns of Cadillac and Rions.

ESPALION, *Aveyron* (5–C6). An endearing small town on the Lot, with a small Renaissance château standing on rocks at the river's edge, a graceful 13th-c. red-sandstone bridge reserved for pedestrians (the modern bridge downstream carries the traffic now), and many old balconied houses hanging over their reflections in the water. There is nothing much else of architectural interest, but it is a favourite resort of artists, and the neighbourhood is full of interest.

On the hill to the SW stand the ruins of a feudal château; still on the S bank, a short walk SE brings you to the little 11th-c. red-stone church of **Perse** with a naive but moving tympanum over the S porch. To the NW, between Estaing and Entraygues (*see entries*), the Lot tumbles through dramatic gorges. To the E, the D6 leads first to the neighbouring fortified village of **St-Côme d'Olt**, full of narrow cobbled streets and ancient buildings, then on towards the barrage of **Castelnau-Lassouts**. The road to Rodez (which you really should visit, only 28km SW – *see entry*) winds uphill to cross the Causse de Comtal; about 10km out of Espalion a turn to the right takes you immediately into the extraordinary little town of **Bozouls** on the edge of a canyon, with a striking modern church in the shape of the bows of a ship.

ESTAING, *Aveyron* (4km NW of Espalion: 5–C6). A quiet, enchanting medieval town on the upper Lot, dominated by the 15th–16th-c. green-clad château of the Estaing family with its immensely tall keep. (The château is inhabited by a religious community, but is usually opened to visitors on application.) A five-arched Gothic bridge of satisfying simplicity spans the river and carries a statue of François d'Estaing, who, when Bishop of Rodez, was responsible for erecting the great tower of the cathedral there. On the first Sunday of every July the town abandons itself, as it has done for hundreds of years, to a fête in honour of St Fleuret, the inhabitants taking part in a colourful procession dressed as saints, angels, pilgrims and historical figures.

ÉVAUX-LES-BAINS, *Creuse* (5–A6). A small spa town 25km SW of Montluçon. There are ruins of Roman baths here, including a marble-tiled floor, and today the same radio-active waters – pouring from 30-odd springs at the rate of a million litres a day – are used in the thermal baths for the treatment of rheumatism and neuro-arthritis. The town itself is rather dull, except for the large Romanesque church and its unique 11th-c. belfry porch in five storeys, the top storey (13th-c.) octagonal and supporting a slender spire. The rest of the church has suffered badly over the ages; it was pillaged and burned in the 15th-c., rebuilt in Gothic style, restored in the 17th-c. after the roof caved in, badly burned in 1942. The latest restoration has been beautifully done, with modern stained-glass windows in marvellously vivid colours.

Recommended excursions: 5km W to Chambon-sur-Voueize for its splendid church (*see entry*), and about 17km N to the Rochebut dam just below the junction of the Cher and the Tardes.

EYZIES-DE-TAYAC, Les, *Dordogne* (4, 5–C4, C5). Well named 'the capital of Prehistory', for it was here in the narrow cliff-lined valley of the Vézère that the discoveries by the Frenchman Lartet and the Englishman Christy, just over 100 years ago, revolutionized the whole approach to the study of early man, and turned it into a science. If you are an enthusiast you should plan to stay here two or three days (there are good hotels and restaurants in the village), but in any case you should at least spend an hour or so in the fascinating museum (remembering that it shuts for lunch at 12 noon sharp) and then visit two or three of the cave sites listed below, all within easy reach.

The museum is housed in the reconstructed ruins of a feudal castle, halfway up the stratified cliff which dominates the centre of the village. Looking up from the main street you can see, under the rock overhang to the left of the museum, the brooding statue of 'Cro-Magnon Man' carved by the sculptor Paul Dardé in 1930. Taken over by the State in 1913, the museum has been steadily enlarged from its modest beginnings until today it is one of the most important of its kind in France. It tells the exciting story of the discoveries, illustrating it with examples of prehistoric skeletons, stone and bone tools, bones of mammoths, actual carvings, and reproductions of cave paintings in Lascaux and elsewhere in the area. Further enlargements to the museum are in progress.

Among the sites well worth visiting are the following:

Grotte de Font-de-Gaume ($\frac{1}{4}$km E on the Sarlat road). A long, narrow passage into the hillside brings you to a series of chambers with prehistoric engravings and coloured drawings on the rock face depicting the reindeer, mammoths and other animals hunted by primitive man.

Grotte des Combarelles (3km E on the Sarlat road). Two cave tunnels, also with rock drawings and engravings of animals of the chase.

La Mouthe ($\frac{1}{4}$km S on the D706, then 2km on a signposted lane to the left). A narrow cave with wall-paintings and drawings of horses, bison, etc. – the first such ornamented cave to be discovered in the region.

Gorge d'Enfer ($\frac{1}{4}$km NW on the Périgueux road). A short walk up a pleasant wooded valley takes you past a rock shelter in the gaping throat of a huge cliff overhang, and through a small open-air zoo of descendants of the bison, red deer, emu, wild boar and other animals who roamed these parts in prehistoric times.

Grotte du Grand Roc and **Grotte de Carpe-Diem** (a few yards further along the Périgueux road) are both cave tunnels with illuminated stalactites, stalagmites and weird crystallizations.

Grotte de Rouffignac (9km NW on the Périgueux road, then signposted to the right). A fascinating, but chilly, trip by a small electric railway through 4km of underground galleries and chambers whose walls are rich in prehistoric outline drawings and engravings of rhinoceros, stags, bison and mammoths. Records show that these caves have been known since the 15th-c., but the rock engravings and drawings were not seriously studied until 1956.

If you are interested in the adventure of cave exploration, visit the Musée de Spéléologie (½km NW on the Périgueux road). The museum occupies four chambers hewn out of the rock (once the fortress of Tayac), and illustrates the techniques of pot-holing along with models explaining the geology of the area.

These are only some of the many places to see in the vicinity of Les Eyzies. For a list apply to the ticket office at the Prehistory Museum.

(*See also the essay on* The Caves of Prehistoric Man *at the beginning of this book.*)

FIGEAC, *Lot* (5–C5). The old centre and the churches of this busy town on the river Célé underwent considerable restoration after being badly damaged during the Wars of Religion. Now ugly modern suburbs surround what is left of the old town. The most interesting building is the 13th-c. Mint (Hôtel de la Monnaie) in the Place Vival, where money was minted at various times for the kings of both France and England; it now houses the tourist office and, upstairs, a museum which has one room devoted to a well-known Egyptologist who was born in Figeac in 1790 – J. F. Champollion, who helped the Englishman Thomas Young to decipher the ancient Egyptian hieroglyphics on the famous Rosetta Stone, now in the British Museum in London; a duplicate of the stone is exhibited here. Other old houses, some dating from the 14th- and 15th-c., are in the Rue Gambetta and the Rue Delzhens.

FOIX, *Ariège* (5–E5). Although capital of the Ariège department, this is a quiet little town with mostly narrow, winding, climbing streets. As you wander through them you get frequent glimpses of the triple-towered château perched romantically on its pinnacle of rock at the edge of the town. The church, which has fine 15th-c. choir-stalls, stands near the junction of the rivers Ariège and Arget, on the site of a former abbey built over the grave of St Volusien, an archbishop of Tours who was martyred in 497. From the church a short walk due W brings you to the winding path up to the château, well worth a visit if only for its marvellous panorama of the Pyrenees. This once formidable castle was built in 1012 by the Vicomte de Carcassonne for his son, who then assumed the title of Comte de Foix. During the 13th-c. Albigensian crusade (*see* Albi) it survived repeated assaults by the dreaded Simon de Montfort, but in 1272, under siege because the Comte de Foix refused to recognize the sovereignty of the King of France, it was forced to surrender when the besieging army of Philip the Bold began to excavate the actual rock on which it is based.

6½km NW is the subterranean river of **La-bouiche**, where you can take a 2km boat journey through an illuminated Aladdin's cave of fantastic limestone formations.

Just S of **Lavelanet**, about 30km SE of Foix, are the grim ruins of the **Château de Montségur**, scene of the last and most horrible episode in the Albigensian crusade. In 1244, after a six-month siege, the heretic defenders were forced to surrender, and 200 of them were burned at the stake.

20km due S of Foix, just beyond **Tarascon-sur-Ariège**, is the **Grotte de Niaux**, a remarkable prehistoric cavern with important cave paintings of the Magdalenian period. For entry, inquire beforehand at the town hall in Tarascon.

If you are travelling west, with time to spare and good brakes, try the *route verte* (D17) which takes you by a narrow winding road over the wooded Massif de l'Arize and then down (sometimes at an 18° angle) into the Arac valley. Breathtaking views all the way, especially near the top where a short walk brings you to the Tour Laffon.

GAILLAC, *Tarn* (5–D5). An old town on the right bank of the Tarn, with many narrow streets of houses built of brick and wood. Now a commercial centre for the Côtes du Tarn and Gaillac wines (red, rosé and sweet white) made from the vineyards on both sides of the river. This was in fact one of the oldest wine areas in France, and continued to be important until the 18th-c. Gaillac has two 13th–14th-c. churches, St-Michel and St-Pierre, and at the S edge of the town the magnificent 17th-c. terraced Parc de Foucauld facing the river, laid out by the celebrated Versailles gardener Le Nôtre.

GAVARNIE, *Hautes-Pyrénées* (4–E3). A great walking, climbing and skiing centre in the most beautiful part of the Pyrenees, 50km S of Lourdes by a good road that climbs through increasingly wild country. Even from the village itself (where there is an interesting 14th-c. pilgrim church) you get a splendid view of the famous Cirque de Gavarnie, but a more dramatic panorama can be obtained by taking a stiff walk to the top of the Pic de Mourgat immediately to the west of the village. Better still, take a walk or a donkey-ride (3 hours there and back), through gorgeous pastoral scenery gurgling with mountain streams, to the Pont de la Neige. Here you are at the centre of the vast amphitheatre of glacial mountains, some of them (on the Spanish side of the frontier) over 3000m high – an awe-inspiring landscape of snow, ice, granite and thundering waterfalls, one of which (the Grande Cascade) is the highest in Europe, plunging over 400m.

GOURDON, *Lot* (5–C5). A hilltop market town which in the Middle Ages was one of the important cities in the *vicomté* of Turenne (*see entry*). The castle which once crowned the hill is no longer there, the site being occupied by an esplanade with a fine all-round view of the town and the rolling country between the Dordogne and Céou valleys. The church of St-Pierre, begun in the

14th-c. and once overshadowed by the castle, now dominates the town; it is large, not very beautiful, but impressively martial with its massive buttresses and the two square towers pierced by arrow slits; a rose-window is partly concealed by a line of battlements. The old town surrounding the church is a descending maze of narrow, winding streets between ancient stone houses, many of them medieval with worn stone-carved doorways, mullioned windows and the occasional turret. A boulevard forms a ring round the foot of the hill, and on the S perimeter is the 14th-c. Église des Cordeliers (Franciscan church), now secularized and used only for concerts in the summer. Beyond, the not very interesting modern town spreads haphazardly outwards.

3km N on the Sarlat road are the **Grottes de Cougnac**, with stalactites and 'columns' and some prehistoric cave drawings of elephants and other wild animals.

GUÉRET, *Creuse* (5–A5). A bustling, mostly modern city set on a high plateau, and once the capital of the old province of Marche. Not much is left of the old town, apart from the handsome late 15th-c. Hôtel des Moneyroux next to the Prefecture (Rue Ferraque), but the municipal museum, housed in a large 18th-c. house in the centre of a large garden on the S edge of the town, is well worth a visit; it contains not only armour, china, paintings and sculpture, Aubusson and Felletin tapestries, and archaeological finds from Celtic and Gallo-Roman times, but above all a magnificent collection of 12th–15th-c. enamelwork from Limoges and elsewhere, including ecclesiastical crosses and shrines – one of which bears a representation of the martyrdom of St Thomas à Becket.

Guéret is a good centre for excursions. An interesting one-day triangular car-trip would be to drive S through the beautiful Forest of Chabrières (lovely for walks and picnics) and on to **Bourganeuf**, where the curious Zizim Tower recalls the exotic Moslem prince who, incarcerated there during the Crusades, nevertheless managed to live a life of 'Arabian Nights' luxury. Then E to Aubusson, and back to Guéret via the Moutier d'Ahun (*see entries*).

HAUTEFORT, Château de, *Dordogne* (22km N of Montignac: 5–C5). Driving S from Limoges, take a right fork off the N20 on to the much quieter D704 through St-Yrieix. About 10km beyond Lanouaille you will begin to catch glimpses to your left of a large and confident château, alternately hidden and revealed as the road twists and turns through the hills and valleys of beautiful farmland. As you turn off towards the village, the château rears proudly on the skyline, dominating the cluster of houses at the foot of its walls.

Hautefort is not at all a typical Périgord château. Most of the thousand or so castles and *manoirs* scattered throughout the region are a blend of defensive severity and domestic fantasy. Hautefort, with its two massive domed towers and the huge, steep-roofed, many-windowed 17th-c. residence set back behind a spacious courtyard, is more reminiscent of the stately châteaux of the Loire.

The original medieval castle on this commanding site once belonged to Bertrand de Born, celebrated in these parts as a troubadour and a soldier (and pilloried in Dante's *Inferno* as a trouble-maker). He made the mistake of taking sides with the ill-fated 'young king' Henry against his father Henry Plantagenet (*see* Martel). This brought him into conflict with his own brother Constantine, who in 1186 seized and destroyed the castle, at which Bertrand renounced the world and retired to a monastery. The present edifice, largely 17th-c., was for a time the home of Marie de Hautefort, whose beauty caught the eye and touched the heart of Louis XIII; unfortunately for the king, she was too bored by him to become his mistress and married one of his generals instead.

In 1968 a disastrous fire gutted the centre of the main building, but the restoration is now complete. From Easter to the end of October the great esplanade, flanked by formal gardens, and the imposing *cour d'honneur* in front of the house, are open to the public, and in the summer months you can visit parts of the château itself. In the round towers are a chapel, a room displaying relics from the 1968 fire, and a museum dedicated to the 19th-c. Dordogne writer Eugène Le Roy.

HENDAYE, *Pyrénées-Atlantiques* (4–E1, E2). The last French town on the Basque coast, and popular seaside resort with beautiful sands and facilities for every kind of water sport. The street names – Avenue des Mimosas, Avenue des Magnolias, Rue des Jasmins – accurately describe the riot of colourful and scented greenery behind the Bd. de la Mer with its casino, and among the hotels, villas and camping-sites. Inland, the Pyrenees begin climbing almost at once.

The little port of the old town, called Hendaye-Ville, faces W across the stretch of water where the frontier river, the Bidassoa, widens out into the Bay of Chingoudy. Opposite, beyond the airport runway, the fortified town of Fuenterrabia beckons you into Spain. South of the old town is the uninteresting modern conglomeration of Hendaye-Gare, where the road and railway bridges cross the river to the frontier posts on the Spanish side.

Up river is the Ile des Faisans, midstream scene of many historic Franco-Spanish events, notably the signing of the marriage contract between Louis XIV and the Spanish princess Marie-Thérèse in 1660, two days before their resplendent wedding at St-Jean-de-Luz (*see entry*).

JUMILHAC-LE-GRAND, *Dordogne* (11km W of St-Yrieix: 5–B5). Every child's dream of a fairy castle, built of stone of many colours – ochre,

Château de Hautefort

amber, red, translucent rose – with a riot of pepperpot turrets, watch-towers, steep roofs and marvellously ornamented Renaissance dormer windows, all topped with flamboyant little figures. The main block – if the word is appropriate for such a light-hearted extravaganza – is 13th–14th-c., but the severe side wings which frame the courtyard were added in the 17th-c. In the N wing is a majestic stone staircase and a huge salon with a remarkable fireplace adorned with sculptures on the theme of the Four Seasons; upstairs, 'La Chambre de la Fileuse' (the spinner), with its thick walls and black-and-yellow hangings, is the room where Louise de Hautefort – so the legend goes – was locked up by her jealous husband for many years; using her own blood as ink, she wrote letters to her lover and let them down on her spinning-thread to the waiting messenger in the street below. Behind the S wing is the village church, formerly the family's private chapel, with an octagonal bell-tower and pretty interior painting. Below the castle, the rock falls abruptly to the river Isle, flowing swiftly through its rugged gorge.

LABRÈDE, Château de, *Gironde* (15km S of Bordeaux: 4–C3). A turning to the W off the N113 leads to this delightful 12th–15th-c. fortified manor house, surrounded by a large moat, where the eminent philosopher and writer Montesquieu (1689–1755) was born and lived. The turreted château, and the park designed by Montesquieu himself 'in the English manner' (he was a great anglophile), are still very much as they were in his

day; and his room and his large vaulted library have been left untouched. Although, like Montaigne (*see entry:* Montaigne, Château de), he played a prominent part in the government of Bordeaux, he too longed for the tranquillity of his library. He spent as much time as possible at Labrède, not only writing the philosophical books which aroused controversy and brought him European fame, but also looking after the management of his estate and its vineyards (he sold a lot of wine to the English). He once said, 'I like being at Labrède because there my money is under my feet.' It is interesting that the château and the domain still belong to his descendants – and that they still bottle an extremely drinkable white Graves. The park and the château are open to visitors most of the year.

LACAVE, Grottes de, *Lot* (8km SE of Souillac: 5–C5). On the S bank of a lovely, sinuous stretch of the Dordogne. A miniature railway and a lift take you down to the start of a 1½km walk through a series of subterranean galleries. Stalagmites, etc., in fascinating shapes and colours, are beautifully lit and often reflected in the running water and standing pools of underground streams.

LANDES, Les (SW of Bordeaux: 4–C3). A huge, triangular area (14,000 square kilometres) of sand dunes, lakes and monotonous pine forests. The base of the triangle is the Côte d'Argent, stretching from the mouth of the Gironde in the north, past the Arcachon basin in the centre, and nearly to

Bayonne and Biarritz in the south. The triangle narrows inland to a point 100km from the sea, not far short of Agen. Thus the Landes occupy nearly the whole of the area bounded by the rivers Garonne and Adour.

Part of the area has been designated a 'Parc Régional des Landes de Gascogne'. It stretches from the SE corner of the Arcachon basin down to **Sabres**. From Sabres a special train journey takes the visitor 4km through the forest to the open-air museum at Marquèze, where the ecology of the region is strikingly demonstrated. Near Arcachon is the 'Parc Ornithologique du Teich', a nature reserve (open to visitors) for the protection of native and migratory birds.

LAVAUR, *Tarn* (5–D5). A pleasant town overlooking the river Agout, 37km E of Toulouse, still haunted by grim memories of the distant past. In 1211 it was besieged by Simon de Montfort during his infamous crusade against the Albigensian heretics (*see* Albi), and after a two-month defence, led by the Lady Guirade in her Château Plo, the town was forced to surrender; the defenders were hanged or burned, and the Lady Guirade was thrown into a well and buried by stones. A few remains of the château are in the garden of Plo on the NE edge of the town. De Montfort's army also destroyed the church of St-Alain; reconstruction of the present brick building with its two massive towers was begun half a century later. It contains a remarkable 15th-c. altar-piece with several panels depicting scenes of the Passion; and on the south façade a painted wooden figure has been striking the hours and half-hours for over 400 years. On the N side of the church the site of a former Bishop's Palace is now an attractive garden with a terrace overlooking the river and the high bridge which spans it.

LIBOURNE, *Gironde* (4–C3). This busy town at the confluence of the rivers Dordogne and Isle has been an important wine centre since the Middle Ages. Its name probably commemorates the English seneschal Roger de Leyburn who built it in about 1270, on the orders of Edward I, as a *bastide* against the French. During the long struggle the town suffered much damage, changing hands many times. The original grid pattern of streets is still there, together with its central arcaded square (Place Abel-Surchamp) and the 15th-c. town hall. The old Tour de Port still stands on the quayside where the two rivers meet, but the site of the old ramparts is now occupied by wide tree-lined avenues. Until the early years of this century the riverside quays were a scene of intense activity as the foreign ships – from England especially – loaded the barrels of wine from St-Émilion, Pomerol and Fronsac, and even from Bergerac and Monbazillac further up the Dordogne. The increasing draught of ships and the development of road haulage have reduced Libourne's value as a river port, but wine shippers still have offices and cellars in the town, and you can sometimes see barrels on the quayside even today.

LIMOGES, *Haute-Vienne* (5–B5). World-renowned for its manufacture of enamels and porcelain, Limoges has grown tremendously since World War II. The incorporation of natural gas into the porcelain firing techniques, the rapid growth of the shoe industry, the development of hydro-electric power, and above all the discovery of uranium near Ambazac (*see entry*), have all contributed to an astonishing post-war expansion. Now there are large industrial zones in the suburbs to the S and NE, a new university campus to the NW and a modern hospital complex to the SW.

The original impetus for the porcelain industry came from the discovery in 1768 of large kaolin deposits at St-Yrieix (*see entry*), 40km S of Limoges, making possible the manufacture of hard-paste porcelain. It was due to the foresight and encouragement of Turgot, the administrator of the region, that a factory was set up in Limoges within three years of the discovery. Most of the porcelain factories today are in the NW quarter; if you would like to visit one, make inquiries at the tourist office (Syndicat d'Initiative) in the Bd. Fleurus on the NE side of Place Wilson. If you are more interested in the end result, visit the MUSÉE NATIONAL ADRIEN-DUBOUCHÉ (just N of the Jardin d'Orsay); its unique collection of over 10,000 pieces of china and porcelain from Europe and the Far East provides a complete history of the subject, ranging from early oriental items to examples of Sèvres, St-Cloud, Dresden, Wedgwood, etc., and the latest products of the Limoges factories.

The art of enamelling, with its various techniques of *cloisonné, champlevé* and *émaux peints*, preceded the porcelain era in Limoges by several centuries. Even today it is still more of an art than an industry, as much the work of individual craftsmen as it was in the 10th-c. In the small streets on the E side of Place Wilson (the Rue des Tanneries and the Rue Raspail, for example) are many little shop windows displaying a fascinating variety of enamel work, and usually at the back of the shop is a craftsman at work who will be glad to let you look over his shoulder.

Limoges is too busy with modern life to be overconcerned with its past. But there was certainly an important town here in Gallo-Roman times, and in 1966 the remains of a large Roman arena were unearthed in the Jardin d'Orsay. Modern history began with the development of two rival townships in the Middle Ages – the 'City' and the 'Town'. A glance at a street map shows the demarcation clearly, for wide modern boulevards occupy the sites of the former ramparts (the French word *boulevard* also means 'rampart'): the Bd. de la Cité curves round the bottom of the hill on which the Cathedral stands, overlooking the Vienne, while the medieval commercial 'Town' is outlined by the Bds. Gambetta, Victor-Hugo, Carnot and Louis-Blanc. Over the centuries both parts of Limoges have had their share of France's nation-wide troubles – the Hundred Years War, the Wars of Religion, plague, the Revolution, and German occupation.

There is a fine view of the City from the opposite bank of the Vienne, just N of the Pont St-Étienne. In the foreground the solid stone bridge with its cut-water embrasures is as good as when it was built some 700 years ago. On the hill behind it, rising above the trees on the N bank, stands the great Gothic Cathedral of St-Étienne, surrounded by flying buttresses and gargoyles, and terminating at the W end in a 62m Romanesque belfry tower, whose spire was destroyed by lightning over 400 years ago and never replaced.

The main entrance to the Cathedral is on the N side, through the St-John doorway – a splendid example of Flamboyant Gothic, with double carved doors and an unusual 'gable' curving upwards from the arch over the doors and narrowing to a point only just short of a large rose-window. The interior is vast, with fluted pillars and tall windows rising towards an immensely high roof of ogive vaulting. Wide side-aisles continue either side of the chancel, and there are few obstructions to the unity of the total space. What is remarkable is that although the Cathedral took 600 years to build (it was not completed until the late 19th-c.) the original design was adhered to throughout – unlike its namesake in Toulouse, which took as long to build but suffered from several changes of plan.

There is a brooding solemnity about this soaring Cathedral, reminiscent of the great Gothic cathedrals of northern France. The stone is a sombre grey granite, and it is something of a relief to turn to the Renaissance rood-screen which used to separate the chancel from the nave but now stands against the W wall at the back of the nave; it is in white stone and ornamented with gay floral decorations and statuettes; at each end a short spiral staircase leads to a little gallery running the full length of the screen; the door under the gallery opens into the narthex and thence to the W door. Other Renaissance ornamental carving is to be found on the marble tombs of 14th- and 16th-c. bishops at the rear of the chancel. But how sad it is that so many of the human figures represented on these tombs, and on the rood-screen and elsewhere in the Cathedral, have been defaced or beheaded, providing chilling evidence of the violent anti-clerical aspect of the Revolution.

On the S side of the Cathedral are the formal gardens of the old Archbishop's Palace. A tree-covered walk leads to a broad terrace overlooking a fine view of the river. Facing down the terrace is the former palace itself, a stiff but elegant building in French 18th-c. style, and now the Municipal Museum. Entrance is free. The interior is well cared for, with superb herring-bone plank floors gleaming with polish. The outstanding items in the collection are the 300 exquisite Limousin enamels dating from the 12th-c. to the present day. There are also sections on Egyptology, local Gallo-Roman finds, early music manuscripts, a basement showing fragments of carved stone (capitals, sarcophagi, inscriptions) and a very good collection of paintings by Limousin artists – including two portraits by Renoir, who was born in Limoges but left it at the age of 4 when his parents moved to Paris.

We move downhill now, NW from the Cathedral, and then uphill again, crossing the Place Wilson and mounting the Rue du Collège towards the focal point of the medieval commercial 'Town' – the Place de la République. This is now an underground car park, out of sight under the spacious marble-paved pedestrian-only square, but for many centuries, until the Revolution destroyed it, the great Abbey of St-Martial had stood here, dominating the life of the town. When the earth was being dug out in 1960 to make the underground car park, the old Crypt of St-Martial was re-discovered at the SW corner. It is open to the public from July to September only, with a recorded commentary and lighting effects; the approach is down an unprepossessing flight of steps, but the crypt is worth the visit, for parts of it go back to the 4th-c., including the tomb of St-Martial himself, who brought Christianity to Limoges.

Close at hand to the SE, at the bottom of a sloping, triangular *place*, is the interesting church of St-Pierre-du-Queyroix with its 13th-c. belfry and 16th-c. façade. The interior is unusual, a large rectangular space whose width exceeds its length. The low vaulted roof is supported on massive 12th-c. round pillars. The extremely wide side-aisles are further extended by the flanking chapels. There is a good deal of beautiful stained glass, the best window being immediately to the right of the chancel, representing the Death and Coronation of the Virgin and made in 1510. To the right of that, a fine 17th-c. gilded retable stands against the E wall.

A narrow street leads uphill and westward, crossing the Rue Jean Jaurès into the steep Rue du Consulat. At the top is an open vegetable-market; to the right a narrow lane winds, still uphill, towards another unusual church, St-Michel-des-Lions, which has recently been undergoing restoration. The lions, frozen in granite, guard the approach to the S door under the belfry; above, the tower ends in a tall, slender spire topped by a copper ball, over 65m from the ground and pierced with holes to reduce its weight. Top-weight seems to have been a problem with this 14th–16th-c. church, for in the sombre interior, which consists of three parallel naves of equal size, the pillars (clearly too slim for their purpose) lean outwards at an alarming angle due to the weight of the roof; this must have happened during the original construction, for the vaulted roof looks safe enough. All the same, it is an unnerving situation and tends to distract the attention from the vividly coloured stained glass, much of it 15th-c., at both ends of the church.

Downhill again, past the meat-market hall in the Place de la Motte, is the oldest quarter of Limoges, a delightful small area of steep, narrow lanes known as LA BOUCHERIE, full of tiny, dark, medieval butchers' shops which are still in business. They seem perhaps a little incongruous now amid the bustling life and traffic problems of a fast-growing commercial and industrial 20th-c. city.

LOUBRESSAC, *Lot* (6km NE of Padirac: 5–C5). High up on the opposite side of the Bave valley from the fortress of Castelnau (*see entry*), Loubressac consists of a small fortified village with narrow streets winding up to a modest château on the very edge of a steep spur. Of the medieval fort which once stood here nothing much remains; the present château with its watch-tower dates from the early 15th-c. but was considerably altered in the 17th. It now houses an odd collection of furniture, prints, and mementoes of the French Revolution. Looking N from the terrace the view is tremendous, and in the foreground the great red fortress of Castelnau broods over the junction of the valleys of three rivers – the Bave, the Cère and the Dordogne.

If you drive down the hill and turn left in the village of La Poujade, the D14 will bring you to a monument on the left of the road. This marks the spot where, in full daylight on 14 July 1944, American aircraft made a pre-arranged drop of 100 tons of arms for the French Resistance forces – with the *tricolore* flying from each parachute.

LOURDES, *Hautes-Pyrénées* (4–E3). Nearly 3 million pilgrims come to Lourdes every year, more than to Mecca or Rome or any other pilgrim centre in the world. Many of the pilgrims are incurably ill, and come here hoping to be cured by the waters of the miraculous spring in the grotto where Bernadette Soubirous, at the age of 14, first saw her vision of the Virgin in 1858.

The Massabielle grotto is now the focal point of a huge Religious City built within the bend of the river, the Gave de Pau. It contains a vast processional esplanade, a gigantic statue of the Virgin, two hospitals (each with 700 beds) and three churches – one of which, the subterranean Basilica of Pope Pius X, was constructed under the esplanade in 1958 to mark the centenary of the miracle, and accommodates 20,000 people under a single unsupported span of roof. The crowds are at their greatest between 15 August and 8 September, when the great esplanade teems with thousands of believers and unbelievers and at night is the scene of torchlight processions. Despite the inevitable commercialization, the accretion of tourist shops, the display of 'religious' trinkets and the activities

of professional photographers, one still cannot help being moved by the massive expression of faith and hope that has made Lourdes what it is today.

The mountain surroundings, too, are impressive. Close to the S edge of the town the river emerges between two dramatic peaks, the Pic du Jer (948m) and Le Béout (790m), reached by funicular or cable-way and affording tremendous views of the Pyrenees. On the E bank of the river, opposite the Religious City, the medieval Château Fort occupies a natural defensive site on its rocky eminence, with a square keep and a perimeter wall 1km in circumference; it houses a fascinating Musée Pyrénéen, and there are good views from the terrace.

A word of warning: in the number of its hotels, Lourdes ranks third in France, but if you plan to stay here during the season you are advised to book well ahead.

12km due W, off the N637 road to Pau, are the well-known **Grottes de Bétharram**, where an underground river has gouged out of the rock a series of descending galleries with extraordinary limestone formations and eroded 'sculptures'. At the end of the 3km tour, which includes a short boat trip, a small train takes you to a cable car which saves you the trouble of climbing back to the start.

LUZECH, *Lot* (12km W of Cahors: 5–C5). A small medieval town on the neck of a tight loop in the river Lot – a smaller version of the one that encloses Cahors (*see entry*). Here the neck is only 200m across, and at one time a canal cut through it. The old castle is a ruin. On the hill to the N of the town is the site known as the Impernal Hill; excavations show that it was occupied as a defensive encampment by prehistoric man, then by the Gauls and Romans, and in the Middle Ages by the French against the English. The square keep on the site is 13th-c. and provides a most agreeable view of the town below and of the Lot snaking through its hilly valley. For a few moments of peace, visit the chapel of Notre-Dame de l'Ile in its isolated riverside setting; it has a rather good Flamboyant doorway and a 15th-c. Virgin which still, it seems, attracts pilgrims in the second week of September.

MARMANDE, *Lot-et-Garonne* (4–C4). On a hill overlooking the Garonne, Marmande is a market town for orchard produce, tobacco and – especially – tomatoes, with a lively cattle market on Saturdays. In the church of Notre-Dame, part of which dates from the 13th-c., there is a fine Entombment (*mise au tombeau*), and from its Renaissance cloisters a splendid view of the Garonne winding through the plain.

MARTEL, *Lot* (12km NE of Souillac: 5–C5). Known as 'the town of the seven towers', this quiet medieval market town, once strongly fortified, lies in the centre of a limestone plateau (or *causse*) just N of a dramatic cliff-girt stretch of the Dordogne river. It was named after Charles Martel (ruler of the Franks, and grandfather of Charlemagne) who, after saving Europe by beating the Moors at Poitiers in AD 732, pursued them southward and finally exterminated them near this spot.

Although its 12th-c. double ramparts survive only in fragments, the old part of the town, grouped around the covered market-place (with its ingeniously constructed roof resting on ugly square stone pillars), retains its medieval character and many of its ancient buildings: notably the elegant Palais de la Raymondie (early 14th-c. and now the town hall), the Mirepoises cloisters (altered in the 18th-c. but retaining earlier features), and the Maison Fabri with its little round tower, reputed to be the house in which the eldest son of Henry Plantagenet died in 1183 in an agony of remorse after plundering the shrine of Rocamadour (*see entry*). The church, partly 12th-c., partly 14th-c., is aggressively military, with watch-towers, battlements, and a huge 50m belfry standing on massive buttresses; the porch has a good, though restored, Romanesque tympanum of the Last Judgment.

7km E, immediately W of Vayrac on the hill called Puy d'Issolud, is what is believed to be the site of **Uxellodunum**, the defensive city where the Gauls made a brave but unavailing stand against Julius Caesar.

MAS-D'AZIL, Grotte du, *Ariège* (23km NW of Foix: 5–E5). Not only a remarkable natural phenomenon but also one of the most important prehistoric sites in the Pyrenees.

15km NE from St-Girons, via D117 and D119, the road suddenly enters a yawning cavern 65m high. This is the entrance to a vast tunnel-cave, bored through the limestone hill by the river Arize – no one knows how many million years ago. The road follows the subterranean course of the river until it emerges into daylight about 400m further on, where the exit is a mere 8m high. The total space in the cave is enormous – no wonder early man lived here. It is worth pulling off the road to visit the prehistoric museum built into a series of galleries in the calcareous rock; it displays a fascinating collection of items of palaeolithic art and artefacts discovered in the excavations. Early Christians, Albigensian heretics and – during a celebrated siege in 1625 – Huguenot refugees, have all found shelter here over the centuries, and during World War II the Germans used the caves for building aircraft.

MÉDOC, Le, *Gironde* (NW of Bordeaux: 4–C3). The greatest wine area in the world lies in a strip roughly 8km wide along the W bank of the Gironde, starting about 20km north of Bordeaux. The very best wines come from the Haut-Médoc, which stretches from Macau in the south to just beyond St-Estèphe in the north; the area to the

north of that, as far as the Pointe de Grave, is known as the Bas-Médoc.

Unfortunately, the scenery of the Médoc is rather uninteresting, being rather flat, but further details of the area can be found in the introductory article on 'The Wines of France' at the beginning of this book.

MERLANDE, Ancien Prieuré de, *Dordogne* (8km NW of Périgueux: 4–C4). Rather difficult to find, but worth the trouble when you get there. The best way is to leave Périgueux by the Angoulême road and soon turn left on to the Ribérac road, the D710, then right for the Abbey of Chancelade (*see entry*), of which Merlande was an offshoot. After visiting Chancelade continue north on the D1 through woodlands for about 5½km and look out for the signposted right turn which brings you to the Ancien Prieuré de Merlande.

The place has the hallowed atmosphere of Round Table legends. The spirit of the Holy Grail seems to hover about the ancient ivy-covered walls, and when you step into the bare, sombre nave you would hardly be surprised to find a knight in armour kneeling on the steps under the archway leading to the choir and the simple altar. Look closely at the capitals on this arch and on the blind arcades either side of the choir; there are marvellous carvings of lion-like monsters twisted in snarling, threatening attitudes, in strange contrast to the air of sanctuary that pervades this 12th-c. priory church. On the NE corner a defence buttress, added in the 16th-c., strikes a discordantly martial note, but behind the church the same quiet spring that led to the choice of this spot for a priory, 800 years ago, still bubbles away with crystal-clear water. There is a crypt below the choir. The only remains of the priory buildings are a large round tower and a lodge, close to a moat.

MILLAU, *Aveyron* (5–D6, D7). A busy crossroads town on the right bank of the Tarn, opposite its junction with the Dourbie. Millau lies at the centre of the wild region S of the Auvergne – a region of semi-barren limestone plateaus (*causses*), dramatic gorges and chaotic rock formations. Here the warmth of the Midi is chilled by the winds from the Massif Central. Thousands of ewes graze on the meagre grass of the *causses*; their milk goes to Roquefort-sur-Soulzon, south of Millau, to make the famous cheese (*see entry*), and their lambs go to Millau to provide skins for its famous glove industry which goes back to the 12th-c. In Gallo-Roman times the town (Emilium Castrum) was widely known for a particular kind of pottery made at La Graufesenque, just S of the town, and examples of it have been excavated at sites as far apart as Pompeii and Scotland. These local industries of ancient pottery-making and the more recent glove-making, are well illustrated in the town's museum in the arcaded Place du Maréchal Foch.

Here is the centre of the old town, where the

most interesting buildings are to be found: notably the curious Belfry in the Rue Droite, part square and part octagonal, sole remnant of a 12th-c. town hall and once used as a prison; an ancient fortified gateway just S of the Place Emma Calvé; and the church of Notre-Dame, dating from the 12th-c. but virtually rebuilt in the 17th-c., and containing some unexpected 20th-c. frescoes.

Millau is a popular centre for exploring the gorges of the two rivers that meet here. The celebrated Gorges du Tarn (*see entry in* Languedoc-Roussillon *section*) are reached by going N on the N9 and then E on the D107n to Le Rozier. For the **Gorges de la Dourbie**, take the picturesque D591n which closely follows the twists and ravines of the river as far as Nant; after that you need a large-scale map!

18km NE on the D110 is the extraordinary Chaos de Montpellier-le-Vieux, where the rocks have been sculpted by nature into fantastic shapes. (*See entry in* Languedoc-Roussillon *section*.)

MOISSAC, *Tarn-et-Garonne* (4–D4). It is well worth making a special journey to visit Moissac, for in the abbey church of St-Pierre are preserved two of the finest works of ecclesiastical art in the whole of France – its cloisters and its S doorway.

It is hard to believe that in the middle of the last century the cloisters were nearly pulled down to make way for a new railway. Thanks to the Beaux-Arts, who stepped in and saved them for posterity, we can still marvel at the artistry and devotion that created this oasis of beauty 800 years ago. The spacious close is framed by long galleries with elegantly proportioned pillars, alternately single and double, in varying tints of marble, and graced by exquisitely carved capitals in a rich variety of ornaments, figures and biblical scenes. A huge cedar in the centre adds to the sense of ageless tranquillity.

The other Romanesque masterpiece, the S doorway, is the finest and best-preserved of the great series of carved doorways created in this region during the 12th-c. by the sculptors of the 'Toulouse School' (*see also* Cahors, Carennac and Beaulieu-sur-Dordogne, for example). The tympanum represents the Vision of the Apocalypse, with a noble Christ in Majesty at the centre, surrounded by symbols of the four evangelists – man, lion, eagle, bull – and seated figures of the elders of the Apocalypse all turning their heads toward Christ. The supporting lintel is carved with eight large foliated roundels. The centre column between the two doors has a design of three pairs of overlapping lions on the front face, with prophets on the side faces. Two scalloped pillars (suggesting Moorish influence) and other carvings flank the door openings. Three slender arches, or covings, richly sculpted with a leaf design, complete the framework of this magnificent doorway.

The lower part of the massive tower is the only other remnant of the original abbey church, the rest being 15th-c. Under the tower, which was

The Cloisters at Moissac

Dr Christopher Tadgell

Château de Monbazillac

clearly built for defence, a vaulted chamber, supported on pillars with decorated capitals, makes an impressive entry porch, but the interior of the church is a great disappointment, with plastered walls crudely decorated (and, alas, only recently restored) with a design that looks like cheap wallpaper. A pity, because in the chapels there are some interesting 15th-c. sculptures, and on the N side of the nave is a moving 12th-c. Christ Crucified carved in wood. If only they had left the walls white!

MONBAZILLAC, Château de, *Dordogne* (6km S of Bergerac: 4–C4). There is a nice but probably apocryphal story of some medieval pilgrims from Bergerac visiting the Pope. 'But where is Bergerac?' they were asked. 'Just north of Monbazillac,' was the reply, at which the Pope raised his hands in benediction, murmuring 'Bonum vinum, bonum vinum . . .'

Certainly they were making their distinctive sweet white wine here long before wine was made in the more celebrated sweet-wine area of Sauternes. The vineyards of four other villages come within the Monbazillac *appellation*, all centring on this sturdy castle on the brow of a gentle hill looking N towards Bergerac and the Dordogne river. Harvesting used to be late here, often going on to the end of November, because the grapes had to be individually picked when they were over-ripe. These days most of the grapes are processed at the great *Cave Co-operative* on the Bergerac–Eymet road, which can be visited by arrangement.

The château, built about 1550 on the site of a medieval village, is really a large house with a medley of steep reddish-brown roofs, with a fat, round, machicolated tower at each corner, capped with a conical roof, to give it a military flavour. The total effect is imposing in a genial sort of way, with a large open courtyard in front under great trees, and views of serried vines in all directions. The interior is worth a visit, though none of the furniture is original; it is now a museum of local Calvinist history and other interests. After your guided tour you can taste and buy the wine in the shop by the gate.

MONFLANQUIN, *Lot-et-Garonne* (14km N of Villeneuve: 4–C4). One of the defensive French *bastides*, strategically built in the 13th-c. on an abrupt hill overlooking the valley of the Lède, a tributary of the Lot. At the top of the town the old market square is unusual in that it still retains all its arcades on all sides; every Thursday it provides the setting for a lively market specializing in poultry. The church, which has undergone considerable restoration, dominates the town with its massive fortifications. There are lovely views of the countryside, and it is altogether a very agreeable old town to wander about in.

MONPAZIER, *Dordogne* (14km S of Beaumont: 4–C4). Although it was frequently attacked and pillaged by both sides in the Hundred Years War, Monpazier remains one of the best-preserved of the *bastides* built by the English and the French during their long struggle in Aquitaine. Begun in

Jean Feuille

Monpazier

1284 by Edward I of England, Monpazier still retains its original rectangular grid pattern of streets, with the fortified church (largely rebuilt in 1550) close to the central arcaded square. Under the covered market is a raised platform on which the fittings for the old bin measures can still be seen; the measures themselves still exist and are sometimes displayed in position. On a hot afternoon the deep shadows under the wide-arched arcades around the square and across the main street give the place the atmosphere of a sleepy little Spanish town at siesta time.

3km S is the Château de Biron, well worth a visit (*see entry*). When Edward I was building Monpazier he found a useful temporary ally in Pierre de Gontaut, lord of Biron – but disagreements soon broke up the alliance.

MONTAIGNE, Château de, *Dordogne* (15km E of St-Émilion: 4–C3). Here the famous essayist Michel de Montaigne (1533–92) was born, lived and died. Even from the gate where you leave your car and buy your ticket (only the gardens and the tower are open to visitors) you get an impression of the sunlit peace of the trees and lawns surrounding the house. The round tower is the only part of the original manor house which survives.

Montaigne's bedroom is on the first floor, over a small chapel, and the library is on the second floor. Alas, the books and original furniture are all gone, but you can still see the Greek and Latin tags inscribed on the beams by his own hand. His duties as mayor of Bordeaux, the anxieties of the Wars of Religion, and his travels abroad, kept him away more than he would have liked, but it was in this tower that he found the solitude he longed for and composed the essays which still speak vividly to us four centuries later.

MONTAL, Château de, *Lot* (1km W of St-Céré: 5–C5). If you take the D673 westward out of the pleasant little town of St-Céré, you soon see to your left, above the road and half hidden by poplars, the seemingly grim silhouette of Montal with its steep roofs and forbidding round towers. But when you turn off the road and approach the castle from the other side the whole aspect of the place changes. Walking up the little path from the car park you will find your first impressions of severity charmed away by the elegance and decorative exuberance of the two wings of the courtyard. Yet it has had a sad history.

At the end of the 15th-c. the Seneschal of Gascony returned from Charles VIII's campaign in Italy dazzled by the splendours of Italian architecture. He bought this rather stark feudal stronghold overlooking the river Bave with the idea of transforming it into a 'castle of ease' in the Italian Renaissance style. His premature death left his daughter Jeanne de Montal, already a widow, with the task of carrying out his dream for the sake of her son, who was himself now fighting in Italy. A woman of courage, perseverance and taste, she employed a large team of masons and artists to enliven the original façade with Renaissance stone-framed windows (the dormers topped with ornate stone gables) and a richly decorated stone frieze above the ground-floor windows, running the full length of both wings. The interior was embellished with carved chimney-pieces and other ornamental stonework and – within the frame of the central square tower – a remarkable three-storey staircase in white Carennac marble, with the under-sides of the steps carved in elegant designs.

Before the work was completed Jeanne de Montal had news of her son's death. Grief-stricken, she ordered the window from which she had watched for his return to be blocked up, and the words *Plus d'Espoir* ('goodbye to hope') carved below it. But she completed the work in hand and commissioned the seven portrait busts which adorn the façade between the first-floor windows, representing herself, her father, her husband, her son and other members of the family – all so lifelike that they might almost be the human originals standing at windows looking down at the courtyard visitors.

During the Revolution, Montal was confiscated as State property, then left to rack and ruin and vandalism. In 1879 it was sold to a demolition speculator. All the beautiful carved stonework – over 100 tons of it – was dismantled (including the windows), auctioned in Paris and dispersed, leaving only the shell of the building and the great staircase. Happily, in 1908 the château was bought by Maurice Fenaille, a wealthy industrialist who determined to restore it to its former glory. He spent a small fortune in tracing the missing stonework; amazingly he succeeded in buying back, at great cost, every item with the exception of one window; this an American museum refused to sell back and it has been replaced by a copy.

Thus restored to what it must have been in Jeanne de Montal's day, the château makes a fitting memorial to a remarkable woman. Beautifully furnished with tapestries, carpets and period family furniture, it has the atmosphere of a home – which indeed it is. For when Maurice Fenaille died he left the château to the State on condition that his family be allowed to go on living in it. It is open to the public every day from March to October (inclusive). Besides the façade and the staircase already mentioned, note also the Guard Room with its vaulted ceiling and marvellous chimney-piece, the Stag Room with the sculptured stag lifting his head above the fireplace, his antlers almost touching the fine beamed ceiling, and the

glimpse of the formal garden from the windows on the second floor at the top of the staircase.

MONTAUBAN, *Tarn-et-Garonne* (5–D5). Set up on a plateau on the right bank of the Tarn, Montauban is an important crossroads and a marketing centre for the district's fruit and vegetable products. Like Toulouse, it is built largely of pink brick. Its heart beats in the Place Nationale, an irregular rectangle lined by four-storey brick terraced houses over double arcades; on market day the place is crowded with stalls and bustling with noisy life. An arched portico at each corner leads out into the surrounding narrow streets, whose rough grid pattern reminds us that Montauban was one of the earliest *bastides*. It was founded in 1144 by the Count of Toulouse – not as a defence against the English but as a new settlement to encourage the productivity of the area.

The W exit from the square leads quickly to the fortified church of St-Jacques, dominated by its battlemented brick tower built 700 years ago. The church used to be the town's cathedral, but in 1739 it was superseded by a vast new cathedral, Notre-Dame, a stone's throw to the SE and not very interesting except that in the N transept is a large painting by Ingres called 'The Vow of Louis XIII'.

This picture recalls the siege of Montauban in 1621, when Louis XIII sent a military expedition to quell the still troublesome Huguenots of SW France. Montauban held out for three months until the king abandoned the siege. Seven years later, having taken La Rochelle, the only other remaining Protestant stronghold, his army returned to the attack, but this time Montauban surrendered to the inevitable, received the king's pardon and dismantled the fortifications.

The painter of the picture in the Cathedral, Ingres (1780–1867), was a native of Montauban. Some 30 of his paintings and 4000 of his drawings (shown in rotation) are to be seen in the fine Ingres Museum, housed in the former episcopal palace, together with sculptures by another son of Montauban, Rodin's pupil Antoine Bourdelle (1861–1929). The palace is a fascinating building, especially in the 14th-c. basement where the former guardroom is still known as the Black Prince's Chamber. From the second floor you get a fine view of the Tarn and the early 14th-c. bridge with its seven brick arches and oval spaces between the arches to allow the passage of flood water. Looking back at the town from the bridge there is a nice view of the episcopal palace and the grand 17th-c. houses standing high above the old quaysides.

MONT-DE-MARSAN, *Landes* (4–D3). Capital of the Landes department, situated on the southern edge of the Landes pine forests, whose resinous scent pervades the town when the wind is in the right direction. The bridge at the end of the Bd. de Candau provides an attractive upstream view of the old quarter of the town at the point where the rivers Midou and Douze merge to become the Midouze. A short walk S leads to the Arena, famous throughout the region as the scene of a local form of bullfighting and – immediately after 14 July – of the *corridas espagnoles*. On the N edge of the town are the airport and a well-known racecourse.

Mont-de-Marsan is a centre for the products of the Landes industries; it has sawmills and resin distilleries, and markets *foie-gras, confits* and poultry. It is also the site of an important military experimental aircraft establishment.

14km SSW is the little town of **St-Sever**, high up on the left bank of the Adour and enjoying tremendous views to the NW across the Landes forests. Its much restored medieval abbey has ancient marble columns and some remarkable 11th-c. capitals.

MONTFORT, Château de, *Dordogne* (6km S of Sarlat: 5–C5). Included here because, although it is privately owned and, at the time of writing, no longer open to the public, it looks romantic and occupies a formidable site. It is best seen from the E. If you are travelling W from Souillac along the D703, which follows the N bank of the Dordogne, soon after the village of Carsac you come round a corner and see the château perched dramatically on a rocky outcrop overlooking a wide bend (*cingle*) in the river.

There seems to be no better reason for the château's name than the fact that in 1214 it was seized and destroyed by Simon de Montfort in the course of his Albigensian crusade (*see also* Beynac-et-Cazenac). Because of its strategic situation it has been besieged, fought over, razed to the ground and rebuilt so often that nothing is left dating from earlier than the 15th-c., and much of it is 19th-c. rebuilding and restoration.

MONTIGNAC, *Dordogne* (5–C5). A bustling little market town on the river Vézère, overlooked by the remaining tower of a ruined castle once owned by the rampageous counts of Périgord. Soon after World War II the town was catapulted into world-wide fame by one of the greatest prehistoric finds in western Europe – the discovery of the paintings in the **Lascaux Caves**, 2½km to the SE. Sadly, not open to the public but a facsimile, Lascaux II, opens late summer 1983.

The caves were found by a small group of local boys in 1940, when this part of France was still unoccupied by the Germans. They reported their find to their schoolmaster, who at once got in touch with the Abbé Breuil, the well-known expert on prehistoric man. He confirmed the importance of the discovery, but not until after the end of the war was it announced to the world. In 1948 the caves were opened to the public. Fifteen years later it was realized that the transparent mineral deposit which had acted as a natural glaze, preserving the paintings for over 25,000 years, was rapidly being destroyed by the atmospheric change caused by the breathing of thousands of tourists in the confined space. So since 1963 the caves have been shut, and only visitors with special permission are allowed in by arrangement.

However, it is still worth visiting the site. The road winds up through woods to a plateau commanding a fine view of the surrounding country. At the entrance to the caves, from 1 July to 15 September, you can see a film show which reproduces on screen the vigorous lines and colours of the wild animals painted on the bare rock by those remarkable artists so many thousands of years ago.

Plans are in hand for the construction of a full-size replica of the caves, but this is a slow, skilful process. At the time of writing the estimated date of completion is late summer 1983.

35km SW is Les Eyzies (*see entry*), known as the 'capital of Prehistory' and centre of a number of cave sites with paintings which *are* open to the public.

MONTRÉJEAU, *Haute-Garonne* (4–E4). A small, ancient *bastide* town astride the east–west N117. It stands on the abrupt edge of a plateau, with a panoramic view of the Pyrenees. From it the N125 points due S into the mountains, towards St-Bertrand-de-Comminges and Luchon, and at the bottom of the hill the river Neste adds its cold mountain water to that of the Garonne.

MOUTIER D'AHUN, *Creuse* (16km SE of Guéret: 5–A5). *Moutier* means 'monastery'. This one has had a chequered history, but the remains of its abbey church, now used as the parish church, are romantic and unusual. The Benedictine monastery was founded in AD 997, but the present church replaced the original one in the 12th-c. Partly destroyed by the English in the Hundred Years War, it was then patiently rebuilt, only to be attacked again 200 years later in the Wars of Religion when, in 1591, the Protestants set fire to the nave, leaving only the W doorway, the chancel and the apse still standing. This time, instead of trying to rebuild the church yet again, the monks decided to make more beautiful what was left. They made a garden where the nave had been, left the 15th-c. doorway as an entrance to it, and commissioned a master carver from the Auvergne, one Simon Bauer, to ornament the chancel and choir. The result, completed in 1681, you can see today. Surrounded by this impressive array of superb carving in black oak, with the screen, the retable and 26 choir-stalls richly adorned with robustly sculptured flowers, animals and scenes, you feel you have strayed into a forest in some three-dimensional tapestry.

At the time of the Revolution, when the monks had to flee, someone – no one knows who or why – covered the whole of the wood-carving in whitewash; perhaps it was one of the monks, trying to disguise it as stone. It required years of

Douglas Dickins

Château de Montfort

patient work by a later parish priest to restore the carvings to their former state.

In the sacristy are relics from the old monastery, including a striking figure of Christ carved in wood.

The village of Moutier d'Ahun, which lies in the valley of the Creuse halfway between Guéret and Aubusson, huddles close to its church. A lovely old bridge spans the river. The little town of **Ahun**, 1km away up the hill, also has a church full of interest, including a chancel with carvings which may have come from the same Simon Bauer

workshop – also an 11th-c. crypt with an ancient reliquary tomb, and, just inside the porch, a really beautiful pietà in many-coloured stone.

NAJAC, *Aveyron* (5–D5). A remarkable little town on a dramatic site in the Aveyron gorges, a few kilometres S of Villefranche-de-Rouergue. Its medieval houses climb steep slopes and straggle along the summit of a narrow ridge which juts out from a plateau and diverts the river in a looping ravine. On the highest point, in a superb defensive position, stands the proud ruin of the 13th-c.

castle. From the donjon tower the view plunges dizzily on three sides to the river. Near the castle, below it to the SW, is the massive but plain Gothic church, built at the same time as the castle but better preserved; the W end has a fine rose-window.

An earlier castle once stood on the site of the present one. But about the year 1200 Najac joined the Albigensian heretics (*see* Albi), and Simon de Montfort's army destroyed that castle and no doubt many of the town's inhabitants as well.

NÉRAC, *Lot-et-Garonne* (4–D4). A pleasant little town on the river Baïse, 30km W of Agen. The old part, with its warren of narrow streets on the slopes of the right bank, is known as Petit Nérac, and is reached across an old Gothic hump-back bridge. At the W end of the 'new bridge', the elegant Renaissance château which was once the court of Marguerite of Navarre and the scene of amorous adventures of her grandson, the young prince who became Henri IV, now survives only in the one remaining wing with an arcaded gallery. In the gardens of the Promenade de la Garenne across the river, the tragic end of one of Henri's *amours* is recalled by the reclining statue of 'Fleurette', a gardener's daughter who, according to tradition, was seduced and abandoned by her royal lover and drowned herself in the very pool by which her image lies.

OLORON-STE-MARIE, *Pyrénées-Atlantiques* (4–E3). A pleasant old town SW of Pau, at the junction of two rivers in the foothills of the Pyrenees. It makes a living from manufacturing berets, shoes, sandals, chairs, and especially chocolate.

After the Roman settlement on the hill was destroyed by the barbarians, a new town sprang up on the W side of the river Aspe. In the Middle Ages the old town revived, and for 500 years or so the two towns developed separately, but in the middle of the last century they were amalgamated under one administration. This dual existence accounts for there being two cathedrals. Ste-Croix was built on top of the hill in the 11th-c., the dome being added 200 years later. Ste-Marie is largely 12th-c.; under its large square tower is a fine Romanesque doorway, carved in Pyrenean marble, which explains its remarkable state of preservation.

From the top of the hill, near the W door of Ste-Croix, a wonderful view of the Pyrenees fills the southern horizon. Due S the N134 climbs the Aspe valley towards the frontier post of **Somport** (55km). If you are going that way, stop off at the little village of **Sarrance** (18km), a pilgrim centre from the 12th-c. onwards, with an interesting old church and cloister. A few kilometres further on, a right turn on to the D239 takes you 5km up a narrow zigzag road which leads to **Lescun** and rewards you with a tremendous mountain panorama.

ORADOUR-SUR-GLANE, *Haute-Vienne* (11km NE of St-Junien: 4–B4). When the Allies landed in Normandy on 6 June 1944, the French Resistance started harrying the Germans all over France. The Germans immediately carried out a series of reprisals against innocent people, especially in SW France, shooting men, women and children in innumerable incidents recorded on village war memorials, plaques on bridges, and other wayside signs. The most horrifying outrage took place here in the village of Oradour-sur-Glane, only four days after the Normandy landings. A Nazi division locked the women and children in the church and the men in other buildings, proceeded to massacre them with grenades, machine-guns, dynamite and fire, and left the village ablaze. Only a handful of the inhabitants survived. The 650 who died are buried in a special cemetery, and the shattered remains of the old village have been preserved untouched as an unforgettable reminder of the horrors of war.

ORTHEZ, *Pyrénées-Atlantiques* (4–D3). 40km NW of Pau in the valley of the Gave de Pau, Orthez is a peaceful little town, but a shadow of its former self. From the 13th-c. to the 15th-c. it was the capital of the Béarn region. The old fortified bridge, with only one of its two towers intact, is still there, but of the castle of the counts of Foix, built in 1292, only the tower remains – the Tour Moncade on the N edge of the town. From the platform at the top you have a good view of the town, the countryside and the distant Pyrenees.

Staunchly Catholic in the Wars of Religion, Orthez was brutally sacked by the Protestants in 1569. Plague completed the decimation of the population. More recently, in 1814, Orthez was the scene of a battle in which Marshal Soult's army was defeated by the forces of Wellington after their victorious campaign through the Iberian peninsula; 2km N on the road to Dax the site is marked by a monument to the French general Foy who distinguished himself in the battle.

PADIRAC, Gouffre de, *Lot* (5–C5). The most remarkable natural phenomenon in the whole of the Dordogne valley. At the height of the season you may have to queue to get in, but the wait is well worth while. (*Caution:* on a hot day it will seem very cool down below – take a jersey with you. And infirm people should not attempt the expedition, which takes about 1½ hours.)

The *gouffre* (or chasm) is an enormous hole in the ground, 100m across and nearly as deep. Lifts take you down to the bottom, whence the view overhead is dramatic enough, but this is only the start of a fantastic underground journey. An easy walk of about 300m along a well-lit winding passage through the rock, under a gradually rising roof, brings you to a little jetty. Here you board a sturdy punt for a magical voyage of over half a kilometre on an underground river which is wide enough to allow the boats to pass in both directions. For thousands of years the river has eroded the sheer rock walls into bold curves and hollows. The water is cool, clear and deep, and the lofty roof is nearly 80m high in places. Finally the boat lands you at another jetty, close to the dripping 'rain lake' and an enormous stalactite which has grown down from the roof until it now almost reaches the water.

On foot once more, you take the narrow passage known as the 'crocodile path' (don't worry, there are no crocodiles) which leads to a wide space where the river breaks up into a series of dams and turquoise pools, culminating in a fairy-like cascade. Here a steep ascent of man-made steps leads you into a vast cathedral-like cavern whose dome is over 90m high (and in fact quite close to surface ground-level). The view, as you climb the stairs around the convoluted rock walls of this enormous subterranean chamber, is tremendously impressive; Gustave Doré himself could not have imagined anything more awe-inspiring. Finally, another twisting, turning passage brings you down to the jetty for the return trip.

The existence of this underground river, which flows NW and eventually comes to the surface just before it joins the Dordogne, has been known for a long time. Indeed it was frequently used as a refuge in troubled times from at least the Hundred Years War onwards. It is only during the last hundred years that it has been professionally explored and gradually opened up for tourists. There are still 8km or so to be explored, and the work continues.

PAU, *Pyrénées-Atlantiques* (4–E3). In the 11th-c. the counts of Foix built a château on the hill above the river, the Gave de Pau, and used it as a hunting-lodge. A village grew up, developed into a town. In the 14th-c. Gaston Phoebus, the most celebrated of all the counts of Foix, and himself an enthusiastic huntsman (he even wrote a book on the subject), enlarged the château, adding the massive brick keep which still dominates it today. Two centuries later, further alterations transformed it into a grand residence for elegant living. When the redoubtable Marguerite of Navarre ('*corps féminin, cœur d'homme, tête d'ange*') was the châtelaine it was a scene of fêtes and balls and became one of the intellectual centres of the day. Her grandson Henri IV was born here; the room and his cradle, along with other royal souvenirs and a fine collection of Gobelins tapestries, can be seen in the part of the château set aside as a museum.

It was Napoleon who inspired the creation of the splendid Bd. des Pyrénées, which runs from the château along the river to the beautiful Parc Beaumont. It provides a famous view of the Pyrenees rising out of the valley towards the snow-capped peaks on the Spanish border.

Once capital of the Béarn, largest of the former Pyrenean provinces, Pau is today the capital of the Pyrénées-Atlantiques department, with an administrative importance that has grown since the discovery in 1951 of huge reserves of natural gas at Lacq, 25km to the NW. Its gentle climate, summer and winter, its agreeable situation above the river, its panoramic views, and its geographical position as a centre for excursions into the Pyrenees, have made it a popular place to stay in – and live in. During the 19th-c. it was 'discovered' by the English, so much so that at one time they comprised some 15 % of the resident population.

The Musée des Beaux-Arts (NW of the Parc Beaumont) contains paintings by Rubens, Corot, Degas, El Greco, etc., and the Musée Bernadotte (just N of the château) is housed in the birthplace of the famous Marshal who served under Napoleon and then founded the present Swedish royal dynasty as Charles XIV.

Across the river is the little town of **Jurançon**, whose vineyards produce well-known red and white wines which have the advantage of travelling well.

PÉRIGUEUX, *Dordogne* (4–C4). Capital of the Dordogne department. The most impressive approach is from the SE, where the road from Brive crosses the river Isle and presents you with a startling view of the huge white Byzantine Cathedral of ST-FRONT, crowning the hill to your right. Five shimmering domes rise above the brown-red roofs of the old town; a dozen elegant minarets point to the sky; and a four-storey bell-tower, surmounted by a short conical stone spire on a *lanterne* of slender pillars, soars above it all. It is an edifice that seems more suited to Venice or Constantinople than to the capital of the ancient region of Périgord.

Park where you can in the tree-lined boulevard which starts at the Place Bugeaud (due W of the Cathedral), walk through the old town and enter the Cathedral by the N door.

The ground plan is a symmetrical Greek cross, and the five domes, one over the centre and one over each arm of the cross, form a lofty roof. The interior is vast, massive, but the effect is cold and somehow uninspiring, perhaps due to the mechanically perfect cutting of the stone which betrays the fact that the Cathedral was virtually rebuilt in the latter half of the 19th-c. Abadie, the architect responsible for the reconstruction, has been much reviled for what he did here (and in other churches throughout the SW), by way of adding extra towers and other unnecessary features, but modern restoration techniques were not available then, and no doubt he had other problems. The previous domed building, erected in the 12th-c. on the site of earlier churches, had been much damaged by Protestants in the Wars of Religion and by successive ill-conceived 're-storations', and by 1850 was in a lamentable state of dilapidation. Certainly what stands here today is a cathedral of great dignity and interest.

The cloisters at the SW corner are of various periods, and in the centre is preserved the upper part of the original belfry. If you are agile and

Périgueux: the domes of the Byzantine cathedral of St-Front

don't mind heights, you can walk about among the domes and turrets on the Cathedral roof and enjoy the views of the old town.

Almost facing you as you leave the Cathedral, again by the N door, is the RUE LIMOGEANNE. In this narrow, winding street, and in the lanes leading off it, is a wealth of 14th–15th-c. houses and shop fronts, with trade signs, courtyards, Renaissance staircases and windows, and many ornamental features. Finally you emerge into the broad Allées de Tourny, and if you turn right you come almost immediately to the PÉRIGORD MUSEUM.

This is well worth a visit. Not only does it house a fine collection of prehistoric finds from the Vézère valley near Les Eyzies (*see entry*), but the end gallery on the ground floor, together with the cloistered courtyard, contains a remarkable assembly of Roman artefacts – mosaic floors, sacrificial altars, statues, portrait heads, jewellery, and hundreds of lapidary fragments with carvings and inscriptions – all unearthed during the excavations of the Gallo-Roman City of Vesunna, 10 minutes' walk to the SW. These Roman relics remind us that the 'old town' by the Cathedral goes back only to medieval times. Vesunna, or Vésone as the French call it, was the old city, and it was there that the history of Périgueux began over two thousand years ago.

Périgueux and the region of Périgord (which corresponds roughly with the modern department of Dordogne) owe their names to the Gallic tribe which first established a settlement here – the Petrocorii. In the last century BC the Petrocorii had to submit to the all-conquering Romans, who proceeded to build here the sophisticated city of VESUNNA, with temples, baths, an aqueduct, a games arena and a forum. For 400 years it was one of the most prosperous cities in SW France, but in the 3rd-c. AD it was sacked by the barbarians as

they attacked one by one the outposts of the crumbling Roman empire. In an unavailing attempt to protect themselves from further onslaughts, the citizens tore down temples and other buildings to form a hastily erected defensive wall – part of which can still be seen adjacent to the ruined 12th-c. CHÂTEAU BARRIÈRE, not far from the site of the Roman arena. The arena itself is now reduced to a few fragments of the outer wall in a public garden.

The best remnant of the Roman city is the 24m Vesunna Tower, or TOUR DE VÉSONE, in the Rue Claude Bernard just S of the railway; one segment of it has fallen, or was pulled down at some stage, but in its original state, when the stone 'brickwork' was faced with marble slabs and bas-reliefs, and it formed part of a temple in the centre of the forum, it must have been impressive indeed.

What the barbarians began, the later destructions of Visigoths, Franks and Normans completed. However, as trade and administration began to revive in the Middle Ages, the 'old city' re-established itself on the Roman site and gradually assumed its responsibility as capital of the province of Périgord. In the 12th-c. it signalized its growing importance by building a four-domed cathedral, St-Étienne (*see below*), just to the SE of the arena.

Meanwhile, on the hill to the NE, a 'new town' was growing up round the monastery of St-Front. This new town, which because of its hilly eminence became known as 'Puy' St-Front, soon outgrew its neighbour, built a larger church and began to usurp some of the old city's administrative functions. The fierce rivalry between them finally ended in 1251 when they united in one community.

ST-ÉTIENNE-DE-LA-CITÉ remained the cathedral of the new conglomerate of Périgueux, but when it was partially destroyed by the Protestants in the Wars of Religion it could no longer fulfil its function as cathedral; despite vain attempts at restoration, it surrendered its status to St-Front in 1669. Today only the two eastern bays still stand, but the interior, under its two remaining domes, retains an aura of grace and faith that is somehow missing from the ponderous cathedral up on the hill. But it is a pity the authorities can't bring themselves to remove altogether the enormous ugly, baroque 17th-c. reredos which at one time obliterated the E wall behind the altar and now leans incongruously against the S wall.

Périgueux has had a chequered history, but today it is a thriving departmental Prefecture, the centre of the great *foie-gras* and truffle industry, of light metal and railway engineering, and more recently the site of a superbly equipped government stamp-printing works.

POMPADOUR, *Corrèze* (15km W of Uzerche: 5–B5). Madame de Pompadour, mistress of Louis XV, never lived in the imposing 15th-c. château which the king gave her, along with the title of marquise, in 1745. Much of the original building was destroyed in the Revolution, but the old gatehouse, the façade and the outer towered walls remain, and the rest has been faithfully restored. Only the terraces are open to the public, for today the château houses the officers in charge of one of the great national studs of France, established by Louis XV in 1761. In the magnificent stables opposite, the famous Puy-Marmont stallions undergo a rigorous training, and if you are interested in horses and horse-breeding they are well worth a visit. In a bowl below the walls of the château is the well-known racecourse, scene of colour and excitement during the meetings held throughout the summer. No wonder that today Pompadour – or Arnac-Pompadour to give it its full name – is known as 'the city of the horse'.

RÉOLE, La, *Gironde* (18km E of Langon: 4–C3). An ancient stronghold on high ground on the right bank of the Garonne. Remarkable for its 12th–14th-c. town hall, one of the oldest in France and still prominent at the top of the town. Unfortunately the castle, its contemporary, is a ruin. Adjoining the much altered 12th–13th-c. church of St-Pierre are the former monastery buildings, now occupied as administrative offices. La Réole is a busy little agricultural market town with attractive narrow winding streets of old houses, and there are good views looking S across the river towards Bazas and the Landes.

ROCAMADOUR, *Lot* (5–C5). A remarkable pilgrim site, famous since the Middle Ages. The easiest approach is from L'Hospitalet, which is off the Martel–Gramat road (N681) and commands a splendid view of the Alzou gorge and Roca-madour itself. The village lies strung out along the foot of a sheer cliff; above it the ecclesiastical city clings to every available shelf in the rock face; and finally, perched on the edge of the cliff summit, is a

19th-c. imitation of a 14th-c. château. From L'Hospitalet you can either drive down and hope to find a parking-space in or near the village, or take the upper road round to the château (where the Rocamadour chaplains now live) and park there.

The straggling village street retains three of its original 13th-c. gateways and a number of old houses (notably the 15th-c. town hall displaying modern tapestries by Lurçat). A few cafés and restaurants with little terraces overlook the valley. Unfortunately the first picturesque impression is spoilt by the clutter of tourist-trinket shops, creating a general bazaar atmosphere which, as at Lourdes, makes a mockery of the pious origins of the place. But don't be put off, for the ecclesiastical city above is more honest and well worth visiting. From the village street it is reached either by lift or by climbing the famous pilgrim stairway, on each of whose 216 steps the genuine pilgrim kneels.

Why do the pilgrims come here? A 12th-c. record states that in 1166 an ancient grave, containing the remains of a man, was unearthed from the floor of a little chapel dedicated to the Virgin. Legend has it that these were the remains of Zaccheus who, fleeing from persecution after Christ's death, came here to end his days as a hermit on the rock. At any rate, the relics were given the name of St-Amadour and placed in a tomb close to the altar, and from that time onward, it is recorded, 'miracles occurred'. The fame of Rocamadour spread throughout Europe. Every year thousands of pilgrims, including French kings and even the English Henry Plantagenet, travelled here to venerate the statue of the Virgin. An abbey and several churches grew up around the chapel, and the shrine accumulated a rich treasure from the donations of the pilgrims, rich and poor. In the poverty-stricken Middle Ages these riches proved too much of a temptation, and the little town was sacked several times. In 1183 the eldest son of Henry Plantagenet, warring against his father but short of money to pay his near-mutinous troops, pillaged the shrine, only to fall mortally ill soon afterwards and die in remorse in Martel (*see entry*). During the Hundred Years War the treasure was frequently robbed – by both sides – but the ultimate disaster came in the Wars of Religion when the Protestants ransacked the shrine, razed most of the churches, broke open the tomb and burned the remains of the hermit saint. The pilgrimages ceased, and have only revived in the last hundred years.

No wonder, then, that most of the buildings of the present ecclesiastical city are the result of the patient reconstruction put in hand during the late 1800s, after the anti-clerical fervour of the Revolution had simmered down. It remains a fascinating place, with its great Fort (formerly the Bishop's Palace) and its seven churches packed together in an amazingly small area, cheek by jowl on different levels, connected by little stair-cases and passageways, and with their outside walls rising sheer from the edge of the rock shelf.

Survivors from the 12th-c. are the Basilique St-Sauveur, with St-Amadour's Crypt below it (containing what are believed to be the saint's charred remains), and the Chapelle St-Michel, built into the overhanging rock and with a 12th-c. painted fresco on its exterior wall.

But the 'holy of holies' is still the Miraculous Chapel of Our Lady of Rocamadour (Chapelle Miraculeuse), rebuilt in the last century on the site of the original chapel. The dark wooden statue of the 'Black Virgin and Child' above the altar, and the bell hanging from the roof (reputed to ring unaided when a miracle is about to occur), are believed by some authorities to be the original sacred objects which somehow survived the Protestant destruction, and they may well be right – certainly both the statue and the bell date from before the year 1000. On the other hand, the great iron sword above the door to the chapel is extremely unlikely to be, as some accounts claim, the original sword 'Durandal' belonging to the legendary Roland.

Despite the disagreeable commercialization, Rocamadour is still a 'must' for the tourist in the area, both for its dramatic situation and for its extraordinary history.

RODEZ, *Aveyron* (5–D6). Former capital of the Rouergue region, now capital of the Aveyron department, Rodez stands on a prominent hill rising to 120m above the river. At the highest point stands the enormous grey-rose Cathedral of Notre-Dame, begun in the 13th-c. and not finished until 300 years later. The severe W front, looking down on the gardens of the Place d'Armes, once formed part of the now vanished ramparts, so it is not surprising that the lower half is almost prison-like; from the ground upwards the walls are virtually devoid of ornamentation, with no porch and no windows; it is not until halfway up that decoration breaks out with a huge rose-window flanked by busy little pinnacles and surmounted by a gable-like classical façade, though the two square towers on either side remain fortress-like to the very top.

On the N side of the Cathedral stands the justly famous belfry tower. Here too the lower half is severely plain, but the upper half, added in the 16th-c. at the personal expense of the bishop, François d'Estaing, is one of the finest examples in France of Flamboyant Gothic and soars high above the rest of the cathedral, reaching a height of 87m. It is visible for miles around.

Entrance to the Cathedral is by the N door. The vast interior is unexpectedly sombre and oppressive: the lofty nave, with side-aisles and ornate side-chapels, is austerely simple, but nobly proportioned. On the S side is an unusual Entombment in painted stone with life-size figures dressed in mid-16th-c. fashion; the colours are still warm and brilliant. Another chapel contains a Renaissance altar with a superb retable which

ranks as one of the masterpieces of 16th-c. sculpture. There is fine wood-carving in the organ-loft in the N transept, and in the S transept a splendid 15th-c. rood-screen (removed from its original position to improve the perspective of the nave). Note the 15th-c. choir-stalls, carved by the same André Sulpice who did those at Villefranche-de-Rouergue (*see entry*), not shown here to same advantage, or perhaps not quite so good. Behind the choir, further chapels contain tombs of early bishops of Rodez.

This is a cathedral to wander in at leisure – there are so many treasures.

Behind the Cathedral, at the E end, is a warren of narrow streets closed to traffic, mercifully free of tourist shops but full of decent *boucheries*, *charcuteries, patisseries* and other purveyors of the delicious edible products of the region. At every turn you catch fresh glimpses of the Cathedral towering above the town. The Place de la Cité has a good Saturday market. The quarter is full of examples of 14th-, 15th- and 16th-c. houses, two of which (off the Place du Bourg) together contain the Musée Fenaille with its archaeological exhibits and sundry works of art (open in summer months only). The Musée des Beaux-Arts (open most of the year) is on the E side of the Bd. Denys-Puech and contains paintings and sculpture.

A good touring centre, full of pleasure and interest.

ROQUEFORT-SUR-SOULZON, *Aveyron* (15km SW of Millau: 5–D6, D7). Over 750,000 ewes (*brebis*) graze on the thin grass of the limestone plateaux (or *causses*) south of the Massif Central, and their milk is brought to the factories of Roquefort to be processed into one of the best – and most expensive – cheeses in the world.

First, the milk is heated, curdled and strained. The curd is then treated with the powdered mould of *penicillium roqueforti* and stuffed into small drums, about 20cm in diameter and 15cm deep. A few days later the surfaces are lightly rubbed with sea salt, and perforated to allow air to penetrate the interior. Finally the drums are stored on racks in vast, vaulted cellars in uniquely favourable conditions created by an accident of nature.

The town of Roquefort-sur-Soulzon is built at the foot of a dramatic limestone formation known as the 'mountain' of Combalou. Here, millions of years ago, a geological fault produced a 'chaos' of tumbled limestone rock, whose crevices allow a flow of ventilation to percolate to the caves below, at a constant cool temperature of 7–8°C. and with an unvarying level of high humidity – conditions which happen to be ideal for the slow maturing of the penicillin. The ripening process takes about three months.

Roquefort cheese was mentioned by Pliny in Rome in the 1st-c. AD. Charlemagne had it delivered to him regularly at Aix-la-Chapelle in the 8th-c. In the 11th-c. the monastery at Conques recorded a gift of Roquefort cheese. And in the

Douglas Dickins

La Roque-Gageac

18th-c. Casanova was seduced by a lady who served him a meal including 'a delicious Roquefort cheese' – which moved him, afterwards, to exclaim: 'Oh, what wonderful restoratives are Roquefort and Chambertin!' Clearly this cheese, with its strong, biting flavour, has been well known for a long time.

The cellars of the Société des Caves are open to visitors all the year round – but remember to wear something warm, even in summer.

ROQUE-GAGEAC, La, *Dordogne* (7km S of Sarlat: 5–C5). A pretty village on a graceful bend of the Dordogne, strung out along the riverside road and bunched up against the great cliff which rears alarmingly behind it. Steep alleyways wind up between the old stone houses, through archways and past odd corners of rock where mimosa and cactus flourish. On the upper level, built on a shelf of rock, is a humble, rather neglected little 12th-c. church with a wide view of the river curving below. Wherever you walk you can't help being aware of the great mass of sheer cliff poised almost directly overhead, riddled with caves and bulging with precariously balanced outcrops of rock. One day not so many years ago a huge piece of rock did in fact break off, causing loss of life and demolishing several buildings; the

patch of fresh ochre surface where the rock split, high up on the cliff face, is clearly visible. The château at the W extremity of the village is a 19th-c. imitation of the 15th-c. style.

ST-AMAND-DE-COLY, *Dordogne* (7km E of Montignac: 5–C5). One of the most remarkable fortified churches in SW France. When the monks of the now vanished abbey built it in the 12th-c., out of blocks of the local yellow-grey limestone, they clearly had in mind not only the glory of God but also the physical defence of the Faith by all military means. They built well, for the church survived the depredations of the English and French soldiery, and in 1575, when the Huguenots seized it and installed a garrison, it took the Governor of Périgord six days of bombardment by cannon to get them out. The abbey was revived, the monks repaired the war damage and lived peaceably until the order was dissolved by the Revolution. After nearly a century of neglect the church was classified as a Historic Monument, and tactful restoration has preserved it in its present austere beauty.

The abbey and the cloisters have vanished, but much of the old ramparts remains. The exterior of the church is impressively severe, the ground plan a simple Latin cross. The walls rise to a great

Photo Zodiaque

St-Amand-de-Coly: the interior of the fortified church

height, with no ornamentation to soften their defensive purpose. From the foot of the bleakly rectangular W tower your eye is carried upward by the tall, pointed, deeply indented arch; high up within the arch is the first sign of the old defences – two rows of corbels, intended to support a platform from which the defenders could fire down on the attackers below. As you enter, the creaking of the door echoes within the bare, lofty nave; the few rush-seated chairs of the parish congregation are the only furniture. No pulpit, no organ, just a starkly simple altar at the top of a wide flight of steps, to which the eye is drawn across the worn stones of the upward sloping floor. High above the choir are the remains of another defensive feature: a gallery, supported on corbels, and connected through small doorways with other galleries round the transept and nave, enabling the defenders to move swiftly to meet a threatened attack from any point of the exterior.

ST-AVIT-SÉNIEUR, *Dordogne* (4km E of Beaumont: 4–C4). Set back off the Cadouin–Beaumont road, St-Avit-Sénieur stands prominently on its isolated hill as a grim and desolate reminder of an unhappy past. It was named after a 6th-c. soldier who, taken prisoner by the Visigoths, was converted to Christianity, created a hermitage here, and on his death was proclaimed a saint. In the 9th-c., Norman soldiers rampaging through the countryside destroyed the hermitage. Two centuries later Benedictine monks founded an abbey here, but in 1214, during the Albigensian crusade (*see* Albi), the abbey was set on fire and destroyed by supporters of the heretics.

The church was fortified and the abbey rebuilt, only to be destroyed again during the Hundred Years War. Rebuilt yet again, in 1577 the abbey suffered its final calamity when a band of roaming Huguenots set fire to it, massacred the monks and ransacked the church. Four centuries have passed. Of the abbey only a few ruined walls remain, and the huge fortified church which failed to defend it is in a state of neglect. A sad place.

ST-BERTRAND-DE-COMMINGES, *Haute-Garonne* (4–E4). Don't miss this if you are touring the central Pyrenees, for here is one of the most beautiful churches in France. A detour of only 1km off the Montréjeau–Luchon road will bring you to this little walled town on its rocky hill with the Cathedral rearing up against a background of mountains.

At the time of Christ it was an important Roman provincial capital. Herod was exiled here not long after Christ's crucifixion. Four centuries later the city was destroyed by the barbarians. On the level ground below the hill you can visit the recently excavated remains of the Roman forum, thermal baths, a theatre and a temple, and the museum up in the town has a collection of prehistoric and Roman objects found here.

Later towns, built on the hill and protected by ramparts, were ravaged by plague or vandalized by warring barons. When, in 1120, Bertrand, Bishop of Comminges, had his vision of building a cathedral here, the place had long been a deserted ruin. He established a chapter of canons, building was started, and the town began to revive.

You enter through a fortified gate in the ramparts and reach the little square below the bell-

St-Bertrand-de-Comminges: the church cloisters

French Government Tourist Office

Denis Hughes-Gilbey

St-Cirq-Lapopie

tower at the W end of the Cathedral. A flight of steps leads up to the 12th-c. doorway, surmounted by a well-preserved tympanum of the Adoration of the Magi. Passing through the porch under the tower, you enter a surprisingly short nave. This end of the church is the original 12th-c. structure (though the pulpit and organ to your left, and the altar on the S wall to your right, are of later dates), and this was the area permitted to the public congregation. A large carved rood-screen, with a railing on either side, firmly bars the way to the much larger 14th-c. extension which contains the enormous choir and was the preserve of the canons. To get to it you must go back through the W door, turn left and, on payment of a modest fee, enter by the cloisters.

Although small, these cloisters are unique, for the whole of the S wall is open to a marvellous prospect of the Garonne valley and the mountains beyond. One cannot help envying the canons in their perambulations here, such is the atmosphere of tranquillity still to be felt within these ancient walls, with their 12th-c. tombstone inscriptions (alas, disfigured by tourist *graffiti*) and the arcade pillars topped with delicate carvings, all so unusually juxtaposed with the beauty of the outside world.

From the cloisters a side door leads you back into the Cathedral – this time into the lofty space of the Gothic extension built in the 14th-c. In spite of its size it has the atmosphere of a private chapel, and so in a sense it was. Half its length is occupied by the great choir created in the 16th-c. The stalls, the bishop's throne and the whole enclosure together form a Renaissance masterpiece of exuberantly sculptured wood, in which representations of piety and devotion mingle with those of malicious satire and robust lewdness.

Behind the high altar is the tomb of the founder, St-Bertrand himself, facing the semi-circle of little chapels which form the chevet at the E end. On the S side of the choir, above the side door, a short flight of steps leads to a small raised chapel from which you get an unusual elevated view of this unforgettable cathedral.

ST-CIRQ-LAPOPIE, *Lot* (18km E of Cahors: 5–C5). Surely one of the most beautiful villages in France, remarkable for its dramatic site high up on a precipitous cliff, with a jagged bowl of rocky hills behind and the Lot flowing directly below. The name (the 'q' is silent) recalls both a 3rd-c. saint, St Cyr, and the local lord La Popie who built the castle (now a ruin) on the peak just over a thousand years ago. A stronghold in such a situation was bound to attract trouble in the stormy centuries to follow. In 1199 Richard Cœur-de-Lion tried to capture it but was repulsed. In the Hundred Years War it was taken and retaken several times. In 1580, in the Wars of Religion, the Huguenot leader Henry of Navarre, having captured and sacked Cahors, took St-Cirq-Lapopie and demolished the castle.

The seigneur moved downhill to the more modest turreted stone house known as La Gardette (now a museum, with an alarming cliff-edge garden); the townspeople, then numbering over 1000, continued with their ancient craft of wood-turning, using the local maple forests for raw material. Throughout the 19th-c. and up to World War I, the town was famous throughout France for making the wooden taps used for wine casks. Mechanization ruined this trade; one small workshop keeps going for the tourists, who today provide the sole income for the 150 inhabitants.

With its castle long gone, the village is dominated by the church. Built in the 15th-c. for both worship and defence, it has a plain high nave flanked by simple chapels, narrow windows, and a double Renaissance doorway surmounted by a square bell-tower, with a round watch-tower built in at one corner. The old houses, of various periods from the 13th- to the 16th-c. jostle each other down the hill, built largely of stone but partly of timber and narrow bricks; many have wooden balconies.

ST-ÉMILION, *Gironde* (4–C3). A historic fortified town, centre of one of the largest and most renowned of the Bordeaux wine districts. It perches invitingly on its hilltop 2km N of the Libourne–Bergerac road, and is well worth a detour. Drive to the top of the town, park by the main church, the Église Collégiale, and walk westward round the church to the little square by the bell-tower. Looking down at the little market square directly below, at the ancient grey and rose-ochre stone buildings, and over the rooftops to the endless vineyards beyond, it is difficult to imagine that this well-preserved, peaceful town has a bloody history. For many years under English

Denis Hughes-Gilbey
St-Emilion: part of the monolithic church

rule, it changed hands several times in the Hundred Years War, was fought over by Catholics and Huguenots, and actively engaged in bitter local struggles at the time of the Revolution. Yet through it all, from Roman times onward, viticulture has triumphantly survived.

A steep cobbled street leads down to the market square, centre of a number of ancient sites, including the CATACOMBS, the CHAPELLE DE LA TRINITÉ, and the supposed HERMITAGE of the 8th-c. St Émilian after whom the town is named. Not to be missed is the interior of the subterranean MONOLITHIC CHURCH, carved out of the solid rock hillside by Benedictine monks around the year 1100 by the process of enlarging existing caves. During the Revolution it was stripped of its altar and tombs, bones and all, and turned into a military saltpetre store, which effectively ruined the frescoes, of which only fragments are visible. Reconsecrated in 1837, it remains a gaunt, impressively foreboding place, with its two rows of massive rectangular rock pillars reaching up to a carved-out, vaulted roof. On a fine morning, the sun streaming down through the deep-set windows casts an ethereal light into the sombre chamber, the largest of its kind in Europe. In the roof can be seen the two holes through which ropes once led up to the bell-tower, built overhead on the upper level of the town at various intervals from about 1100, the spire being completed in the 15th-c.

The ÉGLISE COLLÉGIALE is a large church

constructed at different periods. The exterior is not a harmonious whole, though the 12th-c. W door is very fine; the N door is early 14th-c. but the sculptures were severely damaged during the Revolution. The interior is disappointing, the proportions being ruined by an ugly, intrusive pulpit, and there are the usual tasteless paintings. But the 14th-c. cloister, with its colonnades of elegant double pillars, is beautiful.

Also worth a visit are: the TOUR DU ROI, actually the keep of the King's castle built on the orders of Henry III of England in the 13th-c., from the top of which you get a wide view of the town and the Dordogne valley, and from the foot of which is made the annual proclamation of the opening of the wine harvest; and the COUVENT DES CORDELIERS, the ruins of a 14th-c. Franciscan monastery with a romantic overgrown cloister.

St-Émilion is a thriving town, with traditions of wine culture and management going back beyond the days when Edward I of England promulgated the limits of its jurisdiction, which are exactly the limits of the *appellation contrôlée* today. The vineyards crowd against the ancient battlements of the town, and it is a wonderful experience to drive through the surrounding country in late September or early October when the *vendange* fever is at its height.

ST-GAUDENS, *Haute-Garonne* (4–E4). A busy town almost exactly halfway between the Atlantic and the Mediterranean along the N117, the road which runs along the foothills of the Pyrenees from Biarritz to Perpignan. St-Gaudens' origins lie in Roman times, but it owes its recent resurgence of prosperity to the discovery and post-war exploitation of natural gas centred on St-Marcet, 12km N. Built on the edge of a plateau, it looks S across the Garonne valley to the Pyrenees; for the tourist the view from the Bd. Jean-Bepmale and the public gardens is somewhat marred by the great factory only 2km away which makes 500 tons of cellulose a day and pours white smoke over the valley, but the panorama of mountain scenery beyond, partly wooded, partly snow-capped, is certainly magnificent.

The 12th-c. church on the S side of the Place Jean-Jaurès does not dominate the town, as so many French churches do; it blends with it and stands modestly as the natural centre of daily life. It was considerably damaged when the Huguenots sacked it in 1569, and the exterior, especially the tower, has been much restored, but the N side facing the square is rich in small decorative sculptured features – rosettes, fruits, comic heads, and so on. The interior is impressively simple, with delicate stone carvings at the tops of the pillars in the nave. On the side walls (rather hard to see in the gloom) are three Aubusson tapestries, one of which (on the N wall) is an exuberant design by Rubens.

A good town to stay in, and an excellent jumping-off point for visits to St-Bertrand-de-Comminges, Bagnères-de-Luchon (*see entries*) and other places in the central Pyrenees.

ST-GIRONS, *Ariège* (4, 5–E4, E5). A quiet, rather undistinguished little town which has somehow failed to make the best of its situation astride the river Salat, with its sharply angled weir and the views of the Pyrenees to the south. Halfway between St-Gaudens and Foix, it is a paper-making centre.

At **St-Lizier**, 2km N, is an interesting Romanesque cathedral with a beautiful 12th-c. cloister in two storeys rich in decorated capitals.

ST-JEAN-DE-LUZ, *Pyrénées-Atlantiques* (4–E2). Until the 18th-c., Basque fishermen from St-Jean-de-Luz used to work the Arctic whaling grounds. It is still a thriving fishing port, and in recent times has also become a lively, popular seaside resort and yachting centre. It has a wonderful curving beach, a casino, many hotels, restaurants serving Basque menus, and plenty to do and watch – especially in the evening when the fishing-boats return to harbour and sell their catches of tuna, sardines and anchovies at the quaysides by the Place Louis XIV. This great open space facing the harbour was so named in honour of a royal event which took place here over 300 years ago and which the town can never forget – the sumptuous wedding of Louis XIV and the Spanish princess Marie-Thérèse on 9 June 1660.

All the details are lovingly recorded: the brilliant cortège setting off from the quayside house known as the Maison de l'Infante, the procession to the great church of St-Jean-Baptiste, the three-hour wedding ceremony (the bride wore a silver gown, a purple velvet cloak and a golden crown), and then the return to the bride's house, where from the balcony the King and Cardinal Mazarin tossed commemorative medals to the cheering crowds. Dinner was taken at the nearby Maison de Louis XIV, attended by the whole court, after which the royal couple were escorted upstairs to the marriage bed, where the Queen Mother blessed them, drew the curtains and at last left them alone. After all that, it is sad that the King found his bride rather dull, and later consoled himself with a series of mistresses.

The church where the marriage was solemnized was built in the 13th-c. Typically Basque in style, it has a somewhat severe exterior but is extremely interesting inside, with a nave surrounded by three tiers of galleries where the men (and only the men) of the congregation take their places during certain parts of the service, and an altar raised high and adorned with a magnificent gilded screen and several statues. One senses that Spain is not far away. As you come out of the main door, note the doorway through which the Sun King and his bride passed; after the ceremony it was walled up, and is still walled up, to ensure that no commoner should use it thereafter.

Across the river Nive, on the other side of the

harbour, is the little town of **Ciboure**, now virtually an extension of St-Jean-de-Luz. The quayside which runs from the yacht basin to the outer breakwater is named after the composer Maurice Ravel, who was born at No. 12 in 1875 (d. 1937).

A good excursion is to drive 10km inland on the D918, through the Basque village of Ascain, until you reach the Col de St-Ignace; here a rack railway takes you to the top of **La Rhune**, a 900m mountain right on the Spanish border, with staggering views of the western Pyrenees, the Atlantic, the Basque coastline and, on the northern horizon, the dark line of the great Landes pine forests.

ST-JEAN-PIED-DE-PORT, *Pyrénées-Atlantiques* (4–E2). '*Port*' is a Pyrenean dialect word meaning 'mountain pass', hence the name of this ancient hilltop town at the foot of the Roncesvalles Pass. In the Middle Ages it was an important resting place for pilgrims before they started their daunting journey over the Pyrenees en route for Santiago de Compostella in the extreme NW corner of Spain.

Within its 15th-c. ramparts the old town climbs steeply towards the great citadel which dominates the countryside. Below, on the S bank of the Nive, the 'new town' lies within another wall of ramparts, erected in the 17th-c., and contains the great court and wall of the pelota ground (known as the *fronton*) on which, amid great festivity, the final rounds of the pelota championships are fought out every July and August.

This is a good place to stay for a while. There are several hotels, heated swimming pools, and at least one extremely good restaurant. From 1 July to mid-September the old town provides the background for a fine *son et lumière*. You will certainly wish to explore some of the majestic mountain scenery; here are some worthwhile excursions:

The road to the W takes you through St-Étienne-de-Baïgorry and then winds up the dramatic valley of **Les Aldudes** with its red rocks and turbulent river, the odd château, and everywhere the soaring mountain peaks. The road S from St-Jean involves crossing the Spanish frontier at Arnéguy, but if your papers are in order and there is any romance in your soul it is worth going up to the top, for this is the **Pass of Roncesvalles** where the legendary Roland, one of Charlemagne's generals, was killed in AD 778. Another excursion takes you E out of the town to St-Jean-le-Vieux, then right by the D18 on to a road which becomes increasingly sinuous and brings you to the magnificent **Forest of Iraty** in one of the wildest parts of the Pyrenees.

ST-JUNIEN, *Haute-Vienne* (4–B4). A thriving town on the N bank of the Vienne, manufacturing paper, gloves and leather. The collegiate church is an unusual example of the Romanesque-Limousin

style and contains a masterpiece of 12th-c. sculpture.

The façade has an arched doorway at the top of a flight of steps. At each extremity of the first storey an octagonal turret with a minaret spire creates an unexpected impression, part military, part Byzantine. Between the turrets the façade narrows to form a solid base for the square two-storey belfry, originally designed to extend upwards with two further storeys, octagonal in the Limousin style (as at St-Léonard-de-Noblat) – indeed, on the upper storey, at the foot of the spire, can be seen the bases of the intended Limousin gables. The resulting compromise is surprisingly successful.

The interior has been considerably rebuilt and restored since the church's inception in the 11th-c., especially in this century after the central lantern tower over the transept collapsed in 1922. The church is full of interesting features, including curious 16th-c. statuettes placed about the nave, and the remains of frescoes, but its chief glory is the tomb of St Junien, the hermit saint after whom the town is named and whose bones are shown and revered every seven years. The tomb, situated behind the high altar, is a marvellous example of Limousin sculpture. The principal figure, Christ in Majesty on the east face, is somewhat disfigured, but the carvings of the Old Men of the Apocalypse on the north and south faces are in near-perfect condition. Most appealing of all, perhaps, are the figures of the Virgin and Child framed within a mandorla whose outer corners are ingeniously filled with angels leaping in ecstasy.

At the S edge of the town a 13th-c. bridge with cutwaters spans the river. At the N end of the bridge is the graceful little chapel of Notre-Dame-du-Pont, erected in the 15th-c. and containing a statue of the Virgin of the same date.

The tributary river Glane flows into the Vienne just W of the town; a pleasant walk upstream on the E bank of the Glane leads to a picturesque stretch often painted by Corot, and indeed known as the 'Site Corot'.

10km W on the N141 is the moated **Château Rochebrune**, with four huge medieval towers linked by residential quarters. (Open Easter to early November.)

ST-LÉONARD-DE-NOBLAT, *Haute-Vienne* (18km E of Limoges: 5–B5). Agriculture and small industry are the main activities of this modest hilltop town overlooking the Maulde valley, but it is also known for two delicacies, its macaroons and its *pruneaux confits*. It has long outgrown its medieval quarter, whose interesting old houses huddle close to the church. The town was named after the 6th-c. St Léonard (the 'patron saint of prisoners'), who was a godson of the Frankish king Clovis but rejected a court career to become a religious hermit. His tomb is in the S transept of the church, and the reliquary casket is kept on the altar.

The church, part of which dates from the 11th-c., is a not altogether successful mixture of architectural periods and plans. The three western bays of the nave have no side-aisles, but the next two bays have very narrow side-aisles which continue into the transept and create an awkward narrowing of the perspective. Seven chapels radiate behind the choir. The transept is roofed by three cupolas, one over the crossing and a smaller one over each wing. The most interesting feature is the belfry, considered to be the best example of the Limousin style. Adjoining the exterior of the N wall and forming the entrance to the church, its first three arcaded tiers are built square, supporting three smaller tiers which are octagonal in plan and partly concealed behind four characteristically tall Limousin gables. Over all is a short octagonal spire. Another oddity of the church is the low round sepulchre chapel, now the baptistry, jammed almost as an afterthought between the belfry and the N wing of the transept.

ST-YRIEIX-LA-PERCHE, Haute-Vienne
(5–B5). Perched high on a hill in rich cattle-rearing countryside, St-Yrieix is a lively town well known for its markets and fairs, its chinaware and shoemaking, and the delicious little rum-flavoured sponge-cakes called *madeleines*. It was the discovery here of rich deposits of pure kaolin, just over 200 years ago, that provided the raw material for the porcelain industry which brought world-wide fame to Limoges, 40km N (*see entry*). St-Yrieix itself has two porcelain factories (which can be seen by arrangement), and one of the quarries can be seen about 3km E on the N701.

The busy jumble of narrow streets and small squares on the W side of the town centres round the 12th–13th-c. collegiate church, built on the site of a 6th-c. abbey founded by the saint. This is a large and handsome building, obviously designed with defensive requirements in mind. A remarkable feature is the unique series of decorated corbels whose figures (of knights in armour, etc.) lean out into space from the eaves and seem to grip the roof with their toes; these corbels continue through to the inside of the church, where the ends are carved in a variety of faces, at the same time supporting a narrow gallery which runs most of the way round the church. The nave is simple and uncluttered, giving a restful impression of space and clean lines. On the left of the chancel stands the shrine of St Yrieix, and beside it, in a gloomy niche behind a gilded grille, is the 15th-c. reliquary head of the saint, made of wood and covered with a mask of beaten silver – rather impressive and beautiful.

SARLAT, Dordogne (5–C5).
It would be a mistake to judge Sarlat from the long *traverse* of modern shop fronts as you drive straight through from north to south, or from the boulevards which loop the traffic round the town centre. Either side of the *traverse* (which was slashed through the town

Douglas Dickins

Sarlat: Maison de La Boétie

early in the 19th-c.) lies an absorbing maze of narrow medieval streets with well-preserved ochre-stone buildings from the 12th- to the 17th-c., many of them still with their pebbly grey-stone roofs.

The best of these are on the E side, starting opposite the Cathedral with the Maison de La Boétie, a most beautiful Renaissance house with rich stone carvings on the window frames. This house was the birthplace of Étienne de La Boétie, renowned poet, Bordeaux administrator, and close friend of Montaigne (*see entry*). Montaigne was at his bedside when he died in 1563 at the age of 33, and wrote the famous essay *On Friendship* in his memory.

The Cathedral was built on the site of the 12th-c. Benedictine abbey church around which the town grew up. The entrance porch and the clock tower are an uncomfortable mixture of periods, and the masonry is in a shabby state of disrepair; when you look up at the tower, crowned with its 'bulb' and lantern, the whole thing frankly looks positively unsafe. Restoration is in progress on the main body of the church. The interior, with sturdy pillars, windows set high above the nave, and a newly restored chancel, has noble proportions which impart a sense of space and tranquillity, inviting the passer-by to a few moments of prayer or contemplation.

Adjoining the Cathedral entrance is the former episcopal palace, rather grand in the 15th-c. Florentine style, with a pretty 16th-c. loggia on the upper floor. Opposite, an archway under the left side of the Boëtie house leads into a beautifully restored walk-through of narrow alleys, archways and modest courtyards, one of which has a balcony worthy of Romeo and Juliet. You arrive in the market-place, in front of the 16th-c. house known as the Hôtel de Maleville, with a handsome doorway next to an arched passageway.

The market-place is a large open area in front of the 17th-c. town hall, surrounded by ancient buildings, a wonderful setting for the Saturday morning market which virtually takes over the whole town; even the *traverse* is closed to traffic and lined with stalls offering every kind of produce. The market-place itself is thronged with buyers and sellers who have come in from the surrounding country – a gay, bustling scene which overflows into the crowded little streets that radiate in all directions.

During the Sarlat Theatre Festival (last week of July, first week of August) the market-place is transformed into an open-air theatre; a large auditorium stand is erected in the middle of the square, and a huge stage is built into the north corner; the old houses around it form a superb backdrop when illuminated at night. Well-known companies come here from Paris each summer to perform Molière, Shakespeare and other classics.

Many happy hours can be spent wandering about the old streets of Sarlat. You ought not to miss the Hôtel Plamon, a most carefully restored 14th–15th-c. house in the Rue des Consuls, facing the little square where they have the goose market. Also try the Rue de la Salamandre, which takes you uphill from the market-place under an arch and past many remarkable old houses; it will lead you to the Rue Montaigne, a steep cobbled lane which descends past a curious 12th-c. tower called the 'Lantern of the Dead' (probably a funerary chapel) and returns you finally to the Cathedral.

SAUTERNAIS, Le, *Gironde* (7km W of Langon: 4–C3). A small but important wine area S of Bordeaux on the left bank of the Garonne, immediately W of Langon, where the vineyards of Sauternes, Barsac and – most illustrious of all – Château Yquem, produce the most famous sweet white wines in the world.

Barsac has an unusual early 17th-c. church with three naves, **Budos** the remains of a 14th-c. fortress château, and **Malle** a charming early 17th-c. residential château surrounded by terraced gardens and sometimes open to the public in summer.

SÉGUR-LE-CHÂTEAU, *Corrèze* (10km SE of St-Yrieix: 5–B5). As you enter Ségur, and especially if you happen to do so in the evening light, you may feel you have strayed into one of Tennyson's evocations of Arthurian legend. The ivy-hung ruin of the ancient castle broods above the sleepy village and at first sight seems to be surrounded by a moat, for the river Auvézère almost encircles it with a tight horseshoe bend before departing over a weir. Once the native stronghold of the counts of Limoges, Ségur is one

of those backwaters of history which can still amaze and delight the traveller who is prepared to wander a little off the beaten track.

SOLIGNAC, *Haute-Vienne* (8km S of Limoges: 5–B5). Situated in the pretty valley of the Briance, Solignac is notable for its early 12th-c. church, once part of an abbey that was founded in AD 632 but no longer exists – thanks to the Normans, the Saracens, the English, the Huguenots, and no doubt the Revolution as well.

The church itself has undergone many changes, but what stands here today is a design of satisfying simplicity. The ground plan is cruciform, with three domes in line – two over the nave and one over the transept crossing – supported on bold, pointed arches. From the W porch you enter the nave down a short flight of semi-circular steps; plain high windows flood the space with light and bring out the warm colour of the granite. In the nave and in the transept arms, elegant blind arcades relieve the plain walls and support a little gallery which vanishes behind the massive square bases of the main arches. The transepts are odd, one having an ovoid cupola for a roof, the other having cradle vaulting. In the S transept is a faded 15th-c. fresco of St Christopher.

The chancel is almost circular, with three radiating chapels half hidden behind the choir-screen; here again plenty of light comes from the chapel windows, some with 15th-c. stained glass, and from the semi-circle of small apertures set high in the chevet wall. Richly inventive carving abounds in the 15th-c. choir-stalls, and on the capitals both inside and outside the church.

Well worth a visit if you are staying in Limoges or travelling S on the D704 through St-Yrieix-la-Perche.

5km SE are the daunting ruins of the 12th-c. castle of **Chalusset**, approached by a private path. Occupied by the English during the Hundred Years War, it was used as a base by the Huguenots in the 16th-c. until the Catholics from Limoges launched a full-scale assault, took the castle and dismantled it.

SOUILLAC, *Lot* (5–C5). A busy shopping-centre astride the N20 on the N bank of the Dordogne, remarkable for one thing – the beautiful old abbey church of Ste-Marie at the SW corner of the town, just off the Sarlat road.

From the large open parking-space by the E end of the church there is an impressive view of the compact, rounded masses of the three Byzantine-like cupolas of the roof and the curved walls of the radiating chapels. The former Benedictine abbey suffered terrible damage from the English in the Hundred Years War, and again from the Pro-testants in the Wars of Religion, being rebuilt from the ruins each time. Fortunately the 12th-c. church, though frequently pillaged, has survived, virtually intact except for the addition of the 17th-c. façade at the W end.

The bell-tower and entrance porch are severely simple, almost fortress-like. Immediately inside the inner door is a famous masterpiece of Romanesque sculpture: the original outer doorway which was removed in the 17th-c. reconstruction and placed here facing the interior, safe from further weathering. The complicated story depicted in the stone carving doesn't matter, but the busy scenes, alive with figures of saints, prophets and sundry beasts, are exquisitely chiselled. Most striking of all, to the right of the door as you face it, is the large bas-relief (unfortunately defaced during the religious wars) of the prophet Isaiah in an unexpectedly vigorous, fluid pose, with the left leg twisted forward and the hands deployed in an eloquent gesture.

The church interior strikes the observer with an immediate impression of light and space. The nave has no aisles or side-chapels, but is broad and plain. The high roof, with its three domes in line, adds to the general sense of serenity. A narrow gallery, high up, runs all round the church. Restoration is still needed on the windows behind the simple altar, and in the transept are traces of some not very successful early 18th-c. frescoes. But looking back down the church, with the sunlight casting a golden light on the bare stone walls, one is struck again by the harmonious proportions of the building.

TARBES, *Hautes-Pyrénées* (4–E3, E4). Capital of the Hautes-Pyrénées department and a growing industrial and marketing centre on the left bank of the Adour. Although it was already an important settlement in Roman times, over the centuries it suffered so much from invasions and wars that there is not much left that is old. The Cathedral itself has been much altered and restored since it was first built in the 12th-c.

However, the town makes a convenient and agreeable centre for Pyrenean excursions. In Tarbes itself, just S of the Cathedral, is the celebrated national stud-farm, Les Haras, which was founded in 1806 and is open to visitors most afternoons. A short walk NE from the Cathedral is the delightful Jardin Mussey, with a 15th-c. cloister rebuilt among the trees, and a local museum whose tower affords a panoramic view of the surrounding plain, the Adour valley and the Pyrenees.

TOULOUSE, *Haute-Garonne* (5–D5). Once capital of the former province of Languedoc, the ancient red-brick city of Toulouse ('*la ville rose*') is now France's fourth largest metropolis and its principal centre of aircraft research and construction. It straddles the Garonne, and is within sight of the Pyrenees on a clear day. The old quarter, built largely of the local faded red brick, lies mostly on the right bank. This is still the heart of the city, retaining its individual character despite the post-war spread of industrial suburbs. It has many remarkable churches, aristocratic old houses, a great variety of museums, shaded gardens with fountains, open squares, pedestrian-only streets, glimpses of courtyards. The daily life of the city is enlivened by the students of the University, founded in 1229, now slanted in favour of the Sciences. There are 40,000 students, more than in any other French university outside Paris. At midday and late afternoon the outdoor cafés of the Place Wilson and the Place du Capitole are scenes of leisurely animation. Restaurants abound, some of them not at all expensive, and night life goes on to a late hour.

Two broad shopping thoroughfares traverse the old city: the Rue Alsace-Lorraine from N to S, and the Rue de Metz which runs E from the Pont Neuf. Two ring-roads of wide boulevards carry the main burden of traffic outside the centre. Even so, traffic jams are frequent, especially in summer, and parking is a headache. (Try first the Place du Capitole; as a last resort make for the Allées Jules Guesde, which runs from the Pont St-Michel to the Grand Rond roundabout, 15 minutes' walk from the centre.)

Toulouse has been a human settlement since prehistoric times. The Romans knew it as Tolosa and made it into the third largest city in the whole of Gaul. Capital of the Visigoths in the 5th-c., after the defeat of Alaric it became part of the kingdom of the Franks, but its distance from Paris gave it virtual autonomy under the rule of the Counts Raymond from the 9th- to the 13th-c.

In the early 13th-c. came the Pope's crusade against the Albigensian heretics (*see* Albi); the Count of Toulouse was accused of complicity in the murder of a papal legate near Nîmes, and after defeating the southern heretic army Simon de Montfort entered Toulouse and began a regime of terror and murder. Later, in de Montfort's absence, the Count of Toulouse reoccupied the town; de Montfort returned and besieged it. In the course of the siege, in 1218, de Montfort was killed by a stone from a giant sling – a death mourned by few. Peace followed in due course, though the Inquisition continued to hunt down the dwindling band of heretics until their final massacre in 1244 at Montségur (*see* Foix).

Later, when the daughter and only child of the last Count of Toulouse married the brother of King Louis IX, the *comté* became a royal possession. Toulouse was designated capital of the newly defined province of Languedoc, a region which then stretched from the Pyrenees to the Rhône with a cultural autonomy proudly separate from the rest of France. After the Revolution the province, like the rest of France, was split up into departments more closely linked with the central government.

At the beginning of this century, Toulouse was a pioneer in the field of aviation. It was here, under the inspiration of famous pilots like Saint-Exupéry, that the first steps in French civil aviation were taken. 1919 saw the inauguration of a regular air-mail service to Morocco, 1930 the first commercial air service to South America. Ever since, Toulouse has been the centre of French aerospace research and civil aircraft construction (Caravelle, Concorde, Airbus) and, more recently, the main centre of the French electronics industry.

The city's finest treasure from the past is the ÉGLISE DES JACOBINS, a short walk W from the Place du Capitole. The church of a monastery founded in 1216, it was completed by the end of the 14th-c. At the Revolution it was confiscated by the State, and in 1820 the army appropriated it for use as stables for 500 horses and accommodation for their riders, grooms and vets. Damage and neglect brought it to a state of well-nigh irreparable ruin. In 1865 public pressure got the army out, but it was not until the end of the century that finance was found for serious long-term restoration. The work was completed only as recently as the mid-1970s. The result, as you enter through the S door, is breathtaking.

The vast double nave, divided by a single line of massive pillars, stretches in an unbroken space from the W wall to a semi-circle of apsidal chapels at the E end. The sense of space is emphasized by the huge uncluttered area of floor, all on one level, paved with large slabs of beautiful stone in shades of pink and grey. The Gothic windows are tall and narrow, and go all round the church except the W wall; those flanking the western half of the nave are ablaze with glorious abstract designs by the 20th-c. master *verrier* Max Ingrand – cool colours to the north, to the south warm reds and yellows projected and diffused by the sun over stone pillars and paved floor. The W wall has two high rose-windows, still with their original 14th-c. stained glass; below them, two arched windows have modern stained glass using matching colours.

The only other modern note is struck by the altar: instead of being at the E end, remote from the congregation, it has been placed halfway down the N nave, facing across to the S wall; it consists of a simple white stone table on a dais of shallow steps. A space under the table reveals a gilded casket containing the relics of the great 13th-c. saint, Thomas Aquinas.

The centre line of seven round pillars, made of white stone, enormously thick but so tall they seem slender, carries the eye up to the extraordinary, probably unique roof. From the top of each pillar, eight slim brick arches fan out to form an ogival vaulting with the arches meeting them from the outer walls. At the E end, the last pillar supports no fewer than 22 brick arches, spreading out like the branches of a palm-tree. The only unhappy note is the painted imitation of brickwork between these arches, and elsewhere in the church interior – but that is a minor blemish on what is otherwise a masterpiece of space, light and colour contained within a lofty vessel of great simplicity.

The cloisters, entered through a door in the NW corner of the nave, are a faithful reconstruction of the elegant original destroyed by the army's occupation; some of the 13th-c. capitals were found and have been incorporated. From the W gallery you get a splendid view of the church's austere pink-brick exterior and the great Roman-esque octagonal tower which abuts on to the NE corner of the nave. In the former monastery buildings which make the E wall of the cloisters, are the *salle capitulaire* and a chapel, both opening out on to the cloisters and with fragments of the original frescoes.

The other architectural masterpiece in Toulouse is the basilica of ST-SERNIN, a 5-minute walk N of the Place du Capitole. It is the largest and most perfect Romanesque church in the south of France, scarcely altered since it was built between 1080 and *c.* 1350. Restoration, begun by the architect Viollet-le-Duc in 1855, is still going on.

The exterior is dominated by the enormous octagonal brick tower which rears up from the transept crossing; its five arcaded storeys, each narrower than the one below, end in a balustrade, like a crown, surrounding the base of the narrow spire. The curved walls and shell-like roofs of the five chapels projecting from the chevet form an attractive grouping in stone and brick. The nave and the transept wings are massive, and largely of brick. There is an interesting Romanesque S doorway (the Porte Miégeville) with a modest tympanum of the Ascension and capitals carved with biblical scenes. The W façade, surprisingly, was only completed in the early part of this century.

The interior is vast, 115m from end to end, with a barrel-vaulted roof over 20m above the floor. It was a church designed for pilgrimages and processions; hence the broad nave, the unusually large transepts, the wide ambulatory to provide access to chapels and displayed relics, and the spacious double side-aisles, with a corresponding double line of pillars, on either side of the nave. The inner side-aisles, next to the nave, support a large gallery (or *tribune*), as wide and as high as the side-aisles themselves; it runs all round the church and adds enormously to the spatial effect, pleasing the eye with elegant pillars topped by richly ornate capitals. Throughout the church, the re-mortaring of the brickwork has had the effect – rather pleasing, as it happens – of softening the natural brick colour to a delicate grey-pink. The side-aisles and the gallery, by obscuring the window light, make the nave seem a little sombre, but this only increases the contrast with the greater light in the spacious transepts and in the chancel, where the walls are partly decorated with frescoes in the most delicate colours. The long perspective from the back of the nave, down the lines of pillars, through the carved choir-stalls to the exuberant, gilded Baroque sculpture at the rear of the 11th-c. marble high altar, is deeply impressive.

There is much to see in this splendid church. There are two crypts, containing numerous saintly

Toulouse: basilica of St-Sernin

relics; one crypt is 11th-c., the other was dug out below it in the 13th-c. There are marble bas-reliefs in the ambulatory, a fine 12th-c. figure of Christ in the N transept, carved in wood and plated in copper, and many other treasures. Go and see the basilica of St-Sernin if you possibly can.

Other notable churches: NOTRE-DAME DU TAUR (a few yards N of the Place du Capitole), built on the spot where St Sernin was martyred in AD 250, tied to the tail of a bull; it has a curious flat façade with crenellations and machicolations; inside, it is surprisingly small, and as dark as a Greek Orthodox church, so that it is difficult to see the 15th-c. fresco on the S wall. ST-ÉTIENNE (near the E end of the Rue de Metz) is the city's official cathedral, but it took six centuries to build and is a hotch-potch of changing plans; the nave and the choir are actually on different axes. It was, however, the earliest Gothic church in the south of France, with a single nave and a vaulted roof twice the width of St-Sernin's; unfortunately, though there are many fine individual features in this Cathedral they do not add up to a satisfactory whole. The basilica of NOTRE-DAME LA DAURADE, down by the river by the Pont Neuf, is an 18th-c. church built on the site of a Gallo-Roman temple.

The old quarter is rich in handsome Renaissance houses, including the Hôtel d'Assezat (near the W end of the Rue de Metz), the Hôtel Béringuier-Maynier (36 Rue du Languedoc), the Hôtel de Clary (25 Rue de la Dalbade), and the Hôtel de Bernuy (1 Rue Gambetta).

Dominating the huge central square is the immensely long 18th-c. façade of the Capitole, the city hall. Part red brick, part white stone, its effect is pompous rather than elegant. In the inner courtyard a Renaissance portal supports a contemporary statue of Henri IV, too high up to be properly seen; upstairs are some grandly decorated rooms; behind, in the gardens, is the 16th-c. keep of the earlier Capitole building, with the tourist office on the ground floor.

The city is well served by its museums. Here are some of them: the Musée des Augustins (Rue de Metz), on the site of a former monastery (the 14th-c. cloister is still there), containing a good collection of sculpture and painting, with works by Rubens, Delacroix, Toulouse-Lautrec, etc; the Musée St-Raymond (SW corner of Place St-Sernin), displaying Roman mosaics, pottery and sculpture from local excavations, including an assembly of eminent portrait heads reputed to be the largest collection outside Rome; the Musée Labit (SE of the Grand Rond) containing painting, sculpture and ceramics from the Far East; the Natural History Museum in the Jardin des Plantes; the Museum of Old Toulouse (Rue du May, off the Rue St-Rome); the Musée Paul Dupuy (Rue Ozenne), devoted to applied arts of all ages – metals, wood, stamps, coins, clocks, etc.

Toulouse, then, is a fascinating city – busy, yet with time for leisure, an enjoyable place for a few days' stay. The flat agricultural country around it is not particularly inspiring, but on the other hand it makes a convenient centre for excursions. Each of the following can be managed comfortably there-and-back in a day: SE to Carcassonne; NE to Albi; N to Montauban, Cahors and Moissac; SW to St-Bertrand-de-Comminges; S to Foix. (*See entries*.)

TRÉMOLAT, *Dordogne* (9km SW of Le Bugue: 4–C4). An attractive little village on the Dordogne in the centre of a series of wide S-bends. Its four-domed church is 11th–12th-c. and built like a fortress, with a large defensive belfry, bare walls, arrow-slits and other military features. The roads out of the village to the N and W take you up on to cliffs with good southern views of the 'Cingle de Trémolat', a wide loop in the river which provides a marvellous expanse of calm water for sailing and rowing; regattas are held here in the summer.

TULLE, *Corrèze* (5–B5). The capital of the Corrèze department, and a business and industrial centre. Squeezed into a narrow valley, the town has had to expand along the banks of the Corrèze in the shape of a long snake.

Tulle has had a violent history. In the Hundred

Years War the English took it twice and were twice driven out. In the Wars of Religion it remained Catholic and was brutally sacked by the Protestants under the Lord of Turenne. In June 1944, the town was liberated by the *maquis* to coincide with the Allied landings in Normandy, but the Germans came back, hanged 99 of the inhabitants and deported hundreds of others; a monument records the disaster.

The old quarter clustered on the N side of the Cathedral of Notre-Dame still has something of a medieval atmosphere; the Maison de Loyac is a particularly fine 15th-c. house with stone carvings around the door and windows. The Cathedral was built in the 12th-c., but at the end of the 18th-c. the transept dome and a large part of the chancel collapsed. The remains of the E end were pulled down and the nave closed by a wall. The belfry, with its tall stone spire (70m above ground), was originally 14th-c. but severely damaged in the 17th-c. by lightning; the present structure is an exact replica.

12km NE (via N89 and D53) is the small village of **Gimel-les-Cascades**, with a quiet little church and a spectacular series of waterfalls dropping 140m in a magnificent stretch of wild scenery where the river Montane fights its way through a ravine.

TURENNE, *Corrèze* (11km S of Brive: 5–C5). From earliest feudal times until as late as the second half of the 18th-c., Turenne was a lordship, or *vicomté*, independent of the kings of France, even minting its own money. The most renowned of the Turenne lords was Henri de la Tour d'Auvergne, who inherited the *vicomté* in the 17th-c. and through his military prowess became known as 'The Great Turenne'.

The old houses crowd up against the steep hill as if seeking protection. Unfortunately, the bleak fortress which once dominated the countryside was devastated at the time of the Revolution, and only two towers and part of the outer defences remain. A stepped ramp leads up past the solid rock wall to the guardroom entrance, a large vaulted stone chamber which can't have changed much since medieval times. Above it is the *salle de la monnaie* where the local coinage was minted. The rest of the site is now an attractive garden. At the far end is the 13th-c. Tour de Caesar, consisting of two rooms, one above the other, and a worn spiral staircase leading to an open platform. Here, after your climb, is a literally breathtaking panorama, with an interesting orientation table to identify the landmarks. On a clear day, 90km to the E, you can see the mountain Plomb du Cantal in the Massif Central.

(*See also* Collonges-la-Rouge *and* Castelnau.)

UZERCHE, *Corrèze* (5–B5). A very old town on a prominent hill nearly surrounded by a loop of the river Vézère. Although it is on the N20, 35km N of Brive, happily the road takes the traffic by on the lower level and leaves the visitor in peace to explore the town on foot.

Start at the S and enter by the Porte Bécharie, the only remaining gate of the 14th-c. fortifications. A turn to the right brings you into the Place des Vignerons, then up the hill, past numerous turreted and timbered houses, to the Place de la Libération, where the 11th–13th-c. church of St-Pierre stands at the summit of the hill. Its clock tower is in the typical Limousin style, with the lower storeys square in plan and the top storey octagonal, partly concealed behind narrow gables extending up from the E and W faces of the storey below. Built against the SW corner of the church is a solid, round tower pierced by arrow-slits; this was added in the 14th-c. to guard the main doorway against attacks by the English. The nave has narrow side-aisles and sturdy pillars supporting a barrel-vaulted roof; the 12th-c. chancel contains interesting capitals carved with designs of foliage and animal heads, and below it is a crypt of uncertain age but possibly earlier than the 11th-c. Outside the church, the Lunade Esplanade provides a fine view of the Vézère valley.

Finally, as you pass once more through the Porte Bécharie at the bottom of the hill, look up at the wall to your right, where the motto on the town's coat-of-arms, 'Non Polluta', proclaims its proud boast that Uzerche was never taken – even when, as far back as AD 732, it was besieged for seven years by the Saracens, trying to avenge their defeat by Charles Martel at Poitiers.

VILLANDRAUT, Gironde (14km SW of Langon: 4–C3). Birthplace of Pope Clement V, who brutally suppressed the Knights Templar and moved the papacy from Rome to Avignon. He built this grandiose, massive, rectangular, six-towered fortress as soon as he became Pope in 1305. Now the ruins of his castle dominate the little town on the edge of the Landes forest, while his body lies buried in a white marble tomb in the large Gothic church at Uzeste, 5km SE.

VILLEFRANCHE-DE-ROUERGUE, Aveyron (5–C5, D5). A busy town on the Aveyron, built as a bastide in the 13th-c. The sloping, cobbled market square is surrounded by ancient arcades and dominated by the enormous belfry tower of Notre-Dame which obtrudes into the NE corner with its massive, angled buttresses. The streets framing the square run not only under the arcades but through the base of the church tower, between the buttresses and the doorway. The tower rears over 50m above the square; even the deep pointed arch between the buttresses must be more than 15m high.

On market days the square is an animated and noisy scene. Inside the church all is peace. A vast nave with sombre side-chapels and fluted pillars rises to a soaring roof whose ogive vaulting makes a fluid pattern of arches and curved surfaces. At the E end this vaulting fans out in a semi-circle of slender ribs to join the chevet. Between the ribs, unusually tall and narrow lancet windows flood the chancel with light. In the transept crossing stands a simple, low, stone altar; to its right, on a solitary plinth, is a charming silver-gilt Virgin. A rich background to the altar is the choir, whose stalls are a 15th-c. masterpiece of joyously inventive carvings in dark wood from the hand, or workshop, of André Sulpice (see also Rodez).

A short walk N through the old town soon brings you to the Bd. Haute-Guyenne and the 17th-c. Chapelle des Pénitents Noirs with its elegant double lantern tower. The interior, Greek cross in plan, is richly ornate, with a painted ceiling and a gilt Baroque retable carved with bas-relief scenes of the Passion, separated by twisted columns and flanking the central Crucifixion.

South across the river, on the Albi road, is the remarkable Chartreuse de St-Sauveur, a 15th-c. charterhouse which escaped destruction at the time of the Revolution because it was already serving as the town's hospital and alms-houses, as indeed it still does. It has two chapels, and two cloisters. The small strangers' chapel outside the precincts cannot be visited, but in the main chapel the austere bare-stone nave leads to some fine choir-stalls – also carved by the school of André Sulpice. Next to the chapel is the smaller cloister, a haven of peace with a fountain and a feast of stone carving. The refectory next to it is a fine vaulted room with an unusual stone pulpit built into the wall. Suddenly you come out into the Great Cloister, a vast grass courtyard enclosed within the former apartments of the Carthusian monks. Villefranche-de-Rouergue can be recommended for a few days' stay, exploring the Aveyron gorges upstream and downstream. If you are a fisherman you will want to stay longer.

VILLENEUVE-SUR-LOT, Lot-et-Garonne (4–C4). Like Agen, 30km S, this town straddling the river Lot is a thriving market for plums and dried fruit. It is a former bastide which has long outgrown its original ramparts, but the centre still retains the typical grid pattern of streets and arcaded square. Built by the French in 1253, it must soon have changed hands, because the old bridge, with its uneven arches, was built by the English later in the same century; at its N end chapel of 'Our Lady at the End of the Bridge' is perilously close to the river, which flows sedately through the town between retaining walls. The modern church of Ste-Catherine has some fine 14th–15th-c. stained glass, preserved from the previous church on the site and believed to be from the school of Arnaut de Moles who made those marvellous windows in Auch Cathedral (see entry). Two of the old defence gates still exist: the Porte de Paris, leading to the capital over 600km away, and the Porte de Pujols, from which an old Roman road provides a pleasant walk up to the ancient hilltop walled village of Pujols, only 3km to the SW.

The Massif Central: Introduction

Auvergne

Edward Young

The Massif Central, the highest part of France except for the Alps and the Pyrenees, is a large granite plateau west of the Rhône Valley. Long-extinct volcanic activity has left a weird landscape of peaks and craters that might be described as lunar were it not for the green pastures, the contour-softening woodlands and the clear blue water in the crater lakes. Some of the great rivers of France start their journeys in this *massif* – the Loire, the Cher, the Allier, the Dordogne, the Lot. Before the dams came they thundered through deep, cliff-walled gorges and often burst their banks in the distant agricultural plains; now the hydro-electric *barrages* have controlled their energy. Some of the dams – like those of Sarrans and Bort-les-Orgues – are impressive engineering achievements and there are still long stretches of the Allier, Sioule and Truyère rivers where the gorges are as spectacular as ever.

This section of the book deals with the main central part of the *massif* – the old province of Auvergne, consisting of the modern departments of Allier, Puy-de-Dôme, Cantal and Haute-Loire – though its foothills spread beyond these boundaries: steeply down to the Rhône on the east, gently westward into the Limousin, and in the south continuing into the limestone *causses* of Languedoc and nearly to the Mediterranean. In the very centre of the Auvergne, at an altitude of 400 metres, lies the capital, Clermont-Ferrand. This large city, with its mighty rubber-tyre factories and its thirteenth-century cathedral built of the Auvergne's black lava rock, marks the division between the 'Limagne' – the low-lying fertile valley of the Allier (noted for its salmon) which flows north past Vichy and Moulins through fields of corn, maize, tobacco and vines – and the high volcanic plateaux to the southwest where ewes and cows graze on the windswept pastures and produce milk for some of the finest cheeses in the world (Bleu d'Auvergne, St-Nectaire, Cantal). The high ground begins dramatically, immediately west of Clermont-Ferrand, with the solitary peak of Puy-de-Dôme rearing 1000 metres above the level of the city. But the highest part of the Auvergne lies a few kilometres southwest, on the strange plateau of peaks, valleys and crater lakes known as the Monts Dore, with Puy de Sancy the highest peak at 1885 metres. This is a great skiing area; Super-Besse (above the quiet medieval town of Besse-en-Chandesse) has cable cars and ski-lifts to the upper slopes, and, in the valley below, the long-popular spas of Le Mont-Dore and La Bourboule now double up as wintersport resorts. Further south, in the Cantal, is the other high plateau, the eroded remains of an enormous extinct volcano; its highest peak, the Plomb du Cantal (1858 metres), is accessible by ski-lift from the wintersport resorts of Le Lioran and Super-Lioran.

Le Puy: the Chapel of St-Michel d'Aiguilhe   French Government Tourist Office

In these higher regions the roads are often snowbound from December to April or May, and the winters can be bitter. Even in summer, when it can be very hot at times, the temperature can suddenly drop by twenty degrees or more in a few hours, and the tourist should always have warm clothing handy. Spring is lovely for the flowers and the turbulent river gorges; in autumn there are mists in the warm Allier basins, cool air and bright sunlight on the upper plateaux.

Until comparatively recently the Auvergne, with its poor roads and harsh winters, was a little-known, isolated, secretive province. The Auvergnats had a reputation of being dour, suspicious of outsiders and slow to respond to friendly advances. Perhaps their sufferings in the Hundred Years War and the Wars of Religion had something to do with this. In the last half-century the roads have improved dramatically and the volume of tourists increases steadily. The Auvergnat is after all discovered to be patient, hard-working, economical – taciturn perhaps but certainly not unfriendly. Today he welcomes the tourist. And as the following pages show, there is much for the tourist to see in the Auvergne besides its scenery and its capital – the extraordinary site and the Byzantine cathedral of Le Puy, the superb Romanesque church at Orcival, the romantic setting of the Château de Tournoël, the hot-water springs of Chaudes-Aigues, the old cutlery town of Thiers above its swift river, the ancient brooding abbey church of Chaise-Dieu . . .

Countryside near Clermont-Ferrand

A.F. Kersting

The Massif Central: Gazetteer

Edward Young

AMBERT, *Puy-de-Dôme* (5–B7). A quiet, once fortified little town with a curious round Hôtel-de-Ville and a partly fortified 15th-c. church. The composer Chabrier was born here in 1842. From the 15th-c. to the 17th-c. the town was the centre of a large paper-making industry spread among 300 mills in the surrounding countryside. 5½km E of the town (by N496 and D57) is a resurrected mill, the Moulin Richard-de-Bas, open daily, where you can see paper being made by hand and visit the adjoining historical paper museum.

ARDES-SUR-COUZE, *Puy-de-Dôme* (11km W of Lempdes: 5–B6, B7). Village on the right bank of the Couze soon after it emerges from the gorges of the Vallée de Rentières, in a wild volcanic region. Once the fortified capital of the duchy of Mercoeur (the ruins of the lord's castle are 2km upstream, high above the river). Interesting 15th-c. church.

AURILLAC, *Cantal* (5–C6). Modern city and the tourist centre of the Cantal region. From the Pont Rouge over the river Jordanne is a view of the remaining old quarter with its 15th-c. and 16th-c. mansions. Terrible slaughter took place here during the Wars of Religion, on both sides. Close to the bridge, on the W bank, a statue commemorates the local shepherd-boy genius Gerbert who in the year AD 999 became the first French Pope, Sylvester II; he is also credited with having made an astrolabe and a weight-driven clock, and with the introduction to western Europe of arabic numerals after a visit to Arab-occupied Spain. The nearby 15th-c. church of St-Géraud was built on the site of the medieval abbey church around which the town originally grew.

N of the town centre is the Château St-Étienne; only the 11th-c. keep is original, but the view of the Monts du Cantal to the NE (*see entry*) is superb, and part of the building houses an absorbing permanent exhibition (Maison des Volcans) illustrating the scientific study of volcanoes, the earth in general, and even of space.

BESSE-EN-CHANDESSE, *Puy-de-Dôme* (5–B6). Marvellously unspoilt medieval village and market centre, nearly 2000m up in the volcanic Monts Dore region. Ancient gateway with adjoining belfry, houses of black lava rock. In the sombre Romanesque church stands a much-venerated 'Black Virgin', except between early July and late September when she traditionally rests in the solitary mountainside pilgrim chapel of Vassivière, 8km to the W. To the SW are drives and walks to the crater lakes of Pavin, Chauvet and Montcineyre, and the 1400m peak of Puy de Montchal.

7km W, at 1350m, is the increasingly popular wintersports resort of **Super-Besse**, with covered 25m swimming pool, skating lake, ski-lifts and cable cars to the summit of Puy Ferrand (1846m).

BILLOM, *Puy-de-Dôme* (20km N of Issoire: 5–B7). Old medieval town, now busy with light industry, and an agricultural centre specializing in garlic. But many 15th-c. houses still exist in the narrow winding streets of the old quarter surrounding the Gothic church of St-Cerneuf, a church unusually rich in 13th–15th-c. murals.

9km E on the N side of N497 are the ruins of the once well-fortified hilltop castle of **Mauzun**, with 11 of its 19 towers still standing. Romantically overgrown, and providing panoramic views of the region.

9km NE (via D229 and D10) is the feudal castle of **Ravel**, transformed in the 17th- and 18th-c. into a large and sumptuous residential château, with a garden terrace laid out by Le Nôtre. Fine views looking W over the Allier valley to the Monts Dômes beyond. (Open Easter–1 November.)

BLESLE, *Haute-Loire* (17km W of Brioude: 5–B7). Modest little town in a picturesque valley at the junction of two small rivers. It grew up in the 9th-c. around a wealthy and somewhat exclusive Benedictine abbey. During the Revolution the abbey church, whose vast choir is out of all proportion to its short nave, was taken over as the parish church, though the belfry was demolished. The large square tower W of the church is the sole remnant of an 11th-c. castle.

N from Blesle the N9 wriggles along the dramatic Gorges de l'Alagnon. Shortly after a particularly tortuous bend, the ruins of a 14th-c. fortress, the **Château de Léotoing**, appear perched up to the right of the road, 150m above the river; worth visiting if only for its precipitous views, it can be reached by carrying on to Lempdes and turning S again on D653.

BOURBON-L'ARCHAMBAULT, *Allier* (5–A6). Former walled town, now a pleasantly unpretentious spa. Its waters have been renowned for the relief of rheumatic and arthritic complaints since the days of the Romans. Of the formidable old Bourbon castle only three of the original ten towers are still standing.

On a hill 9km E the former abbey church of **St-Menoux** (11th–12th-c.) has an unusual choir within a semi-circle of massive pillars supporting two tiers of arches, producing a rather sober, Roman-like effect.

BOURBOULE, La, *Puy-de-Dôme* (5–B6). Well-known health resort on the upper Dordogne, 850m above sea-level. Its waters are renowned for the relief of respiratory ailments, skin diseases and allergies. Equable climate, and plenty to do: casino, tennis courts, swimming, riding, a large park, any number of excursions. For example: the dam lake, only a ½-hour walk to the W; the Gorges d'Avèze (18km W); the Roche Vendeix, an abrupt pinnacle of rock which once had a brigand's castle on top (4km S); La Banne d'Ordanche, the 'chimney' of an extinct volcano, with tremendous views (7km NE, altitude 1500m); and from the park in the town a cable car takes you up to the Plateau de Charlannes, also with marvellous views. And Le Mont-Dore (*see entry*) is only 7km to the E.

Since the development of wintersporting in the region around the Puy de Sancy, La Bourboule has become increasingly popular as a winter, as well as a summer, resort.

BRIOUDE, *Haute-Loire* (5–B7). Ancient but busy small market town looking NE over the fertile plain of the river Allier. It is a great salmon-fishing centre, thanks to the dam 2km upstream which stops the abundant salmon from swimming further up river. Centre of the old quarter is the Basilica of St-Junien, largest and finest Romanesque abbey church in the Auvergne. The belfry is 19th-c. reconstruction, but the rest is original – the fine doors, the long nave full of light and warm colour (the walls are a reddish sandstone), finely carved capitals, and a semi-circular apse with five radiating chapels, prettily decorated on the exterior with a band of a mosaic-like pattern of reds and greys. Note on the S side of the nave the strange 15th-c. painted statue of 'Christ the Leper' and the 13th-c. frescoes in the gallery chapel at the W end.

S of the town the D585 follows the writhing **Allier Gorges** to the old town of **Langeac**, just beyond which, on a dramatic promontory, is the ancient fortified abbey church of **Chanteuges**. A further 14km brings you to the village of **Monistrol d'Allier**, perhaps the most beautiful site in the whole valley.

9½km SE of Brioude at **Lavaudieu** are the remains of a Benedictine abbey, with frescoes and a restored cloister of great beauty. 12km N, on a precipitous site above the river, the village of **Auzon** has an interesting 12th-c. church and the remains of a castle and ramparts.

CANTAL, Monts du, *Cantal* (NE of Aurillac: 5–C6). Volcanic mountain region W of Murat (*see entry*). A relief map shows how the valleys radiate in all directions from a rough circle of high peaks grouped around Puy Mary (1787m) and Plomb du Cantal (highest of all at 1858m). This supports the volcanologists' deduction that the whole area is the relic of one enormous volcano, the largest in France and originally nearly twice as high, but gradually worn down by glacial action and erosion.

Five hundred years ago the area was largely covered by forest, but gradual clearing has turned the high plateaux into pastureland. Minerals from the ancient volcano's outpourings of lava have produced a grass which makes the best pastureland in France; on it graze a breed of small reddish-brown cows whose milk is turned into the famous Cantal cheese.

In summer the region provides excursions through a countryside of deep wooded valleys, high cliffs, swift rock-strewn torrents, green prairies, sudden panoramic views and an ever-present skyline of pointed or rounded peaks. Sometimes an unexpected castle rears up on an outcrop of rock, like the 15th-c. **Château d'Anjony** (S of Salers by a circuitous route), with its formidable square keep, its Flemish and Aubusson tapestries, and its chapel with 16th-c. frescoes.

In winter, snow tends to block the roads between Murat and Salers, but road and rail tunnels enable the skiers to reach the wintersports resorts of **Le Lioran** and nearby **Super-Lioran**, whence cable cars and ski-lifts connect with the ski runs around Plomb du Cantal.

CHAISE-DIEU, La, *Haute-Loire* (5–B7). On a cold and windy plateau, over 1000m above sea-level, stands this vast and once powerful abbey church, one of the great monastic edifices of France. The abbey was founded modestly in 1044 by a hermit saint from Brioude; the present church was erected in the 14th-c. by Pope Clement VI, a former monk here. Strongly built to withstand both the bitter climate and possible enemy attack, with a fortified W façade and a great tower at the SE corner with wells and grain-stores in the event of siege, it proved its worth when it was attacked by Huguenots in the 16th-c.; they sacked the church, causing appalling damage, but the monks, locked in the tower with the abbey treasures, survived the siege.

After the Revolution the abbey was suppressed; the church became the parish church, dwarfing the little town. In the huge, gaunt interior are marvellously carved 15th-c. choir-stalls, a series of 16th-c. Flemish tapestries, and a famous mural, 26m long, of the Dance of Death. In the centre of the choir, alone in the empty church, lies the effigy

The main square, Clermont-Ferrand

of the man who built it, Pope Clement VI, recumbent on his battered tomb.

CHAMBON-SUR-LAC, *Puy-de-Dôme* (7km E of Le Mont-Dore: 5–B6). The village, with its 12th-c. church, lies at the W end of the extensive **Lac Chambon**, formed by a shallow crater at an altitude of 875m, and surrounded by volcanic hills. Puy de Sancy, Puy Ferrand and the Vallée de Chaudefour lie to the SW; the formidable red 13th-c. castle of **Murol** dominates the skyline to the E. On the N edge of the lake is a high cliff, remnant of the crater's edge; it is called the Maiden's Leap.

CHÂTEL-MONTAGNE, *Allier* (15km S of Lapalisse: 5–A7). Village in a lovely setting above the river Sobre, surrounded by the wooded hills of the Montagne Bourbonnaise region. A short walk S takes you to the top of the little Puy de Roc, from which you can see the Monts Dore, 100km away on the SW horizon. In the village is a simple but elegant 12th-c. granite church in the Auvergnat Romanesque style.

CHAUDES-AIGUES, *Cantal* (5–C6, C7). The name means 'hot waters'. This celebrated little watering resort, set in a picturesque ravine at an altitude of 750m, has several hot springs beneficial to sufferers from rheumatism and sciatica. One of the springs is so hot (82°C) that since antiquity it has been fed through wooden pipes to provide central heating for most of the town. There are a number of hotels, and it makes an agreeable centre for exploring the nearby gorges of the river Truyère (*see entry*).

CHAVANIAC-LAFAYETTE, *Haute-Loire* (10km NE of Langeac: 5–C7). This huge 18th-c. château just N of the Le Puy–Brioude road (N102, about 35km NW from Le Puy) is of interest to visitors from the United States because it was the birthplace of Lafayette, a hero of the American War of Independence. The château is arranged as a Lafayette museum, and is open most of the year.

CLERMONT-FERRAND, *Puy-de-Dôme* (5–B6, B7). Capital of the Puy-de-Dôme department, geographical and economic centre of the Massif Central. It was the birthplace of the 17th-c. philosopher and writer Blaise Pascal (celebrated for his *Pensées*), and is the centre of the vast Michelin rubber tyre industry, which owes its origin to an early-19th-c. Scotswoman who, married to a local Michelin ancestor, made rubber balls to amuse her children.

400m above sea-level, this lively city of over 160,000 inhabitants lies at the foot of the weird volcanic region of Monts Dômes (*see* Puy-de-Dôme) which extends over the western horizon. To the NE it overlooks a fertile plain crossed by the east-flowing tributaries of the Allier. In the 8th-c., when it was first recorded in history, Clermont was a small town on the site of the present upper, or old, town, built within ramparts on a small hill, itself an extinct volcano. It suffered the usual invasions of Franks, Vikings, Normans, etc., and from the extortions of tyrannous local overlords. It became Clermont-Ferrand in 1630, when it merged with its rival neighbour Montferrand.

The old town of Clermont is full of fountains, ancient houses and narrow streets. Wide avenues have replaced the medieval ramparts. Centre of café life is the Place de Jaude, a spacious tree-shaded esplanade with a statue at each end: one of General Desaix, victor of Marengo and born near Clermont, the other of the great Vercingétorix, who in 53 BC led the Gauls to victory over Julius Caesar 6km S of here on the **Plateau de Gergovie** (a remarkable site, with extensive excavations, reached via the D3 through the suburb of Romagnat).

The great Gothic Cathedral, with its fine 12th- and 15th-c. stained glass, was begun in 1248, and is unique in being built of the local black lava rock, so strong that it enabled the builders to construct unusually slender pillars, thus adding to the effect of lightness and height. The 19th-c. architect Viollet-le-Duc rebuilt the original towers and added the tall spires which are conspicuous for miles around.

NE of the Cathedral is the fine Romanesque Basilica of Notre-Dame-du-Port. Mostly 11th–12th-c., with the typical *tribune*, or gallery, over the side-aisles of the nave, it is remarkable for its richly decorated choir with unusually detailed carvings on the capitals, and its 11th-c. crypt with an altar bearing a small black statue of the Virgin, venerated by pilgrims annually in mid-May. A minute's walk E of this church is the Place Delille where in 1095, in a famous sermon preached from a specially built throne, Pope Urban II set in motion the First Crusade.

The Museum of Art, Ethnography and History is divided between the Musée du Ranquet (2 minutes W of the Cathedral, Rue des Gras) and the Musée Bargoin (on N edge of the Jardin Lecoq). The Musée H-Lecoq is a good Natural History museum, also on the N side of the Jardin Lecoq, which is a large park with a lake and bordered by University buildings.

Clermont-Ferrand has over 20 mineral springs, and supplies a good deal of France's bottled mineral waters. The springs come to the surface just N of the town centre, in the St-Alyre quarter. Here, in the Grottes du Pérou, are many immersed objects in course of petrification through the gradual deposit of iron from the water.

DORE, Monts, *Puy-de-Dôme* (5–B6). Highest region of France apart from the Alps and the Pyrenees. The highest peaks are grouped close together immediately S of the resort of Le Mont-Dore: Puy de Sancy (1885m), Puy Ferrand (1846m) and Puy de la Perdrix (1816m). It is a wild and beautiful area, the result of recurring volcanic activity alternating with periods of glacial erosion or submersion under the sea, a landscape of sharp needles of thrusting rock, heavily wooded slopes, lakes, gorges, waterfalls, deep valleys, with a skyline sometimes jagged, sometimes softened by forest. Carpeted with alpine flowers in spring, and in winter blanketed in deep snow which blocks many of the higher roads from November to April and brings the skiers to Le Mont-Dore and Super-Besse (*see entries*).

The top of **Puy de Sancy** is accessible from Le Mont-Dore by road (N683), then by cable car and a short walk. Immense views of the Monts Dômes to the N, the Monts du Cantal to the S, and even – if you are lucky with the weather – the Alps, some 300km to the E.

ÉBREUIL, *Allier* (8km W of Gannat: 5–B7). Small town on the Sioule at a point where the river slows to a more leisurely pace after its tumultuous passage through the upstream gorges. The church of St-Léger here is well worth a visit for its harmoniously proportioned belfry-porch, the 12th- and 15th-c. frescoes in the nave, and behind the altar the handsome 16th-c. reliquary shrine of the saint.

For a beautiful drive in dramatic river scenery, take the D915 W out of the town and follow the **Sioule Gorges** as far as **Châteauneuf-les-Bains**, a modest spa (altitude 390m) whose waters are said to be good for rheumatism and neuralgia. By continuing W through St-Gervais and then SW on N687 and D62, you come to the 68m-high hydro-electric **Barrage de Besserve** and the nearby **Viaduc des Fades**, claimed to be the highest railway viaduct in Europe.

EFFIAT, Château d', *Puy-de-Dôme* (7km SE of Gannat: 5–B7). Close to the village of Effiat on the Aigueperse–Vichy road stands this handsome edifice of the late Louis XIII period. Surrounded by a large park, it is approached by an avenue of lime-trees and an imposing portal, opening into a spacious *cour d'honneur*. The château was built by one of Richelieu's ministers, but he died at war and never lived here; his son, caught out in a treason plot, was beheaded at the age of 22; another son, an abbot, lived an openly scandalous life, and his grandson was accused of poisoning Louis XIV's sister-in-law. The château is well furnished in the style of the period, and the gardens are a formal design in the Le Nôtre manner – moats, canals, statues, etc.

ENNEZAT, *Puy-de-Dôme* (8km E of Riom: 5–B6). An old town in the fertile valley N of Clermont-Ferrand, with a grid street plan reminiscent of the Dordogne *bastides*. The church is a former collegiate church, partly 11th-c. Romanesque (transept and nave) and the rest 13th-c. Gothic, containing several works of religious art – notably 12th-c. capitals in the nave, a 1420 fresco on the N wall of the choir and an early 15th-c. wax painting of the Last Judgment on the S wall.

GANNAT, *Allier* (5–B7). A small and very old town 25km N of Riom. Its famous ecclesiastical treasure – a medieval *Book of the Gospels*, richly bound – is kept, not in the old church of Ste-Croix, but in a museum in the 12th-c. Château de Veauce (close to the W side of the main N9 road) which was partly demolished in the 16th-c. and then used as a prison from 1833 until quite recently.

ISSOIRE, *Puy-de-Dôme* (5–B7). A busy town which makes gliders, light aircraft and electrical accessories, and claims to have the largest aluminium and light-alloy factory in Europe. The old town, full of narrow streets, lies within the ring of boulevards which replaced the old ramparts. In the Rue des Fours the old Maison des Échevins (magistrate's house) has a permanent exhibition illustrating the town's history – and a nasty, blood-stained history it was throughout the Wars of Religion. Survivor of all its past troubles stands

the splendid 12th-c. church of the once prosperous, now extinct, abbey of St-Austremoine. It is one of the Auvergne's best Romanesque churches. Note the perfect chevet, decorated on the outside with mosaic and zodiac designs, the remarkable capitals in the choir and transept, and the crypt of great simplicity and strength, containing the saint's reliquary shrine.

15km due S, just E of the N9, the village of **Nonette** sits on a high promontory above a bend in the river Allier. A stiff climb of about 15 minutes takes you to the top of the hill, crowned by the ruins of what was the most powerful castle in the Auvergne until it was dismantled in the early 17th-c. on the orders of Richelieu. Marvellous views of the river valley, the Monts Dômes and the Monts Dore.

LAPALISSE, *Allier* (5–A7). A small town 20km NE of Vichy, straddling the river Besbre and dominated by a great château above the E bank. This once rather dour 12th-c. fortress (the northern section, the tower and part of the chapel still remain from the original) was converted in the 15th-c. into a more elegantly residential château in the Italian Renaissance style – a style which had so impressed its owner, Jacques Chabannes, while he was fighting in Italy that he brought back workmen from Florence to do the work. The rooms contain Renaissance furniture and Flemish tapestries, and in the Gothic chapel, which was

Le Mont-Dore

Douglas Dickins

ransacked at the time of the Revolution, are sculptured family tombs.

N from the town the D480 follows the peaceful **Besbre Valley** for 35km, passing a surprising number of 12th- and 13th-c. châteaux (unfortunately not open to visitors) – Chavroches, Vieux-Chambord, Jaligny, Beauvoir (whose gardens *are* open) and Toury – until the river flows into the Loire just beyond Dompierre.

MAURIAC, *Cantal* (5–C6). Small agricultural market town, with houses of local black lava and a notable 12th–13th-c. church, Notre-Dame-des-Miracles, whose doorway is generally accepted as the finest example of Romanesque sculpture in the region. The interior is bare and austere, and at the far end of the choir is a black statue of the Virgin believed to be from the 13th-c.

A good excursion centre, especially for the volcanic Monts de Cantal region to the SE (*see entry*) and the wild Dordogne gorges to the NW; only 11km W is the great hydro-electric **Barrage de l'Aigle**, 90km high and 290m across at the top, with a 'ski-jump' chute which is opened when the dam lake is over-full. For an exhilarating ½-hour walk, climb to the top of Puy St-Mary, just W of the town; magnificent views will reward your effort.

MONT-DORE, Le, *Puy-de-Dôme* (5–B6). At an altitude of 1050m, encircled by mountains and constricted within the narrow valley of the Dordogne (not far from its source here), Le Mont-Dore is full of activity the year round – in summer as a holiday resort and spa whose waters have been relieving asthma sufferers since Gallo-Roman times, and in winter as a wintersports centre, with two cable cars, 19 ski-lifts, and skiing until mid-April. The town has many hotels and restaurants, and a casino with a fine view from its terrace. The surrounding mountains (known collectively as the Monts Dore – *see entry*) are the very top of the Massif Central, the Puy de Sancy (due S) being the highest of all at 1886m. There are any number of walks and drives in gorgeous scenery – lakes, ravines, waterfalls, medieval villages, and the perfect 12th-c. church at Orcival, 17km N (*see entry*). Even invalids can now reach nearly to the top of Puy de Sancy by road and cable car and enjoy its amazing panoramic views.

MONTLUÇON, *Allier* (5–A6). Large industrial town (chemicals, rubber, foundries) on the river Cher, 75km NW of Clermont-Ferrand. On the right bank is a small old quarter with narrow streets sloping up towards a 15th-c. Bourbon castle, which has an esplanade with far-reaching views. The castle also houses a museum illustrating the natural history and folklore of the region, including a unique collection of beautifully decorated hurdy-gurdies, an instrument still used to accompany the traditional folklorique clog-dancing fêtes in hundreds of French villages. The

town has two churches, neither of them of particular architectural interest.

7½km SE is the thermal spa of **Néris-les-Bains**, whose numerous Roman and Merovingian remains show that it has been a well-known health resort for many centuries. Nerves, rheumatism and gynaecological ailments are relieved by the waters here. There is an interesting 11th–12th-c. church.

MOULINS, *Allier* (5–A7). Once capital of the independent duchy of Bourbon, now capital of the Allier department and a busy agricultural market centre. Still retains an air of amiable confidence, and an old quarter with cobbled streets, old houses, and a well-known 'Jacquemart' bell-tower (reconstructed after it was burned down in 1946) with mechanical figures striking the hours and quarters.

The Gothic Cathedral is unusual. A door at the NE corner opens straight into the beautiful choir, square in plan with a flat chevet and an ambulatory lit by marvellous 15th- and 16th-c. stained glass; this end is the old collegiate church from the 15th-c.; the nave, added only in the 19th-c. (along with the two towers) is another square – narrower, but with the pillars in line with those in the choir. Do not miss the sacristy (N side of the choir), for here is one of the masterpieces of 15th-c. French painting – the famous triptych by the unidentified Bourbon court painter known as 'The Master of Moulins'. The centre panel of the 'Madonna and Child with Angels' is an exquisite design of luminous colour and rippling drapery.

12km W is the vast priory church of the former Cluniac abbey of **Souvigny**, founded in the 10th-c. The church is a mixture of the original 11th–12th-c. structure and the 15th-c. enlargement made when the Dukes of Bourbon chose it for their last resting-place. In the lapidary museum under the sacristy is a remarkable 12th-c. calendar of the months, carved on an octagonal column.

MURAT, *Cantal* (5–C6). The grey houses climb the slopes of a great basalt rock, the Rocher de Bonnevie, surmounted by a huge statue of the Virgin. Murat is a small agricultural town (cattle, cheese) on the E edge of the Monts du Cantal region (*see entry*) and only 12km from the wintersports centre of Le Lioran. The church is Gothic with a modern façade, and venerates a 'miraculous' Virgin in black olive-wood. On the other side of the river Alagnon, high on a small volcanic peak with extensive views, is the charming little 11th-c. fortified church of **Bredons**.

ORCIVAL, *Puy-de-Dôme* (12km N of Le Mont-Dore: 5–B6). Small village in the wooded valley of the Sioulet at the foot of the Monts Dore and containing what is probably the most beautiful church in the whole of the Massif Central. It is pure 12th-c. Romanesque, on an extremely simple plan of perfect proportions. The exterior, seen

French Government Tourist Office

Orcival: apse and bell-tower of the 12th-c. church

from the E, is a pleasing arrangement of little chapels fanning out from behind the rounded chevet, their roofs like splayed oyster-shells; behind rises the centre block of the transept crossing, surmounted by an elegant octagonal tower with an octagonal spire rising in two stages, 8m lower than the original spire destroyed in the Revolution. Inside, the plain nave with its two lines of pillars leads the eye to the dome over the transept and beyond to the brightly lit choir and to the enchanting and much-revered 12th-c. Virgin in Majesty behind the altar. Under the choir, and on the same plan, is a spacious crypt, full of light.

3km N (by N683 and D27) is the 15th-c. Renaissance 'manoir-château' of **Cordès**, with solid round cone-roofed towers at the corners and a lovely garden of box and yew hedges laid out (they tell you locally) by Le Nôtre. Open throughout the year.

POLIGNAC, Château de, *Haute-Loire* (3km NW of Le Puy: 5–C7). A flat plateau of rock rises steeply to 100m above the valley; on it stands a formidable square keep surrounded by low ramparts and the remains of 15th-c. castle buildings, once occupied by the lords of Polignac, their retainers and 800 soldiers. The Polignac family produced a crusader, a cardinal, several brigands, a close friend of Marie-Antoinette, and a prince whose political advice to Charles X helped towards that unfortunate monarch's downfall in 1830. In Roman times a temple of Apollo stood on this site and was famous for the oracles pronounced to awed pilgrims, by a ventriloquistic trick, through a huge mask of Apollo (see the collection of Roman remains in the keep). The village lies round the base of the rock, with an interesting Romanesque church containing 15th-c. frescoes.

(The castle is officially open June–September; at other times you might get in if you can find the guardian.)

PUY, Le, *Haute-Loire* (5–C7). A large market town of 30,000 inhabitants on one of the most extraordinary sites in France. Surrounded by mountains, it lies on what was once the bed of a huge lake; volcanic upheavals emptied the lake, shifted the course of the Loire, and thrust up a number of astonishingly abrupt cones, pinnacles and 'chimneys' of lava rock.

On the highest of these, the Rocher Corneille, stands the colossal statue of Notre-Dame-de-France. Erected in 1860 by public subscription, it was made from cannons captured at Sebastopol, and it dominates the town. There is a viewing platform, and in good weather you can climb through the statue to the top and obtain an even finer view of the Le Puy basin.

On the narrowest pinnacle, a sheer 80m from the valley floor, and reached by an exhausting 268 steps, stands the amazing late-11th-c. chapel of St-Michel-d'Aiguilhe with its Romanesque tower pointing skyward like a finger. The final flight of steps leads up to the entrance doorway; the flat façade is almost entirely covered with decorative stonework: a triple arch of swirling arabesques surmounted by horizontal lines of mosaic zigzag patterns reaching nearly to the roof. The complex interior, with a short nave, interesting capitals, and an apse whose ceiling is painted with 12th-c. murals, ingeniously follows the contours of the rock. (Open every day in spring, summer and autumn; but only Sundays, Wednesdays and bank holidays in winter.)

The old town, famous for its handmade lace, and once an important pilgrim centre, is on a lower hill. From the Place des Tables, with its 15th-c. fountain, the road climbs steeply past old houses, flanked by sidewalks mounting in steps, towards the Cathedral standing majestically at the top. The façade is almost Byzantine with its stripes of alternate light and dark stone, and in the interior the oriental impression is confirmed by the line of cupolas along the nave. The main altar stands under the dome of the transept crossing; the organ is against the chevet, behind the choir. A door to the right leads through a 12th-c. porch to the sacristy, which exhibits the Cathedral 'Treasure' (note the celebrated manuscript *Theodolph Bible*). From outside the sacristy there is a neck-breaking view of the many-storeyed Romanesque belfry at the rear of the church. Return through the church to reach the beautiful 12th-c. cloisters on the other side; even here there is a suggestion of Moslem influence.

On the S side of the town the Musée Crozatier, in an interesting collection, contains a display of local handmade lace from the 16th-c. onwards.

PUY-DE-DÔME (5–B6). The highest peak (altitude 1465m) in the extraordinary **Monts Dômes**

area of extinct volcanoes, immediately W of Clermont-Ferrand. A toll road spirals upward for some 3km at a steady angle of 12°. On the summit are an observatory, a TV transmitter, a restaurant, and the foundations of what must have been an enormous Temple of Mercury built by the Romans. The panorama from the viewing platform is stupendous: the volcanic peaks, overgrown with trees and other vegetation, extend for miles in every direction, each with its crater depression at or just below its summit. It is said that there are a hundred of them, that in clear weather you can see into 11 departments of France, and that the best time to see the view is towards the end of the day when the setting sun sets the peaks on fire, the valleys darken, and the shadow of Puy-de-Dôme itself extends swiftly over Clermont-Ferrand, 1000m below.

RHUE, Gorges de la, *Cantal* (W of Condat: 5–B6). From Condat, a pleasant small town to which they say the Auvergnats like to retire after they have made their money somewhere else, the D679 follows the course of the Rhue westward towards its junction with the Dordogne, just below Bort-les-Orgues. The river runs through spectacular wooded gorges, partly tamed now by two dams – the second of which, the Barrage de Vaussaire, not only has its own power station at the foot of the dam but when necessary supplies extra water, through a 12km tunnel, to the dam lake above the Bort barrage on the Dordogne. Between the two dams, at Cornilloux, a ¾-hour walk N brings you to a beautiful waterfall surrounded by forest.

RIOM, *Puy-de-Dôme* (5–B6). A small town full of fountains and ancient history (the site pre-dates the Roman era) and built largely of black lava rock. The old medieval pilgrim town was damaged by an earthquake in the 13th-c., but 100 years later, when the Duc de Berry was also Duc d'Auvergne and built a great palace here, Riom had become the capital of the region.

Although in the 17th-c. the administrative role was taken over by the rapidly growing rival town of Clermont-Ferrand (only 15km S), Riom retained, and still retains, its function as the judicial capital. The Duke's palace is no more, replaced by the 19th-c. Palais de Justice, but his original Ste-Chapelle, with its high roof and marvellous 16th-c. stained glass, has been preserved. It was the wealthy legal dignitaries of the 16th-c. who were responsible for the splendid Renaissance mansions which give the town its present character – the Maison des Consuls, the Hotel Guimoneau, the Hôtel-de-Ville – with their elegant courtyards, staircases and carvings.

The 14th–15th-c. church of Notre-Dame-du-Marthuret contains two statues of the Virgin and Child, one a 'Black Virgin', probably 12th-c. but rather unattractive, the other a celebrated late-medieval 'Virgin of the Bird', a most beautiful piece of naturalistic carving in which the smiling faces of both the mother and the child, who holds a fluttering bird in his outstretched hands, are a touching expression of mutual joy. At one time this statue used to grace the entrance to the church, but at the time of the Revolution, when the mob attacked and damaged the façade, it was hidden in a cellar by the local butchers' corporation; afterwards it was placed for greater safety in its present position inside the church, and it is a copy which now stands at the entrance.

Close to the W edge of Riom is **Mozac**, whose Benedictine abbey was once rich and powerful but now survives only in the 12th-c. church; the capitals in the nave are among the finest examples of Romanesque sculpture, and the 'Treasure' includes some rare Limousin enamelled caskets from the 12th-c. (apply to the sacristy).

At **Marsat**, 3km SW, is another 12th-c. church, the former chapel of a Benedictine priory; here is another 'Black Virgin', very solemn and much venerated locally.

4km S on N9, then 2km W on D15e, stands the partly ruined 14th-c. castle of **Châteaugay**, haunted by ghosts of a murky and violent past. Its great keep is intact, and there are splendid views from the upper platform.

6km NW is the 2000-year-old but agreeably modern health spa of **Châtelguyon**. Its 30 sources of mineral waters have benefited sufferers from liver and stomach troubles from the Romans onward.

7km W are the impressive ruins of the Château de Tournoël (*see entry*).

ROYAT, *Puy-de-Dôme* (3km SW of Clermont-Ferrand: 5–B6, B7). Important thermal resort close to the SW suburbs of Clermont-Ferrand, spread along the banks of a swift and picturesque river. The Romans were the first to construct baths here to enjoy the benefits of the radio-active mineral waters, believed to be good for the heart and the arteries. Many hotels and parks, a casino, plenty of indoor and outdoor amusements. Trips to the top of the Puy-de-Dôme (*see entry*), which is only 6km W and dominates the skyline. In the village is an 11th–12th-c. fortified church. Immediately S is the well-known Circuit Automobile de Royat-Charade with its testing bends and gradients; the great annual meeting, 'Les Trophées d'Auvergne', takes place end-June, early-July.

ST-FLOUR, *Cantal* (5–C6). Old mountain town perched on a steep bluff at an altitude of 880m. Having successfully resisted the English and the Huguenots, after the Revolution it was forced to dismantle its walls. Wandering streets and 16th- and 17th-c. houses climb to the top of the town, where stands a grim Cathedral, started in 1396 and completed a century later, with two massive towers, five naves and no transept; in it is a large 15th-c. Christ beautifully carved in black wood. Next to the Cathedral, in a wing of the former Bishop's Palace, now the Hôtel-de-Ville, is a museum with a good collection of religious art, archaeology, regional folklore, and souvenirs of the wartime Resistance in the Cantal.

ST-NECTAIRE, *Puy-de-Dôme* (5–B6). A health spa specializing in kidney ailments, and home of a famous cheese. 25km E of Le Mont-Dore at an altitude of 760m, inhabited in turn by prehistoric man, the Celts, and the Romans who built baths here, the town extends along a single street in the hollow of a steep, wooded valley. The lower town contains the baths, the hotels, the casino and the shops; above it, 1½km away and out of sight, is the old village with one of the loveliest of the Auvergne Romanesque churches perched on a bluff above it. Facing magnificent views of the Monts Dore, it is renowned especially for the naive but lively biblical scenes carved on the capitals in nave and choir; among its 'Treasure' is a beautiful reliquary casket in copper and Limousin enamel.

ST-POURÇAIN-SUR-SIOULE, *Allier* (5–A6, A7). Small and ancient town on the left bank of the Sioule, just before it flows into the Allier. Surrounded by the vineyards which have for centuries produced its locally renowned wines – red, white and rosé. In the middle of the town is a huge church, parts of which are remnants of the erstwhile abbey of Ste-Croix, founded in the 9th-c.; it is a not altogether happy mixture of various periods from the 11th-c. onward.

SALERS, *Cantal* (5–C6). A gracious old town on a hill at the NW edge of the Monts du Cantal (*see entry*). In the 14th-c. it suffered badly at the hands of the English soldiery, but now in the centre is a large open square surrounded by turreted Renaissance mansions erected by the prosperous judiciary of the 15th-c. and 16th-c. A fountain plays in the middle. The church is 15th-c., with a 12th-c. doorway from the previous church on the site; the interior has interesting sculptures, paintings and tapestries. Splendid views from a promenade at the steep S edge of the town.

THIERS, *Puy-de-Dôme* (5–B7). The 'cutlery capital of France' ever since the Middle Ages, Thiers is an old town rising in terraces from the edge of a rocky promontory, overlooking the ravine of the swift-flowing Durolle. The streets climb steeply, often in steps, between 15th–16th-c. half-timbered houses, with cutlery shops displaying every imaginable shape and size of knife. From the Middle Ages until the advent of electricity the river provided the power which turned the millstones for grinding the knives, a task often performed on the very edge of the torrent. The modern workshops, which produce well over half of all the knives made in France, are still sited down on the river bank, and can be visited by arrangement. The history of the trade, with an astonishing collection of its products, is exhibited in the knife museum in the Rue de Barante, just W

Topham (Picou)

Eiffel's viaduct at Garabit in the Truyère Gorges

of the Place de la Mutualité (open most afternoons, mornings as well in August only).

There are three churches: St-Genès, a much-restored Romanesque church with an un-expectedly large dome over the transept; St-Jean, 15th-c. with some restoration, in an exciting situation overlooking the river; and on the opposite bank the Église du Moutier, the church of the monastery that once stood here – on the site, in fact, of the original town before it was sacked by the Franks in the 6th-c.

TOURNOËL, Château de, *Puy-de-Dôme* (6km W of Riom:5–B6). The romantic hilltop ruins of a once powerful feudal castle, with its *donjon* tower still soaring against the sky and providing panoramic views from the upper platform. The story goes that one of its seigneurs solved his servant problem by filling the place with his illegitimate children and putting them to work; while his wife, no doubt to solve *her* problem, beat him regularly.

1½km S, the town of **Volvic** earns its living by mining the large local deposits of volcanic lava, a dark-grey, nearly black rock which, being easy to work and yet extremely strong and durable, has been widely used for building houses and churches throughout the Auvergne ever since the Middle Ages.

TRUYÈRE, Gorges de la, *Cantal* (5–C6). These dramatic gorges are difficult to follow by road, and you need a good map (e.g. Michelin road map No. 76) to find the places where you can get close enough for the occasional view of the river. A good centre for such excursions is the little spa town of Chaudes-Aigues (*see entry*).

Eastward, upstream and on the N bank, the still splendid remains of the **Château d'Alleuze** stand on a dominant hilltop site overlooking one of the many inlets of the elongated lake created by the Barrage de Grandvet (where the D40 crosses from S to N). This formidable 13th-c. castle was captured during the Hundred Years War by a French mercenary commander fighting on the side of the English; for seven years he created such terror in the neighbourhood that when he eventually withdrew the local French set fire to the castle to make sure that such a situation could never occur again. If you are interested in bridge engineering, return to the S bank and drive E via D13 to the **Viaduc de Garabit**, where both the river and the N9 are spanned by the railway viaduct (450m long) constructed by Eiffel in 1883, six years before he built his famous tower in Paris.

In the downstream direction, the D11 going W from Chaudes-Aigues leads to the **Pont de Tréboul**, a fine suspension bridge which has replaced the 14th-c. bridge built by the English; when the down-river Barrage de Sarrans was built, the lake which formed behind it submerged not only the bridge but the village of Tréboul as well, but the old bridge still reappears, intact, whenever the water drops below a certain level. Beyond the Sarrans dam the river continues through further gorges and *barrages* until it reaches the pleasant little town of Entraygues (*see entry in the* Southwest *section*), where it joins forces with the river Lot.

VICHY, *Allier* (5–A7). Best known and most cosmopolitan of all spas, and seat of the Pétain government from 1940 to 1944. Its hot-water mineral springs, beneficial for liver and stomach complaints, have been widely known from the Romans onward, and Vichy water is bottled in the local state factory for sale all over the world.

Situated on the right bank of a wide bend of the Allier, amid lovely countryside, Vichy first began to be fashionable as a place to relax and 'take the waters' in the reign of Henri IV, but its vogue was really established in the 19th-c. by Napoleon III, who frequently came here for the cure – and incidentally was the instigator of the attractive stretch of garden parkland along the river. The May–October 'season', with its galas, spectacles, cabarets, festivals, concerts, etc., used to be one of the events of the French calendar.

Centre of social life is the Parc des Sources, shaded by its great plane-trees; here, close to hotels, restaurants, fashionable shops and lively cafés, are the famous Great Thermal Establishment (largest in the world) and the Grand Casino. A dam bridge just N of the Palais de Congrès has widened and deepened the river opposite the town to provide an elegant setting for yachting and other nautical sports.

Vichy

French Government Tourist Office

Burgundy and the Rhône Valley: Introduction

H. W. Yoxall

The autoroutes have their advantages, if you are in a rush for the sea or the mountains; but they prevent you seeing Burgundy properly, and confine you to the left bank of the Rhône, and mostly well away from that mighty river. The leisured and civilized traveller leaves the A6 near Auxerre, takes a glance (and a bottle) at Chablis, sees Avallon and the glorious basilica of Vézelay, and makes a northeasterly arc through a series of charming towns and past polite châteaux such as Tanlay, Ancy-le-Franc, Bussy, etc. After Thenissey he turns south to Lantenay and then east to Dijon, a fine city full of ancient monuments, to do the Côte d'Or from its beginning, instead of hitting it amidships, from the A6, at Beaune.

Just south of Dijon begins the narrow strip of wine-land which, broken here and there by soil so rich that it has to be devoted to the lesser crops of cereals, fruit and vegetables, interrupted occasionally by towns, and, centrally, by the great conurbation of Lyon, runs down for 300 kilometres in a succession of famous vineyards from Chambertin to Châteauneuf-du-Pape.

Almost at once after Dijon you should leave even the *route nationale* and wander down the *route des vins*, through those villages where each name is a clarion-call to the wine-lover. You pause, of course, at Beaune, still a fascinating *ville de province*, if only to see the Hôtel-Dieu, or Hospices, one of the loveliest of Gothic secular buildings. But avoid holiday seasons and particularly the third weekend of November, when the Hospices' auction takes place and there is not a free bedroom within 50 kilometres.

From Beaune you meander through great vineyards, towards Puligny-Montrachet and Chassagne-Montrachet. On the Côte de Nuits the vineyards are only about half a mile wide; on the Côte de Beaune they broaden a bit, and in southern Burgundy they bulge; but they still remain only a sliver on the map of France.

The quality of the wine is in inverse ratio to the width of the wine-land as you pass (please, still on by-roads) through the Chalonnais, the Mâconnais and the pretty, rolling Beaujolais; but the local *crus* still have their excellences, and genuine Beaujolais is always a fresh delight, particularly if taken in the region.

But there is more than wine here. Few great houses, but attractive villages, and almost every other one has a noble Romanesque church. Note too how from Mâcon onwards the domestic architecture takes on a southern note. You should detour east to see the basilica at Tournus, and west to Cluny. Here the remains of the once-great abbey are meagre, but it is a neat little town, and the national stud is as fascinating for students of architecture as for lovers of horses. Even those whose archaeological

Hôtel-Dieu, Beaune   Peter Baker

knowledge is vestigial will be excited by the Roche de Solutré, which you cannot miss if you visit the Pouilly-Fuissé vineyards.

By all means go back to the autoroute to avoid the congestion of Lyon, though by doing so you will miss a fine modern city that has preserved numerous beautiful old things. But return to the Rhône at the latest by Vienne, which has an interesting Roman temple and a good cathedral; for here, on the right bank, you find the most elegant Rhône wines, Côte-Rôtie for reds and Condrieu for whites, with the almost unobtainable Château Grillet, the smallest *appellation contrôlée* of France, and perhaps the most individual.

Here too the vineyard-area is narrow, for the vines grow on the precipitous terraced cliffs of the river valley, which is at places almost a gorge, as far as Valence.

But before Valence, at Tain, and now on the left bank, lie the Hermitage fields of 'the manliest French wine' (George Saintsbury), which we do not value as the Victorians did, since we do not give it enough bottle-age. White Hermitage is also a considerable wine. If the weather is baking hot it is worth crossing the stream again at Valence, to take a glass of refreshing *vin mousseux* at St-Péray.

Now the valley widens, the slopes are less acute, till beyond Orange, and its superb Roman remains, you reach a wide plateau of scrub, evergreen oaks and olives, where in fields of large round stones incredibly grow the vines of Châteauneuf-du-Pape. This wine, blended of numerous *cépages*, varies from very good from the right shippers to very bad from the wrong; but anyhow it is enjoyable earlier than Côte Rôtie, let alone Hermitage. Neither should you overlook Tavel, where they make the best *vin rosé* of the world, nor Beaumes de Venise where, if your journey is in winter, which can be bitter, you will enjoy the sweet muscat wine.

From Avignon the Rhône splits into its *bouches*, so for introductory purposes such as this its course may be said to have ended, just as I have not traced its source to Switzerland. But between Vienne and Avignon, dotted here and there beside the hurrying stream, are numerous vineyards of lesser importance that I have been constrained by space-limitations to pass over. And there are almost everywhere occasional fields of the Côtes du Rhône with agreeable everyday wine, while those elevated to the dignity of Côtes du Rhône Villages offer something better, and highly acceptable in these days of inflated prices.

It is well known that you eat well in most wine-lands; and this is certainly true of Burgundy – though, paradoxically perhaps, the better restaurants cluster more thickly as you go south from the fabled Côte d'Or and reach the Mâconnais and Beaujolais. Indeed, the finest are well west and slightly north of the area of the greatest vineyards. Lyon claims, not unjustifiably, to be the gastronomic centre of France, and from there on the three-star restaurants come in rapid succession. Such riches cannot be taken in twice a day. You must choose between your *relais gastronomiques*. But the agony of choice has its compensations. It clearly dictates the necessity of several Rhôneland journeys, till finally you will have sampled all these great tables. So – *bons voyages*, and *bon appétit*.

Burgundy and the Rhône Valley: Gazetteer

Edward Young

ALÉSIA (Alise-Ste-Reine), *Côte-d'Or* (3–E6). Hill site of a famous siege in 52 BC. Here Vercingétorix, heroic leader of the Gauls, made his last stand against Julius Caesar, having previously defeated him at Gergovie near Clermont-Ferrand (*see entry in* Massif Central *section*). After six weeks Vercingétorix was forced to surrender to the besieging army, and the last obstacle to Caesar's total conquest of Gaul was gone.

The excavations of the Gallo-Roman city, as well as the Musée Alésia with its remarkable collection of objects found in the diggings, are open every day from Easter to end-October. A large bronze statue of Vercingétorix overlooks the village of Alise-Ste-Reine below and the nearby village of **Les Laumes** with its interesting modern church.

ANCY-LE-FRANC, Château d', *Yonne* (17km SE of Tonnerre: 3–D5). Classic example of a 16th-c. Renaissance château, designed by the Italian architect Serlio, who was employed at the court of François I. Severe but majestic square inner courtyard; inside, on the first floor, sumptuous apartments and galleries lavishly decorated by Primaticcio; on the ground floor, 12 splendid rooms (including the Chambre des Nudités and the Chambre de Diane) adorned with tapestries and frescoes; also spacious kitchens with copper utensils. Privately owned by descendants of the original owner; open to the public by guided tours every day, strictly on the hour (but shut December–February).

AUTUN, *Saône-et-Loire* (3–E6 and 6–A2). One of the most interesting old towns in the whole of Burgundy. Founded by the Emperor Augustus about the time of Christ, it developed into a city even larger and more important than it is today. Survivors from that age are the two imposing and well-preserved Roman gates with their upper galleries (Porte St-André and Porte d'Arroux), the ruins of a square tower thought to have been part of a Temple of Janus, and the remains of the Roman theatre, believed to have been the largest in Gaul, in a splendid situation facing outwards from the eastern ramparts. After the Romans the city foundered under the onslaughts of the various invaders of the Dark Ages.

Recovery came slowly. The 12th-c. saw the erection, on the S side of the town, of the great Cathedral of St-Lazare to accommodate the influx of pilgrims who came to venerate the supposed relics of Lazarus, brought here from Marseille in the previous century. Most of the original structure remains, including a masterly Last Judgment tympanum over the doorway, signed by its sculptor Gislebert in 1135. The belfry (rewarding view from the top) and the tall spire date from the 15th-c., when the energetic bishop, Cardinal Rolin, set about turning the town into a great religious centre. The two towers above the main doorway are 19th-c. additions. In the interior, note the original 12th-c. capitals carved with biblical scenes; the stained glass is modern, some 19th-c. and some 20th-c.

Near the Cathedral, in a 15th-c. mansion, the Musée Rolin contains a good collection of sculpture from Gallo-Roman to recent times, together with paintings from French and Flemish primitives onward; prize of the collection is the

Porte St-André, Autun

celebrated 'Nativity' by the great 'Master of Moulins' (*see also* Moulins, in the Massif Central *section*).

A tour of the medieval ramparts makes a pleasant walk, with views of the Arroux valley and the surrounding hills. To the W are the Monts du Morvan, the highest part of Burgundy. All around are the forests which supply the wood for Autun's furniture industry.

14km NE, set in a huge park, is the handsome moated Renaissance château of **Sully**. Only the exterior can be visited (from Easter to end-September), but it is worth a diversion if you are travelling towards Beaune.

AUXERRE, *Yonne* (3–D5). Rising up on the left bank of the N-flowing Yonne, Auxerre (the 'x' is pronounced 'ss') is one of the oldest towns in France. Nothing remains of its Gallo-Roman origins (the site of the old ramparts is occupied by a ring of boulevards), but in the two ancient superimposed crypts of the abbey church of St-Germain are some 9th-c. frescoes – the oldest of their kind in the whole of France. Other remarkable frescoes, but dated two centuries later, are in the 11th-c. crypt of St-Étienne Cathedral, a Flamboyant Gothic edifice on the site of the previous Romanesque cathedral. St-Étienne took three and a half centuries to build, from 1215 to 1560 – and even so the right-hand tower of the façade is still incomplete. There is good 13th-c. stained glass in the choir, and a fine rose-window in each arm of the transept.

The former Bishop's Palace, with its handsome Romanesque gallery, has become the Hôtel-de-Ville. Nearby is an unusual 15th-c. clock tower; the clock itself is above an arch over a street and each side has a different face: one tells the time, the other shows the movements of the sun and moon.

Auxerre, now bypassed by the A6 autoroute, is surrounded by orchards and vineyards. Chablis, the wine capital of the region, is less than 20km E (*see entry*). 18km NE, the village of **Pontigny** contains a vast and celebrated Cistercian abbey church, in which Thomas-à-Becket took refuge in 1164 from the wrath of Henry II; later he returned to Canterbury and was assassinated shortly afterwards, in 1170.

AVALLON, *Yonne* (3–E5). Delightful medieval fortified town standing high on a rocky promontory between two ravines. When Louis XIV had no further military use for the town he offered to sell the ramparts to the citizens, who promptly bought them to preserve them for their picturesque beauty. At the S edge of the ramparts a promenade shaded by lime-trees gives lovely views of the river Cousin meandering in its valley below. Within the walls are many gardens, ancient houses and excellent restaurants. At the top of the town stands a 15th-c. clock-tower with a little bell-tower attached. The church of St-Lazare with its fine double doorway dates from the 11th-c. but has

suffered from later reconstructions when the church proved too small; amazingly, a 4th-c. crypt survives under the 11th-c. choir.

BEAUJOLAIS, Le, *Rhône* (S of Mâcon: 6–B3). Surprisingly, Beaujolais was little known in Britain and the United States until after World War II. It is now probably the most popular red wine both in and out of France. The Beaujolais vineyards occupy a narrow belt on the right bank of the Saône (immediately W of the A6 and N6), from just S of Mâcon to the outskirts of Lyon, but it is the northern part of the area (N of Villefranche), known as Beaujolais Villages, that contains those villages whose names on the labels are, for the connoisseur, a guarantee of quality. From N to S they are: St-Amour, Juliénas, Chénas, Moulin-à-Vent (the best of all), Fleurie, Chiroubles, Morgon, Brouilly. Attractive villages in rolling, wooded country, with eastward glimpses of the Jura and the Alps. The 'Route du Beaujolais' is clearly signposted.

BEAUNE, *Côte-d'Or* (3–E6). A very ancient wine town at the heart of the Côtes de Beaune section of the great wine area known as the 'Côte d'Or' (*see entry*). Within its 14th-c. ramparts, most of which still exist, stands one of the outstanding Renaissance buildings of France: the exquisite Hôtel Dieu (les Hospices de Beaune), whose function as a charitable hospital – endowed with the income from some of the most prestigious of the Burgundy vineyards (Pommard and Volnay among them) – has continued unbroken from its foundation in 1443 by Nicolas Rolin, a celebrated chancellor whose son was Cardinal Rolin, Bishop of Autun (*see entry*). In recent years only geriatric cases have been admitted here, the other hospital services having been transferred elsewhere in the town, but the nurses still wear their traditional medieval hooded dress. The building is a Late Gothic masterpiece, with a *cour d'honneur* described ruefully in its day as 'more like a prince's palace than a hospital for the poor'. Inside are splendid rooms, a collection of medieval and later pharmaceutical jars, with pewter pestles and mortars, and a small historical and art-treasure museum; but pride of place goes to the famous polyptych of the Last Judgement by Roger van der Weyden, commissioned for the chapel by the founder.

On the third Sunday of November each year the Hospices de Beaune hold an auction of wine from their vineyards, an event attended by buyers from all over France and from overseas. It is the proceeds from this sale that provide the income for the upkeep of the Hôtel Dieu and the expansion of medical services in the town. The same evening the Confrérie des Chevaliers du Tastevin hold a banquet, the second in a celebrated annual three-day series of feasts known as *Les Trois Glorieuses* (*see also* Clos de Vougeot *and* Meursault).

18km SW is the village of **La Rochepot** with an

imposing feudal château perched above it on a small wooded hill. Built in the 12th-c., it was restored in the 15th-c. The keep was razed to the ground at the time of the Revolution, but the drawbridge is still there and the huge building bristles with pepperpot turrets. The tiled roofs make a striking mosaic effect. (Open March–November.)

BELLEY, *Ain* (6–B4). A peaceful old town at the southern tip of the Jura range, on a plateau surrounded by forests, lakes, waterfalls and mountains. Renowned as the birthplace and home (62 Grande Rue) of Brillat-Savarin (1755–1826), the respected lawyer and judge who achieved immortality as the modest author of the gastronomic classic *La Physiologie du Goût*. The Hôtel Pernollet, in the Ave. d'Alsace-Lorraine, was founded three years before his death and is still there, maintaining a *cuisine* worthy of his memory.

BOURBON-LANCY, *Saône-et-Loire* (6–A2). Small hilltop spa overlooking the Loire valley and the Allier plain towards Moulins. The thermal station is set in pleasant parkland, and its hot-water springs are reputed to alleviate rheumatism and circulatory problems. The 11th-c. church of St-Nazaire is now a museum of local archaeological finds. There are some interesting 15th-c. buildings, including a remarkable wooden house and a fortified gateway with a clock tower. The town specializes in the manufacture of agricultural machinery.

BOURG-EN-BRESSE, *Ain* (6–B3). A thriving market town renowned for its cattle fairs, its animated pre-Christmas poultry market (third Saturday in December) and its restaurants. The 16th-c. church of Notre-Dame contains fine choir-stalls and has a splendid carillon which rings for ten minutes before the hours of 8 a.m., noon, and 7 p.m.

But the pride of Bourg is to be found in **Brou**, its SE suburb. Here is one of the most perfect Flamboyant Gothic churches ever built. Now deconsecrated, it was erected as a monastery church by Marguerite of Austria, daughter of the Emperor Maximilian, in fulfilment of a vow. Started in 1506, it was completed in the amazingly short time of 19 years.

Flamboyant Gothic splendour in the church in Brou, Bourg-en-Bresse

The rich carving of the triangular façade, with a fine tympanum over the Renaissance doorway, makes a powerful first impression. In the interior, on a bright day, the light falling from the high windows on to the white stone walls is almost dazzling. The nave is short and wide; the pillars, each a tight cluster of slender columns, shoot upwards in an unbroken line, fanning out at the top to form the ribs of the vaulted roof. A splendid rood-screen bars the way to the choir, which cannot be entered without a guide; the 74 choir-stalls, formerly reserved for the monks, are a masterpiece of sculpture in wood, with hundreds of figures and lively cameos – all done in two years. At the far end are the magnificent tombs of Philibert of Savoy (centre), his mother Marguerite of Bourbon and his wife Marguerite of Austria, all superbly and extravagantly carved in white Carrara marble.

Other treasures of this unusual church are the stained-glass windows, the chapels (one of which contains a beautiful marble retable) and the cloisters. The adjacent monastery suffered much depredation during the Wars of Religion and the Revolution; in its time it has served as a pig-sty, a prison, and an asylum, but now houses an interesting museum.

BRANCION, *Saône-et-Loire* (9km W of Tournus: 6–A3). A marvellous medieval fortified village on a hill, with ramparts, the remains of a feudal château where the Dukes of Burgundy occasionally resided, a simple Romanesque church, and houses with flowered balconies and outside staircases.

BUSSY-RABUTIN, Château de, *Côte-d'Or* (15km SE of Montbard: 3–E6). A 16th-c. moated residential château that once was the home of Roger de Rabutin, a count of Bussy who was frequently exiled or sent to the Bastille for writing satirical songs and chronicles. It has a Renaissance façade with a round, cone-capped tower at each end; two wings come forward to complete the three-sided courtyard, each with a delicate gallery over an arcade and terminating in a similar tower – one tower being the chapel, the other the keep. The interior decoration and the many portraits (not all originals) of soldiers, nobles and high-born ladies, evoke the artificial elegance of 17th-c. court life.

CHABLIS, *Yonne* (16km E of Auxerre: 3–D5). Centre of the Chablis wine district. Most of the old part of this small town was destroyed by bombs during World War II, but the two round towers of the old town gates, the modest 12th-c. church and the Étoile restaurant beloved of gourmets, have survived. The little river Serein flows gently past the town. The vineyards that produce the celebrated dry white wine (which goes so well with

oysters but few can now afford) occupy a rough circle about 20km in diameter, in an isolated pocket of bituminous clay – a type of soil unknown anywhere else except in England, at Kimmeridge in Dorset.

CHALON-SUR-SAÔNE, *Saône-et-Loire* (6–A3). A large industrial and commercial conglomeration, resulting from its position as a crossroads and rail-junction at the confluence of the Doubs and the Saône and as a terminus of the Canal du Centre. It is also an important river port, the Saône being navigable at this point. Its twice-yearly commercial fairs are renowned, and it is the distribution centre for the wine district that lies W of the town (*see* La Côte Chalonnaise). A statue on the Quai Gambetta reminds us that Chalon was the birthplace of Nicéphore Niepce (1765–1833), the celebrated pioneer of photography – perhaps, as the Chalonnais claim, its inventor.

CHARITÉ-SUR-LOIRE, La, *Nièvre* (6–A1). A bustling market town with a long history, situated on the E bank of the Loire. The river is spanned by an attractive 16th-c. stone bridge that was twice blown up by the Germans in World War II and twice repaired. Until the middle of the 19th-c. the river was a busy navigational highway for goods and passengers, and La Charité was an important river port.

The town's name comes from its 11th-c. reputation for generosity towards the pauper pilgrims who came to worship at the great new abbey church of Notre-Dame. In its day this was the largest church in France after Cluny (*see entry*), but in 1599 a fire destroyed the five western bays of the nave (now occupied by the Place Ste-Croix). The present truncated church, consisting of the original Romanesque choir, the domed transept, the octagonal tower over the crossing, and a nave with only four bays, is still impressive and beautiful with its radiating chapels, its ornamented pillars and carved capitals. The modern stained-glass windows are by Max Ingrand. Of the original façade only the left tower, the Tour Ste-Croix, and a tympanum of Christ in Majesty remain; the old doors are bricked up. In the remnants of the side-aisles on the N side of the vanished nave, the archways have been filled in by a patchwork of dwellings, and very odd they look under the crumbling arches of the old triforium. The old abbey, which once occupied a large area N of the church, has virtually disappeared.

CHARLIEU, *Loire* (6–B2). A quaint old town with many medieval houses and the extensive remains of an ancient Benedictine abbey. Until it was pillaged at the time of the Revolution it was famous as one of the finest examples of Romanesque art. Still extant are the 12th-c. narthex, with its

Vineyards at Meursault, near Beaune, Côte-d'Or (see page 342)   *Guy Gravett*

superb, luxuriantly sculpted doorway, the elegant 15th-c. cloisters and the 16th-c. priory chapel, but the church itself is a sad ruin. Excavations under the choir have revealed the foundations of two previous churches (9th-c. and 10th-c.) on the same site. Nearby stands a fine round defence tower built at the end of the 12th-c. on the orders of Philippe-Auguste. West of the abbey is the site of a former Franciscan monastery that was bought and removed, stone by stone, to the United States; but the Gothic cloisters, with their wealth of carved capitals, are happily still there.

About 17km NW, just E of Marcigny, is the attractive village of **Semur-en-Brionnais**. Set on a small hill above a peaceful countryside of orchards and vineyards, it has a fine Romanesque church, an old priory, a handsome 18th-c. *mairie*, and a castle whose keep is over 1000 years old. There is a *son-et-lumière* here on summer evenings at weekends and on certain other days as advertised.

CHÂTEAU-CHINON, *Nièvre* (3–E5 and 6–A2). A small town with remains of ancient ramparts, capital of the hilly Morvan region W of Autun. The rocky hill above it, at an altitude of over 600m, is a natural strategic site; the Gauls and the Romans in turn used it as a defensive encampment, and there are still traces of the medieval château-fortress that stood here. Now the site is marked by a simple cross and an orientation table. The views from the summit, and from the promenade encircling it, take in the forested heights of the Morvan range to the SE, rising to 900m, and the rolling landscape extending W to the Loire valley. E of the town the infant Yonne flows N towards the great lake formed by the **Pannesière-Chaumard Barrage**, 50m high and 340m across, and well worth a visit; the round trip from Château-Chinon, including a circuit of the lake, is about 40km.

CHÂTEAUNEUF, *Côte-d'Or* (11km SW of Sombernon: 3–E6). An impressive 12th-c. castle W of Dijon, standing on a rocky eminence surrounded by vineyards, close to the N side of the A6. If you see it from the autoroute when travelling SE you have already passed the turn-off, but if travelling NW take the Dijon turn-off to the right (N5) soon afterwards, and then immediately double back on D18 through the villages of Créancy and Vandenesse. If you are driving W out of Dijon on N5, turn off through the village of Sombernon, take the D977 to the SW and follow the signs. It is a splendid fortress with a moat, massive walls, solid round gateway towers, a drawbridge, an interior courtyard, a spacious guardroom, a chapel, and panoramic views.

CHÂTILLON-SUR-SEINE, *Côte-d'Or* (3–D6). Joffre's headquarters from which he repulsed the German advance in September 1914. In World War II the town centre was destroyed by fire after a bombing raid. It is still a charming little town; the Seine, not much more than a stream, wanders through it in a double loop, constantly dividing and rejoining, as if reluctant to leave. At the E side of the town, in a grove below a rocky escarpment, a 'resurgence' like the Fontaine de Vaucluse in Provence issues from the ground at the rate of anything from 600 to 3000 litres per second, depending on the season; it is called the source of the Douix, but within a few metres its waters mingle with those of the Seine.

The museum, which occupies a handsome Renaissance house in the Rue du Bourg, is a fine collection of local Gallo-Roman antiquities and contains an outstanding archaeological treasure discovered in 1953 at Vix, only 7km N of Châtillon: a group of superb Grecian artefacts – in solid gold, silver and bronze – found in the tomb of a Gallic princess of the 6th-c. BC. How they got there no one knows.

CLAMECY, *Nièvre* (3–E5). For three centuries a 'wood port' for the forests of the Morvan mountains. Far up-river the logs were assembled behind a dam; on a pre-arranged day the dam was opened and the logs floated swiftly down the Yonne to Clamecy; here they were arrested by another dam, sorted according to the owners' marks and stacked on great rafts for transport down the Yonne towards Paris. Since 1923 the logs have gone direct from the felling sites by road; but the Morvan forests still support the town, for in the industrial suburbs is the largest carbonization plant in France. The old town, on a hill with lovely views of the valley, has many old houses, a museum with some good paintings (Fragonard, Rubens, Breughel) and a 13th–15th-c. church with a Flamboyant tower and façade.

CLOS DE VOUGEOT, Château du, *Côte-d'Or* (4km N of Nuits-St-Georges: 3–E6). The vignoble was founded by Cistercian monks in the 12th-c. The wall which made it into an enclosure (hence *clos*) was built in 1336 and, though frequently repaired, still stands. The 16th-c. Renaissance château, surrounded by its celebrated vineyards, still preserves its ancient wine-presses. In 1944 it was acquired as the headquarters of the Confrérie des Chevaliers du Tastevin (the 's' is silent) – a society devoted to maintaining the quality and reputation of French wines in general and Burgundy wines in particular. Its banquets, meetings and initiations of new *chevaliers*, held in the medieval Grand Cellar, are characterized by elaborate ceremonies inspired by Rabelais and Molière. One of the important banquets of the year is held on the eve of the Hospices de Beaune wine auction (*see also* Beaune *and* Meursault).

The French Alps: Mount Meije (3983m), 22km SE of Alpe d'Huez (see page 351)   *Picturepoint*

CLUNY, *Saône-et-Loire* (6–A3,B3). A small medieval town NW of Mâcon, containing the remnants of the illustrious Romanesque abbey that was the religious, intellectual and artistic centre of the Middle Ages. The abbey church, built between 1088 and 1130, was the largest in the whole of Christendom – even St Peter's in Rome, built about 500 years later, was only 9m longer. It had five naves, rising to 30m at the highest point, two transepts, five belfries, two other towers and a choir with over 200 stalls. The 12th-c. was the apogee of Cluny's religious power; in the three centuries that followed, the sumptuousness of the abbey life gradually dimmed the spiritual and intellectual flame. In the Wars of Religion the abbey and its church were ransacked, its great library robbed of its most precious manuscripts. At the Revolution the abbey was suppressed, and the great church sold to a demolition contractor. Today there remain only the S arms of the two transepts, the octagonal belfry called the 'Clocher de l'Eau-Bénite' and the smaller 'Clocher de l'Horloge'. Of the great abbey complex little remains but the cloister enclosed by 18th-c. buildings (now a technical college), one wall of which, facing the Place du 11-Août, incorporates a late 13th-c. Gothic façade. The remnants of the abbey library, together with carved stone fragments and other objects rescued from the church, are now in the Musée Ochier, next to the Hôtel-de-Ville, both occupying parts of the former Abbot's Palace.

CÔTE CHALONNAISE, La, *Saône-et-Loire* (about 8km W of Chalon: 6–A3). This relatively small wine district, which produces red and white wines of good but not outstanding quality, lies on the rising ground just to the W of Chalon-sur-Saône, in a strip between the Côte de Beaune and the Côte Mâconnaise. The best-known vineyards are at Rully, Mercurey and Givry.

CÔTE d'OR, La (S of Dijon: 6–A3). Often referred to simply as 'La Côte', this long, narrow strip of vineyards is one of the two most prestigious wine areas of France, the other being the Haut-Médoc of Bordeaux. Sometimes only 2km wide and never more than 10km wide, it lies close to the N74 on the east-facing slopes of a long ridge of hills known as La Montagne. It starts 10km S of Dijon on the D122, at the village of Fixin (N of which the vines belong to the Côte de Dijon) and ends about 50km further S at Santenay, close to Chagny (NW of Chalon-sur-Saône).

The northern part of the area is classified as the **Côte de Nuits**. Producing almost exclusively red wines, it includes the celebrated vignobles of Gevrey-Chambertin, Chambolle-Musigny, Clos de Vougeot (where the *route des vins* joins the N74), Vosne-Romanée and Nuits-St-Georges. From there onwards we enter the southern half of the area, the **Côte de Beaune** (producing both red and white wines), the signposts continuing their

roll of honour with Aloxe-Corton (the 'x' pronounced 'ss'), Beaune, Pommard, Volnay, Meursault, Puligny- and Chassagne-Montrachet (both 't's are silent). S of Santenay the wine road leaves the Côte d'Or and enters the Côte Chalonnaise (*see entry*).

If you are starting your trip through the Côte d'Or from Dijon, note that before you reach Fixin the D122 passes through **Chenôve**, the ancient vignoble shared by the Dukes of Burgundy and the Canons of Autun; it is still divided into the 'Clos du Roi' and the 'Clos du Chapitre' and preserves two huge wine-presses which certainly date back to the 15th-c., perhaps even earlier. Chenôve is also celebrated for its *escargots*.

CREST, *Drôme* (6–C3). 50m above this little town on the N bank of the river Drôme stands a majestic tower keep, all that is left of a fortress that once guarded the way up the valley into the mountains. From the square in front of the church a flight of steps to the left of the Hôtel-de-Ville leads to the approach path. The tower has dark dungeons, vaulted rooms and, from the upper terrace, an impressive panorama of jagged mountain peaks.

CREUSOT, Le, *Saône-et-Loire* (3–E6). A large industrial town specializing in metallurgy. It is the nerve-centre of the industrial basin which straddles the Canal du Centre, including Blanzy to the SW, Montceau-les-Mines to the S, and Montchanin to the SE.

DIJON, *Côte-d'Or* (3–E6). Famous for its restaurants and its mustard, Dijon is the historic capital of Burgundy. After the departure of the Romans from France it suffered the usual fate of most French towns – constant pillaging and rebuilding, and in 1137 it was swept by fire and completely destroyed. Duke Hugues II rebuilt and enlarged it, enclosing it with ramparts and fortified gateways. Its period of greatness began in the 14th-c. under Duke Philippe le Hardi (Philip the Bold) and continued under his son Jean Sans Peur and his grandson Philippe le Bon.

At the height of their power in the 15th-c. the Dukes of Burgundy ruled over a territory that included all the lands between the Loire and the Jura mountains, Lorraine, Luxembourg, Flanders, Artois, Picardy, nearly all Belgium and much of Holland. They were a constant threat to the power of the Kings of France, and at one time even allied with the English against the Crown; indeed it was the Burgundian army that captured Joan of Arc at Compiègne and handed her over to the English (for a huge sum of money). Not until the end of the 15th-c., after the death of Duke Charles the Bold, was Burgundy annexed to the kingdom of France. Though Dijon continued in its rôle as an administrative centre it seemed content to rest on the laurels of its illustrious past, and by the end of the 18th-c. the population was still only about 20,000. But the development of the railways in the

Peter Baker

Dijon

mid-19th-c. turned Dijon into an important communication centre, causing a great expansion into the suburbs and a steady increase in the population. It now numbers over 150,000 inhabitants and is a thriving industrial and commercial city, renowned for its gastronomic specialities.

The hub of the city is the large PLACE DE LA LIBÉRATION, the former Place Royale designed in the 17th-c. by the Versailles architect Hardouin-Mansart, with a semi-circle of elegant arcaded Louis-Quatorze houses facing the DUCAL PALACE. This imposing edifice still recalls its sumptuous past, with its pillared wings flanking the vast courtyard, its monumental staircases, its noble rooms, its eloquent statues, and not least the huge kitchens where the fabled banquets were prepared. Today the Palace is used partly as the town hall and partly as the MUSÉE DES BEAUX-ARTS, one of the best art museums outside Paris, though in some ways the splendour of the rooms – especially the famous Guardroom (Salle des Gardes) built by Philippe le Bon at the height of Burgundian power – tends to overshadow and distract attention from the paintings, sculptures, tombs, furniture, ceramics, etc., which they contain.

Behind the Ducal Palace the picturesque Rue des Forges passes several imposing Renaissance houses (the Hôtel Chambellan, the Maison Milsand, etc.). A turn to the N leads immediately to the fine Gothic church of NOTRE-DAME with its well-known clock tower on which mechanical figures strike the hours and quarters; inside the church is ancient stained glass, a 15th-c. fresco, a modern Gobelins tapestry and, in a chapel to the right of the choir, a very early 11th-c. 'Black Virgin' carved in wood. A short distance E of the Ducal Palace is the church of ST-MICHEL, in a mixture of Gothic and Renaissance styles. The façade (16th–17th-c.) gives an effect of solidity; over a triple porch with rounded arches rise two somewhat graceless square towers, each surmounted by a hexagonal lantern with a pointed dome.

Immediately S of the Ducal Palace is the PALAIS DE JUSTICE, worth visiting because most of the original 16th-c. building and interior has been preserved, including some fine ceilings. From the rear of the building a short walk to the W, along the Rue Amiral Roussin, Rue Piron and Rue Michelet, leads to the CATHEDRAL of St-Bénigne. Though largely Gothic, this early 14th-c. church with its soaring spire has retained in its façade the original doorway from its Romanesque predecessor; the most interesting feature is the 10th-c. crypt, full of pillars and remarkable carved capitals.

Further W, beyond the railway station along the Ave. Albert I, the site of the late 14th-c. CHARTREUSE DE CHAMPMOL, built by Duke Philippe le Hardi as a ducal mausoleum but virtually destroyed in the Revolution, is now occupied by a psychiatric hospital. However, it can be visited; the 15th-c. doorway is still intact, and two of the original works attributed to the Flemish sculptor Claus Sluter have survived – the chapel doorway and a remarkable statuary group of Moses and other biblical figures with striking facial expressions. The magnificent tombs of Philippe le Hardi and other Burgundian dukes which used to rest here are now in the Musée des Beaux-Arts, in the Salle des Gardes.

FLAVIGNY-SUR-OZERAIN, *Côte-d'Or* (18km SE of Montbard: 3–E6). Ancient village perched on an isolated rock, surrounded on three sides by deep wooded valleys. Extensive remains of ramparts, fortified gateways and towers, narrow winding streets. A 13th-c. church with amusing carvings on 16th-c. choir-stalls and some good sculpture. Excavations of the former abbey continue; the abbey church has an 8th-c. crypt with remarkable primitive carvings on the pillar capitals. Flavigny is well known for its centuries-old production of sugar-coated aniseed sweets – *les anis de Flavigny.*

FONTENAY, Ancienne Abbaye de, *Côte-d'Or* (4km NE of Montbard: 3–E6). A celebrated Cistercian abbey and monastery founded in 1118. It reached the height of its fame and prosperity in

The Cloisters, Abbaye de Fontenay

Peter Baker

the 16th-c., after which decline set in, partly through the venal system of appointing abbots by royal favour and partly through the ravages of the Wars of Religion. At the Revolution it was sold and turned into a paper-making factory. Since early in the 20th-c., when it came under new ownership, it has been restored as near as possible to its original state, and now – with its vast and austere abbey church, its cloisters, the dormitory with its superb timberwork, its vaulted chapter house and work-halls – it is one of the finest extant examples of the outer fabric of Cistercian monastic life. (Open all year round.)

The nearby small town of **Montbard**, a port on the Burgundy canal and a metallurgy centre specializing in steel tubes, is notable as the birthplace of the 18th-c. naturalist Buffon, author of the classic *Histoire naturelle.* The gardens he laid out here, and the pavilion in which he did most of his studying and writing, are open to the public at set times, as are the forges he built in 1768 where there is an interesting exhibition.

GRIGNAN, *Drôme* (20km SE of Montélimar: 6–D3). Small town on a rocky eminence between two valleys. Narrow streets huddle below the imposing Renaissance château that was once the home of Madame de Grignan, daughter of Madame de Sévigné the celebrated letter-writer, who loved the place and often stayed here with her daughter. In fact she died here in 1696 and is buried under a marble slab by the main altar in the little church attached to the château. From the terrace is a tremendous panorama: mountains to the NW and NE, Provence to the SE.

JOIGNY, *Yonne* (3–D5). The town rises in a semi-circle on the N bank of the Yonne, radiating outwards from its 18th-c. bridge. Among its old streets and houses stand two fine churches: St-Jean with an unusual wooden Renaissance coffered ceiling; and St-Thibault, whose choir is un-expectedly angled to the left, and whose nave contains religious paintings and a charming 14th-c. stone statue of a smiling Virgin.

18km SW, in the small fortified town of **La Ferté-Loupière**, is a 12th–15th-c. church with a striking early 17th-c. mural of a *Danse Macabre* in which Death shows himself to be no respecter of persons.

LYON, *Rhône* (6–B3). The second largest con-urbation in France after Paris, with over a million inhabitants, and famous for its gastronomic restaurants and its centuries-old silk industry. Today, in addition to textiles, it has many other expanding industries – chemicals, metallurgy, heavy vehicle manufacture, etc. It has an impor-tant University specializing in medicine, a re-nowned annual international trade fair, and enviable sporting facilities, including an Olympic swimming pool and an artificial ski *piste.* It has a great variety of fine museums and (in the Parc de la

Topham (Teddy Schwarz)

Lyon

Tête d'Or) one of the largest rose gardens in Europe. Much of Lyon's 20th-c. advance has been due to the energy of the famous Radical leader Édouard Herriot, mayor of the city from 1905 to 1955.

Throughout history Lyon has been a city of strategic importance due to its geographical position at the junction of two great rivers. The Saône comes gliding down from the N, swerves between Lyon's two famous hills, the Croix-Rousse and the Fourvière, then continues S. The swifter Rhône, full of Alpine water, zigzags in from the NE, almost meets the Saône but, deflected by the high ground of the Croix-Rousse, also turns S. The two rivers now run parallel for about 3km, finally joining forces at the southern tip of the narrow peninsula that lies between them. This peninsula, no more than 600m across, is the heart of the city.

The broad quays on both rivers are tree-lined traffic highways. Those on the E side of the peninsula are bordered by the impressive 16th- and 17th-c. stone houses of prosperous silk merchants. Nearly two dozen bridges, most of them modern, link the peninsula with the opposite banks – on the W side to the old quarter rising steeply up the Fourvière hill, on the other side to the huge modern business complex of the Part-Dieu quarter and the tenement high-rise blocks of Villeurbanne, an ugly suburb that continues to spread E across the low-lying area toward the international Lyon-Satolas airport (opened in 1975). Three autoroutes meet together on the peninsula, in a 'spaghetti junction' just S of Place Carnot – the A6 from the N, slicing through a

tunnel under the Fourvière hill, the A7 from the S, and the A43 from Geneva and Grenoble in the E.

The visitor with little time to spare would do best to start in the middle of the peninsula at the vast PLACE BELLECOUR, one of the largest squares in France, with Louis-Quatorze façades and a great central equestrian statue of Louis XIV. It is a lively scene with its restaurants, cafés and flower-stalls. From its NE corner runs the Rue de la République, a smart shopping-centre and the main street of Lyon, stretching N as far as the grandiose HÔTEL-DE-VILLE. This is a great rectangle of a building, part Louis XIII, with a *cour d'honneur* in the centre; the imposing Hardouin-Mansart W façade, incorporating an equestrian statue of Henri IV high above the central doorway, looks out over the wide space of the PLACE DES TERRAUX and its monumental fountain of four rampant horses. It was here that hundreds of citizens were guillotined during the Revolution, when Lyon's anti-Jacobin policy of moderation aroused the wrath of the 'Terror' and brought violent retribution on the city's inhabitants.

The Place des Terraux is at the centre of the neck of the peninsula. (In Roman times a canal joined the two rivers here.) To the N the ground rises to the Croix-Rousse hill through a curious area known as 'LES TRABOULES', where narrow passage-ways connect with each other by tiny court-yards, up stairways, and through and under houses. One such route wanders NW up to the garden site of the remains of a Gallo-Roman amphitheatre.

On the S side of the Place des Terraux stands the 17th-c. Palais St-Pierre, a former Benedictine nunnery for noble ladies. It now houses the splendid MUSÉE DES BEAUX-ARTS; the inner courtyard has retained the old cloister and displays works of sculpture, including three Rodins; other sculptures are on the ground floor of the building; on the two upper floors is a magnificent collection from all the great schools of painting – Italian Renaissance, Dutch and Flemish, German and Spanish, 17th–19th-c. French, the Impressionists and their successors, right up to contemporary works.

Coming S again, along the Rue Paul Chena-vard, and turning right at the church of St-Nizier (with its two odd spires and, in one of the chapels, a Virgin and Child by the 17th-c. sculptor Coysevox), the visitor faces a good view of the Saône making its wide turn to the S; to the left the Maréchal Juin bridge crosses the river to the old quarter on the lower slopes of the Fourvière hill. Once the thriving centre of the silk industry, LE VIEUX LYON is a warren of passages, narrow streets, excellent restaurants, and many 15th–16th-c. houses, mostly humble but some very grand indeed – notably the Hôtel de Gadagne (which contains a good museum illustrating the history of Lyon) and the Maison du Crible. The main street, Rue St-Jean, runs parallel to the river and leads to the CATHEDRAL, a handsome, mainly Gothic edifice which, though badly damaged in the Revolution, is still impressive with its four square towers, beautiful Romanesque choir and 13th-c. stained glass; in the N transept is a remarkable astronomical clock which at certain hours sets mechanical figures in motion and sounds an unusual chime.

Just S of the Cathedral is the Gare St-Jean, where you can take the funicular railway to the top of the FOURVIÈRE hill. Here, in a dominant position, is the 19th-c. Basilica of Notre-Dame-de-Fourvière. The church is rather undistinguished, but from the terrace alongside is a magnificent view of the whole city and the two rivers with the Alps in the distance. (The view is even better from the top of the church tower.) Nearby are two excavated Roman theatres – the larger of which is equal in size to the one at Arles and is still used for dramatic performances during Lyon's annual arts festival in June and July. The important Roman

Solutré, near Mâcon

Denis Hughes-Gilbey

walled city of Lugdunum occupied this strategic hilltop site; the Roman capital of the whole of conquered Gaul, it guarded the vital river junction and was the centre of a network of military highways radiating to all parts of the country.

MÂCON, *Saône-et-Loire* (6–B3). A quiet but flourishing city on the W bank of the Saône. The river, 200m wide at this point, is crossed by a restored 14th-c. bridge, and at the city end of it are broad quays and old wine cellars. Mâcon is the commercial centre of the **Mâconnais**, the wine area which stretches N and W to Tournus and Cluny and beyond. The French poet and novelist Lamartine was born here in 1790. In the municipal museum, housed in the 17th-c. building of a former Ursuline convent, are the objects excavated at the celebrated prehistoric site of **Solutré**, 8km W of Mâcon, as well as paintings, drawings and engravings by French artists from Greuze to Braque. Nearby are the two towers and other sad remains of the old Cathedral of St-Vincent, which was almost entirely destroyed at the time of the Revolution.

MEURSAULT, *Côte-d'Or* (7km SW of Beaune: 6–A3). Attractive small town in the Côte de Beaune area, renowned for its dry white wine with a slight flavour of over-ripe peaches; a small amount of red is produced as well. The parish church has a tall, slender spire in stone, and the town hall is roofed with Burgundian tiles. There is a *hospice* similar to the one at Beaune, though on a smaller scale. Meursault is the setting of the third of *Les Trois Glorieuses*, the series of feasts held in November by the Confrérie des Chevaliers du Tastevin (*see also* Clos de Vougeot *and* Beaune); this one is a luncheon to which the vineyard owners contribute the best of their own wine.

MONTBRISON, *Loire* (6–B2). Small manufacturing town on the E limit of the Massif Central, with a low-lying area on one side, dotted with lakes and reaching E to the Loire, and to the W the hills rising towards the summits of the Monts du Forez (over 1000m). The Dukes of Forez once had a castle in Montbrison; now only the site remains. The town was ransacked by English troops in the Hundred Years War and by Protestants 150 years later. The church of Notre-Dame-d'Espérance, 13th-c. but recently well restored, has an impressive interior, with a very long nave. Behind the church is a curious building known as 'La Diane', a large hall with a vaulted wooden ceiling of panels painted with armorial designs. There is a lapidary museum here, and in the Bd. de la Préfecture a good doll museum.

Nearby, two fortified churches are worth seeing: at **Champdieu** (4km N), where the machicolated towers and other defence features are both formidable and well preserved, and at **St-Romain-le-Puy** (6km SE), where the priory church is perched on a solitary volcanic hill.

Topham (*Edouard Berne*)

Château de Rochemaure, near Montélimar

MONTÉLIMAR, *Drôme* (6–D3). A fairly modern town famous for its nougat, with some good restaurants. Overlooked by the remains of the 12th-c. castle of Mont-Adhémar, with a fine view from the top. Between Montélimar and the Rhône (4km W) runs one of the bypass canals which form part of the great Rhône Valley scheme for creating hydro-electric power and at the same time controlling the river flow for easier navigation. Across the Rhône, 5km NW by D11, are the ruins of another hilltop feudal castle, the **Château de Rochemaure**, with the remains of a medieval walled village.

NANTUA, *Ain* (6–B4). Small town at the E end of one of the most beautiful lakes in the Jura region, with lovely views of forests and mountains. Before the railways it was an important stage-post for horsedrawn coaches *en route* between Bourg and Geneva; now it has regained popularity as a beauty spot and tourist centre. The 12th-c. church,

survivor from an 8th-c. Benedictine abbey, was sadly mutilated during the Revolution but is worth seeing for its Renaissance chapel. Lakeside and hillside walks, boat tours of the lake, water sports, fishing. Well known to gourmets for its *écrevisses* and *quenelles*.

NEVERS, *Nièvre* (2–E4, E5). Capital of the old dukedom of Nivernais, now of the Nièvre department, and renowned for the manufacture of fine china since the 16th-c., when one of the dukes introduced it from Italy. Nevers is built on high ground facing S across the Loire, which here makes a wide loop to the W before resuming its NW course towards Orléans. To the motorist arriving over the bridge from the S on N7 the town presents an impressive aspect, with the narrow towers of the Ducal Palace and the high square tower and flying buttresses of the Cathedral rising above a huddle of steep roofs.

The huge Cathedral is a mixture of all periods

from the 10th- to the 16th-c. and most unusual in having an apse and choir at each end of the 13th-c. nave, one Romanesque, the other Gothic. The nearby Ducal Palace, now the Palais de Justice, is an elegant Renaissance building in warm ochre stone; a slender central tower carries the main staircase and ends in a pointed roof topped by a delicate bell-tower; two other slim towers at the corners complete the façade.

A short distance W of the Cathedral is the one remaining gateway of the old ramparts, the Porte du Croux, a splendidly deterrent example of 14th-c. military architecture. N of this gateway the Rue Jeanne d'Arc runs alongside the park to the convent of St-Gildard, where after her visions at Lourdes the young Bernadette Soubirous spent the rest of her life as a nun; she was canonized in 1933 and her body is preserved against corruption in a glass casket in the chapel (open to the public every day in daylight hours). The Nevers Museum, a fine collection of faience and enamels, is at present housed in the Hôtel de Vertpré in the Rue St-Martin.

The most beautiful building in the town, though damaged in the Revolution, is the church of St-Étienne, in the eastern quarter. It is pure Romanesque, with an impressive interior of severe simplicity and perfect proportion.

PARAY-LE-MONIAL, *Saône-et-Loire* (6–A2, B2). A small town on the Canal du Centre, with a fine Renaissance Hôtel-de-Ville and a vast church of cathedral-like proportions, the Basilica of the Sacré-Cœur. It was initiated in 1109 by the Abbot of Cluny, and is in fact considered to be a smaller version of what Cluny was before its partial destruction after the Revolution (*see entry*). There are two immensely tall square towers at the W end, an even higher octagonal tower over the transept crossing (all the towers have spires). The nave soars 22m above its floor.

The Musée du Hiéron (shut in winter) has a good collection of religious sculpture, including a particularly fine 12th-c. tympanum that was removed from the doorway of the church at **Anzy-le-Duc** (20km S) to save it from harm at the time of the Revolution; that church is worth a visit, for despite the damage to the façade it remains one of the best Romanesque churches in the area.

PÉROUGES, *Ain* (10km S of Chalamont: 6–B3). Rare example of a fortified hilltop village that has been preserved almost exactly as it was in medieval times, complete with a double line of ramparts, cobbled streets, the two original gateways, and a spacious central square framed by beautiful old buildings. Often used as a setting for historical films.

ROMANS-SUR-ISÈRE, *Drôme* (6–C3). A busy industrial town rising up the N bank of the Isère and well known for shoes and other leather goods. The town museum is largely devoted to the history

of shoes from early Egyptian times to the present day. The old monastery church of St-Barnard contains, besides a number of interesting Romanesque features, a fine series of Flemish tapestries depicting scenes of the Passion.

ST-ÉTIENNE, *Loire* (6–C2, C3). Capital of the Loire department and a vast industrial city with little to recommend it from the tourist point of view. It has been described as *la ville où l'on fabrique de tout* – everything from armaments to ribbons. The main street runs in a straight line for some 5km from N to S, and the tourist would be well advised to use one of the bypasses.

SAULIEU, *Côte-d'Or* (3–E6). Small town at the eastern limit of the Morvan region of hills, forests, lakes and swift rivers. It makes furniture, and supplies Christmas trees to much of France. The bull in the Place de Gaulle is by a local-born 19th-c. animal sculptor; other works by him are in the town museum next to the church. St-Andoche has suffered from mutilation at various times, but it is worth visiting if only for the capitals carved with biblical scenes, superb examples of Romanesque sculpture.

SEMUR-EN-AUXOIS, *Côte-d'Or* (3–E6). A picturesque old town with ramparts and four solid round defence towers, built on a high spur of pink granite and almost encircled by a loop of the river

Sens: Hôtel de Ville

Peter Baker

Château de Tanlay

Armançon. The W end of the spur is now occupied by a hospital in a handsome 18th-c. mansion, but one can walk round the edge of the ramparts and look down at the river in its ravine far below. The 13th-c. church of Notre-Dame stands to the E, at the highest part of the town, with two square towers and a huge porch at the W end, an octagonal tower with a stone spire over the short transept, and an impressive chevet best seen from the garden at the SE corner. Inside, the nave is extraordinarily narrow and so seems even higher than it is; a row of side-chapels extends along the N side only; one of them contains a monumental Entombment in painted stone, and there is some good 13th-c. stained glass, especially in the centre chapel beyond the choir. In the area surrounding the church are several medieval and Renaissance town houses.

SENS, *Yonne* (3–D5). The old part of Sens lies within the oval of well-spaced boulevards which replaced the ancient ramparts. The centre of it is the Place de la République, with a triangular covered market at one end and the soaring Cathedral of St-Étienne at the other. This vast edifice, begun in about 1140, was the first of France's great cathedrals to be built according to true Gothic principles. It was also one of the most

important religious centres of its time; for nearly 500 years up to 1627 its archbishop had jurisdiction over all the sees of northern France, including even those of Paris, Chartres and Orléans.

Despite the unfinished N tower, the W façade is extraordinarily impressive with its huge window of radiating stone tracery over the centre doorway, its array of statuary, and the S tower and bell-tower reaching nearly 80m from the ground. Note also the N and S doorways of the transept, both executed in the Flamboyant style at the beginning of the 16th-c. In the interior the sense of space is overwhelming. The pillars, consisting of slender columns alternately grouped as clusters or in pairs, lift the eye to the ogive-vaulted roof. The high windows were made taller in the century after the original construction, and there is a rich variety of fine stained glass of all periods from the 13th-c. to the 17th-c. The Cathedral 'Treasure' (which can be seen at stated times on application to the sacristy to the right of the choir) is a superb collection of ecclesiastical vestments, tapestries, ivories and gold-work, probably one of the richest in France.

TANLAY, Château de, *Yonne* (9km E of Tonnerre: 3–D5). Handsome mid-16th-c. stately home, built in the true French (post-Italian) Renaissance manner of graceful elegance – with a solid bridge over a wide moat of running water, a monumental entrance porch, domed towers, imposing residential façade and wings looking on to a spacious *cour d'honneur*. The interior has fine sculptured chimney-pieces and is furnished in the style of the period. (Open most days Easter–October.)

TOURNON, *Ardèche* (6–C3). From the upper terrace of the castle (now the Palais de Justice and a Rhône museum) there is a dramatic view of the Rhône and the old town below, with the granite walls of the valley closing in, the Alps on the eastern horizon and, on the facing bank, the twin town of Tain-l'Hermitage, its famous Hermitage vineyards climbing steeply from the river to a height of some 300m. In Tournon itself, close to the river, stands the Lycée Gabriel Faure, a celebrated and influential 16th-c. college of learning founded by a cardinal of Tournon; the original gateway still stands, but most of the present buildings are 17th-c. Tournon is an important market for early vegetables and fruit.

TOURNUS, *Saône-et-Loire* (6–A3). For the motorist travelling on A6 or N6 between Chalon and Mâcon, this small town on the W bank of the Saône makes a convenient and interesting stopping-place. It is very old, with cobbled streets, medieval and Renaissance houses, antique shops, and several good restaurants, some of which are close to the town's outstanding feature – the abbey church of St-Philibert. This is one of the earliest and best-preserved Romanesque churches in France. Older than Cluny (*see entry*), it was begun at the very end of the 10th-c. and completed by the end of the 12th-c. The façade, with two plain square towers joined by a crenellated parapet, has a rather military appearance; within the porch is a large, sombre narthex, severely simple with four

massive pillars and a vaulted ceiling. But the nave, though equally devoid of ornamentation, is by contrast full of light, with plain round pillars of rose-pink stone rising to support rounded arches of alternate white and ochre stone. Beyond the choir, where light falls from plain windows on to white stone, are five radiating chapels; to the left of the choir a flight of steps descends to an unusually spacious crypt which follows the plan of the choir above.

On the S side of the church are the old abbey buildings, which are well worth visiting, including the refectory and cellars. Further S is the Musée Greuze, containing works by the 18th-c. painter, who was born only two streets away, and from the bridge there is an attractive view of the river and the old town, dominated by the great square belfry of St-Philibert.

VALENCE, *Drôme* (6–C3). A large, expanding and animated town on the E bank of the Rhône, with many hotels, excellent restaurants, and a long history going back to the Romans. There was a university here once, and Rabelais was one of its students. The 16-year-old Napoleon spent nearly a year here as a military cadet. Today Valence is a market-centre for fruit and vegetables, and is busy with a variety of light industries. The A7 autoroute runs past it along the river bank. The bridge across the Rhône replaces the one destroyed in World War II; it is an extension of the main tree-lined thoroughfare, the Ave. Gambetta, to the N of which stands the Cathedral of St-Apollinaire, a huge Romanesque edifice that was considerably rebuilt in the 17th-c. There are many interesting old houses. The former Bishop's Palace next to the Cathedral is now a museum. S of the Ave. Gambetta is a vast terrace, the Champ de Mars, with a garden park sloping down below it and a splendid view across the Rhône to **Mont Crussol**

Tournon

French Government Tourist Office

Vézelay

and its ruined cliff-edge castle, from which in the 16th-c. an infamous Huguenot baron terrorized Valence and the surrounding country.

VALLON-PONT-D'ARC, *Ardèche* (6–D2, D3). Starting-point for an exploration by road or water (punt and canoe trips are organized here) of the spectacular canyon-like **Gorges de l'Ardèche.** From the massive natural archway known as the Pont d'Arc the river Ardèche carves its way southeastward between enormous limestone cliffs partly covered in luxurious vegetation. A *route touristique* follows the river's twists and turns as best it can, providing dramatic viewpoints all the way to Pont-St-Esprit near the confluence of the Ardèche and the Rhône.

Vallon-Pont-d'Arc is a good centre for a variety of excursions in the Ardèche region, notably S to the famous **Aven d'Orgnac,** a series of vast caves (one is 250m long) containing a beautifully illuminated subterranean landscape of weird limestone concretions.

VÉZELAY, *Yonne* (3–E5). Travellers on the N6 south of Auxerre should try to find time for a diversion to this marvellous little town on a climbing ridge. Not only is it beautiful in itself, and fortunate in having a very good restaurant (and another at St-Père, 2km SE), but at the top of its

hill stands one of the great pilgrimage churches of northern France – the Basilica of Ste-Madeleine.

Benedictine monks built the original church in the 9th-c., but when the supposed relics of Mary Magdalene were brought here in the 11th-c. it proved too small for the vast crowds of pilgrims and was greatly enlarged. In 1120 a tragic fire swept through the crowded church on the eve of the annual July pilgrimage, killing a thousand pilgrims and destroying the nave. Rebuilding started at once and was completed by 1215. Further disaster, of a different kind, struck at the end of the century: the discovery of other, probably more genuine, relics of Mary Magdalene at Ste-Maximine in Provence (*see entry*). The flow of pilgrims dwindled. Later the church was severely damaged, first in the Wars of Religion, then during the Revolution, and was in fact on the point of collapse when in 1840 the architect Viollet-le-Duc undertook the task of restoring it to its original state.

The exterior façade, considerably restored but with its two towers still incomplete, leads into an unusually large narthex, with side-aisles covered by tribune galleries; it is nearly 20m long and precedes a remarkable interior façade which has escaped the restorer's hand and contains a Romanesque masterpiece, a tympanum of Christ sending the Apostles out into the world to preach the Gospel. Three doors lead into the nave, which astonishes by its length – 10 bays, with side-aisles, high cruciform pillars, marvellously carved capitals, round arches emphasized by the decorative effect of alternate bands of dark and light stone, ogive-vaulting between them – all leading towards the seemingly remote choir and radiating chapels with their Gothic pointed arches and windows.

Behind the basilica is a delightful terrace, shaded by large trees, overlooking a lovely panorama of valleys and hills.

VIENNE, *Isère* (6–B3). A Rhône town 27km S of Lyon, unusually well endowed with Gallo-Roman remains (the Temple of Augustus and Livia, a Roman arch, a Roman theatre even larger than the one at Orange and still used for festival drama) and churches, notably the 12th–15th-c. cathedral with its splendid façade of three portals rich in sculptures and its immensely long nave (nearly 100m), part Romanesque, part Gothic, containing some good stained glass and a wealth of interesting carvings. Two bridges cross the Rhône to the right bank (where Gallo-Roman villas have been excavated): the road bridge is a fine modern design with a central span of over 100m; the old suspension bridge just W of the Cathedral is now reserved for pedestrians only. Vienne also boasts one of the finest and most famous restaurants in the whole of France; it lies on the S side of the town, near the Roman 'Pyramide' after which it is named, and is of course expensive – but well worth it for the meal of a lifetime.

The French Alps: Introduction

Savoie, Dauphiné

Edward Young

This section covers the old province of Savoy (which finally became French as recently as 1860) and the mountainous eastern part of Dauphiné – that is to say the departments of Savoie, Haute-Savoie, Hautes-Alpes, and parts of Isère and Drôme. This is an area therefore of staggering mountain scenery, snow and ice, and winter-sports. Here, amid some of the most extensive and best organized skiing slopes in the world, are some of its finest winter resorts – Chamonix and Megève on the shoulder of Mont Blanc, Val-d'Isère and Tignes, and the new Trois Vallées complex around Courchevel on the Vanoise *massif*, and L'Alpe-d'Huez within easy reach of the technocrats and students of Grenoble. There are many others. But the tourist who comes here in spring, summer or autumn will discover a region of thick forests, rivers abounding in salmon and trout, roaring waterfalls, blue lakes reflecting their mountain surroundings, and remarkable old towns like Annecy, with its canal-side houses and its jewel of a lake, or Chambéry, the ancient capital of the Dukes of Savoy, or remote Briançon, highest town in Europe, or the lakeside watering-places of Aix and Évian.

One of the most dramatic road journeys in Europe must be the 'Route des Grandes Alpes', the mountain road (mostly N202) that runs south from the town of Évian-les-Bains, climbing up to Chamonix, then turning southwest through Megève to negotiate the foothills of the Mont Blanc range whence it follows the Gorges d'Arly to Moûtiers. After Moûtiers the route swings east again along the river Isère to Bourg-St-Maurice where it turns southeast, close to the Italian border, by way of Val-d'Isère and the Col de l'Iseran (blocked by snow, please note, from mid-October to mid-June); thence southwards to Briançon, and further onwards into Provence. This route is tortuous, often steep, and takes a good three days, but the reward is unforgettable views of the awesome majesty of the Alpine panorama. For less arduous motoring, an interesting drive through wild country is the 'Route Napoléon' (N85), which follows the surprise journey made by Napoleon in 1815 during the 'Hundred Days' between his escape from Elba and his defeat at Waterloo. It comes up from Cannes by way of Sisteron and passes through the old towns of Gap and Corps and on to Grenoble.

But wherever you drive in this region you can be sure of breathtaking scenery with thrilling glimpses at every turn of the road – perhaps the unexpected château on a rock pinnacle above a wooded valley, a plunging ravine with a torrent rushing along its stony bed, or cattle grazing on sloping pasture against a background of mountains covered with eternal snow.

Mont Blanc   *Rainbird (Gyger & Klopfenstein Adelboden)*

The French Alps: Gazetteer

Edward Young

AIX-LES-BAINS, *Savoie* (6–B4). One of the most famous and elegant watering-places in the world, beautifully situated on the lower slopes of Mont Revard overlooking the shores of Lake Bourget. Aix became fashionable in the 19th-c., when it was popular with wealthy Americans and the British aristocracy. It still has a Bd. Pierpont Morgan, a Bd. des Anglais, an Ave. Lord-Revelstoke – even a bust of Queen Victoria in the central Place de Revard to commemorate her stay in 1885. Aix is credited with having created the prototype of the 'casino' – which is still here, occupying the Palais de Savoie.

The waters of Aix, taken by sufferers from rheumatism and sciatica, have been well known since the days of the Romans. Evidence of Roman interest is to be seen in the remains of their sumptuous marble baths, still preserved in the S end of the present huge Thermal Establishment; also in the nearby arch of Campanus and, next to the Hôtel-de-Ville, the Temple of Diana, which now houses the archaeological museum. The Hôtel-de-Ville, facing the Thermal Establishment, is in a small restored 16th-c. château, worth visiting for its handsome Renaissance staircase. A short walk along the Rue Davat, past the church of Notre-Dame, leads to the Musée Faure, which has a very good collection of late 19th- and 20th-c. French paintings and sculpture (Corot, Degas, Cézanne, etc.) and some interesting watercolours by Rodin.

Although the baths are open all the year round,

Aix-les-Bains

Barnaby's Picture Library

Annecy

many of the hotels close for the winter. The 'season' at Aix is from April to October, when all sorts of festivals and galas are put on. It is above all a wonderful mountain tourist centre. Chambéry is only 14km S, and Annecy is easily accessible to the NE (*see entries*). There is plenty of sporting activity – swimming, sailing, water-skiing, golf, etc. – and there are boat trips to various beauty-spots around the lake, including an excursion to the Benedictine abbey of **Hautecombe**, whose church contains the tombs of the princes of Savoy and is renowned for its mass with Gregorian chant.

ALBERTVILLE, *Savoie* (7–B5). The main in-terest of this crossroads town lies on the opposite bank of the river Arly, in the neighbouring village of **Conflans**, a charming backwater left behind by the march of progress. From the tree-shaded terrace of 'La Grande Roche' there is a good view S across the confluence of the Isère and Arly rivers. The 'Maison Rouge' is a 14th-c. building that has been a monastery, a prison and now the village museum. The central square with its fountain, the Grande-Rue with its medieval workshops, the old gateways at each end of the village, the quiet church with fine wood-carving on pulpit and altar – all belong to another age.

ALLEVARD, *Isère* (23km SE of Chambéry: 6–B4). A spa whose waters are extremely sulphurous; they are used in inhalation for the alleviation of respiratory ailments. The small town, which has a casino conveniently close to the thermal baths, is at an altitude of 475m, surrounded by forest and mountain, and is well placed for excursions in superb Alpine scenery.

ALPE D'HUEZ, L', *Isère* (6–C4). One of the largest and most popular of the French winter-sport resorts. At an altitude of 1860m it is above the forest line, yet it seems to have more than its fair share of sunshine and its relatively easy slopes attract large numbers of skiers from Grenoble, only two hours away. Many hotels and chalets; plenty of ski lifts; heated open-air swimming pool; Olympic bob-sleigh run. A cable railway connects in two stages with the summit of Pic du Lac Blanc, which at 3327m ranks as one of the higher Alpine peaks and is a stupendous viewpoint; summer skiing is possible on the Sarennes glacier just below it.

ANNECY, *Haute-Savoie* (6–B4). A charming old town, with good hotels and restaurants, at the northern end of one of the most beautiful lakes in the French Alps. The old quarter close to the deep blue lake is full of narrow streets with arcades; quiet canals flow between tall houses with flowered balconies, and under little bridges where no traffic is allowed. On a small island in one of the canals is a so-called 'palace' with turrets, now sometimes used for exhibitions during the season, and to the S of that is a massive château, former residence of the Counts of Geneva and still impressive despite the many changes since it was first built in the 11th-c. Of the several churches the most interesting ·is the 15th-c. St-Maurice, containing old frescoes uncovered in recent restoration, one of them actually dated 1458. Between the town and the lake are gardens with delightful lakeside walks.

Whether you drive round the lake or take one of the steamer trips, you will be surrounded by majestic mountain scenery. The road down the E side, which takes you over the Col de la Forclaz at an altitude of over 1000m, is spectacular; even more so is the D41, due S out of Annecy, which takes you to the top of the Châtillon (1700m), though in places the descent requires strong nerves and good brakes.

On the E shore of the lake, 14½km from Annecy, lies the village of **Talloires**, surely one of the most exquisitely situated lakeside resorts in the whole of France; it is renowned for its first-class hotels and gastronomic restaurants 'avec belle vue sur le lac'.

BOURG-ST-MAURICE, Savoie (7–B5). Small town at an altitude of 840m in the upper Isère valley, on the way to Val d'Isère. It has become more lively since the development of Les Arcs, which lies above the town to the SE and is connected by cable railway; this has opened up a large skiing area on the slopes of a mountain ridge rising to over 2400m.

BRIANÇON, Hautes-Alpes (7–C5). A frontier town at an altitude of 1326m, Briançon claims to be the highest town in Europe. Ever since Vauban, Louis XIV's energetic military engineer, converted this steep rock site into a typical star-shaped citadel, it has guarded one of the most important passes from Italy into France. In 1815, after Waterloo, it successfully withstood a siege by an Austrian army twenty times superior in numbers. The old town is crowded within the imposing ramparts, a double line of irregular walls which cling to the jagged, precipitous rock and jut out at various angles to facilitate cross-fire against an invader. The visitor is advised to park his car at the bottom, outside the ancient gateway, the Porte Pignerol. From here the Grande Rue, with a stream bubbling down the middle of it, climbs steeply between tall houses with balconies and Alpine overhanging roofs. At the highest point of the town stands the old fort, where there is a statue of 'La France' by the celebrated early 20th-c. sculptor Bourdelle and an amazing panorama of mountain, river and forest. The Durance flows below, spanned in one dramatic leap by the Pont d'Asfeld, a fine bridge built 56m above the gorge

over 200 years ago; a footpath winds down to it from the top of the town.

CHAMBÉRY, Savoie (6–B4). The ancient capital of the Dukes of Savoy, who ruled from the huge château which dominates the town with its massive round tower and Italianate chapel. Savoy was an independent state for over 600 years and at one time extended from Lyon to Turin. In 1860, as the result of a plebiscite, it became part of France, with Chambéry as capital of the Savoie department. The great ducal château now serves as the offices of the Prefecture.

Chambéry, only 14km S of Aix-les-Bains, is an old town full of imposing town houses with courtyards, turrets and winding staircases, streets with arcades, and narrow alleys that invite one's curiosity. The principal street is the Rue de Boigne, named after a General who made a fortune in India and left a good deal of it to Chambéry, his native town; he is commemorated by the monumental fountain in the shape of four elephants which stands at the end of the street at its junction with the wide Bd. du Théâtre. The Cathedral began life as the chapel of a 13th-c. Franciscan monastery but was greatly enlarged in the 15th-c., with the addition of the present Gothic façade a century later. In the 15th-c. church of St-Pierre at the N edge of the town is a marvellous 9th-c. crypt and baptistry. The Musée des Beaux-Arts has a fine collection of Italian painting, including Uccello's marvellous 'Portrait of a Young Man'.

Chambéry produces, and gives its name to, one of the best of the French vermouths. It is pale in colour like a very dry sherry and should be taken chilled as an apéritif.

CHAMONIX-MONT-BLANC, Haute-Savoie (7–B5). France's most cosmopolitan all-the-year-round wintersport centre, Chamonix lies at an altitude of 1037m in the most majestic mountain valley in the whole of the Alps. It is equipped with over 20 hotels, several restaurants, a casino, three covered swimming pools, a large indoor skating rink, and facilities for tennis, hockey, curling, riding and even golf. A network of ski-lifts and cableways, giving access to over 100 marked-out ski runs, offers unparalleled opportunities for magnificent skiing.

From the railway station a rack-railway takes you on a 20-minute ride up to Montenvers, where there is a wonderful view across the Mer de Glace, one of the Mont Blanc glaciers. 8km up the valley from Chamonix, from the village of **Argentière**, a cableway rises to the peak of Les Grands Montets (3297m), with stupendous views and all-the-year-round skiing runs. Another cableway leaves from the W edge of Chamonix for the summit of Le Brévent (2526m), whence the view across the valley, taking in Mont Blanc and a whole range of lesser peaks, is a breathtaking panorama.

Most exciting of all is the cable car trip which

A.F. Kersting

Chamonix, with the upper slope of Mont Blanc to the left

starts from the S end of the town and goes via the intermediate station of Plan d'Aiguille to the cable station just below the summit of the **Aiguille du Midi**, a total lift of 2800m. Here, at an altitude of about 3800m, you are only about 1000m below the top of Mont Blanc and at the highest point accessible by cable car anywhere in Europe, surrounded by an awe-inspiring landscape of mountains and valleys, glistening ice and eternal snow. Skiing is possible throughout the year in the Vallée Blanche which lies just below. From the Aiguille du Midi you can continue by another cable railway via Pointe Helbronner into Italy, ending up at La Palud at the Italian end of the Mont Blanc road tunnel. The whole cable car trip from Chamonix to La Palud, which takes roughly two hours and requires warm clothing and sunglasses, is made possible by an amazing feat of engineering; in places the cable is 500m above the ground, and there is one cable span of 3km.

The Mont Blanc road tunnel, another remarkable engineering achievement, was completed in 1965 and (until the recent opening of the new Modane–Bardonècchia tunnel) was the longest road tunnel in the world – 11·6km from end to end. There is a toll station at each end; the customs post is at the Italian end. The French end of the tunnel is about 3km from Chamonix on N506.

CHÂTEL, *Haute-Savoie* (24km SE of Évian: 6, 7–A4, A5). Valley resort close to the Swiss border, S of Lake Léman. Altitude 1235m, surrounded by steep forests; quiet in summer but in winter invaded by skiers. Three cable cars, 16 ski-lifts. 12km W in **Abondance** are the remains of a huge medieval abbey and church, with a ruined cloister containing a remarkable series of primitive frescoes depicting scenes in the life of the Virgin.

CLUSAZ, La, *Haute-Savoie* (6–B4). Wintersports station facing the *massif* of the Aravis range, a mountain ridge exceeding 2000m along most of its length. Three cable cars and 26 ski-lifts give access to good skiing on the NW slopes. Many stimulating excursions.

CORPS, *Isère* (17km SE of La Mure: 6–C4). Small town at an altitude of 937m, with narrow cobbled streets. Welcome stopping-off point at the summit of the most tortuous section of N85, the Route Napoléon between Gap and Grenoble. Napoleon was glad to rest here for an hour or so during his brilliant trek from the Mediterranean at the start of his 'Hundred Days' in 1815. 5km W of the town, on D537, the celebrated **Pont du Sautet** leaps the Drac gorges with a single span of 86m; upstream is the hydro-electric Barrage du Sautet, damming a large lake.

NE from Corps the D212c climbs and twists up a deep valley for 15km to reach the celebrated pilgrimage basilica of **Notre-Dame-de-la-Salette** (altitude 1770m), remarkable for the solitary beauty of its site, 500m below the peak of Mount Gargas and with views in all directions of mountains, valleys and sloping pastureland.

COURCHEVEL, *Savoie* (6, 7–C4, C5). A huge complex of skiing stations at different levels, organized under the direction of a former world champion skier, Émile Allais. 'Courchevel 1850', with its skating rink, swimming pool and a liberal sprinkling of new hotels and restaurants (some of them very good), is the centre of an intricate network of cableways and ski-lifts which can transport 30,000 skiers an hour. Two cableways attain the summit of La Saulire (2630m), where there is a fantastic panorama of majestic peaks, including Mont Blanc 50km to the NE.

A short distance NW along D915 is the small town of **Moûtiers,** the ancient seat of a bishopric. It has a 15th-c. cathedral with a remarkable old carved episcopal throne and a crypt which may date from the 5th-c.

DIE, *Drôme* (6–C4). A small and very ancient town in the valley of the Drôme on the western edge of the Alps, at the S end of the long parallel mountain ridges that make up the Vercors range.

Still visible on the NE side of the town are some of the ramparts erected by the Romans in the 3rd-c. AD, and the town museum (open only in July and August) has a collection of Gallo-Roman objects found in local excavations. Another survivor from that age is the Roman triumphal arch in the SE walls known as the Porte St-Marcel. The Cathedral was almost entirely destroyed by Huguenots in the Wars of Religion; the only parts of the original that have survived in the rebuilt church are the Romanesque porch and the side walls. Edelweiss grows on the mountain slopes to the E, and around the town are the vineyards from which the local sweet sparkling *Clairette* wine is produced.

ÉVIAN-LES-BAINS, *Haute-Savoie* (6, 7–A4, A5). Well-known and fashionable watering-place on the S shore of Lake Léman, the largest lake in Europe, extending for 70km in the shape of a crescent from Geneva in the SW to Montreux in the E. Évian is roughly halfway between them, and directly opposite Lausanne, which is 12km across the lake in Switzerland. Behind, to the S, are the mountains. It is a peaceful resort, with gardens, hotels, villas, casinos and good restaurants, and is famous for its non-sparkling bottled mineral water, sold all over France and believed to be good for the kidneys and arthritis. 9km W along the lake shore is the smaller, more modest resort of **Thonon-les-Bains.**

GAP, *Hautes-Alpes* (6–D4). Although it is the capital of the Hautes-Alpes department, with winter skiing available at nearby Ceüse (1520m), from Gap southward the heights are merely foothills of the mighty Alps and there is a distinct feeling of Provence in the air. The small old centre of the town within the oval of boulevards contains nothing much of architectural interest; the Cathedral is late-19th-c. imitation Gothic, in local stone of various colours. In the Rue de France, near the police station, is the house in which Napoleon spent a night in March 1815 on his way N after escaping from Elba; after his cool reception when he landed on the Mediterranean coast, Gap was the first place on the Route Napoléon to give him a friendly welcome.

GRENOBLE, *Isère* (6–C4). One of the great university cities of Europe, an important wintersports and tourist centre, a metropolis humming with industrial energy and municipal enterprise. In the 19th-c. it was a pioneer in the taming of mountain torrents for hydro-electric power, and its industrial progress has continued ever since. Grenoble's advance since World War II has been spectacular; the population, now over 400,000, has multiplied five times in 35 years and is still

Grenoble   *J.P. Gianada*

growing. Among its new activities are electro-metallurgy, chemicals, heavy industry and, above all, nuclear research.

The first 'must' for any tourist new to Grenoble is to take a trip on the funicular, or *téléphérique*, which starts at the Quai Stephane Jay (where there is a car park) and rises N across the river to the old Fort de la Bastille on top of a high rock promontory. Here, at over 475m, are a café, a restaurant and a stunning view over the whole city spread out in a flat valley between two rivers and closely surrounded by mountains. Mont Blanc can be seen to the NE on a clear day. Directly below, the river Isère winds past the University domain on the E side of the city and sweeps along the quays of the old quarter, continuing W past the nuclear research centre, to be joined by the river Drac coming up from the S. Beyond the old quarter the new Grenoble spreads out in all directions, with broad avenues and skyscraper blocks proclaiming the city's dedication to modernity.

The 1964 Olympic skating championships and the Winter Olympics of 1968 stimulated a flurry of new building, such as the vast Stade de Glace, or ice stadium, and public buildings like the Palais des Expositions, the railway station, the post office and the airport. The Hôtel-de-Ville, in the Parc Paul-Mistral, is the most modern of its kind in France, with plate-glass walls, marble and mosaic patios, a fountain and specially commissioned sculptures.

This forward-looking modernity is fine for the cosmopolitan population of students, technocrats and engineers, but the tourist may prefer the old quarter towards the Isère, centred round the animated Place Grenette. Here the streets are narrower, more intimate, with many historic buildings: the fine Renaissance Palais de Justice, backing on to the river; the Cathedral of Notre-Dame, dating partly from the 10th-c. but much altered and restored since, with five naves and an impressive 15th-c. sculptured canopied shrine (*ciborium*); and the interesting 13th-c. brick church of St-André that was once the chapel of the ruling Dauphins (the Comtes de Dauphiné). Behind the church of St-André the former town hall, facing the municipal gardens, now contains a museum devoted to the writer Stendhal, who was born in Grenoble in 1783; and a short walk to the SE, in the Place de Verdun, is the splendid Museum of Painting and Sculpture, one of the finest collections of 20th-c. art outside Paris.

Old and new, with its long vistas, its many squares and open spaces, its first-class hotels and restaurants, Grenoble is an exciting city to visit. There is something stimulating in the comparative youthfulness of the bustling crowds, the clean mountain air, and the views of forest and mountain at the end of every perspective.

Facilities for skiing are close at hand, notably to the E at L'Alpe-d'Huez (*see entry*), **Les Deux Alpes** and **La Grave**, and to the SW in the neighbourhood of Villard-de-Lans (*see entry*).

MEGÈVE, *Haute-Savoie* (7–B5). Well-known summer and wintersports resort that was established immediately after World War I. Many hotels and restaurants; sports palace, skating rink (which becomes a heated swimming pool in summer), casino, gay and animated *après-ski*. Well served with cableways and ski-lifts. Important ski school. Wonderful Alpine scenery all around, especially from the cableway station at the summit of Mont Arbois (1825m), where there is a magnificent panorama of the whole of the Mont Blanc range to well beyond Chamonix.

MENUIRES-BELLEVILLES, Les, *Savoie* (12km S of Moûtiers: 7–B5). After 19km of twisting and turning, the N515 from Moûtiers reaches the village of St-Martin-de-Belleville, with its solitary domed pilgrimage chapel of Notre-Dame-de-la-Vie. A further 8km up the valley is the recently established skiing station of Les Menuires at 1700m, with cableways and ski-lifts opening up a vast skiing domain in the Vanoise *massif*. The *pistes* here are of widely varying degrees of difficulty, from gentle slopes to ski runs where only experts should venture. Higher still (9km by road) is the even newer, excitingly remote, station of **Val-Thorens**, whose ski-lifts climb to just below the summit of L'Aigle de Peclet (over 3500m). Here the air is cold and the valleys are glaciers.

MODANE, *Savoie* (7–C5). Mountain frontier town at just over 1000m, on the road to the Mont-Cenis pass into Italy. Industrial in a modest way, with only two hotels and little to attract the tourist, though there are ski-lifts up to the nearby skiing slopes at Charmaix and Arrondaz (2200m). Modane is now the N end of the new road tunnel to Bardonècchia which, 12½km long, beats the previous record of 11.6km held by the Mont Blanc tunnel (*see* Chamonix-Mont-Blanc). Before its completion the only way motorists could cross the frontier here in midwinter was by the rail ferry tunnel completed in 1871, the first tunnel ever to pierce the Alps; it was also the first to make use of the compressed-air system invented by the Savoyard engineer Sommeiller, trebling the speed of construction.

MORZINE, *Haute-Savoie* (7–B5). Easily accessible summer and winter resort at 960m, close to the Swiss border in a lovely setting of mountains and wooded valleys. Well equipped with hotels and opportunities for sporting activity: swimming, riding, tennis, etc. For a round trip in beautiful scenery take the D228 from Montriond, past the lake of Montriond and the 30m-high waterfall of Ardent to the lake and ski village of Avoriaz, where the ski-lifts go to the upper slopes of Les Hautforts (2460m); the homeward journey through Super-Morzine (where there is a glimpse of Mont Blanc) ends in a steep drop through a dramatic series of hairpin zigzags. In winter Morzine is one of the busiest of the wintersports centres, with 40 cableways and ski-lifts giving access to a vast area of marvellous skiing.

PRALOGNAN, *Savoie* (7–C5). The D915, which leaves the N90 at Moûtiers and climbs 24km up the twisting, beautiful valley of the Doron, reaches Pralognan and goes no further. Here at 1400m is a quiet mountain village on the W edge of the Vanoise *massif*. Surrounded by steep forests and the perpetual sound of waterfalls, it is renowned as a centre for superb walks in the Parc National de la Vanoise among glaciers and mountain peaks rising to 3500m and more. A cableway from the village to the Mont Bochor plateau gives access to a large skiing area.

ST-GERVAIS-LES-BAINS, *Haute-Savoie* (6, 7–B4, B5). Popular health resort well known for its sulphur springs, its healthy climate and its wintersport facilities. Cableways and ski-lifts connect with all the skiing grounds of neighbouring Chamonix and Megève. In the town itself, where a rivulet meanders through a wooded park, are facilities for skating and swimming, an interesting modern church (Notre-Dame-des-Alpes), and the sulphur baths for those suffering from skin and respiratory troubles. There are endless excursions in the marvellous Alpine scenery all around. In summer the 'Tramway du Mont Blanc' climbs to the 'Eagle's Nest' at 2386m, where there is a close and awe-inspiring view of the Brionnassay glacier on the shoulder of Mont Blanc, here only 6km away.

ST-VÉRAN, *Hautes-Alpes* (7–C5). To find this isolated mountain village, which at an altitude of 2040m is believed to be the highest *commune* in Europe, you need to start from Briançon or Guillestre with a detailed road map. From either direction you have to pass through **Château-Queyras** with its 13th-c. fortress (repaired by Vauban in the 17th-c.). About 14km S, and 650m higher, you come at last to St-Véran, with its little church and its clusters of wooden chalets facing the sun. The village climbs the side of a hill overlooking the steep valley of the Aigue Blanche amid daunting walls of mountains. From St-Véran a track leads further uphill for 6km, passing a disused marble quarry, to reach the solitary chapel of Notre-Dame-de-Clausis (2390m), which attracts pilgrims from both France and Italy every 16 July.

VAL-D'ISÈRE, *Savoie* (7–B5, C5). Together with the neighbouring resort of **Tignes**, this is one of the most celebrated of the French high-altitude Alpine skiing centres, close to the Italian border and with snow until the end of May. Some 40 hotels; animated night-life; over 50 cable lifts to skiing grounds covering a vast area on the higher slopes of the Vanoise *massif*. It is also a popular resort in summer, with access to wonderful scenic excursions by car or on foot in the Parc National de la

Vanoise and to the Col de l'Iseran above Val at 2770m (blocked by snow from October to June). Immediately W of Val, reached by cableway, is the prominent Rocher de Bellevarde (2825m) with breathtaking panoramic views, including Mont Blanc 45km to the N.

VILLARD-DE-LANS, *Isère* (6–C4). Popular winter and summer resort at 1025m, only 33km from Grenoble and especially well equipped for families with children. Numerous mechanical lifts take skiers up to 'La Cote 2000' and other ski areas on the higher slopes of the long N–S mountain ridge known as 'La Montagne de Lans', some of whose peaks exceed 2000m. This is the highest and most easterly of the ridges making up the wild **Vercors** region which was such a stronghold of the French Resistance in World War II; at the N end, at St-Nizier on the SW outskirts of Grenoble, is a memorial cemetery for nearly 100 *maquisards* who lost their lives fighting the Germans. During the summer Villard is a well-known tourist centre for superb excursions in extraordinarily varied scenery; drive westward, for example, through the Gorges de la Bourne to Pont-en-Royans, returning by the dramatic gully called 'Les Grands Goulets'.

VIZILLE, *Isère* (6–C4). Small industrial town 17km S of Grenoble, of no interest to the tourist except for the historical significance of its Renaissance château set in the middle of a park. It was here, in June 1788, that nobles, clergy and commoners sat round a table together, for the first time in French history, and agreed to unite in opposition to the suppression of parliament by the King, Louis XVI; they proclaimed the individual liberty of every Frenchman, and the call was echoed throughout the length and breadth of the country. It was the spark that lit the fuse which exploded in the Revolution a year later. (Château and park are open to the public on most days all the year round, except Tuesdays.)

VOIRON, *Isère* (6–C4). A small town 30km NW of Grenoble, at the western edge of the mountainous **Chartreuse** region which extends N from Grenoble almost as far as Chambéry. Voiron makes paper, linen and skis. It is also the only place where the Carthusian monks still make the famous green Chartreuse liqueur whose secret they have kept for over 300 years. In the Bd. Edgar-Kofler you can visit the *caves* (weekdays only) and watch it being made, but though you may taste it – and buy a bottle of it – you will not learn the secret. It used to be made in the celebrated monastery of La Grande Chartreuse up in the mountains not far from St-Pierre-de-Chartreuse (26 tortuous km N of Grenoble), but though the monks, whose order was founded in the 11th-c., were allowed to return there in 1929 after being expelled by the State in 1901, they allow no visitors to the monastery.

Languedoc-Roussillon: Introduction

George Savage

The area now known as Languedoc-Roussillon comprises the departments of Lozère, Gard, Hérault, Aude, and Pyrénées-Orientales. This is not the historic Languedoc, which disappeared as a political entity during the Revolution. Its eastern boundary has always been the river Rhône, but the northern boundary was once drawn only a few kilometres south of Clermont-Ferrand, and its western boundary took in Toulouse (the Roman town of Tolosa). It enclosed a good deal of the Massif Central and all of the Cévennes within its borders. For many centuries it was virtually cut off from northern France by the Massif Central, and the flourishing civilization which grew up was far in advance of the barbarian north, at least until the time of the Albigensian Crusade. The name, Languedoc, refers to the Provençale language spoken in the region – the language of the Troubadours in which *oc* meant *yes* instead of *oui*. At one time this language was used as far north as the Loire, but it had almost disappeared by the nineteenth century, when, in 1876, it was revived as a literary language by the poet Frédéric Mistral and others.

From the twelfth century, when Henry II of England married Eleanor of Aquitaine, the Languedoc was nominally an English province, and it so remained until 1452. The coastal plains are commonly referred to as the Midi. This is not an exact geographical location, and in ordinary parlance it means the flat lands bordering the Mediterranean from Marseille (the ancient Massilia) to Narbonne (the Roman Narbo) and beyond, bordered in the north and west by the foothills of the Cévennes and the Corbières mountains.

The coastal plains were first settled by the Phocaeans from Greece about 600 BC, who introduced the culture of the vine and the olive. According to the Roman historian, Justinus, the indigenous inhabitants learned to till their fields and wall their towns, and became accustomed to living by law instead of force of arms. 'Their progress,' he wrote, 'in manners and wealth was so brilliant that it seemed as though Gaul had become part of Greece, rather than that Greece had colonized Gaul.' The road from Italy to Spain was traversed by Hercules on his way to seek the Golden Apples of the Hesperides, and in 218 BC Hannibal the Carthaginian general, with an immense army and fifty war elephants, marched through the Midi on his way to defeat the Romans at Lake Trasimene. Some of his men, attracted by the fruitfulness of the country, deserted and planted vineyards in the hills of the Corbières, a region noted for its vineyards to this day. Julius Caesar invaded the Languedoc, and began the history of his campaign with the immortal words, 'All Gaul is divided into three parts.' The Languedoc was then Gallia Narbonnensis, the land inhabited by the Aquitanians who lived south of the river Garonne. The Celts settled the country between the Garonne and the Seine, and the country north of the Seine was inhabited by the Belgae.

Gallia Narbonnensis was densely populated with flourishing towns. The city of Narbo was the birthplace of two third-century Roman emperors, Numerianus and his brother, Carinus. Christianity was brought to the province by St Trophismus of Arles, St Saturnin (Sernin), and St Paul-Serge, of Béziers, but the Languedociens were heretics almost from the first, showing, in early times, a strong tendency towards Arianism. Later this was replaced by Catharism (the Albigensian heresy), and finally by Protestantism, the mountains forming a Huguenot stronghold.

When the Roman Empire began to break up, the Visigoths had already established themselves. They founded the kingdom of Toulouse in AD 412. Angered by the heartless exactions of the Roman treasury, they revolted, took Rome in 410, and pillaged the city in such a curiously respectful way that their alliance with Rome continued unbroken, and they fought beside the Legions to defeat Attila at Châlons in 451. By 478 the Visigoths had conquered Spain, and they held the Midi as far as the Rhône.

Early in the eighth century Saracens invaded Spain from North Africa, and in 718 they poured over the border and penetrated as far as the river Loire. They were decisively defeated at Poitiers and Tours by Charles Martel in 732, and five years later he drove them out of Burgundy and the Languedoc. But their influence still lingers in the Midi. After their defeat individual Saracens remained behind, and in times of peace intercourse between Moorish Spain and the Languedoc continued. At this time the Saracens were, for the most part, a highly civilized people, who had inherited the Greek love of learning and philosophy, and much of the brilliant civilization observable on the French side of the Franco-Spanish border from the eleventh century to the thirteenth was to some extent the product of their influence. During this period the Troubadours sang of love, war, the joys of the wandering life, and the heroic deeds of the great lords who protected them. They disappeared in the thirteenth century with the start of the Albigensian Crusade.

At the end of the eleventh century about 100,000 Languedociens had joined the First Crusade led by Raymond IV, Comte de Toulouse, but their piety did not save them from envious eyes cast on their wealth by less prosperous factions in the north. Their religious loyalty to Rome, and their allegiance to the French crown, were both questionable. Their religion at this time had much in common with the beliefs of the Cathars of Eastern Europe. The centre of the heresy was Albi, and its adherents became known as Albigensians. In the early years of the thirteenth century bishops, prelates, and papal legates joined with acquisitive barons in putting themselves at the head of an army which invaded the south in what has become known as the Albigensian Crusade. The army was commanded by Simon IV de Montfort, father of the English Earl of Leicester, and a campaign of bloody carnage followed, in which the inhabitants of the south were slaughtered and plundered without mercy. Finally Louis VIII led a vast army into the south, and placed seneschals in Beaucaire, Carcassonne, and Béziers, forcibly uniting northern and southern France. To add to the troubles of the Languedociens the country was devastated by the Black Death in 1348. The English Black Prince raided as far south as Narbonne in 1355 but found the region too ravaged to enable him to maintain himself.

Religious disputes broke out again in the reign of Louis XIII. After the sieges of Montauban and La Rochelle, however, Richelieu became conciliatory, and tried to absorb the Huguenots into the administration, encouraging them to devote themselves to trade. Colbert, the astute Finance Minister of Louis XIV, established new industries in the south subsidized by the State. Factories for making cloth were established at Saptes, near Carcassonne, at Villeneuvette and at Clermont l'Hérault. Serge was woven at Montpellier, and a better quality woollen cloth at Castres, Bédarieux, Clermont, and Lodève.

By 1650 over-production of wine started to create problems, and some vineyards went out of cultivation. The situation was saved by the introduction of *eau de vie*, distilled from the *marc de raisin*. This was made in large quantities at Lunel and Béziers. Marc comes from the grapeskins left over after pressing and this potent spirit, still obtainable, was introduced in the 1650s. Large quantities were soon on their way to the peasants of northern France, where they gave rise to difficulties similar to those which attended the introduction of gin into England in the eighteenth century.

Under Colbert many new roads were constructed, both for strategic purposes and to help the trade of the region. These were so well engineered that they astonished Arthur Young when he travelled in the Languedoc in 1789. Coming from England, he confessed he had never seen anything like them. The Canal du Midi (formerly the Canal des Deux-Mers) is some 200 kilometres long, and joins the Mediterranean to the Garonne, and so to the Atlantic. It was completed in 1680. It leaves the river Garonne at Toulouse and joins the Étang de Thau at Agde.

Another religious revolt followed the Revocation of the Edict of Nantes in 1685. This withdrawal of the right to religious liberty granted to the Huguenots almost a century before was followed by the emigration of nearly half a million people, most of them skilled craftsmen and business men. They went to Protestant countries like Britain and the German states. In 1702 the Huguenots of the south, known as the Camisards, took to the mountains, led by Jean Cavalier. Many villages were burned, and the life of the province was severely damaged by the repressive measures which followed.

When the region had recovered from the effects of the revolt the population rapidly increased, new food crops were introduced and the silk industry flourished, particularly at Nîmes and Le Vigan. The novel ideas of Diderot, D'Alembert, Voltaire, Rousseau, Buffon, Montesquieu, and others, circulated widely, and the Languedociens were loud in their clamours for liberty and equality. When English troops entered the Languedoc from Spain in 1814 and marched on Toulouse they were hailed as liberators, and Marshal Soult did not seriously contest the invasion.

The Industrial Revolution reached the Languedoc early in the nineteenth century. The railway from Tarascon to Bordeaux was started in 1839 and completed in 1857. A line from Paris to Toulouse was opened in 1864, which allowed produce to be sent speedily to the northern market. The acreage devoted to the vine had been greatly extended, but disaster struck with the arrival of the phylloxera aphid from America, and the destruction of the vines. The vineyards were re-established with the aid of American phylloxera-resistant root-stock, and by 1906 over-production was again a problem, although the vast consumption of wine during World War I eased the difficulty for the duration of hostilities. By 1930 this familiar

Carcassonne

problem had returned, and today the Languedoc makes a substantial contribution to the 'wine lake'.

After 1940, refugees poured into the region. The Vichy government was opposed by General de Lattre de Tassigny, who commanded a division based on Montpellier. The Germans partially occupied the area in 1942 but found the terrain formidable. The young people took to the mountains, as had the Camisards before them, and organized armed resistance, calling themselves *Maquis*, which is the word used as an alternative to *garrigue* to describe the scrub-bushes covering the stony sides of the southern slopes of the Cévennes. The Cirque de Navacelles became one of their strongholds.

In recent years the French government has supervised the development of the coastline with the object of avoiding the kind of squalor which has devastated the Spanish coast. They began by exterminating the mosquito. For those whose taste is architecture in the modern idiom they have done an excellent job, and the old towns still remain, none of them seriously damaged by modern development.

The Languedoc has been called a land of ruins. These romantic symbols of melancholy and grandeur testify to a long and chequered history. Nîmes boasts what is probably the finest surviving Roman temple, the Maison Carrée of the first century AD. The amphitheatre in the same city is still in regular use.

The landscapes of the region are on the grand scale in the Cévennes, the Massif Central, and the Massif d'Aigoual. A massif is a mountainous mass which breaks out into peaks (*pics*) near the summit. The glaciers of the Ice Ages came down almost to the Mediterranean, and they carved out and deepened valleys and *cirques*. A *cirque* is a valley (or valleys) of glacial origin which ends in a deep rounded hollow. The Cirque de Navacelles is a text-book example.

Between the plateaux of the Massif Central are valleys. The roads wind down the sides, usually in a series of *lacets* (hair-pin bends) which can be difficult on minor roads, sometimes to a point where they are termed *routes acrobatiques*. Most of the plateaux (*causses*) are extremely arid, principally due to the porous nature of the underlying rock, which absorbs water rapidly. Sheep and goats are grazed on them, and livestock is watered by constructing dewponds (*lavognes*). A paved example is to be found at La Couvertoirade. Valleys are fertile, and have been planted with vines and fruit trees. In many places the lower slopes of the mountains are terraced to increase the land available for cultivation, and the terraces have usually been planted with vines, although some of them have been abandoned in recent years. The Languedoc has many caves (*grottes* or *baumes*), and some have been equipped with electric lighting, paths, steps, handrails, and, in one case, a funicular, for the convenience of the tourist. Most are noted for splendid formations of stalactites and stalagmites, and some have underground rivers (as at Bramabiau), streams and pools, or waterfalls and cascades, the more spectacular of which are floodlit. An *aven* is a pot-hole, the best known of which is the Aven Armand. Some surface rock-formations have a curious resemblance to ruined buildings – for instance, at Montpellier-le-Vieux and the Cirque de Mourèze.

Rock is generally igneous granite, metamorphic rock (i.e. igneous or sedimentary rock changed in character by the action of heat, pressure, or water), and such products of volcanic activity as lava. Mineral springs are not uncommon in the region. The popular bottled Perrier comes from Vergèze in Gard; Vernières, similar in its properties and flavour, from Lamalou-les-Bains. Both are naturally aerated. At La Puech (a village just south of Lodève) a sulphurous hot spring (geyser) bursts intermittently from the ground. This is a relatively recent appearance.

The weather in the plains is dry and hot in summer, and the *causses* are bleak in winter. Flocks are driven into the uplands in spring and brought back to the plains in the autumn, a movement known as transhumance. Since the nineteenth century a process of reafforestation has been going on in and around the Massif d'Aigoual. This area had once been denuded of trees and shrubs by grazing sheep and goats, and the felling of trees by the charcoal-burners, but much of the area is now well wooded. In the plains, and at the lower levels, chestnuts, planes, and mulberries grow to large size. The planes are for shade, the chestnuts both for shade and fruit, and the mulberries to feed the silkworms which have sustained the silk industry since the thirteenth century.

As one descends from the *causses* to the coastal plains the climate rapidly changes to Mediterranean. New and more varied plants appear, and the wind blows warm. In the plains fruit and flowers are produced in abundance.

Thunderstorms are not infrequent in the summer. They usually occur at night, and last for several hours in the mountains. Rainfall is often heavy, but it does not last very long, and surface-water drains rapidly. Valleys can be very cold in winter when the wind blows directly off the *causses* and is funnelled down them. Snow often stays on the higher peaks of the Massif, and in the Pyrenees, until late May. In the plains snow comes once in a generation.

Roads of the N classification are well-engineered, but sometimes demand considerable care in the mountains. Gradients are often deceptively steep. D-roads are frequently narrow, with steep bends (*virages*) and *lacets*. The term *lacet*, which means a shoe-lace, was obviously suggested originally by the resemblance of some mountain roads seen from above to a lace carelessly flung down. *Lacet vertigineux*, a sign not often seen even on D-roads, usually refers to a *lacet* which is so steep that it requires at least one reversal of direction to get round it. One side is precipitous, and often there is no retaining wall. A road of this kind, numbered D43, runs from La Malène in the Gorges du Tarn to the Causse Méjean, but usually they are either VO roads or unclassified.

The insects of the Languedoc are more interesting than dangerous, and butterflies and moths are numerous and colourful. The praying mantis is spectacular in its poses. The small black scorpion is comparatively rare, and never seen north of the road from Montpellier to Lodève. Their sting is painful, but not usually dangerous, although medical attention may be helpful. The safest scorpion is a dead one. Lizards are fairly common, colourful, and completely harmless. They are also nervous, and infrequently seen. Adders are sometimes seen on stony ground, but are not dangerous unless stepped on or picked up. Usually they move away quickly if they hear anyone coming. They can occasionally be found asleep on a mountain path, and children should be warned not to meddle with them. If bitten medical attention is essential. The wild boar (*sanglier*) is found in some of the remoter forests of the mountains, but they are too shy to be dangerous. Poachers sometimes shoot them, and the *sanglier* occasionally appears in some restaurants, but not on the menu. *Pâté de sanglier* is recommended. Bears live in the high Pyrenees, and come down to the lower slopes during the winter. They are dangerous, and should not be approached. These two animals, and others, are rigorously protected, and a list of protected animals is usually posted outside the *mairie*. Eagles can sometimes be seen when driving through the mountains, flying above valleys, more or less at the same height as the road. They, too, are protected.

Sheep are principally kept for milk, with which Roquefort cheese is made. Shepherds do not drive their flocks. They, and their dogs, walk on ahead; the sheep follow, usually led by a bell-wether or a goat. Goats are numerous, and kept for milk, cheese, and meat. Oxen and bulls are often used to pull carts and ploughs in the mountains, and since bulls are usually run with the cows they are rarely bad-tempered, although it is wise not to presume too far on their good nature. Hunting-dogs are well-fed and ill-disciplined, but they are friendly animals. Some hunting parties met in the mountains are also friendly, but sometimes dangerous. Guns are frequently carried loaded and unbroken at reckless angles, and newspapers list the dead and injured at the end of each hunting season. The writer has never heard of a case of a rabid animal in the south, and even in the north, where the disease is known to exist, the chance of contracting it, to judge by statistics, is so remote as to be negligible.

The Languedociens are accustomed to meeting foreigners. The local *patois* is a mixture of French, Provençal, and Spanish, and it is not, at first, always very comprehensible. Nearly everyone understands standard French, provided the accent is passable, but in cases of difficulty it is possible to conduct business in writing. Generally, all that is needed is a little patience and goodwill. As a people they are very patient, courteous, and hospitable.

Languedoc-Roussillon: Gazetteer

George Savage

AGDE, *Hérault* (5–E7). This fishing-port is situated about 1km from the mouth of the river Hérault and 22km from Béziers. Its former name was Agathée, and it was founded by Phocaean or Massilian seamen about 500 BC. It was repeatedly sacked by Vandals, Visigoths, Saracens, Franks, and Barbary Corsairs, as well as by the armies of the *Croisades Albigeois.* The Cathedral of St-Étienne looks like a fortress, with walls 3m thick and castellated battlements. It is built of tuff-ash from the ridge of the Cap d'Agde, which is an extinct volcano, and the same material may be seen elsewhere in the town in the construction of houses. The musée Agathois (Rue de la Fraternité) is devoted to folklore. It is open every day.

The Hérault, apart from providing mooring for boats of all kinds, is a venue for the popular French sport of fishing, and anglers line the banks. The Canal du Midi enters the Hérault at Agde, and its prolongation to the Bassin du Thau becomes the Canal de Sète. On either side of the mouth of the Hérault, where it meets the sea, are Le Grau d'Agde and La Tamarissière respectively. In the vicinity of the latter there are

The Cathedral, Agde

tamarisks on dunes of fine sand. For the Cap d'Agde new development *see* Sète.

AIGOUAL, Mont, *Gard* (5–D7). This is the summit of the Massif d'Aigoual, and the second highest point in the Cévennes. It is a little short of 1600m. Mainly of granite and schist, the mountain may be ascended for a considerable distance by car, taking either D986 from Meyrueis by way of the Col de Montjardin and the Col de la Séreyrède, or from Le Vigan on D48 by way of the Col du Minier. On a clear day it is possible to see the Mediterranean from D48. Between November and May the possibility of the road becoming obstructed or impassable because of snow must always be considered. Mont Aigoual is a weather-breeder, trapping clouds from the Atlantic which precipitate their moisture on the plains beyond. Since 1887 there has been a meteorological station at the summit, which can be reached from the Col de la Séreyrède (signposted).

Coming from Meyrueis, on the right of D986 about 5km beyond the Col de Montjardin, there is a small building with a sign **Bramabiau.** This is the starting place for a tour of the remarkable cave of this name (open from June to September), which is noted for a subterranean river. During World War II this region was an important centre of the Resistance in the south.

AIGUES-MORTES, *Gard* (5–D8). The Roman Aquae Mortuae, meaning 'dead waters', which refers to the almost unruffled appearance of the lagoons and marsh pools in the vicinity. The mosquito, once prevalent, has now been eliminated as part of the coastal development. Aigues-Mortes, on the western border of the Camargue, is connected by navigable canals with the sea, and with the Rhône at Beaucaire. There are large salt-pans nearby operated by the Salins du Midi, and the vine is cultivated locally.

The town was once a seaport from which Louis IX (St Louis) set out on his Crusades in 1248 and 1270, but it later silted up. Louis began to fortify the town in 1241, building the massive Tour de Constance, 33m in height with walls 7m thick, in 1248. The ramparts were largely the work of Philip the Bold and Philip the Fair between 1272 and 1300 (*see* Carcassonne). The circuit is about 1750m, the height varies from 9m to 11m, and

Anne Bolt

The Tour de Constance, Aigues-Mortes

there are 15 semi-circular towers and 10 gates. The moat has been largely filled in. There is a car park outside the walls near the Tour de Constance, from the top of which there is a fine panoramic view. In the square is a statue of St-Louis by Jacques Pradier. Informal bull-fights (French style) and cow-races with the noted Camargue cattle are sometimes held outside the walls.

ALÈS, *Gard* (5–D7). Formerly Alais, this town of 40,000 inhabitants is mainly devoted to the manufacture of industrial chemicals. It is situated on the left bank of the river Gardon near a coalfield. It is also a centre for the silk trade, and it was here that Louis Pasteur took his first steps on the road to fame by his work on diseases of the silkworm. There is a bronze monument to him by Noël near the citadel. The Silk Cooperative has a breeding-station here. There is a cathedral, largely 18th-c., a citadel (Fort Vauban) and the Bosquet gardens surrounding it which were laid out in the 18th-c.

AMÉLIE-LES-BAINS-PALALDA, *Pyrénées-Orientales* (6km W of Céret: 5–E6). A spa on the rivers Tech and Mondony, the sulphur springs of which have been known since Roman times. It was formerly Arles-les-Bains, but received its present name in honour of the consort of Louis-Philippe in 1840. The general climate is very favourable. The Gorges du Mondony, and the Fort built in 1670, are both within comfortable walking distance. The Thermes Romaines still retain some parts of the ancient Roman building. The village of Palalda on the left bank of the Tech is the Roman Palatinum Dani. The Mardi Gras Carnival with traditional masquerade takes place in February, and there is an international festival of folk dancing in August.

ANDUZE, *Gard* (5–D7). A small town of 4000 inhabitants situated in a fertile valley, near a gap in the mountain chain known as the Gate of the Cévennes, and in the vicinity of the convergent valleys of the Gardon rivers. It was a Protestant town from the second half of the 16th-c., and it supported the Camisards during their 18th-c. revolt. There is a clock-tower dating from the 13th-c., and some old and narrow streets. Anduze is a pottery-making centre for those interested in the craft. The former park of the Convent of the Cordeliers has some fine trees, notably giant bamboos, and exotic plants of all kinds. Rare Asiatic and American trees, shrubs, and plants, and giant bamboos belonging to 30 different varieties, may be found in the park of Prafrance, about 2km N of Anduze on D129. This park has been used in a number of French films.

ARGELÈS-SUR-MER, *Pyrénées-Orientales* (4km NW of Collioure: 5–E6, E7). A small town with a church in the southern French Gothic style dating from the 14th-c. It was once on the sea, but the Mediterranean is now 2½km away, at Argelès-plage, where there are enormous beaches, forests of pines and cork-oaks, and a fine view of the Albères mountains.

BAGNOLS-LES-BAINS, *Lozère* (13km E of Mende: 5–C7). A small spa of Roman origin. Its season starts on 1 June and ends on 30 September. Built on the lower slopes of a mountain at an altitude of about 900m, it is located on the left bank of the river Lot, which here broadens out. The six hot mineral springs are reputed to be effective in cases of cardiac affection with rheumatic origins, and the equable and salubrious climate makes it very suitable for those suffering from stress and overwork.

BAGNOLS-SUR-CÈZE, *Gard* (5–D8). A town of 16,000 inhabitants which acts as a dormitory for the important Atomic Energy Station at Marcoule, about 8km to the SE on N580. Taking this road, after 5km on the left a smaller road leads through the village of Chusclan and terminates at a viewing point with a splendid panorama of the Rhône and the surrounding country which is well worth visiting. In the Hôtel-de-Ville in Bagnols is a museum (open every day) which contains an interesting collection of Impressionist and Post-Impressionist painting (Monet, Bonnard, Matisse, etc.).

BANYULS-SUR-MER, *Pyrénées-Orientales* (5–E7). A small fishing-port of about 5000 inhabitants, which has a sand and shingle beach with yachting and bathing facilities, a laboratory for the study of marine biology, and an aquarium. Banyuls is noted for its wines, which are naturally slightly sweet (*vins doux naturels*), and there is a Wine Festival in August. The town is also notable as the home of the sculptor Aristide Maillol

(1861–1944), whose 'Three Nymphs' is in London's Tate Gallery. A fine panoramic view may be had from the Cap l'Abeille, 2km E.

BEAUCAIRE, *Gard* (1km W of Tarascon: 5–D8). Twin town to Tarascon on the other side of the Rhône. The two are connected by a bridge about 600m in length. Beaucaire is the Rhône terminal of a canal which goes to Sète by way of Aigues-Mortes. The Foire de Beaucaire, a vast trade fair, was founded in 1217, and at its most prosperous is reputed to have drawn a quarter of a million people annually from all parts of the Mediterranean. The Fair was still important when Arthur Young visited the town in 1789. A smaller version is held annually. The castle on the highest point N, belonging to the Ducs de Montmorency, was built in the 13th-c. and partially dismantled by Cardinal Richelieu in 1632. From the top of the tower there is a good panoramic view of Tarascon and the Rhône. The fine Romanesque Chapelle St-Louis is also worth a visit. The Hôtel-de-Ville, built 1679–83, was designed by Louis XIV's architect, Jules Hardouin-Mansart. The church of Notre-Dame-des-Pommiers belongs to the 18th-c., and the Musée du Vieux Beaucaire (27 Rue Barbès, with limited opening times) contains costumes, Provençal furniture, and material relating to the Fair. Roman antiquities are in the Musée Lapidaire (Rue de Nîmes).

BÉDARIEUX, *Hérault* (5–D6, D7). A small manufacturing town situated on the river Orb. Cloth-weaving was established here by Colbert in the 17th-c. It is a road and rail junction, and in the town centre a road (D35) leads N first to St-Martin-le-Bousquet in the valley of the Orb, and then on D8 to Avène. About 1km SE of Avène, at Bains d'Avène, is a restaurant noted for its specialities. To the N a large lake has been formed by a barrage which supplies water to a hydro-electric station. A dirt-track alongside gives access to the lake, a favourite spot for picnics in the summer.

BÉZIERS, *Hérault* (5–E6, E7). Béziers, the Roman town of Baeterrae Septimanorum and station of the Seventh Legion, is a town of 80,000 inhabitants, situated on a hill which slopes down steeply to the river Orb (the Roman Orobis). A fine view of the river and the surrounding countryside can be obtained from the terrace of the former Cathedral of St-Nazaire. The edifice itself is Gothic in style, the earlier cathedral having been burned in 1209 by Simon de Montfort, when 30,000 of the inhabitants were massacred and the town plundered by his crusading barbarians during the Albigensian wars. There is a fine rose-window in the W façade and some good early ironwork.

The boulevards mark the old walls, and a walk

Béziers

J. Allan Cash

across the old town from the Cathedral by way of the Rue Viennet and the Rue 4-Septembre, leaving the Hôtel-de-Ville on the left, leads to a large shady promenade, the Allées Paul-Riquet, at the N end of which is the theatre, with terracotta reliefs by David d'Angers, and at the S end the Plateau des Poètes, a garden with busts of poets and a fountain surmounted by a bronze Titan by a local sculptor, Injalbert.

Halfway along the Allées, at the Place Jean-Jaurès (where cars may be parked) is a statue by d'Angers of Pierre-Paul Riquet (1604–80), engineer of the Canal du Midi (connecting the Atlantic to the Mediterranean at the port of Sète by way of 134 locks). The Canal meets the river Orb at Béziers, descending 30m through the nine locks of Fonsérannes (2km SW) in 350m to come to the same level. Opposite the Place Jean-Jaurès, on the opposite side of the Allées, lies the Ave. St-Saëns, which leads to the amphitheatre (arènes) about 1km distant. The corrida de muerte is held here in March–April, July, August and September. The French version is also held from time to time (watch out for announcements). To the N of the Allées is the 13th-c. church of St-Aphrodise on an ancient site. Part of the font is the front of a Roman sarcophagus with hunting scenes, and there is a bronze figure of Christ by Injalbert. The Festival of St-Aphrodise, with the Procession du Camel, takes place in March–April.

The Musée des Beaux-Arts (in the Hôtel Fabregut, just E of St-Nazaire) has an excellent collection of Greek vases excavated at Delos, and also some good paintings. The Musée du Vieux Biterrois et du Vin, not far away (Rue de l'Argenterie off the Rue Boussi), is in a former Dominican church and has a collection of prehistoric and Graeco-Roman objects, and costumes and bygones; part of it is devoted to objects relating to viticulture, wine being the principal local trade.

The oppidum of Ensérune (see entry) is easily reached from Béziers (about 14km SW).

BOURG-MADAME, Pyrénées-Orientales (5–E5, E6). A small village on the Franco-Spanish border, the name of which was altered in 1815 in honour of the Duchesse d'Angoulême. The town is situated at the confluence of the rivers Sègre and Raour, and the bridge over the Sègre marks the border. The first town in Spain is Puigcerdá, about 1km W. There is a customs post at the bridge.

CARCASSONNE, Aude (5–E6). An ancient city, the Carcaso of the Romans, now with a population of 46,000. Capital of the department and situated on the river Aude, it was in ancient times the junction of E–W and N–S trading-routes, which gave it particular importance. It is divided into two parts, the Ville Basse (lower town), and

the Cité, which is a heavily fortified area on a hill on the opposite bank. The Aude is crossed by two principal bridges – the Pont Neuf on the Narbonne road, and the Pont Vieux.

Carcassonne first became important under Julius Caesar, and the Visigoths (5th–8th-c.) made it a stronghold. The Saracens besieged it unsuccessfully. From the 11th-c. to the 13th-c. it was held by Viscounts of the Trencavel family. It suffered greatly during the Albigensian crusades, when Simon de Montfort made it his headquarters. It was united to France in 1208; when the town revolted, St Louis besieged and took the Cité, expelling the inhabitants, for whom he built the Ville Basse. The fortifications were enlarged and strengthened by his son, Philip the Bold, and by his grandson, Philip the Fair (see also Aigues-Mortes). The Black Prince looted and burned the lower town in 1355. Carcassonne was an important strongpoint during the 17th-c. war with Spain, but after peace had been restored in 1659 the fortifications were allowed slowly to fall into decay. They were about to be demolished in the 19th-c. when Prosper Mérimée, author of the libretto of Carmen and Inspector-General of Historic Monuments, was able to award the task of restoration to the architect and medievalist, Eugène Viollet-le-Duc (1814–79). As a restorer his work at Carcassonne aroused a good deal of controversy, but now that time has blended old work with new, to a considerable extent his restorations are less offensive than they were. They are, nevertheless, still obvious to the perceptive eye.

As it now stands, the Cité, at a height of about 200m, is the best preserved example of medieval fortification in existence. There are two castellated walls, one inside the other, and the space between them, the lices or lists, was used for tournaments. There are 54 towers, principally the work of the 11th–13th-c., notably by Philip the Bold. There are two gates; the Porte Narbonnaise on the E, and the Porte d'Aude overlooking the Ville Basse. The basilica of St-Nazaire within the walls dates from the 5th-c., was rebuilt in the 11th–13th-c., and drastically restored by Viollet-le-Duc. The Musée de la Cité is mainly devoted to archaeology, and preserves documents relating to local history.

The Ville Basse was also fortified in earlier times, and shady boulevards encircling it mark the original site of the walls. Within the ring formed by the boulevards the streets are narrow and the traffic mostly one-way, so the area is best explored on foot. The Cathedral of St-Michel (late 13th-c.) is Gothic in style, restored after a fire in 1840; it is entered from the Rue Voltaire. The Gothic church of St-Vincent (also end 13th-c.), in the Rue 4-Septembre, has a rose-window. The Place Carnot in the town centre has a marble fountain of 1770 by Baratta depicting Neptune. The Jardin des

Plantes and the Canal du Midi (Bd. Omer Sarraut) are on the N side of the town. Like Toulouse and Castelnaudary, Carcassonne is the origin of a recipe for *cassoulet*, although this speciality of the Midi may be found in good restaurants from Nîmes to Toulouse. The local wines of Corbières and Minerve appear on the *carte des vins* of the local restaurants.

Events in May include the Feast of the Patron St-Gimer, and the Walk of the Donkey, in the Barbacane quarter (beneath the west walls of the Cité). In July there is a Dramatic Art Festival in the Théâtre de la Cité, the patronal feast of St-Nazaire, the Walk of the Donkey, and illuminations of the Cité.

CASTELNAUDARY, *Aude* (5–E5). A town of about 12,500 inhabitants on the road from Toulouse to Carcassonne. It is situated on the Canal du Midi, with a basin in the middle of the town. The town was besieged and burned during the *Croisades Albigeois*, and it was burned by the English Black Prince in 1355. In 1632 the Duc Henri de Montmorency, Governor of the Languedoc, led an uprising of nobles in support of the King's brother, Gaston d'Orléans. Louis XIII and Richelieu defeated and captured the duke at Castelnaudary, and he was beheaded in the courtyard of the Hôtel-de-Ville in Toulouse.

The recipe for *cassoulet* used at Castelnaudary is famous in the Midi; it should not be missed. About 7km E lies the village of St-Papoul, once the seat of a bishop, which has an abbey church, including the cloisters, in the Romanesque style.

CASTRIES, *Hérault* (10km NE of Montpellier: 5–D7, D8). A village on N113 and N110, which should not be confused with Castres (*Tarn*). There is a 16th-c. château and a 17th-c. park designed by Le Nôtre (visits every day except Monday). By taking D26 NW from Castries, and then D109e, the 18th-c. château at Assas may be visited at weekends.

CAYLAR, Le, *Hérault* (14km N of Lodève: 5–D7). A small village on the edge of the *causse*. Here the N9, going S, begins to slope steeply downward towards Lodève and the plains of the Bas Languedoc (usually termed the Midi). The road passes through a gap dynamited in the rock, and the Pas de l'Escalette then lies on the left, with parking places beside the road to admire the view. The name means the steps of a scaling-ladder, and at one time the road ended here in a cliff. Passengers had to dismount and climb ladders spiked to the rock to reach another *diligence* waiting at the top. The transition to a Mediterranean climate is often marked at this point, with appropriate flora beginning here. Stunted olive trees may be seen within about 10km.

CERBÈRE, *Pyrénées-Orientales* (5–E7). A small seaside resort on a rocky coast, and the last town before the Spanish border. It is about 2km from Cap Cerbère which marks the traditional frontier. The name of the resort is taken from Cerberus, the three-headed dog which guarded the portals of Hades.

CÉRET, *Pyrénées-Orientales* (5–E6). A small town near the Franco-Spanish border in a region noted for intensive fruit-growing. There are the remains of fortifications, an early 14th-c. bridge over the river Tech, restored in the 18th-c., which is known as the Pont du Diable, and a 12th-c. church with a Gothic portal. Several of the Fauves group of painters worked here in about 1910, and a Modern Art Museum in the Hôtel-de-Ville (open every day) exhibits work by Picasso, Dufy and others (*see also* Collioure). The Procession of the Resurrection takes place in March–April, and a pilgrimage to the monastery of St-Ferreol, as well as races and a folklore festival, in September. The valley of the Tech narrows at this point and is known as the Vallespir. Amélie-les-Bains is about 8km W.

CÉVENNES, Corniche des, *Lozère* (S of Florac: 5–D7). A picturesque road lying to the NE of Mont Aigoual. It starts S from Florac as D907, becomes D983, and then D9 at Le Rey. Flanked by cliffs on one side and precipitous on the other, the road climbs by a number of zigzags from Florac up to Le Rey, where D9 and the actual Corniche start. There are fine views for most of the way, and an eagle may sometimes be seen more or less level with the road. In the region of the Col de l'Exil there is a signposted viewing point which gives a magnificent prospect of the summit of Aigoual. The greatest height attained by the road along this stretch is about 1000m. Beyond the Col de St-Pierre the road becomes the D260 and drops steeply to St-Jean-du-Gard. Throughout its length the road is narrow and demands care, but it is not unduly difficult.

CLAMOUSE, Grotte de, *Hérault* (2km S of St-Guilhem: 5–D7). This widely publicized *grotte* lies in the Gorges of the river Hérault, S of St-Guilhem-le-Désert (*see entry*) and near the Pont du Diable. It was discovered in 1945 and opened to the public in 1964. There is ample parking-space around the bottom of the steps leading to the entrance. At the top of the steps tickets are sold, as well as light refreshments, postcards, and colour-slides. Conditions for photography inside the caves are poor. The visit takes about an hour, and the principal attraction is a spectacular series of illuminated stalactites and stalagmites at various levels. Part of this series of caverns still remains to be explored and opened up for visitors.

Golfe de Porto, Corsica (see page 443)   Teddy Schwarz

CLERMONT L'HÉRAULT, *Hérault* (5–D7). A small town which is the centre of the local trade in table grapes. There is a ruined château, and the early-Gothic fortified church of St-Paul. The southern shore of the barrage lake of Salagou lies about 5km to the NW. The Cirque de Mourèze is 8km SW, and on the road to it is the interesting little town of Villeneuvette (*see entries*).

COLLIOURE, *Pyrénées-Orientales* (5–E6, E7). A picturesque fishing-port and seaside resort, the former Roman town of Cauco Illiberis. It lies beyond the modern Mediterranean development, which ends at Argelès 6km N. Collioure has been called 'the pearl of the Côte Vermeil' (the Vermilion Coast), but it is less of a pearl than it was before the construction of modern blocks of holiday apartments. Nevertheless, the town, which was the birthplace in 1905 of the movement in painting known as Fauvism, has not seriously changed since Matisse, Derain, Dufy, Picasso and others painted here. The Hostellerie des Templiers is noted for its original atmosphere and a well-known small collection of paintings done by artists who have worked in the district. Hotels situated on the road to Port-Vendres have exceptional views of the old port. There is an ancient château which belonged to the Knights Templar, a yacht harbour, bathing, and camping in the vicinity. The local wine is similar in character to that of Banyuls and excellent in quality. The Festival of the Théâtre Midi takes place in August.

CORBIÈRES, Les, *Aude* (SE of Carcassonne: 5–E6). A spur of the French Pyrenees, lying mainly in Aude between the rivers Aude and Agly, SE of Carcassonne. In effect they join the Pyrenees to the Cévennes. The highest point (1231m) is the peak of Bugarach, 16km E of Quillan. The Corbières are well-wooded, with wild gorges, and vast acres of vineyards producing fruity wine rich in alcohol. The best wine comes from around Tuchan (Aude), and much of the produce of this region is entitled to the VDQS appellation.

COUVERTOIRADE, La, *Aveyron* (20km N of Lodève: 5–D7). This important fortified village is situated about 6km due N of Le Caylar. In the 12th-c. it belonged to the Knights Templar, but when the Order was abolished in 1311 it passed to the Knights of St John of Jerusalem. At one time the ramparts completely encircled it, and included four round towers and two square ones. Today, one of the two gates has been destroyed by lightning, and the ramparts are no longer intact. The castle of the Templars, and their Romanesque church, are now little more than shells, but some of the towers and ramparts are accessible with care, and provide an excellent view over the surrounding Causse de Larzac. Inside the walls many of the houses, some of which date from 1300, are now empty. The village was fortunate to escape the attentions of the architect Viollet-le-Duc in the 19th-c., whose restorations at Carcassonne were so controversial, and it is untouched by anything

La Couvertoirade

Douglas Dickins

Countryside surrounding the Oppidum of Ensérune, near Béziers

but time. When it flourished it provided shelter and protection for bands of pilgrims on their way to the shrine of St James of Compostella along the bandit-infested road between Millau and Lodève (now the N9). The presence of the Knights is also recorded by the villages of L'Hospitalet and La Cavalerie on this road in the direction of Millau. The Knights raised sheep on the *causse*, and just outside the ramparts is a fine stone-paved dewpond (*lavogne*) for watering the flocks. The small charge made for entry to the village helps to defray the cost of repairs, and refreshments are available at a café just outside the walls.

DEMOISELLES, Grotte des, *Hérault* (4km SE of Ganges: 5–D7). The *grotte* was thus called by the peasants, who thought it the abode of the fairies or *demoiselles*. It was discovered in 1770, and explored by the speleologist E.-A. Martel in 1884, 1889, and 1897. It is reached from St-Bazille-de-Putois (a *putois* is a pole-cat) by a one-way road, and near the entrance of the *grotte* is a point from which there is a fine view of the valley of the river Hérault. It is open all the year round, and the charge for admission includes the funicular. It is actually an aven, or pot-hole, as well as a well-illuminated series of caverns notable for fantastic stalactite and stalagmite formations of white calcite. 'La Vièrge et l'Enfant' is a formation so called from its resemblance to the Virgin. The largest cavern is 100m long, 80m wide, and 50m high – dimensions which cause it to be likened to a gigantic cathedral. The visit lasts about one hour.

ELNE, *Pyrénées-Orientales* (12km SE of Perpignan: 5–E6, E7). The ancient Illiberis, situated on a low hill at a height of 52m. It was once on the sea, which is now 5km away. Hannibal camped here after crossing the Pyrenees in 218 BC. It was renamed by the Emperor Constantine after his mother, St Helena. The Emperor Constantius was assassinated here in AD 350. There is a good view of the river Tech from the terrace of the Romanesque cathedral of Ste-Eulalie, which has an altar dated 1069. The façade is of the fortified type, with battlements. There is a tower of stone, and one of much later brick. The Archbishop's Palace has a cloister with sculptured columns of white marble of exceptional quality and interest. The bishopric was removed to Perpignan in 1602. Elne was sacked by the Saracens in the 8th-c. and by the Normans in the 11th-c. It was taken by the kings of France in the 13th- and 15th-c. Only ruins of the fortifications survive. The ancient oppidum is at present being excavated.

ENSÉRUNE, L'Oppidum d', *Hérault* (10km SW of Béziers: 5–E6, E7). The town of **Nissan-lez-Ensérune** is small, with two hotels, and no places of tourist interest except the 14th-c. church. '*Lez*' in place-names, however, means 'near to', and Nissan is only about 4km SE of the oppidum of Ensérune. Ensérune, discovered in 1915, is a hilltop site where excavations have unearthed the remains of a remarkable pre-Roman settlement. It was a Gaulish town of about 10,000 inhabitants and dates from the 6th-c. BC. The museum on the site has some important finds of Greek pottery, beginning with wares of the 6th-c. from Rhodes, proving the existence of a considerable commerce with Greek traders.

The view from the hilltop takes in the Pyrenees, the Cévennes, and the Mediterranean. The Canal du Midi is not far away. Within sight of this hilltop

La Grande-Motte

Hercules passed on his way to find the Golden Apples of the Hesperides; Hannibal, starting from New Carthage in Spain, marched towards Italy with 100,000 men and 50 elephants; later, the Legionaries followed the same road on their way to garrison the towns further south.

FONT-ROMEU, *Pyrénées-Orientales* (5–E5). A wintersports centre, with a casino, near the Franco-Spanish border, 18km from Bourg-Madame. It has a large number of hotels for so small a town. There is a miraculous fountain (the name means 'Pilgrim's Fountain'), and a chapel which is a place of pilgrimage. There are pine forests partially surrounding it, and some magnificent views. In July there is an International Sardane Dancing Festival, another in September, and a regional festival in the monastery.

GANGES, *Hérault* (5–D7). A small industrial town largely devoted to the making of luxury silk and nylon stockings. There is a promenade of fine plane-trees, and the remains of a château. Worth seeing are an octagonal Protestant church and the Cazhilac bridge over the river Hérault. Ganges is a crossroads on the way from Nîmes either to Lodève or Le Vigan, and in August 1944 the Maquis held a column of 3000 German troops who were attempting to cross the Hérault. After ten hours of fighting the Germans retired, leaving about 30 dead and a good deal of equipment.

GIGNAC, *Hérault* (5–D7). A small town lying on N109 about midway between Lodève and Mont-

pellier. There are a number of excellent vineyards locally, notably St-Saturnin (VDQS), and around Montpeyroux and St-Félix-de-Lodez. The local wines are red and rosé VDQS, a natural sweet wine, and a dry, full-bodied Clairette de Languedoc. There is a traditional folklore event in May – the Dance of the Donkey and the Battle of the Simbelet. The Grotte de Clamouse is 10km N.

GRANDE-MOTTE, La, *Hérault* (5–D7). This resort 20km from Montpellier forms part of a 'tourist unit' which is connected by a road along the coast from the Pointe de l'Espiguette to Maguelone, taking in Port-Camargue, Le Grau-du-Roi, La Grande-Motte, Carnon-Plage and Palavas-les-Flots.

L'Espiguette is typical of the Camargue; vast deserted beaches fringed by dunes, notable both for bird-life and bulls. **Port-Camargue** is a new resort and pleasure port, with a holiday village and a camping site. **Le Grau-du-Roi** (a *grau*, in the Midi, is a channel connecting a lagoon or a river with the sea) is a picturesque old fishing town with restaurants noted for *bouillabaisse*, and a bull-fighting arena nearby. The French bull-fight, in which the bull is unharmed, and whatever risk there may be is to the human participants, is amusing and worth seeing. In some of the remoter villages it takes place within an arena of carts, and the tourist is advised not to become unwittingly involved. From Le Grau-du-Roi it is 8km to Aigues-Mortes.

La Grande-Motte is largely new construction in the modern idiom, with pyramid-shaped blocks of flats, many hotels, holiday villages, watersports, and camping-sites for 15,000 people. There are many restaurants, excellent shops, a casino, 3km of beaches, and moorings for 1000 craft. **Carnon-Plage** is an older resort which has been developed in recent times. It is a small port and has a sailing school. **Palavas-les-Flots** is not new, although it has been developed. It was always popular with the people of Montpellier and Nîmes, and it lies at the Mediterranean end of a road from Montpellier which passes the International Airport of Fréjorgues, and provides some excellent views when nearing the sea. Palavas has restaurants, cafés, a casino, and a harbour.

Maguelone is about 2km W of Palavas, and is reached by a narrow road along a strip of land which has the sea on one side and a lagoon on the other. The site is that of an ancient Phocaean port probably dating back to the 6th-c. BC. In the 8th-c. AD it fell into the hands of the Saracens; in 737 Charles Martel threw them out and destroyed the town. A later town on this site was destroyed in 1622 when the Protestant population was evicted by Louis XIII. All that is left is the former cathedral, partly restored in the 19th-c. and built in a mixture of Romanesque and Gothic. Montpellier, another stronghold of Protestantism, was at one time under the Bishops of Maguelone, but the see was transferred to Montpellier in 1536.

The whole of this area is convenient for touring in Hérault, Gard, and the foothills of the Cévennes, and also for visiting some of the towns of Provence (Tarascon, Avignon, Les Baux, Arles, etc.) and the Camargue (Stes-Maries-de-la-Mer).

GRUISSAN, *Aude* (10km SE of Narbonne: 5–E6, E7). This is the most recent of the new Mediterranean resorts, started in 1974. The old fishing village of Gruissan is situated about 2km away at the mouth of the Étang (lake) de Gruissan, and a little to the south is Gruissan-Plage, a chalet development. To the S are salt-pans, the Salins de St-Martin. Nearby is the Montagne de la Clape with some fine views, and Narbonne (for the Étang de Bages) is about 14km NW.

JONTE, Gorges de la, *Lozère* (W of Meyrueis: 5–D7). The Causse Méjean is an irregularly shaped flat plateau which is also an island surrounded by river valleys and gorges, of which the Gorges du Tarn form two of the sides, and the Gorges de la Jonte a third. The area is delimited by Florac, Ste-Énimie, Le Rozier, and Meyrueis, and the Gorges de la Jonte run between the last two. The canyon descends from Meyrueis to Le Rozier, both towns on the right bank of the Jonte, with the cliffs of the Causse Méjean on the right. The Grotte de Dargilan, on the left bank, can only be reached from Meyrueis. About 5km towards Le Rozier are two *grottes*, de la Vigne and de la Chèvre, on the right, in the cliffs of the *causse*. About this point the river disappears underground, returning to the surface at the village of

Les Douzes. Here, on a high rock, is the Romanesque chapel of St-Gervais. A belvedere (i.e. a pavilion on a summit) giving impressive views, is on the left of the road, about 1km beyond Le Truel. At Le Rozier excursions on foot can be made to the Roc de Capluc and the Pas de Loup, both high points with excellent views of the Gorges.

LAMALOU-LES-BAINS, *Hérault* (7km W of Bédarieux: 5–D6, D7). A small spa lying in the mountains which join the Cévennes to the Montagne Noir. The waters are said to be efficacious in cases of rheumatism and afflictions of the nervous system. Lamalou is the source of the bottled mineral water sold as Vernières. An art exhibition is held in July. The Gorges d'Héric are about 10km to the W on D908, the village of Olargues, with a bell-tower and 12th-c. bridge, is about 15km from Lamalou on the same road, and beyond Olargues lie the gorges of the Orb.

LIMOUX, *Aude* (5–E6). A small manufacturing town situated on the river Aude about 23km S of Carcassonne. It is surrounded by vine-clad hills which produced a wine known as 'Blanquette de Limoux' from a local vine known as Blanquette. 'Blanquette de Limoux' is still produced, but now, apparently, from the Clairette vine instead. It is a sparkling wine, but a still wine is also made. The town museum (Promenade de Tivoli) has modern paintings, sketches, and engravings, and is open every day. The church of St-Martin, predominantly Gothic in style, has a Romanesque portal. A little to the N, on the Carcassonne road, is the church of Notre-Dame-de-Marceille, with a miraculous fountain and a black marble statue of the Virgin. It is a place of pilgrimage in September. There is also the Dance of the Fecos in Limoux during February. Nougat is a local speciality.

LODÈVE, *Hérault* (5–D7). A lively market and manufacturing town, the Roman Luteva, situated on N9 at the confluence of the rivers Lergue and Soulondres. It is a busy shopping centre, and the Saturday market offers a wealth of local specialities such as sausages from the mountains and cheese from Roquefort (*see entry in the* Southwest France *section*). Lodève was the seat of a bishop from the 4th-c. to 1790, and the Hôtel-de-Ville is the former Bishop's Palace, which is mainly in the Louis XIV style. The partly fortified former Cathedral of St-Fulcran dates from the 13th-c. and is of considerable interest, although the glass is poor. The Feast of St-Fulcran, with a procession, takes place in May. The town was the birthplace of Cardinal Fleury, Chief Minister of Louis XV, 'who gave Lorraine to France' according to the tablet affixed to the house of his birth in the Rue de Fleury. A sculptor, Paul Dardé (d. 1963), is much esteemed locally, and his rather unsophisticated war memorial is in the open space behind the Hôtel-de-Ville. The ancient Pont de

Montifort across the Soulondres is a bridge with a pronounced 'hump-back' – in French *dos d'âne* (ass's back). The Jacques Audibert Museum specializes in geology, palaeontology, and Stone Age archaeology.

About 8km NW, beyond the village of Lauroux (signposted), is a mountain trout-hatchery and restaurant which is popular during the summer. The new barrage lake of Salagou is about 8km S, just beyond Cartels.

LUNEL, *Hérault* (12km N of Aigues-Mortes: 5–D8). Now by-passed by the A9 autoroute, Lunel is a small town midway between Nîmes and Montpellier on N113, sited near the canal running from Beaucaire to Sète. The local wine from the Muscatel grape is among the best in the region. Traditional events here include the shoeing of the Camargue bulls in May, and the bull-fight (French style) in September.

MARVEJOLS, *Lozère* (17km W of Mende: 5–C7). A small town on the N9 which dates from the 14th-c. and is a *bastide*, or fortified town. Three of the original gates still survive, but little else of the fortifications. Much of the town was destroyed in 1586, but rebuilt later by Henri IV, of whom there is a statue by Auriscote.

The same sculptor was also responsible for a representation of the legendary 'Bête du Gévaudan' (*see* Mende) in the Place des Cordeliers.

MAS SOUBEYRAN, Le, *Gard* (6km N of Anduze: 5–D7). *Mas* is a Provençal word meaning a farmhouse, and the Mas Soubeyran was originally a farmhouse belonging to Roland, one of the leaders of the Camisards. It is now officially the Musée du Désert, and is devoted to preserving relics of the Protestants of the region (of whom over a quarter of a million escaped abroad after the Revocation of the Edict of Nantes in 1685) and in particular of the Camisards, who revolted against the Catholic persecution. It is open every day from March to November. A lapidary museum is housed in the chapel of St-Pierre. There is a procession in September to commemorate the martyrs of the Désert.

MENDE, *Lozère* (5–C7). The chief town of the department, and formerly of the region known as the **Gévaudan**. This region was once densely afforested, but it is less well-wooded than it used to be. This has probably been deliberate policy in the past, when the forests were the haunt of outlaws, religious and criminal, as well as the result of the activities of charcoal-burners. Legend relates it to the ravages of an animal (the 'Bête du Gévaudan'), said to have been a wolf, which killed and devoured about 70 shepherds in the 1760s, and a wolf was shot to prove it. The last wolf was not shot in this region till the 1870s. Since there is no properly attested case of anyone ever having been eaten by a wolf, some other animal, perhaps a

bear, was probably responsible. Bears survive in the Pyrenees, and are rigidly protected but rarely seen. They are dangerous. A list of protected animals and birds, which includes the wild boar (*sanglier*) and the eagle, is posted outside the *mairie* and the post office.

Mende itself lies on the river Lot, at the foot of the cliff of the Causse de Mende, which here rises to 300m or more. There is a 14th-c. Gothic bridge, the Pont-Notre-Dame, and there are picturesque alleys round the Cathedral of the same period. Mende was a Catholic town partly destroyed by the Huguenots during the religious wars, and the Cathedral was rebuilt by one of the bishops soon after 1600, with close attention to the restoration of the original detail. Pope Urban V (1302–70) was born in the region, and was the last of the Popes to reside at Avignon. A bronze statue by Damont is in front of the Cathedral. Above the town is the Ermitage of St-Privat, a resort of pilgrims on the way to Compostella. The Musée de la Société des Lettres, Sciences, et Arts de la Lozère is principally devoted to archaeology, folklore, and bygones. At Chastel Nouvel, about 6km N on N107, is a zoological park with wolves and lynxes, former denizens of the forests.

MEYRUEIS, *Lozère* (5–D7). A small town with several hotels, situated at an altitude of 700m, and an excellent touring-centre for the Massif d'Aigoual and the Gorges de la Jonte. The **Grotte d'Argilan** (about 9km NW) and **Aven Armand** (11km N on D986) are two remarkable pot-holes well worth visiting.

MINERVE, *Hérault* (15km S of St-Pons: 5–D6, E6). An interesting old village on the southern slopes of Le Minervois, a range of hills, partly in Hérault and partly in Aude, which run more or less parallel with, but at a lower level than, the Montagnes de l'Espinouse. The village is best reached from Carcassonne, taking the D610 to Olonzac and then the D10 through Azillat to Minerve. There is an old tower, ramparts, a Romanesque church of the 11th-c., and houses once occupied by the Knights Templar. A museum of prehistory is open every day. An excellent VDQS wine is made locally. St-Jean-Minervois to the NE makes a natural sweet VDQS wine from the local Muscat grape which is among the best of its kind.

MONTPELLIER, *Hérault* (5–D7, D8). Capital of the Hérault department, with about 200,000 inhabitants, and many hotels and restaurants (including a few very good ones). A motel and the Montpellier-Fréjorgues airport are both on the Carnon Road to the S, which leads eventually to the 'tourist unit' of La Grande-Motte (*see entry*).

Montpellier came into existence in AD 737 as a result of Charles Martel's destruction of Maguelone (*see* La Grande-Motte), then in the hands of the Saracens. In the 13th-c. it belonged to the

Kings of Aragon, and until 1349 to the Kings of Majorca, who held it as vassals of the French crown. In the early 16th-c. the bishopric of Maguelone was transferred to Montpellier; by the end of the century the town had become a Protestant stronghold, until it was taken by Louis XIII in 1622. During the 17th-c. and 18th-c. there was a considerable English colony here, although towards 1800 there was a tendency to desert Montpellier for Béziers.

Montpellier is a busy, lively town with disc and meter parking. It is an excellent shopping-centre, notably in the Place de la Comédie (which has a central fountain of 1776 representing the Three Graces), and, just NE, the Esplanade with its fine plane-trees and meter parking (long and short term). NW from the Place de la Comédie runs the Rue de la Loge (more shops) which leads to the Rue Foch.

At the end of this broad street stands the ARC DE TRIOMPHE, erected in honour of Louis XIV in 1691. Two reliefs commemorate the Canal du Midi and the Revocation of the Edict of Nantes (1685). Through the Arch, across a wide boulevard, is the PROMENADE DU PEYROU, the entrance flanked by two stone groups by Injalbert (1883). The bronze equestrian statue of Louis XIV by Debay (1829) is based on an earlier bronze which was destroyed during the Revolution. Flowerbeds flank the broad walk, and at the end of it is the CHÂTEAU D'EAU, the terminal of an aqueduct 20m in height and 1km in length, with two tiers of arches, reminiscent of the Pont du Gard. This was constructed in 1753–66 by Pitot to bring water from a source at St-Clément 14km distant. The Château d'Eau is a small masterpiece. It is a

hexagonal pavilion with Corinthian columns and steps flanked by sculptured reliefs, surrounded by a small reservoir. N of the Promenade du Peyrou is the JARDIN DES PLANTES, the first of such gardens in France and laid out by Richer-de-Belleval (d. 1623) under the patronage of Henri IV; its collection includes the *Victoria regia* water-lily, an orangerie, and Mediterranean flowers in profusion.

Montpellier's medical school, founded in the 13th-c., was world-famous in earlier times. The Faculté de Médecine is housed in the former Bishop's Palace, which adjoins the Cathedral, opposite the Jardin des Plantes. It has the Atger Collection of about 300 drawings, as well as an Anatomical Collection. The Cathedral of St-Pierre is Gothic in style, and dates from 1364. It was restored in 1867, and one of the towers was rebuilt in 1855. The University nearby was founded in 1289. It was visited by Petrarch, and François Rabelais was a student here in the 1530s: he speaks of 'drinking the good wine of Mirevault' [Minerve].

The MUSÉE FABRE (closed Mondays and public holidays) is in the Rue Montpelliéret near the Esplanade; it contains works of art collected in Italy by François-Xavier Fabre (1766–1837), a pupil of Jacques-Louis David, and the donations of other collectors have been added to make this one of the most important provincial collections in France, with works by Courbet, Delacroix, Matisse, etc. The town has also many old *hôtels* (i.e. town houses) to interest the student of architecture, especially in the region of the Rue de la Loge, though the interiors are not normally accessible to the public.

The Château d'Eau, Montpellier

MONTPELLIER-LE-VIEUX, Chaos de, *Aveyron* (11km NE of Millau: 5–D6, D7). This remarkable 'chaos' discovered in 1870, and once the haunt of wolves, may be reached either from Millau, or from Le Rozier and Peyreleau. It is well signposted. It consists of remarkable rock-formations reminiscent of an ancient ruined city, and well deserves the appellation of 'Cyclopean', i.e. a kind of building using large, irregular stones, of which the Lion Gate at Mycenae is the best known example. Many of the rocks have names; one of them is in fact called the Mycenaean Gate (Porte de Mycènes). The Rempart (height about 800m) gives an excellent view over the whole area. Not far from Montpellier-le-Vieux, and best reached from St-André-de-Vézines, is Roquesaltes with a view of Montpellier-le-Vieux, and Le Rojal with a number of curiously shaped rocks.

MOURÈZE, Cirque de, *Hérault* (6km W of Clermont: 5–D7). A chaos of dolomitic rock reached through the small village of Mourèze. Visitors are advised to walk up to the Cirque, since the village streets are steep and narrow, and it may not be possible to turn a car at the top. There is a small café with a car park at the bottom. A visit to the Cirque demands a certain amount of scrambling over rocks, and the place is reminiscent of a lunar landscape, with little vegetation. The ruins of a small château are visible on one of the tallest and most precipitous of the rocks. The village has a small Romanesque church.

NARBONNE, *Aude* (5–E6, E7). The Roman Narbo Martius, founded about 600 BC, and in 118 BC the first town outside Italy to be colonized by Roman citizens; it was the chief city of Gallo Narbonnensis, which approximately corresponded to the Southern Languedoc. In Roman times it was a busy port, and large ships anchored in the lagoon to the south. This has now silted up, and a branch of the river Aude which the Romans diverted to flow past the town returned to its original bed after a severe storm in 1320. The Canal de la Robine, a branch of the Canal du Midi, now bisects the town. Narbonne's magnificent buildings (baths, the capitol, temples, triumphal arches, etc.) were celebrated in the 4th-c. AD by the poet Ausonius, and by Sidonius Apollinaris in the 5th-c. Two emperors of Rome were born here. The Visigoths occupied Narbonne from 413 to 720. The Saracens besieged it for two years before it capitulated, and they defended it against Pépin le Bref for seven.

Later, it came under the rule, first of the Comtes d'Auvergne, and then of the Comtes de Toulouse. The Black Prince turned away from its walls in 1355. Much of the trade of the town was in the hands of a Jewish colony until 1306, when they were expelled. The walls were demolished, to be

The Cathedral of St-Just, Narbonne

replaced by boulevards, in 1867, and the Musée Lapidaire Romaine (Place Lamourguier, open every day) preserves many inscribed stones found at this time. The museum in the former Archbishop's Palace includes an interesting collection of French pottery and porcelain, paintings, prehistoric finds and local antiquities.

The large unfinished Cathedral of St-Just adjoins the palace. It is of the fortified type, was started in 1272, and added to in the 18th-c. and 19th-c. In one of the chapels is a copy by Carle Van Loo of Sebastiano del Piombo's 'Raising of Lazarus', the original of which was purchased from the Cathedral by the Duc d'Orléans and later acquired in London by the banker Angerstein, whose collection eventually became the nucleus of London's National Gallery. The choir and the stained glass deserve attention, and the Treasury is a museum of Christian Art with objects dating from the 7th-c. The church of St-Paul-Serge (Sergius Paulus was first bishop of Narbonne) in the SW part of the town, a little S of the Place des Pyrénées, is early Gothic in style; it is next to a 4th-c. Christian cemetery.

About 14km E is Narbonne-Plage, the nearest seaside resort to Narbonne. The large salt-water lagoon, the Étang de Bages, lies to the S. The village of Bages about 7km S of Narbonne offers excellent views across the lagoon. The white honey of the region has been famous for centuries.

About 15km SW of Narbonne (N113, then left on to the D613) is the **Abbey of Fontfroide** in a picturesque setting in a peaceful valley. Romanesque in style, but restored, with stained glass added in this century, it was an important Cistercian abbey, with a 12th-c. church and a 13th-c. cloister.

NAVACELLES, Cirque de, *Gard* and *Hérault* (13km SW of Le Vigan: 5–D7). This remarkable and important natural curiosity takes the form of a vast hole in the ground with precipitous sides like a crater; it was a stronghold of the Maquis during World War II. It was formed by the river Vis, which leaves the Cirque through narrow gorges. At the bottom lies a small village on a bend in the river. The depth of the hole is about 350m.

It can be reached from Le Vigan on the D48 to Montdardier, thence to Blandas, and then follow the signpost. A road descending into the Cirque on this side was at one time impracticable, but has recently been reconstructed. Inspect before using. Coming from Lodève, take the Millau road (N9), and turn right on to the D25 through Soubès to St-Maurice-Navacelles. Turn left in St-Maurice on to the D130 for the Cirque (7½km). The descent by road on this side is down a gradient of 1 in 4 with several *lacets*. Some may find the descent vertiginous, but the views from the top alone make the visit worth while.

Just E of St-Maurice-Navacelles lies Madières (bear right here for Ganges). In the village, high up on the left, is the 17th-c. Château de Madières with circular engaged towers at the angles of the walls.

George Savage

Cirque de Navacelles

NÎMES, *Gard* (5–D8). Capital of the Gard department, a large town of about 135,000 inhabitants, and a centre of the wine trade and the silk industry. A type of cloth made here was once known as *de Nîmes* and, contracted to 'denim', is a well-known clothing material today.

Nîmes was founded on the site of a large settlement of the Volcae Anocomici tribe, who submitted to Roman rule in 121 BC. Formerly spelt Nismes (the Roman Nemausus, and the 'Rome of France'), it was an important stage on the highway between Spain and Italy. Augustus constituted Nîmes a colony of veterans and gave it numerous privileges; the chained crocodile appearing in the arms of the city commemorates the part played by its Legionaries in the conquest of Egypt during the campaign against Antony. M. Vipsanius Agrippa, who built the Pont du Gard (*see entry*), also built the Temple of Diana and the public baths; he was probably also responsible for the Maison Carrée, the best preserved Roman building of its period extant. The amphitheatre (*les arènes*), still in regular use, is smaller, but in better condition, than the one at Arles.

Nîmes was looted by Vandals in 407, and occupied by the Visigoths, who turned the amphitheatre into a stronghold. The Saracens held it briefly, and were dispossessed by Charles Martel. It passed to the Comtes de Toulouse, and

was garrisoned by Louis VIII during the Albigensian crusades. It was given a university and an art-school by François I. At the time of the Edict of Nantes in 1598 most of its inhabitants were Protestants, and when the Edict was revoked in 1685 large numbers joined the Camisard revolt; the Tour Magne stands on Mont Cavalier, the hill NW of the city named after Jean Cavalier, leader of the Camisards. Among the better known of the sons of Nîmes are Nicot, who introduced tobacco into France in 1564 (hence nicotine), the 19th-c. statesman and historian Guizot, and the writer Alphonse Daudet, author of the humorous classic *Tartarin de Tarascon* (1872).

A ticket taken at any of the monuments covers entry to all of them. To begin at the top of Mont Cavalier, the TOUR MAGNE, a Roman watch-tower, can be ascended by 140 steps. (It was once about 10m higher.) It gives an excellent view of the town and, on a clear day, as far as the Pyrenees. Descending the hill, the remains of the so-called TEMPLE OF DIANA are on the right. It has many fragments of antiquarian interest, and the remains of a vaulted roof should be noted. This building may have been a *nymphaeum* attached to the baths (*thermae*). What is left of the baths is nearby and forms part of the water-garden, the JARDIN DE LA FONTAINE, which is supplied by the same spring as in Roman times. This rises at Sauve in the

Cévennes, and the water filters through beds of limestone lying on impermeable rock. For many centuries, until 1740, the flow was diverted at Sauve, but it was then restored, and the present gardens constructed, taking care to conserve surviving Roman buildings.

The MAISON CARRÉE is nearer to the centre of the city. Arthur Young regarded its proportions as a 'magic harmony'. The tessellated pavement in the interior (which houses a small collection of antiquities) is in excellent condition. Jefferson procured measured drawings of this building as a model for the Virginia State Capitol, so great was the esteem in which it was held during the currency of the neoclassical style. Built by Agrippa about 20 BC, it was restored in 1824.

The AMPHITHEATRE nearby can seat 21,000 spectators, the highest seat being 23m above the arena. It is in a remarkable state of preservation, and Spanish matadors appear here in May and September in the *corrida de muerte*. In Roman times there was provision for the arena to be flooded to enable water-spectacles to be provided.

To the SE is the Esplanade, with a fountain by Jacques Pradier (1792–1852) representing the city of Nîmes above, with figures below representing the Rhône, the Gardon, and the Fontaine de Nîmes. N from the amphitheatre lies the 11th-c. Cathedral of ST-CASTOR, which has a Romanesque W front, the upper part of which is Gothic. There are one or two 19th-c. churches in Nîmes in revived Gothic, which is rare anywhere in the south. The MUSÉE DU VIEUX-NÎMES, housed in the former Bishop's Palace (Place de la Cathédrale), is devoted to bygones and folklore. The MUSÉE DES BEAUX-ARTS (Rue de la Cité-Foulc) has some good paintings and sculptures of the French and Italian schools. The MUSÉE ARCHÉOLOGIQUE (Bd. Amiral-Courbet) has Celtic and Gallo-Roman antiquities. In the same boulevard may be found the PORTE D'ARLES, the lower part of a Roman gate of 16 BC called the Porte d'Auguste, which,

The Amphitheatre, Nîmes

French Government Tourist Office

like the Tour Magne, was once part of the fortifications surrounding the original town.

The many hotels and restaurants make Nîmes an excellent touring-centre for this part of the Midi. The Nîmes-Garons airport is 8km S of the city. The Pont du Gard is 22km NE by way of Remoulins. Arles is 28km SE. Just beyond Uchaud on the Millau road (N113) a turning to the left (D139) leads to the source of the popular mineral water, Perrier, which can be visited.

PERPIGNAN, *Pyrénées-Orientales* (5–E6, E7). Capital of the department, and of the former province of Roussillon, Perpignan is a large and busy city of 108,000 inhabitants, with many hotels, restaurants and places of interest, and a gay Midsummer Festival in June. Less than 30km from the border, it is a city with a distinctly Spanish air.

Most of the places of interest lie within the area bounded by the boulevards, i.e. the old town with its small, narrow streets. Boulevards (the word means, literally, bulwarks or ramparts) always mark the position of former fortifications; in this case they were the work of the great 17th-c. military engineer Vauban, and they were dismantled in 1903 to make way for the growth of the town.

Perpignan dates from Roman times. With the County of Roussillon, it was inherited by the Kings of Aragon in 1172, and they were confirmed in possession by the Treaty of Corbeil in 1258 by Louis IX (St Louis), who renounced his sovereignty. The King of Aragon gave Perpignan to his son, Jaime, King of Majorca, and the Palace of the Kings of Majorca (at the S edge of the inner city) was started in 1276. Built in the Gothic style, it is at present being restored, but it is partly open to the public; there is a fine view from the top of the keep. To the N, nearer the river, Le Castillet (Casa Pairal) is a late 14th-c. red-brick château which is now a museum for the arts and crafts of Roussillon. The nearby Loge de Mer, formerly the Bourse, dates from the 14th-c. and is predominantly Gothic in style but with a Moorish flavour. The Hôtel-de-Ville, ranging in date from the 13th to the 17th-c., has a pebble-covered façade and wrought-iron gates; in the patio is one of Maillol's masterpieces, a bronze nude entitled 'The Mediterranean'. The Cathedral of St-Jean, on the other side of Place Gambetta, was started in 1324 and finished in the 17th-c. It became a cathedral in 1601. The principal style is Gothic, and there are some good early carvings in wood and marble.

The Musée Rigaud is so called because it contains important work by Hyacinthe Rigaud (1659–1743), born in Perpignan, who studied in Montpellier and eventually became Court Painter of portraits to Louis XIV, the Regent, and Louis XV; there are also works by Ingres, Géricault, Tintoretto, Greuze, etc. The Museum of Natural History (Rue Émile Zola), in the old Hôtel de

Cagarriga, has collections of southern French flora and fauna. For collectors, the Joseph Puig Coin Collection (Ave. Grande-Bretagne, closed Saturdays, Sundays, and the whole of August) has some interesting material, including coins from Roussillon and Catalonia.

Local places of interest include the Mas St-Vicens, about 2km E on the Canet road, with an exhibition of Catalan pottery and modern tapestries by Lurçat. **Canet-Plage** (12km E) is a seaside resort with a sandy beach, noted for its nightlife (casino, etc.). **Thuir** (12km SW), on the edge of the Aspres (the foothills of Mont Canigou), is noteworthy for the enormous cellars of the Établissements Byrrh, makers of the popular French apéritif (these are open every day to visitors); the church contains an unusual statue of the Virgin and Child in pewter (*étain*) dating from about 1200. The château and village of **Castelnou**, 5km W from Thuir, are a little-known and well-preserved feudal complex well worth a visit.

Within a radius of about 15km from Perpignan are a number of well-preserved Romanesque churches, including those at Cabestany (4km SE), Toulouges (6km SW), Canohès (7km SW), Pollestres (7½km S), Canet (10km E) and St-Félieu-d'Amont (15km W).

PERTHUS, Le, *Pyrénées-Orientales* (5–E6). Franco-Spanish border village on N9, which becomes N11 in Spain. The village is now bypassed by the B9 autoroute, which has its own separate frontier-post. This is the principal frontier crossing on the Mediterranean end of the Pyrenees. According to tradition the Col du Perthus (altitude 290m) was Hannibal's route into the Midi. Le Perthus is 37km from Perpignan and 6km from La Junquera, the first Spanish town over the border.

PÉZENAS, *Hérault* (5–E7). The Roman town of Piscenae, Pézenas now has about 8000 inhabitants and is situated in a fertile valley devoted to viticulture and market-gardening. Its principal trade is wine. In the past, however, it was one of the most important towns of the region.

The États-Généraux of the Languedoc met here for the first time in 1456, and for a long time the town was the residence, first of the Montmorencies, and then of the Contis, governors of the Languedoc. The now-decayed château of Grange-des-Prés belonging to Armand de Bourbon, Prince de Conti, became known as the 'Versailles of the Languedoc', and here Louis XIII, Louis XIV, and Cardinal Mazarin were magnificently entertained. Molière, whose patron was the Prince de Conti, made his début here in 1655; he lodged with a barber named Gély in the old town, nearly opposite the Tribunal de Commerce. The great days of Pézenas ended with the death of Armand de Bourbon in 1666, and Molière last visited the town in 1657.

Visitors are advised to park their cars in the Place du 14-Juillet, on the E edge of the old town where there is a statue of Molière by Injalbert. Opposite, in the left-hand corner, is the Rue St-Jean, where turn right into the Rue François-Oustrin. On the right is the Hôtel de Lacoste (15th-c.) with Gothic arches, a fine staircase, and a beamed ceiling on the ground floor. In the Rue A.-P. Alliès (turning right from the Place Gambetta), is the Musée Vulliod-St-Germain (closed Tuesday and Friday) which is devoted to archaeology, popular traditions, and items relating to Molière. Returning to the square, the Tribunal de Commerce is on the right, with wrought ironwork ornamenting the façade. A meeting here of the États-Généraux started the revolt in 1632 that ended with the Duc de Montmorency's execution (*see* Castelnaudary). Beyond the Tribunal building on the right is the Rue Alfred-Sabatier leading to the narrow streets of the former ghetto (Rue des Litanies and the Rue de la Juiverie), where the Jewish colony remained undisturbed until the 13th-c., when, with the Cathars, they were classed as heretics. In the opposite direction the Rue de la Foire passes the Hôtel de Wicque, with its Renaissance façade, and then swings left to the former Commanderie of St John of Jerusalem. Opposite the Commanderie is the Sacristie des Pénitents-Blancs with a noteworthy 15th-c. courtyard, and in the Rue Conti (also opposite the Commanderie) are the Hôtels Alfonce and Malibran. Molière's company acted in the former. Events in Pézenas include the 'Sortie de Poulain' (Emergence or Procession of the Foal, the foal being an allegorical animal), and the 'Dance of the Bellows and the Trestle' in February, the Mass of St Hubert and the Blessing of the Dogs in June, a National Drama Festival in July, and another Sortie in August.

PONT-DU-GARD, *Gard* (12km SE of Uzès: 5–D8). One of the best preserved and most majestic of Roman buildings still surviving, the Pont-du-Gard is an aqueduct spanning the river Gardon. It was built towards the end of the 1st-c. BC by M. Vipsanius Agrippa. It consists of three tiers of arches. The lowest tier, of squared honey-coloured stone, has 6 arches; the middle tier, also of stone, 11 arches; and the top tier which carries the water-channel, built of brick, has 35 arches. The span is 275m and the height 50m, and the aqueduct forms part of a conduit 50km in length which formerly brought water from the source of the Eure at Uzès to Nîmes, where it ended at the Castellum Divisorium in the Rue de la Lampèze. On its way to Nîmes this conduit passes through tunnels and over other, smaller aqueducts.

The stones projecting from the face of the masonry presumably supported wooden scaffolding during the actual construction. The road-bridge, which runs level with the bottom tier on the downstream side, was built in 1747. The structure itself, damaged during barbarian invasions, was restored by Questel and Laisné in 1843–57. The Pont-du-Gard is 23km from Nîmes and 3km from Remoulins.

PONT-ST-ESPRIT, *Gard* (5–D8). A town of 7000 inhabitants on the right bank of the Rhône just below its confluence with the Ardèche. The bridge across the Rhône, 900m in length, which carries the main road to Montélimar and Orange, gives a fine downstream view. The Rhône is now wide but shallow, because much of the water has been diverted higher up into the navigable Donzère–Mondragon canal. The bridge was built in the 13th-c. by St Bénézet, founder of the Order of Bridge-building Brothers (the Frères Pontifs) who also built the bridge of which only part remains at Avignon. The Citadel, and the churches of St-Saturnin and St-Esprit, are interesting.

PORT-BARCARÈS, *Pyrénées-Orientales* (5–E6, E7). This is a new Mediterranean resort. There is a yacht harbour with 200 berths, the Centre Méditerranéen du Nautisme with a sailing and skin-diving school, a marina club, and waterskiing at Port-St-Ange 1km S. Port-Barcarès has the usual amenities of a resort, including nightclubs, restaurants, riding, and tennis. To the N is the *Lydia*, a liner beached on sand, which acts as a casino. At the S end of the lagoon (Étang de Leucate) lies the small fishing village and resort of Le Barcarès, and on the W side of the lagoon lies the village of Salses with a château-fort built by Don Sanche of Castille in 1497, worth a visit. Port-Leucate (*see entry*) lies immediately N; Perpignan is about 25km SW.

PORT-LEUCATE, *Aude* (5–E6, E7). One of the new resorts built as part of the post-war Mediterranean coastal development. It lies on a strip of land about 1km wide which separates the lagoon (Étang de Leucate) from the sea, and there are views of the Pyrenees and the hills of Corbières on the landward side. The harbour has over 500 quayside berths. There is a sailing club, a watersports school, and the usual amenities of a seaside resort. The old village of Leucate to the N is not far from Cap Leucate, a headland originally given its name by ancient Greek seamen. Port-Barcarès (*see entry*) is immediately to the S, and Perpignan is about 30km SW.

PORT-VENDRES, *Pyrénées-Orientales* (5–E7). The Portus Veneris of the Romans; a small commercial port and seaside resort between Collioure and Banyuls with a number of hotels open in the season. The harbour is small and landlocked, with about 6m of water alongside the quay. The local vineyards produce an excellent wine akin to that of Banyuls.

PRADES, *Pyrénées-Orientales* (5–E6). A small town in the mountains 43km W of Perpignan, with a Gothic church in the Spanish style containing a

St-Guilhem-Le-Désert

monumental retable of St-Pierre of about 1700. Prades is the most convenient starting-point for a visit to nearby St-Michel-de-Cuxa, an abbey founded about 860, with 12th-c. sculpture and a Lombard-type bell-tower. The annual Prades music festival, held in May in honour of the cellist Pablo Casals, takes place in this abbey. From here the road winds towards the impressive peak of Mont Canigou, though the best approach is from Vernet-les-Bains (*see entry*).

Molitg-les-Bains, 7km NW in the narrow gorge of the Castellane, is a spa with 12 sulphur springs said to be efficacious in the treatment of skin and respiratory diseases, and for beauty treatment generally.

QUILLAN, *Aude* (5–E6). A small manufacturing town of about 5000 inhabitants in the Aude valley, surrounded by forest and the foothills of the Pyrenees. The 18th-c. Hôtel-de-Ville is worth inspection. Quillan is a good centre for excursions in superb scenery. 5km S is the gloomy but impressive Défile (gorge) de Pierre-Lys.

ST-CYPRIEN, *Pyrénées-Orientales* (7km S of Canet-Plage: 5–E6, E7). One of the new resorts, SE of Perpignan, St-Cyprien specializes in golf, with two courses totalling 27 holes which have a view of the Pyrenees as a background. There are facilities for other sports, as well as restaurants, bars, etc.

ST-GUILHEM-LE-DÉSERT, *Hérault* (5–D7). Situated in the Gorges de l'Hérault, it can be reached from Gignac on N109 by way of Aniane or St-Jean-de-Fos and the Pont du Diable (built by monks in 1026), passing the Grotte de Clamouse (*see entry*) on the left. A 13th-c. bridge, and the Hôtel Fonzes on the high bank of the river, mark a turning on the left that leads to the village, which cannot be seen from the road. Cars must be left in the car park at the entrance. The village square is shaded by an enormous plane-tree, and the abbey church of St-Guilhem, a small masterpiece of the Romanesque style, lies on the right. Only a part of the cloister remains: the rest was bought many years ago and shipped to New York, where it forms that part of the Metropolitan Museum collections known as 'The Cloisters'.

The site of the present village was chosen by Guilhem, a valiant and devoted lieutenant of Charlemagne, who made him the governor of Aquitaine. Guilhem defeated the Saracens, who were then occupying much of the Midi, and in doing so became Prince of Orange, in Provence, a principality which centuries later descended to the Stadtholders of Holland (who were named William in memory of Guilhem), one of whom became William III of England. When, in 804, Guilhem founded the abbey he gave it a portion of the True Cross discovered by St Helena, and given to him by Charlemagne who had received it from the Pope. The church was consecrated in 1076. The relic is carried in an annual procession on 3 May.

The village has a few streets of old and picturesque houses. In the vicinity are the ruins of a château which belonged to Don Juan, a Saracen who preyed on the locality until he was slain by Guilhem, who had the tip of his nose cut off in the struggle and was henceforward known as '*Court-nez*'. The land immediately surrounding the village is actually quite fertile; 'Le Désert' in the name refers to the hillsides round about, which are bare except for scrub-bushes, a kind of covering known in the Midi as the *garrigue*, or less often as the *maquis*, from which the war-time Resistance got its name.

Topham

Sète

ST-JEAN-DU-GARD, *Gard* (10km NW of Anduze: 5–D7). A small town situated on one of the rivers Gar or Gardon. It was here that R.L. Stevenson ended his journey with Modestine recounted in *Travels with a Donkey*. It has a 13th-c. bridge, damaged during a violent flood in 1958 and now reconstructed, a Romanesque clock-tower, and the château of St-Jean. The spinning of silk is carried on locally, and there are plantations of mulberries for feeding the worms. It is usually possible to visit establishments of this kind. Inquire locally. In August 1944, largely by courageously bluffing the German commander as to the strength of the forces at his disposal, the leader of the Maquis, a local schoolmaster, obtained the surrender of a regiment.

ST-PIERRE-SUR-MER, *Aude* (15km E of Narbonne: 5–E6, E7). A small resort with large beaches just N of Narbonne-Plage. The Gouffre de l'Oeil Doux (a *gouffre* is a deep chasm or pool), and the caves, are worth visiting.

ST-PONS, *Hérault* (5–D6,E6). A cloth-manufacturing town 51km WNW of Béziers. The 12th-c. cathedral, rebuilt in the 18th-c., has a Romanesque portal, and a N wall which is heavily fortified. St-Pons is situated at the E end of the Montagne Noire, and there are marble quarries in the vicinity.

On the road to Mazamet (N112), at a distance of about 5km, is Corniou and the **Grotte de la Devèze**, which has interesting formations of translucent calcite and aragonite stalactites and stalagmites, which have been likened to threads of glass. A visit takes about an hour, and the *grotte* is open all the year round.

SÈTE, *Hérault* (5–E7). The second largest French Mediterranean port, situated on the long, narrow seaward arm of the Bassin de Thau – the largest lagoon in Languedoc-Roussillon, 55km in circumference.

Sète (formerly Cette) lies at the foot of Mont St-Clair (180m), from whose summit there is a fine panoramic view of the whole area. Colbert, Louis XIV's Finance Minister, provided the money for the construction of the port, and Paul Riquet (responsible for the construction of the Canal du Midi – *see* Béziers) was the engineer. A new basin and an access canal for seagoing vessels were constructed in the 19th-c. and now the deep-water end of the Bassin de Thau has been brought into use as well. Apart from its function as the premier fishing-port of the region, handling most of the sardines and tunny one buys in the Midi, Sète imports a great deal of Algerian wine, to the fury of local vignerons, with whose product it competes. The old port, with its fishing-vessels and sailing-boats and many restaurants, is picturesque. The Musée Paul Valéry has a collection of paintings, drawings, and engravings by Renoir, Cézanne, Toulouse-Lautrec, Matisse, Marquet, etc. The aquarium (summer, closed Monday; winter, open Thursday and Sunday only) is housed in the Station Biologique; it has an excellent collection of Mediterranean fish, crustacea, and molluscs. At various times in the summer Sète puts on its celebrated *Joutes Nautiques* in which young men engage in jousting tournaments from platform extensions on large rowing-boats, each trying to knock his opponent into the water.

In the same area are a number of resorts which have been developed as one of the Languedoc coast 'tourist units'. **Balaruc-les-Bains** to the N is a small spa, with a skin-diving and sailing-centre in the Bassin de Thau. **Bouzigues**, **Mèze** and **Marseillan** are noted for fishing, barrel-making and oysters. Marseillan has a small hotel and restaurant on the quay. The canal between here and the Hérault at Agde is a prolongation of the Canal du Midi, and leads into the Bassin de Thau. The **Cap d'Agde** is a new seaside resort started in 1969 and built on the headland of this name. It is at the base of Mont St-Loup, a former volcano, and Mont St-Martin. The new town has small squares, and streets for pedestrians only, lined with arcades. To the E of it is **Port Ambonne**, a naturist holiday village with accommodation of all kinds, including camping and caravanning facilities. (*See also* Agde.)

TARN, Gorges du, *Lozère* (SW of Ste-Énimie: 5–C7). When tourists first began to visit this part of France 80 years ago, Baedeker described the Gorges as a canyon, and they were only partially accessible by road. A good road now runs their full length, and the drive is spectacular and impressive; there is nothing on this scale to be found elsewhere in the region.

The Gorges du Tarn came into existence when the Alps and the Pyrenees were thrust upwards. These are much newer formations than the mountains of Lozère and the Cévennes. The Gorges are a fault in the earth's surface which separates the Causse Méjean on one side from the Causse de Sauveterre on the other, deepened by the river Tarn, which rises in the mountains of Lozère. Rainfall is relatively low in the Gorges, so cliff-erosion has not been very extensive, and the cliffs remain, for the most part, steep and precipitous.

Florac, 40km S of Mende, is in the centre of the Cévennes National Park and a convenient point at which to begin the journey. Florac lies at the foot of a cliff which marks the edge of the Causse Méjean, on the left bank of the Tarnon, a tributary of the Tarn. It is a pretty town, noted for flowers and early vegetables, and it is a tourist centre for the Gorges and the Lozère mountains. **Ispagnac**, next on the route, is planted with fruit-trees and vines; raspberries and strawberries are cultivated. It lies at the head of the Gorges, which extend to

Le Rozier about 45km SW. There is an interesting Gothic bridge spanning the river between here and Quezac which was largely rebuilt in the 18th-c.

Castelbouc is on the left bank of the river, at the foot of a cliff with the ruins of a château above. Legend refers to a medieval baron, the Seigneur Raymond, who, during the Crusades, was the only man remaining, and therefore greatly in demand among the local women. *Castelbouc*, in Provençal, means the castle of the he-goat, and when Raymond died during a storm his spirit took the form of an enormous goat and disappeared during a clap of thunder. His story is the subject of a *son-et-lumière* during the summer months.

Ste-Énimie is situated on a bend in the river, and it is also a road-junction, with Mende 21km to the N. It has two hotels; a former monastery with a view of the Gorges from its terrace; Le Vieux Logis, a small museum of bygones and folklore; a church with modern ceramic panels by Henri Constans; and a Corn Exchange.

Across the river is the picturesque village of **St-Chély-du-Tarn**, with cliffs and orchards, and a *cirque* of the same name. For the *grotte* enthusiasts there are a number in the vicinity of Ste-Énimie and St-Chély which can be explored with permission. Inquiries should be made locally. A little way downstream from St-Chély, on the road to La Malène, is the rose-red Cirque de Pougnadoires and a village of houses set amid enormous rocks and backing on to them. The **Château de la Caze**, built towards the end of the 15th-c., is attractively sited about 5km N of La Malène, on the river bank. It has a garden, and steps leading to the water. It was built by Soubeyrane Alamand who had eight daughters, all as beautiful as one another, who were known as the 'Nymphs of the Tarn'. The château is now a hotel, but parts are open to casual visitors at certain times.

La Malène itself has two hotels and an *auberge*. The Hôtel de Montesquiou dates from the 15th-c. The village is also a road-junction, and a road on the opposite bank (D43) leads S to the Causse Méjean. This road is steep, very narrow, and has ten *lacets*, some of which need reversing to get round them. Care and skill are needed to negotiate it safely, as the sides are precipitous.

Les Détroits (the straits) are probably the most spectacular and dramatic stretch of the Gorges, but need the sun to be seen at their best. The cliffs are vertical, and often overhang. They are over 400m in height, and the sides approach each other more nearly here than anywhere else in the Gorges. The best view is probably from the river, and boats and boatmen may be hired, but a remark of Baedeker made some 75 years ago is worth quoting – 'not dangerous, but presents various difficulties which distract the attention'. The conditions have not changed.

The **Pas de Souci** is a chaos of rocks which virtually obliterates the course of the river. It is the result of an earthquake about 1400 years ago, but according to legend St Énimie, much troubled by

Satan, chased him along the top of the canyon, calling upon the rocks to stop him from escaping. They answered with a colossal landslide, during which a vast rock, the Sourde, fell squarely on top of him. But, characteristically, he slithered from under it, and made good his escape to Hell.

The Gorges broaden at **Les Vignes**, noted for its wine, and here a road leads to the Cirque des Baumes (*baumes* here means caves) and the Causse de Sauveterre. This road gives splendid views of the Gorges, but the ascent demands care and skill. From here it is 12km to **Le Rozier**, where the road turns to the right for Millau, and left for the Gorges de la Jonte and Meyrueis. Le Rozier is a very ancient town, built at the confluence of the Tarn and the Jonte. The remains of a Roman pottery are in the vicinity. (This region had a considerable reputation for its pottery in the

ancient world. An unopened case of this pottery was found in the ruins of Pompeii.)

Separated from Le Rozier by the Jonte is the village of **Peyreleau**. Its narrow streets are interesting, but all that remains of an old château-fort is a square castellated tower. From here 5km on D29 leads to the corniche of the Causse Noir. Keep left to the end of the road, where a place will be found to park the car. It is a short walk to the Cirque de Madrasse with fine views over Le Rozier, Peyreleau, and the confluence of the two rivers. The first turn right on D29 after leaving Peyreleau leads to Montpellier-le-Vieux (*see entry*).

UZÈS, *Gard* (5–D8). The Roman Ucetia, a picturesque small town on the river Alzon, 25km N of Nîmes. Its ramparts were demolished by

Castelbouc, in the Gorges du Tarn

French Government Tourist Office

Uzès: Tour Fenestrelle

Richelieu about 1630 and boulevards took their place. Uzès, with narrow streets and alleys, gives the impression of a medieval town. On the E side is the former cathedral of St-Théodorat (17th–18th-c.) with a notable organ. The earlier building was destroyed by the Huguenots, and all that remains is the remarkable Tour Fenestrelle (12th-c.), which is a Romanesque campanile 46m in height with six tiers of double windows. On the N side is the Hôtel-de-Ville, a good 18th-c. building, the arcaded courtyard of which leads to the Duché (the only château permitted to be so called) belonging to the Ducs d'Uzès. This dates from the 11th-c. It has a fine Renaissance façade, and the Tour Bermonde (11th-c.) is named after its builder, Bermonde de Crussol. The family are in residence, and only the courtyard is on view. The dramatist, Racine, lived in Uzès in the 17th-c., and the Promenade J. Racine to the SE gives excellent views across the Parc du Duché towards the river. There is now a museum devoted to automobiles and engines.

VALRAS-PLAGE, *Hérault* (5–E7). A small seaside resort on the mouth of the river Orb. It has a casino open in the season, and there is a newly built yacht harbour. The river mouth makes an excellent sailing area. Béziers is 15km to the NW.

VERNET-LES-BAINS, *Pyrénées-Orientales* (5–E6). A spa situated in a fruit-growing area amid dramatic mountain scenery. The waters are reputed to alleviate rheumatism and respiratory diseases. It has in the past been a favourite with English visitors, Anthony Trollope and Rudyard Kipling among them. The old village stands on the slope of a hill, and has a château and a 12th-c. church. To the S, at an elevation of about 400m above Vernet, is the much-restored abbey of St-Martin-du-Canigou, founded in the 11th-c. by a Count of Cerdagne. The summit of **Mont Canigou** (2784m) is only 6km S as the eagle flies, but the approach route is difficult, even dangerous, and the ascent is arduous. The expedition requires a whole day even in good weather, and local advice is recommended. On a clear day the view from the peak is superb.

VIGAN, Le, *Gard* (5–D7). A small town which has been a centre for silk manufacture for centuries. It was also a Protestant stronghold during the religious wars. The town is noted for a promenade of enormous chestnut-trees, and a 12th–13th-c. much-photographed bridge over the river Arre, the arch of which can form a perfect circle with its reflection. The local silk factory may be visited; for times inquire at the Syndicat d'Initiative in the Hôtel-de-Ville. Le Vigan is an excellent centre for exploring the Massif d'Aigoual, and for visiting the Cirque de Navacelles (*see entries*).

VILLENEUVE-LÈS-AVIGNON, *Gard* (1km NW of Avignon: 5–D8). Though geographically belonging to the Languedoc, historically Villeneuve-lès-Avignon is so closely linked with Avignon that its description has been included in the Provence gazetteer section of this book.

VILLENEUVETTE, *Hérault* (3km SW of Clermont: 5–D7). Like most of the 'new towns' in France, this one dates from the 17th-c. It is of considerable interest to the student of industrial archaeology, since it was established by Colbert to weave woollen cloth for the army. The village is entered on foot through a stone arch in the Louis XIV style, bearing the inscription *Honneur au Travail*. Workmen's cottages are grouped around a square shaded by large chestnuts, and there is a central fountain containing goldfish. In a street leading from the square are the factory buildings on the left and the director's house on the right. Steps immediately past the house lead to a rectangular fishpond and a path which goes upwards through the pines. This path terminates in a reservoir, fed by a spring and formerly intended for washing newly woven cloth; it is now often used as a swimming pool. The village has an antique shop, several craftsmen, a restaurant, and an *auberge* open in the season. The Cirque de Mourèze (*see entry*) is about 3km further W. Both places are best reached by D908 from Clermont l'Hérault.

Provence: Introduction

Provence, Côte d'Azur, Riviera

Anne Lockie

Provence: *Provincia* to the Romans, meaning 'The Province'. For them the limit of Italy was the river Var, west of Nice, and the name is symbolic because the Roman imprint on Provence is continual and continuing. Today in the Provençal countryside, in a large complex of farm buildings, where the plough may at any time reveal remains of a Roman villa, or at an abandoned post-stage inn far from habitation, the main entrance is often a large arch; to look at, it could be Roman – in fact it could be Roman, Renaissance or nineteenth century. Except that underfloor heating was forgotten about for at least 1500 years, a lot of the houses are much the same. The way in which the now bare bricks were laid in the curved apse of the Roman Baths at Arles is identical with the way stone was used in the apse of a fifth-century chapel or in innumerable eleventh-century churches. In the atmosphere of the little church of Notre-Dame-de-Brusc near Châteauneuf-de-Grasse one feels the presence of twenty-five centuries of history, and the evolution is seen very simply. The same is true of Arles on a grandiose scale, and in the history of the inhabitants of Hyères. The Romanness of buildings and language has not been much affected by the invasions and other events which have passed over Provence, and if you are with older country people talking among themselves you will often get more of an impression of what they are saying by thinking in Italian rather than in French. Those who farmed near the important east–west road, the N7, which mainly follows the route of the Aurelian Way, recently were still calling it *lou camin aurélian*; 'N7' was newfangled and unnecessary.

Within four centuries (second BC–second AD) three religions were superimposed or grafted upon one another. The sacred places of the original peoples were generally connected with water, like the Goddess of the Green Water in the Gorges du Verdon area, or at springs that to this day may have medicinal qualities or were in strategic positions, like Gréoux and Riez. The Romans in turn had the same reasons for building temples to a god with an attribute linked to its predecessor; and as religious centres they would as naturally become Christian ones later. Buildings were adapted, innumerable Roman altars were (and are) used in Christian churches, old customs were altered, old names stayed in use, and if some of them became 'saint' we must bear in mind that 'saint' only meant good or holy, and not the searching process of canonization that we think of now. So we find Ste Victoire near Marius's victory; St Mitre of Aix, for long thought to be Mithras; the elusive St Siffrein of Carpentras, and the St Mors. Traditionally Mary Magdalene came to La Sainte Baume, and St Anne's body was brought to Apt; authentically St Honorat was at Lérins, and almost certainly St Patrick of Ireland too; St Augustine of

Gorges du Verdon   Douglas Dickins

Canterbury was certainly consecrated at Arles. How can we disentangle mythology, archaeology, legend and history? But an imprint of all this remains in traditional fêtes and place-names. Throughout the centuries the need was recurrently felt for an unswerving quality such as was expressed by the Cistercians: they have left Silvacane, Le Thoronet and Senanque for us to visit, but they are still active in the Abbey at Lérins.

Provence, very roughly, is an oblong with different ranges of mountains running from east to west, separated by valleys of varying widths. Geologically the ranges differ, so there is an amazing variety of skylines and coasts, of trees and wild flowers. At each end of this oblong, speaking even more roughly, is a triangle. In the west the Rhône delta and the Camargue form a unique area, a wild-life reserve with wild white horses and rice-fields. The east, in total contrast, is mountainous; formerly the *comté* of Nice, it was Italian until 1860, when it was ceded to France in return for help in bringing about the unification of Italy. Until then the frontier was still the river Var (on whose delta Nice airport is built) as it had been in Roman times. In 1947 there was another addition to France, the upper part of the Roya valley, where the roads from Nice and Ventimiglia meet to climb towards the present frontier at the Col de Tende, beneath which the road runs through a tunnel on its way to Piedmont and Lombardy, a main road to Turin. If we have used the term 'Italianate' of something prior to 1860 in this area, it should be remembered that it *was* Italian when made or built.

The whole of this triangle is very mountainous (it includes the sinister Mont Bégo, with the Vallée des Merveilles at its foot), and a remarkable aspect of it is the large number of fifteenth- and sixteenth-century paintings and frescoes to be seen in tiny villages and churches apparently perched on inaccessible crags or mountainsides. These villages can be visited by car now, but how hazardous it must have been then. Perhaps the natural dangers with which the villagers were surrounded, in addition to the political hazards, led them to fill their churches with the very best they could, situated as they were on the outer perimeter of the Renaissance in Italy. If the paintings of the Bréas are first encountered from the west of the river Var one might assume they were French, but they are Italian and so were the influences behind them.

Grasse, on the eastern fringe of Provence, was not under the rule of the Counts of Provence until the thirteenth century, having been self-governing, with a *podestà* modelled on Italian city states. The main trade was with Genoa; ruling families were often connected with Savoy and Italy, and to this day many families were originally Italian and still have land and relations in Piedmont. It was a frontier area, with its main connections to the east. The mountains behind have bare stone summits, almost white in the sun, in winter brushed with snow. The hilltop villages are perched against this backcloth – but a few kilometres to the west is the department of Var. Before long cork-oaks appear, the ground becomes more ochre and the light more gold, desolate post-stages have huge Romanesque gateways, and towards Draguignan and all the way to Orange you sense the real Provence. You feel it still at Arles, but then it dies away in the rice-fields and marshes of the Camargue.

Over this rough rectangle, between the sharply contrasted eastern and western triangles, lies a complicated grid of history. Before the Roman era Greeks had traded along the coast, but they rarely colonized inland and had no great effect on the peoples of the country. Ligurian tribes lived along the coast and in Italian Liguria, as it is called to this day. To the north and west were Celtic tribes, and between the two, through trade and inter-marriage, was a band of Celto-Ligurian culture. A network of roads to the Greek settlements on the coast soon developed, and the well graves at Cavaillon show the extent of trade throughout the Mediterranean at that time. When Provence was taken over by the Romans the original tribes became known as Gauls and the evolving culture as Gallo-Roman. The pre-Roman Celto-Ligurian period covered roughly 400 years, almost as long as the Gallo-Roman which began in the second century BC. The Roman occupation began when Marseille asked for help against nearby Celtic tribes, and Julius Caesar's total conquest of Gaul from 59 to 51 BC was followed by 300 years of great prosperity. The Province was born.

The Roman Empire declined slowly, and eventually into chaos. In the fifth and sixth centuries Vandals, Burgundians, Goths and Franks invaded, and from the eighth century onwards the Saracens did far more damage than their predecessors. It is surprising how extensive the Saracen invasions were. Though they were finally expelled from their stronghold at La-Garde-Freinet in 973 by the Count of Provence, coastal raids by Saracens, Barbary corsairs, Moors and sometimes Turks went on into the seventeenth century and beyond, slaving being the major object. Watch-towers, signal systems and the well-known hilltop villages were built.

The tenth-century struggle against the Saracens gave rise to a period of great and austere Christian faith which led to the foundation of many monasteries. Then came the time of the troubadours, the flowering of the Provençal language, and the tradition of courtly love. The twelfth and thirteenth centuries saw the passage of the Crusaders; and during the Albigensian Crusade Louis VIII of France stormed their stronghold at Avignon in 1226. Twenty years later the brother of Louis IX (St Louis), Charles of Anjou, married a daughter of Béranger V, Count of Provence, who left Provence to her in his will, signed at Sisteron. Charles and his successors thus became Counts of Provence. The fourteenth-century popes at Avignon were all French. Following them, the fifteenth-century 'Bon Roi René', René of Anjou, is remembered for the kindness and prosperity of his reign. He left Provence to his nephew, who in 1481 left it to Louis XI, and so to France. But the real Provençal, even today, still regards anyone born north of Valence – some put it further south – as *nordiste*. It seems to be all one whether they come from Lyon, Switzerland, Brittany, Great Britain, Calais or Belgium. Yet this outlook is very kindly to the innumerable foreigners who settle here.

All the same, Provençal history merges henceforth with that of France: the horrors of the Wars of Religion, notably in the Luberon area; Richelieu checking coastal defences; Louis XIV at Marseille; the Amiral de Grasse in a warship from Toulon blockading the British at Yorktown (and another Provençal admiral at Trafalgar); the Revolution and the *Marseillaise*; anti-clericalism accelerating the decay of the abbeys, but awakening interest in the preservation of Roman monuments; Napoleon, so nearly born British, commanding a coastal battery against the British at Toulon, riding across Provence to the Italian campaigns, driving down it to St-Raphaël for Elba, marching up the Route Napoléon in the 'Hundred Days'.

Avignon

There is a whole 'literature' of English eighteenth- and nineteenth-century travellers who kept diaries, who 'wintered', who built villas like palaces from Hyères to Nice; followed by the writers and the painters.* And it still goes on, because Provence is irresistible.

So evocative is the atmosphere that the cultures and events of 2500 years seem present *in* the present. Every few kilometres there is something to be seen from one of these periods; nor can we forget the World War I memorials with their appalling number of names, the Allies' cemeteries of August 1944 and the poignant memorial stones and plaques scattered the length and breadth of Provence marking the places where members of the Resistance were killed.

Medieval villages that had been virtually abandoned are now coming back to life due to better roads, tourism and the revival of craftsmanship. Yet in some ways craftsmanship seems never to have been interrupted. The glass at Biot is bubbly like so much Roman glass, and made with traditional Provençal techniques. At Vallauris pottery and ceramics are produced near the site of Roman kilns. Iron bars were wrought for medieval windows, and are still made for houses. The most modern ships are built on the site of Greek and Roman shipyards at La Ciotat. Wine . . . from Greek amphorae fished up from the sea-bed, from the vineyards of the Popes' Châteauneuf, today from the annual fair at Brignoles.

Plus ça change, plus c'est la même chose, but for one exception – water. The Rhône was always primarily used for transport, but the Durance was known as the 'Scourge of Provence' because of its alternating floods and dryness. The harnessing of this and other rivers, by the building of many beautiful barrages in the mountains and additional canals and reservoirs, has provided adequate water. In regions like Carpentras the once arid soil now produces flowers and succulent vegetables in profusion, and everywhere the hotels have running water.

* On this subject see: Patrick Howarth, *When the Riviera was Ours* (Routledge 1977), and Roderick Cameron, *The Golden Riviera* (Weidenfeld 1975).

Finally there are two Provençal traditions – difficult to put in a gazetteer but entertaining for visitors – which sum up much of the spirit of the people of Provence: the Fêtes and the Christmas Cribs.

Many villages and small towns fête their Patron Saint with the flowers or produce of their livelihood. On a superficial level there is the usual brightly coloured marquee, the shooting alleys, the nougat stalls, the dance music echoing through the night over a long weekend. But the real Fête is on Sunday, and may be as follows. First, mass is said in the marquee with the Patron Saint's statue on an improvised altar; blessed nosegays are distributed; then a brief ceremony at the war memorial followed by an *apéritif d'honneur* in the marquee, and sometimes by the dancing of the *farandole* in Provençal dress (with fifes and tambours, still made at Barjols); and in the afternoon the serious business of the *boules* contests. It is not a money-raising affair, it is the day which brings an often scattered community together to enjoy themselves. In larger towns, like Cannes, elaborate floats loaded with flowers and beautiful girls drive along streets strewn with mimosa. At Menton millions of oranges and lemons are built up on floats to illustrate a different theme each year. The greatest and best known is the *Nice Carnaval* preceding Lent – so enormous, so elaborate, so full of nonsense and gaiety that it really does have to be seen to be believed.

The cliffs near Cassis

Peter Baker

The hilltop village of Èze

Cribs were first made in Italy during the Counter-Reformation to encourage devotion, and were introduced to Provence early in the seventeenth century. Early ones were carved in wood, painted and gilt; followed by movable figures with wax faces and hands, sumptuously dressed over jointed metal forms, in the tradition of puppets and dolls. In the Revolution churches were closed, but a Marseille church sculptor made brightly coloured small clay figures to be set up at home – the Holy Family, angels, shepherds and kings, and also figures from every walk of life in Provençal costume. In churches today they may be arranged in a miniature landscape of the locality and connected electrically, so that houses light up, bakery ovens glow, millwheels turn with water and the church clock strikes midnight. From Christmas to late January it is worth going into any church to see if the Crib is antique, or waiting to be brought to life by a franc in the slot. Here and there, as at Fréjus and Les Arcs, the Crib is in place all the year. Last of all, there are sometimes *Crèches Vivantes.* An ample stable is prepared near the chancel; before Midnight Mass a procession enters the church, led by Mary and Joseph and followed by all the others who will make up the living Crib: the shepherd with his dog and sheep, another with a snowy lamb over his shoulder – and if the market gardener happens to be close behind with his large bundles of everyday vegetables then the lamb may be cautiously nibbling at a leek.

Provence: Gazetteer

David and Anne Lockie

AGAY-LE-DRAMONT, *Var* (7km E of St-Raphaël: 7–E5). The finest natural anchorage on the Estérel coast, the bay of Agay has been used as such since pre-Roman times: amphorae have been found in the bay and the Romans quarried blue porphyry nearby for columns. Rounding a wooded headland from the east, the first impression is of a lake, with the trees growing down to the shore in places and the red mountains rising behind. There is an annual fête at the end of July, with jousting in boats.

Beyond the western headland, the Dramont, a stone commemorates the 1944 landing of troops of General de Lattre de Tassigny and General Patch (commanding the American 7th Army).

AIX-EN-PROVENCE, *Bouches-du-Rhône* (6–E4). In pre-Roman times a federation of Celto-Ligurian tribes had its capital at Entremont, on a plateau 2½km N of Aix – where the excavations are worth visiting, for the town was unusually large and urbanized owing to the civilizing influence of nearby Marseille. In 123 BC, when Marseille appealed to Rome for help against its neighbours, the consul Caius Sextius Calvinus attacked and destroyed Entremont. The following year he established a small settlement of veteran legionaries at a spot nearby, called thereafter Aquae Sextiae in allusion to its many springs. Aix, to give the place its subsequent contracted name, was thus the first Roman settlement in Gaul.

The Romans had come to stay. In 102 BC, when Provence was invaded by a migratory barbarian tribe from N Germany, the Roman general Marius won an overwhelming victory over the invaders near Montagne Ste-Victoire (*see entry*).

Cours Mirabeau, Aix-en-Provence

Douglas Dickins

When Marseille lost its independence in 49 BC, its former territories were divided between Arles and Aix, which soon ceased to be a garrison town and became merely a resort noted for its thermal waters, as it is today. The Musée Granet (*see below*) contains a good collection of both pre-Roman and Roman remains, but visible traces of the Roman town are relatively few.

Occupied and plundered by Visigoths, Franks and Lombards in the 5th-c. and 6th-c., captured by Saracens in AD 731, Aix only began to come to the fore in the 12th-c. when the counts of Provence made it their capital. The university was founded early in the 15th-c. But the golden age of Aix really began with the later years of the reign of 'Good King René' (d. 1480), who encouraged popular festivals and introduced the muscat grape, mulberries and silkworms into Provence. He was a patron of letters, a lover of music and an ornament of chivalry. Nicholas Froment of Uzès was his court painter.

Although Provence was united to France on the death of René's heir (1482), Aix remained its capital and from 1501 to 1790 was the seat of its supreme court of justice, the *Parlement* – hence its many fine 17th-c. and 18th-c. mansions, mostly built by wealthy and ennobled magistrates. Mirabeau (1749–91), also a noble, who gave his name to the Cours Mirabeau, was to emerge as France's leading orator and statesman during the early stages of the Revolution. If Aix stagnated in the 19th-c., when it was a capital no longer, it has grown enormously since 1945, with a new industrial zone and a population of 120,000.

From the Place de la Libération, with its spectacular fountain, runs the celebrated COURS MIRABEAU, a broad avenue shaded by ancient plane-trees on the site of the former ramparts and now lined on one side by excellent shops, open-air cafés and a number of fine 17th-c. and 18th-c. houses. Note the Fontaine d'Eau Chaude and, at the E end, the Fontaine du Roi René. In the Rue Espariat the NATURAL HISTORY MUSEUM (with a notable collection of dinosaurs' eggs) has fine 17th-c. doors and woodwork. Other attractive mansions are in the Place d'Albertas, the Rue Aude and the Rue du Maréchal Foch. The 17th-c. HÔTEL-DE-VILLE, beside a 16th-c. clock-tower, has a fine entrance gate and houses a magnificent library, including King René's *Book of Hours*. The MUSÉE DU VIEIL AIX occupies yet another elegant mansion, while in the MUSÉE DES TAPISSERIES are 19 superb Beauvais tapestries.

The CATHEDRAL, N of the town centre, is an architectural medley ranging from 5th-c. Gallo-Roman to 16th-c. Gothic Flamboyant – a complete contrast to the enchanting Romanesque cloisters. It has particularly handsome W doors and a 5th-c. baptistry. Within, it is like another museum, containing the famous triptych of the 'Burning Bush' by Nicholas Froment, some more pictures of interest, a 5th-c. sarcophagus, a 15th-c. stone retable and, most impressive of all, a series of

Brussels tapestries woven for Canterbury Cathedral in 1511 but sold for a derisory sum during Cromwell's Protectorate.

Among Aix's other attractions the following should not be missed: the MUSÉE GRANET in the 17th-c. Priory of the Knights of St-John of Malta (note also their church, part of which dates from the 17th-c., where some Counts of Provence lie buried), which as well as its archaeological exhibits has a fine collection of French, Italian, Flemish and Dutch paintings, including works by Clouet, Le Nain and Cézanne; the PAVILLON DE VENDÔME, a 17th-c. country residence, containing 17th-c. and 18th-c. pictures and furniture; the ATELIER CÉZANNE, where the painter died in 1906, now both a memorial and a research centre; the MUSÉE PAUL-ARBAUD, with a fine collection of faience and a few good paintings and sculptures; the church of STE-MARIE-MADELEINE (17th-c.), with a 15th-c. triptych; the 17th-c. Fontaine des Quatre Dauphins; and the Fondation Vasarely, devoted to modern architecture.

Aix has a Palais des Congrès (housed in a large former chapel of the Pénitents Blancs), a casino, a theatre (built in the 18th-c.), 14 cinemas, 10 nightclubs, an excellent international music festival (July and August), a large University (Faculties of Letters and Law: the Science Faculty is in Marseille), and both Scandinavian and American university institutes. It is also renowned for its almonds.

ALPILLES, Les, *Bouches-du-Rhône* (14km NE of Arles: 6–E3). This range of miniature mountains, arid and craggy, sometimes ashy-grey, sometimes white, sometimes lilac in colour, seldom rises above 400m and is only 30km long. It is none the less impressively wild, with a peculiar haunting quality like the Cuillins on Skye which adds to the timelessness and mystery of monuments like Les Antiques (*see* Glanum) or places like Les Baux. In the ravines olive and almond trees can be found growing on the lower slopes. More rarely one encounters cypresses. Higher up, trees give way to scrub or coarse grass on which sheep have grazed for centuries. The summits of these miniature mountains are bare rock.

ANSOUIS, Château d', *Vaucluse* (16km SE of Apt: 6–D4). 14km E of Lourmarin (*see entry*), the Château d'Ansouis, a medieval fortress with 17th-c. additions, has the particular interest of a château always owned by the same family. There are beautiful interiors and remarkable hanging gardens. (Open every afternoon.) The Romanesque fortified chapel now used as village church was the medieval Salle de Justice.

ANTIBES, *Alpes-Maritimes* (7–E5). Although a very popular resort with numerous beaches and extensive harbour accommodation, Antibes has managed to retain an agreeable atmosphere of spaciousness, relaxation and dignity. First a minor

A.F. Kersting

Antibes

Greek trading post, then a flourishing Roman settlement, Antibes offers evidence of its prosperity in classical times in a few scattered Roman remains and in the collections in the Musée d'Archéologie (Bastion St-André) and the Musée Picasso, which contains not only the remarkable collection of Picasso's works presented by the painter himself after World War II, but many archaeological remains and Roman potteries. The 13th-c. château Grimaldi in which it is situated (the Grimaldi were lords of Antibes for centuries; *see also* Cagnes) is also the site for classical concerts in the summer.

In late Roman times Antibes became the seat of a bishopric, removed in the Middle Ages to Grasse and now established at Nice. The parish church, largely 17th-c., occupies the possible site of a Roman temple; its altar is believed to be of pagan origin. The church has a Romanesque apse and contains a polyptych of Our Lady of the Rosary attributed to the Niçois artist Louis Bréa.

The old town of Antibes with its tortuous narrow streets is full of atmosphere and interest. Unfortunately only the section of the town ramparts that faces the sea has survived intact

since the 16th-c.; being close to the river Var, then the French frontier, Antibes had by that time become a garrison town of considerable importance – note for instance the 16th-c. Fort Carré guarding both land and sea approaches to Antibes from the N.

On Cap d'Antibes there is a naval and Napoleonic museum. As a promising young artillery officer Napoleon was made responsible for inspecting Mediterranean coastal defences in 1794, and installed his mother and family in Antibes; later, on his dramatic return from Elba in 1815, he landed at Golfe Juan (*see entry*) but despite his efforts the garrison at Antibes refused to admit him. A little further inland the gardens of the Villa Thuret (a magnificent collection of exotic plants and a research centre) have also some historical interest, for it was there that the first eucalyptus seeds were planted when introduced from Australia in the 19th-c. Indeed the whole area inland W and NW of Antibes is famous for horticulture, especially roses, carnations and anemones. On the E side of the peninsula the chapel of Notre-Dame-de-la-Garoupe has been the haunt of sailors for centuries and contains some fascinating ex-votos from landsmen and seamen alike, ancient and modern, which have been offered either to fulfil a vow or in gratitude for deliverance from death. The statue of Notre-Dame-de-Bon-Port is still carried in procession between this chapel and Antibes late in June and early in July.

4km N of Antibes at La Brague, at the junction of the N7 and D4, is 'Marineland', with performing dolphins, sea-elephants, seals and a killer whale.

See also Juan-les-Pins.

APT, *Vaucluse* (6–D4). Apt lies directly over the site of the original Roman town; the Rue des Marchands, the E–W road beside the former Cathedral of St Anne, is about 4½m above the level of the Domitian Way at the main Roman crossroads in the town. The tradition is that the body of St Anne, mother of the Virgin, was brought to Apt, and this was the first sanctuary dedicated to her in France. The 11th-c. church, with a 14th-c. N transept, is built above two crypts (with Roman stonework), the lower containing two tombstones. This is characteristic of very early shrines with relics of particular importance. There are an unusual number of churches and chapels to St Anne throughout Provence. The chapel of St Anne here (NW corner of the Cathedral) was built in 1660 by Anne of Austria; it contains a reliquary bust, and in the sacristy of the chapel is a remarkable treasure of precious objects from the 11th-c. to the 14th-c. S of the church, the cellars of a number of houses, extending over 130m, are formed from a series of large rooms 9m long with huge communicating doors; of Roman construction, they were probably beside the Forum (*see* Arles, 'Crypto-Portiques'). The Baths lie below the Sous-Préfecture building, and a memorial inscription to Hadrian's horse was found in the courtyard of the Bishop's Palace when a well was dug in 1604.

There is an excellent archaeological museum, containing sarcophagi from the four Roman roads which served Apt; from the museum part of the Roman Arena can be visited underground.

Apt is known for its conserved and crystallized fruit, lavender, truffles, and the extraction of ochre.

ARCS, Les, *Var* (20km W of Fréjus: 7–E5). Centre of a wine-producing area, with a Roman bridge and extensive remains of a medieval village and château. The church contains a fine retable by Louis Bréa (1501) and a large, superbly imaginative electrically-operated crib.

3½km NE on the D91, the remains of the former abbey of La Celle-Roubaud are now private property, but the chapel of St Roseline is open to the public. It contains a 16th-c. rood-screen, 17th-c. gilded wooden retables, unusual modern stained-glass windows, and a bronze bas-relief by Giacometti tracing the saint's life.

ARLES, *Bouches-du-Rhône* (6–E3). When you first arrive in Arles, the huge bulk of the Roman Arena seems to block the end of every street. In the time of Julius Caesar, when the power of Marseille was reduced, Arles was chosen as the capital of 'The Province' (Provence). It was an important crossroads. The Aurelian Way from Rome skirted the walls to the N and crossed the Rhône by a bridge of boats, continuing to Nîmes and to conquered Spain. The Agrippan Way led to Lyon and the N, and to the S a canal was built to Fos (near Martigues), where there are vestiges of the Roman port; sea-going ships could pass along it, joining Arles to the sea and turning it into a port. Soon merchandise from the whole known world flowed through Arles. From 46 BC the Romans built on a rocky hillock emerging from the marshes; the Arena, Theatre and 'Crypto-Portiques' (*see below*) date from then. The Baths (originally adjoining the Palace) of Constantine, who spent some time in Arles, are 4th-c. A 75km aqueduct supplied a water-tower near the Arena and distributed water by three conduits: to the Baths, to fountains, and (on a metered system) to private houses.

The Arena, now lacking its third storey which held the posts to support the marquee-like covering (still complete at Nîmes), held 21,000 spectators; though it was an oval of 60 arches, the huge number of corridors and stairs enabled it to be emptied in five minutes. The height of the wall below the lowest seats indicates that there were regular contests with wild beasts, and the tunnels leading from the cages can still be seen. To give the spectators a better view of gladiatorial contests a raised wooden floor was added; the sockets to hold the supports are visible, high in the wall. This movable floor and the marquee-like roof seem incredible in a building about 135m long and over 100m wide. After the fall of the Empire it was transformed into a citadel with about 200 houses and a church inside it, using stone from the Arena. Three defence towers were added in the 12th-c. and these were left in position when restoration started in 1825. Today there are regular seasons of bull-fighting. The modern bull-fight developed directly from the widespread cult of Mithras, authorized by Julius Caesar, and practised in Roman Arles.

Very little remains of the original theatre (*see* Orange), but when you bear in mind that the two soaring pillars behind the stage are only a third of the original total height you realize that the scale was as monumental as that of the Arena. (Note the trench from which the curtain was pulled up.) Seating, constructed in the same way as in the Arena, was for nearly 7000 spectators, and the whole was covered by a similar 'marquee' roof. During the summer there are performances of operas and plays.

In the present PLACE DU FORUM two pillars with Corinthian capitals are seen against the wall of a hotel. The Place is not directly above the Roman

Arles: the Roman Theatre and Arena

Forum, but these pillars are the top of a temple that stood on its northern side. The street beside it leads S across the site of the Forum to the Place de la République, and here stands an obelisk of Egyptian granite, brought from the site of the Hippodrome, SW of the town, where it was used in chariot racing. To the E is a 17th-c. Jesuit church, now a museum of Christian Art (*see below*). Inside descend two storeys, passing 1st-c. water conduits and drains, to three huge galleries (three sides of a rectangle) known as 'Crypto-Portiques', the base of buildings round the Forum. In the northern gallery is the temple, the tops of whose pillars are in the present Place du Forum.

In the huge apse of the remains of the 4th-c. Baths note the now bare brickwork. This technique has been used throughout Provence in stone apses for 2000 years.

To the SE, neither the railway nor the factories can destroy the magical peace of LES ALYSCAMPS.

This wide path, once an important road on either side of which the Romans buried their dead, as was their custom, is bordered with sarcophagi. It was used for burials until the 12-c. The most interesting sarcophagi have gone, but the atmosphere remains. At the end is the church of St Honorat (*see* Iles de Lérins), who became Bishop of Arles.

St Augustine came to Arles to be consecrated as first Bishop of Canterbury in the Cathedral (now church) of ST-TROPHIME (Place de la République). Legend says that St Trophime was sent by St Peter to evangelize Provence, was first Bishop of Arles and lived at Montmajour (*see entry*). Originally Carolingian, the church was transformed in the 11th-, 12th- and 15th-c. The lower part of the façade is recognizably Carolingian, with 12th-c. work above. Superimposed is a remarkable 12th-c. doorway. Enter by the side door into a soaring aisle (rare in Provence): Romanesque nave, Gothic choir, font, 4th-c. sarcophagus, 17th-c.

Flemish paintings, tapestries, and ivories. The 12th–14th-c. cloister is, unusually, elaborately sculptured with saints, biblical scenes and foliated capitals; it has Gothic vaulting and is very beautiful.

Arles suffered terribly from invasions in the Dark Ages and from the Saracens. In the 9th-c. it was capital of the Kingdom of Arles including Burgundy and Neuchâtel, but in the 10th-c. it was bequeathed to the Holy Roman Empire. In the 12th-c. the burgesses chose to join the Counts of Provence and from then on its history became that of Provence.

Van Gogh lived and painted in Arles in 1888 and 1889 before voluntarily going into a mental home near St-Rémy (see St-Paul-du-Mausole). The houses he lived in were destroyed in World War II, but the famous bridge of Longlois has been copied at Port-de-Bouc.

The principal museums are:

MUSEUM OF CHRISTIAN ART (in the 17th-c. Jesuit church just W of the Place de la Cour): sculpture, sarcophagi, etc. found during excavations, thought to be the finest collection after the Lateran Museum in Rome.

MUSEUM OF PAGAN ART (situated in the 17th-c. church of Ste-Anne, in the Place de la Republique): exhibition of excavation finds of non-Christian statuary, mosaics, etc.

MUSÉE RÉATTU (near the river, in the former Grand Priory of the Knights of St John, a 15th-c. building that was part of the medieval wall overlooking the Rhône): 18th-c. paintings; 17th-c. Flemish tapestries; modern paintings, engravings and watercolours by Picasso, Gauguin, etc.; tapestries by Lurçat; sculpture by Zadkine, etc.

MUSEON ARLATEN (in a 16th-c. Gothic town house in the Rue de la République): 33 rooms devoted to all aspects of Provençal life; a museum created by the poet Mistral, who also worked for the restoration of Provençal as a language.

AURIBEAU-SUR-SIAGNE, *Alpes-Maritimes* (9km NW of Cannes: 7–E5). This medieval village perched on a hillock in a valley, clearly visible from D9, remains surprisingly unspoilt. Local handicraft – basket-work. Church 18th-c. with pyramidal tower, fine carved wooden pulpit and 15th-c. reliquary. 6km SW and approached by winding country lanes, the village of **Tanneron** and its environs command views of wooded slopes and valleys overgrown with mimosa. 2km NE on D9, the 18th-c. chapel of **Notre-Dame-de-Valcluse**, a well-known place of pilgrimage, has some interesting votive pictures and magnificent plane-trees.

AURON, *Alpes-Maritimes* (7–D5). Once a mountain hamlet, now a leading ski resort, superbly situated with an attractive 18th-c. church (Romanesque tower). But far more interesting is the Romanesque chapel of St-Érige with its three apses containing astonishing 15th-c. frescoes devoted to the lives of St Mary Magdalene (who, according to legend, settled in Provence), of St Denis (beheaded in Paris in about AD 250 and adopted as their patron by the kings of France) and of St Érige himself (Bishop of Gap in the late 6th-c. and particularly invoked against the plague, from which even a remote mountain village was not immune). These frescoes have an extraordinary primitive vitality. Perhaps the most arresting and powerful of them all is of a stern-looking Christ in Majesty, wearing a fantastic robe decorated with lions, griffins and eagles. (*See also* St-Étienne-de-Tinée.)

AVIGNON, *Vaucluse* (6–D3). Well situated for trade near the junction of Rhône and Durance, the Gallic tribal capital was certainly known to the Greeks of Marseille. In its heyday in Roman times it had an estimated population of 20,000, though it was probably far less important than Orange. External traces of the Gallo-Roman town are few and scattered, but plenty of Roman statuary and pottery has been unearthed – see the Musée Lapidaire in the former 17th-c. Jesuit chapel.

The earliest important sign of medieval prosperity and rebuilding is the ruined bridge, the PONT ST-BÉNÉZET (the 'Pont d'Avignon' of the world-famous song). Only four arches survive, but it was 900m long when it was built (12th–13th-c.) and was then one of the few stone bridges across the Rhône with those at Lyon, Vienne and Pont-St-Esprit upstream. It ended on the W bank by the Tour de Philippe-le-Bel (see Villeneuve-lès-Avignon); on one of its piers is the chapel of St-Nicolas, which is Romanesque below and Gothic above. But the bridge eventually ceased to be worth repairing, and most of it collapsed for the last time in the 17th-c.

The second token of Avignon's great importance in the 14th-c. is the great PAPAL PALACE. In the 13th-c. Avignon was a stronghold of the Albigensian heretics, and was stormed by Louis VIII at the Pope's behest. After their defeat the nearby Comtat Venaissin (see Venasque) became a Papal possession. Early in the 14th-c. intimidation by rival noble families prompted the Papacy to leave Rome, and Pope Clement V was persuaded by the French King, Philippe-le-Bel, to take up residence in Avignon. Clement was the first of seven Popes, all Frenchmen, to reside in Avignon (1309–77), though the city did not become theirs (by purchase) until 1348.

During these years Avignon became both an international capital and the focal point of Christendom. Pope John XXII (d. 1334), who features in Maurice Druon's novel *The She-Wolf of France*, took over and enlarged the episcopal palace, but few traces of these building activities survive owing to the far more ambitious projects of Benedict XII (d. 1342) and Clement VI (d. 1352) on the same site. The Papal Palace in fact consists of two large palaces juxtaposed and built by these two Popes in 20 years; the result is one of the most imposing medieval monuments in existençe.

The architecture of the Old Palace reflects the austerity of Benedict XII, a former Cistercian; that of the New Palace the flamboyance of Clement VI, a true Prince of the Church. Both palaces bear witness to the fabulous wealth of the medieval Papacy, for remember that they are now seen stripped of their past finery – except for some of the frescoes.

Passing through the Porte des Champeaux surmounted by Clement VI's coat of arms, one enters the Great Courtyard, where dramatic festivals are held in July. To left and in front are the wings of the Old Palace. On the ground floor the Salle du Consistoire, where the Pope conferred with his Cardinals and received distinguished visitors, is now hung with Gobelin tapestries; beside it, the chapel of St-Jean has frescoes depicting scenes from the lives of the two St Johns by Matteo Giovanetti, a protégé of the Sienese painter Simone Martini and Clement VI's court painter.

In the magnificent Banqueting Hall on the first floor are examples of Martini's exceptionally fine work, formerly in the Cathedral. Giovanetti's frescoes in the adjoining chapel of St-Martial include an extraordinary heavenly procession welcoming the saint's soul into Paradise. In the Pope's private apartments the study (fine tiling) and bedroom (wall decorations) are especially noteworthy. The Chambre du Cerf, so called because of its gay and lively murals depicting hunting scenes, is part of the New Palace and now thought to have been Clement's bedroom rather than his study. Clement VI's chapel, whose nave is nearly as broad as it is high, contains in the S sacristy casts of the tombs of Clement V, Clement VI himself, Innocent VI and Urban V. The beautiful vaulted Galerie du Conclave led to the Conclave below – the closed room or apartment in which the Cardinals were locked at each Papal election. At the top of the Great Staircase is the Indulgence Window from which the Pope gave his blessing to ·the congregation in the courtyard below. Clement VI's Grand Audience Hall, the most impressive state room in the Palace, is 50m long. Giovanetti's frescoes represent a series of Old Testament figures, mostly prophets. The Small Audience Hall was transformed into an arsenal in the 17th-c., when the murals were also executed.

Palais des Papes, Avignon

Douglas Dickins

Close by the Palace, the CATHEDRAL contains an archiepiscopal throne in white marble, the tomb of John XXII and frescoes by Simone Martini. Beside it the ROCHER DES DOMS, the great crag that dominates the rest of Avignon and commands a magnificent panorama, has been turned into a fine garden. The nearby PETIT PALAIS, whose guests included Cesare Borgia and François I, now houses an important collection of late medieval paintings and sculptures. Thanks to the highly cosmopolitan character of the Papal Court and its position on the trade route linking Flanders and Italy, Avignon developed a school of painting of its own during the 14th-c. After the Popes left Avignon in 1377 and returned to Rome, the city continued to prosper, and the Cardinal Legates, who administered Avignon and the Comtat Venaissin (*see* Venasque) on their behalf, continued their patronage of the arts. This explains the second, 15th-c., school of Avignonese painting, less Italian and more northern in inspiration (for examples outside Avignon *see* Aix *and* Villeneuve-lès-Avignon).

The Cardinal Legates continued until 1790, when Avignon and the Venaissin were annexed to France – hence the 17th-c. Hôtel des Monnaies, also on the Place du Palais, the fine 18th-c. Chapelle des Pénitents Noirs, the attractive 17th-c. mansions in the Rue du Four and Rue du Roi René, and above all the beautiful 18th-c. mansion housing the MUSÉE CALVET – one of the most attractive provincial museums in Europe with a particularly good collection of French paintings across the centuries. The churches mostly belong to earlier periods: St-Symphorien (15th-c.) contains fine painted wooden statues; St-Agricol (14th–16th-c.) has a fine porch; St-Pierre (14th–15th-c.) has superb Renaissance doors. Most worth visiting of them all, not only for its fine 14th-c. frescoes but also for its deeply moving 15th-c. relief of Christ bearing the Cross, is the church of ST-DIDIER. Note the agony upon the Virgin's face. This masterpiece was executed by Francesco Laurana, a Venetian of Dalmatian origin, and is one of the earliest Renaissance sculptures in France.

As a Papal possession Avignon became a natural place of exile for Jacobites, including at times the Young Pretender himself. Inevitably the town and its artistic treasures suffered severe damage from anti-clerical mob violence during the Revolution. It remains, however, a delightful, vivacious city, full of atmosphere. As for its 14th-c. ramparts, almost as well-known and inescapable as its palace and its bridge, their general effect is undeniably impressive, even if parts were rebuilt (rather than restored) in the 19th-c. by the architect Viollet-le-Duc. Innocent VI (d. 1362) would have thought well of them.

BANDOL, *Var* (6–E4). Well-known resort with casino and all other resort activities. Beaches, huge botanical gardens with outdoor and hot-house plants and numerous enclosures of exotic birds. Boat service to **Ile de Bendor**: beach, zoo, a museum of the sea, an exhibition of wines and spirits, and a reconstructed Provençal village.

BARCELONNETTE, *Alpes-de-Haute-Provence* (7–D5). Admirably situated over 1000m above sea-level, the town is said to owe its name to its foundation (1231) by a Count of Provence related to the Counts of Barcelona. From 1388 to 1713 it belonged to Savoy, thereafter to France owing to the prowess of James II's illegitimate son, the Duke of Berwick (1670–1734), in defending France's SE frontiers in the War of the Spanish Succession. (See statue.)

The medieval town layout is still discernible. Two museums. Ski stations at Pra-Loup, Sauze and Super-Sauze (1700m), Ste-Anne-la-Condamine, St-Paul-sur-Ubaye and Larche. To S and E the Cols d'Allos (2240m), de la Cayolle (2326m), de la Bonnette (2800m) and de Larche (1990m), all worth visiting. Mountain flora.

BARGÈME, *Var* (14km SE of Castellane: 7–D5). The highest village in the Var, Bargème huddles inside its medieval walls on a rocky outcrop. The château is mainly ruined; the medieval village was abandoned but is now being intelligently restored. The 12th-c. Romanesque church of St-Nicolas has a 15th-c. retable in low relief, and a 17th-c. wooden retable; also an early altar and font.

BARGEMON, *Var* (12km N of Draguignan: 7–E5). An old town in a green setting which has become very popular residentially, Bargemon still has 12th-c. gateways and part of the town walls which, most unusually, include a church. Shady squares and fountains contrast with medieval alleys. The 14th-c. church of St-Étienne has a doorway in Flamboyant style, a 17th-c. defensive tower, and three 17th-c. retables. The 17th-c. chapel of Notre-Dame-de-Montaigu contains a miraculous statuette of the Virgin brought from Flanders and is a place of pilgrimage.

BARJOLS, *Var* (6–E4). Barjols, beneath its ruined 12th-c. château, is known for its trees, its shady squares and its 33 fountains, of which the most beautiful is in front of the *mairie* shaded by the largest tree. Reputedly the largest plane-tree in France, it is over 12m in circumference. There are remains of the town walls and gates, and interesting buildings. The church, originally a Collegiate Church founded in 1060, was rebuilt in the 16th-c., but the Gothic façade has a remarkable 11th-c. or 12th-c. tympanum. Carved choir-stalls; 17th–18th-c. organ; remains of the cloisters. It is the only church in France where dancing still takes place, for the feast of St-Marcel (16 January) every fourth year. Also the only town to make *tambourins* and *galoubets*, the narrow drums and three-holed flutes or fifes of Provence which accompany Provençal dances.

BAR-SUR-LOUP, Le, *Alpes-Maritimes* (6km NE of Grasse: 7–E5). The birthplace of the Amiral de Grasse (*see* Grasse) to whose family the 16th-c. château belonged until the Revolution, although he was actually born in the château de la Valette in the valley below (private property). But the village is above all worth visiting for its 15th-c. Gothic church. In addition to a fine carved main door and a magnificent retable attributed to Louis Bréa it has a 14th-c. stoup and a 17th-c. painted wooden Crucifixion. Of the various paintings the most striking is the small 15th-c. panel showing the Dance of Death with commentary in Provençal, probably painted during an outbreak of plague.

BAUX-DE-PROVENCE, Les, *Bouches-du-Rhône* (6–E3). Perched on a high spur of Les Alpilles (*see entry*) the ruined castle of Les Baux, first mentioned in a document of AD 981, looks out over a great sweep of plain extending beyond Arles to the Rhône delta, the Camargue and the Crau. But approached by either of the two roads, hemmed in by barren limestone crags, the village remains invisible almost to the last. From the 11th-c. to the 14th-c. the seigneurs of Les Baux were one of the most powerful families in Provence. In its heyday Les Baux was a town of perhaps 3000 people; now it has little more than 300. Yet it was this decaying village which gave its name to bauxite, first discovered in the vicinity in 1822 and now the basic material of the aluminium industry. The local quarries, all within a few kilometres, are mostly no longer exploited.

If in the 13th-c. Les Baux became famous for its Courts of Love and as a meeting place for troubadours, in the late 14th-c. under Raymond de Turenne, Vicomte de Baux, it became a notorious bandits' nest. After a long and sanguinary career he was drowned while trying to escape across the Rhône (1400). In 1426, the

Les Baux-de-Provence

family having died out, the château passed to King René (*see* Aix), and after his death to the King of France.

During the Wars of Religion (1562–98) it became a Protestant stronghold under the de Manville family. In 1632 the castle and ramparts were demolished and the community heavily fined by Cardinal Richelieu who objected to factious and turbulent nobles and their private armies. The eagle's nest had been destroyed and has remained partially in ruins ever since.

Entering the village, note the 16th-c. Hôtel des Porcelets, the picturesque Place St-Vincent with a Romanesque church and the 17th-c. Chapelle des Pénitents Blancs, the former Protestant chapel (1571) attached to the Hôtel de Manville, and the old seigneurial bakery. Up the Rue de Trencat, hewn out of the rock stands the Tour-de-Brau containing the Lapidary Museum. Thence proceed to the end of the spur, the site of a monument to a Provençal poet, from which there is a superb view. On the other side of the spur stands the ruined château with its 14th-c. keep. Below it is the precipitous cliff over which Raymond de Turenne used to hurl those of his victims who could not pay ransoms.

BEAULIEU, *Alpes-Maritimes* (7km SW of Monaco: 7–D6). Its exceptionally sheltered situation was particularly appreciated in the 19th-c. when the British Prime Minister, the Marquess of Salisbury (1830–1903) built the Villa Léonine (planned by himself). James Gordon Bennett (1841–1918) proprietor of the *New York Herald* (who commissioned Stanley to find Livingstone), owned the Villa Namouna and founded the Hôtel Réserve. Note the Villa Kérylos, a painstaking reconstruction of a Greek villa built in 1900 by an archaeologist; it contains marbles, bronzes, mosaics, etc., and is well worth visiting.

BERRE, Étang de, *Bouches-du-Rhône* (6–E3). This vast salt-water lake NW of Marseille whose banks are now partly occupied by petrol refineries has otherwise changed remarkably little, apart from its canals, since prehistoric times when a brisk salt trade was carried on. In the SE note the subterranean Canal du Rove, 7km long and built in about 1920, but no longer used. On the S shore the drive along D5 and D49 beside the sea and across the Chaîne de l'Estaque is recommended. For the W shore *see* Martigues. On the N shore Miramas-le-Vieux with its 15th-c. church and ruined château offers a fine view of the lake, and the Pont-Flavien near St-Chamas is a remarkably fine Roman bridge from the 1st-c. AD. The site called 'Calissanne' or 'Oppidum de Constantine' on a stony hill E of St-Chamas should also be visited for its extensive traces of Ligurian and Roman occupation.

BEUIL, *Alpes-Maritimes* (7–D5). Now a winter-sports resort, Beuil has had a tumultuous history.

It once belonged to the Grimaldi family (14th–17th-c.) and as a result of their intrigues with the kings of France and their quarrels with their overlords, the Dukes of Savoy, one Grimaldi had his throat cut by his barber and another was strangled by two Moslem slaves. The 17th-c. church contains a painting of Louis XIII and religious works of art formerly in the Renaissance Chapelle des Pénitents Blancs.

The D28 road S from Beuil along the **Gorges du Cians** offers 20km of astonishingly variegated and precipitous rock-formations. Scenically they are the finest gorges in the Provençal Alps. 18km from Beuil along this road, a turning left on to D128 brings you by many twists and turns to the village of **Lieuche**, which is not only in a wonderful situation but is above all notable for Louis Bréa's lovely retable of the Annunciation (1499) in the church; the oratory in which Mary is praying is too small for the wings of the Angel Gabriel (clearly female), which are outside the window.

BIOT, *Alpes-Maritimes* (5km NW of Antibes: 7–E5). The clay in the vicinity of this delightful village with its 16th-c. gates and ramparts has made it a centre for pottery and ceramics since Antiquity, which today constitute a flourishing industry. The recently established glass-works can also be visited and purchases made.

The partly Romanesque church contains two fine late-15th-c. retables, one showing the wounded Christ, the other Our Lady of Mercy and treating the subject similarly to the painting at St-Martin-d'Entraunes (*see* Entraunes). The picture of Mary Magdalene in the adjoining panel is of exquisite beauty.

The museum here, specially built for the display of the work of Fernand Léger (d. 1955), is a remarkable piece of architecture designed to catch the maximum of sunlight. It was opened in 1967 and contains over 300 works by Léger, including not only paintings but also tapestries and mosaics.

BRIGNOLES, *Var* (6–E4). On the N7 (the Roman Via Aurelia) Brignoles, now an industrial centre, has been an important settlement since antiquity. Seat of the Comtes de Provence (also styled Kings of Naples, Sicily, Sardinia and Jerusalem) it lies in fertile agricultural land and is the most important centre for Provençal wine. Until the 16th-c. it was also famous for conserved plums, but during the Wars of Religion (when the town was occupied by Huguenots) the mob surged out and destroyed 180,000 plum trees; since then prunes of Brignoles have come from Digne. Latterly it has been the centre of the bauxite trade (*see* Les Baux). The earth and rock are deep crimson: sometimes in large areas, as at Brignoles, or in small isolated patches in a ploughed field or in a vineyard in some small valley.

Candelon marble has been quarried nearby since Roman times, when it was used to face baths and houses. More recently it was used to face the base of the Statue of Liberty in New York.

The old town, which had been abandoned, is being restored. A museum in the Palais des Comtes de Provence, a 10th–11th-c. château rising from the town's ramparts with a fine chapel, includes a famous 3rd-c. sarcophagus from nearby La Gayolle.

BRIGUE, La, *Alpes-Maritimes* (3km SE of Tende: 7–D6). 2½km from St-Dalmas-de-Tende by D43, this 13th–14th-c. mountain village beneath the ruined Lascari castle has typical Ligurian vaulted streets and alleys; a 14th-c. church with Lombard tower; two chapels; pictures by Bréa and Fossano. Ask at tourist office, hotels or M. le Curé for key of the chapel of **Notre-Dame-des-Fontaines**, 4km E, one of the most remarkable in the whole area. It is surrounded by springs, and still a place of pilgrimage. The simple exterior gives no hint of the vigorous 15th-c. frescoes within, the work of Jean Canavesi, a priest from Piedmont.

In the area: sheep rearing and manufacture of sheep's cheese. In July, the Fête of St-Éloi, with caparisoned mules.

CABRIS, *Alpes-Maritimes* (7km W of Grasse: 7–E5). A marvellous site overlooking a superb and extensive panorama. On fine days even Corsica is sometimes visible. Ruined château of little interest and a 17th-c. church that has suffered from modernization. Note medieval octagonal chapel to the W and Chapelle des Pénitents in the village itself. The D4 to St-Vallier runs through weird stony moorland with an ancient stone hut or *borie* (*see* Gordes) concealed in bushes on the E side of the road.

CAGNES, *Alpes-Maritimes* (7km S of Vence: 7–D5). Avoiding the noisy coastal road through Cros-de-Cagnes, the perceptive tourist will turn inland across N7 to the old town dominated by its elegant château, until 1789 owned by the Grimaldi, a branch of the present reigning family of Monaco, but now the property of the town. The original medieval structure was largely transformed in the early 17th-c., but the tower is a (regrettable) 19th-c. addition which does, however, offer a fine view. Both the Place du Château and the triangular interior courtyard deserve to be lingered over. On the ground floor some of the rooms are occupied by a museum devoted to the cultivation of the olive. Note the bas-relief in plaster on the staircase representing François I at the battle of Marignano and the early 17th-c. painted ceiling of Phaeton in the audience hall. The second floor houses a museum of 20th-c. paintings, some of them by artists of great distinction who have lived or worked in or around Cagnes.

At the N end of the picturesque old town, whose ramparts and entrance gates are still partly standing, stands the chapel of Notre-Dame-de-

Protection which deserves a visit, not least to see the apse with its delightfully naive frescoes by an unknown 16th-c. artist depicting scenes from the Life of the Virgin.

It was at Cagnes that the Impressionist painter Renoir (1841–1919) spent the last 13 years of his life, and his house, Les Collettes, reached by the Ave. Auguste Renoir, is now a museum. Standing on the heights opposite the old town and surrounded by olive trees, it contains some sculptures and canvases by the artist, in addition to a bronze Venus in the garden. There are also other more melancholy reminders of the great man who suffered increasingly from rheumatoid arthritis – photographs, his palette and the wheel chair to which he was prematurely confined.

CAMARGUE, La, *Bouches-du-Rhône* (S of Arles: 6–E3). In days of antiquity the Rhône delta's contours were less complex than those of today. It was occupied by countless little rivers and sea ports, traces of which have been found at Albaron on the Petit Rhône and at Fiélouse, La Trinité and Méjanes near the Étang de Vaccarès. This huge salt-water lake was then larger, more inland and

In the Camargue

Barnaby's Picture Library

more navigable than it is now, and the actual sea-coast ran in a more-or-less straight line from Le Grau-du-Roi in the W to Fos in the E. In short, half the present Camargue did not exist, although the area was already famous for its salt pans, and to a lesser extent – as today – for its bulls and horses.

The present-day Camargue, with its apex at Arles, consists of a vast, wide triangle of what was until recently simply salt marsh and lagoon. Now, however, the northern part has been drained, desalinated, irrigated and turned into extensive rice-fields. The southern part is an enormous natural park for bulls and the famous white horses, crossed by a few roads. The area round the Étang de Vaccarès is a reserve for migratory birds (including flamingoes in summer) which only accredited naturalists are allowed to visit, by special permission. The rest is divided into ranches where it is possible to spend a very good holiday

on horseback, preferably in the late spring so as to avoid the summer tourists, the mosquitoes and the winter Mistral.

See also Stes-Maries-de-la-Mer.

CANNES, *Alpes-Maritimes* (7–E5). First dis-covered as a watering-place in 1834 by Henry Lord Brougham, it was after 1860 that Cannes became firmly and permanently established as a fashion-able winter resort, visited by Queen Victoria, Edward VII, the Tsar and other crowned heads of Europe. Since 1890 the population has increased from about 19,000 to some 75,000 inhabitants. It was the British who were responsible for introduc-ing yachting, golf and tennis. The American impact dates primarily from 1918 to 1939, when Cannes became increasingly a summer resort.

The old village, known as Le Suquet and consisting of half a dozen streets straddling the hillock overlooking the main harbour, is domi-

Boulevard de la Croisette, Cannes

Douglas Dickins

nated by its church, Notre-Dame-d'Espérance, which takes its name from the 17th-c. gilt wooden statue of the Virgin, wearing a crown and holding an anchor, over the altar. Another statue, of the Virgin and Child, erected outside the church shortly after World War II, commemorates the town's deliverance from bombardment. There is a fine panorama, both from this spot and from the nearby medieval watch-tower beside what used to be the site of the parish church until the 17th-c. but is now occupied by an ethnological museum.

Modern Cannes stretches for over 6km along the coast, embracing several large harbours for yachts, two casinos and a succession of sandy beaches. The Bd. de la Croisette linking the two casinos may not be beautiful, and is certainly noisy during the tourist season with its incessant traffic, but the sophistication of its flower-borders and palm-trees, its smart shops and large and expensive hotels is undeniably impressive. Halfway along the Croisette, close to the British-owned Carlton Hotel, is the Palais des Festivals where the world-famous film festival is held annually – as are all sorts of other spectacles and activities. Not surprisingly, Cannes is well provided with cinemas. It has also long been associated with painting and the ballet. It is sad that the 19th-c. and early 20th-c. Cannes, which at its best had real charm (exemplified by the old railway station), and even at its worst had at least the merit of architectural individuality, is being obliterated by the relentless advance of purely functional blocks of flats.

Le Cannet, 2km N of Cannes, has partly retained a village atmosphere and a certain old-world charm, although it is linked to Cannes by a modern boulevard. There are some agreeable walks in the vicinity, some 18th-c. houses and – as a *pièce de résistance* – a riotously colourful 16th-c. church dedicated to St Catherine.

The view from the Observatory in **Super-Cannes**, 325m above sea-level and 3km NE by the Ave. Isola Bella, is in some respects rather chastening as well as impressive.

CARPENTRAS, *Vaucluse* (6–D3). Capital of the Comtat Venaissin (*see* Venasque) until the Revolution, and of the Vaucluse department since. The area was made fertile by a canal from the Durance and is now an important agricultural centre. The name comes from the Gallic word for a two-wheeled chariot; it was because of its industry of chariot-making that it was called the Chariot Town. Surrounded by a ring of wide boulevards replacing the ramparts, of which only the fine 14th-c. Porte d'Orange remains, the old town is unusually spacious, with many fine houses. See the beautiful Roman Municipal Arch behind the Palais de Justice (17th-c.), built as the Bishop's Palace, where rooms decorated with paintings (including a Mignard) can be visited. The Bishop's apartments communicated with a gallery in the Cathedral of St-Siffrein (*see* Venasque), who is

also associated with an important relic, the St-Mors ('holy horse-bit') said to have been forged from two nails of the Crucifixion by order of St Helena. The St-Mors is connected with much of the town's history, is its crest and was on the seals by the 13th-c. The Cathedral was begun in 1404; it has a Flamboyant S door (Porte Juive); an unusual classic Renaissance W front; fine gilt carvings, sculpture and paintings; and remains of an earlier Romanesque cathedral beyond the apse.

The Synagogue is the oldest in France. The Jews were financiers to the Popes at Avignon, and it is also thought there was already a Jewish colony here in Roman times. Rebuilt in the 18th-c., the Synagogue has a simple exterior and the magnificent interior can be visited; note the oven for unleavened bread and the purification baths.

There are several excellent museums: the fine 18th-c. Hôtel-Dieu with its original painted dispensary and a collection of Moustiers faience jars; Musée Comtadin (local interests); Musée Duplessis (paintings); Musée Sobirats (furniture and furnishings); Musée d'Archéologie; and an important library with 200,000 books and manuscripts.

To the E, on the N542, is a fine drive to the **Gorges du Nesque**, with a splendid view of the Rocher du Cire.

CASSIS, *Bouches-du-Rhône* (7km NW of La Ciotat: 6–E4). Cassis was much loved by the Provençal poet Mistral (*see* Arles: museums), and is known to many by the paintings of Vlaminck, Matisse, Dufy and Kayser. A typical Provençal fishing village, it is also famous for its fish foods, taken with the white wine of Cassis.

At the nearby Calanque de Port Miou, the white limestone (of which the coast is formed almost to Marseille) is quarried and was used to build certain parts of the Suez Canal.

Les Calanques is the name given to the coast W of Cassis, a *calanque* being equivalent to a fiord. It is a unique coastline of very beautiful and precipitous cliffs, and though it can be reached from inland on foot in 1–2 hours, more can be seen by taking a boat from Cassis or Port Miou.

CASTELLANE, *Alpes-de-Haute-Provence* (7–D5). Approached from the N by the Route Napoléon, N85 (*see entry*), there are fine views down on to Castellane, dominated by its remarkable rock and the spire of the chapel at the summit (glimpsed also when approached from the S). The church of St-Victor (12th-c. with 16th–17th-c. side aisles) was founded by the monks of the Abbey of St-Victor in Marseille. The little pilgrim chapel perched on the rock to the E of the village, Notre-Dame-du-Roc, can only be reached by a 1-hour circuitous walk; first ask for the key at the presbytery in Castellane.

CAVAILLON, *Vaucluse* (6–D3). In an exceptionally fertile plain on the N bank of the Durance,

Cavaillon is the largest market in France for distributing vegetables and fruit, above all melons. In Roman times the reverse of its coins was stamped with a Horn of Plenty. A trading centre only 60km from Marseille, it was in an important position where both the Celtic and, later, Roman N–S and E–W roads crossed the Durance. There was a well-organized ferry service of rafts surrounded by inflated skins: a bas-relief of one of these ferry boats – loaded with Celtic barrels, previously unknown to the Romans – was found to the S of the town (and is now in the Musée Calvet, Avignon). The far-flung nature of the trade at that time can be deduced from the collection in the Musée Archéologique of orange pottery and Egyptian objects found in ancient well graves N of the town. Its importance as a trading centre (surpassing Marseille for a brief period) gave it a privileged status, as can be seen on the Roman Arch in the Place du Clos by the absence of captives and the native Cavares tribesmen wearing the tunics of free men.

The church of Notre-Dame-et-St-Véran, formerly the Cathedral, was originally Romanesque but progressively enlarged from the 14th-c. onwards; the façade is 18th-c. Inside, gilt wood carvings, paintings by Mignard and Parrocel, and 17th-c organ; Romanesque cloister.

CHÂTEAUNEUF-DE-GRASSE, *Alpes-Maritimes* (7km E of Grasse: 7–E5). Perched on a hill close to the D2085 in a landscape reminiscent of Tuscany, this unspoilt village with its stepped streets, alleys, ramparts and bell-tower offers pleasant views in every direction. The 15th–17th-c. church has fine 18th-c. retables. The Chapelle de la Trinité, a place of pilgrimage, is from the 11th-c.

Roses and jasmine are cultivated in the area of Châteauneuf and Opio nearby, which is smaller and less sophisticated, with a well-restored 12th–14th-c. church on a Roman site, and a 17th-c. house that used to be the summer residence of the bishops of Grasse (private property now).

2km S, in the heart of the country, the site of **Notre-Dame-de-Brusc,** one of the most beautiful and peaceful in all Provence, dates back to pre-Roman times as a meeting place and burial ground of the Ligurian tribes, for whom the spring of water, reputed miraculous in Christian times, was of religious importance. There are remains of the wall of a Roman camp, and sarcophagi and steles witness to the continued use of the burial ground. The first Christian church with its separate baptistry dated from 5th–6th-c. and is the only known example in Provence of a baptistry in the countryside, indicating its continued importance as a traditional meeting place and centre of pilgrimage. The church was rebuilt in the Dark Ages, and again in the 11th-c., stones from the earlier churches and Roman remains being used, and the nave and side aisles extended to join the baptistry. In the 17th-c. the baptistry was

converted into a porch, so that its original structure and use are no longer apparent, but as the section of the nave which joined it to the restored part of the church is now in ruins (as are the side aisles), the whole demonstrates remarkably clearly the evolution in reverse of so much religious architecture in Provence over 1500 years. The interior is a good example of 11th-c. austerity, a surprising impression of both width and height deriving from the flattened, rounded arches of the vault and the stilted arches along the side walls. Though these have now been filled in, the masonry of the arches remains, as do the square tapering piers of masonry which support them. The chancel is raised above the crypt and is supported from below by a row of rounded arches on the same square piers, the whole lower half of one of them being a Roman stele with the inscription still clear, but inverted, as was the custom when using pagan inscriptions in Christian buildings, in order to 'neutralize' the words. Other inscribed stones are to be seen in the ruined portion of the nave.

CHÂTEAUNEUF-DU-PAPE, *Vaucluse* (8km S of Orange: 6–D3). The remains of the keep of the Popes' summer residence dominate the vineyards which were their personal property. From it the roofs of the Papal Palace at Avignon can be made out against the jagged skyline of Les Alpilles to the S. In 1923 the vine growers made history by successfully applying to the Courts for definition and regulations in order to have the sole right to call their wine Châteauneuf-du-Pape. This led the way to the organization throughout France of certified designations (*appellation contrôlée*). Wine may be sampled and bought on the spot.

CIOTAT, La, *Bouches-du-Rhône* (6–E4). Originally a Greek port, La Ciotat is now the site of most modern dockyards in France. Happily the charming old fishing port is preserved. Excursions to the Ile Verte. To the W, between Cap Canaille and the Grande Tête, are the highest cliffs in France (about 400m); cliff road with panorama of Les Calanques (*see* Cassis). La Ciotat Plage is 1½km E. Further E, on N559 at St-Cyr, is a Roman villa and an archaeological museum.

CONTES, *Alpes-Maritimes* (11km NW of Monaco: 7–D6). This fortified village, attractively-situated and surrounded by mimosa, should be visited for its Italianate 16th-c. church and its predella (*c.* 1525) devoted to narrative scenes from the life of St Mary Magdalene.

CRAU, Plaine de la, *Bouches-du-Rhône* (NW of Istres: 6–E3). A fascinating bare and stony plain criss-crossed by canals, some constructed for irrigation, others for industrial purposes. Parts of it are planted with fruit trees; like the Camargue, however, it is exposed to the Mistral and hence planted with a great number of cypresses. To see it at its most primeval, take the N568 NW from the Golfe de Fos.

DIGNE, *Alpes-de-Haute-Provence* (6–D4, D5). Capital of the department and a thermal station (especially for rheumatism) roughly equidistant from Marseille, Avignon, Nice and Grenoble. Digne, which is on the Route Napoléon, is the setting of the opening chapters of *Les Misérables* (the bishop's Candlesticks). Note the lavender, local museum, sombre Cathedral.

DRAGUIGNAN, *Var* (7–E5). Draguignan occupies an open position which allowed the building, early in the 19th-c., of wide boulevards with avenues and gardens by two Prefects, Baron d'Azémar and Baron Haussmann, giving it the handsome air of a Préfecture. The town was recently demoted to a Sous-Préfecture (Toulon is now the departmental capital) but the archaeological and other archives happily remain. Its antiquity is shown by Celto-Ligurian sites on nearby hilltops. 1km NW is a remarkable dolmen like a three-legged table 2m high and weighing 40 tons (Pierre de la Fée).

The medieval town clusters below the Tour de l'Horloge with its fine ironwork campanile (not of Roman origin as often thought), on the site of the original keep. Remains of ramparts and two fine gateways: medieval and Renaissance houses. Note the Synagogue with fine 13th-c. façade. Several chapels of varying dates and interest. Museum: archaeology, Italian and Flemish paintings, and a library of manuscripts from the 14th-c.

ENTRAUNES, *Alpes-Maritimes* (13km SW of Auron: 7–D5). Each of the villages of Entraunes, St-Martin-d'Entraunes and Châteauneuf-d'Entraunes, has a church or chapel containing examples of 16th-c. religious painting that make it well worth visiting. In Châteauneuf, despite its remote situation overlooking a wild valley, is a remarkably sophisticated retable of the Five Wounds of Christ, perhaps by François Bréa; most unusually, Christ is represented not on the Cross but standing half naked before it, a red cloak about his shoulders, displaying his wounded hands. The elaborately decorated gold framework adds to the beauty and impact of this astonishing work. The mural at Entraunes in the Chapelle St-Sébastien, depicting the saint's martyrdom, is less accomplished, but its very naivety adds to its charm. The retable at St-Martin devoted to the Virgin, by François Bréa, the most traditional of these three works in its treatment of its subject, shows her being crowned by angels as Queen of Heaven, while on either side of her a pope, bishops and clergy, an emperor, two queens and a king with laymen, are gathered beneath her outspread cloak.

ENTRECASTEAUX, *Var* (18km NE of Brignoles: 6–E4). Medieval village in a valley between wooded hills. Remains of a Gallo-Roman aqueduct, fountain and bridge over the Bresque; also a 13th-c. bridge. Fortified Gothic church with side aisle over vaulted street. The 17th-c. château, with gardens by Le Nôtre, can be visited. Chapels: Ste-Anne, with picture by Van Loo: des Pénitents Blancs, with very old retable; Notre-Dame-de-l'Aube, 12th-c. with 17th-c. retable.

ENTREVAUX, *Alpes-Maritimes* (7–D5). A very spectacular site. Entrevaux is virtually the only fortified strongpoint in SE France to have remained intact since the 17th-c. when the river Var was the frontier between France and the dukedom of Savoy; the impressive fortifications (1695) were the work of Vauban, Louis XIV's great military engineer. Entrevaux was the seat of a bishopric until 1789. The bell-tower of the former cathedral was built by the Knights Templar. Note the fine retable, choir-stalls and wood-carving in the sacristy, all 17th-c. as is the church itself, which has a rich collection of antique silver church ornaments. Picturesque medieval houses, and an interesting historical museum (Musée François I).

ESTÉREL, Massif de l', *Var* (10km SW of Cannes: 7–E5). The view of the Estérel from Cannes is one of the great views of Europe, and one of the most famous. It is beautiful in all weathers, clear-cut, or in silhouette at sunset, or a hazy symphony in grey. This is due to the way in which the particular rock has eroded. The same age as the Massif des Maures (*see entry*), the Estérel is volcanic rock, mainly red porphyry though there are other colours at intervals. In 1964 much of the pine and oak forests were destroyed by fire, and every detail of the extraordinary shapes into which the rock has worn from summit to sea-bed can be clearly seen, thanks to the coastal road N98 built by the Touring Club in 1903. In the interior, with an enormous variety of wild plants, there are vestiges of prehistoric remains, mines and quarries. The Roman Via Aurelia (Rome to Arles) ran along its northern flank and has evolved into the N7, the most important E–W through-road until the completion of the A8 autoroute during the 1970s. For many centuries it was mainly inhabited by highwaymen, thieves and escaped convicts, who could evade capture indefinitely in this rocky wilderness, and it was so dangerous that many travellers preferred to go by sea.

ÈZE, *Alpes-Maritimes* (10km W of Monaco: 7–D6). The most famous example of a Riviera hilltop village which owes its startling situation (over 400m above the sea) to the need for defensive retreats from the Saracen slave-hunting raids. It can only be entered on foot. There are superb panoramas of the Riviera coast but the houses are much restored and everything is very commercialized.

18th-c. church, three chapels, a botanical garden, and small museum. Connected with Èze-sur-Mer by a cliff path.

FONTAINE-DE-VAUCLUSE, *Vaucluse* (5km E of L'Isle: 6–D3). Doubly famous: for the poet Petrarch (1304–74) who lived there for 16 years after he left the Papal Court at Avignon (*see* Senanque), and for the fountain where the river Sorgue emerges from a grotto at the foot of a natural curve in the cliffs. Barred by a ramp of rock and stones, the water percolates through it in the dry season, but it is preferable to visit it in the wetter seasons by afternoon light when the river surges in a tumultuous cascade over the barrier.

There is a *son-et-lumière* in summer; a speleological exhibition with stalactites, etc.; a museum on the reputed site of Petrarch's house containing books by or about him, also engravings; an 11th-c. church; and a fine view of the site from the 13th-c. ruined château of the bishops of Cavaillon. The commemorative Column to Petrarch was erected in 1804, to mark the 5th centenary of his birth.

FORCALQUIER, *Alpes-de-Haute-Provence* (6–D4). Gets its name from its ancient lime-kilns (Latin, *Furnus-Calcarius*; Provençal, *Fourcauquié*). It surmounts a hill surrounded by surprisingly gentle country and has a most charming cemetery descending the hillside, divided by huge clipped yew hedges into terraces connected by arches reminiscent of an Elizabethan garden. The church of Notre-Dame dominates the main square with a museum nearby.

The 12th–13th-c. early-Franciscan monastery (Couvent des Cordeliers) can also be visited. Fine panorama from the modern chapel on the site of a former château. The Observatory of Haute-Provence is 13km SW; the choice of the site was due to the exceptionally pure atmosphere of the region. (It is open to visits occasionally, at advertised times only.)

FRÉJUS, *Var* (7–E5). Founded by Julius Caesar in 49 BC, perhaps as a transit camp during the siege of Marseille, Fréjus owes its transformation into an important naval base to his successor Augustus. It is said that the 140 warships he captured from Antony and Cleopatra at the battle of Actium (31 BC) were subsequently stationed there; but the sea has since receded and the former Roman harbour is now beach or dry land, traversed by a railway. The so-called 'Lanterne d'Auguste' probably marked the S side of the harbour entrance, which was joined to the sea by a canal. On the Butte St-Antoine were, conjecturally, a citadel and a lighthouse, and the remains of baths by the Porte d'Orée, and of quays and walls elsewhere, confirm the existence of a sizeable port with a possible circumference of 2km.

The ramparts of the Roman town, originally colonized by veteran legionaries, had an estimated length of about 3km. The amphitheatre, outside the walls and less impressive than that at Arles, seated approximately 10,000 people. Bull-fights and other spectacles are frequently held there during the summer, in particular on 15 August.

The main street ran from the Porte de Rome to the Porte des Gaules and probably formed part of the Aurelian Way, which followed the coast past Agay before it turned inland after Fréjus and ran up the Argens valley. The theatre (its remains are worth visiting) stood in the NE quarter, while an elevated platform S of the Porte de Rome, where a broad street has been excavated, was the administrative centre and occupied by a garrison. Water supplied by the aqueduct (ruins are close to the N7 near Porte de Rome) came from a spring near Mons (*see entry*), over 40km N.

The 5th-c. baptistry attached to the Cathedral belongs to the late Roman Empire and is one of the most interesting early Christian monuments in France (*see* Aix, Riez *and* Venasque). Baptism was then administered by bishops, like confirmation nowadays, and reserved for adults. Candidates, who were expected to fast and observe a vigil beforehand, would be dressed in a white tunic. Before baptizing them the bishop, following Christ's example, washed their feet and after immersion anointed them with holy oil – all of which explains the baptistry's distinctive features and existence as a separate structure at a time

The Cathedral and baptistry, Fréjus

A.F. Kersting

when St Patrick was perhaps visiting the Iles de Lérins (*see entry*).

The Cathedral, partly 10th-c. but mostly 12th–13th-c., has the same atmosphere of devout simplicity; but there the resemblance ends. Seen through an exceptionally tall and narrow archway, the broad vault above the nave is supported by massive blocks of masonry in contrast to the Roman pillars of the baptistry. Note the Baroque altar-piece with Christ-child wearing a boy's full-skirted dress of the period. Over the sacristy door with a Renaissance lintel is a fine 15th-c. retable. The elegant cloisters, formerly reserved for the canons of the Cathedral, lead to Fréjus Museum, extremely rich in local remains. Other buildings worth visiting include the Hôtel-de-Ville, once the Bishop's Palace, the church of St-François-de-Paule (patron saint), and the chapel of Notre-Dame-de-Jérusalem at La Tour de Mare (4km NE) with frescoes and stained glass by Cocteau. On the N outskirts are a pagoda and mosque built during World War I.

10km N at **Malpasset** in picturesque surroundings is the site of the former barrage which collapsed in December 1959, causing extensive damage to the W part of Fréjus and the loss of over 400 lives. The new barrage is further N at St-Cassien (*see entry*).

For other places of interest around Fréjus, *see* St-Raphaël.

GARDE-FREINET, La, *Var* (14km NW of St-Tropez: 7–E5). Spacious village dominated by its ruined Saracen castle (1 hour on foot, magnificent views from Alps to sea). The Saracens occupied it for almost a hundred years (AD 888–973), and from it they pillaged the surrounding countryside. It was their last stronghold in the Massif des Maures (*see entry*). In compensation they brought an increased knowledge of medicine and introduced the use of the bark of the cork-oak; the making of corks is a principal occupation in the village to this day.

GIENS, *Var* (6km S of Hyères: 6–E4, E5). Separated from Hyères by an isthmus formed by two sand bars, between which are salt-pans and a marshy lake, the peninsula of Giens may have been an island in antiquity. In the centre of it is the small town of Giens, with marvellous views of the surprisingly deserted coast and the Iles d'Hyères (*see entry*) from the site of the ruined château.

Continue SE to the hamlet of **La-Tour-Fondue** (Cardinal Richelieu had the tower built for defence) for the boat service to the island of Porquerolles (crossing 20 minutes).

GIGONDAS, *Vaucluse* (15km E of Orange: 6–D3). Its original name meant 'jocund' – a merry place – from the Latin *jocundum*. The extensive vineyards surrounding Gigondas were developed early in the 14th-c. by the bishops of Orange; generally red, the wine is spirited with a good

bouquet and keeps well (and is for sale here). There is an interesting little 11th-c. chapel.

GLANUM, *Bouches-du-Rhône* (1¼km S of St-Rémy: 6–D3, E3). Glanum is the most extensively excavated classical settlement in Provence. (The site is on the E side of D5, just S of St-Rémy.) Originally built by a Celto-Ligurian tribe, the Glanici, on the site of a primitive sanctuary, it provides a striking example of the cultural influence exercised inland by the Greek colony of Marseille before the Roman occupation. Although never a Greek possession, Glanum was almost certainly developed as a staging post for trade between Marseille and the hinterland, for there are traces of several Greek-style houses and public buildings. But the visitor will have difficulty in distinguishing them from the later and more extensive remains of Roman buildings without consulting the plan in the official guide.

The Roman occupation resulted in the construction of a wider main street and more imposing buildings: baths with courtyard and covered galleries on three sides, as well as a swimming pool; a forum and basilica or public hall, and two temples; a monumental fountain; a temple dedicated in 20 BC by the Emperor Augustus's son-in-law Marcus Agrippa to Valetudo, goddess of Health; and a sanctuary of Hercules with six stone altars.

This flourishing peaceful settlement with its abundant water supply, and built with stone obtained from nearby quarries, makes no appearance in history, probably because it was regarded primarily as a hill station cum health resort. It was destroyed by barbarian hordes in the 3rd-c. AD and later succeeded by St-Rémy (*see entry*).

However, the two celebrated monuments known as **Les Antiques,** on the other side of D5, have miraculously survived, though they were evidently on the outskirts of the town. Both date from about 20 BC. The triumphal arch is certainly the oldest of its kind in Provence, a noble monument even though the top is missing, reducing its height by half. The mausoleum beside it was probably erected by local dignitaries of Roman descent, perhaps the first Romans of noble descent to settle in Glanum. Within, beneath the cupola, are the statues of two male figures wearing togas. Scenes in bas-relief, admirably carved, include tritons and other marine creatures, a cavalry battle, a combat between Amazons, a boar-hunt and an infantry battle around a dead warrior. Note also on the E side the four masques of theatrical comedy (maiden, old man, slave, and young man). It is the most mysterious, evocative and beautiful Roman monument in Provence.

GOLFE-JUAN, *Alpes-Maritimes* (3km W of Antibes: 7–E5). The place where Napoleon landed with about a thousand men on 1 March 1815 on his return from Elba – an event which is

Gordes

commemorated by a memorial beside the harbour and a plaque which marks the starting point of the Route Napoléon (*see entry*).

From the insignificant hamlet which it then was, Golfe-Juan has grown to an important seaside resort with a population of 6000, with a fine beach over 3km long and all the usual seaside amenities. The town forms part of Vallauris (*see entry*), famous for its pottery. The actual gulf is one of the finest roadsteads on the Côte d'Azur.

GORDES, *Vaucluse* (12km E of L'Isle: 6–D3). Built on a picturesque hillside site, with stone houses and streets climbing steeply to a large church and a Renaissance château. The château retains two towers, a gateway and sections of ramparts, and provides a magnificent panorama embracing the ochre hills to the E (*see* Roussillon), the Luberon range and the Durance valley to the S, and Les Alpilles to the SW. A town of character, with a spacious main square.

W of Gordes are a remarkable number of stone huts known as *bories* grouped in hamlets, surrounded by one, two or three walls. Though *bories* may be pre-Roman, it is now thought that these groups may be the 16th–17th-c. equivalent to caravan sites in which town dwellers took refuge from the plague.

GOURDON, *Alpes-Maritimes* (9km NE of Grasse: 7–E5). This astonishing eagle's nest, dominating both the splendid Gorges du Loup (which should be explored N to Gréolières), and a vast panorama S and E to the sea, is linked to Pont-du-Loup across the gorge by a delightful footpath. The 13th-c. château, restored 17th-c., reputedly built on the site of a Saracen stronghold, has a museum and a terraced garden designed by Le Nôtre. The D12 to the NW crosses the fantastic rocky Plateau de Caussols (over 1000m above sea-level), where vestiges of prehistoric dwellings are to be seen.

GRASSE, *Alpes-Maritimes* (7–E5). Although never a Roman settlement, this health resort and world-famous centre of the perfume industry has a long history. From 1138 to 1227 the town was a thriving miniature republic on the medieval Italian model, and throughout the Middle Ages, when its main industry was tanning, Grasse's closest commercial relations were with Genoa. In the middle of the 12th-c. the bishops of Antibes installed themselves in Grasse, which was to remain the seat of a bishopric, except for the French Revolutionary period, until 1823. The town's importance remained unaffected when Provence was absorbed into France in 1482, despite the occasional passage of foreign invading armies, especially during the wars of the 18th-c.

The rise of the Grasse scent industry was closely connected with tanning, due to the 16th-c. fashion for scented gloves. By the 18th-c., when a Grasse perfume manufacturer actually opened a shop of his own in far-away Paris, scent manufacture had replaced glove-making as the main industry. Cultivation of jasmine and the tuberose had already been introduced into the surrounding countryside in the 17th-c.; to these were subsequently added lavender, mint, roses, orange-flower and, more recently, chemicals. Since the 18th-c. Grasse's world supremacy in scent production has never been challenged. Several of the larger scent factories welcome visits by tourists – notably Molinard and Fragonard.

Close to the Fragonard factory is the Musée d'Art et d'Histoire de Provence, in an 18th-c. mansion. The museum contains some fine pieces of faience, notably from Moustiers-Ste-Marie (*see entry*), antique scent bottles and other objects connected with the industry, and, in the basement, an interesting collection of costumes, agricultural implements, kitchen furniture, utensils, etc., illustrative of Provençal life in past centuries.

Nearby to the S is the elegant Villa Fragonard, a late 17th-c. house recently transformed into a museum and containing several examples of the work of the painter Jean-Honoré Fragonard (1732–1806), perhaps Grasse's most famous citizen. There is a charming statue of him in the tiny Square du Clavecin, shaped like a harpsichord, near the Place du Cours, commanding a fine view S. Note also an early religious painting by him in the Cathedral, which contains in addition three canvases by Rubens and a triptych devoted to St Honorat, the patron saint of Grasse, by the Niçois artist Louis Bréa (1443–1520).

Quite apart from these paintings, the largely 12th-c. Cathedral deserves to be visited in its own right. Like Durham Cathedral its dominating site and uncompromising aspect seen from without and the rude massive pillars within remind one of the Church Militant, notwithstanding 18th-c. alterations or additions. In the Cathedral precincts note the Musée de l'Amiral de Grasse* – a remarkable little museum created by private initiative which cannot fail to appeal to anyone interested in naval history, charts, maps, engravings of naval battles, models of 18th-c. ships, etc. De Grasse (1722–88), who was born at Le Bar-sur-Loup (*see entry*), was one of France's most illustrious sailors. He contributed directly to the defeat of Britain in the American War of Independence by blockading the British Army from the sea at Yorktown, Virginia, in 1782, thus compelling it to surrender – an event still commemorated annually in a public ceremony attended by French and American representatives.

Subsequently defeated by Rodney, de Grasse was taken prisoner to London, where he was much fêted and admired.

No visitor to Grasse should omit to explore the old quarter of the town, which is of exceptional interest. Conducted tours are organized during the tourist season by the Syndicat d'Initiative (Place de la Foux). Near to its offices is the recently built Centre International where exhibitions and concerts are sometimes held. 4km NW on N85 is the Maison de Jeunesse et de Culture, with an Olympic swimming pool.

GRÉOLIÈRES, *Alpes-Maritimes* (14km NW of Vence: 7–D5). Although now best known for its ski-station to the N (1340m), Gréolières not only commands fine views over the river Loup and surrounding mountains but is also a village of historic interest. In addition to its ruined château, note the Romanesque church above the village in Haut-Gréolières and, in the parish church, a wooden statue of the Virgin and the 15th-c. retable of St-Étienne. Like Coursegoules to the E, with its prehistoric and Roman remains, Gréolières was on the Roman road Vence–Castellane.

GRÉOUX-LES-BAINS, *Alpes-de-Haute-Provence* (6–D4). The oldest health spa known. Its warm, sulphurous spring is renowned for the treatment of rheumatism, arthritis and breathing difficulties. The spa is reputed to have been in use in pre-Roman times, and the gardens of the modern establishment contain a Roman votive inscription to water nymphs. Views from site of 14th-c. château.

GRIMAUD, *Var* (10km W of St-Tropez: 7–E5). Both the old village and the new port on the gulf of St-Tropez are to some extent show places. Both are well worth visiting.

The ruins of the château dominating Grimaud are at their most impressive when seen from the chapel of Notre-Dame-de-la-Queste, 2km E on the D14. Standing just off the road and surrounded by meadows and trees like a natural park, this ancient chapel (which has a fine retable and a much-venerated statue of the Virgin) is normally closed but remains a place of pilgrimage and, on 15 August, of festivity. In Grimaud itself is a Romanesque church dating back to 1020; close to it stands the arcaded Maison des Templiers. Note, nearby, the superb nettle-trees (*micocouliers*), indigenous to Provence.

Port Grimaud (5½km E on D14), mostly constructed over the past ten years, is an astonishing creation by an Alsatian architect, François Spoerry. In its layout the port is a miniature Venice, built essentially for owners of sailing craft who can afford to have a house built here in accordance with the tradi-

* Plans are in hand to transfer this museum to the Hôtel de Pontèves in the Bd. du Jeu-de-Ballon.

tional Provençal style of architecture but with all modern amenities. The port has its own (interdenominational) church, shops, bank, hotel, cafés, post office, etc., and can accommodate up to 2000 craft. Cars are not allowed in. Each house differs from its neighbour, or is painted in different cheerful colours. Everything, even the lamp posts, is decorative and pleasing to the eye. It shows what can be done even in this tasteless century by an architect with talent, vision, and determination.

HYÈRES, *Var* (6–E4, E5). With its exceptionally mild climate and warm water, Hyères is a resort for winter and summer, and is organized to offer all possible sports on and under water, and on and over land – including parachuting. Surrounded by market gardens and the cultivation of flowers and palms, the town has a comfortable 18th–19th-c. atmosphere, with large shady squares, avenues of palm-trees, gardens and a casino, on level ground below the old town. The Source de la Vierge provides a beneficial mineral water, and health cures can be taken. The spring was known to the Greeks and Romans.

Hyères has a long history. In the 4th-c. BC a Greek trading post was founded from Marseille at Olbia, and in the 1st-c. BC the Romans established a port. In the 7th-c. the population of the area took refuge from marauding raiders on the present site of the old town. The ruined château above has its foundations on a Greek defence wall, showing they had used it also as a strong point. St Louis stayed here on his return from the Crusades in the 13th-c., and it was later made a royal town by Charles I of Anjou. The Knights Templar were established here. In 1564 the young Charles IX was brought here by his mother Cathérine de Médicis and was enchanted by the orange-trees. In the 16th-c. Wars of Religion the château was destroyed and the importance of the town reduced; during the Revolution many of the inhabitants emigrated. In the late 18th–19th-c. French and English took to wintering there. Among the visitors were: Napoleon, Pauline Borghese, Tolstoy, Queen Victoria, and R. L. Stevenson.

Boats to Iles d'Hyères (*see entry*).

HYÈRES, Iles d', *Var* (6, 7–E4, E5). Originally a range of the Massif des Maures (*see entry*), the islands lie opposite the stretch of coast between Le Lavandou and Giens. They are also known as Les Iles d'Or, probably from the golden tone the cliffs take from the sunlight. In the reign of François I the right of asylum was granted to convicts and criminals provided they would populate the islands and defend them against corsairs and pirates. They carried out the former requirement, but as to the latter they became pirates themselves and on one occasion nearly succeeded in stealing a warship from Toulon. They and their successors were not eradicated until the reign of Louis XIV. The islands are a microcosm of southern Pro-

vence, having been successively occupied by Ligurians, Greeks, Romans, monks from Le Thoronet (*see entry*), Saracens, criminals and Turks.

Porquerolles is the most important of the three islands. The name is thought to come from the wild boar that once roamed in the forest which, mainly pine and cork-oak, comes down to the sandy beaches along the northern shore. The small village, which now has villas and hotels around it, was built by the military authorities about a hundred years ago. Almost the whole of the island was acquired by the State in 1971. Beaches, walks to the lighthouse (view over whole of the island), forts and signal station. Boat services from/to: Cavalaire, Le Lavandou, Port-Cros, Hyères-Plage, La-Tour-Fondue (Giens), Toulon.

The **Ile-de-Port-Cros** is private property but open to the public. Camping, fires, smoking, shooting, etc., are forbidden for reasons of safety and because, with the surrounding islets, it is classified as a Parc National and nature reserve for Mediterranean fauna and flora. It is exceptionally green and luxuriant due to the many springs. Lovely walks and panoramas: high cliffs, one or two small beaches. Boat service from/to: Cavalaire, Le Lavandou, Salins-d'Hyères, Port d'Hyères, Ile-du-Levant, Porquerolles.

The **Ile-du-Levant** is now occupied in part by the Navy (no visits) and in part (the W end) by a nudist colony (visits). The cliffs are exceptionally rugged round the entire island. Boat services from/to: Cavalaire, Le Lavandou, Port-Cros.

ISLE-SUR-LA-SORGUE, L', *Vaucluse* (6–D3). The cool greenness that welcomes the visitor to the town comes from its double encirclement by branches of the river Sorgue. The large church is richly decorated in 17th-c. Baroque style with splendid gilt woodwork. Paintings by Mignard, Simon Vouet, etc., a large retable by Levieux, unusual vaulting. The Hôtel-Dieu museum includes 18th-c. carvings and 17th-c. Moustiers faience (*see* Moustiers).

ISOLA, *Alpes-Maritimes* (11km N of Beuil: 7–D5). Situated near the Italian frontier at 870m, at the confluence of two rivers. Magnificent waterfall; surrounded by chestnut-trees. Romanesque tower of old church still standing. Linked by steep twisting road NE with **Isola 2000**, a sophisticated ski-station launched by British enterprise in a superb situation on the frontier at 2000m altitude.

JUAN-LES-PINS, *Alpes-Maritimes* (7–E5). Now the funfair of Antibes, Juan-les-Pins was first created as a resort in the 1920s by the American millionaire Frank Jay Gould. It has a casino and a Palais des Congrès where a jazz festival is held in July. A classical music festival, consisting of five orchestral concerts designed to encourage young soloists, is held in April–May.

LAVANDOU, Le, *Var* (7–E5). Active fishing and sailing port with considerable charm. Sandy beaches and regular boat services to the Iles d'Hyères (*see entry*). Frequented by writers, musicians and painters since the end of 19th-c. In 1942 General Giraud secretly embarked on a British submarine at nearby St-Clair to take command of French Forces in North Africa.

3km NW, in a lovely hilltop setting, is the picturesque village of Bormes-Les-Mimosas (*see* Massif des Maures).

LÉRINS, Iles de, *Alpes-Maritimes* (7–E5). These two islands off Cannes, Ste-Marguerite and St-Honorat, were known to the Ancients as Lero and Lerina. Recent excavations at Fort Ste-Marguerite have revealed native pottery from the 6th–5th-c. BC, and a number of ancient wrecks have been found offshore. It was certainly used by the Greeks as a port of call, and the Romans built a sizeable town here. Traces of their occupation are disappointingly few; the site was later much built over, especially by the Spaniards during their occupation of the islands in 1635–7. The Château Fort, built on Richelieu's orders soon afterwards, and later reinforced by Vauban, was used as a prison by Louis XIV; among his victims were the mysterious 'Man in the Iron Mask' and a number of Huguenot pastors (after the Revocation of the Edict of Nantes), all of whose cells can be visited.

When St-Honorat (*c.* 350–429) landed on Lerina, both islands had been abandoned. The hermitage he founded here quickly became one of the most famous monastic centres of Christendom. Owing to repeated Saracen raids in the 9th-c. and 10th-c. the islands were again temporarily abandoned. Of the buildings erected by the monks after their return to St-Honorat the main survivals are the Chapelle de la Trinité, the 12th-c. cloisters and the medieval fortress on the S coast. The present monastic buildings and church were built by the Cistercians who came from Senanque (*see entry*) in the late 19th-c.; they recreated an active religious centre and recultivated the island.

Regular boat service (15 minutes to Ste-Marguerite) from Cannes. *Son-et-lumière* on most evenings in summer.

LOURMARIN, *Vaucluse* (12km S of Apt: 6–D4). S of the Combe de Lourmarin, through which runs the only direct road across the Luberon (*see entry*), Lourmarin is a pretty town overlooked by the château, partly 15th-c. and partly Renaissance (beautiful fireplaces, etc.), open all the year but p.m. only in winter. The Académie d'Aix-en-Provence, which owns it, organizes international artistic activities here, including a summer festival.

15th–16th-c. Gothic church. The writer Albert Camus is buried in the old cemetery.

LUBERON, Montagne du, *Vaucluse*. A range of beautiful hills to the S of Apt (map 6–D4), extending 65km from E to W and divided by the

D943 road from Apt to Cadenet. The area to the E rises to over 1000m and is called the Grand Luberon; to the W is the Petit Luberon which includes a magnificent forest of cedars. The Luberon range of hills is a nature reserve, and one of the most typical regions of Provence for beautiful drives and views.

Just S of Apt, the valley of Aigue-Brun near Buoux has many palaeolithic cave-dwellings. There are Celto-Ligurian forts on the summits (Buoux, Bonnieux), and huge numbers of stone huts, or *bories* (*see* Gordes). All the villages are worth visiting; particularly: Oppède-le-Vieux, a medieval village coming back to life; Ménerbes, last stronghold of the Protestants in Provence (late 16th-c.); Bonnieux, with a view NE over Lacoste to the colourful ochre hills of Roussillon and Gordes (*see entries*).

Always a natural stronghold, from the early 13th-c. the area was inhabited by members of the Vaudois, followers of Pierre Valdo, an early 'Protestant' who translated the Bible into Provençal. Recently it has been fashionable to concentrate attention on the terrible persecutions in the first half of the 16th-c. under François I, from which some say the Luberon never recovered; but though there was certainly a nucleus of truly religious Protestants among the population, there is no doubt that it was a refuge for brigands and bandits who, in the name of Protestantism, sacked and pillaged throughout the area. (*See* Senanque; Silvacane.)

LUCÉRAM, *Alpes-Maritimes* (25km N of Monaco: 7–D6). Picturesque medieval village built into the mountainside. Ramparts, towers and (in Rue de la Placette) 13th-c. windows. Houses with Ionic columns. The 15th-c church, re-decorated in the 18th-c. in Italian Rococo style, possesses a magnificent 'Treasure', including a 15th-c. silver-gilt reliquary, a 16th-c. monstrance and, above all, six fine retables of the 15th–16th-c. Nice school.

At the oratory of St-Grat (1km S) is a charming mural of the Virgin between St Grat (a 6th-c. bishop of Aosta, here seen holding St John the Baptist's head) and St Sebastian. The chapel of Notre-Dame-de-Bon-Cœur, 2km N of Lucéram, has interesting 15th-c. frescoes, including the Adoration of the Shepherds and of the Magi, all of naive beauty.

MANOSQUE, *Alpes-de-Haute-Provence* (6–D4). Overlooking the river Durance, Manosque is an old, typically Provençal market town. The old quarter lies within a circle of plane-trees lining the boulevards which have replaced the medieval ramparts; the two remaining 14th-c. gateways and the Romanesque church have been considerably restored. This attractive old town is typical of the region which has been much written about by Jean Giono (1895–1970) who made his home here for some years, as have many writers and artists. In recent years Manosque has become an increasingly important agricultural centre, and is still expanding.

MARSEILLE, *Bouches-du-Rhône* (6–E3, E4). The second city of France, Marseille was founded in about 600 BC by Greeks from Asia Minor on the rocky peninsula N of the Old Port. The city's main thoroughfare, La Canebière, was then the bed of a stream, the quays were marshland, the Quartier St-Victor was a cliff occupied by seabirds, and the swampy shore and hinterland were inhabited by primitive Ligurian tribes.

It was the first Greek settlement in Gaul, and commanded the trade route up the Rhône valley by which tin, used for bronze, came overland from Britain. It flourished from the outset and soon aroused the jealousy of Etruscans and Carthaginians. But these commercial rivals could not prevent Marseille from establishing a series of trading posts E to Monaco and W to beyond the Costa Brava. After 237 BC Carthaginian power in Spain began to grow dangerously and in the Second Punic War Marseille was Rome's ally against Hannibal. In return Rome came twice to Marseille's rescue a hundred years later (*see* Aix), thus gaining control of the Rhône's E bank as far as Geneva but allowing Marseille to keep her dependencies along the coast and complete self-government. These prosperous years when Marseille was the chief port and town in Gaul ended in 49 BC when the town backed the wrong side in the civil war between Pompey and Caesar (*see* Fréjus). Marseille was captured after a five-month siege and two naval defeats, and although its powerful ramparts were only partly razed (see the remains beside the Chambre de Commerce), its place was taken by Arles (*see entry*).

According to the 9th-10thc. legend, Christianity was introduced by Lazarus and Mary Magdalene (*see* Stes-Maries-de-la-Mer), who had to take refuge in what is now the crypt of the ÉGLISE ST-VICTOR. This church, first built in the 5th-c. by St-Cassien, does in fact have catacombs, i.e. early Christian burial grounds, and a martyrium as well as a fine series of sarcophagi. Built from the 11th-c. onward on the same site, the present church is the sole remnant of a famous abbey, and looks like a fortress.

Like France's other Mediterranean ports Marseille was ruined and depopulated by the Saracens. It was the Crusades that gave fresh life to the city and marked the beginning of her long commercial rivalry with Genoa and her commercial contacts with the Levant and N Africa. Although formally annexed to France in 1482, Marseille's traditions of municipal independence encouraged an unruly attitude towards French kings. For long its people refused to recognize Henri IV, and the Fort St-Nicolas was expressly built by Louis XIV to keep them in order. In 1789 the Revolution was enthusiastically welcomed, and when war with Austria and Prussia followed

in 1792, it was 500 volunteers from Marseille who, by their rousing singing of a patriotic anthem composed at Strasbourg, earned it the nickname *The Marseillaise*. Royalist under Napoleon I (partly because of the effect of the British blockade), Republican under Napoleon III, Marseille still perhaps feels the occasional impulse to act as champion of the South against the North, despite the motorway linking it to Paris since 1970 and its colossal airport.

Even so, as a stroll down LA CANEBIÈRE, one of the world's great streets, makes abundantly clear, Marseille is highly cosmopolitan. Much of it is also modern – partly replacing extensive damage in World War II, especially around the Old Port and N along the docks, partly the result of recent enlargement and extension of port facilities, new roads such as the Corniche J. F. Kennedy, and new buildings such as Le Corbusier's 'Unité d'Habitation' on the Bd. Michelet.

The 19th-c. neo-Byzantine basilica of NOTRE-DAME-DE-LA-GARDE, with its innumerable ex-votos from sailors, offers a superb panorama. Another fine view is from the PARC DU PHARO, formerly the residence of the Empress Eugénie, overlooking the entrance to the Old Port. On the other side, close to the docks, are the two CATHÉDRALES DE LA MAJOR; the smaller and older is a fine Romanesque church and contains a bas-relief by Luca della Robbia.

Marseille has many excellent museums. The Greek and Roman eras come to life in the MUSÉE DES DOCKS ROMAINS and the MUSÉE D'ARCHÉOLOGIE MÉDITERRANÉENNE. The MUSÉE DES BEAUX-ARTS, with imposing murals by Puvis de Chavannes (1824–98), contains works by Perugino, Brueghel, Rubens and Tiepolo, together with paintings, drawings, etc., by the Marseillais artists Puget (1622–94) and Daumier (1808–79). Nearby, the MUSÉE GROBET-LABADIE contains sculptures, paintings, tapestries, furniture, arms, etc. The Musée du Vieux Marseille, Musée de la Marine de Marseille and Musée Cantini (mainly faience and 20th-c. art including Dufy and Maillol), are all close to the Old Port.

Frequent visits to the Old and New Ports are organized, also to the grim 16th-c. CHÂTEAU D'IF (which owes its fame more to Dumas's *Count of Monte-Cristo* than to the many Huguenots who were imprisoned there), and also to Les Calanques (*see* Cassis).

Note finally that Marseille is the home of the famous soup *bouillabaisse*.

MARTIGUES, *Bouches-du-Rhône* (6–E3). A picturesque village in the 19th-c., a miniature Venice particularly appreciated by Corot and Ziem (see his paintings in the museum) for the quality of the light and for its waterfront, Martigues now has nearly 40,000 inhabitants. Fortunately the petrol refineries responsible for its growth have not destroyed its charm – especially on the Ile Brescon in the centre, surrounded by canals, with its 17th-c. Église de la Madeleine. Note also the Chapelle de l'Annonciade (in Jonquières) and the Gallo-Roman sarcophagi in the museum.

From the chapel of Notre-Dame-des-Marins, just N of the town, there is an exceptional panorama in every direction. Further N, on D5, at St-Mitre-les-Remparts (whose walls date from 1407), turn off NW to the Romanesque pilgrim chapel of St-Blaise; nearby are the remarkable remains of a Greek fortress and settlement, parts of it possibly preceding the foundation of Marseille and thus the earliest in France. There are also traces of Christian occupation from an early date. Further N, just beyond Istres, further Greek-Ligurian remains have recently been discovered at Castellan.

MAURES, Massif des, *Var.* The oldest and most southerly of the E–W ranges of mountains in Provence, mainly of schistous rock, originally part of the huge Tyrrhenian massif which included Corsica and Sardinia and became partly submerged by the later upsurge of the Alps and Pyrenees. The area (map 6, 7–E4, E5) is roughly bounded on the N by N7 (an autoroute) from Fréjus to Le Luc, then by N97 and due S to Puget-Ville and D12 to Hyères, the southern boundary being the Mediterranean. The name comes from the Provençal word *maouro* meaning a dark wood, and probably not from the occupation by the Saracens (Moors) for more than a century.

The area is little populated but the drives and views are of great natural beauty and botanical interest. The road D25 runs from N to S through a cork oak forest, the sombre trunks glowing ochre when stripped, terminating in a huge wood of the increasingly rare umbrella pines at Ste-Maxime. D558 goes N from Grimaud through sweet chestnut forests to the village of La Garde-Freinet (*see entries*).

Cork making and the preserving of *marrons* (sweet chestnuts) are principal industries, as at Collobrières. W from Cogolin (cane chairs, reeds for clarinets, rush-work, corks, pipes and wine) the N98 climbs through plantations of canes and vineyards to chestnut forests, the green of bracken, wild evening primroses and mimosa, to La Môle (air club). The profusion of varieties of wild flowers increases until the ground is rosy with heather beneath the oaks. Arboretum at Col de Gratteloup. The coast road, N559, is exceptionally rich in magnificent trees.

Perhaps the most attractive village in the whole area is **Bormes-les-Mimosas**, just above Le Lavandou. Despite the tourists its medieval appearance and delightful setting, approached from the coastal plain through an avenue of eucalyptus and mimosa, remains unspoilt.

MENTON, *Alpes-Maritimes* (7–D6). The last town on the French Riviera before the Italian border. Founded as a resort by an Anglican clergyman in the late 1850s, Menton was rapidly colonized by the English thereafter. It soon acquired an Anglican church, a club, an English lending library, an English estate agent, and an English newspaper. Queen Victoria visited the town in 1882. However, its reputation as a winter sanatorium had its drawbacks; it used to be said that Cannes was for living, Monte Carlo for gambling, and Menton for dying. However, no one could call it moribund nowadays. Much building is in progress. The biennial International Art Exhibition is held in the 1964 Palais de l'Europe and there is a celebrated Chamber Music Festival in August. Menton's new port with its Cocteau Museum – see also his original decorations in the Salle des Mariages at the *mairie* – enables the town with its two botanical gardens and its fine beaches to accommodate summer visitors of many tastes. The municipal museum contains prehistoric remains, exhibits relating to local history and folklore, works by 15th-c. Niçois painters, and paintings by Vlaminck, Dufy and other modern artists. Graham Sutherland is an honorary citizen of Menton.

The old town, remarkably intact, has exceptional charm. The 17th-c. church of St-Michel, with its 16th-c. retable, and the nearby Chapelle des Pénitents Blancs are among the finest examples of Baroque churches on the Riviera.

The country inland is well worth exploring. 10km N on the winding D22 (reached from Ave. Cernusch) is the mountain village of **St-Agnès** in a superb situation overlooking Menton, over 750m up at the foot of a cliff. Ruined château, allegedly built by a converted Saracen.

MONACO (and **Monte Carlo**), *Independent Principality* (7–D6). This minute sovereign state, occupying an area of only 1½ square kilometres, has a population, including foreign residents, of nearly 25,000. Its citizens (Monégasques) pay no taxes and are not liable to military service. It is visited by innumerable tourists every year and the Casino in Monte Carlo is the most famous in the world.

The Grimaldis, probably of Genoese origin, can claim to be the oldest reigning house in Europe. They acquired Monaco in the 10th- or 11th-c. and thereafter much territory to the W and N, for the family had many branches which provided not only for example, lords of Cagnes and Antibes but also several abbots of Lérins and bishops of Grasse during succeeding centuries. Successively under Genoese, French and then Spanish tutelage, to be followed by a further period as a French protectorate (1641–1814), after which it passed under the indirect control of Piedmont (1815–60), Monaco has nevertheless been ruled by the Grimaldis almost without interruption.

In 1861 Prince Charles III sold Roquebrune and Menton, both in rebellion against his rule, to Napoleon III, reducing the principality from three communes to one. This remaining commune was

Peter Baker

Monte Carlo

situated on a barren rock (named Monte Carlo after the prince) without as yet either hotels or coast road from Nice. The situation was saved by François Blanc (d. 1877), whom Charles invited to open a casino (then forbidden in France) such as he had already directed at Bad Homburg in Germany. Monte Carlo thus came into being on a stretch of wasteland hitherto used for grazing. After the railway reached Monaco in 1868 expansion was rapid: Edward VII's first visit was in 1875, and by 1900 there were 48 hotels.

The Casino is no longer the main source of income. Quite apart from the Opera, the orchestra (one of the first in Europe) and the music festival, there are the Monte Carlo Rally and Grand-Prix, an international television festival, Radio-Télé-

Monte-Carlo (closely linked with advertising), an international dog show, flower shows, congresses, a well-known football team, and last but not least, Monaco's stamps. This list takes no account of Monaco's 'well-to-do' cosmopolitan residents, its banks and connections with large international companies, its numerous holiday attractions, its museums – in particular the world-famous Musée Océanographique and Aquarium directed by Jacques Cousteau, and the Museum of Prehistoric Anthropology – its particularly fine Botanical Garden and Zoo, not to mention the many beaches, gardens and panoramas.

There is an especially fine view from the square on the rock before the Palace, which has a fine 17th-c. main courtyard and a double staircase leading to the 16th-c. Galerie d'Hercule, and to the rooms containing pictures by Breughel, Holbein, Rigaud and others, including portraits of past princes (open to the public July–September). The Historial des Princes de Monaco (waxworks) in the Rue Basse is also worth visiting for those interested in the Grimaldis. Note also the Musée Napoléonien in a wing of the Palace.

The old town, also situated on the rock, includes some pleasing buildings, though, as in the Palace, there has been a good deal of 19th-c. restoration, some of it unfortunate. The Cathedral (19th-c.) contains two fine early 16th-c. retables by Louis Bréa. North of the Casino in a garden with statues by Rodin and Maillol is the Musée National, or Musée Galéa; it displays a remarkable 18th-c. Neapolitan crib and a magnificent collection of 18th–19th-c. dolls and mechanical toys.

MONS, *Var* (17km W of Grasse: 7–E5). A fascinating medieval village at an altitude of over 800m, with a superb view of the countryside and the coast all the way from Menton to Toulon. The church dates from the 13th-c. but was much adapted later. The road southward leads to the little town of **Fayence**. After leaving the town through a 14th-c. gateway a short distance W there is the fine pre-Romanesque chapel of Notre-Dame-des-Cyprès, built on the site of a priory founded from Lérins (*see entry*). 5½km W of Fayence is the unusual village of Seillans (*see entry*).

MONTMAJOUR, Abbaye de, *Bouches-du-Rhône* (5km NE of Arles: 6–E3). Formerly on an island surrounded by marshland gradually reclaimed by the monks across the centuries, this once cele-brated but now ruined abbey on the NE outskirts of Arles was founded through a rich woman's pious generosity, at a time (AD 972) when the Benedictines were the only religious order in western Europe. The little chapel of St-Pierre with its delightful carved stonework and the hermitage to which it leads, associated by legend with St Trophime (*see* Arles), both date from this early time. Nearby the imposing abbot's tower (1369) with crenellations and machicolations and com-manding a fine view, was built for defence purposes – partly against marauding mercenaries, one of the worst scourges of 14th-c. France, and partly against Arles, with which the abbey, now rich and powerful, was not always on friendly terms. The late 12th-c. chapel of Ste-Croix, also outside the precincts, was formerly used as the cemetery chapel. It bears a 15th-c. inscription wrongly attributing its foundation to Charle-magne. The church, also mainly 12th-c. and containing an abbot's tomb, was, like its slightly earlier and unusually fine crypt, never finished. The latter served as a chapel for pilgrims who came in thousands annually from the 11th-c. onwards. The adjoining cloisters have partly Romanesque and partly Gothic capitals of great beauty and interest.

To the W of the medieval abbey, which partly collapsed in the 18th-c., are the impressive ruins of the later buildings which replaced it but are still dangerous to visit. The last (non-resident) abbot, the worldly Cardinal de Rohan, was involved in the affair of the Queen's Diamond Necklace, implicating himself and Marie-Antoinette, and in 1786 the abbey was suppressed. During the Revolution it was sold and the buildings disman-tled. Restoration began slowly only in 1872.

After visiting the remains of two Roman aqueducts and a mill apparently supplied by one of them at Barbegal, a very rare example of a Roman industrial building, a trip 2km further N is worth making to the **Moulin de Daudet**, the windmill associated with Alphonse Daudet's *Lettres de Mon Moulin* (1866). Although Daudet neither lived here nor wrote these famous Provençal stories here, he used to visit the mill and encourage the miller to spin stories. The mill still works and is now a Daudet museum.

MOUGINS, *Alpes-Maritimes* (6km N of Cannes: 7–E5). Since 1918 Mougins has been a highly fashionable place to live, partly owing to its admirable situation and proximity to Cannes, and partly because of its golf course. Fortunately the old village, perched on a conical hill with a 15th-c. gate and some of its ramparts still intact, remains unspoilt, and the 19th-c. restoration of its Romanesque church was not unduly tactless. The *mairie* was formerly a chapel belonging to the Pénitents Blancs. There is still a fine panorama.

Situated on high ground 1km E of Mougins proper is the lovely chapel of Notre-Dame-de-Vie, formerly a hermitage. It is approached by a steep signposted track leading to an avenue of cypresses. Roman and early Christian Mougins stood on this enchanting spot. Note the chapel's 15th-c. stone cross and 17th-c. porch; within the chapel (restored in the 17th-c.) are a 16th-c. gilded wooden retable and two Roman inscriptions. The cemetery was cared for until comparatively recently by the Guinness family. The nearby *mas* of Notre-Dame-de-Vie was subsequently bought by Picasso, and it was there that he spent the last years of his long life, working until the end.

MOUSTIERS-STE-MARIE, *Alpes-de-Haute-Provence* (6–D4, D5). 6km N of the western end of the Grand Canyon du Verdon (*see entry*), the small river Maire forces its way through a cleft in the mountains to join it. Across the chasm hangs an iron chain with a gold star in the centre, about 225m long. It was placed there by a knight in performance of a vow on his return from the Crusades after years of captivity.

Moustiers was founded there in the 15th-c. by monks from the Iles de Lérins (*see entry*). Tradition says that one of the monks came from Faenza (Italy) and brought the secret of the glaze which characterizes the faience made in Mous-tiers, under that name. The great period was that of Louis XIV, when he ordered the melting down of gold and silver vessels for the benefit of the State, and faience became the fashion. There are a variety of handsome Renaissance patterns with mythological beasts, foliage, etc. Production ceased in 1873 but restarted in 1925, and Moustiers faience is now easily available.

The Musée de Faiences is open 1 April–31 October, in the *mairie*. The church has a Romanesque tower and nave and a Gothic choir. The chapel of Notre-Dame-de-Beauvoir, perched above the ravine in the valley of the river Maire, also has a fine Romanesque tower; from its terrace are splendid views of the town and the ravine.

NAPOULE, La, *Alpes-Maritimes* (8km W of Cannes: 7–E5). At the W end of the gulf of Napoule, with 8km of beaches stretching E to Cannes. Large new yacht harbour. The American sculptor Henry Clews (1876–1937) restored château and adapted it, and it contains a large number of his works, including South American type sculptures in the cloister. Concerts and art exhibitions are held from time to time. Open in the afternoons; beautiful gardens with lovely views; the sea on one side and hills covered with wild mimosa on the other.

NICE, *Alpes-Maritimes* (7–E6). The capital of the Riviera and fifth largest town in France. As a summer resort it is admittedly handicapped by shingly beaches, but its large international airport makes it extremely accessible and it has many exceptional attractions for both summer and winter visitors.

The two-week *Carnaval* preceding Lent, descended from Nice's medieval *corsi* but only celebrated on its present prodigious scale since the 1870s, is perhaps the most outstanding popular festival in Europe; with its processions of decorated chariots, fantastic masked figures, brilliant illuminations and fireworks, it is an exhilarating experience. And in summer there are the famous battles of flowers, the open-air theatre, the regattas, etc.

It is certainly a lively town, with its recently established university, its casino, its Palais de la Méditerranée, its Palais des Expositions, its Opera House (recommended for Italian opera, autumn to spring), not to mention its other annual activities – the May Book Festival, the International Dog Festival (June), the Ballet Festival (July and August) when a fine series of concerts is also held in the monastery gardens at Cimiez (*see below*).

At the E end of the front is the rocky plateau where the old Château used to stand; the building was destroyed in 1706 but the site, overlooking the port with its cargo ships, fishing-boats and yachts, is occupied by a fine park with magnificent views. In the Italianate old town below are the celebrated flower market, the 19th-c. Opera House, the Cathedral (1650), several 17th- or 18th-c. Baroque churches, and the 17th-c. Palais Lascaris (starting

point for guided tours of Nice, and worth a visit on its own account).

Nice is well served by its museums: especially the Musée Chéret at the W end of the town (Italian and Flemish primitives and works by the Van Loos, Fragonard, Lawrence, Monet, Sisley, Dufy and Rodin); the Musée Masséna, Rue de Rivoli (Niçois primitives, souvenirs of Marshal Masséna – born in Nice and an able opponent of Wellington – and local history, pottery, jewelry, etc.); the Natural History Museum in the Bd. Risso, near Place Garibaldi (a handsome square named after the Italian patriot, who was born in Nice); the Marc Chagall Museum (Bd. de Cimiez), specially built in 1972 for a permanent exhibition of the painter's works, including his 17 wonderful canvases on Old Testament themes; and finally, in the archaeological museum on the hill site of Cimiez itself, the Musée Matisse, containing about 30 paintings and many sketches, including some for the chapel at Vence (*see entry*).

Cimiez, the NE quarter of the town, was the site of the Roman occupation. Nice itself was founded as a trading post in the 4th-c. BC by Greeks from Marseille, but the Romans, perhaps as early as 154 BC, took over and garrisoned the site of the Ligurian fort up on the hill; though less important than Fréjus, in its Roman heyday Cimiez had perhaps 20,000 inhabitants. It is a site well worth visiting for its small amphitheatre, the remains of the thermal baths, the archaeological museum (containing the Matisse Museum, *see above*) and the monastic church which contains two fine retables by Louis Bréa, dated 1475 and 1512.

Cimiez was largely destroyed by the barbarian and Saracen invasions, and in the Middle Ages it was Nice that came slowly to the fore – first under the counts of Provence, then (from 1388) under the counts (later dukes) of Savoy. Between 1450 and 1550 it was sufficiently important and prosperous to become the centre of a school of religious painting quite distinct from other Italian schools, its best-known artists being Louis Bréa and his nephew François.

Although in 1631 its population was decimated by the plague, Nice evidently recovered quickly, for much of the old town was built in the 17th-c. By the time the British began wintering in Nice in the late 18th-c. it had about 12,000 inhabitants. Among these early British visitors were the novelist Smollett and the traveller Arthur Young, whose account of his journeys through France in 1787–90 does much to explain the Revolution. It was the British colony which in 1822, when the only road W was the present Rue de France, combined to pay for the widening of the path along the shore, now the celebrated Promenade des Anglais.

After the plebiscite of 1860, which led to Nice's annexation to France, and the arrival of the railway in 1864 (note, by the way, the picturesque station), the Russian aristocracy, as well as the

British, began arriving in large numbers – hence the fine Russian Orthodox Cathedral. Edward VII preferred Cannes, but Queen Victoria's favourite place on the Riviera was Cimiez. The great hotels along the Promenade des Anglais belong to this pre-1914 period, when Nice had a population of about 150,000.

OPPEDETTE, *Vaucluse* (17km NE of Apt: 6–D4). A miniature village with a miniature canyon in lavender country near the Observatoire de Haute-Provence, between Forcalquier and Apt (*see entries*). The stone base of the village cross is a Roman altar.

ORANGE, *Vaucluse* (6–D3). Originally a Gallic tribal capital in commercial contact with Marseille, the site of Orange first appears in history when two invading Germanic tribes combined to

destroy a large Roman army here (105 BC). Three years later Marius avenged this defeat near Aix. About 80 years afterwards a town, called Arausio by the Romans, was founded here by Augustus for the veterans of the second legion; it may well be their exploits against the Greek fleet at the siege of Marseille that are commemorated on the N face of the triumphal arch to the N of the town (on the former Via Agrippa linking Arles and Lyon). This is the third largest Roman triumphal arch in existence, and richly decorated with well-preserved sculpture.

To the S of the town, on the hill of St-Eutrope, traces have been found of an imposing capitol and three temples, and also ruins of a medieval château. But Orange's most notable Roman monument (for the baths, amphitheatre, forum and stadium can only be conjecturally located) is its majestic theatre – the finest and best-preserved

The Roman Theatre, Orange

in Europe, in which plays and concerts are held today. The façade is 38m high and 103m long. Near the top of the outer façade are rows of jutting square stone blocks constructed to carry the poles which supported the awning used to protect spectators from the sun. The interior stage wall, which formerly included three tiers of columns and niches containing statues, is dominated by a large statue of Augustus holding his general's baton. Both stage and auditorium, which has excellent acoustics and can seat 10,000 spectators, are impressively large. Beside the theatre are the remains of a temple which probably stood at the end of a vast sports ground and was connected by steps to the capitol. Traces of Roman origin can be seen on the S porch of the former cathedral.

Ravaged by the barbarian invasions of the 4th- and 5th-c., and later occupied by the Saracens, Orange became, after some centuries, a small independent *comté* (11th-c.), and then a tiny principality eventually inherited by William, Count of Nassau in Germany, who led the 16th-c. Dutch revolt against Spanish rule and is known to history as William of Orange, the ancestor both of William III of England and of the present Dutch royal family. The principality was annexed to France by Louis XIV.

The town museum, close to the theatre, contains Roman remains, mementoes of old Orange, some portraits of members of the house of Orange-Nassau and, strangest of all, some paintings by Brangwyn.

PEILLE, *Alpes-Maritimes* (8km N of Monaco: 7–D6). Peille, a medieval village virtually intact except for its ruined château, occupies an impressive situation in a wild and rugged landscape. In the 12th–13th-c. church is a 16th-c. retable and an interesting painting showing what the village looked like in the Middle Ages.

A few kilometres SW, reached by a twisting road, is **Peillon**, the most attractive mountain village near Nice. In the Chapelle des Pénitents Blancs are beautiful late 15th-c. frescoes, probably by Jean Canavesi (*see also* La Brigue). To the N on D21 are the wild Gorges du Paillon.

PEÏRA-CAVA, *Alpes-Maritimes* (12km W of Breil: 7–D6). This former military outpost is now a ski-station and summer resort. Wonderful situation, superb forest 4km N. Mountain footpaths from Pointe-des-Trois-Communes (panorama) connect up with the Vallée des Merveilles (*see* Roya, Haute Vallée de la).

PUGET-THÉNIERS, *Alpes-Maritimes* (7km E of Entrevaux: 7–D5). This is a largely medieval town at the junction of the rivers Var and Roudoule (visit the Gorges de la Roudoule and the Pont St-Léger for marvellous views). The ruined château is

rich in historical associations. The church, partly medieval, partly 17th-c., contains some fine examples of wooden carving and statuary; above all a celebrated retable over the main altar (1525) by an unknown painter but of great pathos and beauty: St James carries a pilgrim's staff and wears a scallop shell on his hat in allusion to the pilgrimages then made from all over Christendom to Santiago de Compostela in NW Spain. In the square is a statue by Maillol (1861–1944).

RIEZ, *Alpes-de-Haute-Provence* (25km E of Manosque: 6–D4). Approaching from the W by D952 through a green valley, it is surprising to see in the fields four columns of grey granite with white marble Corinthian capitals, complete with entablature, the remains of a 1st-c. Roman temple. Across the river is a 5th-c. Merovingian baptistry, square outside, hexagonal inside, with four apses filling the corners, and a circle of eight granite columns with marble capitals surrounding the remains of the font (*see also* Aix, Fréjus *and* Venasque) – key from tourist office in the town centre.

Riez, at the crossroads of the Roman roads Aix–Grenoble and Draguignan–Apt, was a Celtic capital and a religious centre for Celts, Romans and Christians, eventually becoming a bishopric. An attractive old town, now a centre for lavender and truffles.

RIVIERA, Corniches de la. A *corniche* is a road built along the edge of a cliff, and is the name given to the three coastal roads Nice–Monte Carlo–Menton (map 7–D6). The lowest, the Basse Corniche (N559), constructed to help Prince Charles III of Monaco (*see entry*), was built in 1863–78. The Moyenne or Middle Corniche (N7), begun in 1910 to relieve traffic congestion, was completed in 1928; it is the quickest and offers the best views (*see* Èze). The Grande or Upper Corniche (D2564), built by Napoleon in 1806, mainly follows the old Roman road, the Via Aurelia, thus passing through La Turbie (*see entry*); it also leads to the autoroute to Italy. All three are connected with each other at intervals by roads which twist and turn, often with hair-raising hairpin bends.

ROQUEBRUNE-CAP-MARTIN, *Alpes-Maritimes* (1km W of Menton: 7–D6). Roquebrune, the most attractive and interesting medieval hilltop village on the Côte d'Azur, is full of narrow winding lanes which climb by steps and covered passageways under old houses up to the impressive Grimaldi château. Originally built as a defence against the Saracens, the château is believed to date from the 10th-c., but the present structure, which has been well restored, appears to be largely 13th-c. The keep, with walls up to 4m

The view from the Grande Corniche above Menton   J. Allan Cash

thick, dominates the whole site and has a wonderful view. Unusual religious processions, representing scenes from the Passion, wind through the village on Good Friday and 5 August in fulfilment of a vow believed to have averted the plague in 1467.

Cap Martin, with its pines and olive groves, is a millionaire resort. The Empress Eugénie, a frequent visitor, helped to make it widely known in the late 19th-c. J. Pierpont Morgan had a villa here. The painter Van Meegeren, who made a fortune forging Vermeers, was a resident. The poet W.B. Yeats died here in January 1939.

ROUBION and **ROURE**, *Alpes-Maritimes* (5–8km E of Beuil: 7–D5). Attractive villages on the road D30 from Beuil to St-Sauveur-sur-Tinée. At **Roubion**, the chapel of St-Sébastien (1km E) is full of splendidly vivid 15th-c. frescoes, 13 devoted to the saint's life, others representing the Seven Deadly Sins. In **Roure** church are two retables, one of the Assumption (1560) by François Bréa; in the chapel of St-Sébastien above the village are delightfully naive frescoes of St Bernard of Aosta.

ROUSSILLON, *Vaucluse* (9km W of Apt: 6–D4). Var produces relatively little bauxite, but the Vaucluse is an important producer of ochre from the hills between the Plateau de Vaucluse and the Coulon valley. Roussillon is perched on the highest of these hills, and the splashes of varied shades of ochre in the surrounding countryside, and the variety of colour (16 shades) in the Roussillon houses, are not only exceptional but very picturesque. Consequently a large number of artists are attracted to the area and the town has a number of cultural activities, in particular exhibitions of modern pictures.

ROUTE NAPOLÉON (*see* maps 6 and 7, E5 to C4). The official name for the route followed by Napoleon on his march northwards to Grenoble after his dramatic return from Elba in 1815, which ushered in 'The Hundred Days' and ended with his defeat at Waterloo on 18 June. On 1 March he landed at Golfe Juan near Antibes. After his landing, the garrison at Antibes having imprisoned his emissaries and rejected his overtures, Napoleon marched towards Cannes and bivouacked beside the present main Post Office. Anticipating hostile forces if he tried to advance up the Rhône valley to Lyon, he decided to by-pass them by following the route across the mountains: Cannes–Grasse–Castellane–Digne–Sisteron–Gap–Grenoble. This rapid outflanking manoeuvre was completely successful, for although not welcomed at either Cannes or Grasse Napoleon encountered no opposition and found the strongpoint of Sisteron unguarded. In Gap and Grenoble (which he reached on 7 March) he met with an enthusiastic reception.

It was a remarkable forced march, for the state of the road from Grasse to Digne was very inferior to that of the present-day N85, much of it being little more than a mountain track; for large parts of the journey, made under harsh weather conditions, the use of wheeled transport was therefore impracticable. Traces of the old Grasse–Digne road can frequently be seen where the N85 diverges from it, and many places where Napoleon halted *en route* are commemorated. Magnificent scenery.

ROYA, Haute Vallée de la, *Alpes-Maritimes* (7–D6). Of all the gorges descending from Alpine frontiers the upper valley of the river Roya (closely followed by N204) is among the most dramatic geologically, though on a small scale. The heaving turbulence of the primeval earth's crust has petrified into strata of wild chaotic forms: horseshoes, mosaics, vertical sweeps, horizontal layers, pinnacles, chasms, all bewilderingly mixed together. Between the gorges, terraces of olives have been carved out of the mountainside almost to the top. The tenacity of earlier men in scratching a living is awe-inspiring: there are glimpses of old dwellings, chapels and villages at apparently inaccessible heights. From time to time the scene is enhanced by ruined viaducts crossing the river – remains of a railway destroyed during World War II; recently repaired, they have a classic look.

At the Italian frontier the N204 (main road from Lombardy) leaves the Col de Tende tunnel near the source of the Roya and descends to follow its course. The French frontier post and customs are at Tende (*see* entry). At St-Dalmas-de-Tende the D43 turns E to La Brigue (*see* entry) and the remarkable Notre-Dame-des-Fontaines. Westward, the D91 leads in the direction of the **Vallée des Merveilles**, a mysterious prehistoric site in a valley round Mont Bégo, where tribes thought to have been Iron Age or Bronze Age Ligurians have engraved over 30,000 figures, animals and signs on rock faces. (Signposted road to within some kilometres, then choice of many paths; or you can hire special transport from St-Dalmas.)

ST-CASSIEN, Barrage de, *Var* (20km N of Fréjus: 7–E5). The large artificial lake of St-Cassien was constructed after the collapse in 1959 of the barrage above Fréjus (*see* entry). Although parts of the area are rather crowded in summer, it is still less crowded as a whole than most of the seaside resorts and offers pleasant bathing and restricted boating and fishing in agreeably rural surroundings. The dam is at the N end of the lake, which takes its name from the nearby hamlet of St-Cassien-des-Bois; here, in delightful wooded country near a waterfall, is the minute chapel of St Cassien, one of the pioneers of monasticism in Western Europe in the early 5th-c. AD.

ST-CÉZAIRE, *Alpes-Maritimes* (11km W of Grasse: 7–E5). Overlooking the very impressive gorge of the Siagne, which forms the frontier between the departments of Var and Alpes-

Maritimes, St-Cézaire, now a popular place of residence, was already inhabited in prehistoric and Roman times. There are several dolmens and traces of a neolithic burial ground beside the road to St-Vallier.

The well-known local caves off the D613 are worth visiting. In the village itself note the beautifully simple Romanesque chapel containing a Roman sarcophagus. The 18th-c. parish church has a 17th-c. gilded wooden altar.

ST-ÉTIENNE-DE-TINÉE, *Alpes-Maritimes* (3km N of Auron: 7–D5). Magnificently situated summer and winter station, formerly an important religious centre (which explains the frescoes at Auron – *see entry*). 18th-c. church with unusual Romanesque tower, 17th-c. paintings and main altar. The 17th-c. Couvent des Trinitaires contains some amusingly ambitious frescoes commemorating the Turkish naval defeat at Lepanto (1571). Even more interesting are the 15th-c. frescoes in the chapel of St-Sébastien; note the victims cured of the plague (one of the saint's specialities, for which also *see* Auron). At the chapel of St-Maur are yet further frescoes (16th-c. with dog-Latin inscriptions). In superb surrounding countryside (especially in the valley of the Tinée) are 20 oratories.

7½km NW is the highest village in the Alpes-Maritimes, **St-Dalmas-le-Selvage,** in breathtaking scenery. The 17th-c. church contains a fine 16th-c. retable of St Pancras (supposedly martyred c. 304, and buried on the Aurelian Way on the Provençal coast). The D64 leads to Cime de la Bonnette, over 2800m high.

ST-JEAN-CAP-FERRAT, *Alpes-Maritimes* (8km SW of Monaco: 7–D6). A wooded peninsula, 3km long, occupied almost entirely by magnificent private villas. The atmosphere is high-class suburban (St-Jean being the only village on the Cap), with a small but elegant zoo and a large, fascinating botanical garden. Somerset Maugham spent his last years at the Villa Mauresque near the tip. The Villa Ephrussi Rothschild, standing in an extensive garden, is one of the most extraordinary museums in Europe, a once private amateur collection of Renaissance furniture, Sèvres and Dresden china, Oriental carpets, paintings by Tiepolo, Boucher, Lancret, Fragonard, Sisley, Monet, Renoir, etc. – a list which gives an inadequate idea of the variety of its contents.

ST-MARTIN-VÉSUBIE, *Alpes-Maritimes* (7–D5). A summer resort and mountaineering centre, one of the finest in Europe, remarkable both for its situation and its 15th- and 16th-c. houses. The 17th-c. church is admirably decorated, with a richly dressed 14th-c. wooden statue of the Virgin which is taken annually in procession to the 14th-c. sanctuary at Fenestre (15km NW by the D94 through superb scenery; pilgrimages 2

and 26 July, 15 August, 8 September). In the sacristy are two magnificent panels of a retable (possibly by Louis Bréa).

5km N is **Le Boréon** in superb surroundings, point of access (without car, dog or gun) to the National Park of Mercantour.

At **Venanson** (4½km S of St-Martin) is the little chapel of St-Sebastian (1483) whose walls are covered with paintings including 12 episodes from the saint's legendary life.

Immediately SW of St-Martin lies the mountainous area covered by the commune of **Valdeblore,** with varied scenery between the valleys of the Vésubie and the Tinée, both themselves scenically impressive. It includes: La Colmiane (wintersports: ski-lift to Pic de Colmiane (1500m)); St-Dalmas (15th-c. church with three fine retables, 'Treasure' and two 10th-c. chapels in crypt); La Roche and La Bolline (summer resort), both with churches and chapels worth seeing. Note also the extraordinary site of Rimplas.

ST-MAXIMIN-LA-STE-BAUME, *Var* (35km E of Aix: 6–E4). On the Aurelian Way (N7) from Fréjus to Aix, St-Maximin owes its name to the first Bishop of Aix who, according to legend, accompanied the Three Marys to Provence (*see* Stes-Maries de-la-Mer). It was he who had Mary Magdalene buried here (*see* La Sainte Baume), and her remains, together with those of St Trophime (*see* Arles), St Sidonius and St Maximin himself, supposedly lie buried in four fine Gallo-Roman sarcophagi in what was originally the burial vault of a 5th-c. Roman villa but is now the crypt of the Basilica. Whether the most precious relic of all, the skull of Mary Magdalene, now kept in a 19th-c. reliquary made to replace the 13th-c. one lost in the Revolution, is really authentic must be highly doubtful. The burial vault, which may simply have belonged to a rich local family, was covered in during the 8th-c. for fear of the Saracens and not rediscovered till 1279. By this date Vézelay in Burgundy had already been claiming to possess the true relics of the Saint for well over 200 years. The Pope decided in favour of St-Maximin. Vézelay's great days as a place of pilgrimage were thus ended, and the construction of the present Basilica of St-Maximin to replace the Merovingian one began on the Pope's orders under Dominican supervision in 1295.

The Basilica took over two centuries to build and even now the façade is uncompleted. Nevertheless, it is the largest and most beautiful Gothic building in Provence. Fortunately Napoleon's brother Lucien saved it from destruction during the Revolution by turning it into a warehouse.

The 17th-c. choir-screen and fine 18th-c. organ and pulpit are in striking contrast to the austere beauty of the nave with its soaring arches. Among much else of interest note the 16th-c. retable of the Crucifixion showing the earliest known view of the Papal Palace at Avignon.

ST-PAUL-DE-MAUSOLE, *Bouches-du-Rhône* (½km S of St-Rémy: 6–D3, E3). Probably founded in the 10th-c. and named after the nearby Roman mausoleum (1km S, *see* Glanum), St-Paul consists of a large 12th-c. church with 18th-c. façade, a 12th-c. cloister and the buildings of a former monastery used since 1605 as a mental home. In May 1889 Van Gogh arrived here from Arles as a voluntary patient. His cell, now hung with reproductions of his works, has been partly altered since but is worth visiting. Here he remained for a year largely cut off from the outside world and surrounded by neurotics and lunatics with whom intelligent conversation was impossible. He suffered several crises, on one occasion swallowing a quantity of paints. But there are no signs of derangement in the paintings and drawings he executed here – of the head warder, of a sower (particularly famous), of an olive grove, of poplars, of the asylum itself and its luxuriant garden. And about the whole place broods an almost magical atmosphere of peace.

ST-PAUL-DE-VENCE, *Alpes-Maritimes* (2km S of Vence: 7–D5). Largely rebuilt in 1537 by François I (*see* Vence), on a hilltop dominating the river Var, then the frontier, this fortified village is particularly popular with visitors because of its accessibility, its exceptional picturesqueness, its artistic attractions and its good restaurants. Its ramparts are intact and the views of mountain and sea are delightful.

After 1918 St-Paul became very popular with artists and has remained so ever since. One direct consequence of this was the magnificent collection of modern art built up by the perceptive proprietor of the Colombe d'Or. This unique collection includes works by Utrillo, Dufy, Matisse, Picasso and Léger. The Fondation Maeght, erected in 1964 to the NW of the village to house another unique collection, is picturesquely situated among pine-trees and should on no account be missed. Not the least of its attractions are the building itself, a striking example of 20th-c. architecture, and the gardens surrounding it, with the carefully

St-Paul-de-Vence

A.F. Kersting

situated works of art placed therein. Their effect on the visitor is arresting. Even those unsympathetic to modern art cannot fail to sense the mysterious evocative atmosphere they emanate in such surroundings.

The building is devoted exclusively to works by 20th-c. artists. It includes both mosaics and sculpture. Giacometti is particularly in evidence (a whole courtyard is devoted to his bronzes), but few artists of distinction or promise are not represented by some work – e.g. among Anglo-Saxons there are works by Calder, Hepworth and Alan Davie.

Each year special exhibitions are devoted to the work of particular artists – e.g. Matisse 1969, Rouault 1971. The standard of display is always very high. A small cinema shows films on modern art. But the Fondation Maeght does not rest upon its laurels: more exhibition rooms are planned and further areas of garden will be used to display fresh sculptures. In short it continues to do all it can to encourage modern art and to stimulate public interest.

In the village, the 12th–13th-c. church, restored in the 17th-c. contains besides much else of interest an alabaster statue of the Virgin (15th-c.), a painting of St Catherine of Alexandria attributed to Tintoretto, and a fine bas-relief of the martyrdom of St Clement.

ST-RAPHAËL, *Var* (7–E5). In the 19th-c. St-Raphaël was described as 'the Bournemouth of the Riviera', and perhaps the label is still to some extent appropriate despite the considerable difference in size, for not only does St-Raphaël boast an Anglican church which functions during the tourist season but there is also a golf course at Valescure close by dating back to pre-1914 – a product, needless to say, of British enterprise. Even today there is something rather sedate about much of St-Raphaël in contrast to its more free-and-easy younger sister St-Tropez.

Its reputation as a watering-place dates from 1864, helped by the advent of the railway from Marseille, but its existence in Roman times as an adjunct of Fréjus (*see entry*) is attested by the remains found on the site occupied by the present casino.

St-Raphaël, which was liberated by the 36th American Infantry Division in 1944, is well equipped for fishing and sailing (its fine new port is probably the best between Cannes and Toulon), as well as possessing good beaches and a marine archaeological museum. Close to this museum is the interesting 12th-c. church of the Knights Templar, with a watch-tower from which sea-raiding Saracens could be detected.

ST-RÉMY-DE-PROVENCE, *Bouches-du-Rhône* (6–D3, E3). Named after the Archbishop of Reims who converted Clovis, King of the Franks, to Christianity in AD 496 – a momentous date in French history – this charming little town, the successor of the Roman town of Glanum (1½km S, *see entry*), is an important centre for market-gardening and flower seeds. It was also the birthplace of Nostradamus, the 16th-c. doctor and astrologer, celebrated to this day for his rhymed prophecies full of obscure allusions to the future course of world events. The Musée des Alpilles is of local interest; the 15th–16th-c. Hôtel de Sade (formerly belonging to the family of the sadistic Marquis) is a modest archaeological museum with Greek and Roman remains, many of them from Glanum.

Close by to the S is St-Paul-de-Mausole (*see entry*), where Van Gogh spent a year as a voluntary mental patient.

ST-TROPEZ, *Var* (7–E5). Originally a trading post founded by Greeks from Marseille. The name of the town is said to be derived from a Roman officer called Torpes, martyred for his Christian beliefs under Nero, and ever since the late 15th-c. the bust of St Tropez has been carried from the parish church around the town on 16 and 17 May – a procession known as the *bravade* which is very lively, and which no visitor should miss, for it is unique.

The whole peninsula was certainly well populated in Roman times, and in AD 739 the town was sufficiently important to be destroyed by the Saracens. In 1470 a Genoese gentleman undertook to repopulate the ruined town with immigrants from Genoa on the understanding that it would be exempt from royal taxation. St-Tropez continued to exist as a miniature self-governing republic into the 17th-c. Its people were formidable sailors, helping to recapture the Iles de Lérins in 1637 (*see entry*) and repulsing a Spanish attack a month later – an episode commemorated annually on 15 June by a second *bravade*. In view of its maritime traditions it is appropriate that France's greatest sailor, Suffren (1726–88), a formidable enemy to the English during the War of American Independence, should have been a native of St-Tropez, where he is much commemorated.

Unlike the town of St-Raphaël (*see entry*), St-Tropez was not 'discovered' by the British. One of its first distinguished visitors was de Maupassant, followed by a group of post-Impressionist painters, including Matisse, in the 1890s and early 1900s. The idea of going to the Mediterranean coast each summer in order to paint became increasingly fashionable among French artists and has remained so ever since. It is no coincidence that the Musée de l'Annonciade, originally a private collection housed in a deconsecrated chapel and presented to the town by the owner on his death in 1955, is one of the finest collections of late 19th-c. and early 20th-c. works of art in France.

After 1918 the resort began to grow more cosmopolitan and bohemian, a trend which has continued to this day. The damage suffered by St-Tropez and its port in World War II, when forces of the Resistance, parachutists and seaborne troops combined to liberate the town in August 1944, can be studied at the Musée de la Marine.

St-Tropez compensates for its relative quietness in winter by its intense animation during the summer. Despite the hordes of visitors in yachts (there are two large ports) or by land, it remains a little town of great charm situated on a gulf of exceptional beauty with excellent beaches, shops and restaurants. It offers so many varied attractions and distractions (fêtes, *nuits musicales*, folklore festivals, etc.) that detailed description is impossible. To the S, inland, the chapel of Ste-Anne (1km), Ramatuelle, Moulins de Paillas and Gassin are all worth visiting, either for their picturesqueness or for their views.

SAINTE-BAUME, Massif de la (between Aubagne and Brignoles: 6–E4). Although geologically typically Provençal, this impressive range has an awe-inspiring mystery of its own, partly deriving from its magnificent trees (those on its S slopes, said to have been sacred to the Gauls, include, unusually, giant beeches), and partly owing to its Christian associations.

The word *baume* is derived from the Provençal word *baoumo*, meaning cave. According to the 9th–10th-c. legend Mary Magdalene, after landing with her holy companions at Stes-Maries-de-la-Mer (*see entry*) and preaching the Gospel, withdrew to a cave here and spent the rest of her life in total solitude. On her death she was buried by St Maximin (*see entry*). The legend accounts for the exceptional veneration for Mary Magdalene (Ste Madeleine) in Provence, and the grotto at **St-Pilon**, in the centre of the massif, has been visited by thousands of pilgrims over the centuries, including kings and popes, and on 22 July, her feast day, midnight mass is celebrated in the cave. The hostelry at nearby La Sainte-Baume on D80 contains fine 15th-c. statues of Louis XI and his wife and a Renaissance chimney-piece. Superb panorama from St-Pilon.

STE-MAXIME, *Var* (7–E5). An entirely modern resort with a large sandy beach offering all bathing facilities, water skiing, etc.; and a well-equipped harbour for all kinds of boats. In a sheltered position, it is pleasantly situated for many beautiful inland drives in the Massif des Maures and the Estérel (*see entries*).

STE-VICTOIRE, Montagne, *Bouches-du-Rhône* (About 10km E of Aix: 6–E4). A limestone ridge, rising to over 1000m, this is the mountain Cézanne loved and painted so much. Seen from the A8 autoroute and the N7, it lies along the northern horizon as an immense near-white wall of rock for something like 16km. From Aix itself the D17 follows the S slope of the ridge, below the Croix de Provence and continues E to Puylubier, whence the D57d takes you to Pourrières, close to the site where in the 2nd-c. BC the Roman general Marius

won the victory over invading Teutons which probably gave the mountain its name.

The northerly approach is by the D10 from Aix. Leave the car at Les Cabassols, proceed on foot by muletrack to the Chapelle Ste-Victoire and the hermitage, and thence to the Croix de Provence for superb views (whole journey 3 hours there and back).

Near Les Cabassols, at Vauvenargues, the artist Pablo Picasso is buried in the private park of the 17th-c. château.

STES-MARIES-DE-LA-MER, *Bouches-du-Rhône* (6–E3). Van Gogh visited Stes-Maries in June 1888 from Arles. His painting of four brightly coloured sailing boats drawn up on the beach there is now world-famous. He also painted a view of the village (now in the Kröller-Müller Museum, Otterlo, Holland). Since then Stes-Maries has become a seaside resort (the nearest to Arles), with a museum devoted to the Camargue (*see entry*) and, nearby, a large zoo which has flamingoes in its collection. It remains worth visiting, despite its commercialization, both for the legends which make it a place of pilgrimage and for its superb fortified church.

The three Marys who gave their name to the place are: (1) Mary, wife of Cleophas, the Virgin's sister (John 14:25), known as 'Marie Jacobé'; (2) Mary, the mother of James and John, styled 'Marie Salomé'; (3) Mary Magdalene. All three were present at the Crucifixion. According to the 9th–10th-c. legend, they, together with Lazarus and Martha, St Maximin (*see entry*), St Sidonius (the man cured of his blindness) and a black servant named Sara, left Palestine in a boat without sails or oars and landed miraculously at this spot. Lazarus and Mary Magdalene (who later withdrew to La Sainte-Baume – *see entry*), set out to convert Marseille. St Martha went to Tarascon, Maximin and Sidonius to Aix. The two older Marys stayed behind with Sara and built an oratory on the site of a pagan temple. Subsequently a church was raised on the spot. Much later the gypsies, who began arriving in Provence in the 15th-c., adopted Sara as their patron saint.

Stripped of its miraculous details there is nothing improbable about the story of a prominent group of religious refugees coming to Provence from Palestine and landing, whether by accident or design, at a small port in the Camargue rather than at Marseille. By then the whole Mediterranean was a Roman lake. There was certainly a Graeco-Roman settlement at Stes-Maries and possibly a pagan temple too. What makes it difficult to accept the legend as true – despite the researches initiated in 1448 by 'Good King René' (*see* Aix), which led to the discovery or rediscovery of the relics of the two Marys, now kept here in a locked chapel over the apse of the church – is its late emergence. It is also now known that a trinity of mother goddesses was worshipped in the Camargue in pre-Christian times. The fact

Douglas Dickins

The church at Stes-Maries-de-la-Mer

that there was already a church in AD 869, when Saracens are said to have kidnapped the Archbishop of Arles while he was on a visit, certainly shows that it is a Christian site of great antiquity, and the present church, built in 1140–80 as a kind of holy fortress on the very edge of the Mediterranean (the chapel over the apse was originally a watch-tower), has a powerfully supernatural atmosphere. Whether the legend is true or not is of less importance than the centuries of pious belief that it has evoked.

On 23 May, gypsies from far and wide assemble for an all-night vigil in the crypt, which houses the relics of their patron saint Sara and her elaborately clothed statue. (The altar includes a piece of a Roman sarcophagus.) The following day at a special service the reliquary of the two Marys is carefully lowered from the chapel above the apse into the church. On 25 May a procession, including gypsies, Camargue cowboys and fife-players, all in their finery, carries the statues of the saints in the model boat, kept in the church, to the shore. Here they are carried into the waves and the Bishop blesses the sea. The next day is occupied by festivities – Provençal dances, feats of horsemanship, wrestling with bull-calves, etc. – after which the gypsies depart.

SANARY-SUR-MER, *Var* (4km E of Bandol: 6–E4). An all-the-year-round resort, well sheltered from the Mistral by the Gros Cerveau, a ridge to the N of the town rising to over 400m. There is a harbour for yachts and fishing boats, and the chapel on the cliff to the W of it has splendid views of the coast to Bandol and beyond.

To the E of the harbour, close to the N559, is the Fort de Six-Fours, from whose terrace there is a magnificent panorama of Toulon harbour and the coast eastward. The church below contains a 5th-c. chapel on Graeco-Roman foundations incorporated into a 10th-c. church, but the chapel is not easy to identify; there is a good retable, probably by Louis Bréa. If shut, apply for information to the Syndicat d'Initiative in the nearby village of Six-Fours-la-Plage.

SAORGE, *Alpes-Maritimes* (7–D6). The remarkable *village perché* of Saorge is best seen from the S. Hanging high on the mountainside, its streets in tiers one above the other, it appears inaccessible but is in fact easily reached from Fontan (2½km N). The streets tunnel under houses and have many steps, but there is a level square (with Roman inscriptions) in front of the parish church of St-Sauveur (1500). The interior, with much Ligurian Baroque, endearingly run riot, is clearly by local craftsmen who loved their church. NE on a shady belvedere is a peaceful Franciscan convent; the portico to the chapel is in simple 17th-c. Italian style, and there are good wood-carvings, and a small cloister with rustic frescoes. 1km SE, church of La Madone de Poggio, is early Romanesque, with 15th-c. frescoes and an interesting Lombard bell-tower. Privately owned, it may be possible to visit it on request. Other chapels and oratories in the neighbourhood; merino sheep in the countryside.

SÉGURET, *Vaucluse* (6km SW of Vaison: 6–D3). Thanks to working craftsmen and visitors, Séguret is coming back to life. Apparently hooked on to the side of the **Dentelles-de-Montmirail** (so called because the up-ended rock strata towards their summits have worn into a fantastic lace-like skyline), it should be visited on foot. There is a 12th-c. church, a tower, a ruined château, a *table d'orientation* and views W to the Massif Central. Vineyards rise towards the village; the wine has the *appellation* Côtes-du-Rhône-Villages.

SEILLANS, *Var* (22km W of Grasse: 7–E5). Under the Saracen menace the population of Seillans used to gather inside the walls, made by the backs of houses – some of which are still four or five storeys high. The name of the village comes from the Provençal *seilhanso*, the vessels from which boiling oil was poured on to attackers. There are old gateways, a 12th-c. ruined château with keep, narrow paved streets and fountains. Church altered in 15th-c. and 18th-c. Centre for local crafts, scent-making and manufacture of corks.

SENANQUE, Abbaye de, *Vaucluse* (10km E of L'Isle: 6–D3). The site, in a wild and isolated valley over the ridge just N of Gordes, is typically Cistercian. Founded 1148, it is extraordinarily similar in size and plan to its sister abbeys Silvacane and Le Thoronet (*see entries*), the dimensions of the churches varying by only 1–2m.

Senanque had the quietest history of the three, and in the 14th-c. probably inspired part of Petrarch's *Vie Solitaire* (*see* Fontaine-de-Vaucluse). But in 1544 it was attacked by Protestants from the Luberon (*see entry*) who burned it and hanged the monks, only a few escaping. Repaired 1683–1712, from then there were only a few monks. Sold during the Revolution, it fared better than Le Thoronet and Silvacane, for the purchaser appreciated and preserved the splendid buildings. In 1854 it was acquired by Bernadine Cistercians and religious life was resumed until the Expulsions of 1880 and 1903. In later years many of the monks moved to the Abbaye de Lérins (*see entry*). Still the property of the Order, Senanque is a Cultural and Research Centre (lectures, concerts, exhibitions of architectural drawings of the three abbeys and of Cistercian development); Sahara museum.

SILVACANE, Abbaye de, *Bouches-du-Rhône* (4km SW of Cadenet: 6–D4,E4). Probably founded in 1147, Silvacane follows the Cistercian plan, the dimensions of the church varying only slightly from those of its sister abbeys Senanque and Le Thoronet (*see entries*). Sadly awaiting full restoration, it is perhaps the most beautiful of the three abbeys, with the finest masonry. The major differences are that the sanctuary and side chapels are rectangular, not apsidal, with consequent variations in the vaulting; and the fall of the ground obliged the builders to make the floor of the S transept and S aisle five steps higher than the nave; the sacristy is about 1m and the cloister 1½m lower still. The strongly buttressed refectory is lower again; the reader's chair is reached by steps in the thickness of the wall and lit by a small round window (*oculus*). S of the Durance, the site was surrounded by marshes and forests of reeds; hence the name, *silva* (wood) and *cane* (reeds). A group of hermits had settled there to clear the marshes, organize a ferry, and to help and lodge travellers: they became Cistercians. The abbey was founded on the same spot and prospered enough to found another near Apt in 1188.

Its history became the most turbulent of the three abbeys. In the 13th-c. while the Luberon 'Protestants' (*see entry*) were ravaging the countryside, it was ironically not they but

A.F. Kersting

The church at Sisteron

Benedictines from Montmajour (*see entry*) who drove out the Cistercians from Silvacane. An ecclesiastical court at Aix (1229) ordered the abbey's return to the Cistercians. In 1358 it was sacked by a troop of vagabonds, and in 1364 a great frost destroyed the vines, olives and crops, and the abbey was abandoned. Later it became the village church. During the Wars of Religion it changed hands continually. In 1590 it was occupied by brigands who terrorized the countryside until they were besieged and captured without quarter. In the 17th-c. the abbey became a parish church and again it was abandoned. It was sold during the Revolution and used as farm buildings. It is now being restored by the State, and its less perfect condition, compared with Le Thoronet and Senanque, gives it an extraordinary wistful charm.

SISTERON, *Alpes-de-Haute-Provence* (6–D4). Sisteron is sometimes called 'the Gateway to Provence' from Dauphiné. Here the river Durance passes between a huge vertical slab of rock and a cliff on which stands the Citadel, with the picturesque old town below it. The main road S from Gap runs through a tunnel at the foot of the

Citadel, then passes the Romanesque church and three isolated towers, remains of the 14th-c. town walls. The Citadel, 13th–16th-c. (in course of restoration from damage in World War II), can be visited; on the N side of it is an open-air theatre which provides the setting for a festival from mid-July to mid-August, and there is a fine panorama from the viewpoint overlooking the river.

SOSPEL, *Alpes-Maritimes* (9km SW of Breil: 7–D6). Damaged by air raids in 1944 and 1945 because of its strategic position, but since well restored (including the 13th-c. bridge and its tollgate in the middle) and now a popular summer resort. Prehistoric dwellings and caves in the vicinity, traces of medieval ramparts and a château. In the old town are picturesque houses with balconies and an arcaded square, 17th-c. church with a Romanesque Lombard-style tower, and a magnificent retable by François Bréa of the Annunciation with an enchanting landscape. In the Chapelle des Pénitents Blancs is a fine 16th-c. pietà with four kneeling *pénitents* in their cowls.

TARASCON, *Bouches-du-Rhône* (6–D3). Until the death of 'Good King René' in 1480 (*see* Aix), Provence was independent of France, and the Rhône was the frontier between them. This explains the magnificent medieval castle at Tarascon – and the even more commanding site of the ruined fortress across the river at Beaucaire. During the last years of his life René divided his time between Aix and Tarascon, where his castle has miraculously survived intact. The great banqueting hall, the King's and Queen's apartments, the courtyard where miracle plays were performed and minstrels and troubadours would sing, the guardrooms, the chapels – everything is there, together with an astonishing view from the roof-terrace from which Robespierre's supporters were hurled when he fell from power in 1794. Note, too, the half-poignant, half-comic inscriptions on the walls made by English seamen imprisoned here in the 18th-c.

In the town, just below the castle, is the impressive church of St Martha, rebuilt and consecrated in 1197 after the supposed discovery of Mary Magdalene's relics (*see* La Sainte-Baume) had led to the 'discovery' of those of her sister as well. Enlarged in the 14th-c., desecrated during the Revolution, the church was partly destroyed by bombers attacking the nearby Rhône bridge in 1944, but has since been well restored. In the crypt is the singularly beautiful and original tomb of the saint; it is of Genoese workmanship and was commissioned by a 17th-c. archbishop of Avignon. Beneath lie St Martha's alleged relics in a 5th-c. sarcophagus. Halfway up the stairs note the fine Renaissance tomb of Jean de Cossa, King René's seneschal who completed the building of the castle – the work of Francesco Laurana, who was responsible also for a superb retable at Avignon. The church also contains a few primi-

tives, a fine 15th-c. triptych and several 17th-c. paintings.

In late June the town still annually celebrates the legend according to which St Martha tamed a wild dragon and persuaded it to return to the Rhône.

TENDE, *Alpes-Maritimes* (7–D6). First town below the Col de Tende, where the Italian frontier is crossed by a 3km tunnel. The French frontier post and customs are at the N end of the street. The high, slate-roofed medieval houses, clearly built for Alpine winters, cluster below the remains of the 15th-c. château of the Comtes de Tende. 15th–16th-c. church. Market centre for the area. In July the Fête de St-Éloi is celebrated with a cavalcade of mules. Centre for chamoix hunting. Until ceded to France in 1947 the area was the private hunting ground of the King of Italy.

THOR, Le, *Vaucluse* (5km W of L'Isle: 6–D3). Important centre for distribution of grapes in a pretty situation on the river Sorgue. Near the bridge is an unusual 13th-c. church, fine Provençal Romanesque; early Gothic vault, heavy buttresses and Lombard arcading round the apse; interesting doors. Château and remains of ramparts.

3km N, below a ruined château and monastery, and near an interesting Romanesque chapel, the **Grotte de Thouzon** is a 230m cave tunnel filled with delicate stalactites.

THORONET, Abbaye du, *Var* (17km NE of Brignoles: 6–E4). Founded in 1146, at about the same time as its sister abbeys of Senanque and Silvacane (*see entries*), the abbey was probably completed in 40 years. The site, the abbey church, the cloister and buildings form a preconceived whole, unbelievably harmonious and peaceful. This is a direct result of the spirit of the Rule of the newly formed Cistercians, and the austerity, humility and elimination of inessentials in their lives were deliberately communicated to their buildings; functional, solid, unornamented. At the same time, the master-builders of the Order had a deep understanding of proportion, volume and the effect of light, and the simplicity is profoundly moving. Frequently termed Romanesque-Provençal, it is at least as correct to call it Cistercian Architecture.

The church is in the form of a Latin cross with nave and two side aisles. The scarcely pointed arches rest on harmonious piers of masonry (more economical than pillars). The central apse contains three small windows; an *oculus* above; two smaller apses in each transept so that five individual masses could be said. In the N transept, a door leads to the sacristy, and there are stairs to the dormitory; in the N aisle a door leads to a cloister of extraordinary charm and simplicity. In

the centre of the N side is the lavabo, or wash-house, a hexagonal building communicating with the cloister behind it. In the cloister the door to the refectory (the ruins were demolished) was opposite. To benefit from early daylight, communicating with the E side of the cloister are the library, the chapter, the parlour (the only room where heating was allowed) and stairs to the dormitory above. Between the W side and the river is the lay brothers' refectory with dormitory above: to the W of them the guest house. Outside, in the S wall of the church, is a long niche where country people could place their dead.

By 1790 there were only six monks and a brother left; the monastery was in bad repair and in 1791 the monks left for Castellane. Le Thoronet was sold. It was bought by the State in 1854, when it had badly deteriorated; it has been restored brilliantly by the Service des Monuments Historiques, who even reopened the quarry at Cabasse (7km S), from which the stone was brought in the 12th-c., so that it should be identical.

TOULON, *Var* (6–E4). France's most important naval base, with nearly 200,000 inhabitants. In Roman times it was renowned for a purple dye obtained from the murex, a shellfish.

Toulon's rise to importance really dates from the 17th-c. when Richelieu and Louis XIV turned it into a first-class naval base. To be condemned to the galleys at Toulon, like Jean Valjean in *Les Misérables*, was to be condemned to slavery. But prisoners sent there were not only convicts; they included Turks, Negro slaves, and, after 1685, Huguenots.

In 1793 the young Napoleon, then a Captain in the Artillery, leapt to fame at Toulon after the town, in revolt against the Revolutionary government, had welcomed an English fleet. By siting his battery so that it could engage the English gun emplacements at Tamaris (now called Fort-Napoléon), he rendered their position untenable and the English fleet had to withdraw. For a superb evocation of this period read Joseph Conrad's novel *The Rover*.

In 1942 when the Germans invaded Unoccupied France after the Allied landings in N Africa, the French fleet in Toulon was scuttled by its crews to avoid its falling into German hands. The town was liberated after severe damage on 26 August 1944 – see the Memorial on Mont-Faron (which commands fine views), for details of this operation. Other features of naval and historical interest are: the two historic harbours of Toulon, the Darse Vieille (early 17th-c.) and the Darse Neuve (Louis XIV) – although the old buildings there were destroyed in World War II; the Musée Navale and Tour Royale (16th-c.), the latter on a promontory with a fine panorama; the Musée Historique du Vieux Toulon. With the exception of the Tour

Abbaye du Thoronet   *Jean Feuille*

Royale all these are in or near the old town. Note two fine caryatids supporting the town-hall balcony. The Place Puget has a delightful fountain with three dolphins (1782) and the flower, fruit, fish and vegetable markets are lively and colourful – unlike the gloomy Cathedral.

The Museum of Art and Archaeology contains Gallo-Roman remains, some good paintings by Carracci, Fragonard and Vlaminck and others, and fine specimens of Oriental art. Toulon has an opera house, a zoo (on Mont-Faron), and an impressive mountainous hinterland – especially the ridge called Le Gros Cerveau. It is also a good centre for excursions by land or sea. Fine coastal panoramas.

TOURETTE-SUR-LOUP, *Alpes-Maritimes* (4km W of Vence: 7–D5). An attractive unspoilt fortified village with three defensive towers where the outside houses act as ramparts; also a lively centre for arts, crafts, and floral cultivation, especially violets. Restored château with naive frescoes. The 14th-c. church contains (behind the main altar) a pagan altar dedicated to Mercury, also a fine late-16th-c. triptych and two gilded wooden retables.

TURBIE, La, *Alpes-Maritimes* (1½km NW of Monaco: 7–D6). Nearly 500m above sea-level, beside the Grande-Corniche, stands the great Roman monument known as the Trophée des Alpes, built by the Emperor Augustus in 7–6 BC to commemorate his pacification of the troublesome local hill tribes. The original monument, which also served as a fortress, was about 50m high and surmounted by a statue of the Emperor. It was intended as a salutary reminder of Roman military might, the 'Pax Romana', deliberately planted inland on the S limit of wild and mountainous terrain. Later it served as an important staging post on the new road which, leaving the coast near Cap-Martin, climbed to La Turbie and thence ran to Cimiez and Vence. For a time it marked the frontier between Italy and Gaul. Even in Dante's day (1265–1321) it was still remembered as a most celebrated monument. Since then it has been partly dismantled, partly blown up (18th-c.), or simply neglected. Its painstaking restoration to its original condition, although inevitably only partial, has owed much to financial help from an American, Edward Tuck. The museum should also be visited. The views from the terrace are tremendous. The little town is partly medieval, and in the 18th-c. church are 16th-c. gilded wooden carvings, two triptychs, and a pietà of the Bréa school.

UTELLE, *Alpes-Maritimes* (17km S of St-Martin: 7–D5). Unspoilt largely medieval village overlooking the river Vésubie, with 16th-c. fortifications and a church (with Gothic porch and sculptures) containing a late-15th-c. Annunciation. Celebrated above all for the sanctuary of

Madone d'Utelle (1170m), founded 850, rebuilt 1806 (visited by pilgrims on Whit Monday and 16 October), which offers one of the finest views in Alpes-Maritimes.

VAISON-LA-ROMAINE, *Vaucluse* (6–D3). Vaison is three distinct towns: Roman, medieval (the Haute-Ville), and 19th-c. A local civilized tribe, the Voconces, Romanized and prosperous, built a town here – architecturally completely Roman, but not on the typical grid pattern normally imposed when the Romans built in conquered territory. Excavations have not revealed soaring edifices, as at Arles, but rather a way of life. The ground plans of luxurious villas, and the use and disposition of the rooms, are clear, with walls rising to several feet. Two Quartiers have been largely excavated:

(1) *Quartier de Puymin:* the opulent Maison des Messii (an important local family); public gardens, unusual in Provence, called the Portique de Pompée (another important local family), with colonnades and statuary surrounding an ornamental basin of water; beyond it, houses of more ordinary people; to the N the Nymphée, a spring captured in a covered basin from which the town water was supplied; around it, apartment houses; by footpath to the Roman tunnel leading directly to the higher seats of the Theatre. This is on the N slope of the hillock; the tiers of seats descend the natural slope as at Orange (*see entry*). The stage is cut out of rock; note the trench for a curtain as at Arles. (Summer Festival is held each year.) Remarkable museum, near entrance to tunnel, of statuary, murals, mosaics, etc., from excavations and surrounding area. To the W, other buildings, including public latrines similar to Pompeii.

(2) *Quartier de la Villasse* (W of Place du 11 Novembre): Roman Baths below the modern Post Office; part can be seen below. Three others have been identified: one near the station, and two by the river.

La Villasse contains a major road with pavements, a street of shops with colonnade for roof or covering; in it the entrance to the huge and luxurious Maison du Buste en Argent. Beyond it, the Maison au Dauphin. Both have private baths and several gardens.

W of the Villasse quarter stands the former Cathedral of Notre-Dame. From the 3rd-c. onward Vaison was an important centre of Christianity. There are vestiges of a 6th-c. apse to the E of the present apse; the latter is contained in a square block of masonry, with Merovingian arcading inside; the nave is 12th-c. Provençal Romanesque, with a Cistercian simplicity. The charming cloister of the same period houses a museum of Christian Art from the 5th-c.

The medieval town, *La Haute-Ville*, is on the other side of the river Ouvèze. In the 12th-c. the Count of Toulouse seized the church lands and

Jean Feuille

Vaison-la-Romaine: showing the three towns

built a castle on the summit of the rocks to the S of the river to intimidate the bishops in their Cathedral opposite (*see above*). Marauding mercenaries drove the townspeople to take refuge there, and during the 13th- and 14th-c. a new town, with small cathedral, a Bishop's Palace and fine houses, was built below the castle. When the Papacy moved to Avignon, Vaison became Papal territory and the popes strengthened the fortifications. In the late 18th-c. the people began to leave the fortified town and move back to the N side of the river, to build a third town on top of Roman Vaison. The Haute-Ville became deserted, but now people have returned to this part and it is very interesting to visit. Climb to the ruined castle above for superb views.

VALBERG, *Alpes-Maritimes* (5km W of Beuil: 7–D5). Well-equipped ski station and summer resort in attractive site. Notre-Dame-des-Neiges contains interesting examples of modern religious art. Guillaumes (a short distance W), formerly an important market centre, has imposing ruins of a 15th-c. château, a 17th-c. church with earlier bell-tower in Lombard style and a 14th-c. stoup, and an 18th-c. chapel containing a painting representing a fire that ravaged the town. Magnificent views.

VALBONNE, *Alpes-Maritimes* (7km E of Grasse: 7–E5). Quite apart from the nearby golf course Valbonne is worth visiting for its austerely beautiful early 13th-c. church with adjoining monastic vestiges and its 17th-c. arcaded square. It has a well-known grape festival.

VALLAURIS, *Alpes-Maritimes* (3km W of Antibes: 7–E5). On the Plateau des Encourdoules off the road to Grasse are pre-Roman remains, a Roman mausoleum known as La Chèvre d'Or, and other traces of Roman occupation. But Vallauris owes its present fame to Picasso, who in his 10-year residence here revived its moribund pottery and ceramics industry and gave it a worldwide reputation. Two hundred of the ceramics he himself produced are in the Musée Picasso in Antibes (*see entry*) which houses the most important collection of his works in all France.

There are now more than a hundred potters' establishments in Vallauris, together with other arts and crafts, and an international ceramics festival is held biennially.

On the square before Vallauris church is Picasso's bronze of a naked man carrying a struggling sheep, while in a small 12th-c. chapel, now a Picasso museum, his extraordinary paintings of 'War and Peace' testify to the continued exuberance and fecundity of his imagination in old age.

The 16th-c. château has a fine courtyard and staircase. Of the various local chapels the most attractive is the picturesquely situated 17th-c. Notre-Dame-de-Grâce (1km SE).

VAR, River, *Alpes-Maritimes* (7–D5). Until just over 100 years ago the Var marked the frontier between France and Italy. When Nice, Roquebrune and Menton became French in 1860, the E end of the Var department was added to the new territory to form the new department of Alpes-Maritimes, through which therefore the river now flows.

Its source near the Col de la Cayolle (2326m) can be approached from Barcelonnette (*see entry*) through Alpine scenery by D902, which thereafter follows the river as D2202. S of Guillaumes (*see* Valberg) the bright red precipitous Gorges de Daluis, resembling the Gorges du Cian, are of unforgettable grandeur. Just before Entrevaux the river turns abruptly E for 40km, followed closely by N202. At Pont de Mescla, where the river Tinée flows in, river and road swing sharply S into the impressive Défilé du Chaudon, to be joined shortly by the river Vésubie emerging from its own gorges. From then on it is a direct run to the Mediterranean, where the Var flows into the sea on the W boundary of Nice airport.

VENASQUE, *Vaucluse* (10km SE of Carpentras: 6–D3). A small but ancient town between Senanque and Carpentras (*see entries*). It actually preceded Carpentras as the Bishopric and later gave the name to the Comtat Venaissin, a territory which, corresponding roughly to the present department of Vaucluse (but excluding Apt, Orange and Sault), once belonged to the heretical Counts of Toulouse but was appropriated as a Papal possession in 1274 (*see also* Avignon). Beside the 13th-c. church is a 6th-c. Merovingian baptistry (*see also* Fréjus *and* Riez), square with four apses, the arches supported by slim marble columns with classic or Merovingian capitals; the central position of the vanished font is clearly visible. The baptistry and the early date of the Bishopric support the tradition that St Siffrein, patron of Carpentras, was sent from Lérins to evangelize the area.

Just N, on the D4, the sanctuary of Notre-Dame-de-Vie contains the tombstone, with fine Merovingian carving, of Bohetius (d. AD 604), who is believed to have been Bishop of both Venasque and Carpentras.

VENCE, *Alpes-Maritimes* (7–D5). A tribal capital in pre-Roman times, Vence under Roman rule was a place of some importance. The Roman road from the E passed through it and there are traces of a Roman camp; the Cathedral occupies the site of a former temple. Vence also had a bishop as early as the 5th-c.

But Vence's main attractions, apart from its unusually mild climate (which accounts for its English colony and its quaint Anglican chapel), are essentially medieval, ranging from most of its walls, entrance gates and *places* (especially the 15th-c. Place du Peyra with its urn-shaped fountain) to the Cathedral. Although the latter reveals several traces of the earlier pre-Romanesque building, including a 5th-c. sarcophagus and some fine Carolingian strap-work, it is predominantly Romanesque with 17th-c. additions, though its most outstanding feature is the exuberant carving of its 15th-c. choir-stalls. The museum contains some good pieces of church 'Treasure'.

There are some attractive chapels in the vicinity, particularly the seven Chapelles du Calvaire built *c.* 1700; but the most memorable of all is the Chapel of the Rosary, planned and carried out by Matisse for a congregation of Dominican nuns in 1949–51 when in his late seventies and early eighties. The stained-glass windows consist of patterns of blue, green and yellow, and the magical light effects they produce within the white chapel – giving it, as Matisse put it, 'the dimensions of infinity' – make a powerful impact on the visitor. At the time of writing this chapel can unfortunately only be visited on Tuesday and Thursday.

Vence, where D. H. Lawrence died in 1930, is very much an artists' resort, and has a modern art gallery.

VENTOUX, Mont, *Vaucluse* (6–D3). Some of the most astonishing views in Provence – either from the flanks of the Massif or, above all, from the summit (over 1900m), from which can be seen the Alps, the Vercors, the Cévennes, the Luberon, Ste-Victoire, Les Alpilles, Marseille, L'Étang de Berre, the sea, and at night the flashing of lighthouses. The atmosphere tends to be hazy at midday in hot weather. Meteorological observatory, radar and television installations. Snow from December to April: skiing from Chalet Reynard and Mont Serein. Remarkable flora.

VERDON, Grand Canyon du, *Alpes-de-Haute-Provence* (*c.* 16km SW of Castellane: 7–D5). This 21km-long canyon is one of the most extraordinary natural phenomena in Europe, in its scale and its wildness. The cliffs vary in height from about 250m to 700m; the width at the bottom is between 6m and 100m and at the top varies from over 200m to nearly 1½km.

It was originally a natural fault in the limestone plateau. The turbulent river Verdon (tributary of the Durance), runs swiftly in its gorges far below, occasionally disappearing below the rocks; its strong green colour gave rise to the Celto-Ligurian Goddess of the Green Waters. The canyon was first fully explored in 1905 by the early speleologist E.–A. Martel. Roads have since been built along its entire length, with viewing-points at the most dramatic places. It can best be reached from Comps-sur-Artuby, from Castellane or from Moustiers-Ste-Marie.

VILLARS-SUR-VAR, *Alpes-Maritimes* (24km E of Entrevaux: 7–D5). Excellent wine, pleasing situation, picturesque village; of particular interest for its church with superb retables of the Burial of Christ and of the Annunciation, and for a 16th-c. statue of John the Baptist.

VILLEFRANCHE, *Alpes-Maritimes* (1km E of Nice: 7–E6). This old fishing port, once also the naval harbour of the Dukes of Savoy (the port de la Darse), owes its name to the fact that it was founded (early 14th-c.) as a free port (i.e. no customs were payable). With its Italianate architecture and covered streets it is markedly Ligurian and has remained virtually unchanged since the 18th-c. Note the imposing fortress (1560), the 18th-c. port and the late 17th-c. Church of St-Michael with tombs of Knights of St John of Malta. In the Chapelle St-Pierre, formerly a fishermen's chapel, are frescoes by Cocteau.

Villefranche was a base for the American Fleet while France belonged to NATO because of its magnificent roadstead, and it is still sometimes visited by ships of the Royal and American Navies.

VILLENEUVE-LÈS-AVIGNON, *Gard* (1km NW of Avignon: 6–D3). Approaching Villeneuve from Avignon across the river one notices first the Tour de Philippe le Bel (the Iron King of Maurice Druon's novel), built 1293–1307 to survey what was still foreign territory across the Rhône. The second floor and watch-tower, as well as the Fort St-André – an exceptionally fine example of medieval architecture offering superb views – were, however, built later in the 14th-c., by which time the Papacy had moved from Rome to

Avignon, thus putting itself directly under French influence. Avignon had become very over-crowded, and Villeneuve became its high-class residential suburb. Several cardinals lived there, one of whom, a nephew of John XXII, built the church (1333), which contains pictures by the 17th-c. painters Philippe de Champaigne, Vouet and the two Mignards. The 18th-c. main altar has a fine marble relief of Christ Entombed, originally made for the Chartreuse (*see below*); but the church's chief artistic treasure is in the sacristy – a 14th-c. ivory statuette coloured in polychrome, of the Virgin and Child carved out of an elephant's tusk. Note also the 14th-c. Virgin and Child in marble.

Founded in 1356 by Innocent VI, the Charterhouse (or Chartreuse du Val-de-Bénédiction) became the largest house of the austere Carthusian order, whose members spend most of their time in solitary prayer, study and manual work. A plan of the Chartreuse is given in the official guide. In the church is the fine 14th-c. tomb of Innocent VI with its white marble effigy. A sudden view of Fort St-André appears through a ruined apse. The cloisters, both large and small, are intact, unlike the refectory, though even here faint traces of 14th-c. frescoes are visible. Those in the adjoining chapel of Innocent VI, attributed to Matteo Giovanetti and recently restored, are of great beauty. The brothers (as opposed to the monks), who undertook such tasks as cooking and baking for the whole community, had separate cloisters and cells. The 17th-c. hostelry could accommodate 60 people and has fine 18th-c. ceilings. The Charterhouse's woodshed, workshops, stables, etc., are all 18th-c.

In the municipal museum, formerly a 17th-c. mansion, is a fine Crucifixion by Philippe de Champaigne; also a portrait of a bewitching marquise dressed as a Carthusian, which must have been rather distracting for the worthy Carthusians when it hung in their church. But note especially the painting of the Coronation of the Virgin (1453) with St Bruno (who founded the Order in 1084) kneeling in adoration; this masterpiece by Enguerrand-Charenton, who came from Laon but worked in Avignon, has interesting contrasts: the large flat design of the central group is essentially Italian, but the landscape and the city with the Crucifixion and the vision of Hell beneath, are distinctly Flemish.

VILLENEUVE-LOUBET, *Alpes-Maritimes* (9km N of Antibes: 7–E5). This village, a short distance inland, should not be overlooked. Behind the *mairie* the house in which the great chef Auguste Escoffier (1846–1935) was born is now a fascinating museum with a superb collection of old menus, engravings and photographs, recalling not only Escoffier but other celebrated chefs as well. The majestic 12th–13th-c. château was well restored in 1842.

Corsica (Corse): Introduction

Edward Young

The 'Scented Isle', invaded by Phoenicians, Greeks, Etruscans and Romans, was ruled by the Genoese from the Middle Ages until 1768, when it became French, only fifteen months before Napoleon was born in the capital, Ajaccio. It has a thousand kilometres of superb coastline – golden beaches, coves, gulfs, and mountains rising sheer from the sea. Holiday activities include sailing, fishing, climbing, skin-diving in the limpid waters around Cap Corse, canoeing in mountain rivers, skiing at Vergio and Haut-Asco. Geographically the island divides diagonally in two: steep mountain country to the northwest, with Monte Cinto the highest peak at 2700 metres; to the southeast more mountains, gradually descending to the east-coast plains and the stratified cliffs of Bonifacio in the extreme south.

Between the two halves run the spectacular Ajaccio–Corte–Bastia main road and – equally spectacular but more restful – the railway. Both pass secretive old towns, forests of oak, chestnut and *laricio* pine, gorges with raging torrents, upland pastures where cattle, sheep, goats and pigs roam at will. Here the air is scented with resin; crystal water bubbles out of springs; wild strawberries, raspberries, mulberries, mushrooms, cyclamen and the pale-green hellebore flourish according to season. In winter, deep in snow, the forests are silent and unbelievably beautiful. (But a warning to motorists: before leaving the coast for the narrow, steep and winding inland roads, check your car and fill the tank; garages are far apart.)

In the plains the once-prevalent malaria has been eradicated. The *maquis*, a dense undergrowth whose fire risk is a constant threat to the forests, has been brought under control; vineyards, orchards and early vegetables now contribute to the island's economy. A paradise of wild flowers and scented herbs whose perfume carries far out to sea, the *maquis* is a traditional hide-out for bandits – hence the adoption of the name by the French Resistance in World War II.

The Corsican is friendly but hot-blooded. Family quarrels can last for generations (*vendetta* is a Corsican word). Siesta time is sacrosanct. The Corsican's passions are horseracing, football and elections; all provide excuses for festivity, fierce partisanship and short-lived violence. He is a fervent churchgoer, loves festivals and processions – and wedding lunches lasting until early morning.

Corsica is now increasingly popular, yet the beaches (which are free) are never crowded. The best months are May–June, and September–October. Car ferries run from Nice, Toulon and Marseille, and are fully booked months in advance. Air France and Air-Inter operate passenger services from Paris, Marseille and Nice. For up-to-date information, consult travel agencies or the French tourist offices.

Ajaccio: statue of Napoleon   Topham *(Jean-Pierre Benier)*

Corsica (Corse): Gazetteer

Edward Young

NOTE: See Corsica inset on map 7.

AJACCIO. Capital of Corsica and main port of southern Corsica, founded in 1492. It lies on the corner of a protected bay at the head of the Gulf of Ajaccio; on the other side of the bay, 7km by road, is the airport. Viewed from the steamer arriving from Marseille, Toulon or Nice, the town makes an exciting impression – the ancient citadel guarding the point, the old houses and modern hotels, the harbour crowded with yachts, the long curving sandy beach, the boulevards and squares lined with outdoor cafés and palm-trees and, behind it all, the forest-clad mountain rising to a rocky summit.

Ajaccio was the birthplace of Napoleon, and the visitor is not allowed to forget it. There are statues of him in the Place Foch, in the Place d'Austerlitz, in the Place Général-de-Gaulle. The house where he was born is a museum of personal relics. The domed 16th-c. Cathedral contains the font at which he was baptized and a monumental high altar donated by his sister. The Hôtel-de-Ville houses a Napoleon Museum displaying family portraits, his baptismal certificate, a bronze cast from his death mask, etc. In the Palais Fesch, home of Napoleon's uncle, Cardinal Fesch, is the chapel (erected by Napoleon III) in which members of the Bonaparte family are buried (except Napoleon himself – his body lies in the Invalides in Paris). In another part of the same palace is the fine Fesch Collection of 14th–18th-c. Italian paintings.

Ajaccio is an animated town, with crowded open-air cafés and restaurants, a casino, and a daily quayside fish market. For a more peaceful scene, take the coast road 12km W to the Pointe de la Parata; here is a simple 15th-c. defensive tower, with a fine view of the Iles Sanguinaires, especially at sunset. There is also a 3-hour boat trip round the islands from Ajaccio.

13km NW of the town, surrounded by a park with views of the gulf, is the curious late-19th-c. **Château de la Punta**, a reconstruction of a demolished *pavillon* from the Tuileries Palace in Paris; full of remarkable furnishings, including a portrait of Napoleon by David.

ALERIA. In the centre of the narrow strip of east-coast plains, 4km inland from the mouth of the Tavignano in an area of large lakes and long sandy beaches. Aleria was an important colony in Greek

and Roman times, as revealed by the excavations to SW of the present village and by the remarkable collection of local finds in the Jerome Carcopino archaeological museum. For centuries after the departure of the Romans the whole region slumbered in malaria-ridden neglect. Since World War II the malaria has been exterminated and the area is again rich in vines, fruit and agriculture, and – in Lake Diana and Lake Urbino – oysters, mussels and other shellfish.

ASCO. Small village resort in the wild valley of the river Asco, 18km W of Ponte Leccia by a road which passes through steep rocky defiles and gorges. Fishing, walking, climbing. 12km SW is the wintersports centre of **Haut-Asco** (altitude 1450m).

BASTELICA. Old township near the head of the Prunelli valley, 40km NE of Ajaccio, in an area of forest, mountain and upland pasturage, with Monte Renoso (*see* Ghisoni) rearing up to the NE. Good centre for exhilarating excursions in mountain scenery.

BASTIA. The largest, oldest and busiest town in the whole island, Bastia is an important commercial and ferry port set between mountains and sea at the E side of the neck of the Cap Corse promontory. The harbour is divided between the New Port to the N (where the ships come in from Marseille, Nice, Toulon, Livorno and Elba), and the Old Port, used by fishing-boats and yachts, to the S.

Facing the New Port is the vast esplanade of Place St-Nicolas, 300m long, shaded by plane-trees and palms, and lined with outdoor cafés. On a clear day Elba and the mountains of Italy stand out on the eastern horizon. Between the esplanade and the Old Port, a maze of ancient, narrow crowded streets between high balconied houses clusters round the Place de l'Hôtel-de-Ville and two 17th-c. churches.

On the S side of the Old Port, on a steep defensive site, are the ramparts of the old citadel built by the Genoese in 1830. The former Governor's Palace is now a museum, and from it a path leads to the Hanging Gardens with views over the town. Within the ramparts are two old churches, side by side: the 15th-c. Ste-Marie, which was the Cathedral of Corsica until 1801, when the bishopric was transferred to Ajaçcio; it contains a silver statue of the Assumption of the Virgin which is carried in street procession every 15 August; the other is the chapel of Ste-Croix, which has gilded cherubs cavorting on a deep-blue Louis-Quinze ceiling, and a venerated black oak crucifix, the Christ of the Miracles, which was found floating in the sea in the 15th-c. (procession every 3 May). Below the citadel, from the end of the Dragon Jetty, is a fine view of the Old Port with its background of mountains.

A short way inland to the NW, perched on a rock, is the little church of **Ste-Lucie** with a magnificent view of Bastia and the long beach extending southward, with the great Biguglia lake behind it, and Bastia airport beyond, 21km S of the town.

On the SE edge of the airport is the 12th-c. abbey church of **La Canonica**, close to the excavated remains of a 4th-c. basilica.

The N199 road W to St-Florent (*see entry*) climbs the central mountain ridge, reaching its highest point (548m) at **Col de Teghime**, 10km W of Bastia, with superb views of the Mediterranean to E and W. An even finer view can be obtained by taking the D338 north from there to the summit of **Serra di Pigno** (nearly 1000m).

BAVELLA, Col de. One of the most spectacular viewpoints on the island, about 1250m above sea-level. A vast amphitheatre of needle-like rocks, jagged cliffs, wind-stunted pines. Northward the snowy summits of the Monte Incudine range, a glimpse of deep blue sea to the east. In spring an outburst of wild flowers. Southward the road descends through a huge pine forest to the village resort of **Zonza** (9km).

BONIFACIO. The most southerly town on the island, Bonifacio is a medieval fortress built on a most extraordinary site – a plateau of sheer limestone rock 60m high and jutting out into the sea. The ancient city, with its steep approach, its defensive gates, its 13th-c. church, its silos for storing grain against a long siege, the narrow

Bonifacio

French Government Tourist Office

cobbled streets passing under slender arches that channel rainwater into cisterns deep in the rock, and its houses crowding to the very edge of the cliffs, still retains its medieval and military character. Add to all this the radiant whiteness of the sun, the limpidity of the sea and the evident *joie de vivre* of the inhabitants, and one can understand why for many Bonifacio is the most appealing town in the whole of Corsica.

The best views of it are from the lighthouse at Pertusato on the southern tip of the island (whence Sardinia is visible, only 12km away) or from the motorboat which takes you from the harbour quay on a ¾-hour trip round the promontory on which the town is built, passing caves and grottoes, the alarming overhang of the stratified cliffs, and the 187 steps of the 'Escalier du Roi d'Aragon', said to have been cut into the rock in the course of a single night during a 15th-c. siege.

Though Bonifacio itself has no *plage*, there are

Pino, Cap Corse

G.L. Carlisle

sandy beaches within easy driving distance, the nearest being Calalonga (9km E) and Tonnara (10km NW).

Car ferries run daily from Bonifacio to Santa Teresa on the N tip of Sardinia (1 hour).

CALACUCCIA. Mountain resort, facing a new lake formed by a hydro-electric *barrage* across river Golo. Reached by RF9 from Porto through Evisa (*see entries*). Excursions, fishing, climbing, walking, riding. Starting point for the ascent of Monte Cinto (*see entry*). Across the lake, the village of **Casamaccioli** has a striking view of the S face of Monte Cinto, and every 8 September a famous folklorique festival with street procession.

CALVI. An old fortified harbour on the NW corner of the island, and the nearest port to the French mainland. In summer it is crowded with holiday-makers, who come to enjoy its mild climate, its 6km stretch of sandy beach, the protected bay ringed by pine forests and mountains, the lively cafés bordering the palm-shaded quayside, the yachts and fishing-boats moored alongside, and the ancient citadel crowning the dramatic promontory of rock which juts out to protect the harbour from the west.

The citadel, built by the Genoese at the end of the 15th-c., was severely damaged in several sieges – in particular during the Napoleonic Wars in 1794 when the town surrendered to the British Fleet after a seven-week bombardment from land and sea, in which Nelson, then a junior captain, lost the use of his right eye. The ramparts, though often rebuilt, are still intact, and the walk round them is very impressive, with fine views. Inside the walls the old city is deserted, with silent narrow streets and ancient houses. The former Governor's Palace is now a Foreign Legion headquarters. The 13th-c. domed church of St-Jean-Baptiste has a beautifully carved pulpit, a remarkable 15th-c. triptych, an ebony crucifix renowned for its miracles, and other sacred treasures. S of the church the 15th-c. oratory is now a museum of religious art. In the Rue Colombo is a house claiming to be the birthplace of Christopher Columbus; as his parents were Genoese this is just possibly true, but seems unlikely.

CAP CORSE. The name given to the whole of the dramatic promontory which projects 40km northwards at the top of the island. It consists largely of a mountain ridge, with **Monte Stello** the highest point (1300m). The coast road from Bastia to St-Florent (110km) is spectacularly beautiful but slow, with innumerable zigzag bends, especially on the W side where the forests and mountains come steeply down to the sea, giving rise to dizzily situated villages like **Nonza** and **Pino**. The Cap-Corsicans are a race apart, a hardy seafaring people with ancient trade connections with Italy. On the E coast, **Erbalunga** is a picturesque little

fishing harbour. The peninsula abounds in sandy bays, with rocky outcrops in deep clear water, ideal for skin-diving and snorkelling.

CARGÈSE. Small W coast fishing port and summer resort on a promontory at the NW point of the Gulf of Sagone, N of Ajaccio. Founded in the 17th-c. by Greeks fleeing from Turkish rule, it now has two 18th-c. churches facing each other, one Greek Orthodox, one Roman Catholic. High cliffs, a Genoese watch-tower, and sandy beaches within easy reach.

CERVIONE. Small town some 25km N of Aleria on the E coast, elevated about 300m above the coastal plain with fine views across it to the sea; it has an imposing 16th-c. domed cathedral. 1km N is the chapel of Ste-Christine with 15th-c. frescoes. Yacht harbour at Campoloro, 7km E. Inland to the NW the road twists through an area of remote mountainside villages, notably **Piedicroce d'Orezza** and **La Porta** with their unexpectedly ornate Baroque churches.

CINTO, Monte. The highest peak in the island, 2700m and eternally covered by snow, yet only 25km from the sea. The ascent in summer is not technically difficult, providing you are fit and the weather is good and you are prepared to make a dawn start. The best approach is by the SE face from Calacuccia (*see entry*), whence you can drive by road to within 6km of the summit. After that it is hard going, but depending on your fitness and experience you should reach the top in 4–5 hours. Breathtaking views of the whole island, and across the sea to the Alpes-Maritimes, Italy, Elba, etc.

CORTE. The old capital of the island, a fortress from at least the 11th-c. onward, and the largest inland town. Its remoteness from the coast and, in the past, its lack of contacts with the outside world have enabled it to remain more truly Corsican than any other town on the island, and it is closely associated with Paoli (who founded a university here *c.* 1780), Gaffori and other heroes of Corsican independence.

Its situation on a rocky spur dominating the confluence of two turbulent rivers, surrounded by granite mountains, is dramatic. The cobbled streets that climb steeply towards the 15th-c. hilltop citadel have scarcely changed in 500 years; even the marks of 18th-c. gunshots on some of the walls are still there. Fountains add charm to the ancient houses and squares. At the southern edge of the spur, below the walls of the citadel (occupied today by the Foreign Legion), the rock falls sheer to the river 100m below, and the view is tremendous.

Accessible from Ajaccio and Bastia by the N193 or by railway, Corte is a splendid centre for excursions on foot or by car. The best walk is to the W, up the spectacular gorges of the Tavignano, and to the SW is a beautiful drive through the gorges and pine forests of the Restonica. To the E, by a winding road (D14 and D41), is the isolated perched-up village of **Sermano**, whose church has a remarkable medieval fresco.

EVISA. The twisting RF9 road from Porto to Evisa climbs in the space of 23km from sea-level to well over 800m. This mountain village resort lies in a dramatic setting on the edge of the Aitone Forest. An exhilarating 3-hour walk starts less than ½km W of the village, by a path that turns right from the main road; it leads through wild country to a ravine where the torrents of the Aitone and the Tavulella join to form the river Porto; the path now follows the deep and turbulent **Gorges de Spelunca**, arriving eventually at the precipitous village of Ota, where a car service for return to Evisa is available.

Northeastward the RF9 continues its sinuous route towards the **Col de Vergio** (12km). Here, at 1460m above sea-level, you are at the highest point of the highest road in Corsica; the views are tremendous, but it is not the best place for the car to break down in bad weather, and for five of the winter months it is liable to be blocked by deep snow. From the Col the road drops to the wintersports station at **Vergio**, then descends in

twists and turns through the Valdo-Niello Forest to Calacuccia (*see entry*) – 34km from Evisa.

GHISONI. Remote mountain village 650m above sea-level on the RF10 road from Ghisonaccia to Corte. Situated at the foot of two alarmingly high and precipitous rocks in beautiful forest surroundings. 12km E, the RF10 runs above the torrent of the Fium Orbo as it roars through the narrow Stretti and Inzecca gorges. SW stands **Monte Renoso** (2352m), 35km away by road, followed by a long walk to the summit (about 9 hours the round trip); if you aim to reach the top you need good weather and an early start, but once there you have a spectacular view of the whole of southern Corsica and the north of Sardinia.

ILE-ROUSSE, L'. Fashionable resort only 24km NE of Calvi airport. Gets its name from the red-ochre islet of Pietra which has a lighthouse and is connected to the shore by jetty. Yacht harbour, small port, exporting olives, wine and other local produce. Gentle climate, sandy beaches, casino. Good centre for excursions to Calvi, Corte, Cap Corse, etc. Annual fair early September with regattas, etc.

9km W is the ancient fortified port of **Algajola**,

Ota, near Evisa in the Gorges de Spelunca

Peter Brown

Corte

dating back to the Phoenicians. Inland, 5km S of L'Ile-Rousse, is the old town of **Corbara** with Moorish connections and (2½km S) a remarkable 15th-c. monastery. A further 7km S the medieval fortified village of **Sant'Antonino** perches high on a rocky outcrop, with amazing views.

PORTO, Golfe de. This wide gulf on the W coast, midway between Ajaccio and Calvi, is part of the Parc Régional and happily protected from development. Indented by innumerable bays, with mountain foothills reaching out into the sea, their reddish cliffs intensifying the deep blue of water and sky, it is one of the most beautiful stretches of coastline in the whole island.

Porto itself is a small but celebrated resort at the head of the gulf. Here the river Porto emerges into a lagoon anchorage; the hamlet of houses and small hotels nestles behind a rocky outcrop surmounted by an ancient Genoese tower. It makes a delightful centre for exploring this richly varied coastline. The road N gives access to the beaches of Bussaglia and Caspio, then continues to the top of the Col de la Croix; here are superb views and the start of a difficult mule-track (not for cars) which drops down into the tiny village of **Girolata**, beautifully and peacefully situated at the

head of its own smaller gulf; it too is protected by a Genoese tower on a little promontory. (An alternative way of reaching it is by boat from Porto, an absorbing trip along the coast, 3 hours there-and-back.)

W of Porto the road wriggles along the S shore of the gulf, passing first through forests of sweet chestnut, then through a strange area known as 'Les Calanches', a 'chaos' of curiously shaped red and ochre rocks. After **Piana** – a popular hilltop summer resort with marvellous views of the gulf and the distant summit of Monte Cinto – the main road leaves the gulf, turning S to Cargèse (*see entry*). But minor roads return you northward to the coast by a steep descent into Ficajola, with its enchanting little cove, or further W to Capo Rosso, a promontory of rose-red rock, 300m high with a tower at the top, marking the SW extremity of the gulf; from it are unforgettable views of sea and coast, and of the brooding mountains with their ever-changing colours, deepening to orange, crimson and purple in the evening sun.

PORTO-VECCHIO. Thriving little harbour town at the head of a deep fiord-like gulf towards the S end of the E coast. The malarial mosquito which plagued it until the end of World War II has

G.L. Carlisle

Propriano harbour

now been eliminated, and today Porto-Vecchio is one of the most attractive of Corsica's holiday resorts, with a beautifully indented coastline and plenty of sandy beaches, coves and anchorages. High up behind the town brood the remnants of the ancient Genoese citadel, and either side of the N198 is the island's largest plantation of cork-oak, Porto-Vecchio's major export.

PROPRIANO. Known to Phoenician, Greek and Etruscan traders, this little port lies in a marvellously protected position at the head of the Gulf of Valinco. Undisturbed for hundreds of years, it was discovered by tourists in the 1960s. Long sandy beaches, lovely views of sea and mountains, animated beachside cafés, hotels and restaurants, holiday villas, every aquatic sport, and plenty of interest inland.

About 20km NW at **Filitosa**, in the beautiful setting of the Taravo valley, is the most important prehistoric religious site in Corsica, dating from at least 8000 years ago, with remarkable carved and engraved stones, or menhirs. Excavations are still in progress, and there is an explanatory museum.

ST-FLORENT. Former Genoese stronghold at the W extremity of the neck of Cap Corse. The winding narrow streets of the old town, with its ancient citadel (now the *gendarmerie*) and its small harbour, make it a holiday resort full of interest. Close inland is the 12th-c. cathedral church of Ste-Marie, sole survivor of the vanished city of **Nebbio**, destroyed by the Saracens.

SAN-MICHELE-DE-MURATO. Leave St-Florent by the D82 through Oletta. After crossing the **Col de Stefano** (with its far-reaching views to E and W), you come to this extraordinary little church standing alone on a rocky plateau. It is built in different colours of stone, with a tall rectangular tower on two columns of horizontal stripes, and adorned with all manner of charmingly original carvings.

SARTÈNE. Medieval inland Corsican town, in the hills 13km SE of Propriano, with lovely views of sea and coast. Famous for its traditional Holy Week processions. Important prehistory museum of local finds: S and SW the area is rich in megalithic sites, especially at **Cauria** (12km S). 19km NE is the busy little hilltop town of **Ste-Lucie-de-Tallano** where they grow wine and quarry a rare volcanic stone called *diorite orbiculaire* (in Ajaccio they sell paperweights made of it); in the parish church is a charming 15th-c. bas-relief of the Virgin and Child.

VIZZAVONA. Village resort in the wild centre of the island, surrounded by mountains and forests and the noise of raging torrents. Accessible by road and rail from Ajaccio or Bastia. Monte d'Oro (nearly 2400m) dominates the western skyline; the arduous 10-hour walk to the summit and back is rewarded by unbelievable views of mountains, sea, Elba, and the Italian mainland. Other summer mountain resorts nearby: **Bocognano** (12km SW) and **Vivario** (9km N).

Les Calanches, near Porto   G.L. Carlisle

Glossary
of Architectural and Other Terms

Ambulatory. Literally, a place for walking. In cathedrals and large churches it means the area around both sides of the choir and around the main altar, designed to give access to the apsidal chapels, to provide space for processions, and to allow pilgrims to view saintly relics and the Cathedral 'Treasure'.

Angevin Vaulting. *See* Vaulting.

Apse. The semi-circular east end of a church, containing the high altar.

Archivolt. The ornamental decoration or moulding on the face of an arch, following its curve.

Baldaquin, Baldachin. A fixed canopy of wood or stone erected over a tomb, a pulpit, a throne, or an altar. It can be suspended from the roof, supported on pillars, or projected from a side wall.

Barbican. An outer defence post of a castle or fortified town, designed as a guard against attacks on the drawbridge or the main gate.

Baroque. An architectural style developed especially in Italy during the 17th-c. and characterized by a fluid manipulation of forms to produce a deliberately emotional effect, a heightening of spiritual imagination. In France the style was appropriated mainly in secular building for the glorification of King and State.

Bartizan. Small crenellated overhanging turret on the corner of a castle or square tower, giving defenders a cross-view along two walls.

Basilica. Originally, an oblong apsidal building with spacious nave and side-aisles used by ancient Romans for public assemblies. Adapted by the early Christians for their services; in particular, a transept was inserted to separate the nave from the high altar and apse. Later, the apse was moved further east to accommodate the chancel or choir, and the arms of the transept were extended outward, thus completing the cruciform plan in which symbolism and practical requirements so admirably coincided.

Bastides. Small fortified towns built in the southwest by both French and English during the 12th-, 13th- and 14th-c. They marked the approximate frontier between the two sides in their spasmodic and long-drawn-out struggle, and were invariably laid out to the same military pattern – a rectangular grid street-plan surrounded by ramparts and defended gateways, with a fortified church standing at one corner of a central arcaded market square. Tax relief and other privileges were used as inducements to persuade civilians to inhabit the *bastides*. Sometimes the purpose of a *bastide* was not military, but the attempt by a local lord to populate a thinly-inhabited region.

Buttress. Outer support on a wall to take the lateral thrust from interior weight. A **Flying Buttress** is a downward slanting arch which takes the thrust of a wall free-standing to an outer solid pier buttress. The flying buttress is a striking feature of the Gothic style, well exemplified in the Cathedral of Notre-Dame in Paris.

Capital. The carving or moulding at the head of a pillar. In medieval churches the capitals provided the stonemason with an opportunity to express his individuality and imagination in carvings of biblical scenes, grotesque animals, monsters, foliage, and so on, just as the woodcarvers were later able to be creative in the decoration of choir-stalls.

Causses. The area of arid limestone plateaux south of the Massif Central, stretching from the Cévennes in the east to the edge of the Toulouse plain in the west, and southwards almost to the Mediterranean. Limestone being porous, the *causses* have very little top-soil, barely enough to grow a thin, coarse grass. It is a dramatic landscape, created by volcanic action, erosion, and the scouring by a number of torrential rivers to make deep valleys and spectacular gorges.

Chaos. An area of unusually chaotic rock formations resulting from a large cliff-fall or ancient volcanic disturbance.

Chevet. The exterior of the ambulatory at the east end of a church. In Romanesque churches the rounded walls and curved, shell-like roofs of the radiating chapels form agreeable compositional groups. In Gothic churches the main feature of the chevet is usually an array of flying buttresses.

Cirque. An amphitheatre of rock; a concave part-circle of sheer mountainside or high cliffs (e.g. the Cirque de Gavarnie in the Pyrenees, and the Cirque de Montvalent in the Dordogne valley).

Classical. Architectural style embodying the order – proportion, balance, clarity, symmetry – inherent in the architecture of ancient Greece and Rome.

Clerestory. The upper storey of a church, with windows above the level of the aisle roofs providing the main source of light in the nave.

Coffer. Recessed panel, usually square or octagonal, in a ceiling or vault.

Corbel. A block projecting from the face of a wall to support a platform or a gallery, sometimes terminating in decorative carving.

Corps de logis. The main residential section of a castle or château between the towers or partitions.

Crenellation. Square openings along the parapet of a castle or a church tower and enabling defenders to shoot at opponents from sheltered positions.

Crossing. See Transept.

Cupola. A relatively small rounded structure like a dome. See also Dome.

Curtain wall. A non-structural wall linking two towers or other fortifications in a castle, often concealing a watch-path behind crenellation or machicolation.

Diptych, Triptych, Polyptych. Altarpiece painting or relief sculpture consisting of (respectively) two, three, or more than three, hinged and folding panels.

Dolmen. French word for a cromlech, or prehistoric structure of large stones arranged like a table, with one stone supported horizontally on three or four upright ones. See also Menhir.

Dome. A hemispherical or near-hemispherical vault over a circular or polygonal base. Sometimes, as in the Dôme des Invalides in Paris, the dome rests on a cylindrical structure known as the *Drum*. A dome is often surmounted by a small Cupola (*see above*) with windows forming a *Lanterne*.

Donjon. See Keep.

Drum. See Dome.

Flamboyant. In architecture, the term applied to the highly ornate final phase of French Gothic from the late 14th-c. The style is characterized by curvilinear flamelike decorative forms, especially in the stone tracery of windows and open-work.

Flying buttress. See Buttress.

Fresco. (From the Italian word meaning 'fresh'.) A method of painting on a wall or ceiling, using a watercolour medium applied directly to the plaster while the plaster is still wet. The colour is absorbed into the plaster and remains fresh; if applied to dry plaster the paint tends to flake off. The climate of northern Europe is not suitable for the process, but in southern France and in Italy it has been used successfully from the times of Classical Antiquity, reaching its apogee in Italy at the hands of Michelangelo and Raphael in the early 16th-c.

Gothic. Architectural style which originated in northern France in the 12th-c. and dominated the design of cathedrals and churches for some 400 years. It is characterized by the pointed arch, the rib vault and the flying buttress – all of which allowed reduction of the enclosing walls in favour of a frame of soaring arcades, with a great increase in the area of windows.

Gouffre. A large chasm, or deep hole, sometimes the result of the collapse of the roof of a subterranean cave, and often indicating the presence of other such caves in the vicinity.

Groin vaulting. See Vaulting.

Grottes. Subterranean caves caused by the percolating of streams and rivers. Often found in limestone areas like the Dordogne valley, and marked by stalagmites, stalactites and other calcareous formations.

Jubé. See Rood-screen.

Keep. The strong innermost tower of a medieval fortress. The French word for keep is *donjon*, not to be confused with the English word 'dungeon' meaning an underground prison cell, though in practice the lower part of the keep was often used as a lock-up for prisoners.

Lanterne (Lantern). See Dome.

Lapidary museum. A collection of carved or engraved stone fragments found or unearthed on archaeological sites.

Lierne Rib. See Rib.

Loggia. An open-sided room acting as an upper gallery or entrance portico.

Machicolation. A projecting parapet or gallery

with floor openings between the corbels, enabling the defenders of a castle to drop missiles or pour molten lead or boiling oil on the heads of the enemy beneath.

Mandorla. An upright almond-shaped frame, traditionally used in church painting and sculpture to surround a representation of Christ in Glory.

Menhir. Tall monumental stone found placed upright on a prehistoric site. *See also* Dolmen.

Narthex. An inner porch or entrance hall – an 'ante-nave' – found at the west end of some churches, separated from the nave by a railing, screen or wall. In early Christian churches the narthex was reserved for use by penitents and unbaptized converts under instruction.

Nave. The main body of the church where the congregation sit or stand.

Oculus. A small round window (literally, an 'eye'), often incorporated in the upper part of Gothic windows.

Ogee arch. A pointed arch whose sides form a continuous double curve, convex at the top (seen from the inside) turning to concave at the bottom – in profile resembling an 'onion-skin' dome. (Not to be confused with ogive vaulting – *see* Vaulting.)

Ogive Vaulting. *See* Vaulting.

Oppidum. A Gallo-Roman encampment town.

Orders. The classical Greek and ancient Roman forms of post and beam consisting of column (with or without a base), capital and entablature (incorporating architrave, frieze and cornice). The original three Greek 'Orders', distinguished by their specific proportions, mouldings and details, were: Doric, Ionic and Corinthian; to these the Romans added Tuscan and Composite.

Parterre. A level area of a garden laid out as flower beds.

Phylloxera. The insect plague which devastated vineyards throughout France in the late 19th-c. The winegrowers survived by grafting vine cuttings on to American phylloxera-resistant root stock.

Pietà. A representation in painting or sculpture of the Virgin holding the dead body of Christ on her lap. (From the Italian: 'pity' or 'compassion'.)

Polyptych. *See* Diptych.

Renaissance. The great cultural revival that took place in Italy during the 14th-, 15th- and 16th-c., inspired by a new understanding of the artistic and architectural principles of Classical Antiquity. The influence of this revival quickly spread throughout France and the rest of western Europe. At first, however, the new 'Italian style' was merely imitated in a new vocabulary of decorative forms and motifs, and it was only gradually that the underlying principles of order and harmony came to be understood.

Reredos. A decorated screen, or decorated section of the wall, at the back of an altar.

Retable. A decorative structure or framework standing on the rear of an altar, serving as the frame for carved or painted panels, and sometimes acting as a shelf for the cross and other ecclesiastical ornaments.

Rib. Part of the framework of a dome or a vaulted roof (*see also* Vaulting). At first ribs were merely form work reinforcing the edge (or groin) caused by the intersection of curved surfaces in groin vaulting; following the introduction of the pointed arch they became integral parts of the structural skeleton of Gothic building. **Lierne and Tierceron Ribs** are subordinate and largely decorative intermediate ribs in the later variations of ogive vaulting.

Romanesque. The style of ecclesiastical building that was prevalent in France from the early 10th-c. until the advent of Gothic in the 12th-c. The Romanesque style was subject to great regional variations, but the plan was generally cruciform with a semi-circular apse and rounded, radiating, projecting apsidal chapels. The typical Romanesque church has two square towers (often with short spires) at the west end, and a belfry tower (square or octagonal, sometimes a combination of both) over the transept crossing, also with spire. Open-timber roofs, subject to fire risk, were gradually replaced by stone barrel vaulting and, later, by groin and rib vaulting (*see* Vaulting). Walls were thick, with small windows, and naves tended to be sombre. Though basically austere, interiors were often lavishly frescoed and there was great scope for rich and individual sculptural decoration in capitals and façades.

Rood-screen (French: *Jubé*). A decorated screen, of wood or stone, across the full width of the nave, separating it from the east end of the church. A crucifix, or rood, was normally mounted above it in the centre. From the 17th-c. onwards it was felt that the screens were an undesirable separation of the congregation from the choir and altar, and most of them were gradually removed altogether or displaced to the rear of the nave. However, some (as at Albi, for instance) are still *in situ*.

Rose-window. Large circular window, with stained glass in an elaborate framework of stone tracery suggesting the shape of a rose; usually in the centre of the west wall but sometimes at the ends of the transept arms.

Sarcophagus. Stone coffin, usually of an important personage and carved with bas-relief or inscription.

Side aisle. The area either side of, and parallel to, the nave or choir, usually separated by a row of pillars. In Romanesque and early Gothic churches the side aisle was usually surmounted by a gallery.

Tierceron Rib. *See* Rib.

Transept. In a cruciform church, the transverse portion which forms the arms of the cross and separates the nave from the chancel and choir. The word can also apply to each of the arms – i.e. the North and South Transepts. The area in the centre is the **Crossing**, usually surmounted by a dome or a tower, or both.

Tribune. The apse of a basilica or an open gallery, often supported on pillars.

Triforium. An arcaded wall passage below the clerestory, not to be confused with the gallery (or tribune).

Triptych. *See* Diptych.

Tympanum. The semi-circular or triangular space between the top of a door and the arch above it. Frequently used in cathedrals and churches for sculptured representations of Christ in Majesty and similar themes. Some are among the finest examples of Romanesque art.

Vaulting. An arched structure, of stone or brick, forming the roof over a nave, a covered side-aisle, a crypt or any large chamber. The type of vaulting often conditions the architectural style of the whole building, because of the way it transmits weight-load to side-walls or pillars. The main styles of vaulting are as follows, in chronological order:

Barrel vaulting: in the shape of an inverted semi-cylinder, i.e. the simple round arch extended longitudinally over the space to be covered.

Groin vaulting: in square bay compartments over which two barrel vaults intersect at right angles.

Rib vaulting: in the reinforcement of the edges where the surfaces of groin vaulting met by slim arches, or ribs, of stone or brick; later these arches became the ribs of a skeletal construction that was to develop into ogive vaulting.

Ogive vaulting: based on the innovation of the pointed arch, and constructed on a skeleton of pointed-arch ribs, of which two in each bay are the diagonals, intersecting at the centre of the vault; the ribs here express the transmission of weight to piers supported by exterior flying buttresses (*see* Buttress). Later, the basic ogive vaulting became more complicated, with the addition of subsidiary lierne and tierceron ribs (*see* Rib), decorated hanging keystones, and so on.

Angevin vaulting: a variation of ogive vaulting prevalent in the Loire Valley, named after the town of Angers whose cathedral provides the finest example. Whereas in normal ogive vaulting the transverse arches are at the same height as the diagonal arches, forming a continuous ridge of constant height, in Angevin vaulting the diagonal arches rise to a greater height than the transverse arches; thus the vaulting of each bay has a somewhat domed effect.

Voussoires. The wedge-shaped stones used in the construction of an arch. The centre stone at the peak is the Keystone; the bottom stone at each side is the Springer.

Chronology
of Principal Events in French History

BEFORE CHRIST
c. **30,000** BC Cro-Magnon man appears in southwest France. Cave paintings.
c. **3000** BC Evidence of early civilizations from megalithic tombs at Carnac in Brittany and in southern Corsica.
6th-c. BC Celts invade Gaul.
600 BC Foundation of Marseille by Greek traders.
390 BC Gauls invade Italy, sack Rome but fail to capture the Capitol.
2nd-c. BC Romans colonize Provence and consolidate land route to Spain.
59–52 BC Julius Caesar conquers Gaul. Suffers defeat by Vercingétorix at Gergovie (near Clermont-Ferrand), but finally defeats him at Alésia.
44 BC Death of Julius Caesar.

FIRST THOUSAND YEARS AD
3rd–4th-c. Introduction of Christianity to northern Gaul.
c. **250** Martyrdom of St Denis, first Bishop of Paris.
280 Paris (Lutetia, Lutèce) destroyed by Barbarians.
c. **285–365** Series of Germanic invasions.
313 Emperor Constantine grants freedom of worship to Christians ('Edict' of Milan).
451 Attila, king of the Huns, defeated at Châlons by combined forces of Romans and Visigoths.
5th-c. Visigoths establish power in France, with capital at Toulouse.
Late 5th-c. Arrival in Brittany of Celts who emigrated from Britain.
481 CLOVIS proclaimed king of the Franks. Baptized at Reims in 496.
507 Clovis defeats Alaric, king of the Visigoths, near Poitiers.
511 Death of Clovis.
8th-c. Saracen invasions of southern France via Iberian peninsula. The Saracens were active in Aquitaine, Languedoc, the Massif Central, Provence and the Rhône Valley.
732 CHARLES MARTEL (first Carolingian king) gains great victory over the Saracens at Poitiers, driving them south. But the Saracens continued to terrorize the extreme south for a further century or so, especially in Provence.
800 CHARLEMAGNE (768–814), installed at Aix-la-Chapelle (Aachen) in Germany, is crowned Holy Roman Emperor.

814 Death of Charlemagne. His grandsons later quarrel over the succession, finally dividing his empire into three parts by the Treaty of Verdun (843).
9th–10th-c. Central power weakened by continuing series of destructive invasions, especially by Vikings who subsequently settle in Normandy. Local administration taken over by dukes and counts, many of whom establish strong power bases.
987 HUGH CAPET, first of the Capetians, elected king at Senlis, near Paris. Dies in 996.
996–1031 ROBERT II (The Pious).
9th–11th-c. The era of the great pilgrimages to Compostela in northwest Spain, and the building of Romanesque churches.

ELEVENTH CENTURY
1031–60 HENRI I.
1060–1108 PHILIPPE I.
1066 William, Duke of Normandy, invades and conquers England.
1095 First Crusade preached by Pope Urban II, at Clermont-Ferrand.
1099 Capture of Jerusalem.

TWELFTH CENTURY
1108–37 LOUIS VI (The Fat).
1137–80 LOUIS VII (The Young). First husband of Eleanor of Aquitaine.
1152 Eleanor of Aquitaine, divorced by Louis VII, marries Henri Plantagenêt, who becomes King Henry II of England two years later.
c. **1136** Start of construction of Cathedral of St-Denis, later to become the prototype of the Gothic style.
1163 Bishop Sully begins construction of Notre-Dame in Paris.
1180–1223 PHILIPPE II (The August).
1189 Death at Chinon of Henry II of England. Outbreak of struggle between Plantagenets and Capetians.
1195 Richard Coeur-de-Lion starts building of Château Gaillard in Normandy. Killed four years later while besieging Châlus.

THIRTEENTH CENTURY
This century was the great period of *bastide* building.
1204 Normandy united with the French crown.

1205 Philippe II harries the English out of all French territory except for the southwest.

1209–29 The brutal 'Albigensian Crusade', led by Simon de Montfort until his death in 1218, against the Cathars or Albigensian heretics of southern France.

1215 Signing of Magna Carta in England.

1223–6 LOUIS VIII.

1226–70 LOUIS IX (St Louis).

1244 Capture of Montségur, last stronghold of the Albigensian heretics. Garrison slaughtered.

1270 Death of Louis IX at Tunis, and end of the Eighth (and last) Crusade.

1270–85 PHILIPPE III (The Bold).

1285–1314 PHILIPPE IV (The Fair).

FOURTEENTH CENTURY

1307 Suppression of the Knights Templar.

1309–77 The Papacy installed at Avignon. After 1377, until 1403, there were two popes: the Pope, re-installed in Rome, and the anti-Pope in Avignon.

1314–16 LOUIS X (The Quarrelsome).

1316–22 PHILIPPE V (The Tall).

1322–8 CHARLES IV (The Fair), the last of the Capets. On his death Edward III renewed the English claim to the French throne.

1328–50 PHILIPPE VI, the first of the Valois kings.

1337 Outbreak of the Hundred Years War.

1346 English victory at Crécy.

1348 The Black Death.

1350–64 JEAN II.

1356 Battle of Poitiers. Jean II captured by the Black Prince and taken to London, where he died eight years later.

1360 Treaty of Brétigny. French cede Aquitaine to the English.

1364–80 CHARLES V (The Wise). During his reign, inspired by the skilful French general Du Guesclin, the French won back most of the territory they had lost under the Treaty of Brétigny. By 1380 the English had been driven back virtually to Bordeaux and Bayonne.

1380–1422 CHARLES VI (The Well-Beloved).

FIFTEENTH CENTURY

1412 Birth of Joan of Arc at Domrémy.

1415 The English invade Normandy. Battle of Agincourt.

1418–19 Siege and capture of Rouen.

1420 Treaty of Troyes, giving the whole of northern France into English possession.

1422–61 CHARLES VII (The Victorious).

1428 English besiege Orléans.

1429 Joan of Arc relieves Orléans. Charles VII (the Dauphin) crowned at Reims.

1430 Joan of Arc captured at Compiègne.

1431 Henry VI of England has himself crowned King of France in Notre-Dame in Paris. Joan of Arc burned at the stake in Rouen.

1436 Charles VII retakes Paris.

1453 English defeated at Battle of Castillon, near Bordeaux, and withdraw from all France except Calais.

c. **1454** Invention of printing in Germany.

1455–85 Wars of the Roses in England.

1461–83 LOUIS XI.

1480 Death of 'Le Bon Roi René', Duc d'Anjou, Comte de Provence, wise and benevolent ruler of Provence for 46 years. After his death Provence became part of France.

1483–98 CHARLES VIII.

1491 Anne of Brittany marries Charles VIII.

1492 Columbus reaches the New World.

1494 Charles VIII invades Italy. French presence in Italy lasts until 1559. Spread of Italian influence on the arts and architecture of France.

1498–1515 LOUIS XII.

1499 Anne of Brittany marries Louis XII.

SIXTEENTH CENTURY

The early part of this century was notable for the spread of the printed book, growing economic expansion and a rapidly increasing population.

1514 Death of Anne of Brittany. Soon afterwards Brittany was ceded to France.

1515–47 FRANÇOIS I.

1515 French victory over the Duke of Milan at Marignano.

1516 François imposes terms on the Pope, leading to the Concordat of Bologna which gives the French monarchy disposal of the higher positions in the church in France, a right that lasted until the Revolution.

1519 Death of Leonardo da Vinci near Amboise.

1534 Jacques Cartier, French navigator, discovers Canada. Calvin preaches Protestantism in Poitiers. Religious persecutions follow.

1547–59 HENRI II.

1558 Calais, last remaining English possession in France, captured by the Duc de Guise.

1559 Henri II killed in jousting accident. The next three short-lived kings were brothers, the sons of Henri II and Catherine de Médicis. With them expired the line of Valois kings.

1559–60 FRANÇOIS II.

1560–74 CHARLES IX.

1562 Start of the Wars of Religion between Catholics and Protestants (Huguenots).

1572 Massacre of St Bartholomew's Eve in Paris, when thousands of Protestants were murdered during supposed peace negotiations.

1574–89 HENRI III, the last of the Valois.

1580 Publication of Montaigne's *Essays*. Montaigne was Mayor of Bordeaux from 1581 to 1585, and died in 1592.

1589 Henri III murdered while laying siege to Paris.

1589–1610 HENRI IV (Le Vert Gallant), first of the Bourbon kings.

1593 Henri IV proclaims his conversion from Protestantism to Catholicism; the religious wars die down for a time.

1598 The King issues the Edict of Nantes, granting freedom of worship to Protestants.

SEVENTEENTH CENTURY
1610 Assassination of Henri IV. The religious struggle flares up again.
1610–43 LOUIS XIII.
1618 Start of the Thirty Years War in Germany, with the French involved sporadically.
1624 Richelieu becomes First Minister.
1628 The Protestant strongholds of La Rochelle and Montauban surrender to the royal army.
1629 Richelieu orders the dismantling of castles in the Rhône Valley and the Auvergne.
1642 Death of Richelieu. Mazarin appointed First Minister.
1643–1715 LOUIS XIV (The Sun King). The King being a minor, there was a Regency until 1661, virtually under the control of Mazarin.
1648 End of the Thirty Years War. Treaty of Westphalia gives most of Alsace to France.
1648–53 The 'Fronde' (a revolt by nobles and parliament against the centralized power of the monarchy).
1661 Death of Mazarin. Louis becomes King in his own right. Start of the building of Versailles. Rise to power of Colbert.
1685 The King orders the Revocation of the Edict of Nantes. Thousands of Protestants flee the country.

EIGHTEENTH CENTURY
1701–14 War of Spanish Succession. French defeats at Blenheim, Ramillies, etc.
1715–74 LOUIS XV.
Mid-century: Sporadic warfare between France and England over North American colonies. In **1759** French lose Quebec and West Indian possessions.
1766 Lorraine becomes part of France.
1768 Genoese cede Corsica to France.
1769 Birth of Napoleon in Corsica.
1774–92 LOUIS XVI.
1775–83 American War of Independence. France gives active support to the Colonists. Naval war with Britain.
1789 Fall of the Bastille signals the outbreak of the French Revolution.
1792 The Convention proclaims a Republic.
1793 Execution of Louis XVI and Marie-Antoinette.
1794 Fall and execution of Robespierre.
1798 French military expedition to Egypt, Napoleon Bonaparte in command. In August, Nelson destroys the French fleet at Aboukir Bay.
1799 Bonaparte, returned from Egypt, appointed First Consul.

NINETEENTH CENTURY
1803 Renewal of war with Britain.
1804 NAPOLEON crowned Emperor.
1805 Nelson defeats combined French and Spanish fleet at Trafalgar. Napoleon abandons plans to invade England, but defeats a combined army of Russians and Austrians at the battle of Austerlitz.

1808 France invades Spain, and Portugal a year later.
1812 French invasion of Russia, capture of abandoned Moscow, followed by disastrous winter retreat.
1813 Wellington crosses the Pyrenees from Spain.
1814 Allied invasion of France. Paris capitulates. Napoleon abdicates at Fontainebleau and is exiled to the island of Elba.
1815 The 'Hundred Days' begins with Napoleon's escape from Elba and ends with his defeat at Waterloo, his second abdication and final exile to the isle of St Helena, where he dies in 1821.
1814–24 LOUIS XVIII. The Restoration.
1824–30 CHARLES X.
1830 Revolution in Paris. Charles X abdicates.
1830–48 LOUIS-PHILIPPE.
1830–48 Conquest of Algeria.
1848 Further Revolution in Paris. Abdication of Louis-Philippe. Election of Louis Napoleon Bonaparte (Napoleon III) as President. Proclamation of Second Republic.
1848–70 NAPOLEON III. President 1848–52, Emperor 1852–70.
1861–5 American Civil War.
1869 Opening of Suez Canal.
1870 France declares war on Prussia, but suffers a series of defeats. Prussians invade France. Napoleon III surrenders at Sedan. Prussians besiege Paris. Peace treaty gives Alsace and part of Lorraine to Germany.
1871 The Commune in Paris.
1875 The Third Republic.
1876–80 Phylloxera pest devastates French vineyards.
1887–9 Building of the Eiffel Tower.
1889 Paris Exhibition.
1894 The Dreyfus Affair. (French Jewish army officer twice wrongly convicted of treason and sent to prison on Devil's Island; finally proved innocent in 1906.) Bitter political ramifications.

TWENTIETH CENTURY
1904 Entente Cordiale between France and Britain in face of growing German menace.
1914–18 World War I.
1917 Russian Revolution.
1919 Treaty of Versailles. Alsace and Lorraine returned to France.
1923 French occupy the Ruhr, and evacuate it two years later.
1929 Wall Street crash.
1930 Election of over 100 Nazis to German Reichstag.
1933 Hitler becomes Chancellor of Germany.
1935 Italians invade Abyssinia.
1936–9 Spanish Civil War.
1939 Outbreak of World War II.
1940 Germany invades France. French sign armistice. British Expeditionary Force evacuated at Dunkirk. France partitioned, with Marshal Pétain head of Vichy government of Unoccupied France.

1942 Allies land in French North Africa. Germans occupy the whole of France. French fleet scuttles itself in Toulon harbour. October: British victory over Germans at El Alamein.
1944 Allies land in Normandy (6 June) and on the Côte d'Azur (15 August). De Gaulle enters Paris (26 August).
1945 German surrender (8 May); the Western Allies celebrate V-E day (Victory in Europe).
1946 The Fourth Republic.
1951 Pétain dies in prison on the Ile-d'Yeu.
1954 Revolt in Algeria.
1956 France, Britain and Israel make abortive attack on the Suez Canal.
1957 Foundation of the Common Market (EEC) comprising France, West Germany, Italy and the Benelux countries.
1958 French army assumes power in Algeria. Inauguration of the Fifth Republic.
1959 De Gaulle elected President.
1961 Collapse of French army revolt in Algeria.
1962 Proclamation of Algerian Independence.
1968 Students' uprising.
1969 De Gaulle defeated in presidential election. Pompidou elected President.
1970 Death of De Gaulle.
1974 Death of Pompidou. Giscard d'Estaing elected President.
1981 Giscard d'Estaing defeated and François Mitterand (Socialist) elected President.

A Brief Bibliography

Historical and General
ARDAGH, John. *The New France*. Secker & Warburg, London, 1968, and Harper & Row, New York. New edn. *The New France: De Gaulle and After*, Penguin Books 1982; *The Book of France*, Windward, London, 1982.
BRIGGS, Robin. *Early Modern France, 1560–1715*. Oxford University Press, 1977.
CHAMBERLAIN, Samuel. *Bouquet de France*. Hamish Hamilton, London, 1952.
COBBAN, Alfred. *A History of Modern France, 1715–1962* (3 vols.). Penguin Books, London and Baltimore, 1965.
CRONIN, Vincent (General Editor). The Companion Guides to: *Paris* (Vincent Cronin, 1963); *The South of France* (Archibald Lyall, 1963); *The South-West of France* (Richard Barber, 1977). Collins, London, and Harper & Row, New York.
DRUON, Maurice. Novels about medieval France, published in English under the series title, *The Accursèd Kings*. Hart-Davis, London, 1956–61, and Scribners' Sons, New York.
MITFORD, Nancy. *The Sun King*. Hamish Hamilton, London, 1966, and Harper & Row, New York. Also Michael Joseph, London, 1983 and Crescent Books, New York.
OYLER, Philip. *The Generous Earth* (about the Dordogne). Hodder & Stoughton, London, 1950.
WHITE, Freda. *Three Rivers of France* (Dordogne, Lot, Tarn), Faber, London, 1952, and Transatlantic Arts, New York, 1955 (revised 1972). *West of the Rhône*, Faber, 1964. *Ways of Aquitaine*, Faber, 1968, and Norton, New York.

Food and wine
BOCUSE, Paul. *The New Cuisine*. Hart-Davis, MacGibbon, London, 1978.
DAVID, Elizabeth. *French Provincial Cooking*. Michael Joseph, London, 1960, and Harper & Row, New York, 1962 (revised 1977).

FORBES, Patrick. *Champagne: the Wine, the Land and the People*. Gollancz, London, 1967, and Reynal & Co., Clifton, New York.
HALLGARTEN, S. F. *Alsace and its Wine Gardens*. Deutsch, London, 1957, and British Book Center, Elmsford, New York.
OLIVER, Raymond. *The French at Table*. International Wine & Food Society, London, 1967.
PENNING-ROWSELL, Edmund. *The Wines of Bordeaux*. International Wine & Food Society, London, 1968, and Stein & Day, New York.
SIMON, André. *The Noble Grapes and the Great Wines of France*. McGraw-Hill, London, 1957, and New York.
SIMON, André. *The History of Champagne*. Ebury Press, London, 1962.
TOYÉ, Kenneth. *Regional French Cookery*. International Wine & Food Society, London, 1973.
YOXALL, H. W. *The Wines of Burgundy*. International Wine & Food Society, London, 1968, and Stein & Day, New York.

In French
ARTHAUD. *Le Monde en Images*. Beautifully illustrated series of regional appreciations: *Paris, Ville Enchantée*; *L'Auvergne*; *Provence Enchantée*; *Corse, Ile de Beauté*; etc.
HACHETTE. *Les Guides Bleus*. Regional guides.
LES HORIZONS DE FRANCE. Illustrated series of introductions to various regions: *Visages de Poitou*; *Visages de Gascogne*; etc.
MICHELIN. *Les Guides Verts*. Best of the regional guides. Six volumes are issued in English: *Paris*; *Normandy*; *Brittany*; *Châteaux of the Loire*; *Périgord* (Dordogne); *Côte d'Azur*.
READER'S DIGEST. *Les Mille Visages de la Campagne Française*. 1976.
ZODIAQUE. *La Nuit des Temps* (The Mists of Time). Scholarly texts, with fine photographs, on Romanesque churches: *Touraine Romane; Limousin Roman; Bourgogne Romane;* etc.

Tourist Information

Advance Planning

Planning is part of the fun of a holiday. It is hoped that this book will help you to choose the area of France that appeals to you and to note the places you would like to visit. Arm yourself with an up-to-date guide to hotels and restaurants (e.g. the famous red *Guide Michelin*, published annually at Easter and a mine of information, well worth prior study) and a good road map of your chosen area; there are several road-map series available, including the Shell Cartoguides and the *Michelin* 1cm:2km yellow maps. In the height of the tourist season (July–Sept.) it is advisable to book hotels in advance, or at least to telephone ahead (*see* Telephoning *on facing page*).

WHEN TO GO: Any time from Easter to the end of September. In a good autumn, warm sunny weather will last until the end of October. In the north of France the weather is much the same, and as unreliable, as in the south of England. Naturally, the further south you go the warmer temperatures become in general, though it can't be said that fine weather can be guaranteed throughout every summer. For the French, the great holiday rush is July to mid-September. If you can avoid travelling on a summer bank holiday, including the day before and the day after, do so – especially in the approaches to Paris. A list of French bank holidays is given below. The worst time for traffic is the first weekend in August, when every French family seems to be on the move. If a holiday in Paris is your goal, spring and autumn are best: in August, Paris is a dead city.

Driving in France

For the American motorist the drive-on-the-right rule is no problem, and even for the British it is usually no problem after the first five minutes. For the British driver the danger comes with over-confidence; dangerous times are: returning to the road from a car park, a filling station or a picnic spot, turning on to a major road out of a narrow minor road, and turning off a roundabout.

Don't forget the *priorité à droite* in built-up areas. Look out for those inconspicuous roads which come in on your right-hand side. Unless your road is a *passage protégé*, the driver coming in from the right has priority, *and will use it!*

Make sure you are familiar with the International road signs.

TRAFFIC POLICE, especially on main roads at busy weekends, can be tough on motorists who are caught speeding, failing to stop at a red traffic light or a STOP sign, failing to wear seat-belts (obligatory in France outside town limits), and other similar offences.

SPEED LIMITS:

Autoroutes: 130 km.p.h. (80 m.p.h.) – Toll
Dual carriageways: 110 km.p.h. (68 m.p.h.)
Other roads: 90 km.p.h. (56 m.p.h.)
Built-up areas: 60 km.p.h. (37 m.p.h.) – or as directed by signs.

AUTOROUTES: most have periodic tolls (*péages*), and on a long journey they can seem expensive, but you probably save the equivalent in fuel and wear-and-tear. On entering the autoroute you sometimes take a ticket from an automatic machine and pay at the next toll-station. The service areas are usually well managed and of a high standard. Some large modern road bridges (like the Pont de Tancarville near Le Havre) also charge a toll.

The Metric System

The metric measures most likely to be used by the motorist in France are kilometres for road distances, litres for motor fuel, and kilograms per square centimetre for tyre pressures. For motorists not yet used to the metric system, here are some approximate equivalents:

KILOMETRES: 8km equals approx. 5 miles. Thus:

km:miles	km:miles	km:miles
3 : 2	10 : 6	80 : 50
4 : 2½	20 : 12	90 : 56
5 : 3	30 : 18	100 : 62
6 : 3½	40 : 25	125 : 78
7 : 4	50 : 31	150 : 94
8 : 5	60 : 37	175 :110
9 : 5½	70 : 44	200 :125

LITRES: The British (imperial) gallon is just over 4½ litres; the US gallon is about 3¾ litres. Thus:

Litres	British gallons	US gallons
5	1.1	1.3
10	2.2	2.7
15	3.3	4.0
20	4.4	5.3
30	6.7	8.0

Litres	British gallons	US gallons
40	8.8	10.6
50	11.1	13.3
100	22.2	26.7

When you get used to the price of motor fuel (*essence*) in France, you will find it simpler to order in multiples of 10 francs.

KILOGRAMS PER SQUARE CENTIMETRE: To convert lbs per sq.in. to kg per sq.cm., divide by 100 and multiply by 7. Thus:

lbs per sq.in	Approx. kg per sq.cm.
18	1.25
20	1.4
22	1.55
24	1.7
26	1.8
28	2.0
30	2.1
32	2.25
34	2.4

Bank Holidays

Nothing is more annoying than to land in France with no French currency, only to find that it is a bank holiday and that the banks and most of the shops are shut. The following days are bank holidays in France:

New Year's Day . . . . *1 January*
Easter Monday. . . . . *(movable)*
Labour Day . . . . *1 May*
VE Day . . . . *8 May*
Ascension Day . . *6th Thursday after Easter*
Whit Monday . . *2nd Monday after Ascension*
Bastille Day . . . . *14 July*
Assumption . . . . *15 August*
All Saints (Toussaint) . . . . . *1 November*
Armistice Day. . . . . . . *11 November*
Christmas Day . . . . . . *25 December*

Note: If any falls on a Tuesday or a Friday, the day between it and the nearest Sunday is taken as a holiday, being known as the '*pont*' or 'bridge'.

Banks

Banks are shut on Saturdays and Sundays – *except* in towns with a Saturday market, when they open on Saturday and shut on Monday. Banks also close at midday on the eve of bank holidays. Banking hours are normally 8 a.m.–12 noon and 2–4.30 p.m.

When changing travellers' cheques, don't forget to take your passport with you. Unless you are a currency speculator by nature, it is advisable to take French franc travellers' cheques; this avoids fluctuating exchange-rate problems, and makes cashing cheques much simpler. An alternative way of obtaining cash is by use of the Eurocheque system, details of which can be obtained from your own bank. In the height of the season there are often long queues of tourists waiting to cash travellers' cheques, and you may be unlucky if you arrive in the bank at five minutes to noon; since

banks open at 9 a.m. a good time to change your cheques is before breakfast.

Telephoning

The simplest way to telephone is to write the required number on a piece of paper and ask your hotel or a post office to get it for you. However, you may not be in your hotel and there are often queues at post offices, and in any case it is cheaper to use one of the modern coin boxes which are now available in most towns and villages. Slots take 5fr, 1fr, ½fr and 20c. coins. Put plenty of 1frs in the box before you start; the coins needed for the call are automatically taken as the call proceeds, and coins not used are returned to you as you put the receiver down.

Calls within the same department: simply dial the 6-figure number.

Calls to another department: dial 16, listen for the tone change, then dial the area code (2 figures) followed by the 6-figure number.

Calls to the UK: dial 19, listen for the tone change, then dial 44, followed by the UK area code and the number you want (but omit the '0' at the beginning of the area code).

Calls to other European countries: consult a telephone directory.

Transatlantic calls: consult your hotel or a post office.

Although the telephone areas coincide with the department areas, for some reason or other the French area codes are not the same as the departmental post codes (although both consist of two figures). Area codes are listed at the beginning of all telephone directories (they are also shown at the head of each town entry in the *Guide Michelin*).

A sensible precaution when holidaying abroad is to take with you a list of the telephone numbers (including area codes) of anyone you might conceivably need to call in your home country (e.g. relatives, bank, insurance company, etc.)

Shop Opening Hours

These vary according to (a) the season, (b) the type of shop, (c) the size of the town. In most places shops are open on Saturday but may shut on Monday. Food shops (bakers, butchers, small grocery shops) tend to shut later than others, sometimes as late as 7 p.m., and open on Sundays and bank holidays (mornings only), *even on Christmas Day*. On Monday everything used to shut but today you may find several shops open. Generally speaking *all* shops shut for at least two hours, at or soon after *midi*. The French *déjeuner* is sacred. Hypermarkets are open six days a week.

Railways

Today the French railways (SNCF – Société Nationale des Chemins de Fer) are clean, comfortable and reasonably punctual. In the tourist season it is advisable to get tickets in advance (from main stations and many travel agents). Seats can be reserved on all main line trains. Hire-cars can be reserved in advance to await arrival at most large towns. Men over 65 and women over 60 can, on production of their passport, obtain a *carte vermeil* entitling them to a 50% reduction on non-rush-hour trains.

Note: To reduce station staff, obviate fraud and speed-up entry and exit at stations, you must get your ticket, if bought in France, punched *composter* at an automatic (red) machine as you enter the platforms; this dates your ticket. If you omit to do this, the ticket inspector on the train can charge you the price of the ticket again – plus 20%.

Speaking French
Apart from business and the professions, few French people are able or willing to speak English. But they will respect your efforts, however halting, to speak French and will do their best to help you out. Naturally, the better your French the more you will get out of your holiday, and it is well worth brushing up your 'school French' beforehand. Take with you a small two-way dictionary and a phrase-book – also a dictionary of motoring technicalities in case you have to visit a garage for repairs.

Tipping
Most hotels and restaurants automatically add a 15% service charge to the bill (the *Guide Michelin* will tell you whether service is *compris* or not). If you are not sure, don't be shy of asking. If service is not included, something like a 15% tip should normally be given. In hotels, the porter or bell-boy who carries your luggage up to your room, and the 'room service' waiter, will expect a tip; the amount must be left to your own experience and discretion. Museum and château guides should also be tipped as you leave.

Châteaux, museums, etc.: times of opening
Except in a few cases, times of opening have not been included in this book, as they are liable to change. Nor have prices of admission, as in these inflationary days they are bound to have increased between the time of writing and the date of publication. Times and prices are shown in the invaluable Michelin green guides, though even these are not necessarily brought out in new editions each year.

As a general rule, it can be assumed that such places as are open to the public will charge a few francs for admission and will be open at least from Easter to the end of September, including weekends. Museums, especially in large towns, are more likely to remain open all the year round, but many of them shut on Tuesdays even in summer. Hours of opening vary, but will generally include the periods 9.30 a.m.–noon and 2.30–5 p.m.; those with guided tours will cease admission half an hour or so before the morning and afternoon closing times.

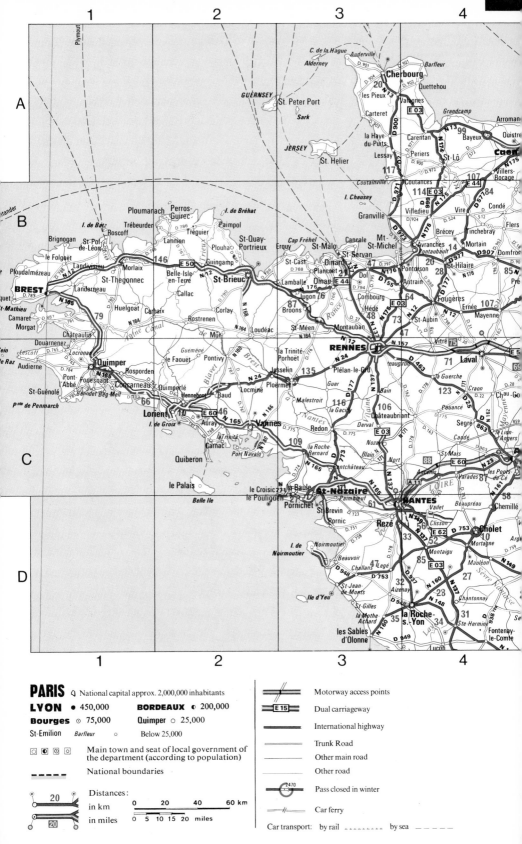

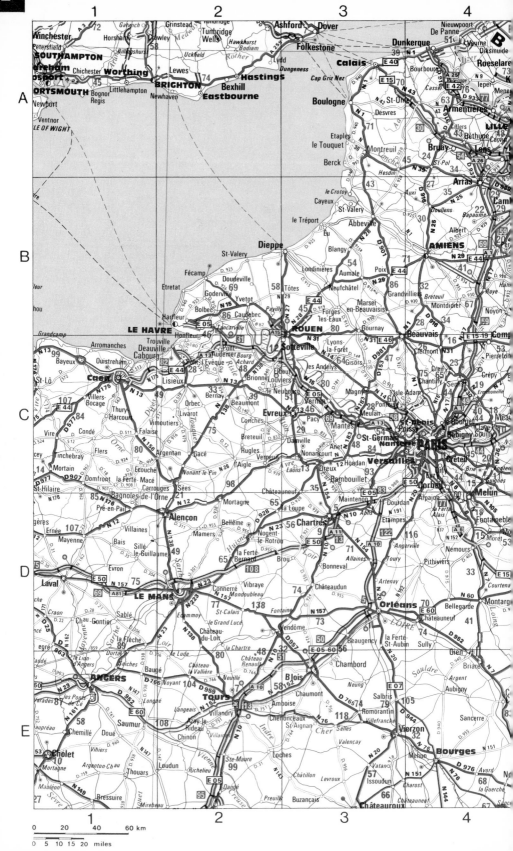

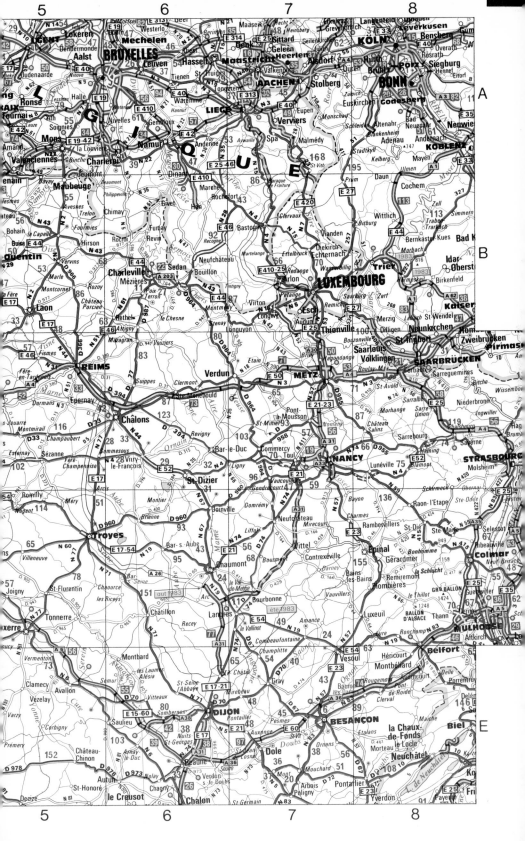

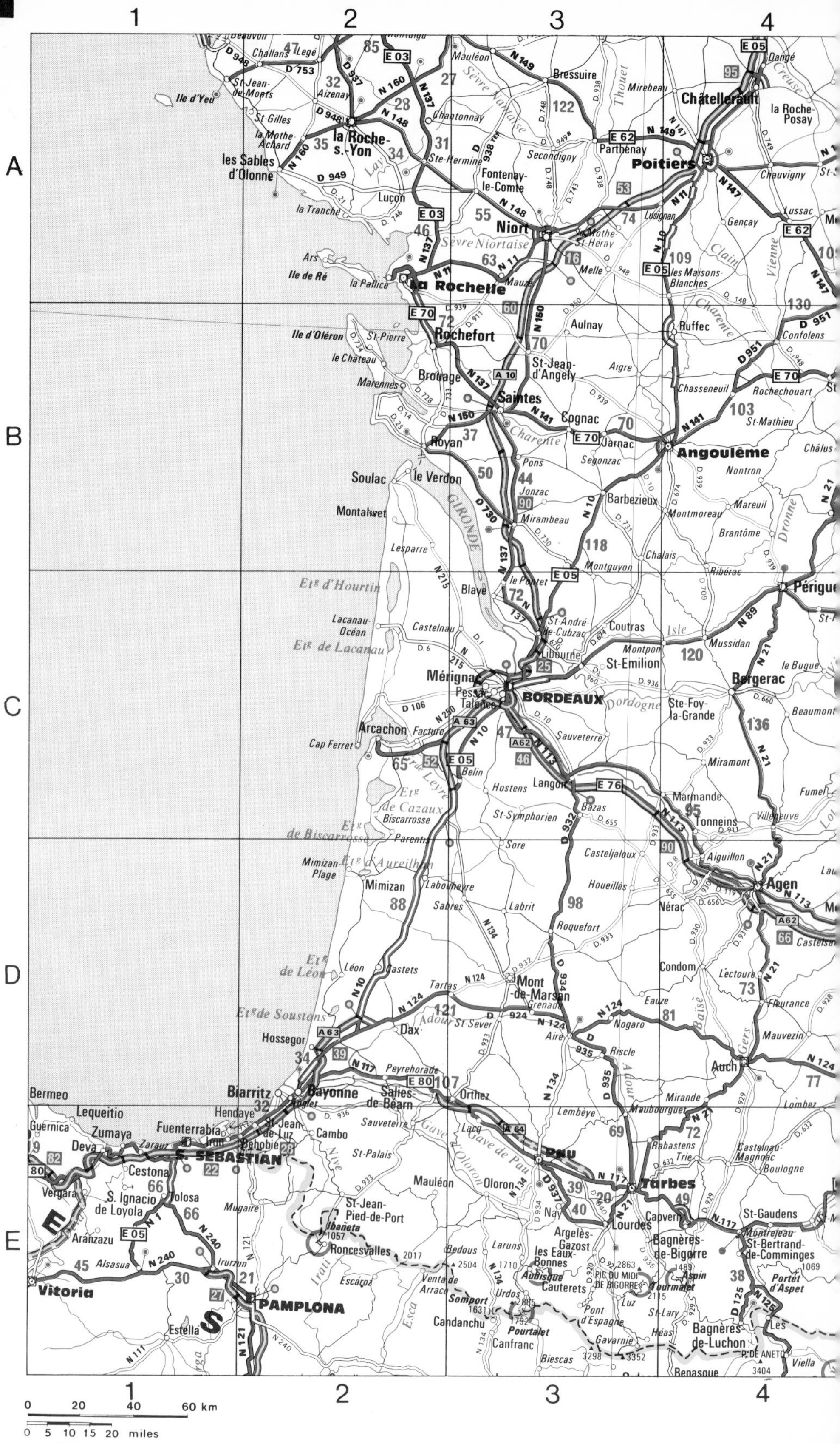

1　2　3　4

A

Beauvoir
Challans Legé
St-Jean-de-Monts
Ile d'Yeu
St-Gilles
la Mothe-Achard
les Sables d'Olonne
la Roche-s.-Yon
Aizenay
Luçon
la Tranche
Ars
Ile de Ré
la Pallice
85
D 753
D 948
D 949
32
63
31
35
34
55
46
D 137
E 03
N 160
N 137
N 148
N 160
27
28
Mauléon
Chantonnay
Ste-Hermine
Fontenay-le-Comte
Niort
Sèvre Niortaise
Maux
Melle
N 149
N 160
938
D 748
122
Bressuire
Mirebeau
Secondigny
Parthenay
Poitiers
la Mothe St-Héray
Lusignan
Gençay
Chauvigny
Châtellerault
la Roche-Posay
Dangé
95
E 05
E 62
E 62
N 149
N 11
N 147
N 10
53
74
109
130
Clain
Vienne
les Maisons Blanches
Lussac

B

Ile d'Oléron
St-Pierre
le Château
Marennes
Brouage
Royan
le Verdon
Soulac
Montalivet
Lesparre
La Rochelle
Rochefort
Saintes
Cognac
Jarnac
Pons
Segonzac
Jonzac
Mirambeau
Angoulême
Barbezieux
Montmoreau
Nontron
Mareuil
Brantôme
Chalais
Ribérac
E 70
E 70
E 05
D 730
D 730
A 10
N 11
N 137
N 137
N 150
N 141
N 10
N 141
72
60
70
70
37
50
44
90
118
103
Confolens
Ruffec
Chassoneuil
Rochechouart
St-Mathieu
Châlus
Charente
Dronne
Aulnay
Aigre
St-Jean-d'Angély
St-André-de-Cubzac
Montguyon

C

Etg d'Hourtin
Lacanau-Océan
Etg de Lacanau
Castelnau
Blaye
le Pouillac
le Pont
Libourne
St-Émilion
Coutras
Montpon
Mussidan
Périgueux
Bergerac
Mérignac
Pessac
Talence
BORDEAUX
Ste-Foy-la-Grande
Beaumont
Arcachon
Facture
Cap Ferret
Belin
Hostens
Langon
Sauveterre
Miramont
Fumel
La Teste
Etg de Cazaux
Biscarrosse
Parentis
Etg de Biscarrosse
St-Symphorien
Bazas
Marmande
Tonneins
Villeneuve
E 05
E 05
E 05
E 76
A 63
A 62
A 62
N 10
N 10
N 215
N 215
N 137
N 113
D 10
D 106
D 200
52
65
47
46
25
72
95
90
120
136
Isle
Dordogne
Gironde

D

Etg d'Aureilhan
Mimizan-Plage
Mimizan
Labouheyre
Sabres
Labrit
Roquefort
Nérac
Condom
Lectoure
Agen
Casteljaloux
Aiguillon
Houeillès
Fleurance
Mauvezin
Auch
Etg de Léon
Léon
Castets
Tartas
Mont-de-Marsan
Grenade
Eauze
Nogaro
Aire
Riscle
Castelnau
Etg de Soustans
Hossegor
Dax
St-Sever
Adour
Biarritz
Bayonne
Salies-de-Béarn
Orthez
Lembeye
Mirande
Maubourguet
N 10
N 10
N 134
N 124
N 124
N 124
N 124
N 113
N 117
N 21
N 21
A 62
A 63
D 933
D 924
D 935
D 932
88
98
81
73
77
121
107
66
39
34
69
72
Baïse
Gers

E

Bermeo
Lequeitio
Guernica
Zumaya
Deva
Vergara
Aránzazu
Cestona
S. Ignacio de Loyola
Tolosa
Mugaire
SAN SEBASTIAN
Fuenterrabia
Hendaye
St-Jean-de-Luz
Cambo
St-Palais
Sauveterre
Mauléon
Navarrenx
Oloron
Ste-Marie
PAU
Tarbes
Lourdes
Argelès-Gazost
Cauterets
St-Jean-Pied-de-Port
Ibañeta
Roncesvalles
Bedous
Laruns
les Eaux-Bonnes
PIC DU MIDI DE BIGORRE
Aubisque
Vitoria
Alsasua
Irurzun
Estella
PAMPLONA
Somport
Urdos
Candanchu
Canfranc
Biescas
Pont d'Espagne
Gavarnie
Bagnères-de-Bigorre
Capvern
Nay
Aspin
Tourmalet
Bagnères-de-Luchon
St-Gaudens
Montrejeau
St-Bertrand-de-Comminges
Portet d'Aspet
Les
Benasque
Viella
PIC D'ANETO
E 05
E 05
E 80
N 111
N 117
N 117
N 113
N 121
N 121
N 124
N 134
N 240
N 240
D 918
D 125
D 125
D 918
D 932
D 933
D 934
D 937
82
80
22
66
45
30
21
32
40
20
39
49
38
9
19
2017
1057
2504
1710
863
2884
1631
1792
1298
1489
2115
3352
3404
1069

1　2　3　4

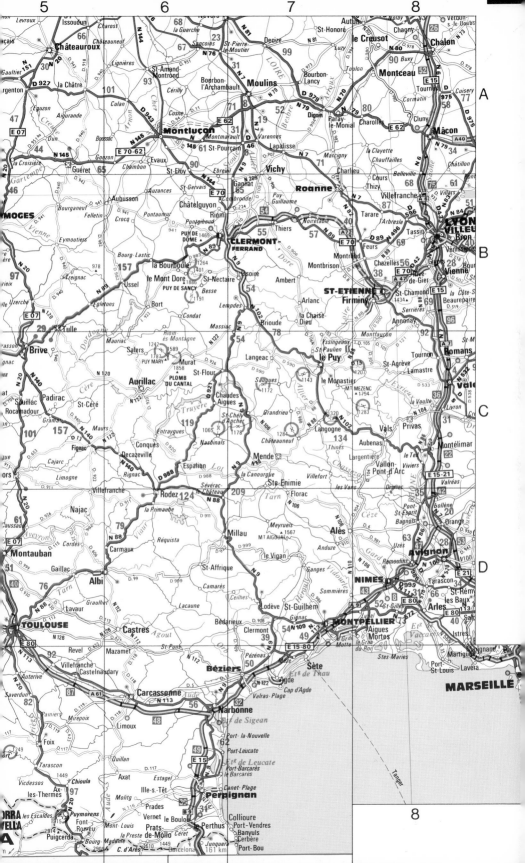

6

1   2   3   DIJON   4

Pontailler

E 17-21

Bourges   N 151   la Charité   Prémery   Corbigny   103   D 980   Nuits-St-Georges   E 17   38   42   Auxonne   E 60   BESANÇON   Éta

N 7   D 976   Avord   152   Château-Chinon   D 978   Arnay-le-Duc   39   E 21   97   St-Jean-de-Losne   38   Ornans   N 83   56   Mo

68   D 977   Nevers   N 81   Autun   D 973   Beaune   A 31   A 36   Seurre   D 973   Dole   36   Mouchard   D 72   Pontarlier

A   67   la Guerche   St-Pierre-le-Moutier   Decize   Luzy   le Creusot   Chagny   Verdun-s-le-Doubs   St-Germain   Arbois   Poligny   Champagnole   51

23   Sancoins   N 81   99   St-Honoré   Montceau   Chalon   26   N 73   N 83   Lons-le-Saunier   Vallorbe

93   St-Amand-Montrond   N 76   31   Moulins   Bourbon-Lancy   Buxy   90   Louhans   E 21   Morez   les Rousses   113

Cérilly   Bourbon-l'Archambault   Toulon   Montceau   52   E 15   Tournus   Cuisery   77   N 83   St-Claude   Bivenne   GEN

Cosne   71   8   52   Digoin   Paray-le-Monial   Charolles   58   Cormatin   975   Cuseaux   89   la Faucille   Gex   1718   39

Montluçon   E 62   31   19   N 79   79   80   Cluny   E 62   Mâcon   N 79   A 40   Bourg   N 83   Nantua   E 62   Bellegarde

62   N 145   61   St-Pourçain   Lapalisse   Marcigny   71   la Clayette   Chauffailles   34   Châtillon   27   E 62   66   Amberieu   A 41   A 40

Évaux   90   Montmarault   N 9   N 7   Charlieu   Belleville   75   61   Pont-d'Ain   Chalamont   Seyssel   Annecy   92

St-Éloy   Ébreuil   Vichy   Cours   Thizy   68   Villars   A 42   51   Aix-les-Bains   du Bourget   47

B   Aizances   N 144   Gannat   E 70   Roanne   N 7   Villefranche   87   A 6   LYON   50   83   Chambéry

Châtelguyon   Combronde   Tarare   l'Arbresle   596   VILLEURBANNE   Belley   N 201

Riom   54   Noirétable   40   Thiers   N 89   A 72   N 89   Feurs   Tassin   Bron   Crémieu   D 517   Bourgoin   28   Vienne   St-Jean   43   A 48   49   les Echelles   57   56

PUY DE DÔME   55   57   E 70   69   Givors   A 43   Moresle   100   Voiron   21   Grenoble

CLERMONT-FERRAND   N 89   Montbrison   Chazelles   56   62   E 70   38   Rive-de-Gier   A 47   Beaurepaire   St-Marcellin   66   les Echelles

la Bourboule   Issoire   Ambert   St-Chamond   69   St-Côte-St-André   Tullins   74   N 532   Chamrousse

le Mont Dore   St-Nectaire   54   ST-ÉTIENNE   Serrières   96   N 85   Villard-de-Lans   GRENOBLE   Alpe-d'H

PUY DE SANCY   Besse   Firminy   Montfaucon   92   A 7   St-Marcellin   E 21   Vizille   le Bourg-d'Oisans

C   Bort   Arlanc   Annonay   Tournon   Romans   96   en-Royans   la Mure   la Bé

PUY MARY   Langeac   St-Paulien   St-Agrève   Lamastre   VALENCE   D 533   le Rousset   2349   97   N 85

Murat   le Puy   MT MEZENC   la Voulte   36   YEYMONT   Croix Haute   103

St-Flour   PLOMB DU CANTAL   Saugues   le Monastier   1283   Livron   Crest   Drôme   Die   1179

Chaudes-Aigues   Grandrieu   Vals   Privas   31   D 93   Baya   Gap   1246

119   St-Chély-d'Apcher   Langogne   N 102   Aubenas   125   993   994   35   N 85

Entraygues   Nasbinals   Châteauneuf   134   Thines   Montélimar   22   Dieulefit   Aspres   Serres   Tallard   44

D 988   Mende   Largentière   le Teil   E 15-21   Valréas   Nyons   N 75   41

Rodez   124   Espalion   la Canourgue   Villefort   Viviers   35   42   Vaison   Sisteron   N 85   106

209   Ste-Énimie   les Vans   Vallon-Pont-d'Arc   Orgnac   Bollène   20   MT VENTOUX   Sault   N 85

D   la Primaube   Florac   N 108   Cèze   Pont-St-Esprit   Orange   1912   Carpentras   Forcalquier   Apt   la Brillance

Réquista   Meyrueis   1567   Anduze   Uzès   63   28   53   l'Isle   Manosque

Millau   MT AIGOUAL   Alès   Remoulins   Avignon   100   Cavaillon   Gréoux   N 96

St-Affrique   le Vigan   Ganges   Gard   Tarascon   St-Rémy   Cadenet   Peyrolles   N 85

Camarès   Sommières   NÎMES   43   999   31   66   les Baux   A 7   Aix   N 7   80

St-Pons   Lodève   St-Guilhem   52   St-Gilles   E 80   Arles   113   Salon   44   Maximin   40

Lacaune   Clermont   39   54   109   MONTPELLIER   49   Aigues-Mortes   Berre   31   56   D 1

Bédarieux   Pézenas   50   E 15-80   la Grande-Motte   le Grau-du-Roi   Istres   Martigues   Aubagne   40

E   Béziers   Sète   Étg de Vaccares   Stes-Maries   Port-St-Louis   Lavéra   A 50   64   TOULON

Carcassonne   N 113   56   Agde   Cap d'Agde   MARSEILLE   la Ciotat   Bandol   la Seyne

48   Narbonne   Étg de Sigean   la Ciotat

62   Port-la-Nouvelle   Port-Leucate

0   20   40   60 km
0   5 10 15 20 miles

1   2   3   4

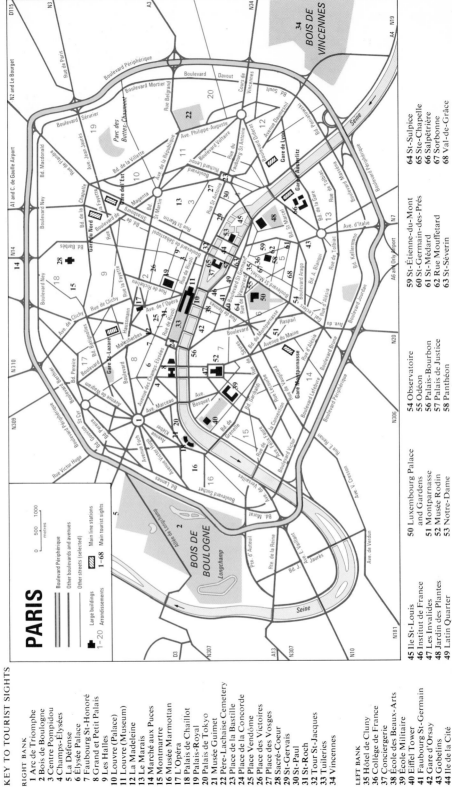

PARIS

Boulevard Périphérique

Other boulevards and avenues

Other streets (selected)

Large buildings

1–20 Arrondissements

Main line stations

1–68 Main tourist sights

0   500   1000
metres

KEY TO TOURIST SIGHTS

RIGHT BANK

1 Arc de Triomphe
2 Bois de Boulogne
3 Centre Pompidou
4 Champs-Elysées
5 La Défense
6 Élysée Palace
7 Faubourg St-Honoré
8 Grand et Petit Palais
9 Les Halles
10 Louvre (Palace)
11 Louvre (Museum)
12 La Madeleine
13 Le Marais
14 Marché aux Puces
15 Montmartre
16 Musée Marmottan
17 L'Opéra
18 Palais de Chaillot
19 Palais-Royal
20 Palais de Tokyo
21 Musée Guimet
22 Père-Lachaise Cemetery
23 Place de la Bastille
24 Place de la Concorde
25 Place Vendôme
26 Place des Victoires
27 Place des Vosges
28 Sacré-Coeur
29 St-Gervais
30 St-Paul
31 St-Roch
32 Tour St-Jacques
33 Tuileries
34 Vincennes

LEFT BANK

35 Hôtel de Cluny
36 Collège de France
37 Conciergerie
38 École des Beaux-Arts
39 École Militaire
40 Eiffel Tower
41 Faubourg St-Germain
42 Gare d'Orsay
43 Gobelins
44 Ile de la Cité

45 Ile St-Louis
46 Institut de France
47 Les Invalides
48 Jardin des Plantes
49 Latin Quarter

50 Luxembourg Palace
   and Gardens
51 Montparnasse
52 Musée Rodin
53 Notre-Dame

54 Observatoire
55 Odéon
56 Palais-Bourbon
57 Palais de Justice
58 Panthéon

59 St-Étienne-du-Mont
60 St-Germain-des-Prés
61 St-Médard
62 Rue Mouffetard
63 St-Séverin

64 St-Sulpice
65 Ste-Chapelle
66 Salpêtrière
67 Sorbonne
68 Val-de-Grâce

Index

The index lists all the places mentioned in the Gazetteers, either as main entries or as sub-entries. These Gazetteer entries are shown in roman type. Numbers in *italic* type indicate either a reference in one of the Introductory Essays or an illustration on a page other than the main entry page. For the convenience of the reader, place-names beginning with St-, Ste- and Stes- have been grouped together at the start of the 'S' section.

KEY TO SECTIONS, REGIONS AND DEPARTMENTS

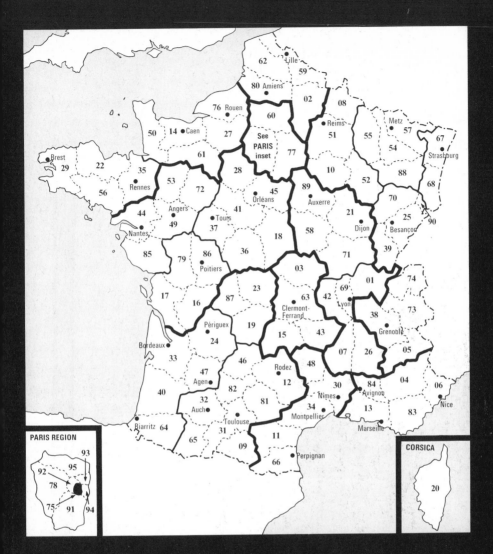

PARIS REGION

93
95
92
78
91 94
75

CORSICA

20